"*much given to Talk and bad Company*"

New-England Runaways,
1704-1754

Compiled by
Joseph Lee Boyle

CLEARFIELD

Copyright © 2020 by
Joseph Lee Boyle

All Rights Reserved.

Published for Clearfield Company by
Genealogical Publishing Company
Baltimore, Maryland
2020

ISBN 9780806359120

INTRODUCTION

The majority of the individuals in this compilation are runaway servants and slaves, but a number are runaway apprentices, both men and women, military deserters, with horse thieves, counterfeiters, burglars, jail breakers, an occasional murderer, and other lowlifes are represented, as well as supposedly errant spouses.

Tracking an individual by name may often lead to a dead end as multiple names were common, and middle names were not often used at this time. Robert Jones ran away from Joseph Turrell of Boston, but Jones "but often changed his Name." Jonathan Lawrence was the victim of a theft by a man who "calls himself by several Names, viz. John St. Ambrose, or John Ambrose, but changes his Name as suits him best."

Some of the runaway Negroes also used multiple names. "Jupeter, but calls himself by the Name of Timothy;" "a tall lusty Negro Fellow named Millet, but calls himself Tom Brown." James Bois advertised for an Indian Man Servant, named "Tobias Peas, but now calls himself James Wicked."

Runaway ladies used multiple names, such as "a Woman who goes by the Name of Elizabeth Richardson, but her true Name is suppos'd to be Mary Rogers, and is a noted Thief, and was committed for several Thefts." Mary Beats of Newport Rhode-Island, "calls herself by several Names."

Some of the multiple names that appear are likely due to spelling or pronunciation errors such as Sabera/Zipporah, Ruggels/Ruggles, and Pepperel/Pepperil/Pepperrell/Pepperell. Names not common in English may have been quite creatively spelled by the advertisers. There are also nicknames such as Venus for Sylvester Charles, an Indian who ran away from Boston in 1741. Negro servant Robin was "but sometimes call'd Christmas." William Young was looking for Thomas Harmon, "he is known by the Name of Fortuneteller."

Multiple spellings of names sometimes appear in the same ad such as Henry Shearbourne/Sherburn/Sherburne who was advertising for William Mandevell. When ads are published in different newspapers or even in the same paper, discrepancies in the ads sometimes appear. If the variations are substantial, the separate ads are included.

The reader should be prepared for phonetic spellings of people they are interested in such as Wamscom/Wombscom, Bargary/Bargery, Flynt/Flint, and Jonson/Johnston/Johnson is always a challenge. In a few cases letters or numerals were indistinct and thus appear in brackets.

Some of the runaways were well skilled. Butchers, bakers, coopers, carpenters, blacksmiths, shoemakers and taylors (tailors) are represented. Skills of others might today be questionable such as that of a corker and silk dyer no longer exist, and have you lately heard of a sailmaker, sugar boyler, or a twine and line spinner.

Advertisers often questioned the supposed skills of people they advertised. John Richardson of New-London advertised for David Robinson who "pretends to be something of a Cooper." John Walker, a hired servant "said he was a Weaver by Trade, and pretends to be a Doctor." Jonathan Dows of Massachusetts was looking for John Yowelen who "pretends to be a Weaver, tho' a Ship-Carpenter when he Runaway."

Scores of ads are for sailors who deserted, most are civilian, and a few Royal Navy. In some ads privateers and privateering are mentioned indicating skills at sailing in the wars of the period.

It is impossible to know how many runaways there really were. No newspapers were published in Delaware or New Jersey for the entire period covered. What are now the states of Maine and Vermont existed as separate colonies, and had no newspapers.

Also printed handbills were often circulated, and some masters may have only advertised with them. Given that so many of the servants appear to be scapegraces, one wonders why their masters spent money to advertise for them, let alone pay a reward for their return. Masters were likely to ignore those who left for a few days of dissipation, particularly planters during the agricultural slow season. Why ads were often delayed can only be guessed at. Jonathan Earl ran away from Rhode-Island on March 23, 1734, but the first advertisement did not appear until January 5, 1735.

Some masters may have not wanted to pay the cost of the ads. Those masters whose servants absconded from more remote parts of the colonies may not have bothered to advertise them. Subscribers who waited lengthy periods to advertise must have greatly reduced the chance of capturing the rogue. Several ads seem to have been intended to let the runaway know how little the master thought of them as very low rewards were posted.

Some of the escapees were rather agile despite physical problems and restraints. Negro servant Cuffe ran away from James Brown in 1733, though "his left Leg is above twice as large as his right, and is attended with running Sores." Taylor John Finly "ran away" from Henry Price of Boston, "He goes lame, with a Crutch, and cannot straiten his Knee. The lame Leg is much less than the other."

Some identifying marks were obvious but one wonders how Evan Mallborn of Newport expected observers to identify runaway Cuff who "has but one Testicle." Whereas Thomas Plaisted advertised a Negro named Brazill who was "well known in Boston by his Legs." James Mitchel sought John Deivo whose "calves of his Legs grows before."

A number of ads were by men for their errant wives such as James Remick for his wife Abigail who "hath for a long Time liv'd in repeated, notorious Breaches of the Marriage Covenant and Duty, and thereby rendered it improper for me to treat her any long as my Wife; she having also in my Absence at Sea, embezel'd and wasted my Estate." Not sentimental, Joseph Brown wrote in 1742, that his wife Rachel "hath eloped (Haven be prais'd) about three Weeks since from me her lawful and tender Husband, and carried off my (reputed) Child contrary to my desire and command."

Several wives countered the statements of their spouses. Sarah Dwyer was advertised by husband James as "eloped from the Dwelling House of said Dwyer, rifled the House by the Assistance of Persons to him unknown, carried away in the Night-Time all the Goods in the House, and secreted the same, as also, a Negro Man named Scipio, about 26 Years of Age, bred among the English, with four Cows, three Horses, and about 26 Sheep." The next week Sarah advertised "in a very little Time after our Marriage he treated me with great Roughness and Violence, frequently with a Whip in his Hand held over me threatning to Horse whip me, afterwards got a Sword, and kept by the Bedside, threatning to run me thro' with it, took from me many valuable Things, and all my Case amounting to some Hundreds of Pounds."

Some enterprising ladies are included such as John Abbot's wife. He was in prison at New-London for counterfeiting and she had "frequently the Liberty of being let into the same to visit him." On February 7, 1732, she went to visit him and "while they were there, they together got off his Fetters, and chang'd Apparel one with another." He then passed out pretending to be her, and "the next Morning *Abbot's* Wife call'd to the Keeper, and desired to be released from her Confinement, which was accordingly done, tho' to his great surprize."

In 1746 an Indian girl named Ruth ran away from Thomas Stone with men's clothing which she had worn before and inlisted in a military expedition against Canada "but was soon discover'd and dismiss'd."

At this time smallpox outbreaks occurred on a regularly, and many did not want to run the risk of inoculation. Quarantine hospitals were established to try and reduce the spread. In 1748, three men who had come to Boston by ship were confined on an island on suspicion of being infected. They took a boat and their things. The public was warned to take "proper Care taken to prevent their Travelling; as there is great Danger to their spreading the Small Pox if they are not stopt, and confin'd in some suitable Place."

A charming fellow was the famous, infamous, notorious Tom Bell who appears in a number of ads was "generally known by his Rogueries throughout the Colonies, and some Part of the West Indies." An Irish servant named Samuel Shaw ran away from James Fairservice was "much given to Talk and bad Company, and apt to get in Liquor. He was lately ransomed from being Shot for Desertion sundry Times from Annapolis Royal Fort."

This work also includes individuals with New England connections who did not run away from those colonies. Irish man servant George Tompson ran away from his New Jersey master John Gordon in 1731, but "He lately Run away from Boston." Newal Coomes was advertised in New York as "an New-England man" who "pretends to be a Doctor" also "often changes his Names in calling himself Thomas Newal Coomes, and sometimes Doctor Pidgeon."

This compilation lists all individuals mentioned. If an individual is listed with more than one name, all the names appear in the index. While many of the Negroes and some Indians are listed as slaves, many are not, so they may have been paid servants. People described as mixed Indian and Negroe blood are indexed under both races. Mulattoes are listed as Negroes with exceptions such as an unnamed "Indian Molatto Man" who ran away in 1745. Those designated as "Mustees" are listed separately when of unspecified mixed races.

I have retained the original spelling, punctuation, and capitalization of the ads. Illegible words or letters are in brackets. Sometimes the ads in different papers are very similar and only the ad which occurs first in time is included, with references to the later ones. Minor differences in the advertisements are considered to be capitalization, spellings such as trousers/trowsers and 7/seven. If the ads are substantially different, each appears at the time it is first run. The majority are advertised in only one paper, some in two.

Newspapers Consulted:

It should be noted that none of these newspapers had a complete run for the period. Also, there were no newspapers published in Delaware or New Jersey for the entire period, colonies where ads for New-England runaways might have appeared. Newspapers from south of Maryland were not consulted.

The American Weekly Mercury
The Boston Evening-Post
The Boston Gazette
The Boston Gazette, And The Country Journal
The Boston News-Letter
The Boston Post-Boy
The Connecticut Gazette
The Independent Reflector
The Maryland Gazette
The New-England Courant
The New-England Weekly Journal
The New-Hampshire Gazette
The New-London Gazette
The New-London Summary
The Newport Mercury
The New-York Evening Post
The New-York Gazette
The New-York Gazette, or Weekly Post-Boy
The New-York Mercury
The New-York Weekly Journal
The Newport Mercury
The Pennsylvania Gazette
The Pennsylvania Journal, or Weekly Advertiser
The Rhode-Island Gazette
The Weekly Rehearsal

1704

LAtely deserted Her Majesties Service at the Castle on Castle-Island, *Jonathan Milburn*, Souldier, a Middle siz'd man, this Visage, dark brown short Hair: Aged about Thirty years: Whosoever shall apprehend and him Convey to the Honourable *Thomas Povey* Esq. Lieutenant Governour of the *Massachusetts-Bay*, shall have Forty Shillings Reward, besides his Charges. And if the said *Milburn* will Voluntarily come in and Surrender himself to the next Justice of the Peace, in order to return to his Obedience, he shall be pardoned his Crime.

The Boston News-Letter, From January 29, to February 5, 1704.

RAn-away from his Master, *Seth Sweetzer* of *Charlstown*, in *New-England*, August 15, 1703. A Young man, named *John Logen*, about 19 years of Age, of a middle Stature, black hair, by occupation at Taylor: He's said to be gone to *Long-Island*, thence to *Pensilvania*: Whoever shall take him up, and convey him safe to his above-said Master, shall have Four Pounds reward.

The Boston News-Letter, From May 29, to June 5, 1704; From June 26, to July 3, 1704.

RAn-away from Capt. *John Aldin* of *Boston*, on Monday the 12th Currant, a tall lusty Indian Man call'd *Harry*, about 19 Years of Age, with a black Hat, brown Ozenbridge Breeches and Jacket: Whoever will take up said Indian, and bring or convey him safe either to *John Campbell* Post master of *Boston*, or to Mr. *Nathaniel Niles* of *Kingstown* in *Naraganset*, Master to said Indian, shall have a sufficient Reward.

The Boston News-Letter, From June 12, to June 19, 1704.

RAn-away from Capt. *Nathaniel Cary*, of *Charlstown*, on *Saturday* the 17th Currant, a well set middle sized *Maddagascar* Negro Woman, called *Penelope*. About 35 years of Age: With several sorts of Apparel; one whereof is a flower damask Gown: She speaks English well. Whoever shall take up said Negro Servant, and her Convey to her above-said Master, shall have sufficient Reward.

The Boston News-Letter, From June 19, to June 26, 1704.

THere is a Negro man taken up supposed to be Runaway from his Master; he said he was a free Negro, and lived at *Bristol*, but upon being sent to Prison, he owned he was a Servant and made his escape from his Master *Matthew Howard* at *Seaconet*, about 5 Weeks ago: he is a Lusty Fellow, says his name is *George*: upon paying the Post-master for this Advertisement the owner may be informed where he is, and also paying the charge and reward for taking him up, may have said Negro again.

The Boston News-Letter, From July 10, to July 17, 1704.

RAN-away on Wednesday last the 8*th*. Currant from his *Master* in *Boston*, a Sirranam Indian *M*anslave, named *Prince*, aged about fourteen years old, black short hair, markt upon his breast with the Letters AP joyned at the foot: has on a black broad Cloth jacket under that a frize Jacket and Breeches, a Crocus Apron, gray yarn Stockings and *M*ittens, and a speckled Neckcloth: Speaks little or no English. Whosoever shall take up and apprehend said Indian Boy, and him Convey to *John Campbell* Post-master of *Boston*, or give any true Intelligence of said Boy, so as his Master may have him again, shall have a sufficient reward.

The Boston News-Letter, From November 6, to November 13, 1704.

1705

RAn-away at Boston about 3 weeks ago from his Master Capt. Samuel Rymes Commander of the Barbadoes Merchant, a Man-Servant named Joseph Ingerson, aged about 22 years, a well-set young man, dark complexion, pretty full fac'd, short dark hair, if not now a Wig. Whoever shall apprehend said Servant, and him safely convey to his Master, shall have Forty Shillings Reward, and reasonable Charges.

The Boston News-Letter, From August 20, to August 27, 1705.

RAn away from his Master, Samuel Niles, of Kingston, in Narraganset; an Indian Man Servant, aged about 26 Years, he is a short and indifferent thick fellow, with a broad flatt Nose, he has had the Small Pox: He has on a grayish Coat, a Castor Hat, Russet coloured Stockings, and old Shoes: Whoever shall take up said Indian, and bring or convey him safe to his said Master, or secure him and send notice of him, shall be well Satisfied for his pains.

The Boston News-Letter, From October 1, to October 8, 1705.

LAtely Deserted Her Majesties Service at Kittery Garison in the Province of Main, David Thomas Souldier, a Welsh-man, aged about 30 years pretty short and thick stature, dark brown coloured hair; hath on a new white Cape cloth Watch Coat, under that an old fad coloured strait bodied Coat and Jacket, grey yarn stockings, and on old black Hat. Whoever shall apprehend said Deserter, and him safely convey to his Post, or to Andrew Belcher Esqr. at Boston, shall have satisfaction to Content, besides his Charges.

The Boston News-Letter, From December 3, to December 10, 1705.

RAn-away from his Master William Pepperil Esqr. at Kittery, in the Province of Maine, a Negro Man-Slave named Peter, aged about 20, speaks good English, of a pretty brown Complexion, middle Stature, had on a mixt gray home-spun Coat, white home spun Jacket and Breeches, French fall shoes, fad coloured Stockings, or a mixt worsted pair, and a black Hat. Whoever shall take up said Negro, and bring him or convey him safe to his said Master, or secure him and send notice of him either to his Master, or to Andrew Belcher Esqr. at Boston, shall be well rewarded for his pains, and all reasonable charges paid besides.

The Boston News-Letter, From December 3, to December 10, 1705. See below.

LAtely Deserted Her Majesties Service in the Province of Main, an Indian Man (under the Command of Cap. Joseph Brown) named Isaac Pummatick, was seen at Newbury, in Company with the above Runaway Negro; he is a short Fellow not very thick, speaks good English, he liv'd formerly with Mr. Samuel Thackster of Hingham; he has on English Cloaths, a fad coloured coat, or else a new light coloured drugget Coat, with buttons, holes and lining of black, black breeches, gray yarn Stockings, a black hat almost new. Whosoever shall apprehend said Indian, & him convey to his said Captain, or to Andrew Belcher Esqr. at Boston, shall have a sufficient reward besides his Charges.

The Boston News-Letter, From December 3, to December 10, 1705. See above.

1706

RAn-away from her Master Nicholas Jamain of New-York Merchant, the beginning of September last, A short thick Indian Girl, named Grace, aged about 17 years, her face is full of Pock holes, very few hairs on her Eyebrows, a very flat Nose, and a broad mouth; she speaks English, Dutch and French, the last best. Whoever shall apprehend and take up the said Servant, and deliver her unto Mr. Andrew Fanueil Merchant in Boston: If taken up in the Provinces of Massachusetes-Bay and New Hampshire; if in Connecticut-Colony, to Mr. John Clark at Saybrook; If at Rhode-Island Colony, to Mr. William Barbutt; In Pensilvania to Mr. Benj. Godfrey; In Carolina to Messieurs Guerard and Pacqueran; If in the Province of New-York at Albany to Col. Peter Schuyler; and other part of said Province to her Master Jamain, 3 pounds, shall forthwith be paid to any one that shall deliver the said Indian Woman to any of the persons above mentioned, besides reasonable Charges.

The Boston Post-Boy, From January 13, to January, 20, 1706; From February 10, to February 17, 1706; From February 24, to March 3, 1706; From March 10, to March 17, 1706.

RAN-away at Boston on the 26th of December last, Samuel Downs, a Man-Servant, aged about 25 years, a spare man, middle Stature, light brown Hair, speaketh broad English; he was in May last at work in Sea-brook in Connecticut Colony, and now adscondeth from said place; Whoever will take up and secure the said Run-away, so that he may be delivered unto John Colman Merchant in Boston, shall be immediately paid Five Pounds, and Charges.
The Boston News-Letter, From June 10, to June 17, 1706.

Ran-away from this Master George Robinson Carver of Boston, on Tuesday last the 16th Currant, A Negro Man-Slave Named Jo, of a middle Stature, well-set, Speaks good English, aged about 32 years, had of a fad coloured Jacket, white Shirt, and Leather Breeches. Whosoever shall apprehend and take up said Runaway, so that he may be delivered unto his said Master, or give any true Intelligence of him, shall have a Sufficient reward.
The Boston News-Letter, From July 15, to July 22, 1706.

Ran-away from his Master Samuel Niles of Kingstown in Narraganset, A Spanish Indian Man-Slave, aged about 28 years, speaks good English, a short fellow, much of the reliques of the small Pox to be seen in his Face, has a broad flat Nose, his teeth are thin before; has on grayish coloured Cloaths much worn. Whoever shall take up the said Indian and bring or convey him to his said Master, or secure him and send notice of him, shall be well rewarded and satisfyed for their pains.
The Boston News-Letter, From July 22, to July 29, 1706.

Ran-away from their Master Nathaniel Niles Junior of Point-Judith in Narranganset, a Negro Woman with 4 small Children, three of them are Molatto's, and the youngest a Negro that sucks or is lately weaned: The Woman is of middle Stature and thick set. The Eldest of the Children is not above 10 or 11 year old, the two eldest are Girls, the other two Boyes. Whosoever shall apphrend the said Negro Woman & her Children, or any of them, and do bring and Convey her or them of any of them to their said Master, or secure her or them, or any of them, and send notice thereof to her or their said Master, shall be sufficient rewarded and satisfied for their pains.
The Boston News-Letter, From October 7, to October 14, 1706.

RAN-away from his Master Col. Nathaniel Byfield Esq. of Bristol, last Monday Evening, the 11th Currant in a Cannooe, James Furdize a Scotch Young man, aged about 19 years, speaks good English, of a middle Stature, fair Complexion, light brown Hair, hath with him a good black felt Hat, two

Jackets, the undermost of Searge lined, the uppermost of Home-spun Kersey dyed of a pretty fad colour, and lined with brown linen called western Tow-cloth, a Flanel Shirt, and leather Breehes. Whoever shall apprehend the abovesaid Servant and bring or convey him safe to his said Master, or secure him, and send any true Intelligence of him, so that his Master may have him again, shall be well rewarded, and all necessary Charges paid besides.

The Boston News-Letter, From November 11, to November 18, 1706.

1707

RAN-away from his Master Capt. *James Pitts* of *Boston*, about a Month agoe, An Indian Young Man, named *Daniel Hump*, aged about 18 years, has on a dark gray Coat, a double breasted Jacket, dark gray Stockings, and a black Hatt; one of his Legs being Sore looks like a Bandy Legg. Whoever shall apprehend and take up the said Servant and deliver him unto his said Master, or Mr. Barnabas Lathrop at Barnstable; or Capt. Simon Davis at Bristol, or Mr. Augustus Lucas at Rhode-Island, shall be sufficiently rewarded and paid, besides all reasonable cost and charges.

The Boston News-Letter, From January 27, to February 3, 1707; From February 3, to February 10, 1707.

RAn-away the Last Spring from her Master John Otis Esqr. of Barnstable, in the Province of the Massachusetts-Bay in New-England, an Indian Girl named Hannah Wapuck, aged about 20 years, middle sized, full fac'd, a comely Countenance, she speaks good English, not very perfect of the Indian Language; had on English Apparel: Whoever shall apprehend and take up the said Servant, and deliver her to her said Master, or give any true Intelligence of her unto John Campbell Post-master of Boston, or unto her said Master so as that he may have her again, shall be sufficient rewarded, besides all reasonable Cost and Charges paid.

The Boston News-Letter, From February 17, to February 24, 1707; From March 10, to March 17, 1707.

RAn-away from his Master Samuel Lyndes of Boston Esqr. The 26th of Febr. last, a Negro Man aged about 20 years, short Stature, bandy leg'd, having of a light coloured gray cloth Coat, a leather Jacket and Breeches, a pair of yarn Stockings; he speaks good English: Whosoever shall apprehend and take up the said Negro, and deliver him to his said Master, or give any true Intelligence of him, so as his Master may have him again, shall have a sufficient reward, besides all reasonable Charges paid.

The Boston News-Letter, From February 23, to March 3, 1707.

RAn-away from her Master Nath. Niles jun. of Point-Judith in Narraganset, a Negro Woman with her Son a Negro Boy about 2 year old, she's of middle Stature & well set. Whoever shall apprehend and convey her either to her Master or John Campbell Post-master of Boston, shall be well rewarded.
The Boston News-Letter, From April 21, to April 28, 1707.

RAn-away from her Master, Nathaniel Baker of Boston, on the 22d of August last, a Tall Lusty Carolina Indian Woman named Sarah, aged about five or six and twenty years; having long straight black Hair, tyed up with a red hairlace, very much mark'd or cut in the hands and face: Had on a striped red blue and white Homespun Jacket, & a red one, a black and white silk Crape Petticoat, a white Shift, as also a blue one with her, and a mixed blue and white Linsey Woolsey Apron: Whoever shall apprehend the said Servant, and her safely Convey to her said Master; or give any true Intelligence of her, so that he may have her again, shall be well rewarded, besides all necessary Charges paid.
The Boston News-Letter, From September 8, to September 15, 1707; From September 29, to October 6, 1707.

RAnaway from his Master, Samuel Wentworth of Boston Merchant, on Saturday the 20th Currant, An Indian Man, Servant, named John Eiles, aged about 23 years, of low Stature, a round well favour'd face, short hair: Having on a round puffe and quilted Cap, a double breasted Kersey Jacket, and round toe'd Shoes; he was bred at Mr. Ebenzer Billings's on the Road between Boston and Rhode-Island, and bought by his Master of Mr. Ephraim Pray. Whoever shall apprehend the said Servant, and him safely convey to his said Master, or give any true intelligence of him, so as that he may have him again, shall be well rewarded, besdies all necessary Charges paid.
The Boston News-Letter, From September 22, to September 29, 1707.

RAN-away at Boston upon Wednesday last the First Currant from his Master Carteret Gillam of Seabrook in Connecticut Colony, Gabriel Jackson, aged about 18 years, he is a slender Young Man, light coloured hair, had on a home-spun Kersey Coat, home-spun Shirt, an old pair of Shoes, home made Stockings, and an old Hat. Whoever shall apprehend the said Servant and him convey to his said Master, or the Post-Master of Boston, or give true Intelligence of him, so that his Master may have him again, shall be well Rewarded, besides all necessary charges paid.
The Boston News-Letter, From September 29, to October 6, 1707.

RAn-away from his Master Mr. John Colman of Boston Merchant the 21st of October last, A Negro man named Primus: Hath on a Homespun Jacket and Breeches, gray yarn Hose, a Hat, a homespun Shirt: Whoever shall apprehend the said Servant, and him safety convey to his said Master, or give any true Intelligence of him so as that he may have him again, shall be well rewarded, besides all necessary charges paid.
The Boston News-Letter, From October 27, to November 4, 1707.

1708

RAn-away from their Master *Nathaniel Niles* of *Kingston* in *Narraganset* the last Winter, an Indian man and his Squaw, who carried with them a Woman Child about two years old, the man formerly belonged to *Cape-Cod*, or that way, and went out under Colonel *Church*, by the name of *John Ame*, he is of a middle Age and Stature; the Squaw's name is *Mary*, a lusty thick far Woman, they both speak English, and partly wears English Cloaths, and commonly a Blanket over them. Whoever shall apprehend the said Servants and Child, or any of them, and he or she safely Convey to their said Master, or give any true Intelligence of any of them, so as that he may have them, or any of them again, shall be sufficiently rewarded, besides all necessary Charges paid.
The Boston News-Letter, From April 12, to April 19, 1708.

RAn-away from her Master *James Berry* of *Boston* Mariner, about Nine a Clock on Sabbath day night, being the 2d Currant, a Young Indian Woman Servant, Named *Pegg*, about 20 years of Age, speaks broken *English*, full Visage, and pretty Tall; She hath a Mark or Branch made in the flesh on her right Arm with Powder, or something else black: hath on two Jackets, one Greenish, and two Petticoats, one Red, yellow Stockings, with Shoes on. Whosoever shall apprehend the said Runaway Servant, and her safely Convey to her abovesaid Master, in Black-horse-lane in the North-End of *Boston*, or to Mr. *Jonathan Mountfort*, Shop-keeper near the North-Meeting-house in said *Boston*, or give any true Intelligence of her, so as that he may have her again, shall have Satisfaction to content, besides all necessary Charges paid.
The Boston News-Letter, From May 3, to May 10, 1708.

ON Monday the 13th of September last, In the Night, A large bay Horse about 11 years old, with a blackish Man and Tail, the Main hanging mostly on the off side, middle paced, Trots mostly; now or late belonging to *James Perry* of Situate, *alias, James Perry* of Rehoboth, Weaver or Brick-maker; was stol'n or Rescoued and unlawfully taken and conveyed away out of the Custody of *Peter Cullimore* of Situate, being then under an Arrest and

Charge of the Law, as the Esate of the said *James Perry*, at the Suit of *Samuel Holmes* of New-port, Merchant, and put to keeping to the said *Peter Cullimore*, by *Isaac Little*, Deputy-Sheriff of the County of Plimouth. Whoever shall give Notice of the said Horse to the said *Isaac Little*, or to the said *Peter Cullimore*, so that he may be recovered again, shall be well rewarded for the same.

The Boston News-Letter, From September 27, to October 4, 1708.

RAn-away from his Master Col. *Nicholas Paige*, of *Rumley*-Marsh, on Tuesday the 2d of this Instant *November*, a Negro Man-Servant, aged about 45 years, call'd *Jack Bill*, of middle Stature, a comely Fellow, speaks good English: He has on a black Hat, black Coat, blew Jacket, a broad cloth pair of Breeches with Livery Lace, and a pair of white Stockings. Whoever shall apprehend the said Runaway, and him safety Convey to his said Master, or unto Mr. *John Geerish*, Gunswith, [sic] at the Upper-End of *Kings-Street* in *Boston*; or give any true Intelligence of the said Negro Man-servant to either of them, so as that his Master may have him again, shall be sufficiently Rewarded, besides all necessary Charges paid.

The Boston News-Letter, From November 8, to November 15, 1708.

RAn-away from his Master *Ambrose Vincent*, Silk Dyer of *Boston*, on Tuesday the 16th of *November* last, an *Irish* Lad call'd *Darby Ragan*, aged about 17 years, he is a short thick Fellow, with very large Leggs, thin dark brown hair, a swarthy Complexion: He has on a black Hat, a loose dark coloured frieze Coat, a light coloured cloth Jacket and Breeches, & a pair of Leather Breeches, gray yarn Stockings. Whoever shall apprehend the said Runaway, and him safely Convey to his said Master, or unto Mr. *Dirick Adolph* at *New-York*, or Mr. *William Bright* at *Rhode-Island*; or give any true Intelligence of him to either of them, so as that his Master may have him again, shall be sufficiently Rewarded, besides all necessary Charges paid.

The Boston News-Letter, From November 29, to December 6, 1708.

1710

Deserted from Her Majesties Brig. Betty at Boston the 26th of February last the following Persons viz. William Moore, a tall Man, brown short curl'd hair aged about 45 years, Speaks Scotch: Robert Arthur, a well set fresh colour'd Man, about 5 Foot 8 Inches high, short brown hair, speaks Scotch, aged about 35 years: John Edwards, a middle Siez'd well set Man, thin short brown hair, aged about 35 years: George Dewy Corporal, a middle Siez'd well set brown Complexioned Man, with a dark brown Perriwigg: William Hide a well set Man, about 5 Foot 7 Inches high, brown hair, fresh colour'd, about 38 years; And Valentine Butler, a slender Man, brown Complexion, light brown hair, about 5 Foot 8 Inches, high, aged about 21 years: If the said Deserters will return to their Duty on board the said Ship Bettey, within six days after the Publication hereof they shall be freely forgiv'n and kindly received. If not, Whosoever shall apprehend the said Deserters, and them safety convey to the Honourable Governour Vetch, Major Walter Elliot, or Capt. Blackmore, Commander of the said Brigt. Or give any true Intelligence of them, so as that they may be had again shall have Forty Shillings reward for each of them besides all necessary Charges paid.

The Boston News-Letter, From February 26, to March 5, 1710.

1711

RAN-away from her Mistress *Sarah Warton* of *Boston* the 13th of January last, a Swiss Servant Woman, named *Anna Maria Barbarie Collier*, aged about 20 years, of a fresh colour, well set, has a lump on her throat under her Chin, has on when she went away a Stuff Gown and Petticoat strip'd with white and fad coloured stripes; but carried also with her other Clothes, she commonly us'd to wear on her head a black velvet Cap, after the Dutch mode. Whoever shall apprehend the said Run-away, and her safety convey to her said Mistress, or to Capt. *John Ballentin* in Anne Street, Boston, or give any true Intelligence of her, and what she carri'd away, so that her Mistress may have her again, shall be well rewarded, besides all necessary charges paid.

The Boston News-Letter, From January 28, to February 4, 1711.

RAn-away from his Master Robert Rumsey at Fairfield in Connecticut Colony, on the 27th of March last, a Negro man call'd Jack, a tall thin fac'd Fellow, exceeding black, a considerable scarr in his face, can play on a Violin, he hath carried his Fiddle with him, and a considerable bundle of Cloaths. Whoever shall apprehend the said Runaway Negro man, and him safety Convey to his said Master, or give any true Intelligence of him, so as his Master may have him again, shall be sufficiently Rewarded, besides all necessary Charges paid.

The Boston News-Letter, From April 7, to April 16, 1711.

RAn-away from his Master Peter Burr Esq: at Fairfield in Connecticut Colony, on the 27th of March last, a Malatto Servant Man, call'd John More, a young well sett smooth fac'd Fellow, of a middle Stature; having on a blewish mix coloured home made flannel Coat, an old gray Kersey Vest, & a new reddish coloured cloth searge Vest Leather Breeches, a good Castor Hat; he speaks & reads English well. Whoever shall apprehend the

said Runaway Servant, and him safely Convey to his said Master, or give any Intelligence of him, so as his Master may have him again, shall be sufficiently Rewarded, besides all necessary Charges paid.
The Boston News-Letter, From April 7, to April 16, 1711.

Ran-away from William Gardner of Kingstown in the Colony of Rhode-Island, on the 28th of May last past A Mollato Man of Middle stature Branded on the Cheek with the Letter G, about five or six & twenty years of Age having A gray Homspun Jacket Linnen Breaches Flannel Shirt, Speakes English well, & a Indian Squa his Wife with a Child. Whoever shall take up & Convey said Runawaise to their said Master or give any Intelligence so that he may have his said Servants again shall be sufficiently Rewarded for their pains besides all Reasonable Charges paid.
The Boston News-Letter, From June 4, to June 11, 1711.

DEserted from Her Majesties Ship the Saphir, Capt. Cockburn Commander, at Boston the 18th day of this Instant June, the following Persons viz. Thomas Barrington, a short well set Man, of a brown Complexion, wearing a Wigg, aged 28 years. John Walters, a Tall well set Man, a dark brown Complexion, wearing wearing his own short brown hair, aged 24 years. James Wilmot, a middle seiz'd Man, of a swarthy Complexion, wearing a Wigg aged about 24 years, John Sullivan, an Irishman, middle seiz'd, well set, of a brown Complexion, wearing his own curl'd hair, aged about 26 years, James Lewis, a short black Man of a black Complexion, wearing a short dark Wigg, aged about 30 years. Whoever shall apprehend the said Deserters, or any of them, and them, or any of them safely convey to their abovesaid Capt. at Boston, or give any true Intelligence of them, so as the said Commander may have them again, shall have fourty Shillings reward for each, besides all necessary Charges paid.

And this is further to give notice to all Masters of Vessels, Masters of Houses, and all others, who shall detain, harbour, or keep the said Deserters or any of them, that they shall be Prosecuted to the extremity the Law admits in that behalf. And if the said Deserters will return to their Duty on board the said Saphir, they shall be freely forgiven.
The Boston News-Letter, From June 18, to June 18, 1711.

DEserted from Her Majesties Service of Capt. Fixhalls Company in the Regiment of the Hon. Col. Kane, a young man named Francis Thompson, aged about 19 years, of a dark brown Complexion, with a black short head of hair, in stature five Foot four Inches being very acute in discourse, with a short lisp on his Tongue; Cloth'd in a blew speckled Shirt, & short white Jacket. Whoever shall apprehend the said Deserter, & him safely convey to his said Commander at Nodles-Osland, or give any true Intelligence of him,

so as his Commander may have him again, shall have Three Pounds Reward, besides all necessary Charges paid.
   The Boston News-Letter, From July 2, to July 9, 1711.

DEserted from Her Majesties Service of Capt. Bridger's Company in the Regiment of the Hon. Col. Kane, John Slapp, Aged 30 years, about six foot high, of a dark brown Complexion, with his own brown Hair, of a thin Visage; Cloathed with the Regiments Cloathing. Whoever shall apprehend the said Deserter, and him safety Convey to his said Commander at Noddles-Island, or give any true Intelligence of him, so as his Commander may have him again, shall have Twenty Pounds Reward besides all necessary Charges paid. And this is further to give notice to all Masters of Ships or Vessels, or Masters of any House, who shall detain, harbour or keep him, shall be prosecuted to the extreamity the Law admits in that behalf. And if the said Deserter will return to his Captain again, he shall be freely pardoned.
   The Boston News-Letter, From July 9, to July 16, 1711.

RAN-away from her Master, John Jenkins of Boston Mariner, the 8th. Of this Instant August, a Carolina Indian Maid-Servant, Named Moll, Aged about 20 years, Speaks good English, a short thick fat Wench, having short Hair, is Lame in one of her Hips and goes Wadling; she has carried away considerable Money, & a bundle of Cloaths, viz. A Pladd Stuff Jacket, a dark colour'd Jersey Peticoat, & a striped Home-spun Peticoat Cotton & Wool; several Cotton & Linnen Shifts, with some others; several pair of Stockings, & several Lace Caps; blue Gloves, and Shoes about half wore out. Whoever shall take up the said Run-away, & her safety Convey to her abovesaid Master, or give any true Intelligence of her, so as her Master may have her again who Live at the North End of the Town in Shipstreet, shall be sufficiently rewarded besides as necessary Charges paid.
   The Boston News-Letter, From August 6 to August 13, 1711; From August 13, to August 20, 1711.

RAn-away from his Mistres, Sarah Gill of Boston Widow, the 5th of this Instant August, at Midnight, a Negro Man Servant, Named Jersey, about six Foot high, Speaks little or no English; his Cloathing is a Soldiers blue Coat fac'd with White, with Pewter Buttons, a dark coloured Watchcoat, a Speckl'd Shirt, with a Hat, and cloth colour'd Cap fac'd with blew. Whoever shall take up the said Run-away and him safely convey to his above said Mistres at the North-End of Boston in Fishstreet, or give any true Intelligence of him, so as his Mistres may have him again, shall have Satisfaction to Content.
   The Boston News-Letter, From August 20, to August 27, 1711.

RAn-away from their Master and Mistress at *Marblehead*, on Wednesday night, the 3d of this Instant *October* the following Indians, viz. from the Honourable *Nathaniel Norden* Esq. An Indian Man, named *Toney*, a thin favour'd Man, of a middle Stature, and pretty elderly Countenance; he carry'd with him a new fad coloured Kersey Coat, not lin'd, a pair of red Breeches, a coloured Cap, cloth Coat and Breeches, a black Hat, a pair of fad coloured yarn Stockings, and new French-fall Shoes.

From Mrs. *Elizabeth Brown* Widow, an Indian Woman, named *Rose*, a thick short Woman, her Neck, Arms and Leggs Marked with Flowers, after the Indian manner, and some streaks in her Cheeks; with a red Jacket, bound with edging, and a white Flannel Petticoat, aged about Forty Years.

Whoever shall apprehend the said Runaways, or either of them, and him or she safely convey to their Master or Mistress, or give any three Intelligence of them, or either of them, so as that their Master or Mistress shall have them, or either of them again, shall be sufficient Rewarded, besides all necessary Charges paid.

The Boston News-Letter, From October 8, to October 15, 1711.

RAN-away from his Master *Joshua Gee* the Ship Carpenter in Back street Boston, On Monday the Fifteenth Currant, a Servant Man named *James Crage*, a North Britain, aged about 22 Years, of a middle stature, well set, brown hair, has on a Kersey Jacket, brass buttons and leather breeches, he return'd on Saturday preceeding from the Late Expedition in Capt *Long*, and belong'd to Capt. *Barker* of the Honourable Col. *Vetch's* Regiment.

Whoever shall apprehend the said Run-away and him safely convey to his said Master, or give any true Intelligence to him; so as his Master may have him again, shall have Five Pounds Reward, besides all necessary Charges paid.

The Boston News-Letter, From October 15, to October 22, 1711; From October 22, to October 29, 1711.

RAn-away from his Master *James Lendall*, in Ann-Street Boston, Merchant, the 24th of this Instant October, a Lusty Young Man named *William Saulter*, aged about 16 or 17 years, speaks West Country, can neither Write nor Read; came from Topsham with Capt. *Robert Keen*, in the Pink Reserve; he hath light Hair, & light Complexion; Had on when he went away, a dark coloured Sea Jacket, blew Breeches, black and white woosted Stockings, a striped blew and white Shirt. Whoever shall apprehend the said Runaway and him safely Convey to his said Master, or give any true Intelligence of him, so as his Master may have him again, shall be sufficiently rewarded, besides all necessary Charges paid.

The Boston News-Letter, From October 22, to October 29, 1711.

A Carolina Indian Woman of a Middle Stature, Speaks very little English, Aged about 40 years, taken up as a Run-away; Inquire at the Post-Office in *Boston*, and know further.
   The Boston News-Letter, From December 10, to December 17, 1711.

RAn-away from his Master *John Oulton*, Merchant, in Marlborough-street, Boston, a Negro Man named *Harry*, of a middle Stature and well sett, with a Leather Jacket. Whoever shall apprehend the said Runaway, and him safely Convey to his said Master, or give any true Intelligence of him, so as his Master may have him again, shall be well rewarded, besides all necessary charges paid.
   The Boston News-Letter, From December 24, to December 31, 1711.
   See *The Boston News-Letter*, From June 22, to June 29, 1713.

1712

RAN-away from his Master the Reverend Mr. *John Wise* Minister of Jabacco, A Servant Man Named *James Holms*, Aged about 19 years, of a short thick body, Sanguin complexion, a grayish eye, light coloured straight hair, not cut on the Crown, nor very long; has on an old felt Hat, a new Home-spun gray cloath Coat, an old Druget Wastcoat, a pair of Home-spun Breeches, dark Sheeps gray coloured Stockings, a new pair of wooden-heel Shoes. Whoever shall apprehend the said Run-away Servant, and himself convey to his said Master at Jabacco, or to Mr. *Joseph Wise* Shopkeeper in Anne-Street Boston, or give any true Intelligence of him to either of them, so as his Master may have him again, shall have Fourty Shillings reward besides all necessary Charges paid.
   The Boston News-Letter, From January 26, to February 2, 1712.

R*U*N-away from *Thomas Palmer* Esq. A Lusty *N*egro man, *N*amed *Lester*, of about 25 years of Age, with a round ful Face, having on a Light coloured broad cloth Coat, Leather Breeches, and yarn Stockings. Whoever can give notice of him so that his Master at Boston may have him again, shall have all necessary charges paid, and well rewarded for their pains.
   The Boston News-Letter, From February 2, to February 9, 1712.

RAn-away from their Master, Capt. *Joseph Swadell*, Commander of the Lake Frigot, now in Boston, two Servant Men, viz. *David Rose,* a North Britain, aged about 18 years, of a short stature, speaks broken English, short black Hair, Sailors Habit, viz speckled Shirt, dark Jacket and Breeches; he Ran away the 21st Currant.
   And the other Servant an Apprentice, named *Joseph Riddell*, a South Britain; Ran-away the 23d Currant, aged about 19 years, a tall man, pretty

much pock broken, short black Hair, a black Wigg: with Sailors Habit, a speckled Handkerchief, and divers sorts of Cloaths.

Whoever shall take up the said Runaway Servants, and them safely convey to their said Master, Capt. *Swadell*, or to Capt. *Ebenezer Wentworth* at Mr. *David Jeffries*, Merchant, in Shrimpton's Lane, Boston, or can give any true Intelligence of them, so as their Master may have them again, shall have Thirty shillings Reward for David Rose, and Five Pounds Reward for Joseph Riddel, besides all necessary Charges paid.

The Boston News-Letter, From April 21, to April 28, 1712.

RAN-away from his Master *Joseph Diamond*, at Boston on Friday the second instant, a Servant Lad named *Robert Hyde*, aged about 17 Years, of a short Stature, very much Pock-broken, Lank hair. Whoever shall apprehend the said Run-away, and him safely convey to his said Master, at the House of Mr. *Florence Maccarty* in King Street Boston, or give any true Intelligence of him; so as his Master master may have him again, shall have Forty Shillings reward, besides all necessary Charges paid.

The Boston News-Letter, From April 28, to May 5, 1712.

RAn-away on Friday the 4th Currant, from his Master, John Jekyll Esqr Collector of Her Majesty's Customs in Boston, a Servant Lad, named James Blair, a North Britain, aged about 15 years: Had on a light Wigg, blew Coat lin'd with yellow. Whoever shall apprehend the said Runaway, and him safely Convey to his said Master, or give any true Intelligence of him, so as his Master may have him again, shall have Twenty Shillings Reward, besides all necessary Charges paid. And all Masters of Vessels, and others are desired not to harbour or entertain the said Run-away, else they shall be prosecuted to the extremity the Law admits of in that Case.

The Boston News-Letter, From June 30, to July 7, 1712.

RAN-away from this Masters in Connecticut Colony the following Negro's and a Spanish Indian, *viz* from Mr. *George Phillips* in Middle-town Two Negro Men one Named *Franklin* aged about Thirty years, of a middle stature, speaks good English, well Apparelled, one finger on one hand Stump'd. The other Negro Named *Harry* aged about 20 years, streight Lim'd, has on a blew Shirt, Red Jacket, Castor Hat, Speaks broken English, and well Apparelled.

Ran-away also from Mr. *Jehiel Hawley* of Durham, A Spanish Indian Man, Named *Peter* aged about Twenty years, of a Middle Stature, a Cheridary Wastcoat, A Soldiers blew Coat fac'd with red, the Cape taken off, he speaks very good English.

And on the 18th of July, Ran-away from Mr. *Ebenezer Hubbard* of said Middletown, a Negro Man nam'd *Peter*, aged about 28 years, a Slim

Fellow, thin fac'd, having a Skare on the back of one of his hands near the Nuckles, with a Slit on one of his Ears, speaks good English.

Whoever shall apprehend said Run-aways or any of them, and him or them safety convey to his or their said Masters, or give any true Intelligence, of them or either of them, so as their Masters may have them again, shall have Fourty Shillings reward for each Servant, besides all necessary Charges paid.

The Boston News-Letter, From August 11, to August 18, 1712.

RAN-away from his Master *John Staniford* of Boston, Tailor, the second of this Instant September, a North British young Man Servant, named *James Watt*, aged about 20 years, broad Spoken, short and well set, light brown straight hair: he had on an old felt Hat, with a hole on one side, a Searge Coat, lin'd with light coloured linen, a linen Jacket with red and white stripes; light coloured Broad Cloth Breeches, gray yarn Stockings, Square to'd Shoes with Steel Buckles.

Whoever shall apprehend the said Run-away Servant, and him safely convey to his said Master at his House in Trea-Mount Street, near the Orange Tree, or give any true Intelligence of him, so as his Master may have him again; shall have fourty Shillings reward besdies all necessary charges paid.

The Boston News-Letter, From September 1, to Septenber 8, 1712.

RAN-away from his Master *Edward Wanton* of Scituate Ship Carpenter, the Second of this Instant September, A Molatto Man Servant, Named *Daniel*, about 19 years of Age, pretty Tall, speaks good English, thick curl'd Hair with a bush behind, if not lately cut off, black Hat, cotton and linen Shirt: he had with him two Coats, one a home-made dy'd Coat, the other a great Coat dy'd a muddy colour, strip'd home-spun Jacket, Kersey Breeches, gray Stockings, french fall Shoes.

Whoever shall take up said Runaway Servant and him safety Convey to his above-said Master at Scituate, or give any true Intelligence of him, so as his Master may have him again, shall have Satisfaction to Content, besides all necessary Charges paid.

The Boston News-Letter, From September 22, to September 29, 1712.
See *The Boston News-Letter*, From May 17, to May 24, 1714, and *The Boston News-Letter*, From August 16, to August 23, 1714.

RAN-away from his Master *Samuel Wenworth* in Ann-Street Boston, Merchant, on Thursday last the 16th of this Instant October, *John Bennet* aged about 30 years, a slender Fellow, thin Fac'd, swarthy Complection, black lank Hair, has on a brow Coat trim'd with black, an old black Hat, he speaks broad west Country.

Whoever shall apprehend the said Run-away, and him safely convey to his said Master, or give any true Intelligence of him so as his Master may have him again, shall be sufficiently rewarded besides all necessary Charges paid.
The Boston News-Letter, From October 13, to October 20, 1712.

RAN-away at Boston about Ten days agoe from the Bristol Gally *John Hillhouse* Master, Two Servant Men, *viz. Edward Bryant*, a middle Statur'd man aged about 25 years, black Complexion, black Hair, had on dark coloured Westcoat & Breeches, yarn Stockings. The other *Thomas Dopson*, a breck Maker by Trade, middle Stature, aged about 35 years, light brown Hair, has a sore upon the Fore-finger of his right hand, light colour'd broad cloth Coat. Whoever shall apprehend the said Run-away Servants or either of them, and him of them safely convey to Capt *Gilbert Bant* at his House in Middle-Street Boston, or give true Intelligence of one or both of them, so as that Capt. *Bant* may have one or either of them again, shall be sufficiently rewarded, besides all necessary charges paid.
The Boston News-Letter, From December 22, to December 29, 1712.

1713

DEserted the 31st of December from the Caswal Frigot *Arthur Savage* Master at Boston, the following Sailors, *viz. Charles Parris*, a tall black thin Visage fellow, with dark hair, about 40 years of age. *Stephen Row* a short thick pock-broken fellow, having but one eye, and no hair, about 23 years of Age. *John Lumbart*, a tall thin pock-broken Youth, light short hair, long Visage, about 20 years of Age. *Peter Riggin*, a thick short black fellow, very fresh Complexion, with black straight hair, speaks very broad West County, about 24 years of Age. *James Letten*, a little short thin fellow, black hair, round shouldred, hard of hearing, about 35 years of Age.

Any Person bringing the said Deserters or any one of them, or giving any true Information to the said *Arthur Savage* that so all or any one of them may be found, shall have all Satisfaction and Charges paid, and Five pounds reward for either *Charles Parris*, or *James Letten*.

If either or all of the other Three, *viz. Stephen Row, John Lumbart*, or *Peter Riggin* will return to their Service on Board said Ship in 8 days they shall be freely Pardoned and their Wages fully run on as if not deserted.
Boston Jan. 2d. 1713.

The Boston News-Letter, From December 28, 1712, to January 4, 1713.

RAn-away on Monday night the 11th of this Instant January at Boston from the Ship Benjamin of London *Thomas Redford* Commander, *Morrice Beals*

Boatswain, aged Twenty four years, of a middle Stature, short dark hair, wears sometimes a Wigg, carried with him his Chest and Bedding. Whoever shall apprehend the said Run-away and him safely convey to his said Commander, or give any true Intelligence of him so as his Commander may have him again, shall have Forty Shillings reward, besides all necessary Charges paid.
The Boston News-Letter, From January 11, to January 18, 1713.

DDserted [*sic*] from his Master Christopher *Redshaw* Commander of the Ship Loyal Bartholomew, at the Long Wharff, Boston, *John Hardin*, A Young Man of about 20 Years of Age, of a middle Size, Blackish Complexion; he has on a black Wigg, and Cinnamon coloured Cloths: Whoever shall take him up or can give Information that his said Master might have him again shall have Forty Shillings Reward.
The Boston News-Letter, From March 1, to March 8, 1713.

RAn-away from Captain *Thomas Elbridg*e out of his Ship which lies near the South Battery in *Boston*, on Friday Night the 19th of this Instant *March, William Netherton* Ship Carpenter, aged about 28 Years; who Stole and carryed away with him Sundry Ship Carpenters Tools, and Merchandizes. He is a Man of a middle Stature, indifferent thin in Body and Face, short Hair, of a Sandy colour, wears an indifferent light Wigg, pretty long pale Visage, has on a light colour'd cloth Coat, trim'd with black and Frogs of the same, a Yellowish cloth Wastcoat, blue Breeches, a white Shirt, black and white mixt Stockings. Whoever shall apprehend the said Run-away, and him safely convey to the said Capt. *Elbridge*, or give any true Intelligence of him, or the Goods he Stole, so as that he may have them again, shall have Fourty Shillings reward besides all necessary Charges paid.
The Boston News-Letter, From March 15, to March 22, 1713.

RAn-away last week from his Master Capt. *John Corney* of Boston, A Servant man named *Benjamin Wallis*, aged about Twenty years, well set, full fac'd, beetle brow'd, pock fretten, brown hair curles at the end; had on a gray cloth Suite trim'd with black; and carry'd with him to the value of Twenty Pounds in Money and Goods. Whosoever shall apprehend the said Run-away, and him safely convey to Mr. *John Frissel* of Boston aforesaid Merchant, or give any true Intelligence of him; or what he carried away, so as his Master may have him or what he carry'd, again; shall have Fifty Shillings reward besides all necessary Charges paid.
The Boston News-Letter, From May 25, to June 1, 1713. See *The Boston News-Letter*, From July 13, to July 20, 1713.

RAn-away from her Master *Thomas Moffet* of Boston Merchant, on Wednesday last the Tenth Currant, a Young Servant Woman, named *Mary Sutton*, of a Low Stature, light hair, had on a light Manto & Pettycoat lin'd with red, or a yellow & white mixt stuffe without lyning; she came over a Servant in the Ship Tiverton Galley from Bristol, and is hereby advertised within three days from the Publishing hereof to return to her former Service, & she shall be forgiv'n, but if otherwise she does not return; Whosoever shall apprehend the said Servant and her safely convey to her abovesaid Master, or give any true Intelligence of her, so as her Master may have her again, shall be sufficiently rewarded besides all necessary charges paid.

The Boston News-Letter, From June 8, to June 15, 1713.

RAn-away on Monday last the 22d Currant from his Master *John Oulton* of Boston Merchant, a Negro man call'd *Harry*, he is short & well set, speaks good English, he hath on a Kersy Jacket lin'd with Red. Whoever apprehends the said Runaway, and him safely Convey to his said Master, or can give any true Intelligence of him so as his Master may have him again, shall have Twenty Shillings reward, besides all necessary charges paid.

The Boston News-Letter, From June 22, to June 29, 1713. See *The Boston News-Letter*, From December 24, to December 31, 1711.

RAn-away from his Master, *Thomas Palmer* Esqr. at Boston on Tuesday last the 23d of this Instant June, a Negro Man named *Lester*, aged about 25 years, of a full round face, having on a light coloured Broad-cloth Coat, and a yellow Broad-cloth Jacket, with Gold Buttons, and a pair of old blue and white linen Breeches, a pair of dark coloured homspun yarn Stockings, round to'd Shoes.

Whoever shall apprehend the said Run-away, and him safely convey to his said Master, or give any true Intelligence of him so as his Master may have him again shall be sufficiently rewarded besides all necessary Charges paid.

The Boston News-Letter, From June 22, to June 29, 1713.

IN our Number 476, the first of *June* last, there was a Advertisement of a Run-away Servant from his Master, Capt. *John Corney* of Boston, the 28th Day of May last, Named *Benjamin Wallis*, aged about 20 years, of a middle Stature, well Sett, full Fac'd, beetle Brow'd, Pock Fretten, brown Hair, curles at the end; had on a new gray Cloth Suit, trim'd with black, and carried with him to the Value of Twenty Pounds in Money and Goods. Whosoever shall apprehend the said Run-away Servant, and him safely convey to his said Master, or to Mr. *John Frissel* Merchant in Boston aforesaid, or give any true Intelligence of him, so as his Master may have

him again, or what he carryed away, shall have Five Pounds reward, besides all Necessary Charges Paid.
The Boston News-Letter, From July 13, to July 20, 1713. See *The Boston News-Letter*, From May 25, to June 1, 1713.

RAn-away at Boston on Monday last the 27th Day of July, from his Master *Adam Brown* Merchant, A North British Servant Man named *Charles Campbell* aged about 17 years, of a fair Complexion, had on gray Cloaths, being a Taylor by Trade. Whoever shall apprehend the said Run-away and him safely convey to his said Master, or can give any true Intelligence of him, so as his Master may have him again, shall be sufficiently rewarded besides all necessary Charges paid.
The Boston News-Letter, From July 23, to August 3, 1713; From August 17, to August 24, 1713.

RAn-away the 19th of this Instant *August* from *William Hirst* of *Salem*, Esqr, a Jersey Boy, named *John Amy*, about 15 years of age, well sett, full Leggs, short brown Hair, Ozenbrigs Jacket and Breeches Cotton & Linen Shirt, a Cap on his head, bare-foot and bare-leg'd. Whoever shall apprehend the said Run-away and him safely convey to his said Master, or to Mr. *Grove Hirst* of *Boston* Merchant, or give any true Intelligence of him so as his Master may have him again, shall be sufficiently rewarded, besides all necessary charges paid
The Boston News-Letter, From August 17, to August 24, 1713.

Lately Run-away at *Ipswich* from his Master *Richard Goss*, a pretty Tall Fellow, Named *William Stone*, dark Hair, has one Leg biger than the other, had on a little Hat, a fad coloured Jacket and a Ticken one under it; he is a North Country man, bought of Capt. *Lake*, and Mr. *Moffat*: Whoever shall apprehend the said Run-away and him safely convey to his said Master, or to Mr. *John Smith* of *Boston* Merchant, or give any true intelligence of him so as his Master may have him again, shall have Twenty Shillings reward besides all necessary charges paid.
The Boston News-Letter, From August 17, to August 24, 1713.

RAn-away on Monday evening last, the 31 day of August, from his Master *John Brand* Watch-maker on the North-side of the Town-house in King-street, Boston, A German Servant Man, named John Copler, aged about 26 years, having a Cast with his Left Eye, with a wildish Look, well set, great Legs being something Lamish in his right foot by an old sore above his Ancle; broken French also; Dutch is his natural Language: He had on a white dowlas shirt, mark'd G C in the bosom, a dark Cinamon coloured Jacket, the skirts lined with red shalloon, Linen Ozinbrigs long Breeches, black Stockings, French fall Shoes. He was seen to carry away other Cloaths, and perhaps may alter his Habit. Whoever shall apprehend the said Run-away, and him safely convey to his said Master, or give any true Intelligence of him, so as his Master may have him again, shall have five Pounds reward besides all necessary charges paid.

The Boston News-Letter, From August 31, to September 7, 1713.

RAn-away on the Third of *September* Currant, from his Master *Richard Draper* of Corn-Hill, *Boston*, Shop-keeper, A Spanish Indian Man-Servant Named *James*, a Tall, Well-sett fellow, about 30 Years of Age: He had on when he went away a course broad-cloth Jacket, with a large Patch in the back, and linen strip'd Breeches.

Ran-away also with him, another Indian Man, Named *Toby*, a Tall Slimb fellow, thin Visage: He had on when he went away a Home-spun strip'd Jacket, leather Breeches, home-spun Stockings, New Shoes.

Whoever shall apprehend the said Run-aways, or either of them, and him or them safely convey to Mr. *Richard Draper* aforesaid, or give any true Intelligence of both or either of them, so as that the said Master *Draper* may have them again, shall have Forty Shillings for each, besides all necessary Charges paid.

The Boston News-Letter, From September 7, to September 14, 1713.

RAn-away from his Master Capt, *Jonathan Dows* of Charlestown, on Monday the 21st of September last, A Servant-Man called *John Yowelen* aged about 18 years, low stature, pretty thick, down look, short thick coloured hair, a little curl'd, had on a turned dark coloured broad cloth Coat, a light coloured pair of Breeches or striped linnen ones, speaks plain English a little upon the West-Country Tone, pretends to be a Weaver, tho' a Ship-Carpenter when he Runaway. Whoever shall apprehend the said Run-away, and him safely convey to his abovesaid Master, or give any true Intelligence of him, so as his Master may have him again, shall be sufficiently rewarded besides all necessary charges paid.

The Boston News-Letter, From October 5, to October 12, 1713.

RAn-away at Boston from the Briganteen Seaflower *Thomas Plaisted* Master, *Thomas Read* a middle sized man, aged 40 years or more, with lank short brownish hair, mixed with gray, he had on a light coloured Fustian Frock, striped Jacket and Breeches, was formerly Master of a Sloop belonging to Antequa. Whoever shall apprehend the said Runaway, and him safety convey to the said *Thomas Plaisted* or Mr. *Adam Beath* in Union-Street Boston, or can give any true Intelligence of him so as he may have him again, shall receive the reward of Forty Shillings, with reasonable charges.

The Boston News-Letter, From October 5, to October 12, 1713.

RAn-away on Tuesday Last the 15th Currant at Boston, from his Master Capt. *Edward Blacket* Commander of Her Majesties Ship Phoenix, A Servant Man, Named *Thomas Wight*, aged about Twenty one Years, a slender fellow, light brown hair, with a Seamans jacket, wearing a cloath Cap. Whoever shall apprehend the said Run-away and him safely convey to *John Jekyl Esqr*. Her Majesties Collector at Boston, or give any true Intelligence of him so as his Master may have him again, shall be sufficiently rewarded, besides all necessary charges paid.

The Boston News-Letter, From December 14, to December 21, 1713.

1714

There is one *Mary Beats*, that lived some time with Mr. *Elkanah Pembroke* of Newport Rhode-island, that is gone from him deeply in his Debt, which calls herself by several Names: This is to give Notice to all Persons whosoever, not to Trust, Credit or Harbour the aforesaid *Mary Beats*, which goes under the Name of *Henaretha Pembroke*, on the account of the aforesaid *Elkanah Pembroke*.

The Boston News-Letter, From January 10, to January 17, 1714.

RAn-away from his Master *John Scott* of Newport Rhode-Island, a Molatto Man named *Daniel* born in New-England, and by Trade a Ship Carpenter, formerly belonging to *Edward Wanton* of Situate, he is about 20 years of Age, indifferent tall, and slender, bushy hair, carried with him white and speckled Shirts, Sea Cloaths and Bedding, and other good Cloaths as a Cinnamon coloured Broad-Cloath Coat trim'd with Froggs, Ticking Breeches, Worsted Stockings &c. Whoever shall apprehend said Runaway and bring him to his said Master, or secure him and give notice to his Master aforesaid that he may have him again shall have reasonable Satisfaction and Charges paid.

The Boston News-Letter, From May 17, to May 24, 1714. See *The Boston News-Letter*, From September 22, to September 29, 1712, and *The Boston News-Letter*, From August 16, to August 23, 1714.

RAn away from Lieut. Col. *Livingston*, the 3d Day of this Instant June, *Thomas Davis* an English Man Servant, of a thick short Stature, having strait Brown Hair, by Trade a Joyner and Carpenter, carried away with him a Blew Coat, Fac'd with Red, with wrought Bath Mettal Butons Gilt, and a Blew Wastcoat, and a light coloured Suit trimed with Black, a Sett of Joyners and Carpenters Tools to a considerable Value; also Stole away with him a Bay Mare, with a small Star in her Forhead, one White Foot behind, Branded on the Shoulder L, and on the Buttock the Letter L with a dash or stroak through it; he also Stole a Silver Spoon, the Crest Graven on it a hare with a bridle & sadle. He sometimes has called himself Thomas Roberts, he has a Red cloth Portmanteau with Buttons to it. Whosoever shall take said Servant and secure him so that his said Master may have him again, or bring him to Mr. John Dixwell Gold-smith in Union Street, Boston: or to New-London to his said Master, shall have Five Pounds Money for a Reward, and have all his Charges born.

The Boston News-Letter, From May 31, to June 7, 1714.

RAn-away from his Master Capt. *Henry Shearbourne* at Boston on Wednesday the 26th of May last, a Servant Man, Named, *William Mandevell* aged about 24 years, a Strong well set man, full fac'd, some pock holes in his Face, gray Ey'd, red Beard, wears a Wigg, and a light cloath Coat, being a Tallow Chandler by Trade. Deserted also from the said Capt. *Sherburn's* Ship, the Sophia, the two following Sailors, viz. *George Vintiman* aged 28 years, a middle seize well set Man, round Visage, Fresh coloured, wearing a light Wigg. The other *James Morris* aged 30 years, a Tall thin Man, pale Fac'd, with long streight black Hair, and a Brown Drugget Coat. Whoever shall apprehend the said Runaways and Deserters or either of them, and him them or any of them safely bring to the said Capt. *Sherburne*, or give any true Intelligence of them or any of them, so at the said Capt. may have them again; shall have Three Pounds reward for each Man, besides reasonable Charges paid.

The Boston News-Letter, From May 31, to June 7, 1714.

RAn-away on Wednesday the 26th Day of May last and Beverly, from his Master *Joseph Tuck*. A Negro Man Servant, Named *Peter*, a slim Fellow not very Tall, goes a little Lane, lost his Fore-upper Teeth, has on a close-bodied Coat, and Pale Copper-coloured Jacket, Coat and Jacket tarr'd in some Place, white Worsted Stockings, Leather Breeches, and French fall Shoes, the heels goes very much back: He was formerly Servant to Mr. *Pepperel* on Kittery, Mr. *Boreman* Tanner in Cambridge, Mr. *Morecock* in Boston, and Mr. *Hubbard* of Middleton.

Whoever shall apprehend the said Run-away, and him safely Convey to his said Master, or to Mr. *Nathan Howell* Merchant in Boston, or give any true Intelligence of him so as his Master may have him again, shall be Sufficiently Rewarded, besides all necessary Charges paid.

The Boston News-Letter, From June 7, to June 14, 1714.

RAn away from his Master *John Bridger* Esq; on Tuesday the 22d of this Instant June, a Scotch Man named *John Grumin*, of a low Stature, Speaks broken English, Long Vizage, light Brown strait Hair, gray Ey'd, white Brows; having on a Cloth Westcoat Tarr'd, a white Shirt, white Ozinbrige Breeches. Whosoever shall apprehend the said Run-away and him safely convey to his said Master in Boston, or give any true Intelligence of him, so as his Master may have him again, shall have Forty Shillings reward, and all reasonable Charges paid.

The Boston News-Letter, From June 21, to June 28, 1714.

RAn-away from his Master *John Cotta* of Boston Taylor, on Thursday last the 5th Currant, a Servant Man Named, *Robert Earland* aged about Twenty years, of a short thick Stature speaks thick West-Country, short brownish Hair, has on an Ash coloured Drugget Coat trim'd with black, Cloth Jacket, stript Ticken Breeches, a new Castor Hat. Whoever shall apprehend the said Runaway and him safely convey to his said Master, or give any true Intelligence of him, so as his Master may have him again, shall have Three Pounds Reward, besides all necessary Charges paid.

The Boston News-Letter, From August 2, to August 9, 1714.

RAn-away from his Master *John Scott*, the 17th of this Instant August, a Molatto Man named *Daniel*, formerly belonging to *Edward Wanton*, of Situate; he is indifferent Tall and Slender, by Trade a Shipwright, but 'tis thought Designs for Sea. Whosoever shall stop, take up, or secure the said Run-away, and bring him or give Notice of him to hs said Master at Newport, Rhode-Osland, shall be well rewarded, and reasonable Charges paid.

The Boston News-Letter, From August 16, to August 23, 1714. See *The Boston News-Letter*, From September 22, to September 29, 1712, and *The Boston News-Letter*, From May 17, to May 24, 1714.

RAn away from his Master *Richard Hall* Perriwigg Maker in Kingstreet, Boston, *Henry Atherton* aged Sixteen Years, had on a Cinnamon coloured cloth Coat, Lank Hair, black Crape in his Hat, slender Body. Whosoever secures him so that he may be had again, shall have Forty Shillings reward and reasonable Charges paid.

The Boston News-Letter, From August 16, to August 23, 1714.

RAn away on Sabbath day Night, the 29th of *August* last past, from his Master *Elisha Odlin* of *Salem*, Innholder, an English Man servant, named *Anthony Pearl*, about Sixteen years of Age, well sett, short bushy black Hair, his Right hand has been burnt, and the fingers drawn up: He has on a Kersey Coat with brass Buttons, a linnen Jacket and Breeches, French fall Shoes. Whosoever shall apprehend the said Runaway, and him safely Convey to his said Master, living at the Sign of the Globe in *Salem*, or to

Mr. *Ezekiel Cleasby*, near the Salutation Tavern in *Boston*, shall have Forty Shillings Reward, and all necessary Charges paid.
The Boston News-Letter, From August 30, to September 6, 1714.

RAn-away last Monday from her Master *Peter Barbour* of Boston a Lusty Tall Servant Maid about 22 Years of Age, Named *Catherine Cayrl*, She had dark black & white Stuff Cloaths on, black Hair. Whoever shall take up the said Run-away and her safety Convey to her said Master, or give any true Intelligence of her so as her Master may have her again shall be sufficiently rewards besides all necessary Charges paid.
The Boston News-Letter, From September 27, to October 4, 1714.

DEserted from His Majesties Ship Success Capt. *Mead* Commander, at *Boston*, of Friday Last the 26th Currant, One *Robert Perry*, an Irish Man, aged 28 Years, having Stollen and Carry'd with him out of the Ship several Goods: He is of a Middle Stature, wears a Light Wigg, has a wound on the right side of his Mouth, has on a dark Frize Coat with Loops. Whoever shall apprehend the said Deserter, and him Safety Convey to the said Commander, or any of the Officers of the said Ship, or give Intelligence of Him, so as the said Commander may have him again, shall have Twenty Shillings reward besides all necessary Charges paid.
The Boston News-Letter, From November 22, to November 29, 1714.

Boston, Our last gave you Account, as 'twas reported at *Piscataqua* of a Vessel being long at Casko Bay, and Four Men saved that were upon the Road to *Boston*, since which we are informed, there was no Vessel lost, but the Report came by one *James Robison*, alias *Stewart*, a Saylor, who had Run away from some Vessel at *Piscataqua,* and Reported not only upon the Road between *Piscataqua* and *Boston*, the one Vessel was Cast-away, bit likewise Reported at *Boston* that there was Two Vessels lost, and being Apprehended upon it at *Boston,* and put into Goal, he Confest himself Guilt to Spreading False Reports, for which he was Sentenc'd according to Law in that Case, and stands committed till it is performed.
The Boston News-Letter, From December 13, to December 20, 1714.

1715

RAn away from his Master, *William Borden* Ship-Carpenter of Newport on Rhode-Island, on the 23d of April last, a very likely Spanish Indian Lad, without any Marks on his Face, had long Hair, looks very like our Indians, named *Caesar*, speaks Indifferent good English, aged about Eighteen Years, had on a brown Kersey Jacket, a pair of old Broad-Cloth Breeches pretty near the same Colour, an old Beaver Hat, and a course Linen Shirt.

Whoever shall apprehend the said Indian Lad, or give any true Intelligence of him, so as his said Master may have him again, shall be Rewarded to their Satisfaction, besides all Necessary Charges paid.
The Boston News-Letter, From May 2, to May 9, 1715.

WHereas *Mary Mason* Wife of Mr. *Alexander Mason* of New-port on Rhode-Island in New England, Vintner, about Eighteen Months ago Departed and Elop'd from her said Husband, and having fail'd in her Attempt upon his Life, continues still to ruine his Estate: Therefore this is to give Notice to all Persons whatsoever that they do not Credt her for the future, for as much as the aforesaid *Alexander Mason* will pay no Debts of her Contracting, he having allows her a sufficient Maintenance otherwise.
The Boston News-Letter, From May 16-23, 1715.

ON Friday last the 17th of this Instant June, Deserted at Marblehead from the Ship Hanibal of London, Capt. *Patrick Aikman* Commander, the following Sailors, viz *Henry Miller* a thick gross Man, much disfigured with the Small Pox, bushy red Hair, several black spots in his Face, aged about Thirty five years. *John Price* a Tall slender Man of a fresh Complexion, with curl'd black hair, aged about Twenty five years. T*homas Bryant* a middle sieiz'd Man of a dark brown Complexion, aged about Twenty years, and *Hugh Chappinter* a short thick Man of a Pale Complexion with brown hair, aged about Twenty three years. Whoever shall apprehend the said Deserters, or any of them, and them or him safely convey to the abovesaid Commander at Marblehead, or to Mr. *Francis Borland* of *Boston* Merchant, or that can give any true Intelligence of the said Deserters, or of any one of them to the said Commander or to Mr. *Borland* so as that they or any one of them may be Apprehended shall receive Three Pounds Reward for each Man, besides all necessary Charges paid.
The Boston News-Letter, From June 13, to June 20, 1715.

RAn away on Friday Morning last the 24th Instant, from their Master, *Samuel Gardner* of Boston, Taylor, Two North-Britain Men Servants, *viz David Magill*, about 19 or 20 Years of age, well Sett, a Fresh Countenance, his Hair lately cut off, and wears a Worsted Cap Speck'd at the Edges. *Alexander Dameeby*, about 19 Years of Age, very short Stature, great Legs, straight Dark Brown Hair; they have Coats alike, of Brown Cloth, Trim'd plain, with five or six Buttons before, one or both has Leather Breeches, Yarn Stockings. Whoever shall take up the said Run-aways, and them safety Convey to their said Master in Fish-Street Boston, near the Old North Meeting-House, or can give any True Intelligence of both or either of them

so as they their said Master may have them again, shall have Three Pounds Reward besides all Necessary Charges.
    The Boston News-Letter, From June 20, to June 27, 1715.

RAn away of Saturday last from his Master John Jekyll, Esq; Collector of His Majesty's Customs at Boston, a Servant Man, named *Thomas White*, Aged about 24 Years, a Lusty Young Fellow, with his own Light Hair. Whoever shall apprehend the said Runaway and him safely convey to his said Master, or give any True Intelligence of him, so as his Master may have him again, shall have Twenty Shillings reward, besides all necessary Charges paid.
    The Boston News-Letter, From July 18, to July 25, 1715; From July 25, to August 1, 1715; From August 1, to August 8, 1715.

RAN-away at *Marblehead* on Wednesday Morning the 10th of this Instant *August*, from his Master *Peter Trevalle*, an English Man Servant, Named *William Lowder*, aged about 20 Years, speaks good English, a well set fellow, thick Streight head of Hair, of a dark colour, had on a blue and white speckl'd Shirt, a home-spun stript jacket, fad colour'd cloth Breeches, mended in the Seat, and on the left knee with a patch on defferent colour, gray yarn Hose, a felt Hat, and a new pair of square to'd Shoes. Whoever shall apprehend the said Runaway, and him safely convey to his said Master at Marblehead or unto *James Marriner* in Dock-square *Boston*, Shop-keeper, or give any true Intelligence of his to his Master, or *Mr. Marriner*, so as they his Master may have him again, shall have *Forty Shillings* Reward, besides all necessary charges paid.
    The Boston News-Letter, From August 8, to August 15, 1715.

RAn-away at Portsmouth, New-Hampshire from his Master *Jonathan Studley*, on Saturday the 27th of August past a Portuguese Molatto Servant Man, aged about 22 Years, a short thick fellow, black Curl'd hair, has on an out-side Jacket fad coloured, old and broken, he speaks but little English: Whoever shall apprehend the said Run-away and him safelyt convey to his said Master, or give any true Intelligence of him so as his said Master, or give any true Intelligence rewarded to Content, besides all necessary Charges paid.
    The Boston News-Letter, From August 29, to September 5, 1715.

RAn away at Newport Rhode-Island, on the 9th of Octoiber in the Night, from his Master *John Jipson*, a North-British Man Servant, Named *Laurence Ross*, a Wigg-Maker by Trade, aged about 20 Years, who speaks broad Scotch, a tall, slim, thin Favoured Fellow, a little Pock-broken, wears a black Campaign Wigg, had on a dark coloured Drugget Coat, Jacket and

Breeches, a Caster Hat, Worsted Stockings of a light Color, square to'd Shoes, and Silver Buckles, and good Linnen on, and now hears that he has Changed his Name, and calls himself *John Blair*. Whoever shall apprehend the said Run-away, and him safely convey to his Master at Newport, or give any true Intelligence of him, so that his Master may have him again, shall have Fifty Shillings Reward, besides all necessary Charges paid.

The Boston News-Letter, From October 10, to October 17, 1715.

1716

RAn-away on the 3d Currant, at Boston, from the Mary Briganteen *George Marshell* Master, a Scotch Servant Lad, Named *Andrew Gibson* aged about Twelve Years, with his own short brown hair, has on Sea Cloths, & all Masters of Vessels and other Persons whatsoever, are hereby notified not to entertain him. Whoever shall apprehend the said Run-away and him safely convey to his said Master, or give any true Intelligence of him; so as his Master may have him again shall be sufficiently rewarded, besides all necessary Charges paid.

The Boston News-Letter, From April 2, to April 9, 1716.

ON the Third Instant one *William Parker* formerly of Cape-Codd, hired a light gray Horse, about 8 years old, 14 hands high, of Mrs. *Emm Peach* at Marblehead, only to go for Salem, but as yet no News of him or Horse, the said *Parker* is of a middle Stature, fresh colour, and dark colour'd Hair, and 'tis supposed he's gone to Rhode-Island. Whoever shall take up said Man and Man and Horse, or either, are desired to give Notice thereof to the said Mrs. *Peach* for which they shall be satisfy'd to Content.

The Boston News-Letter, From May 21, to May 28, 1716.

RAn-away at Boston the 21st of May last from the Ship Hampshire, whereof Capt. *Abel Combs* was late Commander, a Servant Lad named *William Swelling*, aged about 15 years, speaks West-Country, of a dull, freckled Complexion, with short brown hair, has on a gray Sea Jacket, double breasted, with flat white mettle Buttons. Whoever shall apprehend the said Runaway and his safely convey to Mr. *John Powell* at No. 5 Warehouse on the Long Wharffe at the and of King-Street Boston, or give any true Intelligence of him to the said Mr. *Powell*, shall be sufficiently rewarded, besides all necessary Charges paid.

The Boston News-Letter, From May 28, to June 4, 1716.

RAn away on the 25 th of June past at Groton in Connecticut Colony, from his Master the Reverend Mr. *Ephraim Woodbridge*, a Negro Man, named *Pompy*, who formerly belong'd to Mr. *Franklin* late of Boston; he is of a

middle Stature, speaks good English, had on a speckled woolen Shirt, a pair of black Breeches, and a pair of Linen ones underneath. Whoever shall apprehend the said Run-away, and him safely convey to his said Master, or give true Intelligence of him so as his Master may have him again, shall be sufficiently rewarded besides all necessary Charges paid.
The Boston News-Letter, From June 25, to July 2, 1716.

RAn-away on Monday the 30th of July past from his Master *Azor Gale* of Marblehead, a Servant Man named *Thomas Chambers*, Aged about 25 Years, pretty Tall and Spair, thick darkish coloured hair, having a Cast with one Eye, had on a dark coloured Kersey Coat pretty long, Strip'd Jacket and Breeches, Gray yarn Stockings, old Shoes with Strings in them. Whoever shall apprehend the said Runaway, and him safely convey to his said Master, or give any true Intelligence of him, so as his Master may have him again, shall be sufficiently rewarded, besides all necessary Charges paid,
The Boston News-Letter, From July 30, to August 6, 1716.

RAn-away from Mr. *Thomas Selby* in Boston, on the 25th of July last, a North Britain Man Servant, Named *Davie Dowie*, a Perriwig-maker, of a middle Stature, fresh Colour, aged about 24 Years, wears a Perriwig, a Cinamon coloured Coat, Round to'd Shoes. Whoever shall apprehend the said Runaway, and him safely convey to his said Master, or give any true Intelligence of him, so as his Master may have him again, shall have Ten Pounds Reward.
The Boston News-Letter, From July 30, to August 6, 1716; From August 20, to August 27, 1716; From August 27, to September 3, 1716. The scond and third ads show the advertiser's name as Silby.

RAn away from Mr. *David Hillard* of Stonington, a Negro Man, called *Mingo*, aged about Thirty one Years; with an Indian Squaw, called *Milly*, that ran from Mr. *John Swan* of said Town, both speak good English, the Negro Man is of a pale colour, he has on Home-spun Cloathes of a Russel colour. Whoever takes up said Negro Man, and him safely keep, so that his Master may have him again, or give true Intelligence of them, shall have Three Pounds Reward, besides all necessary Charges paid.
The Boston News-Letter, From August 20, to August 27, 1716.

RAn-away from his Master *John Cotta* of *Boston* Taylor, on the 16th Day of *August* last, A Man Servant, Named *Robert Alcock* of Richmond in Yorkshire, aged 36 Years, of Middle Stature, black short curl'd hair, of a very ill Complexion, having lost the sight of his left Eye; has on a Sirtwit Coat with Frogs, drab colour, linen Jacket, and blue knit Breeches, worsted Stockings, and Castor Hat. Whoever shall apprehend the said Yorkshire,

and him safely convey to his Master, or give any true Intelligence of him, so as his Master may have him again, shall have Three Pounds reward, besides all necessary Charges paid.
The Boston News-Letter, From August 27, to September 3, 1716.

RAn away from their Masters in Boston, the 15th of this Instant September, at Night, Three Carolina Indians, viz, Two Men-Servants and One Woman, they speak but broken English, about 30 Years of age or above; one from Mr. *Samuel Adams* Malster, named *James*, well sett, he hath a Leather Jacket, black Stockings. Another of them Servants to Mr. *Nehemiah Yeals* Ship-Carpenter, named *Robin*, with double Breasted jacket, Leather Breeches; they both have other Cloaths with them. The Indian Woman Servant to Mr. *Thomas Salter* Cordwainer, named *Amareta*, pretty Lusty, she had a strip'd home-spun Jacket, blue Petticoat. Whosoever shall take up the abovesaid Runaway Servants, and them or either of them Convey to their abovesaid Masters in Boston, shall have Forty Shillings Reward besides all necessary Charges paid.
The Boston News-Letter, From September 17, to September 24, 1716.

ONe Thomas Wright, about the 18th of October last past, coming to Newport on Rhode-Island, Hired a Boat of Henry Stanton, pretending to go to Stanford in the Colony of Connecticut (one Isaac Johnson Master) and there being several People on Board, they stopt at Oyster-Bay, where in the Night, said Wright with one Man more runaway with the Boat. All Persons where the Man or Boat may be found, are desired to sieze both, and a Reward of Five Pounds shall be made, besides all other charges, by the said Henry Stanton: The said Wright is a Fat Man, of above Forty Years of Age, and wears a Wig; his Head is very Bald, and his Beard very Gray. And for the Boat, her Main-sail is above half worn, and a new Fore-sail; there is some Timber broken under the Cuddy, which is Lined on each side with Planck, and the Boat hath a false Stem, whereon upon the starboard side there is Timber spike on.
The Boston News-Letter, From November 19, to November 26, 1716.

1717

RAn-away from her Master David Melvill of Boston an Indian Woman Servant, Named Ziporah of Low Stature, aged about 28 Years, speaks good English, she had on an old double gown, Dark coloured, and other old clothing, a Camblet ryding hood fac'd with blue. whoever shall apprehend the Run-away Servant, and her safely convey to her said Master, living in Anne Street near to Colonel Checklys, or give any true Intelligence of her,

so as her Master may have her again shall be sufficiently rewarded besides all necessary Charges paid.
The Boston News-Letter, From April 29, to May 6, 1717.

RAn-away from his Master the Reverend Mr. *Peter Thacher* of Milton, on Friday the 3d Currant, A Man Servant, Named Lewis Chapman, aged about 27 Years, short Stature, short Dark Hair, had on a black cloth Jacket wanting the two fore Skirts, a Flanel Shirt, and white yarn Stockings. Whoever shall apprehend the said Run-away & him safely Convey to his said master, or to Mr. *Oxinbridge Thacher* in Marlborough Street Boston at the Sign of the Three Crowns, or can give any true Intelligence of him so as his Master may have him again shall be sufficiently rewarded besides all necessary Charges paid.
The Boston News-Letter, From April 29, to May 6, 1717.

RAn-away from his Master Return Waite of Plymouth, Taylor, about the Twelfth of April last, A White Servant Man, named Thomas Boyles, Aged about Seventeen Years, a slim Youth, not very Tall, dark coloured Lank Hair, pretty Long, has been lately seen at the Fathers House John Boyls Sadler at the South end of Boston. Whoever shall apprehend the said Run-away and him safely convey to his said Master, or unto Mr. Richard Proctor in King-Street, Boston, or give any true Intelligence of him, so as his Master may have him again, shall have Twenty Shillings reward besides all necessary charges paid.
The Boston News-Letter, From May 20, to May 27, 1717.

RAn-away on the 23d of this Instant June, from his Master, *Samuel Bissel* of New-port, Black-smith, an English Man Servant, named *Thomas Richbrook*, aged about 20 Years, a thick short Fellow, full fac'd, brown curl'd hair, very thick Leggs: he had on a brown Kersey Coat, Ozenbrigs Jacket & Breeches, white Holland Shirt, Whoever shall take up the abovesaid Run-away, and him convey to his abovesaid Master in New-port, in Rhode-Island, or to *Francis Miller* in Boston, Worsted-Comer, near the Mill bridge, shall have Forty Shillings *Reward*, and Charges paid.
The Boston News-Letter, From June 24, to July 1, 1717.

RAn away on the 24th of June last, from their Masters Samuel Vernon and William Bourden, both of Newport on Rhode-Island, two Carolina Indian Men-Servants, of about 20 Years of Age each, one of them is a short Fellow, full Fac'd, has on a dark Gray Coat trim'd with black, and Jacket with brass Buttons. Whoever shall apprehend the said Runaways, and them or either of them safely convey to their said Masters, or to Mr. Barrat Dyer in Boston, or give true Intelligence of them, so as that their Master may

have them again, shall have Forty Shillings Reward for each, besides all necessary Charges paid.
The Boston News-Letter, From July 15, to July 22, 1717.

RAN away the 24th of this Instant August, from on Board the Ship Durrell *John Dauvergne*, Commander, A French Man Servant, named *James Larrance*, a lusty Tall fellow, about five or six and Twenty Years of Age, with long Redish Hair, pale Complexion, freckled Face, he had on a dark colour'd Coat, gray Jacket, with red Breeches, and a new Course English Hat, speaks not one word English. Whosoever shall take up said Run away Servant and him Convey to his said Master again, or to Mr. *Thomas Selby* at the Crown Coffee house, Boston, shall have Five Pounds Reward, and all Charges paid.
The Boston News-Letter, From August 19, to August 26, 1717.

RUnaway from the Ship Globe of Dublin, Alexander Douglass, Mr. Laughlin Cojan an Irish Seaman, being Sickly, a Slender man of about 26 Years old, with his own Brown Hair. A young Irish Seaman named Francis Carty of about 18 Years, being a Slender man, full of freckles in his Face, wears his own Curled Bushy Brown hair: If anyone Secures them or any of them and brings them to Mr. John Walker Merchant in Boston, shall have Three Pounds Reward for each of them.
The Boston News-Letter, From September 30, to October 7, 1717.

RAn-away at Boston, on Wednesday Night last, the 16th of this Instant October, from his Master John Mainzies Esq: a Servant Man born in Ireland, Named John Gamble, aged about Twenty-eight Years, a Smith by Trade, and can work something at the Carpenters Trade; a Tall Fellow, of a stammering Speech, inclining to the Scotch Language, straight Hair, of a Yellowish colour; had on a course dark coloured Coat, a white leather Apron, a black Hat, and darkish gray Stockings. Whosoever shall apprehend the said Run-away & him safely convey to his said Master, in Summer Street, Boston, or give any true Intelligence of him, so as his Master may have him again, shall have Three Pounds reward besides all necessary charges paid.
The Boston News-Letter, From October 14, to October 21, 1717. See *The Boston News-Letter*, From November 11, to November 18, 1717

RANaway at Boston, on Wednesday the 16th of October past, from his Master *John Meinzies* Esq; a Servant Man born in Ireland, Named *John Gamble,* aged about Twenty-eight Years, a Smith by Trade, and can work something at the Carpenters Trade; a Tall Fellow, of a stammering Speech, inclining to the Scotch Language, straight Hair, of a Yellowish colour; had on a course dark coloured Coat, a white leather Apron, a black Hat, and darkish gray Stockings, Whosoever shall apprehend the said Run-away and him safely Convey to his said Master, in Summer Street, Boston, or give any true Intelligence of him, so as his Master may have him again, shall have Three Pounds reward besides all necessary Charges paid.

The Boston News-Letter, From November 11, to November 18, 1717.
See *The Boston News-Letter*, From October 14, to October 21, 1717.

RUn-away at Boston about six Weeks ago, from his Master *Edward Goodwin*, Commander of the Ship Friends Adventure, *William Hughes*, born in Ireland, about 28 Years old a Bricklayer, of short Stature, brown complexion, his hair of a blackish brown colour, with the ring Finger on his left hand bent inwards, Whoever discovers the said *Hughes*, so that he may be returned to the Post Master in Boston, shall receive three Pounds Reward besides all necessary Charges to be allowed.

The Boston News-Letter, From November 25, to December 2, 1717.

1718

RAN-away from their Masters Capt. *John Knight* and Mr. *Clement Hughes* of Piscataqua, on the 9th of April Currant, two Marthas Vineyard Indian Women, one Named *Desiah chin*, middle size about Twenty Years Old, her Right Thumb has been hurt; she had on when she went away a black Crape Gown and a striped Stuff Jacket; The other named *Rachel choho*, much about the same Age, something Taller she had on a blew Flannel Petticoat, a dark Estamine Gown and a double striped Gown, Any Person that shall take up and secure them so that their Masters may have them again, or either of them, shall have Three Pounds Reward for each and all necessary Charges Paid, upon their giving Notice thereof to their said Masters.

The Boston News-Letter, From April 7, to April 14, 1718.

RAN-away from his Master *Charles Dickinson*, of *Boston* Neck in *Kingstown*, in *Naragansett*, in *Rhode-Island* Colony. A Negro Man Named *Jack*, aged about 25 Years, who had on him a homespun waistcoat and Breeches of the same cloath, with shoes & stockings on, and an old black torn Hatt. Whosoever shall take up the said Negro and convey him to his master abovesaid, or advise him so that he may have him shall be fully paid & contented for their trouble and are desired to secure him in Irons when apprehended.

The Boston News-Letter, From May 12, to May 19, 1718.

RAN-away from their Master Capt, *William Gibb*, at Marblehead the 20th of May last, A Servant Man Named *John Hurst*, Aged about 25 Years, born in Bristol, in England, a West Comber [*sic*] a tall black Man, lank black Hair, had of a darkish Frize Coat a blue wastcoat and Breeches. And on the 3d Currant another Servant Named *John Maley* a Cooper, Aged about 30 Years, a short Man, with short black Hair, having a Frize Coat, black waistcoat and breeches, having a small bundle with some Cloaths and a Coopers Adge. [*sic*] Whosoever shall apprehend the said Runaways or wither of them, and him or them convey unto the Honble. *Nathaniel Norden* Esq: or to the said Capt. *Gibb* at Marblehead, or unto Messieurs *Steel* and *Betbune* in Boston, or can give any true Intelligence of them, or either of them, so as their Master may have them again, shall receive Three Pounds Reward for each, besides all reasonable Charges Paid.

The Boston News-Letter, From June 2, to June 9, 1718.

RAN-away from *Victorius Looby*, at *Piscataqua*, an Irish servant Named *John Kelly*, aged about 20 Years middle stature, pale Complexion, short black Hair. Whoever shall take up said Ran-away and return him to his Master; or give notice of him so that his Master may have him again, shall be sufficiently Rewarded besides all Charges paid.

The Boston News-Letter, From August 4, to August 11, 1718.

WHereas John Mumford, Cook of the Ship Cumberland John Cumberland Master, hath lately absconded his service on board, this is to give Notice that in case he does not return within a week hence to his duty, he will be treated as a Deserter.

The Boston News-Letter, From September 8, to September 15, 1718.

WHereas *Jacob Jacobs* of the Ship Bacchus, *Francis Franklin* Master, hath lately absconded and abandoned his Service on Board, this is to give Notice, that if he does nto return to his Duty on Board the said Ship at Marblehead in seven Days time he will be treated as a Deserter.

The Boston News-Letter, From September 22, to September 29, 1718.

RAN-away from Mr. *James Palin* in Cornhill, Boston, next to the Post-Office in Boston, on Monday Night last, an Indian Woman Aged 32 Years, named *Sabera*, born at Rhode-Island, she is short and thick, wears a double Stuff Gown, stripped with Blew and White on one side, and Yellow and Red on the other, a bayse Petticoat and a Blew Apron. Whoever brings her home, or gives Notice to her said Master, so as that she may be again restored to her Service, shall be well Rewarded besides all necessary Charges paid.

The Boston-News-Letter, From September 29, to October 6, 1718. See *The Boston News-Letter*, From June 6, to June 9, 1720, for Sabera/Zipporah.

RAN-away at Boston, on Friday Night Last the 24th Currant from the Ship Happy Return of South Hampton, Peter Harvy Master, the following Persons (having taken with them several things belonging to the said Ship and Master) *Viz.* Thomas Story, Tall of Stature amd a fair Complexion Aged about 35 Years, in a light wigg carryed with him a Kersey Watch Coat, of a fad colour, lined with blue Bays. Thomas Cross of brown Complexion, middle size, Aged about 30 years, in light Cloaths, and a light coloured Wigg: and John Taylor of a brown Complexion, short, thick and well set, with a snuff coloured Pee Jacket, and his Hair off. Whoever shall apprehend the said Runaways, and them safely convey to their said Master, or give any true Intelligence of them or either of them so as the said Master may have them again, shall be well rewarded, besides all necessary charges paid.
    The New-London Gazette, From October 20, to October 27, 1718.

1719

WHereas John Guy of New haven in the Colony of Connecticut, Taylor, being called from thence by his necessary Affairs, and, having sufficient Estate to maintain his Wife Anna Guy, notwithstanding she is said to have Run him considerably in Debt at Boston and elsewhere, and has Eloped from her said Husband, both with the Effects and Money to answer the said Debts. This is therefore strictly to Charge and forbid all Persons not to trust her the said Anna with any Goods, whatsoever, for her said Husband will not pay any Debts she shall contract after this Publication.
    The Boston News-Letter, From April 20, to April 27, 1719.

RAN-away from his Master Walter Goodridge of Boston, Marriner, on the 29th of June past, a Negro Man well set, Named Saco, about 26 Years of Age, speaks good English, he had on when he went away, a brown coloured old Jacket lined with blue, and a inside homespun striped Jacket, and a long Ozenbridge pair of Trusers and a Red Cap, no Stockings. Whoever shall apprehend the said Run-away, and him safely Convey to his said Master, at the North End of Town, or give any true Intelligence of him, so as his Master may have him again, shall have Four Pounds Reward, besides all necessary Charges paid.
    The Boston News-Letter, From July 13, to July 20, 1719; From July 20, to July 27, 1719; From July 27, to August 3, 1719.

WHereas John Head a Devonshire Man for Three Years past, Secreted or Absconded himself from his Relations; If therefore the said Head will come to the House of Mr. Andrew Faneuil Merchant in Boston, he had be Informed of what will tend much to his Advantage: Or if any Person or

Persons can give the said Mr. Faneuil any Intelligence of him, he or they will receive a suitable Reward.
The Boston News-Letter, From August 17, to August 24, 1719.

RAN-away from his Master George Webb of Kingston in the Colony of Rhode Island, the Seventh day of August past, A Negro Man called Jethro, a tall well set Fellow, a scar upon his upper Lip, speaks very plain English, has a dark coloured broad cloath Coat, and striped Jacket and Breeches, a Castor Hat, aged about 25 Years; whosoever shall apprehend the said Negro, and him safely convey to his said Master, or secure him in Irons and send his Master Notice, so as that his Master may have him again, shall be well paid for so doing, besides all reasonable Charges.
The Boston News-Letter, From August 29, to September 5, 1719. See *The Boston News-Letter*, From September 21, to September 28, 1719.

Patrick Munden aged about 24 Years a Scotchman who lived some Years in Ireland, of an ordinary stature, thin faced, short darkish yellow Hair not much curl'd, hath a Sagathy Coat and Jacket of a dark mixed colour, with Hair buttons a pair of Leather breeches, also a Jacket and Breeches of stript Fustin, two Shirts, a pair of brownish coloured Stockings, Ran away from his Master John Meinzeis, Esq; on the 11th of this Instant September from Leicester, Deserting his said Service, without rendring an Account of a great Trust committed to his Charge. Whoever shall apprehend the said Deserter and him safely Convey to his said Master at Boston, or give any true Intelligence of him; so as his Master may have him again, shall have three Pounds Reward, besides all necessary Charges paid.
The Boston News-Letter, From September 14, to September 21, 1719; From September 21, to September 28, 1719. See *The Boston News-Letter*, From December 21, to December 28, 1719, and *The Boston News-Letter*, from April 18, to April 21, 1720.

RAN-away from George Webb of Kingstown in Naraganset the 13th of this Instant September, A Negro Man Named Jethro; Aged about 24 Years, a well set tall Fellow, a scar upon his upper Lip; having on a dark coloured Jacket and grey Kersey Breeches and a Felt Hat.
Ran away from Samuel Brown of Kingston aforesaid the 15th Instant, a Negro Man Named Pero; Aged about 24 Years, of a midling Stature and Pox broken very much; white Jacket & Breeches, and whitish coloured Coat, & Hat; the said Negro Men both speaks good English, and are supposed to be both together; and both to have Stockings & Shoes on. Whosoever shall take up & secure said Negro Men & bring or send them, or give Notice to their said Masters; so as they may have them again, shall

receive sufficient Satisfaction & reasonable Charges allowed them
by   George Webb & Samuel Brown.
The Boston News-Letter, From September 21, to September 28, 1719.
See *The Boston News-Letter*, From August 29, to September 5, 1719, for Jethro.

RAN-away from his Master, John Christy of Boston Glover, on Friday the 18th of this Instant December, an Irish Man Servant Named John Carlow, Aged about 28 Years, a short thick well set Man, having black hair and of a dark Complection, he had on when he Ran away, an Irish Frize Coat Jacket and Breeches, a brown pair of Stockings and an old Felt Hat. Whosoever shall take up the said Run away and him safely convey to his said Master, at the Crown and Glove on the Long Wharff in Boston, or give any true Intelligence of him so as his Master may have him again, shall have Fifty Shillings Reward and all necessary charges paid.
The Boston News-Letter, From December 14, to December 21, 1719.

WHereas Patrick Munden a covenant to John Menzeis of Boston Esq; did in September last withdraw from his Masters Service without his knowledge, and since hath been allowed by his said Master to imploy himself in any other service for some time yet to run out, and that his presence is now necessary in order to clear some boundings of property of his Masters only known to him. Therefore it is desired and expected that upon Notice hereof, he do forthwith repare to his said Master at Boston, who shall not detain him above two Days, and also pay all his charges.
The Boston News-Letter, From December 21, to December 28, 1719; From January 4, to January 11, 1720. See *The Boston News-Letter*, From September 14, to September 21, 1719, and *The Boston News-Letter*, from April 18, to April 21, 1720.

1720

RUn away on Wednesday night last, from John Jekyll Esq; his Negro Servant named Caesar, aged about 17 Years, having on a Pea Jacket, and a Child's new Hatt. Whoever brings him to his said Master at the Custom House in Boston, shall have all reasonable Satisfaction.
The Boston Gazette, From January 11, to January 18, 1720.

Whereas Kennet Mackenzie, Servant to John Jekyll, Esq; Collector of His Majesty's Customs at Boston Run away on Monday Night the 2d Currant, taking with him a suit of Black Cloth of his Masters, and a new suit of brown Fustian and other things as is supposed, and taken up Moneys of

others, his Master advertises this to prevent any Bodys being further imposed upon by the said Servant.
The Boston News-Letter, From May 5, to May 9, 1720.

RAn away on the 24th of April last from the Shop Princess Amelia, William Cullen Commander, William Glan an Irish Lad about 18 Years of Age, well sett, short black Hair; had on a dark coloured Pea Jacket, lined with blue Baze, formerly Servant to Mr. Ingram Cooper, and since Servant to Mr. William Spragg of Malden a Miller. If any Person will bring him to the said Master Capt. Cullen, they shall be well rewarded, or if the said William Glan will return he shall be pardoned.
The Boston Gazette, From May 9, to May 16, 1720.

RAN-away from his Master James Palin at the Rain-box Coffee-House in Corn hill, Boston, on Monday the 6th of this Instant June, An Irish Man Servant, Named Richard Evelin, of a middle Stature, about 22 or 23 years old, had on a dark coloured Drugger Jacket, a pair of Leather Breeches, white thread Stockings, but no Coat.

Also went away with said Servant, an Indian Woman, born at Rhode-Island, Named Zipporah, about 30 or 35 Years old, of short Stature, hath on a stuff Gown and Petticoat, also a yellow quilted Petticoat, and a plain round Cap. Whoever shall take up said Servants, or either of them, and bring them to their abovesaid Master, or give any true Intelligene of them, so as their Master may have them or either of them again, shall be well rewarded for their Pains, and all necessary Charges paid.
The Boston News-Letter, From June 6, to June 9, 1720, See *The Boston-News-Letter*, From September 29, to October 6, 1718, for Sabera/Zipporah.

RAn-away the 7th Currant, from his Master Stephen Winchester of Brookline, an Irish Man Servant, named Edward Coffee, about Twenty Years of Age, middle Stature, full fac'd, down Look, flat Nose, a scar in his Forehead about his Right Eye. He had on and carried with him a light coloured broad cloth Coat, a cinamon coloured Camblet Coat, an Ozenbrigs Shirt, and a patch'd Holland Shirt, Cinamon coloured Breeches, with silk puffs tied at the Knees with Ferret Ribbon, gray yarn Stockings, and one pair of worsted, new round to'd Shoes with wooden Heels, a stuff Gown, a Castor and an old felt Hat, a Wig tied with a black Ribbon, a black leather Belt; he carried also away with him a chesnut Sorrel Horse, fourteen hands high, paces well, a round skirted Saddle, with blue cloth Housing, Whoever shall take up said Runaway and Horse, or either of them & Convey to the above said Stephen Winchester at Brookline, or to the Prison Keeper in

Boston, so as his Master may have them both or either again, shall have Forty Shillings Reward, and necessary Charges paid.

The Boston News-Letter, From September 5, to September 12, 1720.

A*Bsented from his Majesty's Ship Rose* John Harris *a Dutch Man, aged* 35 *Years, speaks a little broken English, is pretty Tall, with brown Hair, and a Cast in his Eyes. Whoever shall secure the said* John Harris, *& safely convey him to Capt* Whitney *of his Majesty's Ship aforesaid, shall have Three Pounds Reward.*

The Boston Gazette, From October 3, to October 10, 1720; From October 10, to October 17, 1720.

A*Bsented from His Majesty's Ship* Squirril, William Todd, *about* 6 *Foot* 3 *Inches high,* 46 *Years of Age, wears his own Hair, very gray, is of a black swarthy Complection, long Visage, a long Nose, if with a Coat on 'tis dark coloured, wearing a pair of greasy Leather Breeches, the Buttons covered with Leather. Whoever shall secure the said* Todd *& safely convey him to Capt.* Smart *of His Majesty's Ship aforedaid, shall besides their reasonable Cahrges, have* Forty Shillings *Reward.*

The Boston Gazette, From October 17, to October 24, 1720; From October 24, to October 31, 1720; From October 31, to November 7, 1720.

D*Eserted His Majesty's Service at Castle William on Monday October the* 3*d.* Francis Tharold, *about* 29 *Years of Age, a Tall Man & a black Complection, having on a good Castor Hat, a light Wigg, his own Hair very dark, a gray broad Cloth Coat mix'd with black, or a Red Coat lin'd & fac'd with blue, a strip'd Swan Skin Jacket, a pair of Checker'd Breeches, and a pair of Canvas Trowsers over them, & a pair of gray worsted Stockings. Whoever shall apprehend the said Deserter, & cause him to be deliver'd to the Hon.* William Dummer *Esq; at the said Castle, shall be well rewarded, besides all necessary Charges paid.*

The Boston Gazette, From October 17, to October 24, 1720; From October 24, to October 31, 1720.

R*An-away from the Ship* Lawrence, *Capt.* Peter Blackstone *Commander, now lying at New-Castle in New-Hampshire, viz. Two Men Servants, The one named* Edward Follot, *a tall lusty Man, about* 30 *Years of Age. The other a short Irish Man,* 28 *years of Age. Whoever shall take up the said Runaways, & them safely convey to the said Commander, or to Mr.* John Walker, *Merchant in Boston, shall have Three Pounds Reward for each, all necessary Charges paid.*

The Boston Gazette, From October 31, to November 7, 1720; From November 7, to November 14, 1720.

A*Bout the 20th of this Instant Ranaway from Benj. Bourn Merchant at Sandwich, Richard Holford, an English Boy about* 18 *Years of Age, of middle Stature, light strait hair, had on a Cinnamon colour'd Camblet Coat & short Jacket. Whoever Secures the said Boy, and brings him to Mr. Philip Musgrave Post-Master at Boston, shall have* 40s. *Reward, & all necessary Charges.*
N. B. He is supposed to be at Marblehead or Cape-Ann.
The Boston Gazette, From November 21, to November 28, 1720.

R*UN-away from his Master Col.* William Pepperell *of Piscataqua, a Negro Man called Lymas aged about* 24 *Years, speaks good English he is a Cooper by Trade, and can Read, he is a Large well set Fellow, he has a smooth Face. Whoever shall apprehend said Negro and convey him to his said Master, or at Boston to Mr. Andrew Tyler Goldsmith near the Draw-Bridge, shall have Five Pounds reward, and all necessary charges paid him.* November 17, 1720.
The Boston Gazette, From November 21, to November 28, 1720; From November 28, to December 5, 1720.

RAN-away from his Master George Mayo of King-street, Boston, Block-Maker, on Thursday last, a Servant Lad named John Gullison, aged about 17 Years, of a fresh Colour, round Visage, full fac'd, short truss Fellow, short light coloured Hair; having on a grey knit Cap, a new white Cotton shirt, a strip'd Swan-skin Jacket a new strip'd Searge Jacket lin'd with blue Bayes, and Pewter Buttons, a pair of Cynamon coloured Drugget Breeches, a pair of black Yarn Mittens, a black Hat, a pair of new shoes, round to'd. Whoever shall apprehend the said Runaway, and him safely convey to his Master, or give any true Intelligence of him; so as his Master may have him again, shall be well Rewarded besides all necessary Charges paid.
The Boston News-Letter, From December 12, to December 19, 1720.

THESE are to give Notice That there is lately arrived here at Boston from beyond Sea, a certain Person that wants to speak with one Daniel Pougher an English Man, born at Leicestershire in Old England, a Butcher by Trade, a Quaker by Profession, was marryed at New-York, liv'd some time in Rhode-Island, said to live somewhere in New-England; who is hereby desired to come to John Campbell in Cornhill, Boston, or write him word where he may be spoke with, or if any Person or Persons knows where he lives, they'l do well to inform, that thereby the said Pougher may reap the benefit and advantage intended for him.

The Boston News-Letter, From December 12, to December 19, 1720.

1721

RAN away on the 9th of this Instant March at Falmouth in this Province, from his Master the Revd. Mr Joseph Metcalf, a Servant Man called Joseph Henderson, a Scoth Irish Fellow, aged about 18 Years, of a middle Stature, great bon'd, brownish skin, pretty fair fac'd, big eyes, sharp look, black or dark hair pretty short, speaks good English, of a bold and hasty spirit, can make a fair story, tho' false. He had on a felt Hat about half worn, the brim torn on one side, or sewed up; a strait bodied short Coat, of mixt blew Irish cloath, rent up the back and sewed again; an old mouse coloured cloath Jacket, speckled Shirt, white linnen Breeches, gray yarn Stockings and square to'd Shoes. Whoever shall apprehend the said Runaway, and him safely convey to his Master, or to Mr. John Savell Taylor in Union Street, Boston; or give either of them any true Intelligence of him, so as his Master may have him again, shall have Forty Shillings Reward, besides all necessary Charges paid.

The Boston News-Letter, From March 6, to March 13, 1721.

WHereas Patrick Mundell, Aged about 24 Years, a Scotchman, that lived some Years in Ireland, and some time in this Country, with John Meinzeis of Boston, Eq; and now a Servant and to Nathaniel Thomas of Marshfield, Esq; did on the fifth Day of this Instant April, Desert his said Masters Service: He is a Fellow of an Ordinary Stature, thin faced, short dark yellowish Hair, not much Curled, had on a mix'd coloured Kersey Coat, and Jacket of the same, almost new, a black Castor Hat, half worn. These are therefore desiring all Persons, where he may be found, to apprehend the said Deserter, and him safely Convey to either of his abovesaid Masters, or give any true Intelligence of him, so as either may have him again, shall have Forty Shillings Reward, besides all Necessary Charges paid.

The Boston News-Letter, from April 18, to April 21, 1720. See *The Boston News-Letter*, From September 14, to September 21, 1719, and *The Boston News-Letter*, From December 21, to December 28, 1719.

DEserted His Majesty's Service at Castle William on Saturday the 27th Instant, about Midnight, Archibald Grimes, about 20 years of Age, of Middle Stature, thick set, very much Pockbroken, Redish Face and Hair, generally waring a Strip'd thin Cap, having a Red Coat lined with blue, and round pewter buttons, a serge Jacket and Breeches of a fad Colour, a pair of black Stockings, a new pair in round to'd Shoes, having on one of his Legs an Indian Mark in the shape of a Buck, and on one of his Arms A G.

Sylvanus Bourn about 18 Years of Age, pretty Tall, thin Bodyed and thickish Legs, one of them having an Indian Mark in the shape of a Buck: He is of a fair Complexion, lightish Hair, or wears a dark coloured Natural Wigg, sometimes a thin striped Cap; had on a dark coloured Camlet Coat lined with Red, a short grey Pea Jacket, a pair of Kersey Breeches, or Drugget of a lightish colour, a pair of yarn Stockings, and a new pair of round to'd Shoes.

Joseph Searle about 23 Years of Age, of short Stature and dark Complexion, wearing his own Hair, black, thick and curl'd, prety thick set, having on a dark colour homespun Cloth straight bodyed Coat lined with Red, a Pea Jacket of the same, yarn Stockings and ronnd to'd Shoes, and a great grey homspun Cloth Coat lined with Blue.

Wheover shall apprehend the said Deserters, and cause them to be delivered to the Hon. William Dummer Esq: at His Majesty's said Castle, shall be well Rewarded, besides all necessary Charges paid.

The Boston News-Letter, From May 22, to May 29, 1721.

R*AN-away from his Master Mr.* Edward Watts *of* Winnesimit, *on the Third Instant, a Negro Man Servant, named* Quacco, *about 15 Years of Age, of a middle Stature, his Legs are crook'd, one of his upper fore-Teeth out; He had on when he went away, a dark colour'd Drugget Coat, a doublebreasted Kersey Jacket, wash Leather Breeches, square to'd Shoes. He is supposed to have parted with some of this Cloaths.*

Whoever will take up the abovesaid Run-away, and him safely convey to his abovesaid Master at Winnesimit *shall have* Twenty Shillings *Reward, and all necessary Charges paid.*
Boston, June 13th, 1721.

The Boston Gazette, From June 12, to June 19, 1721.

R*AN-away from his Master Capt.* Richard Brown *of* Newbury, *a middle sized Negro Man named* Mingo, *about 25 Years of Age, having on a Homespun Quakers Coat, with a pair of Square to'd Shoes, with Leather strings, a Blacksmith by Trade.*

Whoever secures the said Negro and brings him to Mr. Philip Musgrave *Post-Master of* Boston *shall have Twenty Shillings Reward and reasonable Charges.*

The Boston Gazette, from June 12, to June 19, 1721.

R**AN-AWAY** the 5th of this Instant September from Mr. Nathanael Kanney, of Boston, Butcher; A Boy named Charles Crouch, Aged about Fifteen Years, small of Stature, white short hair, large Lips, has on a good Felt Hat, a dark gray Coat lin'd with blue baze, a dark and yellow striped pair of Breeches, round to'd Shoes, and has with him several pair of Stockings, and other Cloaths.

Ranaway also at the same time, a Carolina Indian Man named Will, a slim tall Fellow, about Thirty Years of age speaks good English, has a dark spot on one Cheek, has with him a light colour'd broad Cloth Coat, and several Jackets, and several pair of Breeches, and several pair of Stockings & Shoes: He is suppos'd to have a considerable quantity of Paper Money.

Whoever shall take up the said Runaways, and them safely bring to their abovesaid Master Mr. Nathanael Kanney at Boston, or if unwilling to come to Boston, they are desir'd to bring them to Roxbury or Charlstown, or some other near Town, and asend Word, so that they may be had again, and they shall receive Three Pounds Reward, and all necessary Charges paid.

N. B. Whoever takes them up are desir'd to search them.

The Boston News-Letter, From September 4, to September 11, 1721.

R*AN-away on the 9th Instant from Mr.* Wm. Maxwell *of Boston Mariner, A Molatto Boy Named John Bord, aged about* 16 *Years, has black Hair, wearing a new Hat, a Silk Handkerchief, a single breasted Pea Jacket, & a Check Shirt. He is suppos'd to have Forty Pounds in Money with him. Whoever apprehends the said Runaway are desir'd to search him and secure him that his Master may have him again, & they shall have Five Pounds Reward.*

The Boston Gazette, From September 18, to September 25, 1721; From October 2, to October 9, 1721.

D*Eserted from His Majesty's Ship Sea-Horse, about the* 10*th. of July last, an Indian Man named Hector, about* 22 *or* 23 *Years of Age, speaks very good English; wears his own Hair, being of a middle Stature, spare in Body, and thin in the Face. Whoever shall apprehend and safely convey him to the next County Goal, shall have* 5 1. *Reward, and all necessary Charges paid. Note. The said Indian is a very good Seaman, and is suppos'd to be gone to Sea: Whoever can truly discover the Ship or Vessel that carry'd him off, shall have* 20 s. *paid by Capt.* Wentworth Paxton *of Boston.*

The Boston Gazette, From September 25, to October 2, 1721.

1722

B*ROKE out of the Common Goal of Philadelphia, the* 15*th of this Instant February,* 1721, [sic] *the following persons....*

Ebenezer Mallary, *a New-England Man, aged about* 24 *Years, is a middle sized thin Man, having on a Snuff colour'd Coat, and ordinary Ticking Wastcoat and Breeches He has dark brown strait Hair.*

Whoever takes up and secures all, or any One of these Felons, shall have a Pistole Reward for each of them and reasonable Charges, paid them
by John Wilson, *Goaler.*
The American Weekly Mercury, From Tuesday February 13, to Tuesday February 20, 1722; From Tuesday February 20, to Tuesday February 27, 1722; From Tuesday February 27, to Thursday March 1, 1722.

Whereas *on the 29th day of April last, in the Night time, the Shop of* Samuel Porter *of* Hadley *Esq; was broken open, from whence was Stolen & Carried away upwards of One hundred pounds of Bills of Credit, and several Pounds in Silver & Penny's: And whereas there is grounds to suspect one* Robert Parsons *late of* Hadley, *was Guilty of Stealing & Carrying away the same; which said* Parsons *about Five Years since came from Great Britain a Servant, he is now about* 20 *Years of age of Middle Stature, his Hair brown and short, and hath upon one of his hands between his Thumb and his Fore-finger a small round spot coloured (as is supposed) with Powder Artificially Imprinted, and 'tis thought he will speeding make his escape beyond Sea.*
Publick Notice is therefore Given, That whosoever shall apprehend the same Robert Parsons, *and bring him to Justice to answer what shall be Ailedged against him on His Majesty's behalf touching the Premises shall be very well Rewarded for their Service, and besides have all reasonable Charges paid and defrayed.*
The Boston News-Letter, From April 30, to May 7, 1722.

R*UNaway on the* 17*th Instant from Mr.* John Gardner *of Kingston, a French Servant Man, named* Lewis Larbordee, *a thick short Fellow, black Hair, the Scar of a Cutlash wound on one wrist: has an old Hat, a gray Kersey Coat,* 2 *flanel Shirts,* 1 *pair of Linnen Breeches, & another of Orange coloured broad Cloth. A Weaver by Trade. Whoever takes up, said Runaway, and him conveys to his Master, or to Mr.* George Shore *in Boston, shall have Three Pounds Reward, and all necessary Charges paid.*
Boston, June 27. 1722.
The Boston Gazette, From June 25, to July 2, 1722.

RAN-away from Boston or Noddles-Island, on the 4th of this Instant July, from the Service of Mr. David Stoddard, two Irish Men Servants, one went by the Name of William Ryan, a short well-set Fellow, swarthy Complexion, about 23 Years of Age, his Hair cut off; he had on a new hat, a fad coloured Coat, sometime wore long Trouzers, new Shoes. The other went by the name of Richard Roth, a middle siz'd Man, about 26 Years of Age, slim Hair of a sandy colour, a Snuff coloured Coat, also new Hat and Shoes.

Whosoever shall take up the abovesaid Run-aways, and them convey to Mr. David Stoddard at his House in King-Street, Boston, shall have Four Pounds Reward, or Forty Shillings each, and all necessary Charges paid.

The Boston News-Letter, From July 2, to July 9, 1722.

RAN away from his Master Mr. *Joseph Franklin* of *Boston*, Tallow-Chandler, on the first of this Instant July, an Irish Man Servant, named *William Tinsley*, about 20 Years of Age, of a middle Stature, Black Hair lately cut off, somewhat fresh coloured Countenance, a large lower Lip, of a mean Aspect, large Legs and heavy in his going; He had on when he went away, a Felt Hatt, a white knit Cap striped with red and blue, white Shirt and Neckcloth, a brown colour'd Jacket almost new, a Frieze Coat of a dark Colour, gray Yarn Stockings, leather Breeches trim'd with Black, and round to'd Shoes. Whoever shall apprehend the said Runaway Servant, and him safely convey to his abovesaid Master, at the blue Ball in Union Street Boston, shall have *Forty Shillings* Reward, and all necessary Charges paid.

The New-England Courant, From July 2, to July 9, 1722; From July 9, to July 16, 1722; From July 26, to July 23, 1722.

D*Eserted from His Majesty's Castle* William *the* 24*th Instant,* Robert Bayley, *a middle siz'd Man, with black hair, aged about* 21, *Coat Wastecoat & Breecehs of Shuff colour'd Sagathia, & gray Stockings. Whoever will secure the said* Robert Bayley, *& him safely deliver to Mr.* Philip Musgrave, *Post-Master of Boston, or to Capt.* John Gray, *shall have* 40*s. Reward. And if he will return to his Duty in* 3 *day he shall be kindly received, otherwise to be prosecuted as a Deserter.*

The Boston Gazette, From July 23, to July 30, 1722.

RAN-away at London-Derry alias Notheld, in the Province of New-Hampshire, on Tuesday the 7th on this Instant August, from his Master Andrew Todd, A Man-Servant, Named David Kennedy, Aged about 21 Years, born in Ireland, of a middle Stature, speaks a little broad, somewhat Pock-broken, brown Hair, sore Eyes, had on a dark coloured homespun Coat, lined with yellow Linnen, and Breeches of the same, white yarn Stockings, a pair of old Shoes.

Whoever shall take up the said Run-away, and him safely Convey to his abovesaid Master at London-Derry aforesaid, or unto Mr. Jarvis Bethil in Cornhill, [   ], or give true Intelligence of the said Run-away to either of them, so as his Master may have him again, shall have Three Pounds Reward, and all necessary Charges paid.

The Boston Gazette, From August 20, to August 27, 1722.

THESE are to certify, That *Nathaniel Breed*, Master of the Brigantine Happy Return of *Boston, New-England*, from *Boston* bound to *Liverpool*, was Taken on the 18th Day of *May*, 1722, in the Latitude of 41. D. 43. M. about 185 Leagues to the Eastward of Cape Cod, by two Pyrates, a Ship of 30 Guns, and a Brigantine of 14 Guns, who forced away two Men, *viz. Amos Breed*, Mate, a short Man, Pock broken, brown Hair, a Carpenter by Trade, born at *Lyn* in *New-England*, Aged 28 Years, or thereabouts, And also *William Sinclair*, Sailor, a Short Man, short dark Hair, Born in *North Britain*, aged 27 Years or thereabouts.

The New-England Courant, From October 1, to October 8, 1722.

RUN-away from his Master Col. Wm. Pepperel, a Negro Man, Aged about 35 Years, named Sandy, Long Slim Fellow, long Wool on his Head for a Negro, and looks something like a Molatto; He had on a white Woolen Jacket, & a pair of Leather Breeches. Whoever shall apprehend said Negro, and convey him to his Master at Kittery, shall have Forty Shillings Reward, & all necessary Charges paid.

The Boston Gazette, From October 8, to October 15, 1722.

THE Deposition of *William Pitman* Marriner, Master of the Sloop Paradox, and *Edward Richards* Mate of said Sloop, both of Boston in New-England.

These Deponents Testify and Say, That on the Eighth day of July last past, in the Latitude of 18 Degrees, Longitude 46 or thereabouts, West from London; the said Sloop in her Passage from *Boston* to *Surranam*, was taken by a Pirate Ship called the Morning Star, and a Brigantine called the Fortune both under the Command of Capt. *Fiend,* [*sic*] and his Piratical Crew; carried away in the said Brigantine, (under the Subordinate Command of the Quarter Master *Wilks*;) two of the said Sloops Company, viz. *Benjamin Hewes*, a Native of Boston, aged about Nineteen Years, and late Apprentice to Mr. *Barrat Dyre* of said Boston Cooper, and the Deponent *Pitman's* Jersey Boy, aged about Nineteen Years, named *Thomas Symmons*; and the said Pirates utterly refused to release them, and Constrained or Forced them to go along with them, very much against their Wills; and further the Deponents say not.

William Pitman,   Edward Richards.

The Boston Gazette, From October 8, to October 15, 1722; *The New-England Courant*, From October 8, to October 15, 1722. The *Courant* has "*Boston, October* 12. 1722." at the bottom of the ad.

D*Eserted from* Joseph Watson *formerly Master of the Olive branch, now of a new Ship not Launched, two Sailors, viz.* Gilbert Basham & Wm. Lucas, whoever apprehends said Sailors and convey them to said Joseph Watson, or James Sterling, at his Warehouse upon Mr. Belcher's Wharfe, so as they may be obliged to do their Duty in said new Ship or the Olive branch as per Agreement, shall have Ten Pounds reward, or Five Pounds for each with reasonable Charges.

N. B. If they return to their Duty in 14 *Days from the Date hereof, shall have all their Wages as if they had not absented.*

The Boston Gazette, From November 5, to November 12, 1722.

RAN-away on the 17th of October last, from Mr. John Newell of Charlstown, an English Servant Boy, named John Kirby, about 13 Years of Age, fresh colour'd, pretty short brownish Hair. He had on when he went away, a dark colour'd Kersey jacket, a Homespun Wastcoat underneath, and Breeches of the same, Yarn Stockings.

Note, He often changes his Name, and has taken up Money and Goods in Boston, on his Master's Account: All Persons therefore are desired not to trust him.

Whoever shall apprehend the said Runaway, and him convey to his said Master in Charlestown, shall have a reasonable Reward, and all necessary Charges paid.

The Boston Gazette, From November 5, to November 12, 1722.

1723

DEserted from the Ship Benjamin, now lying at the Long Wharff, an Apprentice to the Owners of the said Ship, named Redman Glase, a lusty young Man, with short strait Hair, of a sandy Colour, wearing a dark grey Jacket and speckled Shirt. Whoever shall apprehend the said Runaway, and bring him to Selby's Coffee-House or to the said Ship, shall have 40 s. Reward, and all necessary Charges paid.

The New-England Courant, From December 31, to January 7, 1723.

A Certain Person who goes by the Name of Elizabeth Clark, who absented from Mrs. Mary Archer of Boston the first of this instant January; she speaks thro' her Nose, goes Lame, has dark Hair, something pitted with the Small-Pox; she had on when she went away a Green single Stuff Gown, sorry Petticoats, a Cinnamon coloured Riding-hood, trim'd with black, a pair of course blue yarn Stockings, a Callico Apron. She carried away with her divers other things of considerable Value. Whoever shall take up the abovesaid Elizabeth Clark, and her convey to the said Mrs. Archer in Newbury-Street, over against Judge Sewall's, shall have Satisfaction to Content.

The Boston News-Letter, From January 14, to January 21, 1723.

Whereas John Johnson, Alexander Moore, and William Taverner, Mariners, beling to the Ship Patience and Judith (Henry Clark Master) lying in the Port of Marblehead, did on the 20th Currant absent themselves from their Duty of board the said Ship: These are therefore to desire the said John johnson, Alexander Moore, and William Taverner to Return to their Duty and Service on board the said Ship, within the Space of 20 Days from this Date, otherwise they will be prosecuted as Deserters. Dated at Marblehead the 27th Day of April, 1723.
The New England Courant, From April 22, to April 29, 1723.

On Friday the 26th of *April* last, His Honour the Lieut. Governour & Commander in Chief was pleas'd with the Advice of His Majesty's Council to issue forth a Proclamation for Apprehending Deserters. *viz.*

Whereas divers Souldiers hereafter Named of the Eastern Forces under the Command of Col. Thomas Westbrook, *being sent in a Whale boat from Arrousick to carry Orders from the said Col.* Westbrook *to the Forces on St. George's River, have Deserted His Majesty's Service, viz.* Arthur Low *of Marshfield, Serjeant* Benjamin Lake *of Seconnet,* John Williams *of Norton,* Joseph Peck *of Rehoboth,* Isaac Shute, *of Abbington, Indian; All belonging to the Company of Capt.* Samuel Wheelwright; John Cromwell *of Dover of Col.* Westbrook's *Company,* Matthew Bunn *of Rhode-Island,* Samuel Bunn *of Swanzey, and* John Smith *of Norton: That whosover shall apprehend and arrest the above-named Deserters, or any of them, and deliver them up to Lawful Authority, in case they shall be by Law Convicted of Desertion, shall Receive out of the Publick Treasury a reward of* Ten Pounds *for each of the above-named Deserters so apprehended & Convicted, over & above the Encouragement of* Forty Shillings *Granted & Allowed in an Act of this Province Made & Pass'd at their last Sessions. And all Persons whatsoever are forbid Harbouring, Entertaining, Concealing of Conveying away any of the Deserters, as they will answer the same at their utmost Peril.*
The Boston News-Letter, From April 25, to May 2, 1723.

Ran away from the Ship Seaflower, George Jeanvrin Commander, the following Men, *viz.* John Brock and John Pray the 27th past, Anthony Nicholas, Joseph Jorden, Mathew Varley and Charles Simon on the 14th Currant. If any of the said Sailrs will return to their Duty, on board the said Ship now lying at the Long Wharff in Boston, they shall be kindly received or if anyone will give information where the said Men are so as the said Master may have them again, they shall have a Reward of Twenty Shillings Each.

The New-England Currant, From May 13, to May 20, 1723.

RAN away from his Master Mr. Thomas Byles of New-port on Rhode-Island, on the ninth of this Instant June, a Spanish Indian Man Servant, named Saffidillah, but 'tis thought he will change his name: He is about 21 Years of Age; about 5 Foot 8 Inches high, and pretty Slim; his Hair pretty long, and somewhat curled. He has an Indian mark of Blue across the Temples on the right Side of his Face.

N. B. His Cloaths were found lying by the Water Side on the Day he went away, and 'tis thought he has stole some other Cloaths from on board a vessel.

Whoever shall apprehend the aforesaid Runaway Servant, and him safely convey to his said Master in Newport, shall have Five Pounds Reward, and all necessary charges paid.

The New-England Courant, From June 17, to June 24, 1723.

R*AN-away the* 3*d Instant from his Master* Thomas Lauchlen *of* Boston, *a young Man Servant Named* Peter King, *born in* Ireland, *aged about Seventeen Years, brought up to the Sea, having on a dark coloured Pea-Jacket and Trousers, short dark Hair and smooth fac'd, speaks good English and French. Whoever shall take up the abovesaid Runaway and him convey to his abovesaid Master, or to Capt.* Thomas Steel *of* Boston *aforesaid, shall have a reasonable Reward, and all necessary Charges born him, Dated in* Boston, July 6 *th.* 1723.

The Boston Gazette, From July 8, to July 15, 1723.

Boston, July the 25*th.* 1723.

W*Hereas Lieutenant* John Melledge *of His Majesty's Royal Train of Artillery Arrived here with Eight Matrosses, being for* Annapolis Royal, *and accordingly going to Proceed the Voyage, One of the Matrosses has absented his Duty, whose Name is* John White, *a Thin Spare Man with his own Short Curled Hair, Aged about* 19 *Years, a Painter by Profession, and supposed to be decoy'd by some ill Meaning Persons who wants to make some advantage of him.*

These are to Certifie, that if the said John White *will return to his Duty within the space of Ten Days from the Date hereof, by Surrendring himself to the Honourable Lieutenant Governour, who has promised to procure a Passage for him to* Annapolis Royal; *he shall be pardoned for his fault & misdemeanour, but if the said* John White *do not Comply with this offer, he shall be prosecuted as a Deserter of His Majesty's Service; and whosoever shall be found to have inticed or harbour'd the said Person shall be prosecuted with the Utmost Rigour of the Law.*

John Melledge.

The Boston News-Letter, From July 18, to July 25, 1723; From July 25, to August 1, 1723.

Deserted from the Sloop John and Mary (John Weston Master) Mark Moses and Richard Savage, Sailors: And as the said Sloop is now upon sailing, if the said Sailors do not immediately return to their Duty, they cannot be entituled to their Wages.
The New-England Courant, From July 22, to July 29, 1723.

Ran away on the 14th of this Instant August, Robert Wingham, William Bembridge, and John Jackson, Mariners, from on board the Ship Loyal George, Cornelius Macmanara Master. These are therefore to desire the said Robert Wingham, William Bembridge, and John Jackson to return to their Duty on board said Ship (which is now ready to Sail) on pain of forfeiting their Wages. If any others of the Ship's Company shall absent themselves from the said Ship before or at the Time of her Sailing, they shall be prosecuted accordingly.
The New-England Courant, From August 12, to August 19, 1723.

RAN away from his Master, Mr. Job Bissel of Newport on Rhode-Island, Blacksmith, on the 10th of July last, a Carolina Indian Boy, called Bristow, about 16 or 17 Years of Age, of a short Stature, well set, full Faced, with big Eyes, and thick Lips; he had on when he went away a gray Jacket, and striped Breeches. Whoever shall apprehend the said Runaway, and him safely convey to his abovesaid Master, or give true intelligence so that his Master may have him again, shall have Forty Shillings Reward, and all necessary Charges paid.
The New-England Courant, From August 19, to August 26, 1723.

Marblehead.
WHereas on Sunday the 25th of August last, Ran-away from the Ship Elizabeth and Magdalen Wm Hannay Master, Thomas Butler Cook of said Ship. These are to desire the said Butler to return to his Duty on board said Ship on Penalty of the Forfeiture of his Bond and Wages, he being entituled to Twenty-five Shillings Sterling per Month.
The Boston Gazette, August 26, to September 2, 1723; *The New-England Courant*, From August 29, to September 2, 1723. Minor differences between the papers. The *Courant* has the date of *"Aug.* 29." at the top.

RAnaway on Wednesday the 18th Instant, from his Master Mr. Thomas Wallais of Boston, Blacksmith, an English Man-Servant, named John Hitchburn, about 21 Years of Age, pretty tall and slim, and pretty much

Pock-fretten. He had with him when he went away, a dark colour'd Broad Cloth Suit, a pair of Ozenbrigs Breeches, a Castor Hat, and white Shirt. His Hair is short and dark colour'd, and he had with him a small dark colour'd natural Perrywig.

Whoever shall apprehend the said Runaway, and him convey to his said Master in Boston, shall have Forty Shillings Reward, and all necessary Charges paid: And if any Person or Persons shall entertain the said Servant, they shall be prosecuted according to Law.

The New-England Courant, From September 16, to September 23, 1723.

R*AN-away the* 1*st of September* 1723, *from the Eliz. And Sarah, James Halfall Commander, Robert Scott, John Jones, and Francis Tennant, if they will return in* 10 *Days they shall be kindly received, otherwise they shall be treated as Deserters.*

The Boston Gazette, from October 14, to October 21, 1723.

R*AN away from his Master Mr. Thomas Viorney of New York, a Negro Man named Peter, who is of a middle Size, pale Complection, is Hipshod, crooked Legged, has Scars and Impressions of the Whip on his Back, and was lately seen at Rhode-Island. Whoever shall secure the said Run-away Negro and give advice thereof unto Mr. Joshua Wroe in Boston, shall have full satisfaction for their Charge and Trouble.*

The Boston Gazette, From October 28, to November 4, 1723.

RAn away from his Master, Mr. *James Barbeen* of *Woburn,* on Wednesday the 20th of this Instant November, a Negro Boy about 20 Years of Age, named *Scipio*: He had on when he went away, a brown homespun Shirt, a brown coloured homespun Coat, with Mohair Buttons, a double breasted Jacket made of an old whitish Blanket, with flat Pewter Buttons, a pair of Leather Breeches, gray Yarn Stockings, and a pair of New Shoes with round toes, and low leather heels, also an old felt Hat. *Note*, Said Negro has a lump of Flesh growing on his right Leg, just by his Ancle, about as big as a Coat Button.

Whoever shall take up said Run away, and bring him to his abovesaid Master in *Woburn,* or to Mr. *Wigglesworth Sweetser* in *Boston,* shall have *Thirty Shillings* Reward, besides all necessary Charges paid.

The Boston News-Letter, From November 21, to November 29, 1723; From November 29, to December 5, 1723.

R*AN away from his Master Capt. John Drummey, on the* 21*st Instant, an Apprentice Boy named Michael Marshall, aged about* 18 *Years, Pock-broken and hard favoured, with Black Hair, having on an Orange coloured*

Coat trimmed with the same, and a new pair of *Blew shagg Breeches*, he carried away also with him a *Broad Cloth Coat lined with a Persian Silk*, and a *loose Watch Coat*, with several other things of Value. Any Person that shall apprehend the said Runaway and him safely convey to Mr. Joshua Wroe Merchant in Boston to Major Brown in Newport, or to John Drummey in New-York shall have Five Pounds Reward, and all necessary Charges paid. N. B. If he returns in 10 days time, he shall be kindly received, per John Drummey.

The Boston Gazette, From December 16, to December 23, 1723.

1724

R*AN-away from Mr.* William Walker's *Warehouse at the North End,* Boston, *on Friday the 27th of* December *last, An English Boy, about Seventeen Years of Age, Named* William Horn, *Tall and fresh Coloured; short Hair; having on a Woollen Cap, a Cloth Wastcoat: Any Person that detains the said Boy from the service of said* Walker, *may expect to answer it as the Law directs in such cases. And whosoever shall apprehend and take said Boy and convey him to said* Walker *shall have Satisfaction to Content.*

The Boston News-Letter, from December 26, 1723, to January 2, 1724; From January 2, to January 9, 1724.

RAN-away from Major Nathaniel Sheffield of New-port on Rhode-island, Alexander Higins, an Irish Servant, about 18 Years of Age: he is of a middle Stature, pretty well set, his hair Cut off, and a short Wigg, brown coloured; he had on when he went away a fine home-spun cloath Coat and Breeches, his Coat was buttoned at the hands, both had small wrought mettal Buttons; he had a new felt Hat, a new pair of Shoes, a strip'd Linen Shirt. If any person shall take up the said Runaway and him convey to his said Master at New-port, or secure him so that his Master may have him again, shall be paid to content, with all necessary charges.

RAN-away also from Mr. John Lyon of Rehoboth, being at New-port on Rhode-Island, William Boyes, an Irish Servant, about 19 Years of Age, of middle Stature every way; he has short Red Hair, one fore Tooth broke out; he had on an old felt Hat, an old drugget Coat lined with black, a pair of Ozenbrigs Breeches made long for Riding, and a pair of new thick Shoes. If any person shall take up the said Runaway, and him convey to his abovesaid Master at Reheboth, or to Major Nathaniel Sheffield of New-port, Rhode-Island, shall be paid all Charges, and likewise paid for their trouble to content.

N. B. Both these above-mentioned Man-servants Ranaway together, Feb. 21st. 1723,4.

The Boston News-Letter, From February 20, to February 27, 1724; From February 27, to March 5, 1724.

RAN-AWAY from the Iron Works at *Lamparoel* River, in the Province of *New-Hampshire*, belonging to the Honourable *John Wentworth, George Jaffrey* and *Archibald Macphedris*, Esprs. and Mr. *Robert Wilson*, (supposed to be gone towards Philadelphia) *Robert Dowey* an Irish Fellow middle Stature, strait black Hair, pale thin faced, large Nose with a light coloured Cloth Coat, and *James Millar* an Irishman of about six Foot high, strait dark coloured Hair, with Pimples in his Face, who carried away with him two Coats, one a dark coloured, the other a light brown, they stole from said Owners of the Iron Works, two Horses, one of them a brown Horse, about 13 Hands high, the other a red with a white Main and Tall, of about 14 Hands high. Whoever will apprehend the said Runaways and secure them so as that they may be returned to the said Company concerned in the Iron Works, shall have Five Pounds Reward, and all Charges paid.
The Boston Gazette, From March 30, to April 6, 1724.

Deserted *from the Ship Friend Ship* James Warburton *Commander*, Alexander Spencer, *a Tall slender Man, of a Sandy Complection; And* Arthur Dent, *a Middle siz'd Man with his own Hair, and thick Lips. Whoever gives Notice of them so as they may be had again, shall receive of the said Capt.* Warburton *Forty Shillings reward for each of them. And if their will return to their Duty [they will be kin]dly received.*
N B. They came Passengers [   ]
The Boston Gazette, From March 30, to April 6, 1724.

RAN-away *on Thursday the 2d Instant from* Robert Auchmuty *of Boston Esq; A white Maid Servant, Named* Mary Hefferland, *aged about* 18 *Years, & Cloathed (when she left her said Masters Service) with a Linsey-Woolsey Gown & Petticoat, strip'd with black and blew Stripes. Any Person who shall apprehend said Runaway and bring her to her Master aforesaid, shall have reasonable satisfaction for their pains. And all Persons are hereby forbid to entertain her at their Peril.*
The Boston Gazette, From March 30, to April 6, 1724.

W*Hereas in the Boston Gazette of the* 30 *of March last, there was an Advertisement, That* Thomas Sherrard, Benjamin Millins, *&c absented themselves from their Duty on board the Brigt.* Maremaid, *then lying at* Nantasket, *or they should be prosecuted as Deserters: These are therefore to inform, That they did not Absent themselves from their Duty, no further than the Orders of the Owner and Commander.*
Thomas Shearrer, Benj. Mellens.

53

The Boston News-Letter, From April 2, to April 9, 1724.

R*AN-away the* 27*th of this Instant* April *from* Mr. Obadiah Procter *of* Boston, *A Negro Man Servant, Named* Bristol, *a short thick Fellow with a Kersey Jacket, a strip'd worsted Cap, Linen Breeches, a pair of green worsted Stockings, Cotton and Linen Shirt: He is about* 30 *Years of Age. Whoever shall take up the said Negro Man and him safely Convey to his saud Master in* Boston, *shall have* Forty Shillings *reward, & all charges paid.*
    The Boston News-Letter, From April 23, to April 30, 1724; From April 30, to May 7, 1724.

W*Hereas* James Cox, Richard Smith & William Divers *Mariners, hath deserted from the Ship Peace,* Henry Niles *Commander, if they speedily return shall be kindly accepted, otherwise they shall be prosecuted as the Law directs.* Boston, June 6th, 1724.
    The Boston Gazette, From June 8, to June 15, 1724; From June 22, to June 29, 1724; From June 29, to July 6, 1724.

RAN away from his Master Mr. James Smith, Sugar-Refiner, living near Mr. Colman's Meeting-House, at Boston, a Negro Man named Sambo, about 26 Years old, well set, pretty tall, smooth Skin, with a down Look'd, mark'd with a Whip on his Neck: He carried away with him a Snuff-colour'd Duroy Coat, a blue Camblet Jacket, a light colour'd Sagathee Jacket, with black Buttons, a Pair of Cloth Breeches, a red Cap, a Pair of grey Stockings, a Pair of white Yarn Stockings, a white Linen Shirt, three Cotton and Linen Shirts, a Pair of square and a Pair of round toe'd Shoes. Note, the said Negro formerly lived at Capt. Peter Papillon's Farm at Newtown. Whoever shall apprehend the said Runaway, and him convey to his said Master in Boston, shall have Five Pounds Reward, and all necessary Charges paid.
Note, The said Negro was seen last week at Newtown.
    The New-England Courant, From June 8, to June 15, 1724; From June 22, to June 29, 1724; *The Boston Gazette,* From June 15, to June 22, 1724. Minor differences between the papers. The *Gazette* noes not have the line beginning Note.

Boston, N. E. June 17. 1724.
D*Eserted from the Ship Nevis Frigate, John Hooker Master, John Bridge a squat Man, Pock-broken with black Bushy Hair, aged about* 35 *Years, Cornelius Thompson, a Dean of a middle Stature, well set with Bushy Hair, aged about* 28 *Years, Rodger Shimmans, aged about* 23 *Years, of a dark Complection, with black Hair, Richard Shainton, aged about* 21 *Years fresh*

coloured, wearing a light Wigg, Peter Blee, Edw. Mouleworth, Rich. Cristofor, & Wm. James a Welchman about 50 *Years of Age. Any one that shall apprehend the said Deserters, on any one of them, and conduct him or them to the said Ship lying at Clark's Wharff, shall have* 40 *Shillings Reward & all Charges paid.*
   The Boston Gazette, from June 22, to June 29, 1724.

Ran away on the 22d Instant, from his Master Capt. *Joseph Turrell* of Boston, an English Man Servant, named *Robert Jones,* (but often changes his Name,) about 23 Years old, well set, of a red Complexion, red Hair and Beard, his Hair lately cut off. He had with him when he went away, a Pair of red checker'd Plush Breeches, a striped Flanel Jacket, worsted Stockings, and wooden Heel Shoes.
   N. B. He formely lived with Mr. Miller of Milton.
Whoever shall apprehend the said Run-away, and him convey to his said Master at the North End, Boston, or to Mr. John Sebear, Merchant in Newport, Rhode Island, shall have Forty Shillings Reward, and all necessary Charges paid.
   The New-England Courant, From June 22, to June 29, 1724.

RAn away from his Master, Mr. *John Gibbs,* Painter, in Boston, a Negro Boy, named *Jemy Connungo,* about 12 Years old, well set. He had on when he went away, a speckled Linen Shirt, a Pair of Canvas Breeches, open at the Knees, without Shoes or Stockings. He carried with him a Canvas Jacket, and a Cotton Shirt. Whoever shall apprehend the said Runaway, and him convey to his said Master near Scarlet's Wharff, Boston, shall have Forty Shillings Reward, and all necessary Charges paid.
                                                            Boston, June 27, 1724.
   The New-England Courant, From June 22, to June 29, 1724; Fron June 29, to July 6, 1724; *The Boston Gazette,* From June 22, to June 29, 1724. See *The Boston Gazette,* From July 6, to July 13, 1724.

RAN away from his Master Mr. James Scolley Baker, in Savage's Court in Boston, the 14th of this Instant June, an Irish Man Servant named Francis Flood, about 21 or 22 Years of Age a well-set Fellow, speaks good English, but Grum, with an Irish Tone. He had on when he went away, an old Cloth colour'd Coat, a striped red and white home-spun Jacket, Leather Breeches, scollop'd round the Button-holes; gray yarn Stockings, and round to'd Shoes. Note, Said Servant has short Hair, or else a light Wigg. Whoever shall take up the said Run-away and bring him to his above-said Master, shall have Three Pounds Reward, and all necessary Charges paid.
   The New-England Courant, From June 22, to June 29, 1724.

RAN away at the same time from Mr. *Joseph* Calf of Boston, Tanner, an Irish Man-Servant, nam'd Stephen Cosly, about 19 Years of Age, of a middle Stature, fresh coloured, pretty well set, goes stooping, and has an unusual working with his Shoulders when he walks. He had on when he went away, a grey home-spun Drugget Coat, dyed Leather Breeches, yarn Stockings, wooden Heel Shoes, and an old brown natural Wig. Whoever shall take up said Runaway, and convey him to his abovesaid Master, shall have Five Pounds Reward.

The New-England Courant, From June 22, to June 29, 1724.

RAN away from Mr. *Joshua* Wroe of Boston, Merchant, on the 21st of this Instant, *June*, a white Man Servant, named *John* Mathews, about 18 Years old; well set, of a pail Complexion, has lank dark Hair; had on when he went away, a light coloured Cloth Coat, a Linen *Jacket* and Breeches, and gray Stockings. He carried away with him, a gray Coat, a Holland Shirt, and a Castor Hat, besides the Cloaths he had on. He is an Irish man, but speaks good English. Whosoever shall take him up, and bring him to his said Master, shall have Five Pounds Reward.

The New-England Courant, From June 22, to June 29, 1724.

RAN away at the same time from Mr. *Joseph* Calf of Boston, Tanner, an Irish Man-Servant, nam'd Stephen Cosly, about 19 Years of Age, of a middle Stature, fresh coloured, pretty well set, goes stooping, and has an unusual working with his Shoulders when he walks. He had on when he went away, a grey home-spun Drugget Coat, dyed Leather Breeches, yarn Stockings, wooden Heel Shoes, and an old brown natural Wig. Whoever shall take up said Runaway, and convey him to his abovesaid Master, shall have Five Pounds Reward.

The New-England Courant, From June 22, to June 29, 1724.

Ran away on the 22d Instant, from his master Capt. *Joseph Turell* of Boston, an English Man Servant, named *Robert Jones*, (but often changed his Name,) about 23 Years old, well set, of a red Complexion, red Hair and Beard, his Hair lately cut off. He had with him when he went away, a Pair of red checker'd Plush Breeches, a striped Flanel Jacket, worsted Stockings, and wooden Heel Shoes.

N. B. He formerly lived with Mr. Miller of Milton.

Whoever shall apprehend the said Run-away, and him convey to his said Master at the North End, Boston, or to Mr. Sebear, Merchant in Newport, Rhode Island, shall have Forty Shillings Reward, and all necessary Charges paid.

The New-England Courant, From June 22, to June 29, 1724.

W*Hereas* Thomas Dickings *a Soldier in His Majesty's Castle* William *(under the Command of the Honourable* William Dummer *Esq; being a Tall Man, Thin favour'd, with no Hair, having on a Red Coat, a course Kersey Jacket, Ozenbrigg Breeches, and Cotton Stockings, has lately Deserted His Majesty's Service from said Garrison. If any person shall apprehend said Deserter, and bring him to the said Garrison, shall have Forty Shillings Reward, and necessary Charges paid.*

The Boston News-Letter, From July 2, to July 9, 1724; From July 9, to July 16, 1724.

R*AN-away on the 6th Instant, a Negro Man, named Cesar, about 22 Years of Age, of a middle Stature, and well set. Had on a dirty Cotton and Linnen Shirt, and Ozenbriggs Breeches, open at the Knees. He took with him an old Cherridery Jacket a striped red and White Woollen Cap, without Shoes or Stockings.* Note, *He is wont to hide on board Vessels, unknown to the Commanders, in order to get off.*

Also ran away the 23d of June last, a Negro Boy named Jemmy Connungo about Twelve Years old, well set. He had on when he went away, a speckled Linnen Shirt, a pair of Canvas Breeches, open at the Knees, without Shoes or Stockings. He carried with him a Canvas Jacket, and a Cotton Shirt.

Whoever shall take up the said Run-aways, or either of them, and convey them to their Master Mr. Gibbs *Painter, near Scarlet's Wharff,* Boston, *shall have* Five Pounds *Reward for the Man, &* Ten Pounds *for the Boy, besides all necessary Charges paid.*

Boston *July 9th.* 1724.

The Boston Gazette, From July 6, to July 13, 1724; From July 13, to July 20, 1724; From July 20, to July 27, 1724. See *The New-England Courant*, From July 6, to July 13, 1724.

RAN-away on the 6th Instant, a Negro Man, named *Cesar*, about 22 Years of Age, of a middle Stature, and well set. Had on a dirty Cotton and Linnen Shirt, and Ozenbrigs Breeches, open at the Knees. He took with him an old Cherridery Jacket and Breeches, (a large Piece being out of the Back of the Jacket) a striped red and white Woollen Cap, without Shoes or Stockings. Note, He is wont to hide on board Vessels, unknown to the Commanders, in order to get off.

Also ran away the 23d of June last, a Negro Boy named Jemmy Connungo about Twelve Years old, well set. He had on when he went away, a speckled Linnen Shirt, a pair of Canvas Breeches, open at the Knees, without Shoes or Stockings. He carried with him a Canvas Jacket, and a Cotton Shirt.

Whoever shall take up the said Run-aways, or either of them, and convey them to their Master Mr. John Gibbs Painter, near Scarlet's Wharffe, Boston, shall have Five Pounds Reward for the Man, & Ten Pounds for the Boy, besides all necessary Charges paid.
The New-England Courant, From July 6, to July 13, 1724; From July 13, to July 20, 1724; From July 20, to July 27, 1724. *The Boston Gazette*, From July 6, to July 13, 1724.

R*AN-away from his Master Capt.* Richard Trevett *of* Marblehead, *A Negro Man Named* Pompey, *about Twenty-two Years of Age, a Lusty, Tall Fellow: He had on when he went away, a striped homespun Jacket, Cotton & Linen Shirt, dark coloured Kersey Breeches, grey yarn Stockings round To'd Leather-heel Shoes, and Felt Hat.* Note, *He deserted his Masters Service in the Shallop Ann, at Plymouth. Whoever shall apprehend the said Run away, and him safety convey to his said Master at Marblehead, or to Mr.* Francis Miller *in* Boston, *near the* Green Dragon, *shall have* Fifty Shillings *Reward and all necessary Charges paid.*
The Boston News-Letter, From July 30, to August 6, 1724; From August 6, to August 13, 1724.

R*AN-away from his Master Mr.* John Staniford *of Boston, on the 9th of this Instant September, in the Evening, A Negro Man servant, Named* George, *about* 30 *Years of Age, very slim in the Waste: He had on a dark Coloured Jacket with white Metal Buttons, Leather Breeches and Yarn Stockings. Whosoever shall take up the said Run-away, and him Convey to his abovesaid Master, shall have Forty Shillings Reward, and all necessary Charges paid.*
The Boston News-Letter, From September 3, to September 10, 1724.

RAN away on the 22d Instant, from his Master Thomas Hinkley of Barnstable, a Negro Man named Cuffee, a thick short Fellow, pretty well set, and hath a whitish Place on his right Cheek. Whoever shall take up and secure the said Negro, so that his Master may have Intelligence of him, shall be well rewarded for their Pains.
The New-England Courant, From September 21, to September 28, 1724.

Ran away on the 18th of this Instant November, from his Master Mr, Ebenezer Youngman, Hatter in Boston, an English Man Servant, named Benjamin Jarvis, about Twenty Years of Age: He carry'd with him a new suit of fad colour'd Drugget Cloaths, and a Broad Cloth Coat near the same colour, turn'd.

Whoever shall apprehend the said Runaway, and him convey to his said Master in Boston, shall have Twenty Shillings Reward, and all necessary charges paid.
The New-England Courant, From November 23, to November 30, 1724.

1725

W*Hereas* Anna Clement *the Wife of* Jeremiah Clement, *has at sundry times secretly convey'd away great part of his household Effects, & now of late eloped from her said Husband, & she together with her Accomplices supposed to have convey'd away her said Husband's Books of Accompts, within* 4 *Days, in her Husband's Absence.*

These are therefore to forbid every Person whomsoever, to discount, or pay any Money, give Credit, or any Trust, to the said *Anna Clement* from the Date hereof, for I hereby declare not to pay and Debts she shall contract from the Date hereof.

As witness by Hand, *Jer. Clement.*

Boston, Jan 13th 1724,5.

The Boston Gazette, From January 11, to January 18, 1725.

Ran away on Friday last, the 29th of January, from a Gentlewoman in Boston, an Irish Servant Maid, named Mary Farrel, of a middle Stature, pretty thick sett, and something Pock-broken. She went away with a black Griffet Gown, an old grey Petticoat, and a Pair of Ticken Shoes, with red Heels.

Whoever shall apprehend the said Runaway, and give Notice of her to the Printer hereof, so that she may be convey'd to her Mistress again, shall have a reasonable Reward, and all necessary Charges paid.

The New-England Courant, From January 25, to February 1, 1725; From February 1, to February 8, 1725; From February 8, to February 15, 1725.

R*AN-away from his Master Mr.* Brattle Oliver, *Merchant in* Boston, *the* 11*th of this Instant, A Negro Man Servant Named* Boston, *about Twenty Years of Age, full Face, much Pock-broken, middle Stature: He had on a Cinnamon colour Coat, Leather Breeches, White Stockings. Whoever shall take up the said Run-away, and him Convey to his abovesaid Master, in Milk Street, shall have Satisfaction to Content.*

The Boston News-Letter, From May 6, to May 13, 1725.

R*AN away from his Master John Jeffry of Groton, John Dilling, an Irish Man* 5 *foot* 9 *Inches high well set, wears a Cap or white Wig, a dark*

Coloured pea Jacket, Pale Fac'd flat nosed, went away the 29 *of April and was seen about* 22 *miles distant Enquiring the Road for Boston, he has been to Sea one Voyage and tis thought his design is to Ship himself aboard some Vessel, if he will Return to his Master, he shall be kindly Received, or if any Person will Secure him and give Notice to Mr. James Sterling, shall have Sufficient Satisfaction.*
    The Boston Gazette, From May 10, to May 17, 1725.

RAN away on the 23d on this Instant, May, from his Master Mr. Thomas Ayres of Boston, Cordwainer, an English Man Servant, named Elnathan Dam, a Shoemaker by Trade, about 20 Years of Age, pretty thick and well set, freckled Face, short brownish Hair: He had on a bluish Grey Homespun Coat, a Yellow Duroy Jacket, half worn, Wash Leather Breeches, a new speckled Shirt, Grey Yarn Stockings, new round Toe'd Leather-Heel'd Shoes, and Bath Mettal Buckles. He carried with him some Shoemaker's Tools.
    Whoever shall apprehend the said Runaway, and him convey to his said Master in Union-Street, Boston, shall have Forty Shillings Reward, and all necessary Charges paid.
    The New-England Courant, From May 17, to May 24, 1725; From May 24, to May 31, 1725; From May 31, to June 7, 1725.

RAN away on the 7th of this Instant June, from Mr. Henry Lawton, of Boston, Taylor, a likely Negro Boy, named Jemmy, about 14 Years old: He has on a dark Frize Jacket, Leather Breeches, and Leather heel'd Shoes, but no Stockings, Hat nor Cap.
    Whoever shall takes up the said Negro, and bring him to his aforesaid Master, near the Town-House, shall have Forty Shillings Reward, and all Necessary Charges paid.
    The New-England Courant, From June 7, to June 14, 1725; From June 14, to June 19, 1725; From June 19, to June 26, 1725.

R*An-away from his Master Mr.* William Cranston *of* New-Port *on* Rhode Island, *Shipwright, On Thursday the* 3*d day of this Instant* June, *An Apprentice, Named* Ralph Darwell, *aged* 19 *Years, of a Middle Stature, Dark Complexion, having his own Hair of a dark brown Colour, of Long Visage, Thin Nose, Gray Eyes: He had on when he went away an Ozenbrigs Jacket & Trousers, a Shirt made of Garlix, an English felt Hat and a pair of thick Shoes with Silver Buckles; he carried with him a Seersucker Jacket and breeches, a Cotton & Linnen Shirt, a large strip'd Silk Muslin Handkerchief. Whoever shall take up the said Run-away and him safely Convey to his said Master at* New-Port *aforesaid, shall have* Three Pounds *Reward and all necessary Charges paid.*

The Boston News-Letter, From June 17, to June 24, 1725.

R*AN-away on the* 16*th of this Instant July from his Master* Robert Hadwan *of* Boston *Merchant, a Malatto Man Servant, named* Tony Sampson, *he had on when he went away a Beaver Hat half worn, a Drugget Coat with Brass Buttons, a Black Wastecoat, stript Linsey-woolsy Breeches, worsted Stockings, & round to'd Shoes. About* 21 *Years of Age. Whoever shall take up said Molatto and bring him to his abovesaid Master near the Town-House, shall have Forty Shillings Reward.*
The Boston Gazette, From July 12, to July 19, 1725; From July 19, to July 26, 1726.

D*Eserted from the Ship John & Robert* John Underdown *Commander, now lying at Marblehead, the* 13*th. of this Instant July, Two Sailors, viz.* John Turner, *a Man of middle Stature, black Complection, &* John Masieling *a short well set fellow of a dark Complection: These are therefore to notify that if the said two Sailors will return to their Ship & Commander, they will be kindly received by him, or if any Person will apprehend & convey them to Mr.* George Craddock *Merchant in Boston, or to the said Capt.* Underdown, *shall be well rewarded for their Trouble.*
Marblehead, July 30 20*th.* 1725.
The Boston Gazette, From July 19, to July 26, 1725.

R*AN-away from his Master Mr.* John Dixon *of* Wellington *in Connecticut Colony, the beginning of* July *last, An English Man servant, Named* Edmund Jordin, *(may perhaps change his Name) about Twenty-two Years of Age, of middle Stature, well set, of fair Complexion, short black Hair; an Husbandman; he had when he went away a french Drugget Coat trim'd with blue, and small Pewter Buttons, Breeches and Jacket of a brownish colour, as also a white fustin Jacket: he may also have some other wearing Apparel not mentioned.*
Whoever shall take up said Run away and him Convey, or secure him in some Goal, in any Province or County, and send word to Mr. William Cady *Tavern keeper at the West end of* Warwick, *in Rhode Island, in* Plainfield *Road, or to* Bartholomew Green, *Printer at the South end,* Boston, *shall have* Five Pounds *Reward, and necessary Charges paid.*
The Boston News-Letter, From September 2, to September 9, 1725.

R*AN-away from his Master, Mr.* Adino Bulfinch *of* Boston, *Sail-maker, the Sixth of this Instant,* September, *at Night, A Servant Boy, Named* Thomas Cole, *about Sixteen Years of Age: his Hair is cut off, sometimes he wears a Cap; He had on when he went away a Canvas Jacket and Breeches: has also sundry sorts of Woollen clothing: And Stole from a Fellow Prentice*

Two Suits of wearing Apparel, with a Hat. Whosoever shall take up the abovesaid Servant Boy, and convey him to his abovesaid Master near the Dock in Boston, *shall have* Three Pounds *Reward, and all necessary Charges paid.*
The Boston News-Letter, From September 2, to September 9, 1725.

BOSTON, Sept. 30.
On Saturday Night last, the 25th. Instant, Three Indian Men, (being Captives) Cloth'd in English Habits like Servants, Ran-away from *Dorchester* in a Canoe, Intending (as is suppos'd) to Travel thro' the Country to the Eastward, and by that Means to escape out of the hands of the Government: His Majesty's good Subjects are Desired to enquire after, and if they may be found, to Apprehend and Convey them to His Majesty's Goal in *Boston*; And such Persons shall be rewarded to their Content.
The Boston News-Letter, From September 23, to September 30, 1725.

D*Eserted from the Ship* Berkeley, Robert Watt, *Commander, a Sailor, Named* Henry Archer, *These are to desire him to return to his Duty, otherwise he must expect to be treated as a Deserter.*
The Boston News-Letter, From September 23, to September 30, 1725; From September 30, to October 7, 1725; From October 7, to October 14, 1725.

Ran away on the first of this Instant October, from Isaac Little Esq; at Marshfield, a lusty Negro Man, named Aesop, about twenty-five Years old. Had on a brown Coat, checker'd Woolen Shirt, and grey Yarn Stockings. Whoever shall take up the said Runaway, and him safely convey to his Master, or give any true Intelligence, so as his Master may have him again, shall have Forty Shillings Reward, and all necessary Charges paid.
The New-England Courant, From October 2, to October 9, 1725; From October 9, to October 16, 1725.

D*Eserted from the Ship* Berkely, Robert Watt *Commander*, Anthony Cantey, *a Sailor: These are to desire him forthwith to Return to his Duty, otherwise he must expect to be treated as a Deserter.*
The Boston News-Letter, From November 25, to December 2, 1725.

R*AN-away from the Brigantine Providence,* Philip Viscount *Master, an Irish Man Servant, Named* John Hoyle, *of Middle Stature, pretty fresh Coloured; having with him sundry Clothing, A New Frock and Trowsers, a short Horse hair Bobb Wigg, also a Striped Cap, an Old Jacket Patch'd with Canvas, as also a Coat: Whoever shall Apprehend and Convey him to* *said* Philip Viscount *or to Mr.* Timothy Prout *of* Boston, *shall have Forty Shillings as a Reward, and all Necessary Charges Paid.*

The Boston News-Letter, From December 23, to December 30, 1725; From December 30, 1725, to January 6, 1726; From January 6, to January 13, 1726.

1726

R*A*n-away from his Master Mr. *James Scolley* of Boston, Baker, the 20th of this Instant May, An Irish Man Servant, Named *Arthur Wade,* about 18 Years of Age, speaks good English well set, fresh coloured, with his own Hair: he had on a new Castor Hat, a light coloured Coat, lin'd with red, white Shirt, white Stockings, and wooden heel'd Shoes. Whoever shall take up said Runaway, and him Convey to his abovesaid Master, at Savage's-Court in Cornhill, Boston, shall have Five Pounds Reward, & all necessary Charges paid. *Boston, May* 21 *st,* 1726.

The Boston Gazette, From May 16, to May 23, 1726.

D*Eserted from the Ship Mount Osborne* James Comerford *Commander the* 4th *Instant,* Joseph Demsey, *an Irish Man of a middle Stature, well set & fresh Colour'd about* 20 *Years of Age, he sometimes wears a Wig and sometimes a Cap; sometimes a White and other times a Blew Jacket: Whoever will Secure him, and deliver him on board the said Ship at* Marblehead *or to Mr.* Peter Faneuil *Merchant in* Boston, *shall have Forty Shillings Reward: And if he will return to his Duty in a Week from the date hereof, on Board the said Ship at* Marblehead, *he shall be well received.*
Boston June 20th. 1726.

The Boston Gazette, From June 13, to June 20, 1726.

R*AN away from* Jeremiah Wilcox *of* Dartmouth *the 5th Day of* June 1726, *a Negro Man about Twenty-two Years of Age, named* Jack, *marked with the Small-Pox in his Face, his Cloths are as follows, A Blew Cloth Coat, Home Spun Woolen Breeches Black and White, Two Shirts one Checkerd Woolen, and the other white Holland, Two Pair of Stockens one Black Silk and the other Grey Yarn, a New Pair of square-toed Wooden Heel Shoes, an Old Caster Hat and a Red Silk Handkerchief. The said Negro is supposed to have a Counterfeited Pass with him, and that Justice* Thomas Churche's *and Justice* Silvester Richmond's *Hands are Counterfeited to it.*

Whoever shall apprehend said Run-away and him Convey to his Master or to Arnold Collins *of New-port, or to* Robert Wilcox *of* North Kingstown, *shall have* Five Pounds *Reward and all Reasonable Charges paid.*

The Boston Gazette, From June 27, to July 4, 1726.

R*An-away from his Master, Mr.* John Clark, *Tallow Chandler, the* 12. *of this Instant, August, A Young Man, named* Samuel Holbird, *about* 22 *Years of Age, of a middle Stature, well set, of a brown Complexion, his Face scarr'd, his under Lip very thick, with a hole under his Lip drawn up, with a Scar, his Hair cut close to his Head, a worsted Cap: Had on a white Ozenbriggs Wastcoat, dark fustian Breeches, a pair of worsted Stockings, and a pair of Pumps, with Silver Buckles in them. Whosoever shall take up said Run-away, and him Convey to his said Master, in* Boston, *shall have Five Pounds Reward, and all Reasonable Charges paid.*
  The Boston News-Letter, From August 11, to August 18, 1726.

ON *Monday the* 15*th Instant, Deserted from the Ship Mary, George Kemp Master, now laying at* Marblehead, *Thomas* Cobby, *a lad of about* 17 *Years of Age, with short Hair, of a small Stature and Brown Complexion &c. Whoever will bring the said* Cobby *to his Master at* Marblehead, *shall have* Three Pounds *Reward.*
  The Boston Gazette, From August 15, to August 22, 1726.

D*Eserted from the Ship Joseph & Mary,* Richard Tyson *Master, the following Sailors, viz.* Clousip Baty, Hugh Man, John Prey, *and* Peter Major; *if they'l return to their Duty on board said Ship at* Cape-Ann, *they shall be received Kindly, if not shall be deem'd as Deserters.*
              Boston Sept. 26. 1726.
  The Boston Gazette, From September 19, to September 26, 1726.

R*AN away the* 24th *of this Instant* December *from his Master Mr.* Daniel Johannot *of* Boston, *Distiller, A Negro Man, named* Jupeter, *but calls himself by the Name of* Timothy, *is a Cooper by Trade; formerly belonged to Mr.* Chadock *of* Bradford, *a pretty Tall fellow, speaks bery good English, aged about* 35 *Years; had on a Leather Jacket & Breeches, two pair of arn Stockings, a pair of Square To'd Shoes, a very dark, almost black double breasted frize Jacket, with a white flannel Lining, a very good felt Hat. Whoever apprehends the said Run-away, & him Convey to his abovesaid Master, shall have Forty Shillings reward, and all necessary Charges paid.*
  The Boston News-Letter, From December 22, to December 29, 1726; January 5, 1727.

1727

R*A*n away from the Centry Snow of *Dublin,* John Stewart, *a pretended Sailor, He carried with him Six Pounds* in Money, and some Goods, supposed to be gone to *Rhode-Island,* he is a lusty young fellow; he had on a new Gray Jacket and Speckled Shirt. Whoever apprehends the said

Ranaway and gives notice to Mr. *Peter Luce* in *Boston*, or Mr. *Nathaniel Hatch* in *New-Port*, shall be well rewarded for their Pains.
The Boston Gazette, March 6, to March 13, 1727.

WHereas *William Hazelton*, an indented Servant of Mr. *Robert Auchmuty*, in *Boston*, about the 10th, of March, has Ran-away from his said Master, any Person that can give any Intelligence of him so as his said Master may apprehend him, or shall bring him back to his said Master, shall be sufficiently rewarded and all reasonable cost and charges born.
  N. B. He is of a Ruddy Complection, Middle Stature, wears his own Hair of a Sandy Colour, aged about 45 Years, professes himself a Gardiner, his Apparel when he left his Master was a double breasted drab coloured Coat, a new pair of Leather Breeches, and an Iron gray coloured cloath Jacket.
The Boston Gazette, From May 17, to May 24, 1727; From May 1, to May 8, 1727

D*Eserted from the Ship* Hariot, Joseph Austell, *Commander, the following Persons, viz.* John Davis, Robert Fisher, Francis Turner *and* David Wall; *Notice is hereby given to them or either of them, that if they will return to their Duty on Board said Ship at the Long Wharffe in* 4 *Days, they shall be kindly receive otherwise will be deemed as Deserters.*
The Boston Gazette, From July 10, to July 17, 1727.

☞Ran-away from his Master *Benj. Poole* Esq; of *Reading*, on Friday the 17*th* Instant, a Negro Man named *Pompey*, about 26 Years of Age, a short Fellow, had on a Gray Devonshire Jacket, Sad-colour Leather Breeches, no Stockings or Shoes. Whoever shall take up said Negro, and hin convey to his said Master at Reading, or to Deacon *Gibson* in Boston, shall have Satisfaction to Content.
New-England Weekly Journal, June 19, 1727.

☞Ran-away from his Master Mr. *Benj. Muzzy* of Lexington in the County of Middlesex, on the 11th. of this Instant June, a Spanish Indian Man-Servant, named *Beneto Furnace*, about 26 Years of Age, speaks very good English, and has a Blood-War under the left side of his Nose; is well-set Fellow. Had on when he went away, a Kersey Jacket of a Cinnamon colour, with Pewter Buttons; a pair of gray home-spun Cloth Breeches, with only one Button at each Knee: A Woollen Shirt, black and white Yarn Stockings, round to'd Shoes, but no Hat. He had an Iron Horse-Lock on the small of one of his Legs.
  Note, He was lately a Servant to Mr. *John Muzzy* of Mendon.

Whoever shall apprehend the said Runaway, and him convey to his said Master at Lexington, shall have Five Pounds Reward, and all necessary Charges paid. *Boston, June* 26. 1727.
New-England Weekly Journal, June 26, 1727.

R*AN away from his Master Maj.* Job Green *of* Warwick, *in the Colony of* Rhode-Island, *the* 31*st of* July *past, A Molatto Man, (born of a Negro Woman,) Named* Timothy, *commonly called* Tim, *about* 35 *Years of Age, a well set Fellow, of middle Stature, speaks good English: He had on when he went away, a Cinnamon coloured Camblet Coat, a check'd Cherry derry Jacket, Leather Breeches, a Garlick Holland Shirt, grey worsted Stockings, wooden heel Shoes, and a felt Hat. Whoever shall take up the said Run away, and him Convey to his abovesaid Master, or keep him in Custody so that his Master may have him again, shall have* Five Pounds *Reward, and all necessary Charges paid.*
The Weekly News-Letter, From August 17, to August 24, 1727; From August 24, to August 31, 1727.

☞Ran-away from his Master Mr. *James Lubbuck* of Boston, Chocolate-Grinder, on the 28th of last Month, A Young Negro Man-Servant, about 20 Years of Age, a short Fellow, speaks pretty good English, has thick Lips, battle-ham'd, and goes something waddling: he had on an old Hat, no Coat, a blue baze Jacket, a white Ozenbriggs Shirt, open knee'd long Canvas Breeches, pretty large Shoes, with a slit in the side of one of them. Whoever shall take up the abovesaid Runaway, & him safely convey to his abovesaid Master, living near Mr. *Colman's* Meeting-House, shall have *Three Pounds* Reward, and all necessary Charges paid.
Boston, Sept, 4th. 1727.
New England Weekly Journal, September 4, 1727; September 11, 1727; September 18, 1727. See *The Weekly News-Letter,* From April 25, to May 2, 1728.

R*AN-away the* 11*th Instant in the Evening from her Master Mr.* Thomas Lauchlin, *An Irish Servant Woman, Named* Margaret Smith, *about* 16 *Years of Age, speaks pretty good English, of fresh Countenance, fair Hair, and a good large Stature; She had with her very good Cloathing; She arrived here from* Ireland *about a Month since Whoever shall take up said Run away Servant, and her safely convey to her aforesaid Master in Mr.* Samuel Bleigh's *Yard in* Marlborough Street, Boston, *shall have Three Pounds Reward, besides necessary Charges paid.*
The Weekly News-Letter, From September 7, to September 14, 1727; From September 14, to September 21, 1727.

☞ **Ran**-away from his Master Mr. *Josiah Bacon* of Boston, Sawyer, on the 14th Instant, an Indian Man Servant Named Jo. Daniels, about 20 years of Age, a tall slim Fellow, has strait black Hair, had on an old Castor Hat, a double breasted Orange colour'd Jacket, with a strip'd woollen one under it, a Cotton & Linnen Shirt, an old pair of Leather Breeches, grey yarn Stockings.

Whoever shall take up the abovesaid Runaway, and him safely convey to this abovesaid Master at the North End near the Salutation, shall have *Forty Shillings* Reward, and all necessary Charges paid.

Boston, October 16th. 1727.
New-England Weekly Journal, October 16, 1727.

RAn-away on Wednesday Night last from Mr. *George Skinner, (upon suspicion of Theft)* Thomas Smith, *a short thin Man, of a fair Complection, with 3 large Scars on his Head, he had on when he went away a Worsted Cap of divers Colours, a Blue Camblet Coat cuff'd with red, a short strip'd Jacket run with Yarn, and strip'd Fustian Breeches.*

The Boston Gazette, From October 30, to November 6, 1727.

☞ **Ran**-away from his Master Mr. Robert Leach of Boston Cloathier, on the 2d. Inst. a young Man Servant Named James Pomrey, a wool-Comber by Trade, about 25 Years of Age, of middling Stature, Pock broken, one of his Legs something small then the other, his Toes goes somewhat inward. He took with him a Kersey Coat and Jacket with Brass Buttons an old Druget Jacket and a Striped on also, he has no Hair on his Head but wears a blue or white Cap and a Felt Hat. Whoever shall take up the abovesaid Runaway and him safely Convey to the Exchange Tavern in Boston, shall have Four Pounds Reward and all necessary Charges paid.

New-England Weekly Journal, November 6, 1727.

1728

WHEREAS John Davis *Servant to Mr.* Okeden, *absented himself from his Service on Saturday* March 16. *He is a Thick Clumsey Fellow, wearing his own Hair, and had on a plain Green Livery Coat with Brass Buttons, a Buff coloured Jacket and Breeches, and had with him besides a Brown Fustian Frock and a pair of Strip'd Ticking Breeches. These are therefore to desire all Persons to Stop the said* Davis, *and give Notice to the Post-Office, and they shall have* Three Pounds *Reward, and all necessary Charges.*

And if any Body detains the aforesaid Davis, *he is at their Peril.*

N. B. *He was formerly Servant to Capt.* Austin.

The Boston Gazette, From March 11, to March 18, 1728; From March 18, to March 25, 1728; From April 1, to April 8, 1728; From April 8, to April 15, 1728; From April 15, to April 22, 1728.

RAN-away from Mr. David Chesebrough *of* Newport *Merchant, a Molatto Servant Named* Philip Hall, *a Tall Slim Fellow, aged about* 30 *Years, he had on a dark coloured Druget Coat, Woollen Cap, and a Felt Hat: Whoever shall take up said Ran-away and him Convey to his said Master in* Newport, *or the Mr.* Francis Borland *Merchant in* Boston, *shall have* Three Pounds *Reward, and all necessary Charges paid.*
N. B. *He was formerly Servant to Col.* Wheelwright *of* Wells.
The Boston Gazette, From March 11, to March 18, 1728.

W*Hereas* James Lubbuck *of* Boston, *Chocolate-maker, has lately Absconded & Carried away with him Four* Negro's, *and sundry other Effects to a Considerable Value, and his Creditors having met on said Occasion, do Promise to Reward any Person who shall Secure said* Lubbuck, Negro's, *&c. with* Twenty Pounds, *Money, besides necessary Charges; and in case said* Lubbuck *will Return & Surrender himself & Effects to his Creditors, they Promise to Allow said* Lubbuck *the Sum of* One hundred Pounds *out of his Effects to set him up again, and Suspend any further Prosecution.*
The Weekly News-Letter, From April 25, to May 2, 1728; From May 2, to May 9, 1728; From May 9, to May 16, 1728; *New England Weekly Journal*, May 6, 1728; May 13, 1728. Minor differences between the papers.

☞Ran-away from Mr. *Ephraim Mower* of *Boston*, Cooper, on the 1st. Instant, A Negro Man Servant named *Jemmy*, about 19 Years of Age, speaks good English, of middle Stature, had on a woolen Cap, a thick dark woolen Jacket, a pair of Leather Breeches, Cotton & Linnen Shirt, and yarn Stockings. Whoever shall take up the abovesaid Runaway, and him safely convey to his abovesaid Master living at the North-End, shall have *Forty Shillings* Reward, and all necessary Charges paid.
May 14th. 1728.
New-England Weekly Journal, May 20, 1728; May 27, 1728.

THESE are to give Notice, that one Thomas Paterson, *a Covenant Servant to* Richard Gillam *Marriner, for Years yet to come, hath deserted his service and run-away, he is qualified as a Marriner, a pretty thick, well-bodied Man, of a fresh colour but somewhat tanned; and had upon him an Old ruste Perriwigg, a pair of dark Kersey Breeches, and a Pee-Jacket likewise dark coloured, and a pair of course Stockings mixed colour:*

Whoever can discover the said Thomas Paterson, *and him secure, and give notice thereof at the said* Richard Gillam's *House at the Mill-Bridge, or at the House of* John Menzies *Esq: in summer-street in* Boston, *so as he may be received, shall be honestly rewarded and all charges paid.*
                                             Marblehead, June 1.
   The Boston Gazette, From June 3, to June 10, 1728.

O*N the* 19*th of July last, An Indian Woman, Named* Lydia Charles *Bound by Indenture several Years yet to run, to* John Menzies, *Esq; Deserted his Service from his House in* Boston: *she is a Tall Lusty Woman, and has on a narrow stript Cherrederry Gown, turn'd up with a little flowred red & white Callico, a stript homespun quilted Petticoat, a plain Muslin Apron, & a suit of plain Pinners, and a red & white flower'd Knot. also a pair of green Stone Ear-rings, with white Cotton Stockings. & Leather heel'd Shoes. Whoever shall discover her so as she may be apprehended & delivered to the said* John Menzies *Esq; at his House in Summer Street in* Boston *aforesaid, shall have* Forty Shillings *reward.*
                                       Dated, *Boston, Aug.* 21*st.* 1728.
   The Weekly News-Letter, From August 15, to August 22, 1728; From August 29, to September 5, 1728.

R*AN-away from his Master Mr.* Matthew Sivret *of* Marblehead, *on the* 27*th of* August *last, A Servant Man Named* Samuel Allin, *aged about* 19 *Years, born in* Marblehead, *he is of large Stature, pretty fair Complexion, & of a clumsy Gate, he had on a double striped under jacket, & a light coloured drugget Jacket & Breeches, a new Castor Hat, worsted Stockings & wooden Heel'd Shoes. Whoever shall take up said Run-away & him Convey to his abovesaid Master in* Marblehead, *or to the House of Correction in* Boston, *shall have* Forty Shillings *Reward, and all necessary Charges paid.*
            Matthew Sivret.   Marblehead, Aug 27 1728.
   The Weekly News-Letter, From August 22, to August 29, 1728; From August 29, to September 5, 1728; From September 5, to September 12, 1728.

R*AN-away from his Master Mr.* Abraham Blish *of Boston, A Young Man Servant named* Samuel Waade *a lusty Youth about* 19 *Years of Age, pretty tall & fresh colour'd. He has on a brown woollen Jacket, striip'd homespun Breeches, black Stockings, and leather heel Shoes; a light colour'd Wigg, or otherwise short brown Hair. Whoever shall take up said Runaway, and him convey to his said Master, shall be reasonably satisfied, and all necessary Charges paid.*
   New-England Weekly Journal, September 16, 1728; September 23, 1728.

R*An-away from the* Gray-hound *in* Roxbury, *on the Lord's-Day the* 15th *Instant, A lusty Indian Woman, named* Beriheba Larrens, *she had on a Red flower'd Callico Jacket & Peticoat, a quilted Peticoat. Whosoever shall take up the said Runaway and her Convey to* Roxbury, *shall have* 20 *Shillings reward & all necessary Charges paid.*
  The Weekly News-Letter, From September 19, to September 26, 1728; From September 26, to October 3, 1728.

W*Hereas* Caesar Swift *a Negro Man deserted from Capt.* Marwood, *Commander of His Majesty's Ship* Lyme, *who lately belonged to Capt.* Cornwall, *about five Foot seven Inches high, has 3 Scars on each Cheek, had on when he went away, a Blew Coat, with white Mettle Buttons; Whoever shall apprehend and bring the said Run-away to the aforesaid Capt.* Marwood, *shall have all due Reward.*
  The Boston Gazette, From October 28, to November 4, 1728.

R*An-away the* 6th *of* October *from his Master* Elisha Green *of* Warwick *in the Colony of* Rhode Island, *an Indian Man Servant Named* Simon George, *of a middle Stature and a pale Complexion, he had with him a Cinnamon Coloured Jacket, and a pair of Long breeches, a Woolen Shirt, and a pair of Black Worsted Stockings, and an old Hat: Whoever shall Apprehend said Runaway and him Convey to his abovesaid Master shall have* Forty Shillings *Reward, and all necessary Charges paid.*
  The Boston Gazette, From October 28, to November 4, 1728; November 4, to November 11, 1728; From November 11, to November 18, 1728.

R*an-away on the* 13th. *of* Novemb. *Instant, From their Master* Mahuman Hinsdell *of* Deerfield, *Two Men Servants. The one* John Griffin, *a White young Man about* 16 *Years of Age, something pock broken, short brown hair, had on a Castor Hat, a Kersey Coat, homespun Jacket with Pewter Buttons, leather Breeches, and gray yarn Stockings.*
  The other a Pequot Indian named Peter Put, *alias* Pompey, *of midling stature, hair about* 3 *Inches long, has a remarkable Scar on the midst of his Forehead, had on a blue Broad-cloth Coat, Kersey Jacket with Pewter Buttons, and leather Breeches, speaks good English. They carried away with them* 2 *Guns,* 2 *Silver Spoons, &* 2 *Duffil Blankets.*
  Whoever will take up and convey the said Runaways, or either of them, to their abovesaid Master at Deerfield, *shall have* Five Pounds *Reward for each of them, and all necessary Charges paid.*
  Boston, Novemb. 28. 1728.
  New-England Weekly Journal, December 2, 1728; December 9, 1728.

☞ *Ran-away from* Mr. Daniel Watts *of Winnesimit on the 6th instant, a Negro Fellow named* Primus, *about 25 Years of Age, a tall likely Fellow, speaks good English, & can read well, has a Scar on his right Cheek, & a nub on the second joynt of his Thumbs. He had on a ticken Jacket, blue shag Coat, old Leather Breeches, but he carry'd with him a Mourning Suit; Cinnamon colour'd Coat with brass Buttons, two Hats, 4 Pair of Stockings, and a Gun with a new Rammer. He formerly lived with Mr.* Watt's *deceas'd who kept the Ferry House in Winnesimit.*

Whoever shall take up the abovesaid Runaway, and him convey to his said Master, shall have Forty Shillings Reward and all necessary Charges paid. Boston, Decemb. 7th. 1728.

New-England Weekly Journal, December 9, 1728,

WHereas one George Gray *a Jersey Man, aged about Thirty Years, a Pale looking spare Man of a Middling Stature, having pretended to be a Stranger in the Province, and in an indigent and helpless Condition, and having been under Bodily Distempers, has impos'd himself upon the Town of* Bridgewater, *and then upon the Town of* Sale, *(from whence he is privately gone off as soon as his State of Health allow'd it) in which Towns a considerable Expence has arisen by his Diet, Nursing and Care, and a great Charge has been thereby brought upon the Province; And there is Danger that he may in further Instances impose upon Other Towns, and thereby occasion a further Charge to the Province; For prevention whereof, This is to Notify and Direct the Select-Men of the several Towns, That in case Application should be made to them or any of them by the said* George Gray, *who is an idle, ignorant Fellow, or by any in his behalf for Relief and Maintenance, that they secure him, and give Notice thereof to the Secretary of the Province, and keep him in Custody, till they receive Directions from the Governour and Council concerning him.*

The Weekly News-Letter, From December 12, to December 19, 1728; From December 19, to December 26, 1728.

1729

☞ *Ranaway from his Master Mr.* John Robie *of Boston, Glazier, on the 8th of this instant February, an English Man-Servant, Named* John Clark, *about 19 Years of Age, of middling Stature, he has 4 Blewish Spots on one of his Hands. He had on when he went away, a Chocolate colour'd Drugget Coat, Black Jacket, Leather Breeches, Grey Yarn Stockings, round toed Shooes, Cotton & Linnen Shirt, an old Natural Wig, and a Castor Hat.*

Whoever shall take up said Runaway and him safely convey to his abovesaid Master near the Old North Meeting House, shall have Twenty Shillings *Reward, and all necessary Charges Paid.*

New-England Weekly Journal, February 10, 1729.

*R*AN-*away* on *Tuesday Night last, from his Master Mr.* Samuel Mattocks, *Chair maker, at the Sign of the Cross at the North End of Boston, an Irish Man Servant, Named* Thomas Fennel, *about* 20 *Years of Age, of middling Stature, dark colour'd Bushy Hair, Pock broken round face. He had on when he went away a dark colour'd Pea Jacket, lin'd with white Flannen, dark colour'd Breeches, an old Felt Hat, an old pair of Worsted Stockings, and an old pair of round toed Shoes. Whoever shall take up said Runaway, and him convey to his abovesaid Master at the sign of the Cross, shall have* Forty Shillings *Reward, and all necessary charges Paid.*

And all Masters of Vessels are hereby forbid to Entertain or carry off the abovesaid Servant, as they will answer it at their Peril.

The Boston News-Letter; From March 6, to March 13, 1729. See the *New-England Weekly Journal*, March 17, 1729.

☞Ranaway on Tuesday Night the 11th Instant, from his Master Mr. *Samuel Mattocks*, Chair-maker, at the Sign of the Cross at the North End of Boston, an Irish Man Servant, Named *Thomas Fennel*, Pock broken round Face. He had on when he went away a dark colour'd Pea Jacket, lin'd with white Flannen, dark colour'd Breeches, an old Felt Hat, an old pair of Worsted Stockings, and an old pair of round toed Shoes. Whoever shall take up said Runaway, and him convey to his abovesaid Master at the sign of the Cross, shall have *Forty Shillings* Reward, and all necessary Charges paid.

And all Masters of Vessels are hereby forbid to Entertain or carry off the abovesaid Servant, as they will answer it at their Peril.

New-England Weekly Journal, March 17, 1729; March 24, 1729; March 30, 1729. See *The Boston News-Letter*; From March 6, to March 13, 1729.

Whereas my *Negro Man* Caesar, *has assumed the Name of* John Mallott, *Pretending he was Free-born, and the Son of* John Mallott *a Free Negro in* Jamaica, *and ship'd by the way of* Barbados *here for his Education: This may Certifie the several Persons to whom my said Negro has spread this Report that the same is false & groundless, and that upon Examination before* Habijah Savage *Esq: One of his Majesties Justices, said Negro after being catch'd in Numberless Lies, Confess'd himself Born in* Guinea, *and brought into Barbados for Sale as a Slave, and was Sold accordingly. Also acknowledg'd the Authors of two forged Letters found with him. Now I Desire the several Persons to whom he has Resorted, no longer to Entertain him, and hope no Master of Vessel will Ship him, as he must expect to Answer the same at his Peril.*

Samuel Bass.   Boston, March 22, 1729.
New-England Weekly Journal, March 24, 1729.

WHEREAS Charles Blow, *a thin spare Negro Man about 5 Foot 9 Inches high, 25 Years of Age, has lately deserted from Capt.* Thomas Marwood, *Commander of his Majesty's Ship* Lyme, *the Station Ship here; he had on when he went away a blue Coat lin'd with Red and White Mettle Buttons, an Ash Coloured Jacket lined with Yellow, and Brass Buttons, and formerly belonged to Capt.* Durrell, *Commander of His Majesty's Ship* Sea-Horse, *and afterwards to Capt.* Cornwall, *Commander of His Majesty's Ship* Sheerness: *These are therefore to give Notice, that whoever will apprehend the said* Charles Blow, *and bring him to the said Capt.* Marwood *at the North End of* Boston, *shall have* Forty Shillings *Reward paid by him, and all necessary Charges.*
N. B. *The said* Blow *sounds the Trumpet.*
   The Boston Gazette, From April 7, to April 14, 1729; From April 14, to April 21, 1729; From April 21, to April 28, 1729.

RAN-away on the 20*th of* March *last, from his Master Mr.* Samuel Holmes *of* Newport; *a Negro Boy, Named* Newport, *a small Limb'd Boy and thin Face, about* 15 *Years of Age, speaks good English: Had on when he went away, grey Colour'd Homespun Jacket and Breeches, with Pewter Buttons.*
   Whoever shall apprehend the said Run-away, and him safely convey to his said Master in Newport, *shall have* Five Pounds *Reward, and all necessary Charges paid.*
   The Boston Gazette, From April 21, to April 28, 1729.

   R*an-away from his Master, Capt.* Tho. Foster *of Boston, on the* 28*th. of this Instant May, a Man Servant named* Caleb Cole, *about* 18 *Years of Age of a large Stature, with his short curl'd hair, a down Look, and a brown Complection. He had on a gray double breasted Jacket, and a striped Swanskin Jacket, Trouzers, round to'd Shoes, gray yarn Stockings, a castor Hat; and carried with him a cinnamon colour'd Broad cloth Coat. Whoever shall take up the said Servant, and him safely convey to his abovesaid Master, shall have* 40*s Reward and all necessary Charges paid.*
   Boston May 29, 1729.
   New-England Weekly Journal, June 2, 1729; June 9, 1729.

RAN-away about 8 *Days since from Capt.* Adino Bulfinch *of* Boston, *A Man Servant Named* Jeremiah Jones, *Felt-maker, about* 30 *Years of Age, middle Stature, with a white Shirt and a Speckled one under it, a Swansey strip'd Jacket, a dark coloured Cloth Coat, a narrow brim castor Hat, cut round the Edges his Head being lately Shav'd hath a Cap on. Whoever*

shall take up said Jones, *and him Convey to the abovesaid Capt.* Bulfinch, *Sail-maker in* Boston, *shall have* Forty Shillings *Reward and all necessary Charges paid.*
  The Weekly News-Letter, From May 29, to June 5, 1729; From June 5, to June 12, 1729.

*R*AN-*away from his Master, Mr.* William Ivers, *of* Boston *Rope-maker, on the* 28*th of* May *last, an* Irish *Man Servant, Named* James Hughes, *about* 19 *Years of Age, of a Middle Stature, pale Countenance, and short black Hair: He had on when he want away a new dark colour'd Drugget Coat, a light coloured Drugget Wastcoat, a pair of blew Shag Breeches, Worsted Stockings, and an ordinary Beaver Hat.*
  Whoever shall take up the said Servant, and him safely convey to his abovesaid Master, shall have Five Pounds *Reward, and all necessary Charges paid.*
  The Boston Gazette, From July 2, to June 9, 1729; From June 9, to June 16, 1729.

*W*Hereas Lydia Charles *a lusty well set Indian Woman, about* 25 *Years of Age, Ran away from her Master* William Lambert *of* Boston *Esq; in the* 14*th Instant, and carry'd with her a purple and white Callico Gown and Petticoat, the Gown fac'd with a small checker'd purple and white Callico, a white striped cherryderry Gown and Petticoat, the Gown fac'd with red & white Callico, and sundry other Cloths: she was formerly servant to* [Shu]bal Gorham *of* Barnstable *Esq; and by him disposed of to the Hon.* John Menzies *Esq; deceas'd: If any Person secures her and bring her to the said* William Lambert *in* Boston, *shall have* Forty Shillings *Reward, and all Charges paid.*
18*th of* Aug. 1729.
The Boston Gazette, From August 11, to August 18, 1729.

  Ran-*away from Mr.* John Lucas *Coach-Maker on the* 19*th. Instant, an* English *Servant, named* James Jefferson, *of a middle Stature, about* 24 *years of Age, much pock broken, and goes something Lame. He had on an old Hat, and a woolen Cap striped red & white, a light colour'd cloth Jacket, striped Flannel Wastcoat, blue & white Check Shirt, & yarn Stockings.*
  Whoever shall take up the abovesaid Runaway and him safety convey to his abovesaid Master, at the head of Prison-Lane, Boston, shall have Three Pounds *Reward, and all necessary Charges paid. Boston, August* 25*th.* 1727. [sic]
  New-England Weekly Journal, August 25, 1729; September 1, 1729.

R*AN-away from his Master Mr.* John Dixon *of* Wellington *in Connecticut Colony, the beginning of* July *last, An English Man servant, Named* Edmund Jordin, *(may perhaps change his Name) about Twenty-Two Years of Age, of middle Stature, well set, of fair Complexion, short black Hair; an Husbandman; he had when he went away a french Drugget Coat trim'd with blue, and small Pewter Buttons, Breeches and Jacket of a brownish colour, as also a white fustin Jacket: he may also have some other wearing Apparel not mentioned.*

Whosoever shall take up said Run away and him Convey, or secure him in some Goal, in any Province or County, and send word to Mr. William Cady *Tavern keeper at the West end of* Warwick, *in Rhode Island, in* Plainfield *Road, or to* Bartholomew Green, *Printer at the South end,* Boston, *shall have* Five Pounds *Reward, and necessary Charges paid.*

The Weekly News-Letter, From September 4, to September 11, 1729; From September 18, to September 25, 1729.

R*AN-away from his Master Mr.* Henry Laughton *of Boston, Taylor, on Friday the* 12*th of this Instant September, a tall slim Indian Boy named* Tom, *about* 18 *Years of Age: His Hair is not above half an Inch long, has a Scar of his left Eye, occasioned by a Wound lately cured; also a Scar on each Leg, about the Small. He had on a double breasted Drab Coat with small Buttons and small Sleeves, blue Drugget Breeches, black Stockings, round to'd Shoes, a black Neck-Cloth, and a white Shirt. Whoever shall take up the said Servant and bring him to his said Master, living near the Town House in Boston, shall have Three Pounds Reward, and all necessary Charges paid.* Dated, Boston. Sept. 22.

The Boston Gazette, From September 29, to October 6, 1729; From October 6, to October 13, 1729.

R*anaway from his Master Mr.* John Ham[   ], *of* Dover, *in* New-Hampshire, *the latter of of* September *last, a Negro Man-Servant named* Tom, *about* 24 *Years of Age, of a middling Stature, very strait Limb fellow, he has a hole in each of his Ears, a scar in one of his Cheeks, and one or more of his Teeth our before He speaks good English, He had on when he went away a Grey Homespun Jacket, a strip'd Linen one underneath, a good Holland Shirt, a pair of strip'd Cotten and Wollen Breeches, Yarn Stockings, and round toed Leather heel'd Shoes. He took also a pair of Gold Buttons. Whoever shall take up the abovesaid Runaway, and him convey (or secure) so that his Master may have him again, or to* Timothy Green *of* Boston, *Printer, shall have* Forty Shillings *Reward, and all necessary Charges paid. Boston November 5th.* 1729.

New-England Weekly Journal, November 10, 1729.

R*AN-away from his Master Mr.* John Greenleaf *of* Newbury, *the Twenty fourth of August last, A Negro Man Servant, Named Scippio, about Twenty-three Years of Age, speaks pretty good English, of a middling Stature, he had on when he went away a brownish colour Home made Cloaths, a light coloured Jacket with Pewter Buttons. Whoever shall take up the abovesaid Runaway Servant, and him safely Convey to his abovesaid Master at* Newbury, *or to Mr.* Robert Pateshall *of* Boston, *shall have* Five Pounds *Reward, and all necessary Charges paid.*
The Weekly News-Letter, From November 14, to November 21, 1729.

Ran-away from Mr. Daniel Watts *of Winnesimit on the 6th instant, a Negro Fellow named* Primus, *about 25 Years of Age, a tall likely Fellow, speaks good English, & can read well, has a Scar on his right Cheek, & a nub on the second joynt of this Thumbs. He had on a ticken Jacket, blue shag Coat, old leather Breeches; but he carry'd with him a Mourning Suit; Cinnamon colour'd Coat with brass Buttons, two Hats, a pair of Stockings, and a Gun with a new Rammer. He formerly liv'd with* Mr. Watt's *deceas'd who kept the Ferry House in Winnesimit.*
Whoever shall take up the abovesaid Runaway and him convey to his said Master, shall have Forty Shillings Reward and all necessary Charges paid. Boston, Decem. 7th. 1728.
New-England Weekly Journal, December 9, 1729.

1730

R*AN-away from Mr.* Victorious Looby, (*late of* Boston, *now living at* Newbury) *sometime in the Month of October last, a Negro Man Servant, Named* Roger, *speaks good English, of a middle Stature, well set; he has some signs of the Smallpox in his Face, Branded on his Shoulder* I G. *and a Crows foot: he had on when he went away four Chains of a Scale Beam lock'd about his Neck, a Cotton & Linen Shirt, a black Jacket, a pair of white Bays Breeches; he formerly belonged to Mr.* John Glin *of* Jamaica, *and he served several Years to a Cooper in* New-York. *Whosoever shall take up the abovesaid Negro Servant, and him safely convey to his said Master in* Newbury, *shall have* Five Pounds *Reward, and all necessary Charges paid by* Victorious Looby.
The Weekly News-Letter, From February 12, to February 19, 1730; From February 19, to February 26, 1730; From March 5, to March 12, 1730.

R*AN-away from his Mistress* Lydia Perkins *of* Boston, *on Tuesday Night, the* 10*th of this Instant* February, *a Negro Servant, Named* John Coffee, *lately Servant to Mr.* Thomas Eaton *of* Reading; *he is a pretty thick fellow, speaks good English hath had the Small Pox, hath a Cotton and Linnen Shirt, a Milled Cap, Leather Breeches, a Pee double breasted Jacket, with Brass Buttons, a white Woollen Westcoat lined with brown Ozenbrigs in the Body, yarn Stockings, and old leather heeled Shoes.*

Whosoever shall take up the abovesaid Run-away Servant, and him Convey to his abovesaid Mistress in Marlborough *Street,* Boston, *shall have* Forty Shillings *Reward, and all necessary Charges paid.*

The Weekly News-Letter, From February 19, to February 26, 1730.
See *The Boston Weekly News-Letter*, From November 13, to November 19, 1730.

Ran-away on the 10th of February last from *his Master, Maj.* James Brown *of Newport, a Negro Man, Named* Robin, *but sometimes call'd* Christmas, *about 21 Years of Age, of a middle Stature, and pretty slim: He had with him a Silk Jacket and Breeches, and dark colour'd Callicoe Jacket and Breeches. Whoever will apprehend the said Run-away, and him safely convey to his said Master, shall have* Three Pounds *Reward, and all necessary charges paid.*

The Boston Gazette, From March 9, to March 16, 1730.

Ran-away on the 13th Instant, from his *Master, Mr.* Samuel Frost *of* Piscataqua, *a white Man Servant, Named* Nathaniel Band, *he once belong'd to Mr.* Wallis *of* Boston, *Blacksmith, he had on a grey Kersey Jacket, a pair of new Shoes, and dark Stockings, a castor Hat, a woolen Cap, no Hair, and he is of a midling Stature. Whoever apprehends the said Runaway and him convey to his said Master, shall have* Forty Shillings *Reward, and all necessary charges paid.*

The Boston Gazette, From March 9, to March 16, 1730.

Stolen away from Silvanus Scott of Providence, *on the* 10*th of April last, at Night, a large Red Roan Horse, fourteen hands high, about* 7 *or* 8 *years old, paces very well, and is branded on the near Shoulder with the Letter* S *supposed to be stolen by one* Thomas Lovell, *who formerly liv'd with Mr.* Thomas Debuke *of Boston: If any Person or Persons will bring me the Man and Horse to Providence, shall have* Ten Pounds *Reward, if the Horse only, Six Pounds, as Witness by Hand in Providence*
this 21st Day of April, 1730.   Silvanus Scott.

The Boston Gazette, From April 27, to May 4, 1730; From May 4, to May 11, 1730.

Ran-away from her Master Mr. Samuel Smith, *of Cambridge, Shopkeeper, on the 19th of April last, an Irish Servant Maid, Named* Jenny, *alias* Jane Fitzgerrald, *Aged 18 Years or upwards: She had on when she went away, a Homespun Cinnamon Colour'd Druget Riding Hood, a striped Yard wide stuff Gown, cuf'd and fac'd with Red, and a Yellow and Red quilted Petticoat, and old Shoes patch'd on each Toe: Whoever takes up the said Run-away, and her safely convey to her said Master, or to Mr.* John Blake *Shopkeeper at the South End of* Boston, *shall have* Three Pounds *Reward, and all necessary Charges paid.*
The Boston News-Letter, From April 27, to May 4, 1730.

Ran-away from his Master Mr. Martin *Bremer, of Boston, on the 7th Instant, An Irish Man Servant, named George Shurkey, about* 15 or 16 *Years of Age, a well set Lad, pretty much pock-broken, wears a black Wigg, and has on a dark Duroy Coat, a dark Broadcloth Jacket, Leather, Breeches, Linnen Shirt, white Thread Stockings, and good Shoes. But tis likely he may have changed some of his Apparel. Whoever shall take up the abovesaid Runaway, and him safely convey to his abovesaid Master living at the Head of School-street, near the old Church of England, or to Mr.* Segourney *Distiller, at the North End near Charlstown Ferry, shall have* Forty Shillings *Reward, and all necessary Charges paid.*
The Boston Gazette, From May 4, to May 11, 1730.

*R*AN-*away from his Master, Mr.* William Ivers, *of* Boston *Rope-maker, on the* 28th *of* May *last, an* Irish *Man Servant, named* James Hughes, *about* 19 *Years of Age, of a Middle Stature, pale Countenance, and short black Hair: He had on when he went away a new dark colour'd Drugget Coat, a light coloured Drugget Wastcoat, a pair of blue Shag Breeches, Worsted Stockings, and an ordinary Beaver Hatt.*
Whoever shall take up the said Servant, and him safety convey to his abovesaid Master, shall have Five Pounds *Reward, and all necessary Charges paid.*
The Boston Gazette, From June 2, to June 9, 1730.

*R*anaway *on the 26th Instant* July, *from Mr.* Christopher Phillips *of* North-Kingstown, *a Spanish Indian Man named* Warmick, *about* 24 *Years of Age, of a middle Stature, and Slim, Short Hair, a Tanner by Trade.*
And a Mallagasco Negro Man, Named Cato, *about* 21 *Years of Age, a Thick Short Fellow of a Tawney Complection, long Bushy Hair if he had not since cut it off, a Currier by Trade; They both Speak good English. Whoever shall take up the abovesaid Servants and them convey to their abovesaid Master, shall have* Five Pounds *Reward, besides all necessary Charges paid by*

Christopher Phillips, *North-Kingstown*, July 31, 1730.
New-England Weekly Journal, August 3, 1730.

Robert Boyd, William Boyd & Hugh Leander *Deserted the Ship* Industry *the* 12th *of* September *last, and* Joseph Wattson *the 19th. from the said Ship,* William Shephardson *Commander, arrived from London the* 11 th *of* Sept. *last.*
The Weekly News-Letter, From September 24, to October 1, 1730.

Ran-away the 23d, of this Instant, at *Night, from his Master Mr.* William Wilson, *a Negro Man Servant Named* Boston, *a Lusty Strong Fellow, about* 27 *Years of Age, formerly belong to Mr.* Daniel Henshaw *of* Boston: *Whoever shall take up the above-said Servant and him safely convey to Mr.* George Monk, *near the Crown Coffee-House in* Boston, *shall have* Forty Shillings *Reward, and all necessary Charges paid.*
The Boston Gazette, From October 19, to October 26, 1730.

⁂Ran-away from Col. *Samuel Browne, of* Salem, *two Negro Men, the one Named* Juba, *a tall lusty well set Fellow, with great Lips, formerly belonging to Judge* Lynde: *the other of midling Stature, Named* Ceasar, *liv'd formerly with Major* Merrit *of* New-London, *they both speak good English; and went away on Monday Octo.* 19, 1730. *If any Person will take up said Negros and convey them to their abovesaid Master, shall be well rewarded for Charge and Trouble.*
The Boston Gazette, From October 19, to October 26, 1730; From October 26, to November 2, 1730.

Whereas *Lawrence Faffenback* (a Weaver by Trade) a *Palantine* had engaged to serve a certain time for his Passage from Holland, and went upon Tryal to a Master in Boston, and after a few Days signified his liking; Whereupon the Person who Cloathed him to the expence of *Ten Pounds*, and immediately after he went away and 'tis supposed by Land to Philadelphia. He is of a middle Stature, about 27 Years of Age, speaks no English, and had on a dark coloured cloath Coat and Breeches, a Buff Leather Wastcoat, a chequer'd Shirt and an old like Peruke. If any Person discovers said *Palantine*, it's desired he may be stopt in order to discountenance the like practices, and that Notice may be given to Mr. *Benjamin Atkinson* Merchant in Boston, who is ready to defray all reasonable Charges.
The Boston Gazette, From November 2, to November 9, 1730; From November 9, to November 16, 1730; *The Boston Weekly New-Letter*, From November 5, to November 13, 1730; From November 13, to November 19, 1730.

RAN-away from his Mistress Lydia Perkins of Boston, on Wednesday Night, the 11th of this Instant November, a Negro Man Servant, Named John Coffee, lately Servant to Mr. Thomas Eaton of Reading; he is a pretty thick Fellow, speaks good English, hath a Cotton and Linen Shirt, a Mill'd Cap, Leather Breeches, a Pee double breasted Jacket, with brass Buttons, a white Woollen Westcoat lin'd with brown Ozenbrigs in the Body, yarn Stockings, and old leather heel'd Shoes. Whosoever shall take up the said Runaway Servant, and him Convey to his abovesaid Mistress in Marlborough Street, Boston, shall have satisfaction to Content, with necessary Charges paid.
    The Boston Weekly News-Letter, From November 13, to November 19, 1730; From November 19, to November 26, 1730; From November 26, to December 3, 1730. See The Weekly News-Letter, From February 19, to February 26, 1730.

ON the 17th of this Instant November, Ran away from the Rev. Mr. Cotton of Newton, An Irish Servant, Named John Waughan alias Walker, about 19 Years of Age, had on a gray Coat cuff'd with black Velvet, narrow Sleeves, a striped holland Jacket, cotton & linnen Shirt, a pair of black Callaminco Breeches, a felt Hat, and Cap, his hair Short, and very much curl'd and of a reddish colour; a pair of new Shoes, and yarn Stockings, with white over them; and a silk musling Handkerchief about his Neck; and Shaves well. Whoever shall take up the said Servant, and safely return to his said Master, shall have Four Pounds Reward, and all necessary Charges paid.
    Ran away the same Day, from Mr. Joseph Boman of Newton, with the aforesaid Servant, An Irish Servant, Named, William Walker, about 20 Years of Age, of a middle Stature, a very fresh Countenance; He had on a dark colour'd homespun Coat, narrow Sleeves, with brass Buttons; and Jacket of the same with Pewter Buttons; a fine Shirt with Silver Buttons in the Sleeves, light colour'd drugget Breeches, had on a Cap, his head Sore on the top, a new felt Hat, a pair of yarn Stockings, wooden heel'd Shoes, and a pair of yarn Boots over his Stockings. Whoever shall take up the said Runaway, and safely return to his Master, shall have Four Pounds Reward, and all necessary Charges paid.
    The Boston Weekly News-Letter, From November 19, to November 26, 1730; From November 26, to December 3, 1730.

1731

RAN-away from his Master Mr. Jonas Webber of Newbury, the 7th of July last, a West Country Man Servant, Named, William Godfrey, about 21 Years of Age, a short well set Fellow, speaks broad English, and is much troubled with the Burst: He had on when he went away a Fly Coat, Cotton and Linnen Jacket, with blue and white stripes. Whoever will secure the said Run-away so that his Master may have him again, or convey him to Mr. John Darrell in Boston shall have Five Pounds Reward and all necessary Charges paid.

The Weekly News-Letter, From December 31, 1730, to January 7, 1731; From January 7, to January 14, 1731.

WHereas a Man Servant to Messieurs Merret & Fletcher of Boston Merchants, named Jonathan Aldroyd, otherwise called John, left his said Masters the Second Instant, after having Robbed them of several things.

This is to give Notice, that if any Person or Persons will apprehend him so as he may be brought to Justice, shall be well Rewarded. He is of a middle Stature well Sett, about 30 Years of Age, had on a light coloured Coat, double breasted, lined with Blew.

The Boston Gazette, From February 8, to February 15, 1731; From February 15, to February 22, 1731.

RAn-away from his Master, Mr. Thomas Salter of Boston, Cordwainer, about three Weeks from the Date hereof, A Negro Man named George, about 25 or 26 Years of Age, He is of a middle Stature, but thick and well set, and has a flat Nose, thick Lips, and is very much Pock-broken. He had on when he went away, a great lose Coat of a dark Colour, an old Blue Jacket, and Leather Breeches, but tis Reported that he has been seen of late with a Frock and Trouzers on.

Note, Said Servant can Work very well at the Shoe-maker's Trade.

Whoever shall take up the said Run-away, and bring him to his said Master shall be satisfied to their Content, and all necessary Charges paid. Boston, March 26, 1731.

The Boston Weekly News-Letter, From March 18, to March 26, 1731; From April 8, to April 15, 1731; New England Weekly Journal, March 29, 1731. Minor differences between the papers.

Ran-away from Mr. Joseph Knowlton of Newport on Rhode-Island, Housewright, on the 1st of April last, A Negro Man Servant, named Cuffee, about 28 Years of Age, a pretty tall Fellow, speaks broken English, is of a very black colour, & has several marks in his Face, wears a Cap, & a good Hat, he took with him a large Bundle of Clothing, a broad Cloth Coat lin'd with blue, a dark colour'd Duroy Fly, a light colour'd Duffle great Coat white Flannel Jacket, a Seersucker one a Silk one &c. Whoever shall take up said Runaway, & him safely convey to his said Master at Newport or Mr. Joseph Brown Distiller, near Mr. Waldo's Stillhouse in Boston, shall

have Forty Shillings *Reward, & all necessary Charges paid. Tis suppos'd the said Negro has a forg'd Pass, & designs to get off to Sea.*
New-England Weekly Journal, May 3, 1731; May 17, 1731.

Ran-away from his Master Capt. John Wildman, *on Saturday the 24th. of* April *last, from on board the Sloop Endeavour, then lying at the Town Dock, a Negro Man servant, named* Jack, *about* 30 *Years of Age, Speaks pretty good English, a short thick fellow. He had on when he went away, a Woollen Jacket, Leather Breeches, a homespun Linnen Shirt, a strip'd Woollen Cap, Old Yarn Stockings, he has neither Shoes nor Hat.*
Whosoever shall take up the abovesaid Negro, and him convey to his abovesaid Master at Norwalk, *or to Mr.* Richard Rogers *of* Stratford, *or to Mr.* Samuel Edwards *of* Boston, *shall have* Forty Shillings *Reward and all necessary Charges paid.*
New England Weekly Journal, May 10, 1731; May 17, 1731.

*W*Hereas William Everendine *about* 21 *Years of Age, pretty fat and well set, and short, of a fair Complection, on or about the 25th of* April *last, absconded and Ran-away from Mr.* Pearson, *Cooper, at the North end of Boston; he had on a black cloth Coat, lined with Silk, a grey cloth Wastcoat, with pewter Buttons, has lately cut his Hair, and now wears a fair bobb Wigg: Whoever shall take up the abovesaid Runaway, and him convey to* James Stirling, *of Boston, Mariner (his Master) shall have* Forty Shillings *Reward, and all necessary Charges paid.*
The Boston Gazette, From May 10, to May 17, 1731; From May 17, to May 24, 1731.

*R*AN-*away from his Master Capt.* Richard Brown, *of* Newbury, *on the 15th of* May, *an Indian Man Servant Named* Nero, *about* 22 *Years Old, near six Foot high, well Sett; he had on when he went away, a gray Pea-Jacket, lin'd with homespun, striped Flanel, a Cotton and Linnen Shirt, Leather Breeches, and gray Yarn Stockings. Five Pounds Reward if taken up and convey'd to his Master, and all necessary Charges paid.*
The Boston Gazette, From May 24, to May 31, 1731; From May 31, to June 7, 1731; From June 7, to June 14, 1731.

*W*Hereas William Robinson *has absented himself from His Masters Service, Major* Cope, *if he will return to Mr.* John Carnes *Merchant in Boston he will be forgiven, or if any Person will bring him to the said Carnes shall have Three Pounds Reward.*
The Boston Gazette, From May 31, to June 7, 1731.

R*AN away from* Josiah Jones *Master, sometime in the Month of* November *last, A Man Servant, Named* James Finney, *A Scotch Man speaks a little on the Scotch Tone, Aged near Forty Years, professes a Miller & Millwright by Trade, but went to Sea* 16 *Months since with his said Master, was in* Boston *last Tuesday. Whosoever shall take up said Servant and him Convey to Mr.* George Monk, *in King Street, shall have* Forty Shillings *Reward, and all necessary Charges paid.*
The Boston Weekly News-Letter, From June 3, to June 10, 1731.

RUN away the 18th of *July* last, from *John Gordon* of *Freehold* in *East-New-Jersey*, in the Township of *Middleton*, an *Irish* Servant Man named *George Tompson*, by Trade a Shoemaker, aged about 21 Years, of a pale Complexion, short lightish Hair, of Sature [*sic*] Tall and Slender, had on when he went away an old brown Ratteen Coat, an Ozenbrigs Shirt and an old Felt Hat, old Shoes and no Stockings. He Writes well and is much inclined to Reading and Smoking.

Whoever takes up and secures the said Servant, so that his Master may have him again, shall have *Thirty Shillings* as a Reward, and all reasonable Charges, paid by me *John Gordon.*

N. B. *He lately Run away from* Boston, *and pretends to have served his Time in* Boston *or* Rhode-Island.

The American Weekly Mercury, From Thursday July 22, to Thursday, July 29, 1731; From Thursday July 29, to Thursday, August 5, 1731; From Thursday August 5, to Thursday, August 12, 1731.

RAN-away from *Bond* and *Blowers*, on Thursday last a Negro Man named Tom, about 22 Years old, he is a tall well shap'd Fellow, he had on a Swanskin Jacket, speckled Shirt and Ozenbrigs Trowsers. Whoever will take up said Negro, and bring him to said *Bond* and *Blowers*, shall be satisfied to content.

The Boston Gazette, July 26, to August 2, 1731; From August 2, to August 9, 1731.

Tuesday Evening last a lusty new Negro Fellow that can speak little or no English, was missing and has not been since heard of, and 'tis tho't he has lost himself by his going without the least provocation. He had on a dark dueroy Jacket, Cotton & Linnen Shirt, Ozenbrigs Breeches, he has three long Cuts from his Temple downwards on each side his Face. Any Person that can give any account of him to the Printer hereof, shall have Thirty Shillings *Reward, and all necessary Charges paid.*

New-England Weekly Journal, August 9, 1731; August 16, 1731.

Ranaway from his Master Capt. John Bulkley *of* Boston, *on the Ninth of this Instant* August, *a Negro Man Servant, Named* Will, *about* 30 *Years of Age, a well set Fellow, Pock broken, Speaks good English. He had on when he went away, a striped Worsted Cap, Cotton & Linnen Shirt, a striped Flannen Wastecoat, Linnen Breeches, and Yarn Stockings. Whoever shall take up the abovesaid Runaway, and him convey to his abovesaid Master living in Queen Street, near the Town House, shall have* Forty Shillings *Reward and all necessary Charges paid.*

New-England Weekly Journal, August 16, 1731.

DEserted from the Ship Hannah, George Allen Master, Daniel Haberson, William Bonnett, James Steward, More Chorceman, and John Tompson; it they will return to the said Ship they shall be received.

The Boston Gazette, From August 23, to August 30, 1731.

Ran-away on the 2d of this Instant August, from his Master Mr. Comfort Carpenter, *of* Rehoboth, *a Spanish Indian Man Servant, named* Caesar, *about* 23 *years of Age, of a middling Stature, his Hair Lately cut off. Had with him when he went away, an old Felt Hat, a Cloth colour'd Serge Coat, black Calaminco Jacket, Ozenbrigs Shirt & Trousers, and strip'd Cotton Breeches. He had Iron Pothook about his Neck when he went away, and has a Scar on his right Elbow. Whoever shall apprehend the said Runaway & him convey to his said Master, or secure him in any of His Majesty's Goals, shall have* Three Pounds *Reward & all necessary Charges paid.*

New-England Weekly Journal, August 30, 1731.

R*AN away from Capt.* Pethuel Whiting *Master of a Ship now in* Marblehead, *the* 21*st of this Instant* September, *a Negro Man Servant Named* John Cuffee, *about Twenty Six Years of Age, speaks pretty good English, but something lisping: He had on a light coloured Duffel Coat, black Buttons, and black Velvet Cuffs to his Coat, strip'd Linnen Jacket, and Leather Breeches. He formerly belong'd to the Rev.* George Pigott, *late of that Town. Whoever shall take up the said Run away and him convey to his abovesaid Master, shall have* Five Pounds *Reward, and all necessary Charges paid.*

The Boston Weekly News-Letter, From September 16, to September 23, 1731. See *The Boston Gazette,* From July 23, to July 30, 1733.

R*AN-away from his Master, the Rev. Mr.* Johnson *of* Stradford, *in* Connecticut, *Sept.* 17*th. an Indian Man named* Pallas, *aged about* 18 *Years, a good looking Fellow, with short Hair, and a worsted Cap, a good grey homemade plain cloath Coat full trim'd with black, and linnen Breeches,*

speaks pretty good English, and had with him two Bags with some Provision in them, marked with Ink S I. *If any one shall secure the said Indian that he may be recovered by his said Master, shall have* Four Pounds *Reward, and all necessary Charges paid.*
    The Boston Gazette, From October 4, to October 11, 1731; From October 11, to October 18, 1731; From October 18, to October 25, 1731. See *The Boston Post-Boy,* June 2, 1740.

    Ran-away *from his Master Mr.* Samuel Jones *of Boston, Black-smith, on the 25th Instant, a Jersey Man Servant, named* Nicholas Cobbet, *about 21 years of Age, a short Fellow with his own black Hair, down look, squint ey'd, had on tis suppos'd when he went away a broad Cloth Coat yellow colour, woolen Breeches with Shammey Lining, but has Stol'n & carry'd with him sundry sorts of Cloathing, as Wollen, Linnen Sheeting and Shirting, Bedding, Peter Silver Buckles, a Silver Spoon & Scizirs, Chain, & divers other things to the Value of about* 50 *or* 60 pounds And thought to be with a French Fellow of Capt. Greenough's *who Stole and Run-away some time since. Whoever shall take the abovesaid Thief & Run-away, & convey him to his abovesaid Master living at the North End of the Town, shall have* Five Pounds *Reward, & all necessary Charges paid.* Octob. 18.
    New-England Weekly Journal, October 18, 1731.

    *R*AN-away *from* Ebenezer Eastman *of* Pennycook *on the 29th of November last, An Irish Man Servant called* John Henderson, *about* 18 *Years of Age, of Middle Stature, of a dark Complexion: he has a large Mold on one of his Cheeks. And a Cutt on one of his Leggs, leather Breeches, with a black Wasteband, a great blew Coat & a Bever Hat. Whoever shall take up the said Runaway and him safely convey to Mr.* Nathanael Peaslee *in* Haverhill, *shall have* Forty Shillings *Reward, and all necessary Charges paid by said* Peaslee.
    The Boston Gazette, November 29, to December 6, 1731; December 6, to December 13, 1731.

1732

    *R*AN *away from his Master Mr.* Edward Langdon *of* Boston, *Wigmaker, living near the Salutation Tavern, (early this Morning it being the* 12*th of* February,*) a Young Negro Man-Servant, named* Jack, *about* 18 *Years of Age, of a middling Stature, well set, something Pock-broken, his upper Teeth are artificially made sharp, Speaks English. He had on when he went away, an old Felt Hat, an old Kersey Coat with close Sleeves of a lightish Colour, an old Cloath Jacket something lighter than his Coat, a Leather* *pair of Breeches, grey Yarn Stockings, and an old Pair of Shoes. He has a hole in one of his Ears.*

Whoever shall take up the abovesaid Negro Servant, and him safety convey to his abovesaid Master, shall have Five Pounds *Reward, and all necessary Charges paid.*

N. B. *'Tis suppos'd he was entic'd by some ill minded Person in order to be carry'd out of the Country.*

This is therefore to desire all Masters of Vessels to take Notice that there is a great Penalty in the Law for carrying away any such Servant.

The Boston Gazette, From February 7, to February 14, 1732; From February 21, to February 28, 1732. See *The Weekly Rehearsal*, February 14, 1732.

☞*Ranaway from his Master Mr.* Edward Langdon *of* Boston, *Wiggmaker, on Saturday the* 12*th Instant, a Young Negro Man-Servant named* Jack, *about* 18 *Years of Age, of a middling Stature, well set, something pock-broken, his upper Teeth artificially made sharp, and has a hole bor'd in one Ear, speaks English. He had on when he went away, an old Felt Hat, an old Kersey Coat of a lightish Colour, an old Cloth Jacket something lighter than his Coat, a Leather pair of Breeches, Yarn Stockings, and an old Pair of Shoes. Whoever shall take up the abovesaid Negro Servant, and him safety convey to his abovesaid Master, living next door to the Salutation-Tavern, at the North End of* Boston, *shall have* Five Pounds *Reward, and all necessary Charges paid.*

Note, 'Tis suppos'd the said Negro has been by some ill-minded Person entic'd away in order to be carry'd off to the Sea, this is therefore to desire all Masters of Vessels to take notice of the Penalty the Law in that Case has made & provided, and all others are hereby warn'd against concealing or detaining of him. Boston, Febr. 14, 1731,2.

New-England Weekly Journal, February 14, 1732; February 21, 1732; February 28, 1732; *The Weekly Rehearsal,* February 14, 1732. See *The Boston Gazette,* From February 7, to February 14, 1732.

R*AN away on Saturday Evening last, from Mr.* Shirley *in King Street,* Boston, *a Molatto Negro Boy, Named* Jack, *about Nineteen Years of Age, of a Middle Stature, his Head close shaved, with three or four little Scars under the corner of one of his Eyes: He went off without a Hat, in a worsted Cap, a brown Suit of Cloaths, with white Strings in his Breeches Knees, and a Ring on one of his Fingers. He liv'd before he came to the said Mr.* Shirley *first with Mr.* Joshua Winslow *of* Boston *Merchant, and then with Mr.* Leavitt *of* Hingham. *Whoever shall secure him, and bring him to his said Master in King Street, shall have all reasonable Charges allow'd, and* Twenty Shillings *for his Trouble.*

The Boston Weekly News-Letter, From February 10, to February 17, 1732.

☞ *Whereas* Ruth Brown *the Wife of* Patrick Brown *of* Charlestown *hath Eloped from her said Husband, and run him in Debt greatly to his damage: These are therefore to Warn all Persons against Trusting the said* Ruth Brown, *for that I will not pay any Debt she may Contract after this Publick Notice given against the same.*
PATRICK BROWN,   February 21. 1731,2.

New-England Weekly Journal, February 21, 1732.

We hear from *New-London,* That one *John Abbot* was committed to Goal there, for Counterfeiting the last Emission of Five Pound Bills of Credit, of the Colony of *Rhode-Island*; and we have further Account, That as the said *Abbot* was in close Prison, his Wife had frequently the Liberty of being let into the same to visit him, and on Monday Evening the 7th, of this Instant *February,* she being let in as usual, while they were there, they together got off his Fetters, and chang'd Apparel one with another; after which *Abbot* call'd to the Keeper to let out his Wife; and the Door being open'd, he came out with her Apparel, and went thro' a Room where was several Persons sitting, making them the usual Complements of a Woman, and pass'd off undiscovered; the next Morning *Abbot's* Wife call'd to the Keeper, and desired to be released from her Confinement, which was accordingly done, tho' to his great surprize. There has been diligent Search made for said *Abbot,* but nothing cou'd be hear'd of him on Wednesday the 9th Instant.

The Weekly Rehearsal. February 21, 1732.

R*AN-away from his Master, Mr.* Nath. Dole *of* Newbury, *the 26th of* January *last, A Spanish Indian Man Servant, Named* James, *about 26 Years of Age, speaks good English, Middling Stature, with streight black Hair, not very long, & a Scar in his Forehead: He had on when he went away, A dark coloured Homespun Pee Jacket, with round Pewter Buttons, a pair of Long Trowsers over his Leather Breeches, a good Felt Hat, a pair of Yarn Stockings, and round to'd Shoes.*

Whosoever shall take up the abovesaid Runaway, and him safely Convey to his said Master at Newbury, *shall have* Forty Shillings *Reward, and all necessary Charges paid.*

The Boston Weekly News-Letter, From March 2, to March 9, 1732; From March 9, to March 16, 1732; From March 16, to March 23, 1732.

RAN away from Philip Arnold *of* Warwick *in* Rhode-Island *Colony on the 29th of March last past, An hired Man Servant, Named* John Barnes, *alias* Henry Barnes, *about* 30 *or* 40 *Years old, of a middle stature, fresh colour, has short dark Hair: He hath taken with him from his said Master, a grey Kersey Coat, a brownish Kersey Jacket, a Cotton Jacket, a Linnen Jacket, all without lining; a pair of Leather Breeches with Pewter Buttons, also a pair of Woollen Breeches, a felt Hat, a pair of white cotton Gloves, one pair of Yarn Stockings, two pair of worsted Stockings, one cotton and two woollen Shirts, three pair of round to'd Shoes: A yellowish or rather an Orange coloured Riding Hood with Arm-holes, a worsted Gown, and a pair of Woman's Shoes. He hath also taken with him a large Silver Watch mark'd with the Letters* S. A. *at the Key-hole, a round pair of Gold Buttons; a Gold Shirt Buckle of a Heart shape, two Gold Rings, a Silver Scissars Chain, marked, with the Letters* S. G. *a pair of Silver Shoe Buckles with double Tongues, Two Razors and a Hone, a Linnen Bolster Case, and an Ivory headed Cane.*

Whosoever shall apprehend said Servant, and him safely Convey to his said Master in Warwick, *shall have* Ten Pounds *Reward, and all necessary Charges paid,* Philip Arnold.   Providence, April 6, 1732.
The Weekly Rehearsal, April 10, 1732; April 17, 1732,

RAN-away from on board the Sloop Five Brothers, William Pattin *Master, on Friday the 7th of April last, an Irish Servant Boy named* William Sharp, *about sixteen Years old, has a small stopage in his Speech he had on when he went away a Brown Pea Jacket and blue Jacket and Cap.*

Whosoever shall take up the said Runaway and bring him to William Patten *shall have* Thirty shillings *Reward and all necessary Charges paid.*

N. B. *All Masters of Vessels and others are hereby Cautioned against harbouring said Servant.*
The Boston Gazette, From April 10, to April 17, 1732; From April 17, to April 24, 1732.

RAN-away from Henry Sherburn, *Esq. of* Portsmouth *in* New-Hampshire, *on the 17th of* April Currant, *an Indented Man-Servant, a Mason by Trade, named* Zebulon Salter, *he is a portly lusty fresh coloured young Fellow of twenty three or four Years old, & had on a double worsted Cap, a light coloured cloth or Kersey pea Jacket, seam'd & bound with Oznabrigs, a pair of Oznabrigs Trowsers, a pair of yarn Hose, & a ragged Shirt. He took with him sundry valuable Goods of his said Masters, and it is thought went towards* Rhode-Island.

Whosoever shall apprehend the said Servant, and him safely convey to his said Master at Portsmouth *aforesaid, shall be amply rewarded & have all necessary Charges paid.*

The Weekly Rehearsal, April 24, 1732; May 1, 1732; May 8, 1732.

Boston, June 1, 1732.
*R*an-away *early this Morning from his Master Mr.* Samuel Smith *of* Cambridge, *Shopkeeper, a Scotch Man Servant named* Neal Taylor, *about 18 years of Age, he is a short well set Fellow, has a full Face much Pitted with the Small Pox, and has thick brown curl'd Hair. He had on a homespun brown colour'd Coat, strip'd Jacket and Breeches, yarn Stockings, and a Felt Hat, beside a bundle of Cloaths.*

Whoever shall take up the said Neal Taylor *and return him to his abovesaid Master, at* Cambridge, *shall have* Forty Shillings *Reward and all necessary Charges paid.*

The Boston Gazette, From May 29, to June 5, 1732.

*R*an-away *from Mr.* Nathan Cheever *of* Rumney-Marsh, *in the Township of* Boston, *on Monday the 5th Instant, a Negro Man-Servant named* Portsmouth, *about 24 or 25 Years old, a pretty short well set Fellow, speaks good English, and can Write pretty well. He had on when he went away, an old Hat or Cap, a greyish homespun Coat, with Mettle Buttons, a homespun Jacket, a speckled homespun woollen Shirt, a pair of Ozenbrigs Trouzers, yarn Stockings, and old round toed Shoes. Note, Said Negro has been used to go in a Boat, and 'tis tho't will endeavour to get off to Sea; therefore all Masters of Vessels and others are forbid entertaining him, as they will answer it in the Law. He plays upon a Violin, & is suppos'd to have one with him. Whoever shall take up the abovesaid Negro, & bring him to his abovesaid Master, or to Mr.* Joshua Cheever *at the North End of* Boston, *shall have* Three Pounds *Reward, & all necessary Charges paid.*
Boston, June 10*th.* 1732.
New England Weekly Journal, June 12, 1732.

*R*an-away *on the* 11*th of this Instant* June, *from Mr.* Jonathan Sever *of* Roxbury, *an English Servant Boy, named* Wm. White, *he is about 15 or 16 years of Age, of middling Stature, has short brown Hair, and goes very shambling with his Feet. He had on a dark colour'd Fly Coat, Black Jacket, an old pair of Drugget Breeches, a pair of black or gray worsted Stockings, a fine Linnen Shirt, & an old felt Hat.*

N. B. *He took a quantity of Silver Money with him.*

Whoever shall take up the said Runaway and him convey to his abovesaid Master at Roxbury, *or to Mr.* George Skinner *in* Boston, *shall have* Five Pounds *Reward, and all Necessary Charges paid.*

New England Weekly Journal, June 12, 1732.

DEserted from the Ship Vine, *Capt.* William Moverly, Stephen Newing, *a tall young Man: whoever shall apprehend him shall have* Twenty Shillings *Reward.*
 The Boston Gazette, From June 26, to July 3, 1732; From July 3, to July 10, 1732.

☞ *Broke out of Bridewell on Monday the 7th Currant, a Negro Servant Man named* Tom, *he is about Twenty-five years of Age, a tall, comely well shap'd Fellow, he had a strip'd Swan skin Jacket, and is suspected to have taken some other Cloaths with him: He was seen on a Horse the 9th Instant riding towards* Braintree. *Whoever shall take up said Negro, & bring him to* Pyam Blowers *Merchant in* Boston, *shall have* Three Pounds *Reward, and all necessary Charges paid.*
 New-England Weekly Journal, August 14, 1732.

R*anaway from* Wm. Follangsby, *Commander of the Sloop John & Mary, now lying in the Harbour of* Boston, *on the 13th Instant, Two Irish Men Servants, the one named* Henry Welch, *a pretty short Fellow, aged* 23 *Years, black bushy hair, speaks good English, he went away in a Sailors Dress. The other named* Edmund Burran, *of a middling Stature, aged about* 21, *short brown hair, has the brogue on his Tongue. He had on a speckled Shirt, full trim'd Coat, a frize pair of Breeches. Whoever shall take up the abovesaid Runaways, & them safely convey to their abovesaid Master, or to the Keeper in his Majesty's Goal in* Boston, *shall have* Five Pounds *Reward for either of them, or* Ten Pounds *for both, and necessary Charges paid.*
 Boston, August 16th, 1732.
 New-England Weekly Journal, August 21, 1732.

R*an-away from his Master Mr.* Jarvis Bethell *of* Boston, *the 27th Instant, an Irish Man Servant named* Martin Conner, *about Twenty-five years of Age, speaks broken English, of a middle Stature, dark Complection, something pock-broken, short brown hair, and had on a bluish gray Suit of Duroy, a new Cotton and linnen Shirt, an old Checker'd Silk Handkerchief round his Neck and old Castor Hat, a new pair of Shoes, with several Nails drove in the heels both inside the Shoe and out, light colour'd Stockings, darn'd at the heels Whoever shall take up said Runaway, and him safely convey to his abovesaid Master, next Door to the sign of the Royal Oak at the North End of* Boston, *shall have* Three Pounds *Reward, and all necessary Charges paid.* Boston, August 30th, 1732.
 New-England Weekly Journal, September 4, 1732.

Newport, October 3, 1732.
Ran away on the 1st of this Instant October from his Mistress Mrs. Elizabeth Cole of South-Kingstown, a Spanish Indian Man named James, about 20 Years of Age, somewhat round shoulder'd, of a short Stature, pale Complection, and speaks very good English: Had on when he went away a Beaver Hat, a Silk Muslin Handkerchief, a light Grey Coat, with long Pockets, and a dark Grey Camblet Jacket, Tow Cloth Breeches and Shirt, and Grey Yarn Stockins.

Whoever takes the said Indian, and conveys him to his said Mistress, shall have Five Pounds Reward, and all necessary Charges paid.

The Rhode-Island Gazette, October 4, 1732. See *The Boston Weekly News-Letter,* From October 12, to October 19, 1732.

RAN-away on the first of this Instant from his Master Nathanael Wheeler *of* Boston *Blacksmith, an Irish Man Servant, named* Patrick White, *a short thick Fellow about* 22 *Years of Age, mark'd* P. W. *on one of his Hands with Powder, he wears short dark Hair, or a white Wigg or Cap, a light colour'd drugget Coat, and Jacket of the same patch'd in the Flaps, Leather Breeches and Yarn Stockings. He also took with him a gray Coat lin'd with blew.*

Whoever shall take up the said Servant and safely convey him to his Master, shall have *Five Pounds* Reward and all necessary Charges paid.

The Boston Gazette, From October 9, to October 16, 1732; From October 16, to October 23, 1732.

RAN-away on the first of this Instant October *from his* Mistress Elizabeth Cole *of* North Kingstown, *a* Spanish Indian *Man named* James, *about* 20 *Years of Age, the back part of his Head something flat, of a short Stature, somewhat round shoulder'd, pale Complection, speaks very good English: Had on when he went away, a Beaver Hat, a Silk Muslin Handkerchief, a light Grey Cloth Coat, with long Pockets, and a dark grey Camblet Jacket, Tow Cloth Breeches and Shirt, and grey yarn Stockings. Whoever takes up the said Indian, and conveys him to his said Mistress, shall have* Five Pounds *as a Reward, and all necessary Charges paid.*

The Boston Weekly News-Letter, From October 12, to October 19, 1732; From October 19, to October 27, 1732; From October 27, to November 2, 1732. See *The Rhode-Island Gazette,* October 4, 1732.

*R*AN-*away from* Thomas Porter, *on Tuesday the* 17*th of this Instant* October, *a Negro Woman named* Bess. *Whoever shall conceal or keep her must Expect to be Prosecuted as the Law provides in such Cases.*

The Boston Weekly News-Letter, From October 12, to October 19, 1732.

RAN-away from his Master Mr. John Sale, *of* Boston, *on the* 22 *of* October *at Night, an Irish Man Servant named* Francis Mc Genissy, *he had on when he went away a duroy Coat, a loose Red Coat, a natural Wigg, new Shoes, he goes somewhat Stooping, he had a Watch in his Pocket. Whoever takes up the said Runaway and him convey to his Master at the Three Horse Shoes, shall have* Forty Shillings *Reward and all necessary charges paid.*
    The Boston Gazette, From October 16, to October 23, 1732; From October 23, to October 30, 1732.

ABsconded from the Service of Mr. *James Smith Sugar-Baker, his Indented Servant* Samuel Grice, *a Sugar Boyler, a Man aged about* 35 *Years; whoever will take up or secure the said* Grice, *so that his said Master may have him again, shall receive* Five Pounds *Reward, and all necessary Charges paid: All Masters of Vessels are hereby forbid carrying off the said* Grice, *under the penalty of the Law in that Case made and provided, and those that knowingly Entertain him will be prosecuted in the Law.*
    The Boston Gazette, From November 20, to November 27, 1732; From November 27, to December 4, 1732.

R*AN-away from Capt.* Thomas Steel, *in* Hanover Street, Boston, *A Negro Boy called* Bass. *He is a tall slender Boy, has a smooth Face, stammers in his Speech, Aged about eighteen Years: Whoever takes him up, and sends him to his Master shall be rewarded for their Trouble; and his Master requests that none entertain him.*
    The Boston Weekly News-Letter, November 23, to November 30, 1732; From November 30, to December 7, 1732.

    On Saturday the 16th Instant, as Capt. *John Hubbard* of this Town, was in his way home from Connecticut, near Hewes's he was seized with the Numb Palsy; and just after was Robb'd of a large Sum of Money, by *John Harris* alias *John James*, who made his Escape; but on Monday was apprehended in this Town and committed to Prison.
    The Boston Gazette, From December 18, to December 25, 1732.

1733

    □R*Anaway last Thursday Morning, the* 22d *of this Instant* February, *from his Master Mr.* Aaron Blanchard *of* Medford, *an Irish Man servant, named* Moses Hood, *about* 17 *Years of Age, a short thick fellow, short Hair, much Red freckled, he waddles as he walks. He had on when he went away, an old Grey great Coat without Cuffs, a stone grey Jacket with flat Pewter Buttons, Leather Breeches, Grey Yarn Stockings, & round to'd Shoes worn out at the Toes. And 'tis tho't he took with him, a Natural Pacing Bay Mare,*

about 4 *Years old, she has a Star in her forehead, and the hair on her right Shoulder is worn off; with Bridle & Saddle. Whoever shall take up the above said Runaway and him safely convey to his abovesaid Master, shall have* Three Pounds *Reward and all necessary Charges paid.*
                                                                    Boston, Feb. 24. 1733.
    New-England Weekly Journal, February 26, 1733.

WHereas four Men, belonging to the *Fane* Frigate, *Samuel Marshall* Master, viz. *George Barclay, John Barclay, Peter Higgins* and *John Foster*, have for Three Days past neglected their Duty, and absented themselves from the said Ship without leave. THIS may Certify them, If they will return to their Duty, they shall be favourably received; otherwise they must expect to be treated as Deserters.
    N. B. Whoever will advise where the said Hands are, so as they may be taken up, shall have Forty Shillings Reward, provided they don't return voluntarily in Twenty four Hours after this Date.
                                                          Boston, Feb 28, 1732,3.
    The Boston Weekly News-Letter, From February 22, to March 1, 1733.

                                                            Boston April 16. 1733.
WHereas sundry hands belonging to the Fame *Frigate, Samuel Marshall Master, have absented themselves without leave from on board said Ship, and neglected their Duty. This may inform them, that notwithstanding their Desertion (provided in Twenty Four Hours after this Date, they or any of them do return to their Duty) they shall be favourably receiv'd: Otherwise must expect to be treated & deem'd Deserters.*
    The names of the Deserters are as follows, viz.
    John Holland, Isaac Chapman, Archibald Lyndsie, William Simons, George Banclay, John Banclay, John Rintoul, David Thompson, James Brown, John Forrester, Humphry Noble, David Nucall, & Peter Higgins.
    The Boston Gazette, From April 9, to April 16, 1733.

W*Hereas Three Sea-men deserted from the Ship* Union, *Capt.* John Homans *Commander, viz.* Thomas Martin, Joseph Stokes *and* John Smith, *on Sunday last: These are to Notify them, that if do forthwith return to their Duty on board the said Ship. They shall be favourable received, otherwise they must expect to be treasted as Deserters.*
                            Hampton, *In the Province of* N. Hampshire, April 13.
    The Boston Weekly News-Letter, From April 12, to April 19, 1733.

ON the 18th Instant Run-away from his Master Mr. *Richard Long*, of Salisbury, a Negro Man, about 24 Years of Age, a lusty thick set Fellow, had on a brown homespun Coat & Waistcoat, and a new pair of Shoes.

Whoever secures the said Negro, so that his Master may have him again shall receive as a Reward *Three Pounds*, besides being paid all necessary Charges.
   The Boston Gazette, From May 14, to May 21, 1733; From May 21, to May 29, 1733.

DEserted from the Ship *George*, Jacob Ayres Commander, lying in the Harbour of *Marblehead, George Exeter, John Lafagette, George Anderson* and *David Harris*, Marriners, belonging to said Ship.
   There are therefor to give Notice, that if they will return to their Duty in a Weeks time from this Date, they shall be received; otherwise deem'd at Deserters.
   The Boston Gazette, From May 21, to May 29, 1733.

WHEREAS *John Richardson* & *Elijah Harris*, Marriners & Foremast Men, belonging to the Brigt. Success, *Samuel Staples* Master, had for several Days absented from the Service of said Vessel. These are thereore to Notify them forthwith fo Return to their Duty on board, where they shall be kindly receiv'd; otherwise they will be treated as Deserters.
   The Boston Gazette, From May 21, to May 29, 1733.

RAN-away the 22d *of this Inst. at Night, from on board the Ship* Yoemans *and* Sawcolt, Nicholas Wadge *Master, a Servant Man Named* John Mason, *a Husbandman, about* 20 *Years of Age, a thin spare fellow, of middle stature, brown Complection, calls himself a Warwickshire Man, smooth Face, very short Hair, has the Irish brouge on his Tongue, had on when he went away, a brown Coat, a white Flannel Waistcoat, a white Silk Handkerchief, a white pair of Stockings, a check Shirt, an old Sea Hat, an old pair of thick sole Shoes.*
   Whoever shall apprehend the abovesaid Run-away and him convey on board the said Ship, now lying at Clark's *Wharf at the North End, or to Capt.* Phillip Dumerisq; *Merchant in Boston shall have* Three Pounds *Reward and all necessary Charges paid.*
   The Boston Gazette, From May 21, to May 29, 1733; From June 4, to June 11, 1733.

RAN away *on the 20th of May last, from his Master* James Brown, *Esq; of* Providence, *a Negro Man servant, named* Cuffe, *about* 30 *Years of Age, a thick well sett Fellow, a pretty large Stature, his left Leg is above twice as large as his right, and is attended with running Sores: He had on when he went away, a new dark homespun Jacket, an Ozenbrigs Shirt and a pair of Linnen Breeches. Whosoever shall apprehend the above Run-away and him*

convey to his said Master in Providence, *shall have* Twenty shillings *reward, and all necessary Charges paid.*
Providence, June 14. [sic] 1733.

The Boston Gazette, From June 4, to June 11, 1733; From June 18, to June 25, 1733.

R*AN-away from his Master, Mr.* Joseph Williams *of* Roxbury, *on Tuesday the* 19*th Instant, an Irish Man Servant, named* Patrick Ambrose, *about* 24 *Years of Age, Tall and thin Visag'd, has short brown Hair, peaks broad:* [sic] *He had on a check'd woollen Shirt, double breasted Jacket, long Trowsers, old Shoes, and an old Felt Hat. Whoever shall take up the said Servant, and convey him either to his said Master at* Roxbury, *or to Mr* Henry Howell, *Blacksmith in* Boston, *shall have* Five Pounds *Reward; and all necessary Charges paid.*

The Boston Weekly News-Letter, From June 14, to June 21, 1728; From June 21, to June 28, 1733; From June 28, to July 5, 1733.

R*AN-away from the Rev. Mr.* Pigot *of* Marblehead, *a Negro Man Servant, Named* Cuffy, *who had on a broadcloth Jacket lined with black, a pair of black Leather Breeches lined with shamy, an Ozenbrigs Shirt, a bouble* [sic] *worsted Cap, and a silk Handkerchief. He is distinguished by an oblong Wen over his left Eye. Whosoever shall secure said Negro shall receive* Forty Shillings *reward, with reasonable Charges.*

The Boston Gazette, From July 23, to July 30, 1733. See The Boston Weekly News-Letter, From September 16, to September 23, 1731.

R*AN-away from her Master, Mr.* Samuel Allaen *of* Newbury, *the* 17*th of July past, an Indian Maid-Servant, named* Keziah Wampum, *about* 19 *or* 20 *Years of Age, a tall, lusty Wench, speaks good English, but Stutters. She had on when she went away, a striped homespun Gown and Coat, a pair of black Shoes with wooden Heels, She took with her also a new striped bought Stuff Gown, and a Silk Crape quilted Coat. Whoever shall take up the abovesaid Maid-Servant, and her convey to her said Master at* Newbury, *or to Mr.* Boylstone *of* Charlestown, *shall have* Forty Shillings *Reward, and all necessary Charges paid.*

The Boston Weekly News-Letter, From August 2, to August 9, 1733.

Three Months ago Ran away from *her Master Mr.* Henry Tripsack, *from* Pemaquid, *an Irish Servant Woman, named* Hannah Smyth, *aged Thirty Years or thereabouts, pretty tall, and much mark'd with the Small Pox, very hard featur'd, she had on when she Run away, a striped Stuff Gown, and has been lately seen here in* Boston, *she has stole from her said Master a Diamond Ring. Whoever shall take up the abovesaid Run away*

Maid Servant, and her safely convey to Mr. Charles Apthorp *Merchant in Boston, shall have for their Reward Five Pounds and all necessary Charges paid.* Boston, Aug. 17. 1733.
The Boston Gazette, From August 13, to August 20, 1733.

R*AN* away from Mr. *Thomas Salter* of *Boston,* Cordwainer, on the last Commencement Day, a Negro Man Servant named *George,* about 26 or 27 Years old, a lusty well set Fellow, with thick Legs and thick Lips, and very much Pock broken, He had on a brown Cloth Coat with small Cuffs, Leather Breeches, and white Stockings. *Note,* He can work well at the Shoemaker's Trade. *Note* also, he now goes by another Name, and says he belongs to the Man of War. Whoever shall take up the said Servant, and bring him to his above-said Master in *Boston,* shall have *Forty Shillings* Reward, and all necessary Charges paid.
The Weekly Rehearsal, August 20, 1733; August 27, 1733; September 3, 1733. See *The Boston Evening-Post,* October 20, 1735 for George.

Whereas *Richard Dickson, Jordan Willson & Richard Ednale Marriners, belonging to the Ship* Mary *now in the Harbour of Boston,* John Lithered *Master, have absented from said Ship's Service, and taken away their Chests and Bedding, on Friday night last; notwithstanding if they or any of 'em will return to their Duty within three Days from the date hereof and proceded the Voyage, they shall be kindly receiv'd, otherwars will be proceeded against as Deserters.*
The Boston Gazette, From August 27, to September 3, 1733.

R*AN away from his Master Capt.* John Hayes, *Keeper of the Light House, the 29th of August last, an English Man Servant named* John Elwood: *He had on when he went away, a striped Homespun Jacket, a Cotton and Linen Shirt, a pair of Cinnamon coloured Plush Breeches, with Trousers over them.* Note, *he is a short well set Fellow, with a broad red Face, pretty much Pock broken. Whoever shall take up the said Runaway, and bring him to his said Master, or to Capt.* Philip Dumaresque *in* Boston, *shall have* Forty Shillings *Reward, and all necessary Charges paid.*
The Weekly Rehearsal, September 3, 1733; September 10, 1733; September 17, 1733; September 24, 1733.

R*UN-*away from the Ship *Stephen,* Stephen Jeudwin *Master* Simon Griffin, *a Foremast Man, contrary to his Agreement of Shipping; nevertheless if he will return to his Duty on Board in 3 Days time he shall be kindly received, otherways deemed as a Deserter.*
The Boston Gazette, From September 17, to September 24, 1733.

RAn-away from his Master, Mr. William Spikeman of Boston, Baker, on Saturday the 6th of this Instant October, a Negro Man Servant named Caesar, of a middle Stature but well set, between Thirty and Forty Years old, is splaw Footed, has thick Lips, and speaks good English. He had on when he went away, a thick blue Jacket, and a thin blue Jacket under it, a pair of Leather Breeches, and has with him a Suit of Black with other Cloathing. Note, The said Negro formerly lived with the Reverend Mr. Thayer of Roxbury. Whoever shall take up the abovesaid Run-away, and bring him to his said Master in Boston, shall have Forty Shillings Reward, and all necessary Charges paid.
    The Weekly Rehearsal, October 15, 1733; October 29, 1733; November 5, 1733. The second and third ads show a reward of Five Pounds. See The Boston Gazette, From October 15, to October 22, 1733, and The Boston Weekly News-Letter, From December 6, to December 13, 1733.

Ran-away from his Master, Mr. *William Spikeman* of *Boston*, Baker, on *Saturday* the 6th of this Instant *October*, a Negro Man Servant named *Caesar*, of a middle Stature but well set, between 30 and 40 Years old, is splaw Footed, has thick Lips, and speaks good *English*. He had on when he went away, a thick blue Jacket, and a thin blue Jacket under it, a pair of Leather Breeches, and has with him a Suit of Black with other Cloathing. *Note*, The said Negro formerly lived with the late Reverend Mr. *Thayer* of *Roxbury*. Whoever shall take up the abovesaid Run-away, and bring him to his said Master in *Boston*, shall have *Five Pounds* Reward, and all necessary Charges paid.   *Newport, October* 17. 1733.
    The Boston Gazette, From October 15, to October 22, 1733; From October 22, to October 29, 1733. See The Weekly Rehearsal, October 15, 1733, and The Boston Weekly News-Letter, From December 6, to December 13.

RAN-away on the 17th of this Inst. October, *a Negro Man named* Harry, *about* 40 *Years of Age, belonging to Mr.* John Gooch, *Sugar Baker, he is a very lusty Fellow had on an old pair of Leather Breeches, Oznabrigs Frock and Trousers, a great [ne]w duffel Coat. Also a Negro Girl named* Phillis, *about* 14 *Years old, belonging to Capt.* Roger Dench, *She is a short well set Girl, having on a dark coloured serge Jacket, a blew and white checkt cotton Coat, she carried away with her several other things as Sh[if]ts and Coats, &c. Whoever shall apprehend the said Runaways and bring them to Mr.* John Gooch, *shall be well satisfied for their Trouble and have all necessary charges paid.*
    The Boston Gazette, From October 22, to October 29, 1733.

RAN away from his Master, Mr. *John Tarp*, of *Kennebeck* River, about the middle of *September* last, an *Irish* Man-Servant named *Daniel Danworth*, about 28 or 30 Years old, of a middle Stature and brown Complexion, with Chesnut coloured frizled Hair. He had on when he went away, a red Jacket, a speckled Cotton and Linen Wastcoat, blue Breeches, yarn Stockings, and round toed Shoes. Whoever shall take up the abovesaid Run-away, and bring him to Mr. *Andrew Hunter*, Peruke-Maker in *Union-Street, Boston*, shall have *Three Pounds* Reward, and all necessary Charges paid.

The Weekly Rehearsal, November 12, 1733; November 19, 1733.

Ran-away from his Master, Mr. *Wm Spikeman* of Boston, *Baker, on the 6th of* October *last, a Negro Man Servant named* Caesar, *of a middle Stature, well set, between* 30 & 40 *Years old, he has a Mole on one of his Cheeks, thick Lips & Splay footed, speaks good English: He had on when he went away, a Blue thick Jacket, and a thin one of the same Colour under it, and a pair of Leather Breeches. He took with him besides, a Suit of Black and other Cloathing.*

Note, *The said Negro formerly lived with the Rev. Mr.* Thayer *of* Roxbury.

Whoever will take up the abovesaid Run-away, and bring him to his said Master in Boston, *shall have* Ten Pounds *Reward, and all necessary Charges paid.*

The Boston Weekly News-Letter, From December 6, to December 13, 1733. See *The Boston Gazette*, From October 15, to October 22, 1733, and *The Weekly Rehearsal*, October 15, 1733.

1734

*W*Hereas John Rackwood *Apprentice to* Weeks *and* Cannington *has absented himself several Days from his said Master's Service; Aged about* 19 *Years This is to forbid any Person to Negotiate any Business with the said* John Rackwood *on said* Weeks & Cannington's *Account; and further to apprehend the said* John Rackwood *and bring him to his said Masters, and they shall be well Rewarded, and have all necessary Charges paid.*

The Boston Weekly News-Letter, from April 11, to April 18, 1734; *The Weekly Rehearsal*, April 29, 1734; May 6, 1734. Minor differences between the papers.

A Servant Boy belonging to a Gentleman in *Boston*, has Absented from his Master's Service ever since the Day of General Election; he is a well set Boy about 12 Years old, and had on when he went away, a dark Duroy Suit of Cloaths, he wears his own Hair but above his Forhead a good part is

shav'd off. Whoever secures the said Boy and gives notice to the Printer hereof shall be satisy'd to Content.
   New-England Weekly Journal, June 10, 1734; *The Weekly Rehersal*, June 10, 1734.

R*AN away from Mr.* Joseph Parsons *of* Boston *Merchant, seven Days ago, a Negro Girl named* Violet, *aged about sixteen Years; She had on when she went away a white Jacket, a fad colour'd Petty coat, a Chain about her Right Leg, if not taken off is Pock-broken, a black rough Nail upon her Left Thumb. Whoever shall bring said Negro to her Master, at his House, or at* Parson *and* Adam's *Ware-house near the* Swing Bridge, *shall be well Rewarded for their Trouble.*
   The Boston Weekly News-Letter, From July 4, to July 11, 1734; From July 11, to July 18, 1734; From July 18, to July 25, 1734.

Ran-away on the second of this Instant *July*, from his Master Mr. *George Tilley*, Shop-keeper in Kingstreet *Boston*, a Negro Man Servant named *Cuffee*, about 35 Years of Age, of middling Stature. He had on when he went away, a Cotton and Linnen Shirt, Oznabrigs Frock & Trouzers, Old Shoes, a pretty good Hat; Speaks good English, and has had the Small Pox. Whoever shall take up the abovesaid Run-away and him convey to his abovesaid Master, shall be well rewarded for the Pains and Trouble, & all necessary Charges.
   New England Weekly Journal, July 15, 1734; *The Weekly Rehearsal*, July 15, 1734; July 22, 1734; July 29, 1734. Minor differences between the papers.

R*AN-away from* Timothy Keeler *of Ridgfield in the County of Fairfield in Connecticut, about the last of June, a Negro Man named* Mingo, *a likely well grown Fellow, thick set, speaks good English, can read and write, two of his little Toes is missing he is about* 28 *Years of Age. He had on a good duroy Coat of a lightish colour, a striped Caliminco Vest and Breeches, good Shoes and Stockings, a plain cloth Home-made great Coat with Brass Buttons, he had (as I am inform'd) a false Pass, a Pocket Compass, and several Books. Whoever shall take up said Fellow and convey him to Capt.* Samuel Keeler *at Norwalk in Connecticut, shall have* Seven Pounds *Reward and all necessary charges paid,*
                By me   Timothy Keeler.
   The Boston Gazette, From July 25, to July 29, 1734; From July 29, to August 5, 1734; From August 5, to August 12, 1734; From August 12, to August 19, 1734.

RAN-AWAY from his Master Mr. *Cornelius Campbel*, of *Boston*, Nailer, the third of this Inst August, an Irish Man-servant, Named *Daniel Mc Nemarer*, about Eighteen Years of Age, he has short brown Hair, if he has not shav'd his Head all over, a long Nose, a wide Mouth. He had on when he went away, a homespun strip'd Jacket, blue Buttons, a blue Coat with high crown'd white metal Buttons, a pair of white Plush Breeches, a Cotton and Linnen Shirt a square darn in the back it it, a pair of dark colour'd yarn Stockings, a Castor Hat almost new, and a pair of new round to'd Shoes, with white metal Buckles. It is suppos'd that he has taken sundry Goods from his said Master; and it's tho't he will change his Name.

And all Masters of Vessels &c. are hereby warned against concealing and carrying off said Servant, on Penalty of the Law in that Case made and provided.

Whoever shall take up the abovesaid Runaway, and him safely convey to his abovesaid Master, shall have *Six Pounds* Reward, and all necessary Charges paid. Boston, August 5*th*. 1734.

New-England Weekly Journal, August 5, 1734.

R*AN away from Mr.* Samuel Miller *of* Boston, *Gun-Smith, on Wednesday the* 14*th of this Instant* August*, an Irish Man-Servant named* Patrick Tomy*, who formerly went by the Name of* John Tomy, *and now calls himself a* New-England *Man born. He is about* 16 *or* 17 *Years old, a thick well set Lad, with very thick Legs, and wears a Cap, but has no Hair on. He is much Pock broken, and as lost the Sight of his left Eye. He had on when he went away, a dark coloured Kersey Fly Coat, with flat Pewter Buttons, a striped homespun Jacket, Leather Breeches Indian Dress, Yarn Stockings, and Calf Skin Shoes about half worn. Whoever shall take up the said Servant, and him safely convey to his abovesaid Master, in Draw Bridge Street,* Boston, *shall have* Three Pounds *Reward, and all necessary Charges paid. Note, The said Servant went from* Marblehead *to* York, *in the Eastern parts of this Country.*

The Weekly Rehearsal, August 19, 1734; August 26, 1734.

RAN-away on the 17*th.* Instant, From his Master Mr *Cornelius Cambpell* of *Boston*, Nailer, an Irish Man Servant named *Alexander Claton*, but 'tis thought he will change his Name, he is a short Fellow with short Arms and small Face, his Hair is very short if he has not shav'd it off, and has sundry scars in his Head, and he Writes pretty well, he had on a new brown strip'd homespun Jacket, a cotton Shirt, a pair of brown Shag Breeches pretty off and patch'd a pair of dark gray yarn Stockings, a pair of round to'd Shoes almost new. Whoever shall take up the abovesaid Runaway, and his safely convey to his abovesaid Master in *Boston*, shall have *Six Pounds* Reward, and all necessary Charges paid.

New-England Weekly Journal, August 26, 1734; September 2, 1734.

Newport, Aug, 16. We are informed that a Quarrel happened on the 3*d* of this Instant, between *William Manchester* and *William Teber*, both of *Dartmouth*, which arose to such a Heat of Passion that *Teber* struck *Manchester* with the Handle of a Mop over the Head, that he was carried home, he died on Tuesday last of his Wound.—*Teber* has since made his Escape, notwithstanding the 1000 *l.* Security he had given for his Appearance to answer to the said Fact.

The New-York Weekly Journal, August 26, 1734.

Ran-away from their Master Mr. William Wall *of* Prudence Island, *the beginning of this Month, a Welsh Man Servant Named* William Jones, *a well set Fellow, a short thick Neck, great Head, bushy brown Hair, about 25 or 30 years old, he had on a homespun mix coloured blue drugget Coat, greyish camblet Breeches, long linnen ditto, 2 cotton Shirts and one linnen a castor Hat, he carried away several things of value. Also Ranaway a Negro Man Named* Cuffee, *about 24 Years of Age, middle Stature, speaks pretty good English, slim bodied, had on a beaver Hat, Ozenbrigs Waistcoat, he carried away several Shirts both of linnen and woolen, a cinamon coloured Coat flat pewter Buttons long linnen Breeches, Shoes and Stockings. Whoever shall take up said Runaways and convey's them to their Masters shall, have* Six Pounds *for the white Man, and* Four *for the Negro, with all necessary Charges*
    paid by William Wall.

All Masters of Vessels are warn'd not to carry off the abovesaid Servants at their Peril.

The Boston Gazette, From September 9, to September 16, 1734.

RAN away from his Master *John Benkier,* Esq: *an Indented* Irish *Servant named* Alexander Gregory, *he is a Taylor by Trade, a short thick black Man, about 25 Years of Age; had on when he went away, a blue Coat lined with black, and black Horse-hair Buttons to it, and a small Cape lin'd with black Velvet, a light colour'd Cloth Coat, Waistcoat and a pair of Linnen Breeches. Whoever secures the said* Gregory *and brings him to the Post-Office in* Boston, *shall have* Five Pounds *Reward paid by said Benkier.*

The Boston Gazette, From September 9, to September 16, 1734.

RAN-away from his Master Mr. *John Hoorl of* Boston *Shipwright, on the* 11*th Instant at Night, a Negro Servant Lad named* Ben, *about 18 Years of age: He had on when he went away, a white Coat with brass Buttons, dark colour'd Breeches, a speck'd Shirt, a pair of new Shoes, but no Stockings. Whoever shall take up said Run away and him*

convey to his said Master near the Sign of the Bull, *shall have* Three Pounds *Reward and all necessary Charges paid.*
   The Boston Gazette, From October 14, to October 21, 1734.

                    RAN-AWAY from their Master, Capt.
James Woodside *of* Fredricks Fort,, *two Irish Men Servants, Named* David Roach, *and* John Kennelly, *they carried with them a Gun.* Roach *is aged about* 40 *Years,* Kennelly *about* 19 *and speaks good* English, *but* Roach *very broken. Whoever shall secure said Servants, and make the same known to their said Master, or to Mr.* Wheelwright, *or Mr.* Frederick Hamilton *of* Boston, *(so as that their said Master shall have them) shall have* Eight Pounds *Reward, and all necessary Charges paid.*
                                      Boston, Octob. 19th. 1734.
   The Boston Gazette, From October 14, to October 21, 1734. See *The Weekly Rehearsal,* October 21, 1734, and *The Weekly Rehearsal,* March 31, 1735.

R*AN away from their Master, Capt.* James Woodside *of Fredrick's Fort, about Three Weeks ago, two Irish Men Servants,* David Roach, *and* John Kenneiy, *they carried with them a Gun,* Roach *is aged about* 40, *Kennely about* 19 *Years:* Kenneiy *speaks good* English, *and* Roach *very broken. Whoever shall secure said Run-aways, and make the same known to their said Master, or to Mr.* John Wheelwright, *or Mr.* Frederick Hamilton *of* Boston, *(so as that their said Master shall have them) shall have* Eight Pounds *Reward, and all necessary Charges paid.*
                                      Boston, Octob. 19th. 1734.
   The Weekly Rehearsal, October 21, 1734; October 28, 1734; November 4, 1734. See *The Boston Gazette,* From October 14, to October 21, 1734, and *The Weekly Rehearsal,* March 31, 1735.

RAn-away the 29th of Octob. past, an Indented Servant to *John Corbett,* but assigned over to *George Webber,* at present residing in *Boston,* a White Woman Servant named *Mary Grenane,* about 22 years of Age, a tall swarthy Woman, has broad Teeth and thick Lips. She stole her Indentures and carry'd them with her. Whoever shall take her up and bring her to Capt. *Thomas Lowlor* on *Bronsdon's* Wharfe, Boston, shall have 5 *l.* Reward, & necessary Charges paid.
   New-England Weekly Journal, November 4, 1734.

    Ran-away from his Master *Stephen Sawyer of Newbury, the* 7th *of April last, an Indian Man Servant named Peter, of middle stature, upwards* *of* 30 *Years, he has a small bunch in his Forehead, speaks with small Voice. He had on when he Ranaway, a Homespun brownish plain Coat, a homespun sea-green Jacket with pewter Buttons, a speckl'd woolen Shirt, Trowzer Breeches, yarn Stockings, and good Shoes. Whoever will take up above said Ranaway and him convey to his said Master, shall have* Ten Pounds *Reward, and all necessary charges paid them.*

The Boston Gazette, From November 4, to November 11, 1734; From November 11, to November 18, 1734.

On the 5th Instant Ran away from his Master Mr. *Daniel Collins* of *Charlestown, Denies Mohegin* (commonly called *Ned*) about 18 Years of age, of a middling size, short dark Hair, thin visaged, freckled, and thin Lips, he had on a grey Coat, shammy Leather Breeches, Canvas Trowsers, grey Yarn Stockings, new Shoes, a Felt Hat, besides blue Riding Coat which he stole and has been seen with it on his Back in Boston.

Whoever secures him so that his said Master may have him again shall receive Forty Shillings Reward, over and above defraying all necessary Charges.

The Boston Gazette, From December 2, to December 9, 1734; From December 9, to December 16, 1734; From December 16, to December 23, 1734.

On the 27th of *July* last, *John Herrald, an Indented Servant Ran away from his mistress mrs.* Elizabeth Hubbart, *and is not yet Return'd, he is by Trade a Hatter, and has about* 2 *Years to serve; as to his person he is a pretty lusty well set young man of a fresh Complexion, wears no Hair, he carried with him a suit of grey Cloaths trim'd with black, it's supposed he goes in a Wastecoat and Trowzers, and bound for* New-York.

Whoever will secure him so that his mistress may have him again, shall receive Five pounds *Reward besides Necessary Charges.*

The Boston Gazette, From December 2, to December 9, 1734; From December 9, to December 16, 1734; From December 23, to December 30.

Simon Elwerthy, William Whaley & Robert Taylor, Mariners, belonging to the Ship *Priscilla, Christopher Rymes* Master, have absented themselves from the Service of the said Ship.

This is therefore to Notify them or either of them, that if they will return to their Duty within three Days from the date hereof, they shall be kindly received by the said Master, otherways will be deem'd Deserters.

The Boston Gazette, From December 2, to December 9, 1734.

1735

Run away on the 23*d* of March, 1734, from *Joseph Earl,* of *Portsmouth* in *Rhode-Island,* an English Servant Man, named *Jonathan Earl,* about 22 Years of Age, about 6 Foot high, has with him when he went away, an old Hat, a grayish coloured homespun Coat, Jacket and Trowzers, 2 woolen Shirts, and a fine one, and a Pair of Leather heel'd Shoes; his Hair was then lately cut off, and he has a Scar on one of his Legs. Whoever takes up the said Servant, and secures him so that *William Lawrence* of *Shrewsbury* in *East-Jersey,* or *Joseph Earl* of *Portsmouth, Rhode Island,* may have him, shall have 3 Pounds as a Reward, and all reasonable Charges.
The New-York Weekly Journal, January 5, 1735; January 12, 1735; January 19, 1735; December 1, 1735; December 8, 1735; December 15, 1735; December 22, 1735.

D*Eserted on Friday last from the Ship Samuel and James,* David Orrok *Commander, the seven following Sailors, viz.* Christopher Boman, Peter Peterson, James Douia, John Young, James Tomson, Robert Tomson, *and* Robert Young, *If the said Deserters will immediately return to their Duty on board the said Ship they shall be received, otherwise they shall be treated as Deserters.* January 25th. 1734,5.
New England Weekly Journal, January 27, 1735.

RAN away on Tuesday last *Thomas Denham an Irish Indented Servant, a Taylor by Trade, about sixteen Years of Age, with short Hair, having no Toes.*
Whoever can tell where said Run-away may be found and secure, shall receive Forty Shillings *Reward from the Publisher hereof.*
The Boston Gazette, From February 24, to March 3, 1735.

ON Saturday Night the eighth of Feb. past, the Shop of Samuel Belden of Norwalk in Connecticut, was broke open, and sundry Goods stolen out of the same, viz. Three Pieces and half of Chince, or fine Callico, one of them the ground word skie colour sprig'd with Red; another the Ground green, flower'd with red and white; another, spotted with red and dark purple, and the half Piece purple and white, spotted with red and the flowers bold; One Piece of striped Lutestring, One Piece of Flowered striped Lutestring, Four Pieces of Camblets, One Piece of Muslin, One piece grey Duroy, One piece of Diaper, several pieces of Ribbon, Men's grey Stockings, and Women's blue Stockings with white Clocks, some of the Clocks Silk and some Worsted; half a piece of light colour'd East India Sattin, raised Work upon it of the same Colour, which spotted it all over; a parcel of Men's Shoes and

sundry other Goods. This Felony is supposed to be committed by two Irish Men, viz. John MacNeil and William MacKeel, said MacKeel is a well set Man, of darkish Complexion, pockfretten, and has dark sandy Hair. MacNeil is a Man of middle Stature, full faced, with a Flat Nose. These two Men go under the pretence of Pedlars, and have Goods in their Packs. One has a sort of Leather Port Mantua, and the other has a Bag. They have been pursued to the City of New York, where they have disposed of some of said Goods, and 'tis supposed are in the Jerseys or Pennsylvania, or gone towards Maryland. Whoever shall apprehend and secure any Person or Persons with the said stollen Goods, and give Notice to the said Samuel Belden, so that such Person or Persons may be brought to Justice, shall have Ten Pounds as a Reward, and Reasonable Charges,
    paid by Samuel Belden.
The Pennsylvania Gazette, March 11, 1735.

R*AN away from their Master, Capt.* James Woodside *of* Fredrick's *Fort, the* 28*th of* February *last, two Irish Men Servants,* David Roach, *and* John Kennely. Roach *is aged about* 40 *Years, a short thick Fellow, speaks very broken* English. *He had on a white Freeze Jacket, a blue under Jacket of Linsey Woolsey Homespun, blue and white striped Breeches of Homespun Woolen.* Kennely *is aged about* 23 *Years, speaks pretty good* English, *had on a dark brown under Jacket of Freeze, a blue under Jacket of Linsey Wooley Homespun, and Leather Breeches. They have both short Hair, and wear Caps. Note,* Roach *speaks* Latin, Kennely *is a Shoe-maker. They had with them each Man a Blanket, and two checker'd Woollen Shirts.*
 Whoever shall secure said Run-aways, (so as their Master may have them) shall receive Sixteen Pounds *Reward, and have all necessary Charges paid. Inform Messieurs* John Wheelwright, Rowland Houghton, *or* Frederick Hamilton, *Merchants in* Boston.
         Frederick's Fort, *March* 12, 1734.
The Weekly Rehearsal, March 31, 1735; April 7, 1735. See *The Boston Gazette,* From October 14, to October 21, 1734, and *The Weekly Rehearsal,* October 21, 1734.

R*An-away* from their Master Mr. *William Owen* of *Boston,* Taylor, on the 11th Instant, two young Men Servants, the one named *John Maxwell* (not *Maxfield* as it's in the Printed Advertisement,) about 20 Years of Age, a tall slim Fellow, has a down look, wears a light natural Wig, dark colour'd fly Coat, took with him a blue Jacket, and a striped home spun one. The other named *John Saltar,* about 19 Years of Age, a very small, slim Fellow, had on a dark natural Wig, a dark gray fly Coat trim'd with black, a dark colour'd Jacket with brass Buttons. They took with them some other Cloathing besides what they had on. Whoever shall take up the abovesaid

Runaways, & them safely convey to their said Master near the Market at the Town-Dock, shall have *Six Pounds* Reward for both, or *Three Pounds* for each, and all necessary Charges paid.

New-England Weekly Journal, April 21, 1735; May 5, 1735. See *New-England Weekly Journal*, May 12, 1735, for Saltar.

*R*UN-*away from his Master, on Monday the* 28*th of* April *past, A Lusty Servant Man, whose Name is* William Hugh*s: He is a Welch Man; talks very broken English; is of a fair Complection; He had on, an old Fustain Coat and an old Kersey Jacket over it, very much Moth eaten: One of his Fore Fingers is very sore, and bundled up with Rags: Whoever will take up the said Servant, and bring him to his Master on Board the Sloop Two Brothers, now lying at the Town Dock, shall have* Three Pounds *Reward, with reasonable Charges; as Witness my Hand this* 1*st of May* 1735.
Robert Wing.

The Boston Weekly News-Letter, From April 24, to May 1, 1735; From May 1, to May 8, 1735.

*R*An-away from his Master Mr. *William Owen* of *Boston*, Taylor, on the 11th past, a young Man Servant, named *John Saltar*, about 19 Years of Age, a very small, slim Fellow, had on a small dark natural Wig, a dark gray fly Coat trim'd with black, a dark colour'd Jacket with brass Buttons. He took with him some other Cloathing besides what he had on. Whoever will take up the abovesaid Runaway, and him safely convey to his said Master near the Market at the Town-Dock, shall have *Five Pounds* Reward, and all necessary Charges paid.

New-England Weekly Journal, May 12, 1735; May 19, 1735. See *New-England Weekly Journal*, April 21, 1735; May 5, 1735.

*D*eserted *from the* Booth Friday, *Capt.* Thomas Douglass, *now in* Marblehead *Harbour:* Charles Mcalkin, *a lusty fresh coloured Man aged about* 21 *Years: and* Thomas Ward, *of a Brown Complexion, aged about* 22 *Years: If the abovesaid Persons or either of them shall Return to their Duty within Seven Days shall be received kindly.*
Boston, June 4. 1735.

The Boston Weekly News-Letter, From May 29, to June 5, 1735.

RAN-away the 8th instant, from Capt. *Joseph Ladd* of *Little-Compton*, Marriner, an Irish Man-servant, named *William Fitzchgerald*, about 16 or 17 Years of Age, well set, Light Hair, a Blemish in one of his Eyes, much Pock broken, Speaks broken English. He had on when he went away a torn Felt Hat, a striped Cotton Shirt, a Kersey Jacket lin'd with Blue, with Pewter Buttons, a pair of long Tow Trouzers, a Barcelony Silk Hankerchief,

a pair of peeked toed Shoes and a pair of Brass Buckels. Whoever shall take up said Runaway and him convey to his Master or Mistress, shall have *Six Pounds* Reward, and all necessary Charges paid,
    by *Joseph Ladd.*   *Little-Compton, June* 21.
New-England Weekly Journal, June 30, 1735.

Whereas *Ann* the Wife *of Lewis Sharpe, of Boston, Marriner, is lately Elop'd from her Husband, and gone off with one* Francis Rowlandson *of* Boston *aforesaid Shipwright, and she has convey'd away all the Houshold Goods of her said Husbands: This is to desire those that have any of the Goods in their hands to give Notice to the Printer and they shall be satisfied. Also all Persons are hereby warned not to Entertain or Credit her, not to deliver any of the aforesaid Goods as they will answer it at their Peril.*   Lewis Sharpe.
The Boston Gazette, From July 7, to July 14, 1735; From July 14, to July 14, 1735

THese are to signify to all Persons whatsoever, That I Daniel Martin *of* Rowley, *in the County of* Essex, *and Province of* Massachusetts-Bay *in* New-England, *Cordwainer, Do forbid, forwarn and deny* Rebeccah *my Wife of taking up upon my Account, any manner of Goods or any thing else, or to run me in Debt with, or to any Person or Persons: For as she through the Instigation of others, and by her own Unadvisedness taking up therewith has absented herself from me, and refuseth to return; had she not so done, I should always been ready and willing to afforded her all necessary Things as my Capacity could admit of; but I shall utterly refuse to pay any Debts she shall make on my Account hereafter.*
    Daniel Martin.   Dated *June* 30th. 1735.
The Weekly Rehearsal, July 14, 1735; July 21, 1735.

R*An away from his Master, Capt* Robert Sharples *of* Boston, *Mariner, on the* 17*th Instant, a Servant Boy named* Joseph Rathwell, *born in Ireland about* 17 *Years old, a thin spare Lad, with light brown Hair. He had on a Rateen Pee Jacket a speckled Shirt, and a pair of Trowsers, and speaks with the Tone. Whoever shall take up the said Run-away, and bring him to his said Master, living at the North End of the Town, shall have a very handsome Reward.*
The Weekly Rehearsal, July 21, 1735; July 28, 1735.

ON the 21st of *July* past deserted from the *Ship* Mary, Thomas Homans *Commander, the three following Men, viz.* Daniel Durham, Thomas Grennings, *and* William Gibbins. *Now in case either or all of them shall*

return to their Duty on board said Ship in five Days from time of this Date, they shall be kindly received, otherways shall be deemed as Deserters.
The Boston Gazette, From July 28, to August 4, 1735.

RAn away from the Sloop *Martha* and *Elizabeth,* lying at *Clark's* Wharfe, *Nathanael Owen* Commander, on the 30th of *July* last, a Negro Man Servant, Named *Sam*, about 28 Years of Age, a lusty well set Fellow; he had on when he went away, a Frock & Trowsers, and a Worsted Cap. Whoever shall take up said Runaway and him convey to the abovesaid Sloop, or to the House of Mrs. *Barnsdale* at the North End of *Boston*, shall have *Three Pounds* Reward, and all reasonable Charges
paid by   Nathanael Owen.
New-England Weekly Journal, August 4, 1735.

Ran away from his Master *Humphry Hicks,*
Commander of the Tagus *now lying in the Harbour of* Marblehead, *a Portugueze Boy named* Antonia, *about 17 Years old, of a very dark Complexion, and short dark Hair: He had on when he run-away, an old Felt Hat, an old dark Camblet Coat, a pair of Drawers and a pair of Greek Slippers.*
Whoever brings the said Boy to his Master, shall be well rewarded, and all necessary Charges paid.   Marblehead, Aug. 8.
The Boston Gazette, August 4, to August 11, 1735; From August 11, to August 18, 1735.

R*UN-away from Capt.* John Corney's *Ship lying at* Cape Ann, *an Indian Man Servant named* Silas Quanomp, *belonging to Mr.* Samuel Staniford *of* Ipswich: *He is a well-set Fellow, has a large Scar on his Right Cheek down towards his Chin: His Hair is newly cut off. The said* Staniford *hereby forbids all Masters of Vessels from carrying off the said Indian on the Penalty of the Law.*
The Boston Weekly Post-Boy, August 11, 1735; August 18, 1735; August 25, 1735; September 1, 1735; *The Boston Gazette,* September 8, 1735.

RAN-away from Capt *Peter Bliss of* Boston, *on Monday the* 11*th Instant, an Irish Man-Servant named* Alexander Mc'Gregor, *of about* 24 *Years of Age, a Taylor by Trade, of a short Stature, is pitted with the Small Pox, a full Face, with short black Hair, had on a Cloth coloured Frise Coat, and has taken with him sundry other Cloaths.*
Whoever shall take up the abovesaid Run away, and him safely convey to his said Master living in Newbury-street, *shall have* Five Pounds *Reward, and all necessary Charges paid.*

The Boston Gazette, From August 11, to August 18, 1735; From August 18, To August 25, 1735.

RUN-away from his Master Mr. *Cornelius Campbell* of *Boston*, Nailer, on Saturday the 6th. Current, an Irish Man-Servant named *John Hickie*, ('tis tho't he will change his Name) he is about Thirty Years of Age, a well set Fellow, a full Face. He had on when he went away a felt Hat, Grey bob Wig, speckled Shirt, and a white one over it, a white Stock, a coarse brown under Jacket, an old whitish Duroy Coat, a pair of Leather Breeches, and a pair of Trousers over them, black Yarn Stockings, round to'd Shoes, and large Brass Buckles. He can work well at the Blacksmith's Trade. All Masters of Vessels and others are hereby warned against entertaining him on the Penalty of the Law. Whoever shall take up the abovesaid Run-away and him convey to his said Master, shall have Thirteen Pounds Reward, and all necessary Charges paid.

New England Weekly Journal, September 30, 1735; October 7, 1735.

RAn-away from his Master Mr. *Ephraim Copeland*, of *Boston*, Tayler, on the 22*d.* of *September* last, an Irish Young Man Servant named *Alexander Walker*, about Seventeen or Eighteen Years of Age, a strait Limb Lad, with a full light Eye: He had on a strip'd homespun Jacket, blue Linnen Breeches, yarn Stockings, Cotton & Linnen Shirt. Whoever shall take up the abovesaid Runaway, and him convey to his abovesaid Master in *Boston* aforesaid, shall have *Forty Shillings* Reward, and all necessary Charges paid.

New England Weekly Journal, October 7, 1735; October 14, 1735; October 21, 1735; November 4, 1735; November 11, 1735.

R*AN-away from his Master Mr.* Abijah Wheeler *of* Ipswich, *on the 7th Instant, a Spanish Indian Servant named* Jack, *about Thirty Years of Age, a well set stubbed Fellow, full-fac'd, long thick black Hair, but may have cut it off, speaks very good English: He had on a good Felt Hat, an Orange colour'd Jacket, thick Leather Breeches, with a patch in the Crotch, of Shoe Leather, checker'd woollen Shirt, light gray Stockings, with tops sew'd of another sort, and pretty good Shoes. He took with him a course Bag with some Provisions in it.*

Whoever shall take up the said Runaway, and convey him to his abovesaid Master, at Ipswich, *shall have* Five Pounds *Reward, and all necessary Charges paid.*

The Boston Weekly News-Letter, From October 2, to October 9, 1735; From October 9, to October 16, 1735. See *New-England Weekly Journal*, October 14, 1735.

RAN-away from Mr. *Abijah Wheeler* of *Ipswich*, on the 7th Instant, a Spanish Indian Man, named *Jack*, about 30 Years of Age, a well set stubbed Fellow, full-face, long thick black Hair, wears an Orange colour'd Jacket, thick Leather Breeches, with a Patch in the Crotch of Shoe Leather, Checker'd Woollen Shirt, light gray Stockings, with tops sew'd on of another sort, pretty good Shoes, and a Felt Hat. He took with him a coarse Bag, with some Provisions in it. He speaks good English.

Whoever takes up the said Runaway, and him convey to his Master, at *Ipswich*, shall have *Five Pounds* Reward, and all necessary Charges paid.

New-England Weekly Journal, October 14, 1735. See *The Boston Weekly News-Letter*, From October 2, to October 9, 1735.

R*AN-away on the* 8*th Instant from his Master, Capt.* Thomas Lawton *of* Bristol, *a Molatto Slave named* Caesar, *about* 32 *Years of Age: Had on when he went away, a double breasted Jacket of a greyish Colour, and Breeches of the same, a white Flannel Shirt, and Castor Hat.* N. B. *He is thick and well set, with bushy Hair, a down look and surly Countenance. Whoever shall apprehend the said Run-away, and him convey to his said Master, shall have* Five Pounds *Reward, and all necessery Charges paid.*

The Boston Weekly News-Letter, From October 9, to October 16, 1735; From October 16, to October 23, 1735; From October 23, to October 30, 1735.

RAN-away from Mr. *James Ellis* of *Providence*, an Irish Man Servant named *George Cooper*, about 21 Years of Age, a middle siz'd Fellow, pale dull Look; wears a gray Pea Jacket with Pewter Buttons, Trowsers, gray Stockings, round to'd Shoes, a Felt Hat, and worsted Cap, but sometimes wears a Wigg. Whoever takes up the said Runaway, and him convey to his Master at *Providence*, or to Mr. *Matthew Ellis* at *Cambridge*, shall have Five Pounds Reward, and all necessary Charges paid.

All Masters of Vessels are hereby admonish'd against entertaining or caraying off said Servant, that they may prevent the Penalty of the Law.

New England Weekly Journal, October 14, 1735.

R*AN away from Mr. Thomas Salter of Boston, Cordwainer, about the beginning of September last, a Negro Man-Servant named George, a sturdy well set Fellow, aged about 26 or 27 Years, with thick Lips, a flat Nose, large Legs, is very Black, and much Pock broken. He speaks good English, and is a Shoe-maker by Trade. He had on when he went away, a Woollen Jacket, Leather Breeches, and a Capt, but no Coat or Hat, Stockings or Shoes.*

R*AN away at the same Time, from Mr.* John Billings *of Boston, a Negro Woman named* Dinah, *about 24 Years old, a handsome likely Wench,* *of a middle Stature, with a Callico Jacket, a blue Bays Petticoat, blue Stockings with white Clocks, and high heel'd Shoes.*

Whoever will take up the abovesaid Servants, and bring them to their respective Masters in Boston, shall have Three Pounds Reward, or Thirty Shillings *for either of them, besides all necessary Charges paid.*

The Boston Evening-Post, October 20, 1735; October 27, 1735; November 3, 1735; *The Boston Gazette,* From October 20, to October 27, 1735; From October 27, to November 3, 1735; From November 3, to November 10, 1735. See *The Weekly Rehearsal,* August 20, 1733, for George.

RAN away from on Board the *Schooner Elizabeth,* John Giles *Master. a tall slim young Man named* Joseph Hyat, *aged about* 18 *Years, has a black Mole on one of his Cheeks, had on when he went away, a Cap, an Olive coloured Coat and Breeches: He took with him a Moidore and an English Crown, a pair of English made Shoes, two light coloured natural Wigs, which he stole out of a Chest on Board.*

Whoever shall secure said Runaway and Thief, and bring him to Mr. Thomas Hutchinson, *jun.* Merchant in Boston, shall have Three Pounds Reward, and Five Pounds *if they secure the Goods and Money, and necessary Charges.*

The Boston Gazette, From October 20, to October 27, 1735; From October 27, to November 3, 1735; From November 3, to November 10, 1735.

RAnaway on Monday the 13th Instant from Mr. *John D'Coster* of *Boston,* Mason, living in Milkstreet, a Negro Woman named *Rinah,* she is lusty and well-set with a round full Face pretty much Pock broken, her Nose somewhat Flat, and her Lips thick; she speaks tolerable good English; she had on when she went away, a Cinamon colour'd Camblet Cloak, and yellow colour'd Head, a strip'd red and green Stuff Robe, a red and white quilted Callico Petticoat, and under blue and Linsey Woolsey Petticoat, with others, Cotton and Linnen Shift, blue yarn Stockings, and red Shoes. Whoever shall apprehend said Negro and her covey to her said Master, shall have Forty Shillings Reward, and all necessary Charges paid.

N. B. All Persons are hereby forbidden Entertaining said Negro under the Penalties of the Law.

New-England Weekly Journal, October 28, 1735; November 4, 1735; November 11, 1735.

R*An away from Mr.* Nicholas Sprague, *jun. of* Billerica, *on the* 16*th of* August *last, a Covenant Man Servant named* William Smith, *a Cloathier by Trade He is a tall well set Man, about* 45 *Years old, with a full Face, and* *of a black Complexion. He had on a white Horse-Hair Wigg, a dark brown double breasted Coat, with Brass Buttons, a striped jacket, light coloured Kersey Breeches, black Worsted Stockings, and square toed Shoes. Whoever will take him up, & bring him to his said Master in* Billerica, *or to Mr.* John Tucker, *near* Charlestown *Ferry in* Boston, *shall have* Three Pounds *Reward, and all necessary Charges paid.*

The Boston Evening-Post, November 3, 1735; November 10, 1735; November 17, 1735; November 24, 1735.

R*AN away from Mr.* Thomas Keighley *of* Boston, *Twine and Line Spinner, on the* 30*th of October last an* English *Servant Boy named* John Long, *about* 17 *Years old, well set, of a black Complexion, with a large Head, a wide Mouth, and large Ears. He had on an old dark coloured Jacket, a pair of Trouzers, a Cotton and Linen Shirt, yarn Stockings, and old Shoes. All Masters of Vessels and others, are hereby forbid to harbour, conceal or carry off the said Servant, as they will avoid the Penalty of the Law in that Case made and provided.*

Whoever brings the said Servant to his abovesaid Master, shall have Forty Shillings *Reward, and all necessary Charges paid.*

The Boston Evening-Post, November 10, 1735; November 17, 1735; November 24, 1735.

RAN-away from on board the Snow Batchelors Hall, *John Beard* Master, a middle sized young Man named *George Andoyer*, Aged about 19 Years, of a brown Complection, he had on when he went away, a light coloured plush Cap, two short double breasted blue Jackets, a blue & white check't Shirt, dark brown yarn Stockings, old Shoes, and a pair of Trowsers, his Hands were very tarry. These are therefore to desire all Masters of Vessels &c. not to carry off or entertain him at their Peril. Whosoever will secure and bring him to the Bunch of Grapes in *Boston* shall have Forty Shillings Reward, and all necessary Charges
    paid by *John Beard.*

The Boston Gazette, From November 10, to November 17, 1735; The Boston Weekly Post-Boy, November 17, 1735; November 24, 1735. Minor differences between the papes. The *Post-Boy* spells the runaway's name as Audoyer.

Ran-away from Mrs. *Grizel Cotton, on Wednesday the* 3*d Inst. an* Indian *Girl Named* Jenny, *about* 16 *Years of Age, lusty and well set, remarkable for her Limping as she walks she had on a stript homespun Jacket and Petticoat, a Cap, Shoes but no Stockings, 'tis suppos'd she's entertain'd somewhere in this Town. If any Person will discover and secure*

said Runaway, so as her Mistress may have her again shall have Three Pounds *Reward, and all necessary Charges paid.*
The Boston Gazette, From December 15, to December 22, 1735.

Marblehead, Dec. 23, 1735.
RAN-*away from the Snow* Sherburn, Obed Hussey *Master, now lying at* Marblehead, *an Indian Man about Twenty two Years old, an Irish Lad about Twenty Years old, both indented Servants to the said* Hussey: *They took with them the Snow's Long-Boat, with two Masts and Sails, a Case of Bottles, with Rum, sundry Cloaths, &c.*
Whoever shall convey the said Run-aways, Boat, &c. to the said Hussey *at* Marblehead, *shall have* Five Pounds *Reward, and all necessary Charges paid, by*   Obed Hussey.
The Boston Weekly News-Letter, December 12, to December 25, 1735.

1736

Whereas *Thomas Becks of Ireland, an Indented Servant to* John Peagrum, *Esq, of Boston, has absented himself from his Masters Service, and it's suppos'd he'l endeavour to get off by Sea. This is therefore to forwarn any Master of a Vessel from carrying off the said Servant; and if any Person or Persons can give any Intelligence where the said* Thomas Becks *is so that he may be secured or brought to his said Master again, shall Receive as a Reward* Five Pounds *from the Publisher of this Paper, besides reasonable Charges. He had on when he went away a blue stuff Coat, a lac'd Hatt, and Leather Breeches, is low in Stature, well sett, and about 22 Years of Age.*
The Boston Gazette, From December 29, 1735, to January 5, 1736.

RAN-away on the 19*th* Instant, from Mr. *Thomas Cradock* of Milton, Nailer, an Irish Man Servant, named *Edmund Ryan* (but 'tis suppos'd he will change his Name and Cloaths) He is about Sixteen or Seventeen Years of Age, of middling Stature, has thick Legs, grey Eyes, speaks pretty good English, but has something of the Irish Tongue, he has short Hair, and wears a Cap He had on when he went away, a Check'd Cotton Shirt, a striped homespun Jacket with Pewter Buttons, a dark colour'd Coat and Breeches of the same, a Felt Hat, Yarn Stockings, a good pair of Shoes with plain brass Buckles.

Whoever shall take up the abovesaid Runaway and bring or convey him to his abovesaid Master at Milton, or to *Kneeland & Green* in Queen-street over against the Prison in Boston, shall have *Three Pounds* Reward, and all necessary Charges paid.

And all Masters of Vessels and others are hereby warned against entertaining or carrying off the said Servant, on Penalty of the Law.
Boston, January 20*th.* 1735,6.
New-England Weekly Journal, January 20, 1736; January 27, 1736.

Thursday Night last, 3 Prisoners in his Majesty's Goal in this Town, found Means to break Prison, and make their Escape, *viz. William Mortimore,* on Suspicion of Counterfeiting the Bills of Credit on the Colony of *Connecticut. John Hayes,* from breaking open the Warehouse of Mr. *John Phillips,* and *John Joyce* for deserting one of His Majesty's Forts at the Eastward. Mr. *Trescott,* Keeper of the said Prison, has offered a Reward of *Ten Pounds,* to any Person who shall apprehend the said *Mortimore,* and bring him to the said *Trescott,* and *Forty Shillings* for each or either of the other Two Prisoners, besides necessary Charges.

The Boston Evening-Post, February 2, 1736. See *The Boston Weekly Post-Boy,* February 2, 1736.

B*Roke from His Majesty's Goal in* Boston, *on* Thursday *Night the 29th of* January, *Three Prisoners, viz,* William Mortimore, John Hayes *and* John Joyce: *The first, viz.* Mortimore, *is an Irish Man of middle Stature, a black swarthy Complection, something pock-broken, wears a black Wigg, and had on a loose blue Duffle Coat, and has plain Silver Buckles in his Shoes. The next, viz.* Hayes, *is a pretty tall Fellow, an Irish Man, and has the Irish Brogue; he had on a gray Coat, white Shirt, a white Wigg, and a good Beaver Hat. The other, viz.* Joyce, *is a little Man, thin fac'd, poorly cloath'd, but took with him a good blue great Coat, double Cape, with brass Buttons: He is a Taylor by Trade.*

Whoever shall take up the abovesaid Mortimore, *and him bring or safely convey to Mr.* Zechariah Trescot, *Keeper of His Majesty's Goal in* Boston, *shall have* Ten Pounds *Reward, and all necessary Charges paid; and* Forty Shillings *Reward for each or either of the other Two, viz,* Hayes *and* Joyce, *and all necessary Charges.*

The Boston Weekly Post-Boy, February 2, 1736; February 9, 1736; February 16, 1736; *New-England Weekly Journal,* February 3, 1736. Minor differences between the papers. See *The Boston Evening-Post,* February 2, 1736.

W*HEREAS* Isaiah Verry *about Forty-five Years of Age, born in* Boston, *has been absent from his Friends about Eighteen Years, but was seen in* Boston *last* July, *tho' he did not then make himself known to his Friends living here: Now if the said* Isaiah Verry *be yet living, he is desired to make himself known, or send Letters thereof to* John *and* Richard Billings, *at their Dwelling-House in Hanover-Street,* Boston, *the House that was formerly*

Deacon Tay's, *Deceased, or at their Shop on the Town-Dock; who can give him an Account of his Mother Mrs.* Elizabeth Ruggels, *Widow, now living in* Roxbury, *but very ancient, who is very desirous of seeing him, and has also an Estate of a considerable Value, that will immediately come into his hands, upon his making himself known to the said* John *and* Richard Billings: *This is also to desire all Persons upon the Sight hereof, to make inquiry for the said* Isaiah Verry, *who 'tis tho't lives in some part of* Maryland *or* Virginia.

The *Boston Weekly Post-Boy*, February 9, 1736; February 16, 1736; *The Boston Weekly News-Letter*, February 12, 1736; *The Boston Evening-Post*, February 16, 1736; March 8, 1736; June 7, 1736. Minor differences between the papers. The *Post* spells his mother's name as Ruggles.

R*AN*-away on the 13th Instant from his Master Mr. *George Holmes* of *Boston*, Hatter, an English Man-servant named *Joseph Johnson*, about 18 Years of Age, a tall Lad, wears a Cap or Wig, had on when he went away a Yellowish Broadcloth Coat, and took with him also a Blue Broadcloth Coat, had on a Black Cloth Jacket, and Leather Breeches with Brass Buttons, carry'd with him divers pair of Stockings, and sundry Shirts, speckled and white.

Whoever shall take up the abovesaid Runaway and him safely convey to his abovesaid Master in Boston shall have *Ten Pounds* Reward, and all necessary Charges paid.

And all Masters of Vessels are hereby warned against carrying off the said Servant, on pain of suffering the penalty of the Law.

New-England Weekly Journal, March 23, 1736.

R*AN-away from Mr.* Robert Jenkins *of* Boston *Perriwigg-maker, on Tuesday the* 23d *Instant, an Irish Man-Servant named* Dennis Donovan, *aged about Twenty One Years, of a tall Stature, but goes somewhat stooping, of a fair complexion and fresh colour'd; He had on when he went away, a light colour'd Drugget Coat with Mohair Buttons, a Jacket of the same with Brass Buttons, a pair of old light colour'd Broad Cloth Breeches, and yarn Stockings: He took with him a light old Bob Wigg, a light Tail-Wigg, and a dark brown Bob-Wigg.*

All Master of Vessels are hereby cautioned against harbouring, concealing, or carrying off said Servant, as they will avoid the Penalty of the Law in that Case made and provided.

Whoever shall take up the said Servant and bring him to his abovesaid Master, shall have Three Pounds *Reward, and all necessary Charges paid.*

The Boston Weekly News-Letter, From March 18, to March 25, 1736; From March 25, to April 2, 1736.

RAn-away from Mr. *Thomas Esmond* of *Newbury*, Sawyer, on Monday the 19th of this Instant *April*, an English Servant Lad named *John Loyd*, born in the West County, about Eighteen Years old, pretty tall but slim, and goes stooping; he is full fac'd and fresh colour'd, and has strong black Hair: He had on when he went away, an old Frize Coat, and two Jackets under it, one a dark Cloth, and the other a dark striped Homespun; an old speckled Cotton and Linen Shirt, and checker'd Plush Breeches. All Masters of Vessels and others are hereby cautioned against harbouring, concealing or carrying off the said Servant, as they will avoid the Penalty of the Law in that Case made and provided. Whoever shall take up the said Servant, and bring him to his above said Master in *Newbury*, shall have *Three Pounds* Reward and all necessary Charges paid.

New-England Weekly Journal, April 27, 1736.

RAN-away on the 12th of Instant from his Master Mr. *Alexander Hunt* of *Boston*, Shipwright, an English Man Servant, named *John MacMillon*, about nineteen Years of Age, a lusty, strong, hearty fill Fac'd, fresh colour'd young Man. He had on when he went away, a Cap, a good pair of Leather Breeches, a striped Homespun Jacket, Yarn Stockings, single sole Shoes: He took with him a Cloth Coat of a Dove colour, a striped Holland Jacket, and two or three pair of Shoes. He can work well at the Shipwright's Business, and has taken some Tools that belongs to said Business. Whoever shall take up the abovesaid Runaway and him safely convey to his said Master, Mr. *Alexander Hunt*, living near Fort Hill, shall have *Ten Pounds* Reward, and all necessary Charges paid.

New-England Weekly Journal, May 18, 1736. See *New-England Weekly Journal*, June 22, 1736.

Deserted from Capt. *Ellys Bennett*, Commander of the Brigt Six Brothers, lately arriv'd from Cadiz, a Sailor named *Richard Fox*, about 34 Years old, of a middle Stature, but slim and thin favoured. He had on when he went away, a lightish gray coloured Watch Coat, a red Jacket, and a pair of cloth Breeches & a Hat with very narroe Brim, and all Tar'd over. All Masters of Vessels and others are hereby cautioned against harbouring, concealing or carrying off the said Servant, as they will avoid the Penalty of the Law in that Case made and provided. Whoever shall take up the said *Richard Fox*, and bring him to his said Master living at the North End of *Boston*, shall have *Three Pounds* Reward, and all necessary Charges paid.

The Boston Gazette, From May 24, to May 31, 1736.

RAn away on the 12th of *May* last from his Master Mr. *Alexander Hunt* of *Boston*, Shipwright, an English Man Servant, named *John MacMillon*, about nineteen Years of Age, a lusty, strong, hearty fill Fac'd, fresh colour'd young Man. He had on when he went away, a Cap, a good pair of Leather Breeches, a striped Homespun Jacket, Yarn Stockings, single sole Shoes: He took with him a Cloth Coat of a Dove colour, a striped Holland Jacket, and two or three pair of Shoes. He can work well at the Shipwright's Business, and has taken some Tools that belong to said Business. Whoever shall take up the abovesaid Runaway and him safely convey to his said Master, living near Fort Hill, shall have *Ten Pounds* Reward, and all necessary Charges paid.

N. B. When he run away some time ago he chang'd his Name to *Joseph Stevens*, and 'this tho't he has done so now.

New-England Weekly Journal, June 22, 1736. See *New-England Weekly Journal*, May 18, 1736.

DEserted from the Brig. *William*, Nariar Vaughan Commander, being his Servant, on the 2d Instant, an Irish Boy named Mauris Fitzgerald, of about Eighteen Years of Age, Freckled in the Face, narrow Visage and small: He had on when he went away, a dark colour'd Pea Jacket trim'd with blue, a striped Wastecoat, speckled Shirt, a Worsted Cap or Felt Hat. Whoever will take up the said Runaway, and convey him to his said Master in Prince Street near Charlestown Ferry, or to Messi. Merrett and Harris, Merchants in Boston, shall have Three Pounds Reward, and all necessary Charges.

New-England Weekly Journal, July 6, 1736.

WHEREAS Catherine Dove, *Wife of* Henery Dove, *now of* Boston, *Merchant, has Eloped, and for a considerable Time absented her self from her said Husband, without any just Cause, and has taken with her Money and Goods of her said Husband's to a considerable Value, without his Leave or Privity: These are therefore to forbid all Persons whatsoever from trusting the said* Catherine Dove, *or letting her have any sort of Victuals, Cloaths, Good, Wares or Merchandize, on Account of her said Husband, he being determined not to pay any Debts contracted by her after the Date of these Presents.*

    Henery Dove.   Boston, *July* 19. 1736.

The Boston Evening-Post, July 19, 1736; July 26, 1736; August 2, 1736.

DEserted from the Ship *Hannah* in *Boston, William Bennet* Master, two Sailors, viz. *Mical Manning*, a swarthy Man with bushy Hair, about twenty-eight Years of Age, *Thomas Alsted*, is a short thick Man, about the same Age with the forementioned. If the said Deserters will return to their Duty on board the said Ship, they shall be kindly received, otherwise treated as Deserters. And all Masters of Vessels are caution'd against taken on board

their Vessels or carrying off the said Men, on penalty of the Law in that Case made and provided.
New England Weekly Journal, July 20, 1736.

R*AN away from Mr.* Thomas Cutler *of* Lexington, *on the* 8*th of this Instant* August *at Night, an Irish Man-Servant named* George Kelley, *about* 18 *Years old, of a middle Stature, but thick and well set, and goes something stooping; he is also fresh coloured, and has a full Face. He has also short black Hair, and had on when he went away, a coarse Linen Short, a small striped Cherriderry Jacket, homespun Trouzers of Towe-Cloth, and a small Felt Hat, but neither Shoes or Stockings. Whoever shall take up the abovesaid Servant, and bring him to his said Master in* Lexington, *shall have* Five Pounds *Reward, & all necessary Charges paid.*
Note. *All Masters of Vessels and others are hereby forbid to harbour, conceal or carry off the said Servant, as they will answer it in the Law.*
The Boston Evening-Post, August 9, 1736; August 16, 1736; August 23, 1736.

RAN-away from his Master Mr. *Joseph Mansfield* of *Lynn*, Shipwright, on the 22*d of July* past, a Spanish Indian Man Servant, named *Peter*, about 26 Years of Age, a sturdy well set Fellow, of middle Stature, speaks good English, has lately clipt off his Hair, & wears a black Natural Wigg; had on a good Castor Hat, Cinnamon colour'd Coat pretty short, a striped linsey woolsey Jacket, white homespun Trousers, Yarn Stockings, and a good pair of single sole Shoes with flat Pewter Buckles therein. Whoever shall take up the abovesaid Runaway and him safely convey to his abovesaid Master at *Lynn*, shall have *Four Pounds*, Reward, and all necessary Charges paid.
New-England Weekly Journal, August 10, 1736.

R*AN-away from* Elisha Dyre *of* Boston, *a French Servant Named* John Shotoro, *on the* 18*th of this Instant August: He speaks but little English; and took with him a sorrel colour'd Mare Cot, branded with a 4 on the near Shoulder, and her Main is cut off close to her Neck on the off side, is sho'd all round, and has a lightish colour'd hunting Saddle, and a light colour'd Bridle: The said Servant is of a low Stature, with black Hair, dark Skin, black Eyes, with a Scar over one of his Eye-brows; He had on when he went away, a light coloured streight bodied Coat with a small Cape, a speckled Shirt and Neckcloth, a pair of old leather Breeches, grey yarn Stockings and a pair of old Shoes: he also took with him a light coloured great Coat, a white Shirt and several Pair of worsted Stockings, &c.*
Whoever shall take up the said Run-away, and safely convey him with the said Mare and her Furniture, to his Master living in Newbury-Street *at*

the South End of Boston, *shall have* Ten Pounds *Reward, and all necessary Charges paid by* Elisha Dyre.
The Boston Weekly Post-Boy, August 23, 1736; August 30, 1736.

WHEREAS *on the* 17th *of last Month* July, *One* John Hobbs, *Marriner* (*with others*) *ship'd himself to go to* Newbury, *for there to enter as a Sailor on board the* Dolphin Snow, Philip Butler *Commander, and received as advances of Wages of Messi.* John Merrett *and* Robert Harris, *of* Boston, Merchants l. 6 10 s. *This Money, and immediately deserted: He is of a middle Stature and fair Complexion, about* 25 *Years of Age.*
    Also *on the first Instant, one* William Ross, *Mariner, ship'd himself as a Sailor on board the St.* George *rigateen* [sic] Christopher Pate *Commander and received as advanced Wates of the said Messi.* Merrett *and* Harris l. 5. *This Money, and immediately deserted, he is a full made well-set Man, of a brown Complexion and about* 40 *Years of Age.*
    Also *on the 5th Instant the said Capt.* Christopher Pate, *redeemed out of the Prison of* Boston (*on Paying his Debt of* Ten *Pounds*) *one* John Mason, *Mariner, the said* Mason *having before ship'd himself, as Sailor on board the aforesaid Briganteen, who about Midnight following went from the said Vessel, then lying near* Nantasket, *in a Moses of about Nine Feet and half long, with a Long Boat Oar of Eighteen Feet long, and has not been since heard of: He is about* 23 *Years of Age, black Hair, Mark'd with the Small-Pox.*
    Whoever *can give any intelligence of all or either of the said Sailors* (*so as they may be secured*) *unto the said* John Merrett *and* Robert Harris, *shall have* Forty Shillings *Reward for each Sailor, and all necessary Charges. Also* Forty Shillings *Reward for the Moses.*
John Merrett, Robert Harris.
The Boston Weekly Post-Boy, August 23, 1736.

RAN-away from his Master *John Horsewel* of *Little-Compton*, on the 17th of *July* last, a Molatto Fellow named *Isaac*, thick, well set and full Fac'd, about twenty-one Years of Age, who was advertis'd in *July* last, and taken up on the Advertisement the 12th of this Instant *August* and made his Escape from the Person that took him up, was pinioned on the 15th following at *Stoughton*, and was cloath'd with a light colour'd short Coat, almost worn out, and patch'd up the Back, long Breeches, strip'd Worsted Cap, Linen Shirt, and Shoes with Brass Buckles. Whoever shall apprehend the said Molatto Fellow, and convey him to his said Master in *Little-Compton* aforesaid, or to any of his Majesty's Goals, or to Mr. *Benj. Williams* in *Boston*, or Mr. *Samuel Atherton* at *Rehoboth*, shall have *Five Pounds* Reward, and necessary Charges
          paid by   *John Horsewel.*

New-England Weekly Journal, August 24, 1736; September 7, 1736.

WHEREAS *Mary Oldcraft* a bought Servant *of* Robert Auchmuty, *Esq'r; has lately Stolen sundry Things from her said Master, and now conceals herself. Whoever shall apprehend her so as she may be brought to Justice, shall be well rewarded, and all persons are forbid to give her any Credit on her Master's Account.*
The Boston Gazette, From August 23, to August 30, 1736.

RAN-away from his Master Mr. *Ephraim Doane* of Province Town on Cape Cod, an Irish Man Servant named *Robert Stack*, lately arrived from Ireland in Capt. *Boyd*, [*sic*] about 20 Years of Age, of middling Stature, or a pretty red Complexion, short reddish colour'd Hair, a Mole on his Face, speaks pretty plain English, he had on a blewish Coat pretty much faded, a white Linnen Shirt, black Camblet Breeches, dark yarn Stockings, and old Shoes. Whoever shall take up the abovesaid Runaway, and him convey to his abovesaid Master, or the Mr. *Robert Thompson* Taylor in King-street Boston, shall have *Three Pounds* Reward, necessary Charges paid.
Boston, Sept. 7th. 1736.
New-England Weekly Journal, September 7, 1736; September 14, 1736.

R*AN away from Mr.* Benjamin Astills, *now of* Boston, *on Friday the* 17*th of September Instant, a Negro Man named* Cajo *about* 21 *Years old, with an Iron Collar about his Neck, with the Name of his Master engraven upon it in Capital Letters. He had on a double breasted Jacket of a greenish Colour, an Oznabrigs Frock and Trouzers, but no Hat or Cap, Shoes or Stockings. Whoever shall take up the said Negro, and bring him to Mr.* James Gordon, *Merchant, living in Cornhill in* Boston, *shall have* Twenty Shillings *Reward, besides all necessary Charges paid.*
The Boston Evening-Post, September 20, 1736; September 27, 1736; October 4, 1736.

Ran-away from his Master *Jableel Brenton of* Newport *on* Rhode Island, *the* 10*th Instant, a Negro Man named* Melech: *He had on when he went away a grey Kersey Coat with flat metal Buttons, a pair of linen Trousers, a white Shirt made of tow Cloth; he is about six feet high, of a yellow Complection, of about* 23 *Years of Age, he was born and bred in the* Jerseys *near* New-York. *Whoever shall apprehend said Servant and bring or safely convey him to his said Master at* Newport *aforesaid, shall receive for his trouble* Ten Pounds *Reward, and all necessary Charges paid by me* Jableel Brenton. *Newport, October* 15*th,* 1736.

The Boston Gazette, From October 11, to October 25, 1736; From October 18, to October 25, 1736.

LAST Monday Night I had my Shop broke open, and a parcel of English Goods taken out, to the value of 150 l. *and have great Reason to Suspect one* William Mc'Gee *an* Irishman; *a very large Man, he had a dark coloured Coat on, shabbily dress'd. His Companion is a short thick Man, with a red Coat double Breasted, and very much Pockbroken. There was taken away a blue Piece of Camblet, a black and white Crape, two pieces of Drugget, one Cinamon colour'd, the other dark blue; Garlix, Chints, and sundry other Goods unknown. Who soever shall take up the aforesaid Men, and secure them, shall have* Five Pounds *Reward, and all necessary Charges paid by me.* Edward Flint.

The Boston Gazette, From October 18, to October 25, 1736; From October 25, to November 1, 1736; From November 1, to November 8, 1736.

BROKE *out of Bridewell on* Friday Night *last* Thomas Hunter, *a Covenant Servant belonging to Capt.* Thomas Homans: *He is of a middling Stature, a pale Complexion, with short brown Hair, a North-country Man, of about 25 Years old, wears a blue Wastcoat and a white and blue strip'd Shirt, who undoubtedly conceals himself in this Town. Whoever will discover him and bring him to his said Master shall have* Five Pounds *Reward. N. B. All Masters of Vessel and others are hereby forwarned of entertaining or carrying him off, on Penalty of the Law in such Case provided.*

The Boston Gazette, From October 18, to October 25, 1736; From October 25, to November 1, 1736.

RAn-away away from Mrs. *Margaret Steel* of *Boston*, on Saturday the 23 Instant, a Negro Man named *Tom*, alias *Tom Scipio*, aged 36 Years, is of a middle Stature, much pitted with the Small Pox, his Eyes are small, and much sunk in his Head, he speaks good English, born in this Country, has been used to the Sea: He had on when he went away a speckled Shirt, a Kersey Jacket lined with white Woollen, an Ozenbrigs Frock, a Woollen Cap, a pair of square to'd Shoes with Wooden Heels. Whoever shall take up said Negro, and deliver him to his abovesaid Mistress at her House in Hanover street, shall have *Five Pounds* Reward, & all necessary Charges paid. All Persons are hereby forbidden entertaining, or imploying said Negro, & from carrying him off to Sea.

New-England Weekly Journal, October 26, 1736.

W*Hereas* Zachariah Blood, *of* Concord, *Husbandman, was committed to His Majesty's Goal in* Cambridge, *upon several Executions which were issued out upon Judgements obtained against him for divers Sum of Money, amounting to several hundred Pounds, but by Means of a Steel Saw conveyed to him by some Evil minded Person, he cut through the Iron Bars of the Prison Window, and hath made his Escape on* Tuesday *the* 26*th of* October *past, in the Night Time.*
These are therefore to give Publick Notice, That whosoever shall apprehend and bring the said Zachariah Blood *to me the Subscriber, or commit Him to the Under-Keeper of the said Goal, namely Mr.* John Morse, *such Person or Persons shall have a Reward of* Ten Pounds,
    and be paid all necessary Charges by me,
        Richard Foster, *Sheriff of the County of* Middlesex.
The Boston Evening-Post, November 1, 1736; November 8, 1736.

ON Tuesday the 12th of *October,* Ranaway *from his Master* Ebenezer Brenton *of* South Kingston, *in the Colony of* Rhode-Island, *a Mustee Man-servant named* Abel, *aged about 23 Years, a short thick set Fellow, something stooping in his shoulders, bare Leg'd, short Hair a little Brown, he shews something of white in his Complection ('tis supposed that his Father was a Dutch man, his Mother a Spanish Indian) He had on when he went away, a Grey Kersey Great Coat & Jacket, Linnen Frock & Trousers, New Felt Hat, and New Shoes; he took with him a Gun, Whoever shall apprehend said Runaway, and convey him safe to his Master shall have* Ten Pounds *reward & all necessary Charges*
      paid by   Ebenezer Brenton.
The Boston Gazette, From November 1, to November 8, 1736; From November 8, to November 15, 1736; From November 15, to November 22, 1736.

1737

John Simpson *Marriner, beginning of last Month Deserted from the service of the Ship Dragon,* John Paterson *Master; whoever will secure him and give notice thereof at Mr.* John Erving's *Warehouse No* 4 *on the Long Wharfe, shall have* Forty Shillings *Reward.*
The Boston Gazette, From December 27, 1736, to January 3, 1737.

R*AN-AWAY from his Master* Jonathan Seaver *of* Roxbury, *on the 25th of* December, *an English Man Servant named* William White, *about Twenty Years of Age, a short well set Fellow, with short brown Hair, fresh colour'd, he had on a dark colour'd homespun Coat, Jacket and Breeches, with metal Buttons, a loose Great Red Coat with brass Buttons, two Shirts,* a Garlick and a Cotton & Linnen one, two pair of Stockings, one grey Yarn the other dark Worsted, a small brim'd Castor Hat, and a Silk Handkerchief about his Neck. He goes shambling with his Feet, his Legs something turning out. Whoever takes up the abovesaid Runaway and him safely convey to his abovesaid Master, shall have Forty Shillings *Reward,* and all necessary Charges paid.

The Boston Weekly News-Letter, From December 30, 1736, to January 6, 1737; January 6, to January 13, 1737; January 13, to January 20, 1737.

RAN-away from Mrs. *Pullen* on Saturday Morning last, the 22d Instant, a Negro Woman of middling Stature named Cuber, about five & thirty Years of Age, with a Scar over her right Eye, a pair of Gold Ear Kings [sic] in her Ears, and had on when she went away a light coloured Riding Hood and a striped homespun Jacket & Petticoat, having with her a large Bundle of wearing Cloaths. Whoever will apprehend & take up the abovesaid Runaway, and her safely convey to the abovesaid Mrs. Pullen *living in Corn Court near the Town Dock Marker in Boston, or to the Publisher hereof shall be well rewarded for their Trouble.*

This is likewise to forewarn all Persons whatsoever to Harbour the abovesaid Runaway, and Masters of Vessels to carry her off on Penalty of the law. Boston January 24th. 1736,7.

The Boston Gazette, From January 17, to January 24, 1737. See *The Boston Weekly Post-Boy,* April 30, 1744, *The Boston Weekly Post-Boy,* July 9, 1744, and *The Boston Weekly Post-Boy,* August 6, 1744.

RAN-away from *Edward Williams* of Boston, Currier, on the 31st of January last, *Jonathan Reed,* an Irishman lately come from *Dublin,* but speaks pretty good English, about 32 Years of Age, a short well set Man, round Fac'd, black Beard, round Shoulder'd, his Legs leaning a little in, wore a blue Cloth Coat & Jacket, brown Breeches, & brown Wig, a Currier by Trade, but can work at the Shoemaker's Trade. Whoever will take up said *Reed* and him safely convey to his said Master in *Boston,* shall have Five Pounds Reward, and all reasonable Charges paid.

Boston February 2d. 1736,7.

New-England Weekly Journal, February 8, 1737.

Whereas *Joseph Whetstone* Carpenter of the Ship Cumberland, William Oliver, *Master, has absented from the Service of said Ship, and cannot be found by the Marshal of the Court of Admiralty either on Board said Ship or any where else: This is therefore to Notify him to appear at a Court of Admiralty to be holden at* Boston *to morrow at 0 o'Clock in the forenoon, to show cause, if any he have, why his Wages*

ought not to be forfeited agreeable to the prayer of a Complaint files against him by said Oliver.
The Boston Gazette, From February 28, to March 7, 1737.

Deserted from the Ship Jane Galley, *Jer. Fones Master,* Adam Dixon and Richard Wreggon, *Mariners; Notwithstanding if they return immediately to their Duty they shall be kindly received, otherways shall be treated as Deserters.* Boston, Mar. 9th, 1736.7.
The Boston Gazette, From March 7, to March 14, 1737.

Newport, March 24. Last Night his Majesty's' Goal in this Place was broke open, and sundry Prisoners made their Escape, viz. *Dennis Daugherty* and *John Hamilton,* two Criminals, for stealing sundry goods from Capt. *John Brown* of this Town; as did likewise at the same Time, *William Cuthbertson, Joseph Olivey* and *Patrick Downing,* Debtors; and *John Ford,* a Servant to the Widow *Jackson* of Boston: The manner of their Escape was this, they first pull'd down part of a Chamber Chimney, and took the Iron Bar out, and rip'd up the Chamber Floor, and then rip'd up the lower Floor and dug through the under Pinning; but before they went away, they wrote of the Floor of the Prison with Chalk, (that the Prison keeper should not forget them.)
"Fare you well *Davis,* your Prisoners are fled,
"Your Prison's broke open while you are in Bed.
The Sheriff of this County offers a Reward of Three Pounds for each, besides all necessary Charges, for apprehending them, or any of them, that they may be bro't to this Town for Justice.
The Boston Evening-Post, March 28, 1737.

*R*AN-*away early on Sunday Morning the 24th of this Instant, from her Master Mr.* Benjamin Astill *now residing at the South End of* Boston *near the great Elm Trees, (but lately from* Jamaica) *A Negro Woman called* Mimbo, *aged about 26 Years, she is a likely Wench of a middle Size, and had on when she went away, a dark colour'd Bays Gown, and over that a blue and white strip'd Holland Petticoat with a red one under it; she also took with her a strip'd Callimanco Jacket with a blue Ferret round the Bottom, a pair of low heel'd old Shoes, and generally wears an Handkerchief on her Head, she is mark'd on one of her Shoulders with the Letters* K. S. *but pretty well worn out. Whoever shall take up the said Runaway, and convey her to her abovesaid Master at* Boston *aforesaid, shall have Forty Shillings Reward, and all necessary Charges paid. This is also to caution all Masters of Vessels and others from carrying off said Servant, upon the Penalty of the Law in that Case provided.*
Boston, April 8, 1737.

The Boston Weekly News-Letter, April 21, to April 28, 1737.

R*AN-away from his Master Mr.* Samuel Foster, *of* Boston, *Clothier, on Tuesday the Third of this Instant* May, *at Night, an Irish Man Servant named* Florence Carty, *about* 20 *Years old, of a middle Stature, and fresh coloured. His Hair is cut off, and he wears a Cap, and he had on when he went away, a dark Blue Coat, a striped Jacket, Blue Plush Breeches and Yarn Stockings.*
N. B. *He is a Worsted Comber by Trade.*
Whoever shall take up the said Servant, and bring him to his abovesaid Master living in Newbury-Street *at the South End of* Boston, *or secure him and give Notice thereof so that he may be had again, shall have* Five Pounds *Reward, and all necessary Charges paid.*
The Boston Weekly News-Letter, From April 21, to April 28, 1737; From April 28, to May 5, 1737; From May 5, to May 12, 1737.

R*anaway from his Master* John Corney *of* Boston, *A Jersey Servant Man named* Thomas Lefeaver, *aged about* 17 *Years a short squat Fellow, fresh colour'd and full fac'd speaks pretty good English, but very thick, had on when he went away a white Shirt and a long Jacket Olive colour'd, short Hair. The Person who will give any Intelligence of him so that he may be secured, shall have* 40 *s. Reward, and all reasonable Charges. And all Masters of Vessels are forbid carrying him off at their Peril.*
The Boston Gazette, May 30, to May 6, 1737.

Worcester, *April 29th.* 1737.
R*AN away from his Master, Mr.* Oliver Wallis *of* Worcester, *an Irish Man Servant named* Cornelius Murfee, *a short well-set Fellow, with a Red full Face, hollow Eyes, and hanging Eye-Brows. He had on when he went away, a White coarse Shirt, a Red Jacket, a Brown strait Bodied Coat, and had with him a Woollen Cap and a Wigg. Whoever shall take up the said Servant, and convey him to his said Master, or confine him in some of his Majesty's Goals so that his said Majesty may have him again, shall have* Three Pounds *Reward, and all necessary Charges paid.*
The Boston Evening-Post, May 9, 1737; May 16, 1737.

R*AN* away from her Master *Isaac White* of Boston *Shipwright, a Negro Wench named* Juno.
Whoever shall bring the said Negro to her Master, or give any Intelligence of her, shall be very well satisfied for their Trouble.
The Boston Gazette, From June 6, to June 13, 1737; From June 13, to June 20, 1737.

R*AN away from Messieurs* John Dollinson *and* Richard Sutcomb *of* Boston, *Periwig Makers, on Monday the* 13*th Instant, a Servant Lad named* Henry Doset, *about* 16 *Years old. He had on when he went away, a dark coloured Kersey Jacket, lined with blue Bays, an old pair of Leather Breeches, and Yarn Stockings. He has also Bandy Legs. Whoever shall take up the said Run-away, and bring him to his abovesaid Masters, at the lower end of King-Street, near the Long Wharf, shall be Rewarded to their Content, and have all necessary Charges paid.* Note, *All Masters of Vessels and other Persons are hereby cautioned against harbouring, concealing or carrying off the said Servant, as they will avoid the Penalty of the Law in that Case provided.*
The Boston Evening-Post, June 20, 1737.

WHEREAS *Elizabeth* the Wife of *John Smith,* jun. *of* Rochester *aforesaid, Yeoman, (said* Smith *being formerly a Trader in* New-York *Government) is departed from him against his Consent, and supposed to be now in* New York *Government: And for preventing the said* Elizabeth *running her said Husband in Debt be the said* John Smith, *doth hereby forbid any one from giving her Credit of his Account, for he will not pay and Debt contracted by her since her Departure. In Witness whereof he hath hereunto set his Hand,* John Smith, *jun.*
The Boston Gazette, From June 20, to June 27, 1737. See *The New-York Weekly Journal,* November 30, 1741.

These are to give Notice that Capt. *Job Almy of* Newport, *took up a Runaway Negro Boy, about* 18 *or* 19 *Years old, on the* 8*th of* July 1737, *who on Examination confessed that he belonged to Lieut.* Hopkins *of the* Scarborough *Man of War, he the said Negro told his Name was* Emanuel *before he said he belonged to the said* Hopkins, *& afterwards he was named* Charles. *Whoever shall make a lawful Right and Title to the abovesaid Negro shall have him again, paying all necessary Charges, who in now secured in Goal till a true Owner appear.*
The Boston Gazette, From July 4, to July 11, 1737.

Deserted from the Ship London, *Thomas Hoare Master, on the* 4*th Instant, a Sailor named* John Hoskins *of midling Stature, black Complexion, and a black bobb Wig. If said Sailor returns to his Duty on board said Ship, he shall be kindly received, otherwise treated as a Deserter.*
The Boston Gazette, From July 4, to July 11, 1737; From July 11, to July 18, 1737; *New-England Weekly Journal,* July 12, 1737. The *Journal* spells the master's name as Hoar.

Ran away from his Master *Job Townsend* of Newport *on* Rhode Island, *an Apprentice Boy about* 19 *Years of Age, named* Samuel Allin, *of middle Stature, dark curl'd Hair, dark gray Eyes, speaks quick and thick, and sputters in his Talk, and has wrought at the Ship Joyners Trade some Years, he had on when he went away, a dark blue Homespun Coat, a strip'd Cotton and Linnen Jacket, blue and white; & dark coloured Leather Breeches with Pewter Buttons, and a pair of blue Worsted Stockings. Whoever shall apprehend the abovesaid Runaway, and convey him to his aforesaid Master, shall have a Reward of* five Pounds New England Currency, *and all reasonable Charges paid thankfully by me* Job Townsend.

Newport, July 4th, 1737.

The Boston Gazette, From July 4, to July 11, 1737; From July 11, to July 18, 1737; From July 18, to July 25, 1737.

Ran-away from his Master *Samuel Cooper of Boston, Tailer, a French Man Servant named* James Fellet *he is a short well set Fellow with his own black Hair, speaks broken English; he had on when he went away a light colour'd Cinnamon Cloth Coat with slit Sleves, light colour'd Saggathe Breeches, yarn Stockings, speckled Shirt, and Bever Hat, and carried with him a Holland Coat with slit Sleeves, and Holland Jacket.*

Whosoever shall take up the abovesaid Servant & him convey to his said Master shall have five Pounds *Reward and all necessary Charges paid.*

N. B. All Captains of Vessels and others are hereby notified not to entertain said Servant under the Penalty of the Law.

Boston, July 18*th*, 1737.

The Boston Gazette, From July 11, to July 18, 1737; From July 18, to July 25, 1737; From July 25, to August 1, 1737.

Some days past, *Charles Child, Benjamin Wiggan, and Louis Williams, Mariners, left the Ship* London, William Hoar, *Master, This is to Notify 'em that if they or either of them will return to their Duty in 3 days time they will be receiv'd again, or otherways threated as Deserters.*

The Boston Gazette, From July 25, to August 1, 1737; From August 1, to August 8, 1737.

ON the 19th Instant ran away from his Master *John Walton of Norwich, a servant Man named* Thomas Edderige, *he is either an old England Man, or an Irish Man, aged about* 27 *Years, he is a thin tallow fac'd slim body'd Fellow, hath a small Beard, and is of a middling height, his Hair is newly cut off, he wore when he went away a new felt Hat, a worsted Cap, a grey coarse Jacket, a fine old Short, both much too big for him, he had old woollen Breeches, old Shoes, and no Stockings.*

Whoever shall convey said Servant to his said Master, shall have Five Pounds *Reward, and all necessary Charges paid, by me* John Walton. New-London, July 22. 1737.

The Boston Gazette, From July 25, to August 1, 1737; From August 1, to August 8, 1737; From August 8, to August 15, 1737.

*R*AN *away on the 6th of* July *last from his Master* Henry Gibbon, *an Irish Man-Servant named* John McCormrick *alias* John Harvey, *about Twenty-five Years of Age, a short well-set Fellow, his Hair is cut off, and he has a Scar under one of his Ears, as if he had formerly the King's Evil: He had on when he went away, a Felt Hat, a gray broad Cloth Coat, strip'd homespun Jacket and Breeches, a white Linnen Shirt, if not a Cotton and Linnen one besides, gray Yarn Stockings and a pair of pretty good Shoes. Whoever shall take up the abovesaid Run-away, and bring him to the said Mr.* Gibbon *near the Great Trees at the South End of* Boston, *shall have* Forty Shillings *Reward, and all necessary Charged [sic] paid.*

The Boston Weekly News-Letter, From July 28, to August 4, 1737.

*L*AST *Night went away from Major* Mascarene'*s House, a Negro Lad aged about Sixteen Years, pretty tall and slim; he had on a dark homespun Kersey Coat, with red Buttons and Button holes, a light Drugget pair of Breeches with Metal Buttons, and a light pair of Worsted Stockings. Whoever shall take up the said Run-away and safely convey him to his said Master, Major* Mascarene, *shall have all necessary Charges paid, and be rewarded for his Pains, and all Masters of Vessels and others are hereby caution'd not to entertain or convey away the said Negro, as they will avoid the Penalty of the Law.*
N. B. *The said Negro's Name is* Harry. Monday, August 8*th,* 1737.

The Boston Evening-Post, August 8, 1737; August 15, 1737.

RAn-away on the 7*th.* Instant from his Master *Israel Hearsey* of *Boston*, Carman, an Irish Man Servant named *Dennis Crowley,* about 19 or 20 Years of Age, a short well-set Fellow, short Hair, and 'tis suppos'd he had on a Cap or a Wigg, and had on when he went away a greenish Cloth Coat with Buttons of the same colour, a black Jacket much worn, a pair of Snuff colour'd Plush Breeches, yarn Stockings, a Castor Hat, and a fine Shirt.

Whoever all take up the abovesaid Runaway, and him safely convey to his said Master at the North End of *Boston* aforesaid, shall have *Three Pounds* Reward, and all necessary Charges paid.

And all Masters of Vessels are hereby warned against carrying off said Servant on Penalty of the Law in that Case made and provided.

Boston, August 8th. 1737.
New-England Weekly Journal, August 9, 1737; August 16, 1737; August 23, 1737.

BROKE out of the Goal of *Burlington* in *New Jersey*, a certain Man, named *John Crues*, of middle Stature, hollow mouth'd, (that is) his Nose and Chin inclining to meet, a Weaver by Trade, but pretends to be a *Quaker-*Preacher; he took with him two Coats, one a light colour'd Camblet or Duroy, the other a brown homespun Stuff, both very plain, a Searsucker Jacket and Breeches, and a pair of patch'd leather Breeches, two fine Shirts, a half worn Beaver Hat, thread Stockings, and peek'd toed Shoes, his Garters have his name wove at full length; he had also with him a pair of Saddle Bags. He's suppos'd to be gone to *New-England* near *Boston*, to Preach again where he has Preach'd before.

Whoever takes up and secures the said Man, in any Prison, giving Notice to *Charles Tonkin*, Under-Sheriff of *Burlington* aforesaid, shall have *Three Pounds* Proclamations Money as a Reward,
        paid by me.   *Charles Tonkin*, Sub-Sheriff.   *Aug*, 4. 1737.

The Pennsylvania Gazette, From August 4, to August 11, 1737; From August 11, to August 18, 1737. See *The New-York Gazette*, From August 22, to August 29, 1737, and *The Boston Gazette*, From September 5, to September 12, 1737.

A Negro Man named *Caesar* belonging to *Mr.* Thomas Pearson, *Ginger-Baker, in this Town, is Runaway from his Master; he formerly belong'd to Mr. Lee, Lime Burner, a well set Fellow, Middle Stature: Having on an Ozenbrigs Jacket and Trousers, and blew Worsted Stockings; Aged about Twenty Eight Years, speaks but Ordinary English. Whoever secures said Negro and brings or give Notice to his said Master, so that he may be had again, shall have* Forty Shillings Reward. *All Masters of Vessels are hereby forbid carrying him off at their Peril.*

The Boston Gazette, From August 22, to August 29, 1737.

BROKE out of the Goal of Burlington in New-Jersey, a Man named John Crues, he is of middle Stature, hollow mouth, (that is his Nose & Chin inclining to meet) a Weaver by Trade, but pretends to be a Quaker Preacher. He took with him two Coats, one a light Colour'd Camblet or Duroy, and the other a brown Home-spun Stuff, both very plain, a Seasucker Jacket and Breeches, two fine Shirts, a half worn Bever Hat, thread Stockins, and peeked toe'd Shoes; his Garters have his Name woven in them at large; He had also with a pair of Saddle Bags. It is supposed he is gone into New-England near Boston to preach again where he has been before. Whoever takes up and secures this said Man in any Prison, gives Notice to Charles

Tonkin, under Sheriff of *Burlington* aforesaid, shall have Three Pounds Proclamation Money, as a Reward,
                paid them by   *Charles Tonkin*, Sub Sheriff.
    The New-York Gazette, From August 22, to August 29, 1737; From September 12, to September 19, 1737. See *The Pennsylvania Gazette*, From August 4, to August 11, 1737, and *The Boston Gazette*, From September 5, to September 12, 1737.

               W*HEREAS* Elizabeth *the Wife of* Nathaniel Kall
of Boston, *hath absented her self from his Husband; and in a clandestine Manner, in her said Husband's Name, Trafficks about, which may tend to his great Detriment: These are therefore to forbid all Persons to Trust her the said* Elizabeth Kall, *or to buy any Thing of her—And to assure them he will not pay any Debt which she shall contract.*
    The Boston Weekly News-Letter, From August 25, to September 1, 1737; From September 1, to September 8, 1737; From September 8, to September 15, 1737.

RUN away from *Edward Williams* of *Boston*, Currier, on the 31st of *January* last, *Jonathan Reed*, an Irishman lately come from Dublin, but speaks pretty good English, about 32 Years of Age, his Name is mark'd with Ink on one of his Hands, a short well set Man, round fac'd, black Beard, round Shoulder'd, his Legs leaning a little, wore a blue Cloth Coat and Jacket, brown Breeches, and brown Wig, but 'tis suppos'd he may have chang'd his Cloaths; he is a Currier by Trade, but can work at the Shoemaker's and Brushmaker's Trade. There was in Company with him *John McCarrol*, an Attorney at Law.
    Whoever shall take up said *Reed*, and him safely convey to his said Master in *Boston*, shall have *Five Pounds* Reward and all reasonable
                Charges paid by.   *Edward Williams*.
    Note. The said *Reed* sells Playbooks and Pamphlets, and is suppos'd to be gone towards *North Carolina*.
    The Pennsylvania Gazette, August 25, to September 1, 1737; September 1, to September 8, 1737.

BROKE out of the Goal of *Burlington* in *New-Jersey, a certain Man named* John Crues, *of middle Stature, hollow Mouth'd, (that is) his Nose and Chin inclining to touch each other, a Weaver by Trade, but pretends to be a Quaker Preacher; he took with him two Coats, one a light colour'd Camblet or Duroy, and the other a Brown homespun stuff, both very plain, a sear sucker Jacket and Breeches, and a pair of patch'd leather Breeches, two fine Shirts, a half worn Beaver Hat, Thread Stockings, and picked toed Shoes, his Garters have his Name wove therein at large; had also with him* *a pair of Saddle Bags, he is suppos'd to be gone into New-England, near Boston, that he may preach again where he has preach'd before.*

Whoever takes up and secures the said Man in any Prison, giving Notice to John Boydell, *or* Charles Tonkin *the Under-sheriff of* Burlington *aforesaid, shall have* Three Pounds *Proclamation Money, as a Reward, paid by me.* Charles Tonkin, *s sher.* Dated Aug, 4th. 1737.

The Boston Gazette, From September 5, to September 12, 1737; From September 12, to September 19, 1737. See *The Pennsylvania Gazette*, From August 4, to August 11, 1737, and *The New-York Gazette*, From August 22, to August 29, 1737.

R*AN away from Messieurs* Beteille *and* Price *of* Boston, *on Saturday Night the* 10th *Instant, an* Irish *Servant Man named* Morris Roch, *about 21 Years of Age, and about five Foot six Inches high, well set and Pock broken. He had on when he went away, a Blue Cloth Coat with Silver Thread Buttons, a striped Cotton Jacket, dark colour'd Cloth Breeches, a pair of blue Grey Ribb'd Stockings, also a Hat and Wigg. N. B. All Masters of Vessels and other Persons are hereby caution'd against harbouring, concealing, or carrying off the said Servant, as they will avoid the Penalty of the Law in that Case made and provided. Whoever shall take up the said Servant, and bring him to his abovesaid Masters, living in King Street, or secure him and give Notice thereof so that he may be had again, shall have* Ten Pounds *Reward, and all necessary Charges paid.*

The Boston Evening-Post, September 19, 1737; September 26, 1737. See *The Boston Gazette*, From September 12, to September 19, 1737.

R*AN away from his Master, Mr.* George Glen *of* Boston, *Taylor, on Saturday Night the* 10th *Instant, an* Irish *Man Servant named* Anthony Kentey, *about 20 years old, a pretty tall lank Fellow, with strait black Hair, but 'tis suppos'd he has cut it off. He has a long Vissage, a little Pock broken, and speaks pretty good* English. *He had on when he went away, and carried with him, a Grey Drugget Coat with slit Sleeves, and trim'd with Black, an old brown Camblet Jacket, brown Holland Breeches, a Castor Hat, two pair of Shoes, a pair of Grey Worsted Stockings, and two pair of Yarn, three white Shirts, and one Checker'd. He is a piece of a Taylor, and his left Hand fore Finger is much prick'd with the Needle. N. B. All Masters of Vessels and other Persons are hereby caution'd against harbouring, concealing, or carrying off the said Servant, as they will avoid the Penalty of the Law in that Case made and provided. Whoever shall take up the said Servant, and bring him to his abovesaid Master, shall have* Three Pounds *Reward, and all necessary Charges paid.*

The Boston Evening-Post, September 19, 1737; September 26, 1737.

*R*AN-away from his Master Nathanael Holbrook *of* Sherburn, *on Thursday the* 15*th of September Instant, an Indian Lad about Sixteen Years of Age, named* John Pittome, *he is pretty well set and full Fac'd:* He had on an old grey Coat, a new dark grey Jacket with large Brass Buttons, white Linnen Breeches, no Stockings, old Shoes and an old Felt Hat. Whoever shall take up the abovesaid Runaway and bring him to his Master at Sherburn, *shall have* Forty Shillings *Reward, and necessary Charges paid.*

The Boston Weekly News-Letter, From September 15, to September 22, 1737; From September 22, to September 29, 1737.

RAN away from Messi. *Reteille* and *Price* of Boston, *last Saturday Night, the* 10*th Instant, an Irish Servant Man named* Morris Rock, *about* 21 *Years of Age, & about five Foot six Inches high, well set & Pock broken.* He had on when he went away, a Blue Cloth Coat with Silver Thread Buttons, a striped Cotton Jacket, dark coloured Cloth Breeches, a pair of blue Grey-Ribb'd Stockings, also a Hat and Wigg. N. B. *All Masters of Vessels and other Persons are hereby cautioned against harbouring, concealing, or carrying off the said Servant, as they will avoid the Penalty of the Law in that Case made and provided. Whoever shall take up the said Servant, & bring him to his abovesaid Masters, living in Kingstreet, or secure him and give Notice thereof so that he may be had again, shall have* Ten Pounds *Reward, and all necessary Charges paid.* Sept. 12, 1737.

The Boston Gazette, From September 12, to September 19, 1737; From September 19, to September 26, 1737; From September 26, to October 3, 1737. See *The Boston Evening-Post,* September 19, 1737.

RAN-away from *Peter Weare* of *North-Yarmouth, a stout Negro Man, about* 26 *Years of Age:* he had on a Cotton and Wool Shirt, a brownish Fustion Coat: a light colour'd Cloth Jacket: an old Pair of Trousers and a pair of strip'd Cotton & Wool Breeches under them, an old Felt Hat, gray Stockings, and a new pair of Shoes: Note, He speaks good English. *Whoever shall take up said Negro and him convey to his said Master, shall have* Five Pounds *Reward and all necessary Charges paid him by Peter Weare.*

The Boston Gazette, From September 19, to September 26, 1737.

RUN away from *John Belden* of *Norwalk,* a lusty Negroe Fellow, named *Jack,* aged about Eighteen Years, full fac'd, stammers in his Speech, had on when he went away, a Linsy Woolsy Coat with flat Peter Buttons, a white Fustain Jacket, Leather Breeches with Brass Buttons, Tow Shirt, White Stockings, Shoes with a large pair of Pewter Buckles and old Beaver Hat, he took with him an Olive coloured Broad Cloath Coat, something old and turn'd and a very good Holland Shirt. Supposed to be Seduced by one *John*

Davison alias *William Mackgee Suppos'd to be seduced by an* Irish *Fellow named* John Davisson, alias *William Mackgee, an Irish* Fellow and an Indented Servant to *Samuel Belden* of *Norwalk,* who hath deserted his Service, and run away from his said Master, and taken with him the said Negroe Fellow. The said *Davison* alias *Mackgee,* is a Weaver by Trade, aged about Thirty five Years, a lusty full fac'd Fellow of a pale Complection, something Pock-broken, wears his own Hair of a brownish Colour, his Cloathing was a light gray Duroy Coat, an old Brownish colour'd Cloth Coat, striped Holland Vest, yellowish Camblet Breeches, Linnen Trousers, speckled Shirt, and a Homespun Linnen Shirt, Worsted Stockings, and a new Castor Hat. Whoever takes up the abovesaid Runaways, so that their Masters may have them again, shall have *Ten Pounds* Reward for both or *Five Pounds* for either of them, with all reasonable Charges paid by John Belden.
Samuel Belden.

The New-York Weekly Journal, September 26, 1737; October 3, 1737; October 10, 1737. See *The Boston Evening-Post*, October 3, 1737.

R*An away from his Master, Mr.* John Belden *of* Norwalk, *a lusty Negro Fellow named* Jack, *about* 18 *Years old, full faced, speaks good* English, *but stammers or stutters in his Talk. He had on a Linsey Woolsey Coat with flat Pewter Buttons, a white Fustian Jacket, Leather Breeches with Brass Buttons, a Tow Shirt, Yarn Stockings, & Shoes with large Pewter Buckles. Has also taken with him an Olive coloured Broad Cloth Coat, turn'd and something worn, and a good New Holland Shirt. Suppos'd to be seduced by an* Irish *Fellow named* John Davisson, *alias* William Mackgee, *an Indented Servant to Mr.* Samuel Belden *of said* Norwalk, *who is also run away, and taken said Negro with him.* Davisson *alias* Mackgee *is a lusty Fellow, full faced, of a pale Complexion, wears his own Hair of a brownish Colour, is something Pock broken, suppos'd to be about thirty five Years of Age, and a weaver by Trade. His Cloathing was a new Duroy Coat, of a light Gray Colour, an old brown Cloth Coat, a striped Holland Jacket, Camblet Breeches, Tow Trowsers, a speckled Holland Shirt, and homespun Linen Shirt, Worsted Stockings, Shoes with white Mettal Buckles, and a new Castor Hat. Whoever shall take up the said Run-aways, or secure them so that their said Master may have them again, shall have a Reward of* Ten Pounds *for both, or* Five Pounds *for either of them, with necessary Charges,* paid by John Belden. Norwalk, Sept. 16, 1737.

The Boston Evening-Post, October 3, 1737; October 10, 1737. See *The New-York Weekly Journal*, September 26, 1737.

R*AN-away from their Master Capt.* William Mirick *of Boston, on Tuesday the* 27*th of this Instant September, Two Servant Men, one a Negro named*

Peter, *about 27 Years old, of a middle Stature, but rather short. Had on when he went away a blue Jacket, two pair of old Trouzers, and a Hat painted of several Colours.* N. B. *His Hair is longer than Negro's Hair commonly is, and he talks food French and Spanish, and pretty good English.*

The other is an English Man named Daniel Davis, *about 19 Years old, of a middle Stature, with smooth Face and large Eyes, and is pretty slow of Speech. He has short light Hair, and had on when he went away, a light colour'd Kersey Jacket, spotted with Tar, Leather Breeches, speckled Shirt, a pair of ribb'd Yarn Stockings, old Shoes and a very good Beaver Hat, and has with him a short light colour'd natural Wigg.* N. B. *All Masters of Vessels and other Persons are hereby cautioned against harbouring, concealing or carrying off the said Servant, as they will avoid the Penalty of the Law in that Case made and provided. Whoever shall take up the said Servants, or either of them, and bring them to their abovesaid Master, living at the North End of Boston, shall have* Five Pounds *Reward for each, and all necessary Charges paid.*

The Boston Weekly News-Letter, From September 22, to September 29, 1737; From October 6, to October 13, 1737; *The Boston Gazette*, from September 27, to October 3, 1737; From October 3, to October 10. 1737. Minor differences between the papers.

RAN-away on the 26th of this Instant *September, from Mr.* John Smibert *of* Boston, *Painter, a Negro Man Servant named* Cuffee, *who formerly belonged to Capt.* Prince, *and understands something of the business of a Sailor, he is about 22 Years of Age, and speaks good English, a pretty tall well shap'd Negro, with bushy Hair, has on a large dark colour'd Jacket, a pair of Leather Breeches stain'd with divers sorts of Paints, and a pair of Blue Stockings. Whoever shall take up said Runaway, and him safely convey to his abovesaid Master in* Boston, *shall have* Three Pounds *Reward, and all necessary Charges paid. All Masters of Vessels are hereby warned against carrying off said Servant on Penalty of the Law in that Case made and provided.* Boston, *Sept.* 30th. 1737.

The Boston Gazette, From October 3, to October 10, 1737; From October 10, to October 17, 1737. *New England Weekly Journal*, October 11, 1737; October 18, 1737; October 25, 1737. Minor differences between the papers.

Ran away on the 21st Instant in the Night, *from their Master Mr.* Amos Wood *of Unity Furnace in the Gore of Land between this Government and the Colony of* Rhode Island, *Two English Men Servants, one named* William Coleman, *aged about 22 Years, of middle slim Stature, proportionably shap'd, hook nosed, pitted a little with* the Small Pox. He has on when he went away a new Kersey Wastcoat of a light drab colour, with mettal Buttons, a pair of Deer Skin Leather Breeches, the colour changed by being daub'd with Tar in many Places, a new worsted Cap lin'd with blue, a Felt Hat, also a good Broad Cloth Coat and Wastcoat, of a deep brown colour, an Oznabrigs Frock and Trowsers, and two or three white Shirts, his Head lately shaved, and one of his Fingers on his left Hand has been lately hurt, and by Occupation a Gardner.

The other named George Blackmore, *a lusty portly young Fellow, aged about* 19 *or* 20 *Years, but not very tall, is round Fac'd, and has short dark curl'd Hair, he had on when he went away a Kersey Wastcoat of the same Cloth and Buttons as the above, a new pair of Sheep Skin Leather Breeches, a Felt Hat, he is a little knock knee'd, he has with him a plush Coat with Gold Vellum button holes, and Gold wash'd mettal Buttons, and a pair of Breeches the same as his Wastcoat, a Frock and Trousers, and a speckled Shirt and a white Shirt.*

Whoever shall take up the said Runaways, and them safely convey to the said Amos Wood *at the Furnace aforesaid, or to Mr.* Robert Thomlinson, *Merchant in* Boston, *or keep then in Custody so that they may be had again, shall have* Three Pounds *Reward for each of them and all necessary Charges paid.*

All Masters of Vessels are caution'd against carrying them to Sea least they incur the Penalty enjoined by Law.
N. B. *They have with them a small Ticken Bed Sack for a Wallet.*
The Boston Gazette, From October 17, to October 24, 1737.

RAN-*away from his Master,* James Fry *of* Andover, *on the* 14th *of this instant* October, *a Negro Boy about* 19 *Years old named* Cuff, *of a middle Stature and speaks good English. He had on when he went away, a brown coloured homespun Coat with Mettal Buttons, brown homespun Breeches with Knee Buckles, and took with him two Shirts, one Cotton & Linnen, the other fine Linnen, also two pair of Stockings, one Worsted and the other Yarn, two Worsted Caps and a Felt Hat, and round to'd Shoes with large flowered Pewter Buckles. Whoever shall take up the said Negro and bring him to his abovesaid Master, or to Mr.* Benjamin Harrod, *Brazier, at the North End of* Boston, *shall have* Forty Shillings *Reward, and all necessary Charges paid.*

The Boston Weekly News-Letter, From October 20, to October 27, 1737.

RAN-away from his Master Mr. *Thomas Craddock* of Milton, Nailor, on the 30th Instant, an Irish Man-Servant, named *Edward Murphy*, about 17 or 18 Years of Age, of middling Stature, has the Irish Brogue on his Tongue,

of a down leering Look, and blear Ey'd, short Hair, and wears a Cap. He had on when he went away, a dark colour'd Coat with open Sleeves, a white Flannel Jacket, a good pair of light colour'd shagg Breeches, a blue & white Handkerchief, two Shirts, one check Woolen, the other check Linnen, gray yarn Stockings, a Felt Hat, and a strong pair of round to'd Shoes. Whoever shall take up said Runaway and him safely convey to his abovesaid Master at *Milton*, or to Mr. *Edward Jackson* Brazier in *Boston*, shall have *Three Pounds* Reward, and all necessary Charges paid. And all Masters of Vessels are warned against carrying off said Servant, on Penalty of the Law in that Case made and provided.   *Boston, October* 31, 1737.
    New England Weekly Journal, November 1, 1737; November 8, 1737.
    See *New England Weekly Journal*, November 22, 1737, and *New England Weekly Journal*, March 21, 1738.

RAn-away at *Boston* from his Master Dr. *Joseph Franklin* of *Portsmouth*, on the 26th Instant, an Irish Man Servant, named *Charles Cavenagh*, about 24 Years of Age, 5 Foot & 10 Inches high, and pretty well set, very much pock-broken, and ill look'd Fellow, wears a Wigg of pale Hair, had on when he went away, a dark frize Coat trim'd with black Mohair, a black Wastcoat, the fore part Callamanco, and the back part black Damask, a pair of old shag Breeches, a Sawyer and Clifts Man by Trade.
    Whoever shall take up said Runaway, and him safely convey to his said Master at Portsmouth, or to Dr. *Sylvester Gardner*, Mr. *John Franklin*, or Mr. *Carrel Tabs*, Shoemaker in *Boston*, shall have *Three Pounds* Reward, and all necessary Charges paid.
    All Masters of Vessels are caution'd against carrying him off, least they incur the Penalty of the Law in that Case made and provided.
    Boston, October 31, 1737.
    New England Weekly Journal, November 1, 1737; November 8, 1737.

STollen from Mr. Richard Bethel *of* Salem, *Innholder, on Saturday the 5th of this Instant* November, *sundry Goods, viz. a Gray broad Cloth Jacket, a dark coloured broad Cloth Coat, with white Mettal Buttons, with other Things to a considerable Value. The above mentioned Goods were carried away by a Man who calls himself* Francis Spaulder, *alias* Turner, *a Dutch Man, a tall slim Fellow, with black curled Hair, about 30 Years old, Pock broken, full Mouth, flat Nose and white Eyes, and speaks broken* English. *He had on the above mentioned Cloaths, and a pair of blue and white striped Ticken Breeches, and light Gray or white Stockings. Whoever shall take up the said* Francis Spaulder, *alias* Turner, *and bring him to the above-named* Richard Bethel *in* Salem, *or to* William Winter *in* Boston, *shall have* Ten Pounds *Reward, and all necessary Charges paid.*
    The Boston Evening-Post, November 14, 1737; November 21, 1737.

Ran-away from his Master Mr. *Benedict Arnold of Newport, the 7th Instant, his Apprentice* William Kelly, *aged about twenty Years, a little Fellow, he had on when he went away a blue Jacket bound with Black. Whoever shall take up said Runaway and convey him to his Master shall have* Three Pounds ten Shillings Reward *and all necessary Charges paid.*
   The Boston Gazette, From November 7, to November 14, 1737; From November 14, to November 21, 1737.

RAn-away from his Master Mr. *Thomas Craddock* of Milton, Nailor, on the 18th Instant, an Irish Man Servant named *Edward Murphy*, about 17 or 18 Years of Age, of middle Stature, has the Irish Brogue on his Tongue, of a down leering Look, and blear Ey'd, short Hair, & wears a Cap. He had on when he went away, a dark colour'd Jacket, and an under woollen Jacket, woollen Trousers patch'd on the Knees and Seat with Pieces of another colour, check Shirt, gray yarn Stockings, and a strong pair of round to'd Shoes. Whoever shall take up the abovesaid Runaway, and him safely convey to his said Master in Milton aforesaid, or to Mr. *Edward Jackson* of Boston, Brazier, shall have *Three Pounds* Reward, and all necessary Charges paid. And all Masters of Vessels are hereby warned against carrying off said Servant, on Penalty of the Law in that Case made and provided. *Boston, Novemb.* 19*th.* 1737.
   New England Weekly Journal, November 22, 1737. See *New England Weekly Journal*, November 1, 1737, and *New England Weekly Journal*, March 21, 1738.

R*AN-away from his Master Mr.* Thomas Bentley *of* Boston, *Boat builder, on the 21st of November past, An English Servant, Named* Thomas Moore, *about Twenty Years of Age; A short well set Lad with short Hair, but commonly wears a Cap; He had on an old Kersey Jacket, something patch'd, a new homespun Jacket with Pewter Buttons, dark coloured Drugget Breeches, yarn Stockings, round to'd Shoes, with an old Felt Hat painted Red.*
   Whosoever shall take up the said Runaway, and convey him to his Master, shall have Three Pounds *Reward, and all necessary Charges paid.*
   All Masters of Vessels are hereby cautioned against harbouring or carrying off the said Servant, as they would avoid the Penalty of the Law.
   The Boston Weekly News-Letter, From November 24, to December 1, 1737; From December 1, to December 8, 1737; From December 8, to December 15, 1737.

Boston, *December* 23*d.* 1737.
R*AN away from his Master, Capt.* Nicholas Luce *of* Boston, *on Saturday the* 17th *Instant, an Irish Man Servant named* Gilbert Kilby, *about* 21 *Years*

of Age, a Cooper by Trade, of middle Stature, full ey'd, short dark colour'd Hair; he had on a Hat, a worsted Cap, a dark Snuff colour'd Fly Coat, a blue grey Jacket without Buttons but was Lac'd, a speckled Shirt, Yarn Stockings, and old double sol'd Shoes. He also carried with him a brown Cloth Pea Jacket, a pair of Trouzers and a Frock. Whoever shall convey the said Servant to his abovesaid Master in Summer Street, Boston, *shall have* Five Pounds *Reward, and all necessary Charges paid. If the said Servant has been ship'd on board any Vessel and carry'd off, the Master of said Vessel, upon his Return, is desired to bring him to his Master; which if he does, he shall be clear from any Damage of the Law, otherwise must expect to be prosecuted.*

The Boston Evening-Post, December 26, 1737; January 2, 1738; *New-England Weekly Journal,* December 27, 1737; *The Boston Weekly News-Letter,* December 27, 1737. Minor differences between the papers.

1738

Ran-away the 4th Instant from Mr. Newton, at *the South End of Boston, his Servant* Richard Williams, *a Welchman about 25 Years of Age, a fresh colour'd, short well set Fellow, had on when he went away, a dark colour'd cloth double breasted Coat, and a Doe Skin pair of Breeches, and a black Perriwig. Whoever shall discover the said* Richard Willams *to his Master, so that he may be apprehended, shall receive* Five Pounds *Reward.*

The Boston Gazette, From January 2, to January 9, 1738; From January 9, to January 16, 1738; From January 16, to January 23, 1738.

R*An away from his Master, Mr.* Andrew Gilman *of* Exeter, *on the* 18*th of* November *last, an* Indian *Man Servant named* Covy, *about 27 Years of Age: He is a short thick Fellow, has a very grum Voice, and smooth Face, speaks very good* English, *can both Read and Write, plays on a Viol. He hath a large Scar on one of his Knees, and a Scar on the upper part of one of his Feet. He had on when he went away, two Jackets, one a dark coloured Kersey, the other a blue and white woollen Cloth, a white woolen Shirt, a new Felt Hat, a pair of Indian dress'd Leather Breeches, a new pair of gray Yarn Stockings. Whoever takes up said Runaway, and conveys him to his said Master, shall have* Five Pounds *Reward, and all necessary Charges paid.*

Andrew Gilman. Exeter, December 26*th*, 1738.

The Boston Evening-Post, January 23, 1738; January 30, 1738; February 6, 1738.

RAN away from his Master, Mr. *Samuel Capen* of *Dorchester*, on Friday the 23d Day of *December* last, a Negro Man named *Jo*, upwards of Forty Years old, of a middle Stature, but well set, was born in *Boston*, and speaks very good *English*. He had on when he went away, a brownish coloured Drugget Coat, a blue Jacket, a speckled Woollen Shirt, old Yarn Stockings, and a pretty good Hat.

    N. B. All Masters of Vessels and other Persons are hereby cautioned against harbouring, concealing, or carrying off the said Servant, as they will avoid the Penalty of the Law in that Case made and provided.

    Whoever shall take up the said Servant, and bring him to his abovesaid Master, living in *Dorchester*, shall have *Forty Shillings* Reward, and all necessary Charges paid.

    New England Weekly Journal, January 31, 1738; February 7, 1738; February 14, 1738; February 21, 1738.

R*AN-away from her Master, Mr.* John Wilson *on Friday the* 13*th of* January *past, An Indian Woman, named* Ann Warwick, *about* 22 *or* 23 *Years of Age, speaks good English: She had on when she went away, A homespun Gown, strip'd Blue and Grey, Cotton and Linnen Shift, blue Stockings and wooden heel Shoes. She had also with her, an English Stuff Gown strip'd White, Green and Red. Whoever shall take up the said Indian Woman and convey her to the abovesaid Mr.* Wilson *in* Roxbury, *shall have* Three Pounds *Reward and all necessary Charges paid.*

    The Boston Weekly News-Letter, From January 26, to February 2, 1738; From February 2, to February 9, 1738; From February 9, to February 16, 1738; From February 16, to February 23, 1738.

R*AN-away from his Master Mr.* Jonathan Pue *of* Roxbury, *on Tuesday Morning last, an indented Servant Lad, named* John Gahoit, *about* 16 *Years of Age, of a ruddy Complexion, round Visag'd, and wears his Hair: He had on when he went away, a good Hat, a double breasted blew Cloth Coat with Brass Buttons, and over that a great blue Cloth Coat. Whoever shall convey the said Run-away to his Master at* Roxbury *shall be well Rewarded for their Trouble: And whoever shall conceal or carry off the said Servant must expect to be prosecuted as the Law directs.*

N. B. *He took with him a Gun, and wore Boots.*

    The Boston Weekly News-Letter, From March 2, to March 9, 1738.

R*AN away from his Master, Mr.* Christopher Askin *of* Boston, *Tanner, on the 5th of this Instant* March, *an Irish Servant Man Servant named* John Bryan, *about* 21 *Years of Age, of a midling Stature, but slim, has a Cast with one of his Eyes and has got black bushy Hair, and speaks but broken English. He had on when he went away, an old speckled Shirt, a gray*

Drugget Jacket, a brown Cloth Fly Coat, with flat Pewter Buttons, a pair of brown coloured Breeches, Yarn Stockings and round toed Shoes, and al old Felt Hat with a Slit on the Crown. N. B. *All Masters of Vessels and other Persons are hereby caution'd against harbouring, concealing, or carrying off the said Servant, as they will avoid the Penalty of the Law in that Case made and provided. Whoever shall take up the said Servant and bring him to his abovesaid Master, living near the Rev. Mr.* Checkley's Meeting-House, at the South End of Boston, *shall have* Three Pounds *Reward, and all necessary Charges paid.*
   The Boston Evening-Post, March 13, 1738; March 20, 1738; March 27, 1738.

RAN-away on the 17th Instant from Mr. *Thomas Craddock* of *Milton*, Nailer, an Irish Young Man Servant, named *Edward Murphy*, about 18 Years of Age, of middling Stature, has the Irish Brogue on his Tongue, and of a down leering Look, had on a woollen Cap, a Felt Hat, and took with him a light colour'd Wigg, had on a dirty Flannel Jacket, light colour'd Shagg Breeches, and a pair of Trousers over them, check'd woollen Shirt, brown yarn Stockings, strong Neat Leather Shoes pretty much crack'd in the upper Leather. He had on also a dark colour'd Frize Jacket with Pewter Buttons. Whoever shall take up the abovesaid Runaway Servant, and him convey to his said Master at *Milton*, or the Mr. *Edward Jackson* of *Boston*, Brazier, shall have Three Pounds Reward, and all necessary Charges paid. And all Masters of Vessels and others, are hereby caution'd against concealing or carrying off said Servant, on Penalty of the Law in that Case made and provided. *Boston, March* 17, 1737,8.
   New England Weekly Journal, March 21, 1738. See *New England Weekly Journal*, November 1, 1737, and *New England Weekly Journal*, November 22, 1737.

RAN-away from his Master Mr. *Thomas Choat* jun. of *Ipswich*, the 19th Instant, an Indian Man Servant, named *Primus*, about Thirty Years of Age, middling Stature, well set, full Face, wears his Hair; He had on when he went away, a Homespun double-breasted gray Jacket, his Breeches of the same, bluish yarn Stockings, check'd Drugget Shirt, and Felt Hat almost new, round to'd Shoes. He can Read pretty well. Whoever shall take up the abovesaid Runaway Servant, and him convey to his said Master at *Ipswich* have *Five Pounds* Reward, and all necessary Charges paid. And all Masters of Vessels and others, are hereby caution'd against concealing or carrying off said Servant, on Penalty of the Law in that Case made and provided.
Boston March 21*st*. 1737/8.
   New England Weekly Journal, April 4, 1738; April 11, 1738.

BRoke out of Bridewell in *Boston*, the 26th of *March* last, at Night, an Irish Young Man, Servant to Mr. *Francis Richey* of *Boston*, Wharfinger, the said Servant's Name is *Hugh Mc Can*, about 20 Years of Age, of a pale complection, long dark Hair, had on a grayish Fly Coat with Brass Buttons, coarse white Shirt, gray yarn Stockings, and Shoes with Brass Buckels in them. In his Speech he has something of the Irish Brogue There were Three others that broke Bridewell with him, and may be in his Company. Whoever shall take up the abovesaid Runaway Servant, and him convey to his said Master at the North End of *Boston* near Scarlett's Wharffe, or to Mr. *Henry Dyre* at the Alms House in *Boston* aforesaid, shall have *Five Pounds* Reward, & all necessary Charges paid. All Masters of Vessels & others, are caution'd against concealing or carrying off said Servant, on Penalty of the Law in that Case made & provided.
New England Weekly Journal, April 11, 1738.

R*AN from his Master* James Sisson *of* Portsmouth, Rhode-Island *the* 17*th Instant in the Evening, an Irish Man Servant, named* John Reynolds, *about* 22 *Years of Age speaks pretty good English, of middling Stature, has very short Hair: He had on when he went away, a worsted Cap, an old Felt Hat, which had been bound, but the Binding was rip'd off, a red Cloth Jacket speckled Shirt, a blew great Coat and long Oznabrigs Breeches. Whoever shall take up the said Run away Servant and convey him to the said* James Sisson *at* Rhode-Island, *shall have* Five Pounds *Reward, and all necessary Charges paid.*
The *Boston Weekly News-Letter*, April 20, to April 27, 1738; From April 27, to May 4, 1738.

Ran away from *Thomas Malony*, on Mr. *Luce's Farm near* Dedham, *A Servant Man, named* William Mc Kenny *or* Ken, *a short Swarthy Fellow, with long black Hair, much like an Indian, he had on when he went away, a Brown Homespun Coat with Pewter Buttons: whoever secures the said Runaway, and brings him to the Printer hereof; shall receive* Three Pounds *Reward and all necessary Charges.*
The *Boston Gazette*, From April 24, to May 1, 1738.

RAN-away on the 14th Instant from Mr. *Thomas Craddock* of *Milton*, Nailor, an Irish Servant Man Servant, named *Edmund Ryan*, about 18 or 19 Years of Age, of middle Stature, well Featur'd, freckled Face, gray Eyes, very thick Legs, he took with him a new woollen check Shirt, & a new white Shirt, a good brown homespun Drugget Jacket and Breeches, a Suit of new fad colour'd Duroy, & took with him several Silk Handkerchiefs & Caps, and a Felt Hat. He works well at the Nailer's Trade. There went away with the said Runaway, and 'tis suppos'd is in Company with him, one

Edmund Butler, a good Scholar, who speaks English, Latin, Greek, French &c. a thin looking Fellow, of a middle Stature, and had on a ruffled Bosom Shirt, an old flowerd bluish Silk Jacket trim'd with Silver, and a dark homespun Jacket, an old black and white Crape Coat the fore Skirts worn away, and a pair of old Trowsers over an old pair of Breeches. Whoever shall take up the abovesaid Runaway Servant and the said *Edmund Butler*, and them bring to the said *Craddock* at *Milton* aforesaid, or to Mr. *Edward Jackson* of *Boston*, Brazier, shall have *Five Pounds* Reward for each or either of them, and all necessary Charges paid. And all Masters of Vessels are hereby warned against carrying off said Servant, or the said *Edmund Butler*, on Penalty of the Law in that Case and provided.
New England Weekly Journal, May 16, 1738; May 23, 1738. See *New England Weekly Journal*, June 20, 1738.

R*AN away from his Master, Mr.* James Barton *of* Boston, *Rope-maker, on the* 16th *of this Instant* May, *an* Irish *Man named* John Gradey; *he is a short thick Fellow, has a pretty grum Voice, and black short Hair, that grows over his Forehead, and is a little Bushy; he holds his Head a little on one side. He had on a Woollen speckled Shirt, a red Jacket pretty well worn and patch'd, a dark blue Coat with a striped Stuff Lining, the Coat is pretty much patch'd and worn; a pair of Leather Breeches almost new, and he took with him also a new blue Kersy Coat and Breeches with Brass Buttons, and Four of his Master's Holland Shirts that are new. N. B. All Masters of Vessels and other Persons are hereby cautioned against harbouring, concealing, or carrying off the said Servant, as they will avoid the Penalty of the Law in that Case made and provided. Whoever shall take up the said Servant, and bring him to his abovesaid Master in* Boston, *or secure him in any of his Majesty's Goals, and give Notice thereof to his Master, shall have* Four Pounds *Reward, and all necessary Charges*
paid by me   James Barton.
The Boston Evening-Post, May 22, 1738.

D*eserted on Tuesday Night the* 9th *Instant, from on board the Ship* New-England Galley, Stephen Hall *Commander, Three Sailors, viz.* John Titmarsh, *a lusty Fellow, swarthy Complexion, about* 25 *Years of Age, and wears a Wig.* John Binham, *a small Fellow, with his own Hair.* Robert Robertson, *a short round fac'd Fellow. Whoever shall take up the said Sailors, and bring them to the abovesaid Commander, shall have* Twenty Shillings *Reward for each.*
The Boston Weekly News-Letter, From May 18, to May 25, 1738.

R*AN away from his Master, Mr.* Christopher Askin *of* Boston, *Tanner, on the* 5th *of this Instant* March, *an* Irish *Man Servant named* John Bryan,

about 21 *Years of Age, of a midling Stature, but slim, has a Cast with one of his Eyes, and has got black bushy Hair, and speaks but broken* English. *He had on when he went away, an old speckled Shirt, a gray Drugget Jacket, a brown Cloth Fly Coat, with flat Pewter Buttons, a pair of brown coloured Breeches, Yarn Stockings and round toed Shoes, and an old Felt Hat, with a Slit on the Crown.* N. B. *All Masters of Vessels and other Persons are hereby caution'd against harbouring, concealing, or carrying off the said Servant, as they will avoid the Penalty of the Law in that Case made and provided. Whoever shall take up the said Servant and bring him to his abovesaid Master, living near the Rev. Mr.* Checkley's *Meeting-House, at the South End of* Boston, *shall have* Three Pounds *Reward, and all necessary Charges paid.*
    The Boston Evening-Post, May 27, 1738.

R*AN-Away from his Master* Ebenezer Moody *of* Farmington, *on the* 17*th of this Instant* May, *A white Man Servant between twenty and thirty Years of Age, calls his Name* Lewis Williams, *and saith he's a Welch-man: He is of a dark Complection, black Hair but cut off, of a middle Stature, a well set Fellow, great Leggs and Feet, a very heavy moulded Man; Had on when he went away, a checker'd Cotton Shirt, blew Duroy Vest, dirty colour'd Cloth Boat, an old pair of Linnen Trousers much patch'd, Yarn Stockings footed with a different Colour, a new Felt Hat, sharp to'd Shoes. Whoever shall take up said Run away and convey him to his said Master in* Farmington, *shall have* Three Pounds *Reward and all necessary Charges paid.*
        Ebenezer Moody.   *Dated in* Farmington, May. 20. 1738.
    The Boston Weekly News-Letter, June 1, to June 8, 1738.

B*ROKE* out of Bridewell, last Night the 18*th Instant, an Irish Man Servant named* Jeremiah Maccowloss, *about* 25 *Years of Age, of middle Stature, Pale Countenance, Black Hair, something Pock broken, he goes a little stiff with his Left Hip, & something stooping. He had on when he Ran away, a light colour'd Kersey Coat, Black Breeches very ragged, broken Shoes and Stockings. Whoever shall take up said Runaway, and commit him to Goal, & inform the Printer hereof, shall have* Forty Shillings *Reward, and all necessary Charges paid.*
    The Boston Gazette, From June 12, to June 19, 1738. See *New England Weekly Journal*, June 20, 1738.

B*ROKE* out of Bridewell on the 18th Instant, an Irish Man Servant, belonging to Mr. *Thomas Cradock* of *Milton*, Nailor, named *Edmund Ryan*, about 18 or 19 Years of Age, of middle Stature, well Featur'd, freckled face, gray Eyes, very thick Legs, short sandy Hair, had on a good brown homespun Drugget Jacket and Breeches, and a Felt Hat. He works well at

the Nailor's Trade. Whosoever shall take up the said Servant and him convey to his said Master at Milton, aforesaid, or to Mr. *Edward Jackson* of *Boston*, Brazier, shall have Five Pounds Reward, and all necessary Charges paid. All Masters of Vessels and others, are caution'd against concealing or carrying off said Servant, on Penalty of the Law in that Case made and provided. Boston, June 19. 1738.
New England Weekly Journal, June 20, 1738. See *New England Weekly Journal*, May 16, 1738.

BROKE out of Bridewell on the 18th Instant at Night, an Irish Man Servant named *Jeremiah Maccowloss*, about 25 Years of Age, of middling Stature, pale Complexion, black Hair, something Pock-broken, he goes a little stiff with his left Hip, and something stooping. He had on when he Ran away, a light colour'd Kersey Coat, black Breeches very ragged, broken Shoes and Stockings. Whoever shall take up said Runaway and commit him to Goal, and inform the Printer hereof, shall have *Forty Shillings* Reward, and all necessary Charges paid.
New England Weekly Journal, June 20, 1738. See *The Boston Gazette*, From June 12, to June 19, 1738.

R*AN away from his Master, Ensign* John Knigh*t of* Newington, *in* New-Hampshire, *on the* 22d *of* June *past, an* Irish *Servant Man named* Timothy Madden: *He is a short thick Fellow, pock broken, with a large Scar under his Chin; black curled Hair, of a considerable Length. He had on a light coloured Kersey Coat, a yellowish Jacket much worn, white Worsted Stockings, or gray homespun, a Felt Hat, and a pair of Tap'd Shoes, half worn. N. B. All Masters of Vessels and other Persons are hereby caution'd against harbouring, concealing or carrying off the said Servant, as they will avoid the Penalty of the Law in that Case made and provided. Whoever shall take up the said Servant and bring him to his abovesaid Master in* Newington, *shall have* Three Pound*s Reward and all necessary Charges paid.*
The Boston Evening-Post, July 10, 1738; July 17, 1738.

R*AN away from his Master, Mr.* Cockrell Reeves *of* Salem, *on the* 10*th of this Instant July, a Negro Man Servant named* Will, *a tall strait Limb'd and well looking Fellow, who talks good* English. *He carried away with him, two Coats, one a dark Homespun, the other white Fustian, a pair of Ozenbrigs Breeches, and several other Garments. His wool is lately cut off. There went away with him a short Negro Fellow belonging to Mr.* William Browne, *who was dress'd in Black. The said Negro plays well on the Violin. They Stole and carried away with them, one large Bay Horse, with a large Star in his Forehead, that Paces and Trots, but chuses to Gallop. Also a*

Bay Mare about Thirteen Hands and half high, that paces well, and has been wrenched behind. [sic] N. B. They are suppos'd to be gone towards New-York. *Whoever shall take up the said Negro* Will, *and secure him so that his said Master may have him again, shall have* Five Pounds *Reward, and necessary Charges, for the Horse, and Mare* Forty Shillings *each with necessary Charges.*
    The Boston Evening-Post, July 17, 1738; July 24, 1738; July 31, 1738.
    See *The Boston Evening-Post*, July 24, 1738, for the unnamed Negroe.

RAN-away from Mr. *Samuel Waldo*, of *Boston*, Merchant, about the 7th Instant, *Edward Glashine*, an Irish Man servant, about 20 Years of Age. He had on when he went away, a black Wig, white Woollen Jacket, an old ragged dark colour'd Coat, Woollen Shirt, dark colour'd Yarn Stockings. Whoever shall take up said Runaway, and him convey to Mr. *Samuel Waldo's* at *Boston*, aforesaid, shall have Forty Shillings Reward, and all necessary Charges paid: Or any Person inclining to purchase said *Glashine's* four Years Service, may have the same on reasonable Terms.
    New England Weekly Journal, July 18, 1738; July 25, 1738.

R*AN away from this Master,* William Browne, *Esq; of* Salem, *on the Tenth of this Instant* July, *a short Negro Fellow named* Maximus, *dress'd in Black, who can play well on a Violin. Whoever shall take up the said Negro, and bring him to his said Master in* Salem, *or secure him so that he may be had again, shall have* Five Pounds *Reward, and all necessary Charges paid.*
    N. B. *The said Negro went away in Company with a tall strait Lim'd Negro Fellow named* Will, *belonging to Mr.* Cockrell Reeves *of said* Salem. *They stole and took with them a large Bay Horse with a large Scar in his Forehead, and a Bay Mare that has been wrenched behind. [sic] They are cunning crafty Fellows, and are suppos'd to be gone towards* New-York.
    The Boston Evening-Post, July 24, 1738; July 31, 1738. See *The Boston Evening-Post*, July 17, 1738.

R*AN away the* 4th *Instant from Mr.* George Tilley *of* Boston, *a Negro Fellow, named* Bristol, *aged about* 35 *Years, he is tall and slim, walks very upright, speaks broken* English, *he had on when he went away, a Felt Hat, a homespun striped Jacket, and striped Linen Breeches, a Cotton and Linen Shirt, no Stockings, pair of old Shoes.* N. B. *He has lately been seen with a Frock and Trouzers on. Whoever shall take up the said Runaway, and him safely convey to his abovesaid Master in* Boston *aforesaid, shall have* Twenty Shillings *Reward, and all necessary Charges. And all Masters of Vessels are hereby cautioned against concealing or carrying off said Servant on Penalty of the Law in that Case made and provided.*

The Boston Evening-Post, July 24, 1738; *New England Weekly Journal*, July 25, 1738. Minor differences between the papers. The *Journal* shows a reward of Forty Shillings.

R*AN-away from his Master* John Willis *of* Medford, *a Negro Man Servant named* Quaco, *aged about Twenty-five Years. He is a handsome, likely, sensible Fellow, and speaks extraordinary good English. He carry'd away with him two or three Suits of Cloaths, so that it is uncertain what he will have on. He has a Scar in his Forehead, and the little Finger of his Right hand is crooked and bends inwards. He us supposed to have a Sum of Money with him. Whoever shall take up the said Negro, and bring him to his Master shall have* Five Pounds *Reward, and all necessary Charges paid by* John Willis. Medford July 11. 1738.
The Boston Weekly News-Letter, From July 20, to July 27, 1738.

R**an**-away on the Third Instant, from his Mistress
Mrs. Margaret Payne, *a Negro Man named* Jack, *between* 40 & 50 *Years of Age. He had on when he went away a strip'd homespun Jacket, a pair of dark colour'd cloth Breeches, with brass Buttons, blue worsted or yarn Stockings: He speaks very broken English, and has a Film in one Eye. Whoever shall secure said Negro and bring him to his Mistress at her House at the South End near the Fortification shall have* Forty Shillings *Reward, and all necessary Charges paid.* Boston, July 19th. 1738.
The Boston Gazette, From July 24, to July 31, 1738.

R**A**n-away from *Martineco* sometime in *June* last, and lately came to *Boston*, and on Saturday last went from hence, a Molatto Servant, named *John Peter*, about 45 Years of Age, he has gray Hair or Wool on his Head, speaks nothing but the French Tongue, and is wrinkled in the Face, wears a white Callico Cap, an old Beaver Hat, a dark colour'd double breasted Jacket, a white Shirt, a Silk muslin Handkerchief round his Neck, a blue & white ditto in his Pocket, and worsted Stockings.
New England Weekly Journal, August 8, 1738.

R**AN**-away from his Master *Jaques Nolan* of Boston, Merchant, on the 22d of August past, a French Man Servant named *Philip Danbruuil*, aged about 40 Years, of a low Stature, but pretty thick and well set, and broad over the Shoulders, of a black Complection, has short black Hair, a round Visage, and chearful Countenance, he had on when he went away a white Draper Cap, a coarse Flannel Jacket, a check Linnen Shirt, a pair of old light colour'd Fustian Breeches very greasy, gray yarn Stockings: He speaks very broken English, mixing therewith French & Dutch. He is a Weaver by

Trade, and 'tis possible may incline to reside at Plymouth, towards which place he was seen travelling the 24th of August from Barnstable.

Whoever shall take up said Servant, & return him to his said Master in Boston, shall have *Five Pounds* Reward, and all necessary Charges paid,
Per *James Nolan.*   *Dated Boston, Sept* 15*th* 1738.
New England Weekly Journal, September 19, 1738; October 10, 1738.

BROKE out of His Majesty's Goal in *Boston,* the last Night, nine Persons, as follows, *viz. Thomas Dwyer,* an Irish Man, being a lusty full fac'd Fellow, of a pale Complection, having long strait Hair; he had on when he went away, a dark blue Coat, about 25 Years of Age.

John Maccarty, a tall slim pock-broken Fellow with a Scar upon his right Temple, about 30 Years of Age, he had on a green double breasted Jacket with Mettal Buttons.

Michael Hair, about 25 Years of Age, of middle Stature, short black Hair, down look, he had on a dark colour'd Coat; a Turner by Trade.

Alexander Maccarty, about 20 Years of Age, a likely Fellow, wears a light Wig, and a Cloth colour'd Coat.

One —*Hambleton,* about 30 Years of Age, wears his own Hair, his fore locks are White, and is a short Fellow small Face, he had on a dark colour'd Coat, This fellow together with the aforegoing are Irish Men.

Thomas Mayby alias *Thomas Manning,* an English Man, a lusty well set Fellow, about 40 Years of Age, he had on a dark colour'd Coat & Great Coat.

And one *Elizabeth Decoster,* about 30 Years of Age, a very likely Woman, she had on a strip'd Callimanco Gown.

An Indian Fellow named *John Baker,* a short Fellow, and who has but one Arm.

A Negro Fellow named *Jocco,* about twenty Years of Age, a well set Fellow, speaks very good English, and is Servant to Capt. *Sigourney.*
Whoever shall apprehend the said Absconded Prisoners, and bring them to the said Prison, shall have Three Pounds Reward for each or either of them,
paid by me,   *William Young.*
New England Weekly Journal, September 26, 1738. See *The Boston Evening-Post,* October 2, 1738. See *New England Weekly Journal,* December 26, 1738, for Mayby/Manning and Jocco/Jack.

Last Monday Night the following Prisoners broke out of the Stone Goal in this Town, viz. *Thomas Dwyer,* (Velvet Merchant) *John* and *Alexander Mccarty, Michael Hair,* —*Peter Hamilton, Thomas Manning, Elizabeth Decoster, John Baker,* (an Indian) and a Negro Fellow named *Jocco.* The first of these Fellows, viz *Thomas Dwyer,* tho' in nothing else worthy our Imitation, yet is certainly a Pattern of Frugality and good

Husbandry, if we may depend upon what is affirmed in the Advertisement for apprehending him; after his Person is described, 'tis said, *He had on when he went away, a dark blue Coat, about* TWENTY FIVE *Years of Age.*
The Boston Evening-Post, October 2, 1738. See *New England Weekly Journal*, September 26, 1738.

RAN-away of Lord's Day the 24th of *September* from his Master Mr. *Jonathan Raymond*, of *Lexington*, an English Man Servant named *James Clarke*, about 25 Years of Age, he has a Roman Nose, and light colour'd Hair: He had on when he went away a light colour'd double breasted Jacket and a red Jacket trim'd with black underneath, a pair of Green Plush Breeches, a pair of bluish Yarn Stockings, a fine white Shirt, he is short of Stature, but well set.
Whoever shall take up the abovesaid Runaway and him safely convey to his abovesaid Master at *Lexington*, or to Mr. *John Greton*, Housewright in *Boston*, shall have *Three Pounds* Reward and all necessary Charges paid.
New England Weekly Journal, October 3, 1738.

W*ENT away from his Father Mr.* James Beal *of* Needham, *on Monday the 25th of* September *last,* William Beal, *about Twenty Years of Age, a well set Youth with black Hair, his Face broke out with Pimples: He had with him, a grey Linsey-woolsey Coat pretty much worn, a dark Homespun Coat, a strip'd Cotton and Linnen Jacket, Linnen Breeches, blue Yarn Stockings, and round to'd Shoes: He took with him a Gun, two Hatts, one new Beaver, the other Felt pretty much wore. Whoever takes up said* Beal, *and conveys him to his Father Mr.* James Beal *abovesaid shall have* Three Pounds *Reward, and necessary Charges paid.*
The Boston Weekly News-Letter, From September 28, to October 5, 1738.

RAN-away from *John Ledyard,* Esq; of Groton, *a Negro called* Pompey, *about* 25 *Years old, a well made Fellow, has a Sore on one of his Legs, and has with him a Fiddle and a Bundle of Cloaths. Whoever brings him to his Master, or secures him, and advises where he may be had shall be well rewarded and paid all necessary Charges.*
N. B. He has been secure in South Kingston *Goal, and made his Escape from the Person who was bringing him Home the* 30th *September last.*
The Boston Gazette, October 2, to October 9, 1738; October 9, to October 19, 1738.

RAN away from the Rev. Mr. *Samuel Allis* of *Somars* in the County of *Hampshire*, a Negro Man about 34 or 5 Years of Age, named Coffe, well built, of a middling Stature, talks very good English. He took away with him all his wearing Apparel consisting of sundry good Cloaths, viz. a plain Cloth Coat of a brownish Colour with brass Buttons, another Coat of plain Cloth being black and white with large pewter Buttons, a Jacket of blue Camblet, with two pair of Linnen Breeches, two pair of Stockings, the one of black Worsted, and another of white Cotton, with a pair of Yarn leggins, a pair of round to'd Shoes, the Heels of them being fill'd with Horse Nails, he had two Hatts, the one a Felt, and another of Leather, he took away with him his Master's Gun of several Pounds Value, being neatly rigg'd with Brass, the top of which Gun hath had its Stock broken off about four or five Inches, and it is splic'd with Brass, he had with him several Pounds of Money. Whoever shall take up the said Runaway and convey him to his Master in *Somars* aforesaid, or to Mr. *Jonathan Dwight* at the Sign of the Lamb in *Boston,* shall have Three Pounds Reward, and all necessary Charges paid. All Masters of Vessels and others, are hereby caution'd against concealing or carrying off the said Servant on Penalty of the Law in that Case made and provided. *Somars, October* 4. 1738.

New England Weekly Journal, October 10, 1738; October 17, 1738. See *The Boston Weekly News-Letter*, From December 7, to December 14, 1738.

RAN-away last Night from his Master Mr. *Edward Gray* of *Boston*, Ropemaker, a Scotch Boy about 17 Years of Age, named *Andrew Stewart* of a tawny Complexion, & small Stature: He had on when he went away, a new bluish Kersey Jacket, white Shirt, Ticken Breeches, white Stockings, a new Hat and Shoes

Ran-away at the same Time, An Irish Servant belonging to *Caleb Joseph Gray*, Rope maker, named *James Mitchel*, about 19 Years of Age, speaks good English, fresh Complection, thick Legs & clumbsy set: He had on two Jackets, one thick white Woollen, the other homespun: He either wears a Cap or Wigg.

Also, An Irish Servant belonging to *Philip Mortimer*, Ropemaker, about 17 Years of Age, named *John Odinell*, a tall slim fellow, smooth Fac'd, he had an Impediment or Lisp in his Speech, & talks broad in the Irish Dialect; He had on when he went away a brown Kersey Pea Jacket, homespun Wastecoat, Kersey Breeches, Oznabrigs Trousers, Check woollen Shirt, worsted Cap, gray yarn Stockings and old Shoes and Breeches.

Whoever shall take up the abovesaid Servants, and convey them to their Masters at *Boston*, shall have *Forty Shillings* Reward for each, and all necessary Charges paid

All Masters of Vessels are hereby caution'd not to carry off the said Servants, as they would avoid the Penalty of the Law. *October*, 11. 1738.

New England Weekly Journal, October 17, 1738.

RAN-away from her Master *George Boldeare* in Connecticut, on the 18th Instant in the Night, an Indian Woman named *Pegg*, about 25 Years of Age, she is of a middling Stature, pretty thick set, very much pock-broken, has a small Mole on her Neck, has a waddling Gate, speaks good English, stutters a little when talking earnestly, she can read and write well: She carried away with her a check'd Cotton and Linnen Shirt, and two fine Garlick Shirts, a large grey Great Coat of a brownish colour with large flat mettal Buttons, a pair of Mens sharp to'd Calf Skin Shoes, a pair of large Steel Buckles: She is suspected to have changed her Woman's Dress to Mans's; or dress'd with Blankets, Indian like, she having run away once before, and was found in a Man's Apparel.

Whoever shall take up said Run-away, and bring her to her said Master, shall have *Five Pounds* Reward, and all necessary Charges
     paid by   *George Dolbeare*.   *New London, October* 19. 1738.
New-England Weekly Journal, October 24, 1738.

R*AN away from his Master, Capt.* Samuel Carlton *of* Salem, *Mariner, on Tuesday the* 10*th of this Instant* October, *a tall lusty Negro Fellow named* Millet, *but calls himself* Tom Brown, *about six Foot high, with the letters* **L B** *branded on his Breast, and talks good* English. *He had on or took with him when he went away, a dark coloured double breasted Jacket of Homespun, a striped homespun under Jacket, and an old thick Jacket of a Purple Color, but faded, and mended much the same at both Elbows; a white Shirt, and an old Ozenbrigs Shirt, homespun dark coloured Breeches, and a pair of Purl Yarn Stockings, with old Shoes. He is a Shoemaker by Trade, and carries his Tools in a Bag. N. B. All Masters of Vessels and other Persons are hereby cautioned against harbouring, concealing, or carrying off the said Servant, as they will avoid the Penalty of the Law in that Case made and provided:*

Whoever shall take up the said Servant, and bring him to his abovesaid Master in Salem, *shall have Five Pounds Reward, and all necessary Charges paid.*
     The *Boston Evening-Post*, October 25, 1738. See *The Boston Evening-Post*, December 17, 1739.

Ran-away on the 29th of October last from his Master Mr. Foxcroft *of* Boston, *a* Negro Man *named* Cambridge, *a lusty well looking Fellow, some of his fore Teeth worn down with his Pipe, and speaks but broken English: Went away without Hat, or Cap having on only an Oznabrigs Jacket and Breeches, yarn Stockings and square toe'd Shoes, if any. Also missing for some Time and supposed to be stolen, a large Silver Porringer,*

mark'd F
T A
with the Maker's Name K. Leverett, *and an old Silver Spoon with only the two first Letters of the Maker's Name* J. C.

Whoever shall take up the said Negro, or discover the said Plate, *shall be well rewarded.*

The Boston Weekly News-Letter, From October 26, to November 2, 1738; From November 2, to November 9, 1738.

D*Eserted from on Board the Ship* Thomas & Diana, James Nelson *Commander* Slack Vickerman, *Boatswain of said Ship: If he will return to his Duty on board in Two Days he shall be received otherwise deem'd as a Deserter.*

The Boston News-Letter, From November 9, to November 16, 1738.

RAN-away on Thursday Evening the 23d Instant from Mr. *Thomas Pearson* of *Boston*, Ginger-bread Baker, two Irish Man-Servants, one named *Michael Dullowin*, a slim Fellow, thin Visage, pale Complection. He had on when he went away, a light colour'd Coat with brass Buttons, a brown Nappey Jacket with Mettal Buttons, a white Shirt, a light colour'd short Wig, Sheep Skin Breeches, dark Yarn Stockings, & new Shoes with brass buckels. He has the Brogue on his Tongue. The other named *Patrick Shangasseys*, a short well set Fellow, fair Complection: He had on a white Cloth Coat, dark Drugget Jacket and Breeches, a white Shirt, gray worsted Stockings, and new Shoes with brass Buckles. They also took away with them an old light colour'd Great Coat, a dark colour'd Jacket and breeches with brass Buttons.

Whoever shall take up the said Runaways, and them convey to their Master at the Wheat-Sheaff in *Boston* aforesaid, shall have 5 l. Reward, and all necessary Charges paid. All Masters of Vessels &c. are hereby caution'd against concealing or carrying off said Servants, on Penalty of the Law in that Case made and provided. *Boston, November* 27. 1738.

New England Weekly Journal, November 28, 1738.

A Negro Man being brought before a Justice by *Nathaniel Fellows*, as a Run-away, said his Name is *Cuffee,* That his Masters Name is Mr. *Samuel Allis,* Minister of *Somers,* in the Province of the *Massachusetts Bay*; That he left his said Master in *September* or *October*: This is to notify the Owner or the Master of said Negro, that he is now confin'd in *Portsmouth* Goal, ready to be deliver'd up on paying the necessary Charges.

The Boston Weekly News-Letter, From December 7, to December 14, 1738. See *New England Weekly Journal*, October 10, 1738.

BROKE out of His Majesty's Goal in Boston, the Night following the 13 of this Instant December, 6 Persons (who were Committed to Goal for Stealing and other Criminal Actions;) Named and Described as follows, *viz.*

John Fitz Gerrald, about 30 Years of Age, a well set Fellow, much Pock broken, he draws his Mouth on one side when he speaks, & has Letters mark'd on each of his hands; he had on a Red double Breasted Jacket, with Mettal Buttons, a pair of Trousers, & a Red Mill'd Cap.

Patrick Fisher, about 35 years of Age, of a Sandy Complexion, much Freckled, Redish Hair, he has an Impediment in his Speech; he had on a dark Brown Coat, Green Jacket, & Blue Breeches.

James Kapen, about 25 Years of Age, short Stature, a down look, he has a Blemish in one of his Eyes, he had on a Red Shag Coat, a dark colour'd Coat underneath. These three above are Irish

Thomas Mayby, alias *Thomas Manning* about 42 Years of Age, a lusty well set Fellow; he had on a dark colour'd Coat & Great Coat; he is an English Man.

A Negro Fellow named Jack, about 20 Years of Age, a well set Fellow, speaks good English, Servant to Capt. Sigourney. This Negro stabb'd his Master about 3 Months ago. He had on a red Great Coat, and a dark colour'd Pea Jacket underneath.

A Negro Fellow named Thomas Harmon, about 40 Years of Age, that is lame in one of his Arms, he is known by the Name of Fortuneteller, and used to white wash in this Town, he has large thick Lips, large Eyes, and goes stooping, and is of a pale Complexion.

Whoever shall apprehend the said absconded Prisoners, and bring them to the said Prison, shall have Three Pounds Reward for each or either of them, paid by me,   *William Young.*

New England-Weekly Journal, December 19, 1738; December 26, 1738; January 2, 1739. See *New England-Weekly Journal*, September 26, 1738, for Mayby/Manning and Jocco/Jack.

1739

DEserted from the Sloop *Mary, Josiah Thacher* Commander, on Wednesday last the 31st of *January*, an Indian Man named *John*, about 22 Years of Age, of middling Stature, short Hair. He had on a grey Kersey double breasted Jacket with flat Mettle Buttons, Breeches of the same, and a speckled Woollen Shirt. Whoever shall take up the abovesaid Indian Fellow and bring him to Dr. *Stephen Greenleaf*, in *Boston*, or to Mr. *Hezekiah Usher*, of *Newport*, or to the abovesaid *Thacher* at *Norwalk*, shall have *Forty Shillings* Reward, and all necessary Charges paid.

Boston, Feb. 6, 1738,9.

New-England Weekly Journal, February 6, 1739.

RAN-away Yesterday Morning from his Master Samuel Hollowel *of* Boston, *Shipwright a Servant Lad named* William Miller, *between seventeen and eighteen Years of Age, of middling Stature, and a smiling Countenance. His left Thumb is cut close off. He has with him divers Cloaths. Whoever shall take up said Servant and convey him to his Master near Mr.* Hollowel*'s Ship Yard shall have* Fifty Shillings *Reward, and necessary Charges.*

The Boston Weekly News-Letter, From February 1, to February 8, 1739; From February 8, to February 15, 1739.

Monday 5th of this Instant, Ran away from *his Master* William Fountain *of* Norwich, *then in* Boston, *a Likely Negro Man commonly called* Tom the Fidler, *about* 20 *Years of Age speaks Good English, he had on when he went away a Light Colour'd great Coat no Buttons nor Button holes to it and a Dark Colour'd Close Body'd Coat with Mettle Buttons, and a Green Cloath Westcoat a Worsted Cap and a very narrow Brim'd Hatt. Whoever takes up said Negro and carrys him to Mr.* Clear's *at the sign of the White Horse at the South End of* Boston *shall have* Three Pounds *Reward, if any ways in the Country shall have* Five Pound *Reward and necessary charges paid.*

The Boston Gazette, From March 5, to March 12, 1739; From March 19, to March 26, 1739; The Boston Weekly Post-Boy, March 19, 1739; March 26, 1739; April 2, 1739. Minor differences between the papers.

Taken up and brought to Salem *Goal, a likely young Negro Man about 22 Years old, who says his Name is* Cuffe, *and belongs to a Widow Woman in* Boston, *named* Bethiah Tucker, *he was taken up last Monday was Se'n night.* Salem, *March* 1739.

The Boston Weekly Post-Boy, March 19, 1739; March 26, 1739; April 2, 1739.

Absconded from her Master *John Wass* of Boston, *a Negro Girl named* Letitia *formerly bought of Mr.* James Gordon. *Whoever will take up the said Negro, and bring her to said* Wass *at the South End of* Boston, *shall be satisfied for their Trouble.*

N. B. *All Persons are being caution'd against entertaining said Negro on Penalty of the Law.*

The Boston Gazette, From March 26, April 2, 1739; From April 2, to April 9, 1739.

RAN-away from his Master John Karr *of* Chester, *on Monday the* 16*th of last Month an Irish Man Servant named* Dennis Coughlan, *aged about* 18 *Years; a short, stout well set Fellow, red Face and light colour'd Hair: He*

had on when he went away, a dark colour'd Coat of fine Kersey, a lightish colour'd Wastecoat of Broad Cloth, a pair of strong Wash Leather Breeches with round Pewter Buttons: He speaks good English, but with the Brogue, Whoever shall take up said Runaway, so as his said Master may have him again, shall have Five Pounds *Reward, and all necessary Charges paid by* John Karr.
The Boston Weekly Post-Boy, April 2, 1739; April 9, 1739; April 16, 1739.

RAN-away from their Master Mr. *Edward Carter of* Boston *Silk Dyer on the* 30*th of* March *last past, two Irish Men Servants, one named* John Browne *alias* John Corkerry; *the other named* James Rogers *formerly a Butcher: Said* Browne *is a short thick wellset Fellow, about* 20 *Years of Age, with a down Look, treads smart, walks upright, wears a Wig, went away dress'd in Black. Said* Rogers *went away in a light Drabb Coat, homespun Jacket, black Kersey Breeches: He is a stout well set Fellow, short brown Hair mixt with gray, if not shav'd, grey Eyes, thick Lips, with Tobacco in his Mouth. Their Nails stain'd with Dying if not scrap'd, their Cloths may be chang'd, not knowing what they have taken with them of other Persons.*
Whoever takes up said Runaways, and them safely conveys to their said Master, shall have Five Pounds *Reward for each, and all necessary Charges paid.* E. Carter.
The Boston Gazette, From April 2, to April 9, 1739.

*DE*serted *from on board the Ship* Francis *and* William, James Flucker *Commander, now lying at the Long Wharf in* Boston, *on Wednesday the* 11*th past, three Persons, One of them named* John Baker, *a Corker by Trade, the other two Sailors named* Samuel Cheney *and* Francis Ellis. *Whoever shall take up the above Deserters shall be well rewarded.*
The Boston Weekly News-Letter, From April 12, to April 19, 1739; From April 19, to April 26, 1739; From April 26, to May 3, 1739. See New-England Weekly Journal, April 24, 1739.

RAN-away from Mr. *Pierson Richardson* of *Woburn*, on the 30th of March past, a Negro Man Servant, named *Jim*, about 29 Years of Age, middling Stature, ready to talk, and speaks good English, had on when he went away a grey colour'd homespun Coat, flat Pewter Buttons, a Cape on the Coat, strip'd Wastecoat, Breeches strip'd blue and white, old Shoes, Felt Hat.
Whoever shall take up the said Runaway, and him safely convey to his said Master at *Woburn*, shall have *Forty Shillings* and all necessary Charges paid   Boston, April 10 th. 1729.
New-England Weekly Journal, April 24, 1739.

DESERTED from on board the Ship *Francis* and *William, James Flucker* Commander, now lying at the Long Wharf in *Boston*, on Wednesday the 11th Instant, three Persons, One of them named *John Baker*, a Corker by Trade, the other two Sailors named *Samuel Cheney* and *Francis Ellis*; If they will immediately return to their Duty they shall be kindly received, otherwise treated as Deserters.
    See *New-England Weekly Journal*, April 24, 1739. See *The Boston Weekly News-Letter*, From April 12, to April 19, 1739.

RAN-away from their Master Mr. *Chambers Russel* of *Concord*, on Monday Night the 9th of this Instant *April*, 2 Irish Men Servants, the one named *John Lambert*, about 23 Years of Age, a tall well set Fellow, short air, He took with him several Cotton & Linnen Shirts, a light colour'd Coat with close Sleeves, trim'd with the same colour, a dark colour'd Pea Jacket, yellow BuckSkin Breeches, Yarn Stockings, and round toed Shoes. The other named *David Regane*, about 22 Years of Age, of middling Stature, short curl'd Hair, he has a Scar under his Left Jaw, He had on when he went away, a light colour'd Pea Jacket, Leather Breeches, Cotton & Linnen Shirt, yarn Stockings, and round toed Shoes. Whoever shall take up the abovesaid Runaways, & them safely convey to their abovesaid Master, or to the Hon. *Charles Chambers,* Esq; at *Charlestown*, shall have *Five Pounds* Reward, or *Fifty Shillings* for either of them & all necessary Charges paid.
                                                               Boston, April 13th 1735.
    New-England Weekly Journal, April 24, 1739.

Ran-away from her Master *William Wall* of *Prudence Island*, on the 20th of *March* last, an Indian Woman named *Mary*; she had with her when she went away two Gowns, one of a homespun Drugget of red and yellow Colour, the other of a striped Flannel and black Duroy quilted Coat and a blue Callico Apron; she hath lost her Toes on one Foot. Whoever shall take up the said Runaway, and bring her to Dr. *Aaron Bourne* of *Bristol*, or to her Master on *Prudence Island*, shall have 40 s. Reward, & all necessary Charges paid.
    The Boston Gazette, From May 7, to May 14, 1739.

D*Eserted from the Brigantine* Elizabeth, William Fowler *Commander, now lying in* Boston *Harbour, on the Third of this Instant* June, *a Sailor named* John Goble, *about* 35 *Years old, of a middle Stature, and has dark coloured Hair. If the said* John Goble *will return to his Duty on board the said Brig, he shall be kindly received, otherwise he must expect to be treated as a Deserter.*
    The Boston Evening-Post, June 4, 1739; June 11, 1739; June 18, 1739.

155

RAN-away on the 29th of last Month from his Master *Edward Carter* of *Boston*, Silk Dyer, an Irish Man Servant, named Thomas Manning, alias *Carter*, he is a lusty well set Fellow; had on when he went away, a black Cloth Jacket, blue Kersey Breaches trim'd with black, suppos'd to have Trowsers, yarn Stockings, good Shoes, cotton and linnen Shirt, new Beaver Hat, dark colour'd natural Wigg or Cap; he speaks thick, rolls his Eyes, stoops a little, treads firm, speak smartly to him and he'll repeat your Words again. His Nails somewhat stain'd, if not scrap'd. He is a Sheerman, Presser, &c. at the Cloathers Business. Whoever shall take up the abovesaid Runaway, and his safely convey to his abovesaid Master, shall have *Five Pounds* Reward, and all necessary Charges paid. All Masters of Vessels are hereby caution'd against concealing or carrying off said Servant, on Penalty of the Law.

The Boston Weekly Post-Boy, June 4, 1739; June 11, 1739; June 25, 1739.

RAN-away from his Master *Nathaniel Messervey* of *Portsmouth* on the 6th Instant, a white Man Servant, named *John Force*, about 20 Years of Age, a lusty well set Fellow, had on when he went away a Ratteen Coat of a light colour, a blue broad Cloth Jacket, light colour'd Plush Breeches, with Trowsers over them, but took with him divers other sorts of Cloathing and so may change his Apparel: He is a Ship Carpenter by Trade, and 'tis likely will endeavour to get such an Employment. The said Servant was taken up last Tuesday Morning, and committed to *Newbury* Prison, but broke out the same Night. Whoever shall take up said Servant and convey him to his said Master in *Portsmouth*, or to the Prison-keeper at *Newbury*, or to any of his Majesty's Goals in this Province, shall have *Three Pounds* Reward, and all necessary Charges paid.   Boston, June 1st. 1739.

New England Weekly Journal, June 5, 1739.

W*Hereas* Elizabeth *the Wife of Dr.* James Howard *of* Stoughton, *has at several Times Sold sundry Things of his Property, without his Knowledge or Consent, and also unreasonably absented herself from him and his Family, which is to his great Detriment: These are therefor to Notify all Persons not to receive any Things of her in a Way of payment or Barter, not to Trust or give Credit to her upon his Account for he hereby declares his Intention not to pay any Debts contracted by her, without special direction from himself.*

The Boston Weekly News-Letter, From May 24, to June 7, 1739.

STOLEN from off the common High-Way in *Abbington* on Tuesday Night the 5th Instant, An Iron Gray Mare, belonging to *Daniel Read* of said Town: She is about 13 Years old, 14 Hands and an half high, not enclining to Pace; the inner Part of her off Fore Foot somewhat defective; the Hair is worn off the near Fore Foot, the fore Part, by the Fatter-Lock, and a hard Piece of Skin grown up. 'Tis supposed she is carry'd off by *Jabez Allen* alias *Mead* he having been lately seen in those Parts with a whitish Horse, which was fond near where the Mare was stolen. Whoever shall take up the said Mare, and bring her to the Owner in *Abbington* shall have *Forty Shillings* Reward, and all necessary Charges paid.

The Boston Weekly News-Letter, From June 7, to June 14, 1739; From June 14, to June 21, 1739; From June 21, to June 28, 1739; From July 12, to July 19, 1739.

Boston, June 11, 1739 Ranaway from the *Bunch of Grapes & Three Sugar Loaves in Kingstreet, a Molatto Wench, called* Mercy, *she had on when she went away a white jacket with a variety of Petticoats, some Silk, some Callico; she is well set, of a middle Stature. Whoever secures the said Runaway and conveys her to the above place, shall be rewarded to their satisfaction.*

The Boston Gazette, From June 11, to June 18, 1739.

RAN-away on Saturday the 9th Instant from his Master Capt. *Alexander French*, a Negro Man Servant, named *Jack*, about 22 Years of Age, formerly belonged to Capt. *Durell* ard since [sic] to Capt. *Warren*, a tall slim Fellow, speaks good English, he had one when he went away a short red Jacket with Mettal Buttons, a pair of Trousers, a pair of round to'd Shoes with large carv'd Buckles, a worsted Cap, a small Beaver Hat with no Loops. Suppos'd he is in *Boston*.

Whoever shall take up said Runaway Servant, and him safely convey to his abovesaid Master in Queen-Street near the Prison in *Boston*, shall have *Forty Shillings* Reward, and all necessary Charges paid.

And all Masters of Vessels are hereby warned against carrying off said Servant, on Penalty of the Law in that Case made and provided.

New England Weekly Journal, June 19, 1739.

R*AN-away the Ship* Betty, William Forster *Commander,* James Nichols *and* Peter Hobson*, both Indented Servants: Whoever secures said Servants, and brings them to their Master on board said Ship, lying at the Long-Wharff, shall have* Five Pounds *for each of them.*

N. B. *All Masters of Vessels are forewarn'd carrying off said Servants under Penalty of the Law.*

The Boston Weekly News-Letter, From June 14, to June 21, 1739; From June 21, to June 28, 1739.

Ran-away on the 13d instant from Mrs. *Mary Hamilton, Tallow Chandler, at the North End of* Boston, *an Irish Man Servant named* Thomas Burch *of a short thin Stature, pale Face, with a rim round his white Eyes. He had on a knit worsted Cap, no Hat, a dark colour'd Pea Jacket, a narrow strip'd homespun Wastecoat a Cotton Shirt, dark Cloth Breeches with red Puffs if not taken out, and yarn Stockings. He took with him 3 Cotton & Linnen Shirts, a light bob Wigg, a pair of blue and white homespun Breeches. Whoever shall take up said Runaway, and bring him to his said Mistress, shall have* 40s. *Reward, and all necessary Charges paid. And all Masters of Vessels are warned against carrying off said Servant, on Penalty of the Law in the Case made & provided.* Boston, June 25th 1739.

The Boston Gazette, From June 18, to June 25, 1739; From June 25, to July 5, 1739.

R*AN away from Mr.* James Jeffs *of Boston, Painter, on the* 22*d of this Instant* June, *a Negro Boy named* Scipio, *aged about* 16 *Years, pretty short for his Age, but very well set. He has three Scars on the middle of his Forehead, and a Sore on one of his Shins. He had on when he went away, a Cotton Shirt, and a Frock and Trouzers, pretty much painted. All Masters of Vessels and others are hereby cautioned against harbouring, concealing or carrying off the said Negro, as they will avoid the Penalty of the Law. And whoever shall take up the said Negro, and bring him to his abovesaid Master, living near* Clark's *Ship Yard, at the* North End, *shall have* Forty Shillings *Reward and all necessary Charges paid.*
Boston, June 25. 1739.

The Boston Evening-Post, July 9, 1739; July 16, 1739; July 23, 1739; August 1, 1739.

R*AN away from his Master Mr.* Nathanael Brown *of* Salem, *on Wednesday the* 4*th of this Instant* July, *a Negro Fellow named* Cuffe, *about* 20 *Years of Age, a strait limb'd & handsome Fellow of a middle Stature plays upon a Violin, and dances pretty well. He carried away with him a Gray Woollen Coat, a brown Holland Coat, a striped Jacket and Breeches, a pair of white Trowsers, sundry pair of Stockings, one of which is Blue, and a new Felt Hat. All Masters of Vessels and other Persons are hereby cautioned against harbouring, concealing, or carrying off the said Servant, as they will avoid the Penalty of the Law in that Case made and provided. Whoever shall take up the said Servant, and bring him to his abovesaid Master in* Salem, *shall have* Five Pounds *Reward and all necessary Charges paid.*

The Boston Evening-Post, July 9, 1739; July 16, 1739; July 23, 1739.

R*AN away from his Master, Mr.* John Newell *of* Boston, *Caulker, on Thursday the* 29*th of* November *past, an Irish Servant Man named* Robert

Long, *about* 19 *or* 20 *Years old, of a middle Stature, and had black Eyes and short Hair. He had on when he went away a dark coloured Drugget Coat and Breeches, a blue and white striped Cotton and Linen Jacket, Gray Worsted Stockings, a white Garlix Shirt, and a Felt Hat. Whoever shall take up the said Servant, and bring him to his abovesaid Master, living near Dr.* Cutler's *Church at the North End, shall have* Five Pounds *Reward, and all necessary Charges paid.*

N. B. *All Masters of Vessels and other Persons are hereby cautioned against harbouring, concealing, or carrying off said Servant, as they will avoid the Penalty of the Law in that Case made and provided.*

The Boston Evening-Post, July 9, 1739. See The Boston Evening-Post, December 3, 1739.

R*AN away from his Master, Mr.* John Woods *of* Groton, *on Thursday the* 12*th of this Instant* July, *a Negro Man Servant named* Caesar, *about* 22 *Years of Age, a pretty short well sett Fellow. He carried with him a Blue Coat and Jacket, a pair of Tow Breeches, a Castor Hat, Stockings and Shoes of his own, and a Blue Cloth Coat with flower'd Metal Buttons a white flower'd Jacket, a good Bever Hat, a Gray Wigg, and a pair of new Shoes of his Master's, with some other Things. It is suspected there is some white Person that may be with him or design to make Use of his* Master's Apparel *above described.*

Whoever shall take up the said Servant, and bring him to his abovesaid Master in Groton, *or be a Means of convicting any Person or Confederate with said Servant as above suspected, shall have* Five Pounds *Reward for each of them, and all necessary Charges paid.*

The Boston Evening-Post, July 16, 1739; July 23, 1739; July 30, 1739.

Ran-away from the Rev. Mr. *Pigot of Marblehead,* Robert Wilson, *a Dutchman, an Indented Servant, aged about* 35 *Years, of a middle Stature, spare and thin, wears a black Jacket, a homespun speckled Shirt, long Trowsers, and a woollen Cap. Whoever secures him and gives Notice to Mrs.* Pigot, *shall be Rewarded to Content.*

The Boston Gazette, From July 23, to July 30, 1739; From July 30, to August 8, 1739.

Boston, Aug 5. 1739.

WHEREAS Ann *the Wife of* James Flood, *jun. of* Boston, *Cooper, has absented her self from her Husband, and carried off sundry Things of his Property to a considerable Value, without his Knowledge & Consent.*

These are therefor to Caution all Persons not to receive any Household Stuff or other Things of her in any way of Barter or Payment, not to Trust or give Credit to her on his Account, for he hereby declares his Intention

not to pay any Debts Contracted by her without special Direction from himself. *James Flood,* jun.
The Boston Gazette, From July 30, to August 8, 1739.

WHereas *Elisabeth,* the Wife of *John Tolman* of *Dorchester*, has absented her self from her Husband, and carried off sundry Things of his Property, to a consiberable Value, without his Knowledge and Consent: These are therefore to caution all Persons not to receive any Household Stuff or other Things of her in any way of Barter or Payment; not to trust or give Credit to her upon his Account; for he hereby declares his Intention not to pay any Debts contracted by her without special Direction from himself.
John Tolman.
The Boston Weekly News-Letter, From August 2, to August 9, 1739.

W*Hereas* Mary *the Wife of* Joseph Macres *of* Salisbury *in the Province of the Massachusetts Bay has eloped from him and is gone into the Province of New Hampshire, where she lives in open and manifest Violation of the holy Marriage Covenant, and persists in an obstinate Refusal of returning to the said* Joseph *her lawful Husband, tho' he hath sundry Times kindly invited here thereto, with a Promise of Forgiveness for her past unlawful Seperation and Absence;*

These are therefore to Warn all Persons against giving any Trust or Credit to the said Mary *on the Account of her said Husband, he the said* Joseph *publickly declareth that he will pay no Debt contracted by her after the Date of these Presents.* Dated the 2d Day of July. 1739.
The Boston Weekly Post-Boy, August 13, 1739.

RAN-AWAY from his Master *Joseph Cundall* of Portsmouth on Rhode-Island, *an Indented Servant about the beginning of* July *last,* named Richard Comber, *a Bricklayer by Trade. He had on when he Ranaway a Frock & Trousers, and a Woollen Cap. He is about Forty Years of Age, he has a cut in his under Lip, and one of his fore Teeth is out. Whoever shall secure said Run-away, and send word to his Master, shall have* Five Pounds *Reward, and all necessary Charges*
paid by Joseph Cundall.
The Boston Gazette, From August 13, to August 20, 1739; From August 20, to August 27, 1739; From August 27, to September 3, 1739. See *The Boston Weekly Post-Boy,* August 20, 1739.

R*AN-away from his Master* Joseph Cundall *of* Portsmouth *on* Rhode-Island, *the beginning of* July *last, an Indented Servant named* Richard Combes, *a Bricklayer by Trade: He had on when he went away, a Frock and Trousers and a Woollen Cap has a Cut in his Under-Lip, on one Tooth out before,*

about Forty Years of Age. Whoever shall secure said Runaway and send Word to his Master, shall have Five Pounds *Reward and all necessary Charges paid.*
    The Boston Weekly Post-Boy, August 20, 1739; August 27, 1739; September 3, 1739; September 17, 1739; September 24, 1739. See *The Boston Gazette*, From August 13, to August 20, 1739.

RAN-away from his Master Mr. *Nathanael Thwing* of *Boston,* on the 23d Instant, an Irish ManServant named *Michael Bourk,* of middle Stature: He had on when he went away a blew Drugget Coat and Breeches of the same, and a pair of Trousers, a strip'd Swanskin Jacket.
    Whoever shall apprehend the said Servant, and bring him to his abovesaid Master, shall have *Five Pounds* Reward, and all necessary
            Charges paid by   *Nath. Thwing.*
New-England Weekly Journal, August 28, 1739.

R*AN away from his Master, Mr.* James Fairservice *of* Boston, *Trader, on the* 13*th of this Instant* September, *an Irish Man Servant named* Samuel Shaw, *a tall slim Fellow, about* 40 *Years of Age, Pox broken and of a pale Complexion, much given to Talk and bad Company, and apt to get in Liquor. He was lately ransomed from being Shot for Desertion sundry Times from* Annapolis Royal *Fort. He works well at the Weavers and Clothiers Trade, and has a good Faculty at Pedling. He had on when he went away, a pair of Check Trowsers, dirty light coloured Yarn Stockings, half worn Shoes, large Bath Metal Buckles, a Felt Hat, short black Hair mix'd with Gray, a white Shirt, an old striped Stuff Jacket, an old light Camblet Coat full trim'd, with Scarlet Lining; he had a choice Cain in his Hand and several sorts of Pedlers Ware with him.*
    Whoever shall take up the said Run-away, and bring him to his aforesaid Master, living in Middle Street, Boston, *or to Capt.* Watt *near the Swing Bridge, shall have* Five Pounds *Reward, and all necessary Charges paid.*
    The Boston Evening-Post, September 17, 1739; September 24, 1739.

RAN-away from *Edward Bridge,* of *Roxbury,* Esq; on Sabbath Day the ninth of this Instant *September*, an Irish Man servant named *James Murphy*, about 18 Years of Age, a well set Fellow, with short sandy Hair, pretty clear Skin. He had on when he went away, a dark colour'd Cloth Coat and Breeches, a Speckled Shirt, Gray Yarn Stockings, round toed Shoes with Brass Buckles, and a Felt Hat with narrow Brims.
    Whoever shall take up the abovesaid Runaway Servant, and him safely convey to his abovesaid Master shall have *Three Pounds* Reward, and all necessary Charges paid.

New England Weekly Journal, September 18, 1739.

RAn-away on the 12th Instant from Mr. *John Box* of *Boston*, an English Man Servant named *Daniel Johnson*, about 19 or 20 Years of Age, a well set young Man, has a large Scar down his Forehead, wears a Wigg or Cap, and took with him a Coat and Jacket with broad flat Mettal Buttons, a homespun Wastecoat, and a white Shirt.

Whoever shall take up the abovesaid Runaway above Servant, and him safely convey to his abovesaid Master in *Boston* aforesaid, shall have *Five Pounds* Reward, and all necessary Charges.

New England Weekly Journal, September 18, 1739.

R*AN-away from his Master* Nathanael Holbrook *of* Sherburn, *on Wednesday the* 19*th of* Sept. *last, an Indian Lad of about* 18 *Years of Age, named* John Pitteme: *He is pretty well sett and of a guilty Countenance, and has short Hair: He had on a grey Coat with Pewter Buttons, Leather Breeches, an old tow Shirt, grey Stockings, good Shoes and a Felt Hat.*

Whosoever shall take up the said Servant, and convey him to his Master in Sherburn, *shall have* Forty Shillings *Reward, and all necessary Charges paid. We hear the said Servant intended to change his Name and Clothes.*

The *Boston Weekly News-Letter*, From October 4, to October 11, 1739; From October 11, to October 18, 1739.

*T*HE *Governour's Negro* Juba, *being Run-away, its desired whoever may see him would seize him and send him home. He has on a Woolen Cap, a bound Hat, a Linnen Jacket, and Leathern Breeches.*

The *Boston Weekly News-Letter*, From October 4, to October 11, 1739.

R*An away from Mr.* John Little *of* Boston, *Gardner, on Tuesday the* 9*th of* October *Instant, a Covenant Servant Man named* James Maxwell, *about* 30 *Years old, a lusty stout Fellow, with a small Mouth, and has red Hair. He understands Gardning very well He had on when he went away, an old whitish Wig, a Castor Hat, a blue broad Cloth Coat and Jacket, a whitish Coat with Metal Buttons, a grey broad Cloth Jacket with Metal Buttons, Leather Breeches, and a pair of Trouzers; he has also with him three white Linen and two speckled Woollen Shirts, round toed Shoes, and blue Worsted Stockings. Whoever shall take up the said Servant, and bring him to his abovesaid Master, living in Milk-Street, shall have* Three Pounds *Reward, and all necessary Charges paid.*

The *Boston Evening-Post*, October 22, 1739; October 29, 1739.

BRoke out of His Majesty's Goal in *Boston*, the 28th Instant at Night, Seven Prisoners, Named and Described at follows, Viz.

Gideon Braydon, about 26 Years of Age; he had on a dark Fustian checkered coat, a Green Jacket, and a light Wigg.

John Call, about 21 Years of Age, of middling Stature, a stammering Speech; He had on a Great Coat, a Green Jacket, a pair of Trousers, and an old Hat.

John Rullo, about 20 Years of Age, a lusty young Fellow; he had on a yellowish colour'd Coat, and a white Cap.

Thomas Manuel, a free Negro Man, about 50 Years of age, Gray Headed; He had on a dark colour'd Great Coat, a strip'd Jacket, and worsted Cap.

Lawrence Hoar, about 30 Years of Age, a lusty well set Fellow, has sore Eyes, short black Hair; He had on a Red Jacket, and a pair of Trowsers.

Thomas Weeks, about 23 Years of Age, a short thick well set Fellow; He had on a dark colour'd Great Coat, a strip'd homespun Jacket, and a woollen Cap.

Carter McCarty, about 23 Years of Age, a short thick well set Fellow; He had on a Red Jacket, Wash-Leather Breeches, yarn Stockings, an old pair of Shoes, and a Leather Apron.

At the same Time, Ranaway from his Master *John Gorman*, of *Boston*, Locksmith, an Irish Man Servant, named *William Lenox*, of middling Stature, pale thin Face, about 21 Years of Age; he had on a light colour'd Coat with a Cape, and Mettal Buttons, a dark colour'd Jacket, red Cloth Breeches with white Mettal Buttons, speckled Shirt, Felt Hat, gray worsted Stockings; tho' 'tis thought he has chang'd his Cloaths.

Whoever shall take up the abovesaid Runaways, and them safely convey or bring to His Majesty's Goal in *Boston* aforesaid, shall have *Five Pounds* Reward for each or either of the four first named Persons, and *Three Pounds* to each or either of the other Persons Named and Described as above, paid by   William Young.

Boston, October 29th. 1739.

New-England Weekly Journal, October 30, 1739.

On Tuesday last a Proclamation was issu'd out for apprehending *Peter Knox* and *Samuel Cockrain*, the two Persons concern'd in the Murder of Mr. *Peter Brown*, as mention'd in our last. *Knox* is an Irishman between 20 and thirty Years of Age, a comely well set Man, low of Stature, has lately had a Blow to one eye, wears short Hair, and light colour'd Cloathing. *Cockrain* is an Irishman of the same Age, of middling Stature, has a Cast of his right Eye, wears a Wig, and a blew Coat with white Mettal Buttons.

The Boston Gazette, From November 19, to November 29, 1739.

R*AN* away from Ichabod Soule *of* Scituate, *on the* 15th *of this Instant* November, *a Molatto Man Servant, named* Toney Samson, *a well set Fellow, of about* 33 *Years of Age, he had on an old Felt Hat, a Worsted Cap, a blue Broadcloth Coat, a black and white Flannel Jacket, a white Flannel Shirt, a pair of Trousers, and old Stockings and Shoes. Whoever shall take up the abovesaid Runaway, and convey him to me at* Scituate, *shall have three Pounds Reward and all necessary Charges paid by* Ichabod Soule.

All Masters of Vessels are hereby caution'd against carrying off said Servant, to avoid the Penalty of the Law.

The Boston Weekly News-Letter, From November 22, to November 30, 1739; From November 30, to December 6, 1739; From December 13, to December 20, 1739.

R*AN* away from his Master, Mr. John Newell *of* Boston, *Caulker, on Thursday the* 29th *of* November *past, an Irish Servant Man named* Robert Long, *about* 19 *or* 20 *Years old, of a middle Stature, and has black Eyes and short Hair. He had on when he went away, a dark coloured Drugget Coat and Breeches, a blue and white striped Cotton and Linen Jacket, Gray Worsted Stockings, a white Garlix Shirt, and a Felt Hat. Whoever shall take up the said Servant, and bring him to his abovesaid Master, living near Dr.* Cutler's *Church at the North End, shall have Five Pounds Reward, and all necessary Charges paid.*

N. B. *All Masters of Vessels and other Persons are hereby cautioned against harbouring, concealing, or carrying off the said Servant, as they will avoid the Penalty of the Law in that Case made and provided.*

The Boston Evening-Post, December 3, 1739; December 10, 1739. See The Boston Evening-Post, July 9, 1739.

R*AN* away from Harrison Downing *of* Kennibunk *on the* 4th Current, *an Irish Man Servant named* William Beetle, *about twenty two Years of Age, of a middling Stature, well set, had a bluish Mole in one of his Cheeks, and a Scar in his Face: He had on when he went away, a light colour'd coarse Broad Cloth Coat, a Drugget Jacket, Leather Breeches, Yarn Stockings and a new pair of Shoes with a Strap from the Quarter down to the Sole. Whoever will apprehend the said Run-away, and safely convey him to his Master* John Downing, *jun. of* Newington *in the Province of* New-Hampshire, *or to the said* Harrison Downing *at* Kennebunk *shall have* Five Pounds

The Boston Weekly Post-Boy, December 3, 1739; December 10, 1739.

R*AN* away from his Master, Capt. Samuel Carlton *of* Salem, *on the* 6th *of this Instant* December, *a lusty, tall, likely Negro Man, named* Millet, *but*

calls himself Tom Brown. *He has the Letters* L D *branded on his Breast, and had on when he went away, an old Cotton speckled Shirt, mended at the Elbows, a Felt Hat, an old Homespun Jacket of a darkish Colour, dark coloured Homespun Breeches, with Pewter Buttons, a striped red and black and white under Jacket. Gray Yarn Stockings, and a pair of thick Shoes. He is a Shoemaker by Trade. Whoever shall take up the said Servant, and bring him to his abovesaid Master in* Salem, *shall have Three Pounds Reward, and all necessary Charges paid.* N. B. *All Masters of Vessels and other Persons are hereby cautioned against harbouring, concealing, or carrying off the said Servant, as they will avoid the Penalty of the Law in that Case made and provided.*
    The Boston Evening-Post, December 17, 1739; December 24, 1739.
    See *The Boston Evening-Post*, October 25, 1738.

RAN-away from his Master Mr. *Alexander Hunt* of *Boston*, Shipright on the 16th Instant, an Irish Man Servant named *Charles Cartee*, about 26 Years of Age, a thick well set Fellow, he has a Blemish in one of his Eyes. Had on when he went away a blue Coat, trim'd with the same Colour, a pair of Leather Breeches, yarn Stockings, and round to'd Shoes. Whoever shall take up the abovesaid Runaway, and him safely convey to his said Master near Fort-Hill (so called) in *Boston* aforesaid, shall have *Forty Shillings* Reward, and all necessary Charges paid.   *Boston, Decem.* 17th 1739.
    New England Weekly Journal, December 18, 1739.

WHEREAS *Bethiah*, the Wife of *Daniel Lawrence* of *Wrentham*, hath unjustly absented herself from him, and hath disposed of some of his Goods, Provisions, &c. and run him in Debt at divers Places, without his Knowledge or Consent, and to his great Damage: These are therefore to warn all Persons, not to Trade or Traffick with the said *Bethiah Lawrence*, nor to trust her upon her Husband's Accompt; for he hereby publickly declares, he will not pay any Debt so contracted by her, from the Date hereof.
    The Boston Weekly News-Letter, From December 20, to December 27, 1739.

1740

RAN-away from his Master Mr. *Caleb Richardson* of *Boston*, the 18th ult, a Jersey Boy named *Elias Hooper*, aged about 17 Years, of low Stature, fresh Complexion, and speaks very good English: He had on when he went away, a Copper colour'd Jacket & Breeches with flat Pewter Buttons (the Jacket lin'd with red Baze, Breeches had Knee Straps & Buckles) a pair of blue seam'd Stockings, a single worsted Cap, & a small old Hat. Whoever

shall take up said Servant, & him safely convey to his abovesaid Master, shall have *Forty Shillings* Reward, & all necessary Charges paid.
New-England Weekly Journal, January 1, 1740.

R*AN* away from his Master Mr. *David Haward* of *Bridgwater* on the 25th of *December* last. A French Man Servant named *John Deno*, about 38 Years of Age, of a short or middle Stature, both his Legs have been broke; He had on when he went away, a kersey Coat and jacket of a brownish Colour, with mettal Buttons, a white Shirt, a Castor Hat, black Calamanco Breeches, grey yarn Stockings, and round to'd Shoes. Whoever shall take up the said Servant, and convey him to his Master at *Bridgwater*, shall have *Forty Shillings* Reward, and all necessary Charges paid.

All Masters of Vessels are hereby cautioned against carrying off the said Servant, as they would avoid the Penalty of the Law.

The Boston Weekly News-Letter, From December 27, to January 3, 1740; From January 10, to January 17, 1740.

R*AN* away from her Master, Mr. John Norton *of* Boston, *Mariner, on Wednesday the 9th of this Instant* January, *a Negro Woman named* Phillis, *about* 24 *Years old, of a middle Stature but well set, and her Teeth both upper and lower are filed Sharp. She he on when she went away, a striped homespun Jacket and Petticoat, and took with her a Callico Jacket and Petticoat, and two pair of Stays, one of which is new, belonging to her Mistress.*

Whoever shall take up the said Negro, and bring her to her abovesaid Master, living near Oliver's *Bridge, shall have* Three Pounds *Reward and all necessary Charges paid.*

The Boston Evening-Post, January 14, 1740.

T*Aken up in a Canoe, the* 16*th Day of* December *last Two Leagues South of* Block-Island, *A Negro Man about Twenty Years old, who says his Name is* Quomino *and his Master was* John Rothman *belonging to the aforesaid* Block-Island, *and that he had ran away because he was to be whip'd next Bay for stealing; said Negro is now in* Salem *Goal put in by me* Richard James *of* Marblehead, *who was Master of the Vessel that took him up. Whoever shall appear to be his Master, and pay all Charges may have said Negro again.*   Salem, N. England, *For* Richard James,
January 10, 1739,40.   James Jeffry.
The Boston Weekly Post-Boy, January 21, 1740; January 28, 1740.

WHEREAS *Rachel* the Wife of *Joseph Brown* of *Dorchester*, Taylor, has eloped from her said Husband, and refuseth to live with him: These are

therefore to warn all Persons not to trust her the abovesaid *Rachel*, for he will not pay any Debts she shall contract after the Date hereof.
    Joseph Brown.   Boston, Jan, 29. 1739,40.
New-England Weekly Journal, January 29, 1740; February 5, 1740.

RAN-away from *William Sanford* of *Dartmouth*, on the 28th of Jan. last, a Negro Man aged 21 Years, named *Daniel*, a well set Fellow, of a middle Stature talks English, had on when he Ran-away a felt Hat almost New, a Coat and a pair of Breeches of full'd Cloth of a brown colour and knotted. Whoever shall take up said Negro, and bring him to his Master in Dartmouth, or to Wm. Sanford of Rhode-Island, shall have Five Pounds Reward paid by said Sanford.
The Boston Weekly Post-Boy, February 4, 1740; March 3, 1740.

DEserted from the Ship *Caesar*, Capt. *Jonathan Crawford* of Portsmouth, on the 22d Instant, *Samuel Sunderland*, a thin Faced, sandy Complexion'd Man aged about 40 Years: Whoever apprehends him and brings him to Mr, *Charles Apthorp* Merchant in Boston, or Capt. *James Roche* at Portsmouth, shall have Five Pounds Reward and all necessary Charges paid.
             Dated Portsmouth Feb. 25. 1739,40.
The Boston Weekly News-Letter, From February 21, to February 28, 1740; From February 28, to March 6, 1740.

RAN-away from Capt. *Anthony Moseley* (in *Boston,* Master of the Brigt. Pretty Betty, cast on shore at *Billingsgate,* the 3d of Jan last) an Irish Servant Man Named *Anthony Hall*, of middle Stature, a thin spare Man about 26 Years of age, much Pock-fretten, sandy Complection, short Hair, wears a Cap or Wig, has a blemish in one Eye; he had on a brown colour'd Great Coat, brown Pea Jacket, an Irish Frize Coat, good Stockings and Shoes.
  Whoever takes up the said Ran-away, and safely conveys him to Capt. *William Fletcher*, living near the Draw Bridge in *Boston*, shall have *Three Pounds* Reward.
  All Masters of Vessels are hereby cautioned not to carry off said Servant, as they would avoid the Penalty of the Law.
The Boston Weekly News-Letter, From February 28, to March 6, 1740; From March 6, to March 13, 1740; From March 20, to March 28, 1740.

R*AN away from his Master Mr.* Alexander Parkman *of* Boston, *Mast-maker, on Wednesday the 5th of this Instant March, a Negro Man Servant named* Caesar, *about 25 Years old, of a middle Stature his right leg a little Bandied, and is apt to smile when he is spoke to. He had on when he went*

away, a light coloured Kersey Jacket and Breeches, a speckled Woollen Shirt, gray Yarn Stockings, old Shoes, and has with him a Leather Jockey Cap, and a striped red and white milled Cap. Whoever shall take up the said Servant, and bring him to his abovesaid Master, living near Fort Hill, shall have Forty Shillings *Reward, and all necessary Charges paid.* N. B. *All Masters of Vessels are hereby cautioned against harbouring, concealing, or carrying off the said Servant, as they would avoid the Penalty of the Law in that Case made and provided.*
  The Boston Evening-Post, March 10, 1740. See *The Boston Evening-Post,* August 18, 1740.

RAN-away from his Master Mr. *Isaac Brewer* of Springfield, sometime in *May* last past, a certain Negro Man Servant Named *Anser*, aged about 30 Years; he was a slim Fellow, midling for height, speaks good English, and is very handy and ingenious about almost any sore of Husbandry work, as also he is well acquainted with work within Doors, especially about Cooking and Dressing of Victuals: He had on when he went away, a grey drugget Coat something faded, a striped Callaminco Waistcoat, a good pair of Leather Breeches, a fine Shirt, a fine pair of Yarn Stockings, a Felt Hat, and a good pair of Shoes, but it is suppos'd his Cloaths are most of them worn out. Whosoever can find said Negro, and safely convey him to his said Master, shall have *Ten Pounds* Reward, and all necessary Charges paid.   Isaac Brewer.   Springfield, Feb. 29. 1739.40.
  The Boston Weekly News-Letter, From March 6, to March 13, 1740; From March 13, to March 20, 1740; From March 20, to March 28, 1740.

Ran-away the 10th of this Instant from his Master Mr. William Phips *of* Cambridge, *an Irish Man Servant, named* Andrew Blake, *a stout well set Fellow, about twenty Years of Age, and of a dark Complecion: He had on when he went away a coarse broad Cloth Jacket, a woollen strip Shirt, yarn Stockings and a woollen Cap. Whoever will take up said Runaway and his safely convey to his aforesaid Master, shall have* Forty Shillings *Reward, & all necessary Charges paid.*
  The Boston Gazette, From March 17, to March 24, 1740; From April 7, to April 24, 1740.

RAn away from Lieut. *James Mitchel* of Haverhill, on the 8th of this Instant, two Men Servants, named *John Deivo* and *Philip Granding: John Deivo* is about forty Years of Age: He had on when he went away his own short Hair but sometimes wears a Cap, a speckled woollen Shirt, a red Duffel Coat with a blue Kersey Cape, a Pea Jacket, and blue Camblet Breeches: He is of middling Stature, speaks broken English, and chews

Tobacco; the calves of his Legs grows before. *Philip Granding* is a Jersey Boy about 17 Years of Age, of middling Stature, round Visage, light Complection, has short Hair, and wears a Cap, had on a woollen Shirt, a blue broad Cloth Coat, a red Duffel great Coat, and Duroy Jacket and Breeches.

Whoever shall take up the said Runaways, and convey them to their abovesaid Master at Haverhill, shall have *Five Pounds* Reward, and all necessary Charges   paid by   *James Mitchel.*

New-England Weekly Journal, April 22, 1740.

RAN-away from his Master Capt. *Benjamin Soper* of *Boston*, on the 23d Inst. a Scotch young man Servant named *James Lacey*, a short thick Fellow, about 19 or 20 Years of Age; wears a new Beaver Hat, a striped worsted Cap, and sometimes a Wig; he took with him a double breasted Jacket something mended, and bound over the Button Holes with another Sort, and a blue and white striped one under it, a pair of new blue Breeches, with neither Strings nor Knee-Straps to them, a dark speckled blue and white Shirt, a red Handkerchief spotted with white, a dark pair of stock'd worsted Stockings, a new pair of Shoes, a Silver Buckle in one, and a Metal one in the other. Whoever shall take up said Runaway, and him safely convey to his abovesaid Master in *Boston* aforesaid, shall have *Four Pounds* Reward, and all necessary Charges paid. All Masters of Vessels are hereby warned against carrying off said Servant on Penalty of the Law.

New-England Weekly Journal, April 29, 1740.

RAN-away seven Days since from her Master, Andrew Sigourney, *jun. a likely Negro Wench Named* Janto *purchas'd of Mr.* Edmund Quincy: *she had on her Head a speckled Handkerchief; a striped Woollen Jacket, a white Oznabrigs Petticoat. Whoever shall apprehend and safely convey her to her Master shall have Twenty Shillings Reward, and all necessary Charges paid.*

The Boston Weekly News-Letter, From May 8, to May 15, 1740; From May 15, to May 22, 1740.

*W*Hereas *Abiall the Wife of Ebenezer Smith, late of* Bellingham, *but now of* Holliston *in the County of* Middlesex, *hath by her great Mismanagement obliged her said Husband to break up House keeping: The said* Ebenezer Smith *does therefore hereby caution all persons against Trading with, or trusting his said Wife, upon his Account; and gives publick Notice, that he will pay no Debt she shall contract from the Date hereof.*

May 11. 1740.

The Boston Weekly News-Letter, From May 8, to May 15, 1740; From May 15, to May 22, 1740.

169

RAN *away from his Master* John March, *Esq; at* Newbury *on the* 8*th Day of* May *Instant an Indian Man named* Primus, *a short Fellow, about* 40 *Years of Age, speaks very good English, and can read and write very well: He had on when he went away, a yellowish Coat with Brass Buttons, and a dark brown Coat with Pewter Buttons, a strip'd Wastcoat, and Leather Breeches.*

Whoever shall take up said Indian and convey him to his aforesaid Master shall have Forty Shillings Reward and all necessary Charges paid by John March. Dated *at* Newbury, May 17*th*, 1740.
The Boston Weekly Post-Boy, May 19, 1740; May 26, 1740. See *The Boston Weekly Post-Boy*, November 3, 1740.

GOD save the *KING*.
*W*Hereas *divers Seamen belonging to His Majesty's Ship* Astraea, *under my Command, have absented themselves and deserted His Majesty's Service. I do hereby Command them forthwith to return to their Duty promising in case they return by the twenty second of* May *Instant, to Pardon their Offence; and assuring them if they do not return in that time and be afterwards taken, they shall by Punished with the utmost Severity. And for the Encouragement of all Persons to apprehend the said Men or any of them; I do hereby promise a Reward of* Ten Pounds *the Currency of this Province, for every one of the said Seamen they shall bring and deliver aboard the said Ship, or into the Hands of* Charles Paxton, *Esq; Marshal of the Vice Admiralty.*

The Names of the said Seamen and the Description of them are as follows, viz.

John Jollif, a tall thin young Man and freckled Face.
Nicholas Morris, a short fat Man, curl'd brown Hair.
Talburt Williams, a tall thin Man, brown Complection, about 23 Years of Age.
Christopher Livingston, a tall thin Man, wears a Wig.
Edward Turner, a short well set Man, speaks very broad North Country.
John Gardner, a tall young Man, with Pimples in his Face.
John Nichols, a thin Man, swarthy Complection.
Thomas Bright, an Elderly Man, limps when he walks.
James Raby, a short Man brown Complection.
F. PERCIVALL.
The Boston Weekly Post-Boy, May 19, 1740.

RAN *away from his Master, Mr* Alexander Parkman *of* Boston, *Mast-maker, on Friday the* 30*th of* May *last, a Negro Man Servant named*

Caesar, *about* 25 *Years old, of a Middle Stature, his right Leg a little Bandied, speaks pretty good* English, *and is apt to smile when spoke to. He had on when he went away, a pair of light coloured Kersey Breeches, a speckled Woollen Shirt, Yarn Stockings, and thin Shoes, also a thin Canvas Apron, but had neither Hat or Cap. It is supposed he has since taken with him his dark coloured Coat lined with Red, and has Brass Buttons. Whoever shall take up the said Servant, and bring him to his abovesaid Master, living near Fort Hill, shall have* Forty Shillings *Reward, and all necessary Charges paid.*

The Boston Evening-Post, June 2, 1740.

*W*Hereas Rachel Bumpass, *the Wife of* James Bumpass *of* Middleborough, *in the County of* Plimouth, *has lately eloped from her Husband, having first rifled his House, and run him into Debt at sundry Places; These are to forbid all Persons from Trusting or entertaining her, for he will pay not Debt she shall contract. And all Persons are hereby caution'd from contracting Matrimony with her, or any other Act which may tend to the Violation of the Marriage Covenant.*

Dated at Middleborough, May 19. 1740.

The Boston Evening-Post, June 2, 1740; June 9, 1740.

John Bedgood, Carpenter, having Deserted on *The* 28th *ult. from the Ship* Britannia, Jeremiah Fones *Master: He is hereby warned to return to said Ship in three Days from the Date hereof, otherwise he will be treated as a Deserter.* June 2d 1740.

The Boston Gazette, From May 26, to June 2, 1740.

*R*AN-*away from his Master the Rev. Mr.* Johnson *of* Stratford, *a pretty handsome Indian Man named* Pallas Worrison, *about* 27 *Years old; He speaks good English, is apt to get in Drink, and then affects much to be thought a Scholar, and to talk about Religion, and Preaching to the* Indians: *He had on a white Linnen work'd Cap, a brown Camblet Coat lined with red, a lightish Drugget Jacket, and Tow Breeches, and had with him a good Fiddle on which he delights to play. Whoever shall take up the said Fellow, and bring him to his said Master, shall have* Four Pounds *Reward and all necessary Charges paid.*

The Boston Post-Boy, June 2, 1740; June 9, 1740; June 23, 1740. *The Boston Gazette*, From June 2, to June 9, 1740; From June 16, to June 23, 1740; From June 23, to June 30, 1740. Minor differences between the papers. See *The Boston Gazette*, From October 4, to October 11, 1731.

R*AN away from his Master Capt.* James Oliver *of* Boston, *on Monday the second of this Instant* May, *a Negro Fellow named* Cambridge, *about* 22 *Years old, who is short but well set, Pock broken, and speaks very good* English. *He had on when he went away, a good* Bever Hat, *a Neck with a Silver Clasp, a Garlick Shirt, a Blue Kersey Jacket, with broad Metal Buttons, a pair of broad Cloth Breeches, with a Leather Lining, and over them a pair of Trouzers, a pair of Gray Worsted Stockings, a pair of handsum Pumps, with large work'd Metal Buckles in them. Whoever shall take up the said Servant, and bring him to his abovesaid Master, living hear Fort Hill, shall have* Forty Shillings *Reward, and all necessary Charges paid.* N. B. *If the said Negro should be taken up at* Rhode-Island, *it is desired he may be confined in His Majesty's Goal and Notice given to his Master.*
The Boston Evening-Post, June 9, 1740. See *The Boston Evening-Post,* October 17, 1743, and *The Boston Evening-Post,* January 9, 1744.

R*AN away from Mrs.* Bethia Tucker *of* Boston, *Widow, some Time in the Month of May last, a Negro Fellow named* Cuff, *about* 23 *Years old, and is tall and slim, and very black. He speaks very good* English, *and had on when he went away, a light coloured Cloth Coat, red Breeches, and a pair of Trouzers over them, Yarn Stockings, and a pair of large Brass Buckles in his Shoe. He had also on a Purple Cloth Cap, bound with black velvet.* N .B. *He is a Shipwright by Trade. Whoever shall take up the said Negro, and bring him to the aforesaid* Bethia Tucker, *shall have* Five Pounds *Reward, and all necessary Charges paid.* N. B. *All Masters of Vessels and other Persons are hereby cautioned against harbouring, concealing or carrying off the said Servant, as they would avoid the Penalty of the Law.*
The Boston Evening-Post, June 16, 1740; June 23, 1740.

WHereas *Mary* the Wife of *Charles Cox,* Rope-maker, hath from time to time, run him in Debt and continues so to do (that he is much reduced) which obliges him to publish this Notification To warn all Persons not toe Trust her the said *Mary,* for he will pay no Debts she shall Contract after the Date hereof.   As Witness my Hand,
      Charles Cox.   June 17th, 1740
 New-England Weekly Journal, June 17, 1740.

RAN-away from *Andrew Davis* of *Groton* in *Connecticut,* the 16th Day of March, last, an Indian Man Servant, Named *James Wright,* a well set Fellow of a midling Stature, he had on when he went away, a yellowish Coat and Jacket, a new Beaver Hat, a worsted Cap, a fine Holland Shirt, a pair of thread Stockings, his Hair cut off. He Stole a white Mare, Bridle and Saddle. Whoever shall take up said Fellow and convey him to the said

Andrew Davis at Groton, or secure him so that his said Master may have him again, shall have *Ten Pounds* Reward, and all necessary Charges
paid by me   *Andrew Davis.*
The Boston Weekly Post-Boy, June 23, 1740.

R*A*n-away from Capt. *John Downing*, jun. of *Newington* in the Government of *New-Hampshire,* on the 5th of *June* last, two Irish Men Servants named and described as follows, one of them is about 21 Years of Age, a short thick Fellow, very short Neck, named *Terrence Forgerty,* he had on when he went away, a reddish colour'd Homespun Coat, with large round Brass Buttons, Duroy Jacket of a dark Colour, dark colour'd Homespun Breeches, a pale Wigg, and a Beaver Hat half worn. The other nam'd *George Beasley,* about 18 Years of Age, of middling Stature, the Fingers on one of his Hands has been broke, and are much crooked, had on dark colour'd jacket and Breeches, a Felt Hat, and dark Hair, if he has not cut it off. Whoever shall take up the abovesaid Runaways, and them or either of them convey to their abovesaid Master, shall have *Five Dollars* Reward each, & all necessary Charges paid.
All Masters of Vessels are hereby caution'd against carrying off said Servants, on Penalty of the Law.   *Boston, July* 2*d.* 1740.
New-England Weekly Journal, July 8, 1740.

R*AN away from Mr.* Joseph Josselyn *of* Hanover, *on the* 11*th of this Instant* July, *an* English *Man Servant named* Richard Simmons, *about 23 or 24 Years old, of a middle Stature, round Visage, fresh coloured, something round Shoulder'd, and has a down Look. He had on a white Woollen Shirt, two old Homespun Jackets, lightish coloured Duroy Breeches dark Blue Worstead Stockings, double soal'd Shoes, and a Castor Hat. Whoever shall take up the said Servant, and bring him to the abovesaid* Joseph Josselyn *in* Hanover, *shall have* Forty Shillings *Reward, and all necessary Charges paid.* N. B. *All Masters of Vessels and other Persons are hereby cautioned against harbouring, concealing or carrying off the said Servant, as they would avoid the Penalty of the Law.*
The Boston Evening-Post, July 14, 1740; July 21, 1740; July 28, 1740.

R*AN away from his Master, Mr.* Ebenezer Knap *of Boston, Collier, on Tuesday the* 15*th of this Instant* July, *an Irish Man Servant named* John Fowler, *about* 20 *Years old, of middle Stature, but slim and thin favour'd, his Hair cut off, and wears a Cap. He had on or took with him a Duroy Coat & Jacket, also a Homespun striped Jacket, four speckled Shirts, two Bever Hatts, a Thrum Cap, and a Worstead Cap, two pair of Yarn Stockings, and one pair of Worstead, round toed Shoes, with very thin Soles, and plain Metal Buckles. Whoever shall take up the said Servant, and*

bring him to his abovesaid Master, living near Fort Hill, shall have Twenty Pounds *Reward, and all necessary Charges paid.* N. B. *All Masters of Vessels and other Persons are hereby cautioned against harbouring, concealing, or carrying off the said Servant, as they will avoid the Penalty of the Law.*
   The Boston Evening-Post, July 21, 1740; July 28, 1740; August 4, 1740.

R*AN away from his Master Mr.* Zephaniah Basset *of* Boston, *Ship-wright, on Tuesday the* 15*th of this Instant* July, *an Irish Man Servant named* Patrick Mograch, *about* 21 *Years old, of a middle Stature, with a very flat Nose, and speaks broken* English. *He had on when he went away, a Homespun striped Jacket a pair of Trousers, Yarn Stockings, and round toed Shoes. He also carried away with him a blue Drugget Coat and Breeches a striped Holland Jacket, and sundry Shirts. Whoever shall take up the said Servant, and bring him to his abovesaid Master, living near Fort Hill, shall have* Six Pounds *Reward, and all necessary Charges paid.*
   N. B. *All Masters of Vessels and other Persons are hereby caution'd against harbouring, concealing or carrying off the said Servant as they will avoid the Penalty of the Law.*
   The Boston Evening-Post, July 21, 1740; July 28, 1740; August 4, 1740.

R*AN away* Thomas Baldwin *of* Portsmouth, New-Hampshire, *on the* 13*th of this Instant* July, *an Irish Man Servant named* John Casady, *aged about* 26 *Years, a short thick set Fellow, a little pitted with the Small Pox; speaks but indifferent English, and wears dark brown Hair. He had on when he went away, a brown outside Jacket, with a narrow red Lining to the Cape, a short blue inside Jacket, a white Shirt, a new pair of thin Canvas Trousers, sew'd with tar'd Twine, and a pair of new Shoes and Stockings. Whoever shall take up the said Fellow, and convey him to the said* Thomas Baldwin *at* Portsmouth, *or secure him so that his said Master may have him again, shall have* Ten Pounds *Reward, and all necessary Charges paid,*
        by me   Thomas Baldwin.   Portsmouth, July 17. 1740.
   The Boston Evening-Post, July 21, 1740; July 28, 1740; August 4, 1740. See The Boston Post-Boy, July 21, 1740.

R*AN-away* Thomas Baldwin *of* Portsmouth, New Hampshire, *on the* 13*th of* July, *an Irish Man Servant named* John Casady, *aged about* 26 *a very short thick set Fellow, a little pitted with the Small Pox; speaks but indifferent English, wears dark brown Hair: He had on when he went away a brown out side Jacket, with a narrow red lining to the Cape, a short blew inside*

Jacket a white Shirt, a new pair of thin Canvas Trousers sew'd with tar'd Twine:

Whoever shall take up said Fellow, and convey him to the said Master, or secure him so that his said Master may have him again, shall have Ten Pounds Reward, and all necessary Charges paid by me,   Thomas Baldwin.

The Boston Post-Boy, July 21, 1740; August 4, 1740; August 11, 1740. See The Boston Evening-Post, July 21, 1740.

RAN-away from his Master Mr. Benjamin Hallowell, of Boston, Shipwright, a Spanish Negro Man Servant, Named JACK, speaks pretty good English, has a short Neck and is Pock broken, he had on when he went away, a blue Cloth Jacket with red Button Holes and Brass Buttons, and a homespun Jacket, a checkt woollen Shirt, and a pair of black Breeches, light blue yarn Stockings, and a pair of double Channel Pumps with large Brass Buckles, and a Beaver Hat. Whoever shall take up the abovesaid Run away and him safely convey to his abovesaid Master shall have Forty Shillings Reward, and all necessary Charges paid.

The Boston Weekly News-Letter, From July 17, to July 24, 1740.

RAN away from Lieut. George Brownell of Little Compton, in the County of Bristol, on the 27th of July last, a Negro Man named Hector, about 26 Years old, of a middling Stature, born in the said Town, speaks very good English, is very confident, and does not scruple a Lye. He has a broad flat Nose, thick Lips, very white Teeth, and his Face is longish: When he talks or smiles he shews his Teeth much; is well Shouldered, has small long Legs, great Feet, and walks lubberly with his Feet. He had on when he went away, a greenish coloured Coat, a Linen and Woollen striped Jacket, gray full Cloth Breeches, a Linen and Tow Shirt, and a Felt Hat. Whoever shall take up the said Servant, and bring him to his Master in Little-Compton, or to the Printer of this Paper, shall have Three Pounds Ten Shillings Reward, and all reasonable Charges paid. N. B. All Masters of Vessels and other Persons are hereby cautioned against harbouring, concealing or carrying off the said Servant, as they will avoid the Penalty of the Law.

The Boston Evening-Post, August 11, 1740.

DESERTED from Capt. Samuel Dunn, Commander of one of his Majesty's Companies enlisted at Rhode Island, on the intended Expedition against New Spain, one Benjamin Whiting, a tall slim thin favour'd Man aged about 38 Years; who had on when he went away a blewish homespun Coat; born in Connecticut Government: Whoever shall apprehend and secure the

aforesaid Whiting *in any of his Majesty's Goals or bring him here to the aforesaid Capt.* Dunn, *shall have* Ten Pounds *in Money Reward, and all necessary Charges paid by* Samuel Dunn.
   The Boston Weekly Post-Boy, August 11, 1740; August 18, 1740.

R*AN away from his Master Mr.* Alexander Parkman *of* Boston, *Mastmaker, last Night, being the 17th of this Instant* August, *a Negro Man Servant named* Caesar, *about 25 Years old, of a middle Stature his right leg a little Bandied, speaks pretty good* English, *and is apt to smile when he is spoke to. He had on when he went away, a light coloured Kersey Jacket, a dark coloured Homespun Robin, a pair of light coloured Homespun Breeches, a pair of open Knee'd Trouzers, a speckled Woollen Shirt, a new pair of Yarn Stockings, and a pair of Worstead Stockings, and a pair of old thin Shoes, with large Brass Buckles. Whoever shall take up the said Servant, and bring him to his abovesaid Master, living near Fort-Hill, shall have* Forty Shillings *Reward, and all necessary Charges paid.* N. B. *All Masters of Vessels and other Persons are hereby cautioned against harbouring, concealing, or carrying off the said Servant, as they would avoid the Penalty of the Law.*
   The Boston Evening-Post, August 18, 1740. See *The Boston Evening-Post,* March 10, 1740.

R*AN-away from his* [sic] *Master Mr.* Arthur Noble *of* Boston, *Trader, on Sabbath Day, the 10th Instant, A Negro Woman, named* Mary, *about 30 Years old, of a middle-Stature, buy streight, slim and well shap'd of a Pale Complection can speak good English; she formerly belong'd to Mr.* John Dolbeare, *deceas'd, who purchas'd her of a West-India Gentleman at* Salem. *She carried with her a strip'd Homespun Jacket and a White Holland one; a blue and white Holland Gown, and a paned Callico one; Two Linnen and Two Cotton and Linnen Shifts: One Pair Blue Stockings; several Caps and sundry other Things yet unknown. Whoever shall take up the said Negro, and convey her to her abovesaid Master, living near the Red Lion, shall have* Five Pounds *Reward, and all necessary Charges paid.* N. B. *All Masters of Vessels and other Persons are hereby cautioned against harbouring, concealing or carrying off the said Negro, as they would avoid the Penalty of the Law.*
   The Boston Weekly News-Letter, From August 14, to August 21, 1740; From August 28, to September 4, 1740. The second ad shows her name as Mary Ann.

   Supposed to be carried off in a Boat or Sloop, *from Newport, Sunday the* 27th *of July, a Fantan Negro Man belonging to* John Banister, *named* Quoddy; *a well set strait Fellow, pleasant Countenance, of a middling*

Stature, about 30 *Years of Age, Imported in May last in Capt.* Wickham *from the Gold Coast.*

Whoever shall give Intelligence so that his Master may have him again, or the Person who stole him brought to Justice, shall have as a Reward Forty Pounds *and Reasonable Charges paid by* John Bannister.

The Boston Gazette, From August 25, to September 1, 1740; From September 8, to September 15, 1740; *The Boston Weekly Post-Boy,* September 8, 1740. Minor differences between the papers.

RAN-away from Mr. *James Bois* of Raynhan, in the County of Bristol, on the 24th of *August,* an Indian Man Servant, named *Tobias Peas,* but now calls himself *James Wicked,* about 20 Years of Age: He had on when he went away a brown Coat with brass Buttons and large Cuffs turned up above the Elbows, the fore Parts lin'd with Shalloon, the Body with Toe Cloth, a striped double breasted Jacket, coarse white Linnen Shirt, Toe Trousers something short, blue worsted Stockings, round to'd single sol'd Shoes, white Linnen Cap, small Beaver Hat with a hole in the Brim about as big as a Musquet Bullet: He is a tall Fellow, with a full Face, goes something stooping, has a down Look, a smiling Countenance. Whoever shall take up said Runaway, and him convey to his said Master, shall have *Five Pounds* Reward, and all necessary Charges paid. All Masters of Vessels are caution'd against carrying off said Servant, on Penalty of the Law.

New England Weekly Journal, September 2, 1740.

Boston, September 5, 1740.

RAN away an Indian Man Servant, named *Paul Abraham,* of whitish Complexion, short black Hair, and a good set of Teeth, about Thirty Years of age, speaks pretty good English, a middle statured Fellow, He had on when he went away, a striped spotted Swan Skin red and white Jacket, a new blue and white Linen Check Shirt, a Pair of old Trouzers, a Cinnamon or Chocolat colour'd pair of Cloth Breeches, with Linen Linings, and flowered yellow Mettle Buttons, very handsome ones, Worstead Stockings, new Shoes, and White Mettle Shoe-Buckles. He was seen on the Road going towards *Barnstable.*

Whoever takes up the said Runaway, and conveys him to his Master *Caleb Philipps* on Dock-Square in *Boston,* shall have Five Pounds and all Charges paid by *Caleb Philipps.*

His is a subtle Fellow, and may change his Cloaths with some other Indian.

The Boston Weekly Post-Boy, September 8, 1740; September 22, 1740.

RAnaway on Sabbath-day Night last being the [ ] of this Instant *September*, from his Master Mr *Thomas Bennet* of Boston, an Irish Man named *Thomas Ryan*, about 24 Years of Age, a well set Fellow, has very much of the Irish brogue, he limps something as he walks. He wears a Wig or Cap, and has taken with him two good white Shirts, two white Caps, a Felt Hat, a green Ratteen Jacket, a dark Ratteen Coat and Breeches of the same, with Mohair Buttons, a good pair of new Shoes, with a pair of plain Iron Buckles.

At the same Time Ranaway from Mr. *James Gardner* of *Boston*, an Irish Man Servant named *Timothy Gary*, about 19 or 20 Years of Age, a slim Fellow, and wears a Cap or Wigg, freckled Face, has much of the brogue on his Tongue, he took with him a green Ratteen Jacket and dark Ratteen Coat & Breeches, with Mohair Buttons, a Felt Hat, a Flannel under Jacket, and old Shoes.

Whoever shall take up the abovesaid Servants, and them convey to their abovesaid Masters in *Boston*, shall have *Five Pounds* Reward for each or either of them, and all necessary Charges paid.

Boston, September 16th 1740.
New England Weekly Journal, September 16, 1740.

RAN-away from Mr. *Thomas Norton* of Boston, the 10th Instant, an Indian Man Servant named *Silas Charles*, about 35 Years of age, a tall well set Fellow, can speak good English: He had on when he went away an old Hat bound and painted red round the Button in imitation of a Cockade, has short Hair, and has an old Wigg with him, two short Jackets, a pair of old Trousers tarr'd and something colour'd with red Paint, a pair of yarn Stockings, and a pair of English Shoes half worn.

Whoever shall take up said Runaway Indian, and shall convey him to Mr. *William Baker*, at the South side of the Town House in *Boston*, shall receive *Ten Pounds* Reward, and all necessary Charges paid.

Boston, September 15*th* 1740.
New-England Weekly Journal, September 16, 1740.

R*AN-away from his Master, Capt.* Edward Stewart *of* Newport *on* Rhode-Island, *the 27th of this Instant September, an Indian Man Servant named* Moses Thomas, *about 25 Years old, of a middle Stature but slender, and a good looking Fellow, that speaks very good* English, *and has short Hair. He had on a brown Drugget Coat, a pair of striped Breeches and a pair of Trouzers over them, an Oznabrigs Frock, and a Felt Hat, but neither Shoes, Jacket, Shoes or Stockings. Whoever shall take up the said Servant, and bring him to Mr.* Martin Howard *in* Newport, *or to Mr.* John Tuckerman *in* Boston, *shall have* Three Pounds *Reward, and all necessary Charges paid.* N. B. *All Masters of Vessels and other Persons are hereby cautioned*

against harbouring, concealing or carrying off the said Servant, as they will avoid the Penalty of the Law.
The Boston Evening-Post, September 29, 1740; October 6, 1740.

RAN-away from his Master *Edmund Perkins* of *Boston*, Chair-maker, on the 30th of *September* past, a Negro Man Servant named *Jack*, about 26 Years of Age, of middling Stature, hath a Scar, above one of his Eyes, speaks good English; He had on when he went away, a double breasted Kersey Jacket, lin'd with striped Homespun, a pair of old Shoes, a new Felt Hat bound round with Thread on the Edge thereof. Whoever shall take up the abovesaid Runaway, & him safely convey to his abovesaid Master at *Boston*, or secure him so that his Master may have him again, shall have *Ten Pounds*, Reward, & all necessary Charges paid. All Masters of Vessels & others are hereby caution'd against concealing or carrying off said Servant on Penalty of the Law.   *Oct.* 14th 1740.
New-England Weekly Journal, October 21, 1740.

T*AKEN up by* John Leach *of* Salem, *in his Cornfield, the* 13*th of* October *Instant, a Negro Man about* 45 *Years of Age clothed with a Blanket and a pair of striped Breeches, a double breasted Woollen Jacket with Pewter Buttons, a good Holland Ruffled Shirt, all which Cloathing he says he took because he was cold: He is a tall well proportioned Fellow, talks little* English, *but by what he can inform People he came from* Virginia *or* Maryland, *Seven Moons past in a Canoe. The said Fellow is now in* Salem Goal, *where whoever may be the Owner may repair, pay for taking up, Charges, &c. He says his Name is* Peter, *and his Master's Name is* Arthur Jean.   John Leach.   Salem, Oct. 18. 1740.
The *Boston Evening-Post*, November 3, 1740; November 10, 1740; The *Boston Weekly Post-Boy*, November 3, 1740. Minor differences between the papers. The *Post-Boy* shows the advertiser's name as both Leach and Leech.

R*AN-away from* John March, *Esq; at Newbury, An Indian Man named* Primus: *He had on when he went away, a brownish Coat with Pewter Buttons and Leather Breeches: He is a short thick Fellow, about Forty Years of Age: He speaks very good English can write and read, and is handy at all Husbandry Work, and can work at the Sadlers Trade. I hear the said Indian since he went away calleth himself* Kilborn; *and that he was in* Connecticut *Government in a Place called* Wallingford.
Whoever shall take up said Indian Fellow and secure him or bring him to his Master, shall have Five Pounds *Reward, and all necessary Charges paid. The said Fellow ran away the* 8*th Day of* May 1740.
John March.

The Boston Weekly Post-Boy, November 3, 1740. See *The Boston Weekly Post-Boy*, May 19, 1740.

BROKE out of his Majesty's Goal in *Boston*, on Tuesday Night the 4th of this Instant *November*, a Negro Fellow nam'd *Pompey*, he is about 30 Years of Age, a well set Fellow, part of one of his Ears has been cut off, he is a Blacksmith by Trade, speaks very good English: He had on when he went away, a bluish Jacket, a Holland Shirt Ruffled, &c.

The above Negro Fellow belongs to Mr *Francis Cogswell* of Ipswich; and whoever shall take up the abovesaid Negro, and convey him to his said Master at Ipswich aforesaid, or commit him to the nearest Goal, and inform his abovesaid Master thereof, shall have *Three Pounds* Reward, and all necessary Charges paid. *Boston, Nov.* 11, 1740.

New England Weekly Journal, November 11, 1740. See *The Boston Weekly Post-Boy*, January 11, 1742.

RAn-away the 27th of *October* past, from *Gyles Russell* of *Marblehead*, a Negro Boy named *Sharper*, about sixteen Years of Age, a well set Fellow, speaks broken English, he has a Cast with one of his Eyes, and something bandy-Legg'd. He had when he went away a striped Under-Waistcoat, a Cotton and Linnen Shirt, a dark colour'd Jacket lin'd with red, with brass Buttons, a pair of Leather Breeches, a woollen Cap, worsted Stockings, and an old pair of Shoes.

Whoever shall take up the abovesaid Runaway, and him convey to his abovesaid Master at Marblehead, or to *Kneeland* and *Green* in Boston, shall have *Forty Shillings* Reward, and all necessary Charges paid.

Boston, Novemb. 7th, 1740.

New-England Weekly Journal, November 11, 1740.

THE Governours Negro Man *JUBA* having
broke Goal: This is to forewarn all Persons from harbouring him, and to desire he may be return'd by any Person that may him him: He has a Grey Coat, and a Linnen Wastecoat and Breeches.

The Boston Weekly News-Letter, From November 6, to November 14, 1740; From November 14, to November 20, 1740.

WHEREAS John Toole and Thomas Campbell, *belonging to the Ship Elizabeth,* Lewis Turner, *Master, have for some Time past absented themselves from the Service of the said Ship; This is therefore to inform the said* Toole *and* Campbell, *that is they will return to their Duty they shall be accepted, otherwise they will be deem'd Deserters.*

The Boston Evening-Post, December 1, 1740.

RAN-away from Mr. *Thomas Valento*n, sometime ago, a Negro Man Servant nam'd *Briton*, about 40 Years of Age, speaks broken English, a tall strait limb'd Fellow; He had on when he went away an old black Coat with a slit Sleave, a black Jacket, a blue Jacket with mettal Buttons, a pair of black Leather Breeches, he had on grey yarn and black worsted Stockings, a worked Cap, cotton Handkerchief, a cotton and linnen and one Holland Shirt, an old Beaver Hat that has been split and sew'd up again, he had with him a pair of strip'd Trousers; and 'tis said he's one of the Negroes seen in *Needham* Woods, and 'tis suppos'd he had chang'd Cloaths.

Whoever shall take up said Runaway and him safely convey to the Jail in *Boston*, shall have *Five Pounds* Reward, and all reasonable Charges paid by *James Gooch*, jun. of *Boston*.
New-England Weekly Journal, December 2, 1740.

Boston, December 4. 1740.
Deserted *from the Ship* Mary *and* Jane *of* Londonderry (*now in the Harbour of* Boston) Robert Blacklock, *Master, on the* 23*d of* November *past, the following Seamen,* viz. William Ackin, *Mate,* John Thompson, *Boatswain,* William Bratten, *Cooper,* Robert Dyer *and* Joseph Wilson. *Now if the above-named Deserters will return to their Duty on board the said Ship, any Tine within Fifteen Days from the Date hereof, they shall be kindly received, and have the same Usage as heretofore; but if they do not, they may expect to be treated with the utmost Severity of the Law.*
The Boston Evening-Post, December 15, 1740.

RAN-away from his Master *Josiah Cotton* of *Plymouth,* Esq; and supposed to be now in *Boston*, a Negro Man named *Quomina*, between thirty and forty Years of Age, he had on a Homespun great Coat, black and blue mixt colour's Coat, and Jacket of the same, and a pair of Leather Breeches. He speaks Engish well.

Whoever shall take up the said Runaway Servant and convey him t he abovesaid Master at *Plymouth* aforesaid, shall be well rewarded
by *Josiah Cotton.*
New-England Weekly Journal, December 16, 1740.

*W*Hereas Hannah Alfrey *the Wife of* Godfrey Alfrey *of* Dighton, *absented herself from her Husband the* 17*th of* January 1738,9 *and carried off with her Goods of considerable Value, and continues to live separate, assuming her Maiden Name, which was* Hannah Clifton, *and has also hired all use and carrys on Traffick in her said Name: These are therefore to warn all Persons not to countenance or give Credit to the said* Hannah; *for he will not pay any Debt she shall contract during such Separation.*

The Boston Weekly News-Letter, From December 11, to December 18, 1740.

1741

RAN-away from Mr. *William Dunn* of Boston, Shipwright, on Friday last the 30th ult a Scotch Man Servant named *William Cobb* about 23 Years of Age, small Stature, a Distiller by Trade. Had on when he went away an old Blew Great Coat, a white close bodied Coat with a large Cape of the same; he took with him a new broad Cloth Coat and Breeches of a bluish Colour. Whoever shall take up said Runaway, and him convey to his said Master, shall have *Three Pounds* Reward, and all necessary Charges paid. And all Master of Vessels are hereby caution'd against concealing or carrying off said Servant on Penalty of the Law.   *Boston, Febr*, 3d 1740,

New-England Weekly Journal, February 3, 1741; February 10, 1741; February 17, 1741.

RAN away from his Master Mr. James McHard *of* Haverhill, Merchant, a Welch Man Servant named Benjamin Williams, *about seventeen or eighteen Years of Age, a short well set Fellow with black short Hair: He had on when he went away, a short Shagg Waistcoat, a pair of Duck Trowsers, and a speckled Shirt: He carry'd off with him, three Duroy Coats, and a black Cloth Coat, besides sundry other Goods. Whoever shall take up the abovementioned Servant, and bring him to his Master at* Haverhill *aforesaid, or to Mr.* Samuel McClewer *of* Newbury, *shall have* Three Pounds *Reward, and all necessary Charges paid.*

                                                 Haverhill, Feb. 2. 1741.

The Boston Weekly Post-Boy, February 9, 1741; February 23, 1741.

Deserted from the Ship *Pegasus, John Connolly Master, on Friday last,* William Wotton, Philip Thomas, Matthew Magrath, *and* Alexander Mack Daniel, *Mariners, belonging to said Ship, who also carried off the said Ships Long Boat: Whoever shall inform said* Connolly *of the aforesaid Deserters so that they may be brought to Justice, shall have* Five Pounds *Reward for each one of them, and necessary Charges paid.*

    The Boston Gazette, From February 23, to March 2, 1741; From March 9, to March 16, 1741; From March 23, to March 30, 1741.

WHEREAS Jane, *the Wife of* John Wilson *of* Roxbury *has entertained some of her Country People at his House, to his great Cost and Damage, and also threatens to sell his Household Goods, and run him in Debt as much as she can; These are therefore to caution all Persons not to purchase any Houshold stiff, or other Things of the said* Jane; *nor to trust her upon any*

Account whatsoever, without her Husband's consent; for he is resolved to prosecute such Persons in the Law, for the Recovery of any of his Goods so illegally sold and will not Pay any Debt she shall contract, for the Date hereof. John Willson, Cordwainer, in *Roxbury*.
   The Boston Weekly News-Letter, From February 27, to March 5, 1741.

RAN-away from his Master *Thomas Story*, Commander of the Snow Nottingham; *Thomas Brown*, a Scot's Man, middle Stature, short Hair, Pockbroken, red Beard, had on a loose white Coat tarry about the middle, a blue Jacket, and a pair of Trousers. Whoever shall take up said Runaway, & bring him to his said Master, or to Mr. *Ralph Inman*, shall have *Five Pounds* Reward.
   New England Weekly Journal, March 10, 1741; March 17, 1741.

RAN away from his Master Mr. Daniel James *of Portsmouth on Rhode Island, the 23d of January, an English Man Servant named* John Flowers, *a Taylor by Trade; he is a short middle set Fellow of a ruddy Complexion, with a red Beard and a Bunch on one Side of his Head under his Cap or Wigg. He had on when he went away, a blue strait bodied Coat with black velvet Buttons and black Button Holes, a bluish silk camblet Jacket, a fine white Shirt, with Ruffles at Bosoms and Wrists, Cloth Breeches, worsted Stockings, new Calf-Skin Shoes with Mettle Buckles, a blue Shagg great Coat, a Beaver Hat, and a Linnen Cap.*
   N. B. It is suppos'd he has chang'd his Name and Cloaths. He is a great Drunkard.
   Whoever shall apprehend said Runaway and convey him safe to his said Master shall have Ten Pounds Reward, and all necessary Charges paid. Dated Newport, March 9. 1740,1.
   The Boston News-Letter, From March 12, to March 19, 1741; From March 19, to March 26, 1741; From March 26, to April 2, 1741.

Deserted from the Ship *Caesar, Wm. Clarke* Commander *at* Portsmouth New-Hampshire, *the following Mariners, viz.* James Power *of a middle Stature swarthy, has black bushy Hair, and had on a blue Coat and a red Rugg Watch Coat,* Patrick Goff, *a lusty Fellow, of a dark Complecion, with black Hair, having on a blue Coat. Whoever shall give Notice of the said Deserters, so as that they may be secured shall have* Three Pounds Reward, *and necessary Charges paid them by the said* Clarke *at* Portsmouth, *or Mr.* John Hutchinson *at* Boston.
   N. B. All Masters of Vessels are hereby caution'd against carrying off said Mariners, as they would avoid trouble.
   The Boston Gazette, From March 23, to March 30, 1741.

RAN away from her Master John Bazin, *the 8th [   ] an Indian Woman named* Betty Paun, *about 25 Years of Age a pretty lusty well-set Woman, has several Scratches in her Face which she got by Fighting. She had on when she went away a red and white Callicoe Gown pretty much wore, a coarse Tow-Cloth Shift, an upper Petticoat of a brownish Colour, patch'd with an ironing Cloth, and a blue Duffle under Petticoat.*

Whoever shall apprehend said Run-away and convey her to her said Master in Newport *shall have* FORTY SHILLINGS *Reward and all Necessary Charges paid*   Newport, March 10. 1741.
The Boston Weekly Post-Boy, April 6, 1741.

RAN-away from his Master Capt. *John Connolly,* on Friday the 3d Instant, an English Man-Servant about 17 Years of Age, five Foot six Inches high, thin Visag'd, has a pretty long Nose, and wears his own short Hair: Had on when he went away, two blue Jackets, a pair of Shagg Breeches, and a pair of Silver Buckles in his Shoes. Whoever shall apprehend said Servant and bring him to his said Master on board the Ship Pegasus, or the Warehouse of Mess. Gerrish and Barrel, shall have *Five Pounds* Reward, and all necessary Charges paid. All Masters of vessels and others, are hereby cautioned against concealing or carrying off said Servant, as they would avoid the Penalty of the Law.
The Boston Weekly Post-Boy, April 6, 1741.

RAN away from his Master, Capt. Benjamin Kent *of* Boston, *Mariner, the 12th of this Instant* April, *an* English *Servant Lad named* Thomas Jannerkins, *about 17 or 18 Years old, of middle Stature, and of a pale Complexion. He had on when he went away, a Garlick Shirt, a Suit of dark blue Cloth Cloaths, a pair of light blue Worstead Stockings, a pair of single soled Shoes, a brownish coloured Wigg, and a Bever Hat about half wore. Whoever shall take up said Servant, and bring him to his Master again, living in* Bromfield's *Lane, shall have* Four Pounds *Reward, and all necessary Charges paid.*

N. B. *All Masters of Vessels and other Persons are hereby cautioned against harbouring, concealing or carrying off the said Servant, as they will avoid the Penalty of the Law.*
The Boston Evening-Post, April 20, 1741; May 4, 1741.

RAN for on board the Ship Experiment, now in Newbury, William Curtis Master, the two following Men, *viz.* John Lakeman, suppos'd to be between 26 and 30 Years of Age, thin favour'd, wears his own Hair which is dark and strait; he is of a blackish Complection: Also Mark Pitman, fresh colour'd, has dark curl'd Hair, one of his Toes turns in against the other, and his Heels point to go foremost: he wears a Soldiers Red Coat: They are both married Men. Whoever shall apprehend the said Marriners, and them safely convey to said Curtis shall have Five Pounds Reward, and all necessary Charges   paid by me   *William Curtis.*

All Masters of Vessels & others are hereby caution'd not to entertain, conceal, any ways employ, or carry off the said Sea-Men, as would avoid the Penalty of the Law.

The Boston Weekly News-Letter, From April 24, to April 30, 1741; From April 30, to May 7, 1741.

RAN-away from his Master *John Green* of *Warwick,* in the County of *Providence, April* 26, 1741, A Mollatto Man-Servant born of a Negro Woman, aged about 48 Years, speaks good English, and is a well-set Fellow: He had on when he went away, a new Flannen Shirt, one Olive-green colour'd Jacket and another of a greyish Colour, both of thick Cloth, a great Coat of the same with the grey Jacket, with Buttons cover'd with the same; gray Yarn Stockings, & Strings in his Shoes. The said Servant is called *Tim;* He plays well on a Violene. Whoever shall take up said Servant, and him safely convey to his said Master, shall have *Ten Pounds* Money Reward, and all necessary Charges
    paid by his Master,   *John Green.*
The Boston Weekly Post-Boy, May 4, 1741; May 11, 1741.

RAN away from his Master, Joseph Perry *of* Sherburn, *An Indian Servant named* Joshua Waban, *about* 19 *or* 20 *Years old, of middle Stature: He had on when he went away, a white woollen Shirt with a cotten Collar, a Bluish colour'd Cloth Coat, a brown Linnen Jacket, blue yarn Stockings, a Pair of new double sol'd Shoes, and a Castor Hat not much worn. Whoever shall take up said Servant and bring him to his Master again, shall have all necessary Charges paid. All Masters of Vessels and other Persons are hereby cautioned against harbouring, concealing or carrying off the said Servant, as they would avoid the Penalty of the Law. He left his Masters Service the 15th Day of April last.*

The Boston Weekly News-Letter, From April 30, to May 7, 1741; From May 7, to May 14, 1741.

RAN away on the 4th of *May* Inst from Jonathan Norris of Exeter, a Negro Man nam'd Nero, about [ ] Years of Age, of middle Stature and well set, pock-broken, speaks good English: He had on a blue upper and a plaid under Jacket, and a French felt Hat: He carried off with him in a Bundle, a blue Broad-cloth Coat trim'd plain, several brown Holland Jackets and Breeches, also three Guineas and two Moidores.

Whoever takes up said Negroe and secures him, so that his Master may have him again, shall have Five Pounds Reward, and all reasonable Charges paid, by   Jonathan Norris.
The Boston Weekly Post-Boy, May 11, 1741; June 1, 1741; June 8, 1741.

WHereas *Abigail White* Wife of *Benjamin White* of *Dudley in the County of Worcester*, Husbandman, has behaved her self in such a Manner that he is obliged to part from her: These are therefore to forewarn all Persons not toe Trust of give Credit to her, with a View or Expectation of their receiving Pay for the same of him, for he will pay no Debt contracted by her after the Date hereof.   *Benjamin White.*   *Dudley May* 6. 1741.
New-England Weekly Journal, May 26, 1741.

RAN-away from their Masters Col. Paul Gerrish *and Mr.* Jeremiah Rawlings, *both of Dover in New-Hampshire, A Negro Man named* Jupiter, *and a Negro Woman named* Venus. *The Negro Man is of middling Stature, about* 35 *Years of Age, had on, or with him, when he went away, a striped Calamanco Jacket and Breeches, a double breasted gray homespun Jacket, a strip'd homespun Jacket, one fine Shirt, and several others, and several Pair of Stockings, The Negro Woman carried away with her, a strip'd light colour'd Coat and Jacket, a Callico Coat and Jacket, a Pair of Bone Stays, cover'd with green Shalloon, and many other Garments, Aprons, Caps, Handkerchiefs, &c. She is by the best Computation that can be made between* 35 *and* 40 *Years of Age; she usually wore Rings on her Fingers, her Ears were bored, and she had Gold Earings in them, she usually carried her Hair, and tied it up like an English Woman.*
    Whoever shall take up said Negroes, and them safely convey to their respective Masters in Dover, shall have Five Pounds Reward for each, and all necessary Charges paid.
    N. B. The Negro Woman was Servant to Gerrish, and the Negro Man to Rawlings.
    The Boston Weekly Post-Boy, June 8, 1741; July 6, 1741.

R*AN away from his Master, Mr.* John Colson *of* Boston, *Trader, on Wednesday the* 3*d Instant, an* English *Man Servant named* John Gravel, *about* 40 *Years old, of a middle Stature, a well set fleshy Man, a round Face, red Complexion, short black Hair very thin, and he speaks West Country.*
    He had on when he went away, a good Cotton and Linnen Shirt, a Felt Hat, an old brownish coloured Coat, a Frock and Trouzers, a pair of striped Cotton and Linen Breeches, a pair of Diamond bluish coloured Stockings, old Shoes, and a blue Silk Handkerchief sta[   ] *a pale Blue,*

Whoever shall take up said Servant, and bring him to his said Master again, living at the North End of *Boston, shall have* Five Pounds *Reward, and all necessary Charges paid.*

N. B. All Masters of Vessels and other Persons are hereby cautioned against harbouring, concealing or carrying off the said Servant, as they will avoid the Penalty of the Law in that Case made and provided.
Boston, June 13, 1741.
The Boston Evening-Post, June 15, 1741; June 22, 1741; June 29, 1741.

RAN-away from *Thomas Cradock* of Milton, *Nailor,* on the 18th Instant at Night, two Irish Men Servants; their Names, Ages and Discriptions as follows, *viz. James Twehee,* (who when he run away before call'd himself *James Hart,*) about 18 or 19 Years of Age, of midling Stature, round Shoulder'd, goes something stooping, stutters when he speaks hastily, has a large Roman Nose, short Hair, had on a check woollen Shirt, an old brown homespun Coat, and Trousers. The other named *Thomas Heley,* about 19 Years of Age, a short good looking Fellow, with grey Eyes, pretty thick Leggs; had on a check'd woollen Shirt, a working Jacket, and Trousers, one of his Shoes has a Patch on the top of it.

Whoever shall take up the abovesaid Runaways & them or either of them convey to their said Master in *Milton,* shall have *Three Pounds* Reward for each or either of them, and all necessary Charges paid.

All Masters of Vessels and others are hereby caution'd against concealing or carrying off said Servants on Penalty of the Law in that Case made and provided.

New-England Weekly Journal, June 23, 1741.

ON the 15th of *November last, a Man who call'd himself* Samuel Lee, *but is supposed to be* Jonathan Ingersol, *a Sadler, late of* Jabaco *in the County of* Essex, *hired a Horse of the abovesaid* Watts, *but has neglected to return him. Also on the 8th of this Instant July, one who call'd himself* Delaney, *but is supposed to be* Thomas Bell, *who is lately arriv'd from* Barbados, *hired a Mare of said* Watts *to go to* Salem, *but upon Enquiry cannot be heard of. Any Person who will give Information of the abovesaid Horse, so that the said* Watts *may have him against, shall have* Five Pounds, *and for the Mare* Ten Pounds *by said* Watts.

N. B. *The Horse is a Bay Horse, about thirteen Hands high with a white Face, branded with a* C *on the near Shoulder, is a natural Pacer. The other is a Bay Mare, about fourteen Hands and an half high, is a natural Pacer.* July 17, 1741.

The Boston Weekly Post-Boy, July 20, 1741; July 20, 1741; August 3, 1741. The advertiser was Samuel Watts.

WHOEVER shall take up *Ann Flood*, (who was forcibly taken out of the Officer's Hands as he was carrying her to Bridewell last Thursday Night) and deliver her to Justice, shall have *Three Pounds* Reward.
July 27. 1741.
   The Boston Evening-Post, August 3, 1741.

D*Eserted from on board the Snow* Friendship, Nicholas Cooney *Master, now lying at the Long Wharff, the Mate of said Snow, named* John Cottom, *who if he returns to his Duty by to Morrow Morning shall be forgiven, otherwise shall be deem'd a Deserter: And likewise a Servant Boy, named* Joseph Poor, *about* 19 *Years of Age, who had on when he went away, a dark colour'd Wigg, a brown Frize Coat, a blew Jacket, with white Fish-Bone Buttons, and black Breeches: Whoever shall take up the said* Joseph Poor, *and him convey to the said* Nicholas Cooney, *or* James Bowdoin, *Esq; in* Boston, *shall have* Five Pounds *Reward, and all necessary Charges paid.*
   The Boston Weekly Post-Boy, August 3, 1741; August 10, 1741.

DE*serted from the Ship* Hannah, John Evers *Commander, now lying in* Boston *Harbour, the following Sailors, viz.* Thomas Hughes, *aged* 23 *Years, of middling Stature, and of a brown Complexion, wearing a Wigg.* William Nush, *aged* 21 *Years, short of Stature and well set, and of a brown Complexion, also wearing a Wigg.* Thomas Stott, *aged* 20 *Years, tall and slender, of a fair Complexion, likewise wearing a Wigg. If the said Deserters will return to their Duty on board the said Ship within Three Days from the Date hereof, they shall be kindly received and forgiven their past Offence; but after that Time, whoever shall take all or any of them up, and bring them to the said Commander on board his Ship, shall have* Five Pounds *Reward for each of them, and all necessary Charges. N. B. All Masters of Vessels and other Persons are hereby cautioned against harbouring, concealing or carrying off the said Sailors, as they would avoid the Penalty of the Law in that Case made and provided.*
Boston, *July* 31. 1741.
   The Boston Evening-Post, August 10, 1741.

RA*N away from his Master, Capt.* John Leech *of* Salem, *on Thursday the* 6th *of this Instant* August, *a Negro Man named* Peter, *about* 40 *Years old, a tall well proportion'd Fellow, but can speak very little* English. *He had on when he went away, a Woollen Shirt, a short striped black and white homespun Jacket, with Pewter Buttons, Tann'd Leather Breeches, and a Felt Hat. Whoever shall take up the said Servant, and bring him to his abovesaid Master, living in* Salem, *shall have* Three Pounds *Reward, and all necessary Charges paid.*

The Boston Evening-Post, August 10, 1741; August 17, 1741.

RAN away from his Master Mr. *Richard Billings* of *Boston*, Taylor, on the 24th of *July* last, a Negro Man Servant, named *Exeter*, of a short Stature and yellow Complection; had on when he went away a colour'd Canvas Coat pretty long, a blew Jacket with brass Buttons not lined, and a Cloth colour'd pair of Breeches; He has likewise a Mould on the right side of his Face: He works well at the Taylor's Trade, and formerly lived with Mr. *John Hill* at *Narragansett*.

Whoever shall apprehend said Runaway, and convey him to his said Master in Boston, shall have *Five Pounds* Reward, and all necessary Charges paid by   RICHARD BILLINGS.

All Masters of Vessels and others are caution'd against concealing or carrying off said Servant.

New England Weekly Journal, August 11, 1741; August 18, 1741; August 25, 1741. See *The Boston Evening-Post*, August 24, 1741.

Ran-away from his Master Mr. *John Pinder of North* Kingstown, *in the Colony of* Rh. Island, *on* June 22d, 1740, *a Negro Man Servant named* Plumb, *about* 25 *Years of Age, a thick well set Fellow, middling Stature, full fac'd, has a bump on the inside of his right Thumb; and he can play on a Fiddle.*

Whoever shall take up the abovesaid Runaway, and him safely convey to his said Master, shall have Ten Pounds *reward, and all necessary Charges paid by me* John Pinder.

The Boston Gazette, From August 10, to August 17, 1741.

RAN-away Yesterday the 16th Inst. from his Master Mr. *John Graton* of *Roxbury*, Innholder, an Irish Man Servant nam'd *Matthew Morris*, about 20 Years of Age, a lusty pale fac'd Fellow, brown Complection. He had on when he went away, a double breasted dark colour'd Coat with a large Cape of the same, the Coat fac'd with green, a pair of Leather Breeches and a pair of bluish Yarn Stockings, a Cotton Rug Cap and a brown Wigg. Whoever shall take up the said Run-away Servant, and him safely convey to his abovesaid Master in *Roxbury* shall have *Three Pounds* Reward, and all necessary Charges paid. All Masters of Vessels and others, are hereby warned against carrying off said Servant on Penalty of the Law.

Aug, 17. 1741.

New-England Weekly Journal, August 18, 1741. See *The Boston Weekly Post-Boy*, August 31, 1741, and *New England Weekly Journal*, September 1, 1741.

Ten Pounds
To be Receiv'd.

O*N the* 24th *of* July *last, Ran away from his Master, Mr.* Richard Billings *of* Boston, *Taylor, a Negro Man Servant, named* Exeter, *of a short Stature, yellow Complexion; had on when he went away, a colour'd Canvas Coat pretty long, a blue Jacket not lined, with Brass Buttons, and a Cloth colour'd pair of Breeches; he has likewise a Mould on the right side of his Face: He formerly liv'd with Mr.* John Hill *at* Narragansett. *He works well at the Taylor's Trade; and is suppos'd to be at Work in some Country Town, and to have chang'd his Cloaths.*

Whoever shall apprehend said Runaway, and convey him to his said Master in Boston, *shall have* Ten Pounds *Reward, and all necessary Charges paid by* Richard Billings.

All Masters of Vessels and others are caution'd against concealing or carrying off said Servant, as they would avoid the Penalty of the Law.
Boston, August 21st. 1741.

The Boston Evening-Post, August 24, 1741; August 31, 1741; *The Boston Weekly News-Letter,* From August 20, to August 27, 1741; *The Boston Weekly Post-Boy,* August 31, 1741. Minor differences between the papers. The *News-Letter* and *Post-Boy* do not have the location and date at the bottom of the ad. See *New England Weekly Journal,* August 11, 1741.

W*HEREAS* Bridget Southworth, *the Wife of* Edward Southworth *of* Middleborough, *in the County of* Plimouth, *Yeoman, about Four Years ago, hearkening to the Counsel of some of here wicked Neighbours, absented herself from him, and continues so to do, which is a Breach of the Marriage Covenant; These are therefore to forbid all Persons from harbouring, entertaining or trusting her, as they will answer the same at the utmost Peril of the Law, and the Loss of all such Sums as any Person or Persons shall trust her.* Edward Southworth.
The Boston Evening-Post, August 31, 1741.

RAN away about a Fortnight since, from his Master Mr. *John Graton* of *Roxbury,* an Innholder an Irish Man Servant named *Mathew Morris* about 21 Years of Age, a pale Fac'd Fellow, brown Complection. He had on when he went away a brown Holland jacket, a new dark colour'd Coat, double breasted, fac'd with green, which has a large Cape, a pair of Buck Skin Breeches, bluish yarn Stockings: He has also on a brown Wigg, or a white Cotton thrum'd Cap. Whoever shall take up the abovesaid Runaway, and convey him to his Master in *Roxbury,* shall have *Five Pounds* Reward and all necessary Charges paid.

All Masters of Vessels and others, are hereby warned against carrying off said Servant, on Penalty of the Law in that Case made and provided.
August 31, 1741.
The Boston Weekly Post-Boy, August 31, 1741; September 7, 1741; September 14, 1741. See *New-England Weekly Journal*, August 18, 1741, and *New-England Weekly Journal*, September 1, 1741.

RAN-away on the 16th of *August* past, from his Master Mr. *John Graton* of *Roxbury*, Innholder, an Irish Man Servant nam'd *Matthew Morris*, about 20 Years of Age, a lusty pale fac'd Fellow, brown Complection. He had on when he went away, a double breasted dark colour'd Coat with a large Cape of the same, the Coat fac'd with green, a pair of Leather Breeches and a pair of bluish Yarn Stockings, a Cotton Rug Cap and a brown Wigg. Whoever shall take up the said Run-away Servant, and him safely convey to his abovesaid Master in *Roxbury* shall have *Five Pounds* Reward, and all necessary Charges paid. All Masters of Vessels and others, are hereby warned against carrying off said Servant on Penalty of the Law.
Sept 1*st*. 1741.
New England Weekly Journal, September 1, 1741. See *New England Weekly Journal*, August 18, 1741, and *The Boston Weekly Post-Boy*, August 31, 1741.

RAN away from Rhode-Island, the 4th of Sept. a likely portly young Mollatto Fellow about 25 or 30 Years of Age, about 6 Foot high, and calls himself a Negro, he had on a dark coloured Jacket, a black Wigg, white Shirt, a pair of worsted & silk Stockings, and Shoes; had with him an Indian Squaw which he called his Wife, she had on a straw Hatt: Whosoever shall apprehend the aforesaid Malatto and bring him to Newport Goal, shall have Five Pounds Reward, New-English Currency, and all necessary Charges payed by Robert Lawton of Portsmouth on Rhode-Island.
The Boston Weekly Post-Boy, September 14, 1741; September 21, 1741.

RAN-away from his Master Capt. *Henry Pigeon* of Boston, a Negro Boy named *Port*, about 20 Years of Age, pretty thin, and not very tall, has large Lips, speaks good English; had on when he went away an old Cotton & Linnen Shirt, a dark blue under Jacket, broad Cloth, a Buck Skin pair of Breeches, and Trowsers over them, dark Stockings, and good Shoes, an old Hat and Cap. Whoever shall take up said Runaway, and safely convey to his said Master, shall have *Five Pounds* Reward, and all necessary Charges. And the same Reward shall be given to any Person that can convict any one, with full proof, of concealing or carrying off said Negro.
Boston, October 5th 1741.

New England Weekly Journal, October 6, 1741.

*R*AN *away from his Master, Capt.* Peter Williams *of* Boston, *Mariner, on the 9th of this Instant* October, *an Irish Man Servant named* Michael Newman, *but sometimes calls himself* Michael Mitchel. *He is about 20 Years old, short of Stature, but very thick, has sandy coloured curl'd Hair, and is mark'd with the Small Pox. He is a Taylor by Trade. He had on when he went away, a blue Pee Jacket with Horn Buttons, black Friz'd Breeches, and has Shoes ty'd with Strings. Whoever shall take up the said Servant, and bring him to Mr.* James Day, *Distiller, as the South End of* Boston, *shall have* Five Pounds *Reward, and all necessary Charges paid.*
The Boston Evening-Post, October 12, 1741.

WHEREAS I the Subscriber have been prodigiously hurt and injured by my Wife Mary Nichols *and sundry other Persons, and in divers Places, by taking up Goods on my Credit, without my Leave or Knowledge, and still persist so to do;*
THESE are therefore to Notify all Persons whatsoever from the Date hereof, not to Credit, Trust or Deliver any Manner or Sorts of Goods or Commodities to the said Mary, *or any other Person or Persons whatsoever, without a written Order under my own Hand, on Penalty of never being paid for the same.*
            John Nichols, *jun.*   Boston, October 14. 1741.
The Boston Gazette, or, New England Weekly, October 20, 1741; October 27, 1741.

*R*AN-*away from their Master* Nathanael Niles *of* South Kingston *in* King's County *in the Colony of* Rhode-Island, *&c. Esq; in the Evening of the* 1[6th] *of* October *Instant, Two Negro Men, namely* York *and* Pompey, *between 24 and 25 Years of Age;* York *is of a middle Stature, and of a pleasant, smiling Countenance, but* Pompey *is a thick well-sett Fellow and of a downish Look and surley Countenance; and they carried with them Two great Coats of Homespun Cloath the one being White and other of a darkish Colour, with Shoes and Stockings, and sundry other wearing Apparel. Whoever shall take up said Negro Men or either of them, so as to convey them safely to their aforesaid Master shall have* Five Pounds *Reward for either, and other necessary Charges paid   per* Nathanael Niles.
The Boston Weekly Post-Boy, November 2, 1741.

WHEREAS *Mary,* Wife to *John Stuart* of *Boston* hath eloped from her Husband, and tho' requested refuses to dwell with him; These are therefor to caution all Persons against harbouring, entertaining or trusting the said *Mary* on any Account whatsoever, as they will answer the same at their

Peril, and he hereby declared that he will not pay any thing for her Maintenance for the Time past, or any Debt which she may commit for her Maintenance, or otherwise for the Time to come.

And all Persons who are any ways indebted unto, or may have any Accounts with the said *John Stuart*, are hereby forbid paying any Money upon the same to her, as it shall not be allowed unless paid to himself, or some others appearing by a lawful Power from him executed after this Day.

John Stuart.   *Dated, Nov.* 21, 1741.

The Boston Weekly Post-Boy, November 23, 1741.

A Negro Fellow who calls himself *Cato*, was taken up at *Brooklin*, last Week, and his Master, not being known, was committed to Bridewell in *Boston*, where the Owner may have him: Upon his discharge the said Owner is desire to repair to the Printer hereof, in order to pay such Charges as shall be thought reasonable.

The Boston Weekly News-Letter, From November 19, to November 26, 1741.

*R*AN *away from his Master Capt.* Stephen Eastwick, *A Negro Man named* Jack, *about* 35 *Years old: He had on when he went away, a double breasted blew Pea Jacket, a speckled Shirt, a white cloth pair of Breeches, a pair of white Stockings, and a pretty good Bever Hat: He is very well known in* Rhode-Island: *He was Cook to Mr.* Keys *the Collector of* New-Port *several Years: Whoever takes up said Negro, and brings him to Mr.* John Brown *of* New-Port, *or Mr.* Charles Apthorp *of* Boston, *shall have* Five Pounds *Reward, and all necessary Charges paid. All Persons are hereby caution'd not to Harbour or Entertain said Negro; as they would avoid the Penalty of the Law in that Case made and provided.*

The Boston Weekly Post-Boy, December 14, 1741; December 21, 1741; December 28, 1741; January 11, 1742; January 18, 1742; January 25, 1742; February 15, 1742. See *The Boston Weekly Post-Boy*, May 31, 1742.

WHEREAS *John Smith*, formerly of *New-York*, Trader, but now an Inhabitant of *Rochester* in *New-Hempshire*, Advertised in the Year 1737, that no Body should Trust his Wife *Elizabeth* upon his Account, She having then elop'd from his Bed and Board, and still persists in her evil Course; and as he is now inform'd that she Endeavours to get Credit upon his Account, he thinks proper to give this further Publick Notice that she may not impose upon any Body, not to give her any Credit upon his Account, for that he will not Pay any Debts, that she hath or many contract.

The New-York Weekly Journal, November 30, 1741; December 14, 1741. See *The Boston Gazette*, From June 20, to June 27, 1737.

R*AN* away from Mr. Daniel Ballard *of* Boston, *on the Sixteenth of* December, *an* Irish *Servant Boy named* James Mc Clean, *about* 18 *Years of Age, who had on when he went away, a Worsted Cap, with Holes in it, a new Check Shirt, a pair of Camblet Breeches, Yarn Stockings, and a coarse Coat. Whoever shall take up the said Servant, and bring him to his abovesaid Master, living in* Marlborough-Street, *shall be well satisfied for their Trouble, and have all necessary Charges paid.*

The Boston Evening-Post, December 21, 1741; December 28, 1741; January 4, 1742.

R*AN away from his Master* Francis Cogswell, *Esq; of* Ipswich, *on the* 30*th of* Nov. *last, a Negro Man named* Pompey, *a Blacksmith by Trade, had on when he went away a grey Kersey Jacket, old Breeches and Trowsers, check'd drugget Shirt, he carried away with him a blew broad cloth Coat, has part of his left Ear cut off: Whoever shall take up the above Negro and commit him to the nighest Goal shall have* Forty Shillings *Reward and all necessary Charges paid: And all Masters of Vessels are required not to carry off said Negro, as they will answer the Penalty of the Law in that case made and provided.*

The Boston Weekly Post-Boy, December 21, 1741; December 28, 1741; January 4, 1742; January 11, 1742. See New England Weekly Journal, November 11, 1740.

R*AN away from* James Holt *of* York, *in the County of* York, *on the* 30*th of* Nov. *last, an Irish Man Servant named* John Ryan *of about* 26 *Years of Age, fair Complection, brown bushy Hair, thin Fac'd, and a big Nose, he had on a broad-cloth Coat & jacket of a dark Cinnamon colour, a Pair of Leather or Orange colour'd Plush Breeches, and a good Beaver Hat: His working Dress is a blew Pee-Jacket, and an under homespun striped Jacket with Trowsers.*

Whoever shall take up the abovesaid Servant and bring him to said James Holt, *or secure him so that said Holt may have him again shall have* Three Pounds *Reward, and all necessary Charges paid by* James Holt*: All Masters of Vessels, Housholders and others are hereby warned against entertaining or concealing said Fellow on Penalty of the Law in such Case made and provided.*

The Boston Weekly Post-Boy, December 21, 1741; December 28, 1741; January 11, 1742; The Boston Weekly News-Letter, From December 24, to December 31, 1741; From December 31, 1741, to January 7, 1742. Minor differences between the papers.

1742

RAN away from his Master Capt. George Ruggels *of* Boston, *on the* 1st *Inst. an Indian Man Servant, named* Sylvester Charles, *alias* Venus, *about* 22 *Years of Age, a tall lusty Fellow, with short Hair, had on a Seaman's Dress. Whoever shall take up said Runaway and him safely convey to his abovesaid Master in Wings Lane,* Boston, *shall have* Five Pounds *Reward, and all necessary Charges paid. All Masters of Vessels are hereby caution'd against carrying off said Servant, on Penalty of the Law.*
    The Boston Weekly News-Letter, From December 31, 1741, to January 7, 1742; From January 7, to January 14, 1742.

    James-Town, Rhode-Island, January 1, 1742.
RAN away from John Martain, *the Officer having him in Custody, an Irish Man, named* John Burk, *a Rope-maker by Trade; he is a thick stout Fellow, with a thick Cloth Jacket and a coarse Shirt and Trowsers over his Breeches: He had a felt Hat and a new Pair of single sol'd Shoes. The said Officer hath paid* Eight Pounds *already in* June *last, for taking up said Fellow and Charges. His said Master being at* Philadelphia, *the said Officer would not put said* Burk *to Prison, least put his Master to more Charge than he had already been. Whosoever shall apprehend said Fellow, and bring him to the abovesaid Officer, or secure him in any of his Majesty's Goal,* [sic] *shall have* Ten Pounds *Reward, paid* John Martain.
    The Boston Weekly Post-Boy, January 11, 1742; January 18, 1742.

RAN away from the Sloop Prosperity, *lying at the Long Wharf,* David Allen *of Pemaquid Master, on the* 3d *of this Instant February, an Irish Servant named* John Dear, *about* [ ] *Years old, a short well set Fellow, of a fresh Complexion: He speaks pretty good* English, *and had on when he went away, a brownish coloured upper Jacket, and a red Cloth under Wastcoat, a Snuff coloured pair of Breeches, and a Worsted Cap. Whoever shall take up the said Servant, and convey him to his abovesaid Master* David Allen, *or to Messiers* George Glen, *or* Peter Pelham *in* Boston, *shall have* Five Pounds *Reward, and all necessary Charges paid.*
    N. B. *All Masters of Vessels and other Persons are hereby cautioned against harbouring, concealing or carrying off the said Servant, as they will avoid the Penalty of the Law.*   Boston, February 4th. 1741.
    The Boston Evening-Post, February 8, 1742; February 15, 1742.

RAN from on Board the Ship *Experiment, William Courtis*, Master, now in *Nantasket*-Road, on the 11th Instant, *William Lloy*d, a thin, grim Complexion'd Man' something Pock-broken. He having once before run from Said Ship and stole away a seven Oar Boat, was catch'd and convicted by Col. *Savage* for said Fact, and afterward clear'd by the said Master, on his promise to return to the Ship and Duty again; but the same Day ran away again, and has not came to the Ship or Master since; These are therefore to assure said *Lloyd*, that being deem'd a Deserter, he shall be treated as such wherever he can be found. And whoever takes him up and conveys him to his Master, so that he may be brought to justice, shall have *Forty Shillings* Reward, and all necessary Charges paid.

All Masters of Vessels, Tavern-Keepers, Innholders, Victuallers, and all others, are strictly forbid to harbour said Deserter, as they will answer th Damage, according to the Law made and provided in that Case.

   Wm. COURTIS.   *Boston, Feb.* 16. 1741.2.

The Boston Weekly News-Letter, From February 11, to February 18, 1742; From February 18, to February 25, 1742.

R*AN away from his Master, Mr.* Alexander Chamberlain *of* Boston, *Sail maker, on the* 20*th of this Instant* February, *a White Servant Lad named* George Clarke, *aged 17 Years, of middle Stature, is full faced, has large grey Eyes, but no Hair. He had on when he went away, a striped woollen Cap, a large red Silk Handkerchief, a dark Kersy Jacket and Breeches, a striped Homespun under Jacket, gray Yarn Stockings, and a new pair of Shoes. Whoever shall take up the said Servant, and bring or send him to his abovesaid Master in* Boston, *shall have* Five Pounds *Reward, and all necessary Charges paid.*

N. B. *All Masters of Vessels and other Persons, are hereby cautioned against harbouring, concealing or carrying off the said Servant, as they will avoid the Penalty of the Law.*

The Boston Evening-Post, February 22, 1742; March 1, 1742.

RUN-away from his Master *William Bulfinch* of *Boston* Sail:Maker, on the *21*st of *February* Instant, a white Servant Lad, named *Joseph Christophers*, aged about nineteen Years, of middle Stature, light Countenance, ruddy Complection; had on when he went away, Pea-Jacket, with large Plate Buttons, a blew great Coat and a black Wigg.

Whoever shall take up said Servant, and bring or send him to his abovesaid Master in *Boston*, shall have *Five Pounds* Reward, and all necessary Charges paid.

N. B. All Masters of Vessels and other Persons are hereby caution'd against harbouring, concealing or carrying off said Servant, as they will avoid the Penalty of the Law.

The Boston Weekly News-Letter, From February 18, to February 25, 1742; From February 25, to March 4, 1742.

RAN *away from their Master,* Francis Willet, *Esq; of* North Kingston, *on the* 10*th of* February *last, a Negro Man named* Jack, *of a middle Stature, well set, and about* 24 *Years of Age. He had with him three Coats, a Gray fulled Cloth, a dyed Cloth of a brown Colour, and a Duroy, all homespun. Also a Negro Woman named* Jean, *about* 30 *Years of Age, pretty tall; she had two striped Homespun Gowns, besides considerable other Cloaths. Both speak good* English. *It's thought they went off in a Fishing Boat. Whoever shall apprehend said Runaways, and convey them to their aforesaid Master, shall have* Ten Pounds *Reward, and all necessary Charges paid.* March 4. 1741-2.

The Boston Evening-Post, March 8, 1742; The Boston Weekly Post-Boy, March 8, 1742. Minor differences between the papers.

W*Hereas...the Ship* Ann, *Capt.* John Phillips *Commander....*William Baker, *a Sailor belonging to the said Ship* Ann, *is deserted, and* Edward Dungen, *an* Irishman, *Servant to the said Commander, is run away: These are to caution all Masters of Vessels and others, against harbouring, concealing or carrying off the said Deserter or Servant, as they will avoid the utmost Severity of the Law.*

The Boston Evening-Post, March 8, 1742

RAN *away from Mr.* Josiah Woodberry *of* Beverly, *a Negro or Mulatto Man-Servant named* Obed, *about* 43 *Years old, and upwards of six Feet in Stature. His Head bows forward towards his Breast, and carries his Toes outwards when he Walks. He had on when he went away, a white woollen Shirt, a woollen under Jacket striped black and white, a double breasted Jacket of a mix'd Colour, the fore part lin'd with red Bays, and trim'd with Brass Buttons; also a mix'd coloured great Coat, with Buttons of the same Cloth, a pair of Breeches made of tand'd Horse Hide, gray Yarn Stockings, and large Shoes better than* 12 *Inches long, a Felt Hat, and a red Bilboa Handkerchief. Whoever shall take up the said Servant, and bring him to his aforesaid Master in* Beverly, *shall have* Twenty Shillings *Reward, and all necessary Charges paid.*

The Boston Evening-Post, April 26, 1742.

RAN*-away from his Master Mr.* Tho. Plaisted, *a Negro Man about* 23 *Years of Age, named* Brazill, *well known in Boston by his Legs had on a blew Jacket, and has often been seen about Boston; and also going to his Whore, who lives at Mr Gibson's at New Town. Whoever sees him, is desired to bring him to his Master at Mrs. Beat's at the Deck Head. Boston.*

The Boston Weekly Post-Boy, April 26, 1742. See The Boston Weekly Post-Boy, May 3, 1742.

RAN-away on Saturday Night last the 11*th Inst. from Mr. Gershom Flagg of Woburn, a Negro Man Servant, Indented for* 7 *Years named Pompey York, about* 35 *Years of Age, speaks good English, of middle Stature; He had with him, two old cotton & linnen Shirts much patch'd a grey Broad Cloth great Coat fac'd with Yellow, a blew Camblet Coat all trim'd, a blew Jacket made of divers Pieces, light Cloth Breeches patch'd with a brown Cloth in the Seat, two Pair of grey Yarn Stockings, one Pair New, a Pair of old Shoes which had a Patch upon each Side, an old Hat patch'd on the Crown. He had also a Spoon and Dial Mould and other Tinker's Tools. Whoever shall take up the said Negro and bring him to his Master shall have Twenty Shillings old Tenor, if he is found within Twenty Miles, of above then Forty Shillings Reward, and all necessary Charges. All persons are caution'd not to conceal or harbour the said Negro as 'tis suspected some do, as they would avoid the Penalty of the Law.*

N. B. The said Negro can read and write well, and is very deceitful, pretending to be a new Convert, and is very forward to mimick some of the Strangers that have of late been preaching among us.

The Boston News-Letter, From April 22, to April 29, 1742; From April 29, to May 6, 1742. See *The Boston Weekly News-Letter*, March 31, 1743.

RUN-away the 25th Instant from his Master *Joseph Plaisted*, Esq; at *York*, a Negro Man named *Jo*; aged about Forty Years: Had on when he went away, a grey Pee Jacket, an old Bever Hat, a woollen Shirt: He is of an old Look, and speaks good English. Whosoever shall take up or secure said Negro, or send him to his said Master, shall have *Five Pounds* Reward, and all necessary Charges paid.

Jos. Plaisted. April 29th 1742.

The Boston Weekly Post-Boy, May 3, 1742; May 10, 1742.

RAN away from his Master Mr. Tho. Plaisted, a Negro Man about 23 *Years of Age, well known in Boston by his Legs had on a blew Jacket, and has often been seen about Boston, and also going to his Whore, who lives at Mr. Gibson's at New Town. Whoever sees him, is desired to bring him to his Master at Mrs. Beath's at the Deck Head, Boston.*

The Boston Weekly Post-Boy, May 3, 1742. See *The Boston Weekly Post-Boy*, April 26, 1742.

BRoke out of Bridewell last Saturday Night, and ran away, a Negro Man named Tom, belonging to Mr. John Becham *of* Boston, *Victualler, a short well set Fellow, about 32 Years of Age, of a Tawny Colour. Whoever shall discover the said Negro, so as his Master may have him again, or any Person concealing him, shall have* **Three** Pounds *Reward. And all Masters*

of Vessels or others are forbidden to convey the said Negro off, as they will answer the same in the Law. Or if any Person pretending a Title to dispose of him, shall be discovered, the above Reward shall be given.
                                                        Boston, May 24. 1742.
   The Boston Evening-Post, May 24, 1742; May 31, 1742.

THIS *is to certify all Persons, that my Wife Jane Kimbel has unjustly and without any Reason absented herself from me the Subscriber; and all Persons are hereby forbid to give, trust, or Credit unto the said Jane Kimbal on pain of loosing any or all Debts that she shall contract, for I do solemnly forbid and warn all Persons trading with her or crediting her on my Account; and all persons are forbid to entertain the said Jane Kimbal as they will answer it at the peril of the Law.*
              Jonathan Kimbel.   *Bradford May* 12. 1742.
   The Boston Weekly Post-Boy, May 24, 1742.

Ran-away from his Master Capt. Stephen Eastwick, *A Negro Man named* Jack, *about* 35 *Years old: He had on when he went away, a double breasted blew Pea Jacket, a speckled Shirt, a white Cloth Pair of Breeches, a Pair of white Stockings, and a pretty good Bever Hat: He is very well known in* Rhode-Island: *He was Cook to Mr.* Keys *the Collector of* New-Port *several Years: Whoever takes up said Negro, and brings him to Mr.* John Brown *of* New-Port, *or Mr.* Charles Apthorp *of* Boston, *shall have* Five Pounds Reward, *and all necessary Charges paid. All Persons are hereby caution'd not to Harbour or Entertain said Negro; as they would avoid the Penalty of the Law in that Case made and provided.*
   The Boston Weekly Post-Boy, May 31, 1742; June 14, 1742; June 21, 1742; June 28, 1742; July 5, 1742; July 12, 1742. See *The Boston Weekly Post-Boy,* December 14, 1741.

BRoke *out of Bridewell, a Servant Boy, belonging to Capt.* Benjamin Hammet, *named* William Taylor, *about* 19 *Years of Age: He is fresh colour'd; and had on a blew Jacket, and stuters in his Speech. Whoever shall bring him to his Master abovesaid, shall be well rewarded. All Persons are hereby notified not to entertain said Servant, or carry him off, as they would avoid the Penalty of the Law.*
   The Boston Weekly Post-Boy, May 31, 1742; June 14, 1742; June 21, 1742; June 28, 1742; July 5, 1742.

W*Hereas* Obadiah Mors, *late residing in* South Kingston, *in the County, of* King's County, *and Colony of* Rhode-Island, *&c. Goldsmith,* alias *Painter, made his Escape in the Night of the twenty-sixth Day of* May *past, out of his*

Majesty's Goal in Newport, *in the County of* Newport, *and Colony aforesaid; and for the apprehending of him again, the Honourable* RICHARD WARD, *Esq; Governour of said Colony, has issued a Proclamation of the twenty seventh Day of said May, promising therein a Reward of* Five Hundred Pounds *in Bills of publick Credit of said Colony, to any Person or Persons that shall perform said Service, and deliver him to any of the proper Authority of said Colony, so as he may be committed to his Majesty's Goal in* Newport *aforesaid: The said* Obadiah Mors *is of low Stature, pretty round Visage, a full dark Eye, and black Beard, full breasted, being about twenty six Years of Age, and well proportioned.*
      John Easton, *Deputy Sheriff.* Newport 4th June, 1742.
  The Boston Evening-Post, June 7, 1742; June 14, 1742; June 21, 1742.
  See *The Boston Evening-Post,* June 28, 1742.

R*AN away from a Farm in* Hopkinton, *belonging to the Rev. Mr. Commissary* Price *of* Boston, *on the* 31*st of* May *past, a* Scotch *Man Servant named* James Carey, *about* 30 *Years old, of a midling Stature, but well set. He speaks broad* Scotch, *his Hair is lately cut off, and he had on when he went away, a striped* Woollen *Cap, a light coloured Coat, a white Jacket, and Trouzers of Tow-Cloth. Whoever shall take up the said Servant, and bring him to* Thomas Fleet, *at the Heart and Crown in Cornhill,* Boston, *shall have* Three Pounds *Reward, in Bills of Credit of the Old Tenour, and all necessary Charges paid.*
  The Boston Evening-Post, June 7, 1742; June 14, 1742; June 21, 1742.

R*AN-away from his Master* James Gooch *of* Hopkinton, *the* 8*th of* June, *an Irish Man Servant, named* Daniel Carrel, *a short, well set Fellow about* 24 *Years of Age; a Shoemaker by Trade and a good Workman; he had on when he went away, a dark cloth Coat half trim'd, Horse-hair Buttons of the same Colour, and a light colour'd Cloth Jacket, both lined with Red, a Pair of Red chequered woollen Breeches: He had also with him a Dimity jacket and several fine Shirts, with ruffled Bosoms, white Stockings; he wears a dark Bob Wigg. Whoever shall apprehend said Servant, and bring him to his said Master of to Mr.* John Gooch *Merchant in* Boston, *shall have* Five Pounds *Reward and all necessary Charges paid.*
  The Boston Weekly Post-Boy, June 14, 1742; June 21, 1742; June 28, 1742; July 5, 1742.

R*AN away from his Master* Hugh Scott *of* Cambridge, *on the* 19*th Instant, a Negro Man named* Nevis, *he formerly belong'd to Mr.* Brewster *the Chocolate-Maker: Whoever shall take up the said Negro, and bring him to Capt* James Williams *in Common-Street, shall be handsomely Rewarded, and all Charges paid.*

The Boston Weekly News-Letter, From June 17, to June 24, 1742.

W*HEREAS* Obadiah Mors *has lately made his Escape from his Majesty's Goal in* Newport *aforesaid, and thereupon a Proclamation has been issued out by his Honour the* GOVERNOUR, *promising a Reward of* Five Hundred Pounds *to any Person or Persons that should apprehend the said* Obadiah Mors, *and him safely deliver to any proper Authority in this Colony,* &. This Assembly approving of His Honour's Conduct, do hereby confirm said Proclamation, and further enact, That a Fine of *Four Hundred Pounds* in passable Bills of publick Credit, be laid on every such Person as shall conceal the said *Mors*, or convey, or assist in conveying said *Mors* out of this Colony, or over Sea, in any Boat or Vessel, or by any other Ways or Means whatsoever; one half to the Informer, and the other half to be paid into the General Treasury, and to be recovered by Bill, Plaint or Information, in any Court of Record in this Colony; and that a Proclamation be forthwith issued out by his Honour the GOVERNOUR agreeable thereto; and that this Act be inserted in the publick Prints three several Times. True Copy, Teste. *Ja. Martin*, Secr.

The Boston Evening-Post, June 28, 1742. See *The Boston Evening-Post*, June 7, 1742.

RAN away from his Master Aaron Bourne of Bristol, on the first of July instant, A white Boy named George Hanes, about 14 Years of Age, well set, with short black Hair; he had on when he went away, a rusty Hat, the Brims cut narrow, a jacket and Breeches made of Tow Cloth with Pewter Buttons: Whoever shall apprehend the said Boy, and bring him to his Master at Bristol, or secure him so that his Master may have him again, shall be well rewarded, and have all necessary Charges paid. All Masters of Vessels and others are caution'd against concealing or carrying off said Servant, as they would avoid the Penalty of the Law.

The Boston Weekly Post-Boy, July 12, 1742; August 9, 1742.

RAN-away from his Master Mr. *James Monk* of *Boston*, Merchant, an Irish Man Servant, named *Timothy Brennon*, he went away the 11th Instant at Night, and had on a dark grey Coat, much torn under the Arms, every where else looks very well, a pair of green Breeches, and a pair of Trousers: He carried with him an old blue Livery Coat lin'd with yellow, and brass Buttons. He is about 22 Years of Age, has red Hair and freckled Face, well set, great Legs, and about 5 Foot 4 Inches high.

Whoever shall take up said Runaway, and bring him to his Master, shall have *Three Pounds* Reward, (old Tenor) and all necessary Charges paid.

The Boston Gazette, or Weekly Journal, July 13, 1742.

RAN-away from his Master, Capt. *John Guynn* of *Boston*, Mariner, on Thursday the 8th of this Instant *July*, a Spanish Indian Slave named *John Francis* alias *Jaun Francisco*, about 26 Years of Age, short well set Fellow, short Hair, speaks pretty good English; he had on when he went away a blue Waistcoat, Oznabrigs Frock and Trousers, Worsted Cap, Felt Hat, a reddish Handkerchief, a new Pair of grey Yarn Stockings, and a Pair of large Shoes.

Whoever shall take up the abovesaid Runaway, and bring him to his said Master, in *Boston*, shall have *Three Pounds* (Old Tenor) Reward, and all necessary Charges paid.

All Masters of Vessels and others are hereby caution'd against concealing or carrying off said Servant, on Penalty of the Law in that Case made and Provided.

The Boston Gazette, or Weekly Journal, July 13, 1742.

RAN-away the 11th Instant, from his Master Mr. *Samuel Emmes* of *Boston*, Blacksmith, an Irish Man Servant named *Darby Crowly*, about 16 Years of Age, of middling Stature, had on when he went away a green Broad Cloth Jacket, a Check Shirt, Cloth pair of Breeches, yarn Stockings, and a Beaver Hat.

Whoever shall take up said Runaway, and him safely convey to his Master in *Boston* aforesaid, shall have *Three Pounds* Reward and all necessary Charges paid.

All Masters of Vessels are hereby warned not to carry off said Runaways. [*sic*]

The Boston Gazette, or Weekly Journal, July 13, 1742.

R*AN away from his Master, Mr.* Samuel Hendly *of* Charlestown, *on Commencement Day last, a Negro Fellow named* Nero, *about 25 Years old, he is short but strong and well set, and speaks good* English. *He had on when he went away, and probably has yet, a striped homespun Jacket, Leather Breeches, and black Stockings, but his other Cloaths are uncertain.*

The Boston Evening-Post, July 19, 1742; July 26, 1742.

R*AN-away from the Schooner* St. Joseph, (*the Spanish Privateer lately brought into* Rhode-Island,) *A Negro Man who can't speak English; and it is suppos'd he came towards* Boston. *Deserted also at the same Time an Irish Man named* James Seeth, *who was Prisoner on board said Privateer. Whoever takes up the above Negro & Man so as to convey him to Capt.* John Freebody, *or to Capt.* John Holnans *in* Boston, *shall have* Ten Pounds *old Tenor Reward for each of them, and all necessary Charges paid.*

N. B. *The said Negro is mark'd all on his Breast, with their Country Cuts.*

The Boston Weekly Post-Boy, July 19, 1742.

W*Hereas* Mary *the Wife of* Leonard Bazin *hath elop'd from her Husband, and run him in Debt several considerable Sums, almost to his Ruin, these are therefore to forewarn all Persons whatsoever from harbouring or entertaining her, upon the Penalty of being prosecuted according to Law, and also to advertise all Persons not to trust or credit her upon any Account whatsoever, declaring that he will not pay any Debts she shall contracts after this Time.*
      Leonard Bazin.   Newport, August 3d. 1742.
 The Boston Evening-Post, August 9, 1742.

RUN-away from *Caleb Godfrey* of *New-Port, Rhode-Island*, on Friday the 23d of *July*, a Negro Man, named *Mingo*, a lusty well-set Fellow, about Thirty five Years of Age, has been but on Day in the Country, has some gray Hairs in his Head, speaks but poor English, had on an old Flannel Wastcoat, no Shoes, Stockings, nor Hat: Whoever shall apprehend said Negro, and convey him to his abovesaid Master, shall have *Five Pounds* current Money of *Rhode-Island* Reward: And whoever shall entertain or conceal said Negro, must expect to be dealt with as the Law directs in such Cases.
 The Boston Weekly Post-Boy, August 9, 1742.

RAN-away from his Master *Joseph Callender*, the 13th of *June* last, a Negro Man named *Coffy*, middle Stature: He had on when he went away, a check'd woollen Shirt; he changed his Name to *Sambo*; he formerly liv'd with the Rev. Mr. *Waldron* deceas'd: Whoever shall take up said Negro, and convey him to his Master, shall have *Forty Shillings* Reward, and all
    necessary Charges paid by *Joseph Callender.*
 The Boston Weekly Post-Boy, August 16, 1742; August 30, 1742; September 6, 1742; September 27, 1742; October 25, 1742; November 8, 1742. Last two ads have "Boston, Oct. 21. 1742." at the bottom.

RAN-away from the Rev. Mr. *Samuel Moody* of *York*, about the middle of last Month, an Indian Woman named *Dinah*, about 44 Years of Age, speaks good English, short Stature, well set, she had on when she went away, a new Cotton Shift, with Silver Buttons in her Sleves; two homespun quilted Coats, the under Coat black and white strip'd, the upper blue and white.
 N. B. It's thought she was seen on the Road between *Greenland* and *Hampton.*
 Whoever shall take up the abovesaid Runaway and bring her to her said Master, or to the Printer hereof, shall be well rewarded.

The Boston Gazette, or Weekly Journal, August 24, 1742; August 31, 1742.

BRoke out of Bridewell last Lord's-Lay was sev'nnight a Negro Man Servant belonging to the Rev. Mr. *Gee* of *Boston*, named *Tom*, supposed to be about 29 Years of Age, he is of a lively and active Disposition, and is well known in *Boston*: Whoever shall take up the said Servant, and bring him to his said Master shall have 3 £. as a Reward, and all necessary Charges paid.
The Boston News-Letter, From August 26, to September 2, 1742.

WHEREAS *Rachel* the Wife of Me the Subscriber, living in *Dorchester*, hath eloped (Haven be prais'd) about three Weeks since from me her lawful and tender Husband, and carried off my (reputed) Child contrary to my desire and command. This is therefore to caution all Persons to beware of said *Rachel*, and not to trust her; for I hereby declare off from Matrimony, and against paying any Debts that she has or shall contract from the 7th of *August* last past, that being the last Day I have to do with her.
    Witness my Hand, *Joseph Brown.*
The Boston Weekly News-Letter, From August 26, to September 2, 1742.

DESERTED from the Brigantine Industry, *John Williams* Master, lying in *Portsmouth* Harbour, two Sailors, named *Henry Colthurst* and *Robert Lane*, short thick sett Men, of about Twenty six Years of Age, yellowish Hair. Whoever will apprehend said Deserters, and bring them to *Jacob Royall* or *Benja. Bagnall*, shall be satisfied for their Trouble, and all necessary Charges paid.
The Boston Evening-Post, September 6, 1742; September 13, 1742.

R*AN away from his Master, Mr.* Thomas Rogers *of* Newbury, *Baker, on the 6th Day of this Instant* September, *a white Boy named* John Johnson, *of about fifteen Years old.* He had on when he went away, a check'd Woollen Shirt, a long striped red and white Cotton and Woollen Jacket, a pair of wide Ozenbrigs Trouzers, a pair of gray Yarn Stockings, an old pair of Shoes, and a Felt Hat. He has light coloured short Hair, and is of a light Complexion.
  Whoever shall take up said Boy, and safely convey him to his said Master, shall have Forty Shillings Reward, Old Tenor, and all necessary Charges paid.
    Thomas Rogers.   Newbury, September 11, 1742.
The Boston Evening-Post, September 13, 1742; September 27, 1742.

Deserted from the Ship *Clifton, Francis Coates,* Commander, lying at *Portsmouth* in *New Hampshire,* two Transports from *Ireland,* viz *Darby Coulney* and *John Bacon: Darby Coulney* is about 5 Feet 8 inches, of a dark Complexion, wearing a Wigg, a black Coat, a blew Waistcoat, and Leather Breeches: He cannot speak a Word of English. *John Bacon* is a well set Man, a red Beard, and much freckled in the Face and Body, wearing a Wigg, and speaks English well. If therefore any Person or Persons will secure the two Persons, or bring them to *Francis Coates,* at *Portsmouth,* they shall receive *Ten Pounds* old Tenor, and all necessary Charges paid by *Fran. Coates. Portsmouth, Sept.* 10. 1742.
The Boston Weekly Post-Boy, September 27, 1742.

D*eserted from the* John *Galley,* Capt. Craige *Commander, now lying in* Boston *Harbour, on Thursday last, the Three following Sailors, viz.* John Lock, Thomas Billingsly *and* John Murfey, *If the said Sailors don't immediately return to their Duty of board the said Ship, they will be treated as Deserters.*
The Boston Evening-Post, October 4, 1742.

RAN away from his Master, Capt. *John Aves* of *Boston,* on the 5th of this Instant *August,* a Negro Man named *Phillip,* about 28 Years old, much pitted with the Small Pox, and speaks pretty good *English* and *Portuguise.* He is used to the Sea, and 'tis supposed will endeavour to get off in some Vessel, having carried away his Sea Bedding and all his other Cloaths; therefore all Masters of Vessels and other Persons are hereby cautioned against concealing or carrying him off, as they will avoid the Penalty of the Law. And whoever shall take up the said Negro, and bring him to his abovesaid Master, living near Dr. *Cutler's* Church at the *North* End of the Town, shall have *Five Pounds* Reward *(Old Tenor)* and all necessary Charges paid.
The Boston Evening-Post, October 11, 1742; October 25, 1742.

RAN-away from *Nehemiah Allen* of *Sturbridge,* on the 5th Day of *September* last, An Indian Man Servant, named *Coocbuck,* about 20 Years of Age: He is a slim spare Fellow: Whosoever shall take up said Run away, and bring him to his said Master shall have *Twenty Shillings* Reward, old Tenor.
N. B. All Masters of Vessels and other Persons are forbid concealing or carrying off said Servant, as they would avoid the Penalty of the Law.
The Boston News-Letter, From October 7, to October 14, 1742.

R*AN away from his Master,* Shadrach Keen *of* Bristol, *a Negro Man named* Ben, *about* 29 *Years old, small of Stature, and very full faced. He had on* *when he went away, a red Cloth double breasted Jacket, with a few Brass Buttons, but without Lining, and an old striped Flannel Shirt, a pair of Tow Cloth Breeches, a pair of bluish Yarn Stockings, a pair of old Shoes, and a Felt Hat with the Brim cut, and carried with him a Fiddle. He ran away on the 9th Day of this Instant* October. *Whoever shall take up the said Servant and bring him to his abovesaid Master in* Bristol, *shall have* Five Pounds *Reward in Old Tenor.* October 14. 1742.

The Boston Evening-Post, October 18, 1742; October 25, 1742; November 15, 1742.

RAN-away from his Master *Job Lewis,* the 13th Inst. a Negro Man named *Cato,* about 25 Years of Age, speaks good English, a short well-set Fellow, he had on when he went away a blew Jacket with brass Buttons, strip'd cotton Breeches, grey yarn Stockings, since has been seen with a frock & Trowsers: whoever shall apprehend the said Negro and bring him to his Master shall be well rewarded and all necessary Charges paid.

All Masters of Vessels and other Persons are forbid concealing or carrying of said Servant as they would avoid the Penalty of the Law.

The Boston Weekly Post-Boy, October 18, 1742; October 25, 1742.

RAN-away from Mr. *James Kenney* of *Dorchester,* on the 21st Inst. an Irish Man Servant, named *Edward Hakney,* about 22 Years of Age, of middling Stature, well sett, red short Hair, and wears a Cap, a Felt Hatt, a dark Pea Jacket, and Breeches of the same colour, a pair of large Trowsers, striped under Jacket, a speckled cotton & wool Shirt, freckled Face, has pretty much of the Irish Brogue. Whoever shall take up the abovesaid Run-away, and him safely convey to his abovesaid Master at *Dorchester,* shall have *Ten Pounds* old Tenor, Reward. All Masters of Vessels are caution'd against carrying off said Servant, on Penalty of the Law.

The Boston Weekly News-Letter, November 25, 1742; December 2, 1742.

RAN-away from his Master Mr. James Adams of Boston, Block-maker, on the 26th Instant, a Negro Boy named *Cicero,* about 17 Years old, spare and thin, of a tawney Complexion, and has a Scar in his Lip, speaks good English; had on a double breasted Jacket with white mettal Buttons, a Cotton and Linnen Shirt, Leather Breeches, short Trousers, yarn Stockings, and old Shoes.

Whoever shall take up said Runaway, and him safely convey to his said Master in *Boston,* shall have *Five Pounds* Reward Old Tenor, and all necessary Charges paid.

All Masters of Vessels are caution'd against carrying off the said Servant, on the Penalty of the Law.

Boston, November 30. 1742.
The Boston Evening-Post, December 6, 1742; December 13, 1742; *The Boston Gazette, or Weekly Journal,* January 4, 1743; January 11, 1743. Minor differences between the papers. See *The Boston Evening-Post,* January 3, 1743.

RAN-away from his Master *Paskee Whitford* of *North-Kingston, Rhode-Island Government,* on the 22d of September last, an Indian Boy, named *James,* about 17 Years of Age, and suppos'd by some to be part White, of a middle Stature, about five Feet and an half high: He has had one of his great Toes cut off and joined on again, and stands some thing crooked: He had on when he want away, a thick Kersey cinnamon coloured Jacket, a pair of black and white stripd'd Breeches, a Flannel Shirt, new Shoes, yarn Stockings folded half way up his Leg, and a new felt Hat. Whoever will take up said Run-away Boy, and secure him in one of His *M*ajesty's Goals; or deliver him safely to his Master, shall have *Six Pounds,* old Tenor, *Rhode-Island* Currency Reward, and all necessary Charges
    paid by   *Paskee Whitford.*
The Boston Weekly Post-Boy, December 13, 1742; *The Boston Weekly News-Letter,* December 16, 1742.

Newport, Rhode-Island, December 3. 1742.
W*Hereas Sarah* the Wife of *John Bazin,* eloped from his House by the Enticement of some ill minded Persons, he being absent from Home, and carried away almost all his Linen, Money, Bonds and Notes of Hand, and sundry other Things, to his great Ruin and Damage, who was obliged to hire a Woman to take Care of his House, which may cause unthinking People to give them a bad Name. *These are therefore to forewarn all Persons whatsoever to harbour, entertain or Credit her, upon the Penalty of being prosecuted according to Law, and not to trust or credit her on any Account whatsoever; declaring, that I will not pay any Debts she shall contract after this Time; and also if any Person conveys her Home, and the Things above-mentioned, or part of them, they shall have* Ten Pounds *in Cash,* Old Tenor,   John Bazin.
The Boston Evening-Post, December 20, 1742; January 3, 1743.

1743

RAN away from his Master, Mr. *Lewis Vassall* of Brantrey, a Negro Man named *Cuffy,* a short thick well set Fellow. Whoever shall take up said Negro, and him safely convey to his aforesaid Master, shall have *Three Pounds* Reward, Old Tenor.

The Boston Evening-Post, January 3, 1743; January 17, 1743.

RAN away from his Master Mr. *James Adams* of *Boston*, Block-maker, on the 26th of *November* last, a Negro Boy named *Cicero*, about 17 Years old, spare and thin, of a tawney Complexion, and has a Scar in his Lip, speaks good English; had on a double breasted Jacket with white mettal Buttons, a Cotton and Linnen Shirt, Leather Breeches, short Trouzers, yarn Stockings, and old Shoes. Whoever shall take up the said Runaway, and him safely convey to his said Master in *Boston*, shall have *Ten Pounds* Reward, Old Tenor, and all necessary Charges paid. All Masters of Vessels are cautioned against carrying off the said Servant, on the Penalty of the Law.
Boston, Jan. 3. 1742-3.
The Boston Evening-Post, January 3, 1743; January 17, 1743. See *The Boston Evening-Post*, December 6, 1742.

R*An-away from Capt.* Timothy McDaniel *of* Boston, Henry Barodell, *a Servant Lad about* 16 *or* 17 *Years of Age, fair Countenance, was born in* London; *had on a red Jacket, and an under blue ditto; whoever takes him up and brings him to Mr.* Chargles Apthorp, *shall have* 40s. *Reward, old Tenor.*
The Boston Gazetter, or, Weekly Journal, January 25, 1743.

R*AN away from his Master, Mr.* Elisha Jones *of* Weston, *the beginning of* December *last, an* Irish *Man Servant named* Darby Slattery, *about 23 Years old; a short thick well set Fellow, that can speak but very little* English. *His hair is cut short and he wears a Cap, and the Hair on one side of his Head is white and the other black. He had on when he went away, a close bodied Coat of mix'd homespun, a Jacket of a greenish Cast, a speckled Linen Shirt, Leather Breeches, gray Yarn Stockings, and blue Buskins over them, and a pair of strong Shoes. Whoever shall take up the said Servant, and bring him to Mr.* Anthony Bracket *in School-Street in* Boston, *or to his above-said Master in* Weston, *shall have* Three Pounds *Reward,* Old Tenor, *and all necessary Charges paid.* January 31. 1742-3.
The Boston Evening-Post, January 31, 1743; February 7, 1743; February 14, 1743; February 21, 1743.

RAN-away from the Ship Leghorn-Galley, now lying at the Long-Wharff, *David Ellis* Commander, an Apprentice Boy, about Eighteen Years of Age, of a dark Complection and a middle Stature, named *John Lowder* alias *John Tompson*: He had on when he went away a Cinnamon colour'd Coat, with a light-colour'd Velvet Cape and Brass flat Buttons, a Leather Cap, a dark colour'd Wigg, with light-colour'd Kersey Breeches. Whoever will take up the said Apprentice Boy, and bring him to Capt. *David Ellis*, on board said

Ship, or to *John Row* at his Warehouse, shall receive *Five Pounds* old Tenor; and whoever detains said Apprentice from his Service, or carried him clandestinely away, shall be prosecuted to the utmost Severity of the Law.

The Boston Weekly News-Letter, February 3, 1743; February 10, 1743.

R*AN away from the Sloop Elizabeth, Stephen Eastwicke, Commander, on the 18th of* January *past, the two following Servants, viz. One named* James Blake, *a West Country Fellow, about* 20 *Years old, and has a Cast with one of his Eyes. He had on when he went away, a pair of check'd Plush Breeches, an under Jacket, and a Red Bays upper Jacket, a check'd Shirt, and new Stockings and Shoes. He formerly liv'd with Mr. Gray, Ropemaker.*

The other is an Irish *Lad named* Andrew Barns, *about 19 Years old, and had on a new Kersey double breasted Jacket, and a red Bays Jacket under it, check'd Plush Breeches, and a mill'd Cap. He lately liv'd with Capt.* Temple.

Whoever shall take up the said Fellows, and bring them to the said Eastwicke *in Boston, or in his Absence to Mr.* Charles Apthorpe, *Merchant in said* Boston, *shall have* Ten Pounds *Reward* (old Tenor) *for each of them, and all necessary Charges paid.*

N. B. *All Masters of Vessels and others are hereby cautioned against harbouring, concealing or carrying off the said Servants, as they will answer the same in the Law.* Boston, Feb. 7, 1742-3.

The Boston Evening-Post, February 7, 1743; February 14, 1743.

R*AN-away from his Master Mr.* Elias Robinson *of* Boston, *Shipwright, om Tuesday the* 15*th Instant, a Scot's Man Servant named* Thomas Mathers, *about* 17 *Years of Age, a short well set Fellow, fresh Complexion, blink Ey'd; he had on when he went away a blue Coat, black Jacket, cloth colour'd Breeches, Yarn Stockings, and an old Pair of Shoes. Whoever shall take up the abovesaid Runaway, and him convey to his said Master, shall have forty Shillings Reward, (old Tenor) and all necessary Charges paid.*

The Bost Gazette, or, Weekly Journal, February 22, 1743.

R*AN away from his Master Mr.* Andrew Le Mercier *of* Boston, *an* Irish *Man Servant about one and twenty Years old, pretty tall, of fair Complexion, and pale; hath pretty light Hair, wears sometimes a Worsted Cap, and sometimes a light Wig. He is pretty much pitted with the Small Pox. He had on when he run away, a great blue Coat almost new, with flat Pewter Buttons, a whitish Cloth Jacket, a black one under that, and hath carried away a black pair of Breeches and another of coarse brown Cloth,*

a pair of Yarn Stockings, 2 Cotton and Linen Shirts. Whoever shall apprehend the said Runaway Servant, named David Merkey, and shall convey him to his Master Mr. Le Mercier, shall have Five Pounds Reward, Old Tenor, besides their Charges paid. All Masters of Vessels and others are desired not to conceal or carry away the said runaway Servant.
The Boston Evening-Post, February 28, 1743; March 7, 1743; March 14, 1743.

Newport, Rh Island, March 10. 1743.
RAN away from his Master the 6th or 7th Inst. a tall well set Spanish Negro Man, about 26 Years of Age, is something of a yellowish Complexion, and bow leg'd, talks little or no English, and had on when he ran away, a Castor Hat, a grey homespun double breasted short Jacket, with Metal Buttons, old Breeches and Stockings. All Persons are cautioned against harbouring or entertaining the said Fellow, and whoever takes him up, and brings him to the Subscriber, or conveys Intelligence so as he may come at him, shall have Three Pounds Reward, old Tenor, and all necessary
Charges paid by   Patrick Grant.
The Boston Gazette, or, Weekly Journal, March 15, 1743.

RAN-away on the 15th Instant from Wm Watt of Deer-Island, an Irish Man Servant named Michael Rian, aged about 28 Years, a short young Man with black Hair: He had on when he went away an old black Coat & Jacket, with Hair Buttons, black Breeches with Trousers over them, yarn Stockings, old Shoes with Strings in them.
Whoever shall take up said Runaway and convey him to his said Master, shall have forty Shillings Reward, old Tenor, and all necessary Charges paid.
All Masters of Vessels and others are hereby caution'd against carrying off said Servant on Penalty of the Law.
The Boston Gazette, or, Weekly Journal, March 22, 1743.

RAN-away from his Master Gershom Flegg of Woburn, on the 21st Instant at Night; a Negro Man-Servant, indented for 7 Years, named Pompey York, about 38 Years of Age, of middling Stature, speaks good English, can read and write: He had on, or with him when he went away, a grey homespun Coat turn'd and piec'd flat metal Buttons; a blew Jacket, with metal Buttons, an old Camblet one without Sleeves; also an old blue Shag loose Coat, and a brown Holland one; two good cotten and linnen Shirts, a pair of Leather Breeches with metal Buttons, grey Yarn Stockings, thick strong Shoes, two Castor Hats, one old, the other almost new, sundry Wigs, and a striped Cap. He has also with him Spoon Moulds, and other Tinkers Tools. He walks stooping and waddles as he goes. On his right Hand there are several Specks like Warts. He sometimes undertakes to Exhort, and sometimes to tell Fortunes.

N. B. He had a Manumission of Freedom from *Seth Ross* and *William Crosby* of *Billerica*, before he was indented as aforesaid.

Whosoever shall take up the said Servant and bring him to his Master, or secure him in *Boston, Cambridge*, or *Charlestown* Goal, shall have *Eight Pounds* old Tenor Reward, and all necessary Charges paid.

All Masters of Vessels and others are caution'd not to harbour, conceal or carry off the said Servant, as they would avoid the Penalty of the Law. *Dated March* 25, 1742,3.

The Boston Weekly News-Letter, March 31, 1743; *The Boston Weekly Post-Boy,* April 11, 1743. See *The Boston News-Letter,* From April 22, to April 29, 1742.

R*AN away from Mr.* Benjamin Hallowell *of* Boston, *Shipwright, on Tuesday the 5th Instant, A Negro Boy about* 19 *Years old, named* Paul, *(who formerly belong'd to Major* Lockman*) well set, with a Scar in his Face. He had on when he went away, a blue Jacket, Breeches and Stockings, a striped Cap, and had Brass Buckles in his Shoes. Whoever shall take up the said Negro, and bring him to his abovesaid Master, shall have* Five Pounds Reward, *Old Tenor, and all necessary Charges paid.*

The Boston Evening-Post, April 11, 1743; *The Boston Gazette, or, Weekly Journal,* April 12, 1743; April 19, 1743. Minor differences between the papers.

R*An away from the Ship* Neptune, Andrew Dewar *Commander, lying in the Harbour of* Salem, *on the 5th of this Instant* April, *the three following Sailors, viz.*

William Tanton, *about 5 Feet 8 Inches high, pretty jolly and of a red Complexion, aged about* 26 *Year, and had on a Cap and Hat, a Flannel Jacket trim'd with Black, and a white Pee Jacket and Trouzers.*

John Phillips, *aged about 19 Years, about 5 Feet and an half high, wears a Hat, with a red and green Cap, a white Pee Jacket, a green Wastcoat, a pair of Trouzers, checkered Shag Breeches, and is of a fair Complexion.*

Thomas Keebler, *about five Feet high, is well set, wears a red Jocky Cloth Cap, and a kind of Greigo Watch-Coat.*

Any Person or Persons that shall bring the said Sailors, or any of them, to Mrs. Pratts, *at the Ship Tavern in said* Salem, *or to Messieurs* Gerrish *and* Barrel, *Merchants in* Boston, *shall have* Five Dollars *Reward, Old Tenor, for each of them.*

      And. Dewar.   Boston, April 6. 1743.

The Boston Evening-Post, April 11, 1743.

R*An away from his Master Mr.* Nathaniel Wate *of* Leicester, *on the 5th Day of this Instant* April, *an Irish Man Servant named* George Mc Culluch, *about* 18 *Years old, of a middle Stature, and Pock-broken. He had on when he went away, an old gray Coat and Jacket, a speckled Linen Shirt, with white Wrist-Bands, and one white Shirt; two pair of Yarn Stockings, a pair of Leather Breeches patch'd, a pair of thick Shoes, a new Felt Hat, and a white Cap, and has short Hair. Whoever shall take up the said Servant and bring him to his abovesaid Master, or secure him in any Goal so that his Master may have him again, shall have* Ten Pounds *Reward, Old Tenor, and all necessary Charges paid.* N. B. *All Masters of Vessels and other Persons are hereby cautioned against harbouring, concealing, or carrying off the said Servant, as they would avoid the Penalty of the Law in that Case made and provided.* Dated April 6. 1743.
The Boston Evening-Post, April 18, 1743; April 25, 1743.

DEserted on Thursday the 14th Instant, from the Brig *Industry*, now lying in the Harbour of *Boston, Andrew Gardner* Commander, and [sic] Indian Man named *Eli Moses*, about 30 Years of Age of middle Stature, long Hair, speaks good English. He had on when he went away a bluish colour'd Coat &c. Whoever shall take up said Deserters and bring him to Mr. *Samuel Jackson* on Minots T shall have *forty Shillings* (old Tenor) Reward.
The Boston Gazette, or, Weekly Journal, April 19, 1743.

D*Eserted from the Sloop* Charles, Robert Goulding *Master, lying at the Long Wharf, bound for* Maryland, *two Servant Men, viz.* John Carr, *aged about 42 Years, full Face, talks thick, walks lame, and has swell'd Legs. He had on an old great Coat and a Cap.* Peter Langley, *a young Fellow about* 21 *Years old, with short Hair, and had on an old Great Coat and Cap. He is splaw-footed and walks lame, and can talk good* French. *Whoever shall take up said Deserters, and convey them of board said Sloop, or to* Ebenezer Swan, *at his Warehouse No.* 11 *on the Long Wharf, shall have* Fifteen Pounds *Old Tenor for each and all necessary Charges paid.*
N. B. The Men are both *London* born.
The Boston Evening-Post, April 25, 1743; May 2, 1743.

R*AN away on the 25th of* November *last past from his Master Mr.* Caleb Bennet *of* Portsmouth *on* Rhode-Island *an Indian Lad named* Absalom Jennings, *about* 16 *Years of Age of a middle Stature and well set; had on when he went away a dark mors-colour'd Wastcoat, another grey Wastcoat, with Flannel Sleeves, striped red and blue, a flaunel Shirt strip'd blue and White, a Pair of Breeches made out of a Sheep-Skin, a Pair of Trowsers, a Pair of good Stockings; near the Colour of his upper Wastcoat, and an old Hat cut round like a jockey Cap: He has a Scar upon the out-side of one of* his Legs, about half way from his Knees to his Ankle, right across his Leg. He can work at the Weaver's Trade. Whosoever shall apprehend the said Run away, him safely convey to his said Master, or secure him in any of his Majesty's Goals so that his said Master may have him again, shall have *Five Pounds* Reward old Tenor, and all necessary Charges paid.

Portsmouth, April 22d 1743.

The Boston Weekly Post-Boy, May 2, 1743; May 9, 1743; May 16, 1743.

RAN away from Capt. *John Cunningham*, Commander of the Ship *Peggy*, lying at the Long Wharf in *Boston*, on the 5th of this Instant *May*, the following Servants, *viz.*

Morgan Swiny, a young Lad of a fair Complexion, pretty much freckled, and wears a Wig. He had on when he went away, a dark coloured Frize Coat: He speaks good *English*.

Mary Mansfield, aged about thirty Years, of a brown Complexion, wearing a striped Stuff Gown. She speaks pretty good *English*.

Catharine Fitzgerald, of a black Complexion, pitted with the Small Pox, between 30 and 40 Years old. She had on a blue Stuff Gown when she ran away, and can speak but little *English*.

Elioner Connor, of a black Complexion, and pretty tall. She had on a black Stuff Gown when she ran away, and can speak but little *English*.

Whoever shall take up the said Servants, or any of them, and bring them to their aforesaid Master on board the said Ship, or secure them in any Goal so that he may have them again, shall have *Five Pounds* Reward for each, Old Tenor, and all necessary Charges paid.

N. B. All Masters of Vessels and other Persons are hereby cautioned against harbouring, concealing, or carrying off the said Servants, as they would avoid the Penalty of the Law in that Case made and provided.

Boston, May 7. 1743.

The Boston Evening-Post, May 9, 1743. See *The Boston Evening-Post*, June 6, 1743; June 13, 1743, for the three women. See *The Boston Gazette, or, Weekly Journal*, May 15, 1744.

R*AN away from Mr.* Zachariah Johonnot *of* Boston, *Distiller, on the* 18*th Instant, an Irish Man Servant named* Patrick Shaw, *but calls himself* Patty Sha, *about* 18 *Years old, is a thick short Fellow, with short dark bushy Hair, and speaks pretty good* English. *He had on when he went away, a short blue Jacket, a pair of new Trouzers, gray yarn Stockings, and a good Bever Hat. Whosoever shall take up the said Servant, and bring him to his said Master, living at the South end of* Boston, *shall have* Ten Pounds *Reward, Old Tenor, and all necessary Charges paid. N. B. All Masters of Vessels and other Persons are hereby cautioned against harbouring,*

concealing or carrying off the said Servant, as they would avoid the Penalty of the Law in that Case made and provided.
⁂ *He is full faced and fresh coloured.*
The Boston Evening-Post, May 23, 1743; May 30, 1743.

RAN-away from Mr. *Thomas Johnson* of *Boston,* Joyner, a young Man Servant named *Thomas Clark,* about 19 Years of Age, is well set and of a middling Stature, fine spoken: He carried with him a brown Broad Cloth Coat and Breeches, Dark or Mouse Colour, and one Coat light gray, with large Copper Buttons, one white and several speckled Shirts, one pair gray Hose new, one pair Pumps, one Beaver Hat, one Brownish Wigg, one Cream colour'd stamp'd plush Jacket. He is of a smooth Countenance.
The Boston Gazette, or, Weekly Journal, May 24, 1743.

STolen from *James Macknall* of *Union* in *Windham* in *Connecticut, May* 18th 1743, at Night, a brown Mare, about fourteen Hands and Half high branded with a double **R** (one in the other) on the near Thigh, eight Years old, paces well, *eighty Pounds* Value. The Person suspected to have stolen said Mare, was a Lad named *John Stacy,* about 18 Years of Age, a short well set Fellow, had on a strait bodied Coat, the Collar lin'd with red, brown woollen strait bodied Coat, with white Mettal Buttons, green Jacket, bound round with white Cord, a Pair of Leather Breeches, a new Felt Hat, two Shirts the one coarse the other fine, two Pair of Stockings, a white Linnen Cap.

Whoever shall take up said Lad or Mare, or both of them, and convey them to the aforesaid *James Macknall* of *Union,* shall have *Five Pounds* (old Tenor) Reward, and all necessary Charges
    paid by me, *James Macknall.*
The Boston Gazette, or Weekly Journal, May 31, 1743.

Boston June 3, 1743.
RAN away from Capt. *John Cunningham,* Commander of the Ship *Peggy,* lying in the Harbour of *Boston,* a few Days ago, the three following Women Servants, *viz.*

Mary Mansfield, aged about thirty Years, of a brown Complexion, wearing a striped Stuff Gown. She speaks pretty good *English.*

Catharine Fitzgerald, of a black Complexion, pitted with the Small Pox, between 30 and 40 Years old. She had on a blue Stuff Gown when she ran away, and can speak but little *English.*

Elioner Conner, of a black Complexion, and pretty tall. She had on a black Stuff Gown when she ran away, and can speak but little *English.* Whoever shall take up the said Servants, or any of them, and bring them to their aforesaid Master on board the said Ship, or secure them in any Goal so that he may have them again, shall have *Five Pounds* Reward, Old Tenor, and all necessary Charges paid.

N. B. All Masters of Vessels and other Persons are hereby cautioned against harbouring, concealing, or carrying off the said Servants, as they would avoid the Penalty of the Law in that Case made and provided.

The Boston Evening-Post, June 6, 1743; June 13, 1743. See *The Boston Evening-Post*, May 9, 1743.

RAN away from Capt. *John Henderson* of *Boston*, on the first Instant, a Negro Man named *Charles*, a tall well shap'd Fellow, with a Scar from the lower Part of his Nose through his upper Lip. He had on when he went away, a speckled Shirt, a pair of Trouzers and a Cloth Jacket. Whoever shall take him up, and convey him to his said Master in *Boston*, shall have *Forty Shillings* Reward, Old Tenor, and all necessary Charges paid. All Masters of Vessels and others are cautioned against entertaining or carrying off said Negro, as they would avoid the Penalty of the Law.

The Boston Evening-Post, June 6, 1743; June 13, 1743.

RAN-away from Capt. *John Bulkey* of *Boston* on the 25th of last Month, a Negro Girl named *Billah*, about 18 Years of Age, short of Stature, and well dress'd. Whoever takes her up and brings her to her said Master, shall be satisfied to Content. And all Persons are hereby caution'd against entertaiing, concealing or carrying off said Servant on Penalty of the Law.

The Boston Gazette, or, Weekly Journal, June 7, 1743. See *The Boston Gazette, or Weekly Journal*, November 3, 1747, and *The Boston Gazette, or Weekly Journal*, September 27, 1748.

R*UN-away from* Josiah Browne *of* Sudbury, *on the 6th Day of* June *Instant, A Negro Man named* Sampson, *about 23 Years of Age; middling Stature; has a pretty large Leg, walks light & spritely on the Ground: Had on when he went away, a Castor Hat, a Cap, a dark coloured Coat all Wool, with plain white Metal Buttons, a blue Cloth Jacket, with brass Buttons filled out with Wood & Catgut Eyes, a Cotton & Linnen Shirt, Leather Breeches, white cotton Stockings, a Pair of double-sol'd turn'd Pumps; and took with him a Pair of large Silver Buckles, a dark colour'd Silk Handkerchief. Whoever shall take up said Run-away and him safely convey to his abovesaid Master at* Sudbury, *shall have* Five Pounds *old Tenor Reward.*

The Boston Weekly News-Letter, June 23, 1743; June 30, 1743.

Philadelphia, June 16. 1743.
BROKE out of Prison, on the 11th Instant, at Night, the NOTED and NOTORIOUS TOM BELL, born in New England, generally known by his Rogueries throughout the Colonies, and some Part of the West Indies, and

often changes his Name and Cloaths; he is a slim Fellow, of thin Visage and pale Complexion: Had on when he broke Prison, a dark blue cloth Coat, black silk Jacket, black cloth Breeches, black silk Stockings, new Pumps, with black steel Buckles; and grey Wig; he stole a Great Coat of lightish brown Colour, with brass Buttons. Whoever apprehends the said Bull, and secures him, in any Goal, so that he may be brought to Justice, shall have Five Pounds Reward, and reasonable Charges,
   paid by THOMAS CROSDALE, Sub Sher.
The Pennsylvania Gazette, June 23, 1743. See *The Pennsylvania Gazette*, July 14, 1743, *The Boston Weekly Post-Boy*, August 22, 1743, *The Boston Gazette, or, Weekly Journal*, September 20, 1743, *The Boston Evening-Post*, December 12, 1743, *The Boston Gazette, or Weekly Journal*, May 22, 1744, and *The Boston Weekly Post-Boy*, April 8, 1745, and *The Boston Weekly Post-Boy*, October 5, 1747.

New-Port, July 22. 1743.
RUN-away from Mr. *Philemon Howard* of *New-Port* Barber, on Sunday last the 17th Instant, one *John Walford*, is of low Stature and thin favour'd, had a large Ring-Worm on his Right Cheek; He had on a black Wigg and a Felt Hat, a brown Holland Jacket, a white Linnen Shirt, a Pair of Homespun Linnen Trowsers, grey worsted Stockings, thick Shoes and white Metal Buttons. Whosoever shall apprehend the said Run away, and secure him in any of His Majesty's Goals, and send the aforesaid *Howard* Notice of it, shall have *Forty Shillings* Reward old Tenor paid by me *Philemon Howard.*

All Masters of Vessels are warned not to carry off the aforesaid Servant, as they will answer the same at their Peril.
The Boston Weekly Post-Boy, July 25, 1743.

RUN-away from his Master *John Heulet* of *Scituate*, in the County of *Providence*, in the Colony of *Rhode-Island*, on the First of this Instant *July*, a Molatto Man-Servant, named *Felix*, aged about Twenty-four Years; he is a lusty well-set Fellow, of a middling Stature, pretty square shoulder'd, one of his upper Teeth is out before. He had on when he went away two Jackets, one blue the other Cloth-colour'd, two Shirts, one Linnen the other Flannel, two Pair of Linnen Breeches, a Felt Hat, and a Pair of Homespun Stockings. Whoever shall apprehend the said Run-away Servant, and bring him either to his Master in *Scituate,* or to *Stephen Hopkins*, Esq; in *Providence*, shall have *Five Pounds* old Tenour Reward, and all necessary Charges
   be paid. John Heulet.
   Dated in Scituate aforesaid, July 15. 1743.
New-Port, July 22, 1743.
The Boston Weekly Post-Boy, July 25, 1743.

William Osgood, a stout well set Man, about six Foot high, had on a Cloth Coat and Jacket, a light Wigg, he is of a brown Complection.

John Cunningham, a tall stout Man about six Foot three Inches high, he had on a Cap, cinnamon colour'd Coat or Plaid Banyan, he is about fifty Years of Age, he lived as a Cook formerly with Mr. *Smith* at the Grey Hound Tavern in *Roxbury*.

Robert Stirman, a well set Man about five Foot four Inches high, wears his own Hair, and a red Beard, pock broken, he had on a cotton & linnen Shirt, he is forty Years of Age.

Richard Sylvester, of black Complexion, about five Feet six Inches high, he had on a brown Jacket and a cotton and linnen Shirt: He belongs to *Braintree*.

Whoever shall take up the said Persons, and bring them to the said Goal, shall have *Ten Pounds* for *William Osgood*, and *Five Pounds* for each or either of the rest, (old Tenor) by *William Young*.

The Boston Gazette, or, Weekly Journal, June 28, 1743; July 5, 1743; July 12, 1743.

WHereas *Jean* the Wife of *Joseph Hooker* of said *Westford*, has eloped and absented her self from her said Husband: These are therefore to notify all Persons not to harbour or entertain the said *Jean* upon any Account whatsoever, nor to trust her on any Pretence, for he will not pay any Debt of her contracting: And if the said *Jean* will return and dwell peaceably with her said Husband, she shall be well received. Witness my Hand the Day above said *Joseph Hooker*.

A True Copy of the Original, per *Nath. Russell.*

Cambridge, June 14. 1743.
The Boston Gazette, or, Weekly Journal, June 28, 1743.

RAN-away from on Board the Snow *Katharine, John Pharour* Master, a lusty Negro Fellow named *Robin*; he had on when he went away a speckled Shirt, and a pair of Ozenbrigs Trousers, Whoever shall take up said Runaway and bring him to his Master on Board said Snow lying at *Hutchinson's* Wharfe, shall have *six Pounds* old Tenor Reward, and all necessary Charges paid.

The Boston Gazette, or Weekly Journal, July 12, 1743.

NEW YORK, July 11.
Yesterday was sevnnight the notorious Tom Bell, who lately made his Escape from Philadelphia, was at the Ferry opposite this City: He cross'd over from this side early in Morning in a Pettyauger, without either Coat or Waistcoat, and went to a Publick House there, where having breakfasted, he called for Pen, Ink and Paper, and pretended he was going to write to some

of the most considerable Gentlemen of this City, with whom he was well acquainted, but could not see them till he was provided with Cloaths to appear in, and said he was lately come from Sea, where he had met with Misfortunes and had lost upward of 600 l. and insinuated he was a Son of a Gentleman of Fortune at the East End of Long Island; but being soon known and challenged, he denied that he ever heard of such a Man as Tom Bell; yet said that whoever Tom Bell was, he was a Man that deserved Compassion; and taking his Hat, thought fit to make the best of his Way out at the Back Door, and is no doubt gone to play his Pranks where he is not in so much Danger of being known.

The Pennsylvania Gazette, July 14, 1743. See *The Pennsylvania Gazette*, June 23, 1743, *The Boston Weekly Post-Boy*, August 22, 1743, *The Boston Evening-Post*, December 12, 1743, *The Boston Gazette, or Weekly Journal*, May 22, 1744, *The Boston Weekly Post-Boy*, April 8, 1745, and *The Boston Weekly Post-Boy*, October 5, 1747.

B*Roke out of Bridewell Yesterday, and made his Escape, a lusty, stout and comely Negrow Fellow, named* Dorus, *belonging to Mr.* James Griffin, *Merchant in* Boston. *He had on a Leather Cap, a blue Sailor's Jacket, with Canvas Seams, a pair of Trowsers, and a pair of Shoes. Whoever shall take up the said Negro, and bring him to his abovesaid Master, living in Summer-Street, shall have* Ten Pounds *Reward, Old Tenor, and all necessary Charges paid.*
N. B. *He is suppos'd to be gone towards* Braintree.

The Boston Evening-Post, July 25, 1743; August 1, 1743.

RAN-away the 14th Instant from *Thomas Parkes* of *New-Castle* in the Province of *New-Hampshire*, an Indian Man, named *Samuel Cozens*, a thick set Fellow, with short Hair: He had on when he went away, a strip'd homespun Jacket, long Trowsers, a new Felt Hat, Jersey knit Stockings: Any Person that shall take up said Run-away and convey him to the Goal of said Province, or said *Parker*, shall have *Six Pounds* Reward old Tenor.
   Thomas Parkes.   New Castle, July 14*th* 1743.
The Boston Weekly Post-Boy, July 25, 1743.

WHereas *Abigail* the Wife of *Thomas Gilpen* of *Boston,* Marriner, having been convicted of being found in Bed with another Man; these are to warn all Person not to entertain or trust her on his Account, for he will pay no Debt she may contract.
   Thomas Gilpen.   Boston *July* 22*d* 1743.
The Boston Gazette, or, Weekly Journal, July 26, 1743.

TAKEN away from Mr. *James Dolebeare* of *Boston,* Brasier, some few Days ago, a Negro Female Child called *Rose,* aged about five Years, had on a green Petticoat, and a white Wastecoat, and has a large Scar on one of her Breasts. If any Person can give Information to said *Dolbeare,* where said Negro may be found; it being apprehended that she is concealed by some ill minded and malicious Persons, the Person that makes the Discovery shall be suitable rewarded. And all Persons are hereby fore warned from entertaining the said Negro on any Pretence whatever at their Peril, even
          Mr. *Benjamin Babbidge* himself.
   The Boston Gazette, or, Weekly Journal, August 2, 1743.

RUN-away from *Robert Morris,* now residing in *New-Port, Rhode-Island,* Marriner, on the 3d of *August,* a Servant Man, named *Thomas Hutchinson,* a very lusty Fellow of a red Complection, his Face and Hands much freckled; had on a new double breasted red Jacket and red Breeches, a blew Rug great Coat; a brown Jacket without Sleeves; one Pair of Shoes, half wore, the upper Leathers very smooth; a new Frock and Trowsers, and several Pair of old Stockings: He carryed a Bagg with him, in which he put some of the Things mentioned. Whosoever shall apprehend the said Runaway. and bring him to said *Morris* in *New-Port,* shall have *Five Pounds* old Tenor Reward, and reasonable Charges
        paid by   *Robert Morris.*
   The Boston Weekly Post-Boy, August 15, 1743; August 22, 1743.

        Portsmouth, New-Hampshire, August 19.
   Notice is hereby given to the Publick to be upon their Guard for in all probability, the famous, or rather infamous *Tom Bell* is upon the Line" A Person exactly answering his Character (had from many Places) has this Week broke open a Chest, and carried off considerable Moneys and Goods of value from several Persons, He says he has been Prisoner at St. Augustine 9 or 10 Months, and that he came from Eustatia: He is very shy in telling his Name; tho' to some he said it was Winslow. He went hence Yesterday at Noon, had on a blue riding Coat, strip'd Holland Shirt, a white Cap and Handkerchief. The Catchpole is after him; and if he can haply lay his ample Hand upon his Shoulder, his Body obsequious to the touch, will be convey'd to our inchanted Castle, Francis *T*ucker Commandant: The above Chap is very grave & serious, has a ready invention, with a good Elocution; and he has ('tis tho't) already deceived many here.
    The Boston Weekly Post-Boy, August 22, 1743. See *The Boston Gazette, or, Weekly Journal,* September 20, 1743, *The Boston Evening-Post,* December 12, 1743, *The Boston Gazette, or Weekly Journal,* May 22, 1744, *The Boston Weekly Post-Boy,* April 8, 1745, and *The Boston Weekly Post-Boy,* October 5, 1747.

RAN-away from Mr. *Daniel Jent Tuckerman,* of *Boston,* Taylor, on the 20th Instant *August,* an Irish Man Servant, named *Francis Mc'Coy,* about 19 Years of Age, a tall well set Fellow, of a pale Complection; he had on when he went away, a blue Cloth Coat, trim'd with the same Colour, and with red Lining, an Olive-coloured Cloth Jacket, and light colour'd Cloth Breeches, white Stockings, and a new Pair of Shoes, he took with him two Wigs, one dark the other Light.

'Tis tho't he is gone away with another young Fellow.

Whoever shall take up the abovesaid Runaway and him safely convey to his said Master, shall have *Five Pounds* (old Tenor) Reward, and all necessary Charges paid.

The Boston Gazette, or, Weekly Journal, August 23, 1743.

WHEREAS a Negro Fellow about 40 Years of Age who calls his Name *Quan,* a stout well set Fellow, large Eyes, speaks broken English, who says, he was formerly a Servant to Mr. *James* at *Casco* but is now free, and goes about seeking Employ at Farming; and for that purpose came to Mr. *Wm Cheney* of *Roxbury,* on the 25th of last Month, where he now is; but it being suspected he might be a Runaway Servant, This publick Notice in given, that his Master or Owner (if he has any) may repair to said *Cheney,* and take him away paying Charges.

The Boston Weekly News-Letter, September 1, 1743; September 22, 1743.

W*Hereas my Wife* Eleanor Lovett *has eloped and is now in the Town of* Woodstock, *and refuses to return; These are to forewarn all Persons from trusting or crediting her the said* Eleanor, *or giving any Credit on my Account; for I do hereby declare, that I will not pay one Farthing for any Debt which she shall contract. In Witness whereof I have hereunto set my Hand, this* 19 *Day of* August, Anno Domini, 1743.

     Joseph Lovett.

The Boston Evening-Post, September 5, 1743.

W*Hereas* Ann Linard, *the Wife of me the Subscriber,* Henry Linard, *of* Boston, *Turner, hath for some Time past absented herself from my House, and is entertained by some ill minded Persons: This is to desire the said* Ann *to return home to me, where she shall be kindly entertained; and also give Notice to all Persons not to entertain or harbour her, as they will answer the contrary at their Peril. And further, that I will not pay any Debts heretofore or since her absenting, or hereafter to be by per contracted.*

    Henry Linard. *Dated* 12*th* September 1743.

The Boston Evening-Post, September 12, 1743.

R*Anaway from Capt.* Thomas Frankland, *Commander of His Majesty's Ship* Rose, *a Negro Man Servant named* Joseph Green, *about 5 Feet 6 Inches high, speaks good English, had on a light coloured Cloth Jacket and a pair of Trowsers, is about 22 Years old.*
    Whoever takes up said Negro and brings him to the Collector Henry Frankland, *Esq; in* Boston, *shall have* five Pounds *Reward, old Tenor, and all necessary Charges.*
    And all Masters of Vessels are forbid carrying off said Servant on Penalty of the Law.
    The Boston Gazette, or, Weekly Journal, September 13, 1743.

R*AN away from Mr.* James Clark *of* Biddiford, *at the Eastward, about two Months ago, a Negro Man named* Quambe, *about* 40 *Years old, He has a Hurt on two of his Fingers, and his Face is a little on one side. Whoevr shall take up said Negro, and bring him to Mr.* Benjamin Mathes *or* Joseph Sias *at* Durham *in* New-Hampsire, *shall have* Five Pounds Reward, Old Tenor, *(or secure him and send them Word) and all necessary Charges paid.*
    The Boston Evening-Post, September 18, 1743.

A Certain Person came to the House of Mr. *James Hay* of Charlstown on Friday Night last to lodge, and call'd his Name *Woodbridge*, and tarry'd till last Night; he has stole from said *Hay* a Piece of black Velvet, a Piece of Chints, some coin'd Money, and sundry other Things: If they should be offer'd to Sale, it's desir'd they may be stopt: The said Person is tho't to be the famous *Tom Bell*; he had on when he went away a new red Ratteen great Coat with a red Velvet Cape.   Charlstown, Sept. 19. 1743.
    The Boston Gazette, or, Weekly Journal, September 20, 1743. See *The Boston Weekly Post-Boy*, August 22, 1743, *The Boston Evening-Post*, December 12, 1743, *The Boston Gazette, or Weekly Journal*, May 22, 1744, *The Boston Weekly Post-Boy*, April 8, 1745, and *The Boston Weekly Post-Boy*, October 5, 1747.

WHereas *Martha* the Wife of *Joseph Tidd* of *Woburn*, hath eloped from her said Husband, and hath run him considerable in Debt: These are therefore to warn all Persons against trusting her on her said Husband's Account, for he will not pay and Debts she shall contract after the Publication hereof.
    Joseph Tidd.   *Woburn, Sept.* 26. 1743.
    The Boston Gazette, or, Weekly Journal, September 27, 1763.

R*An away from Capt.* Benjamin Waldo *of* Boston, *on the 26th of this Instant* September, *an* Irish *Servant Lad named* William Poor, *about* 17 *Years old, of a midling Stature, with fair Complexion, and had short light*

Hair. He had on when he went away, a blue speckled Shirt, a woollen Jacket, Leather Cap, and Silver Buckles in his Shoes. He had also sundry other Clothes with him.

Whoever shall take up the said Servant, and bring him to Mr. Charles Apthorpe, *Merchant in* Boston, *shall have* Three Pounds *Reward, and all necessary Charges paid.* N. B. *All Masters of Vessels and other Persons are hereby cautioned against harbouring, concealing or carrying off the said Servant, as they would avoid the Penalty of the Law in that Case made and Provided.*

The Boston Evening-Post, October 3, 1743; October 10, 1743.

WHEREAS *Sarah*, the Wife of *Philip Jenkins* of *Brunswick* in the County of *York*, hath eloped from her said Husband, and run him very much in Debt:

This is therefore to warn all Persons against trusting her on my Account, for I will pay no Debts contracted by her after this Day.

    As witness my Hand,
          Philip Jenkins.   Brunswick Oct. 8. 1743.
The Boston Gazette, or, Weekly Journal, October 11, 1743.

W*Hereas the under-mentioned Persons have deserted from his Majesty's Sloop* Hawk, *under my Command, and some of them rob'd the said Sloop of her Boat: These are to give Notice, that whoever shall give Intelligence of the said Persons, or any of them, so that they may be apprehended and delivered to Capt.* THOMAS FRANKLAND, *Commander of his Majesty's Ship* Rose, *shall have* Five Pounds Old Tenor *for each Man deliver'd, and all reasonable Charges. And whoever shall entertain or give Encouragement to any of the said Deserters, shall be prosecuted with the utmost Severity of the Law.*
ARTHUR FORREST, Hawk Sloop, Octob. 12th. 1743.

The Names of those who stole the Boat, are as follow.
Thomas Burkell, George Harris, Timothy Parkeson, John Whitworth, John Brown, *and* John Carso.
The other Deserters are,
John Anderson, Stepen Reed, Daniel Plastead, *and* David Marchell.

N. B. *The Boat is* Deal *built, Clinch Work,* 17 *Feet Long, new, and has a Box abaft for a Cockswain, and this* ↑ *Mark upon her Stern.*
The Boston Evening-Post, October 17, 1743; October 24, 1743.

W*Hereas* Cambridge, *a Negro Man belonging to* James Oliver *of* Boston, *doth absent himself sometimes from his Master; Said Negro plays well upon a Flute, and not so well on a Violin. This is to desire all Masters and Heads of Families not to suffer said Negro to come into their Houses to each their*

Prentices or Servants to play, nor to any other Accounts. All Masters of Vessels are also forbid to have any thing to do with him on any Account, as they may answer it in the Law.

N. B. *Said Negro is to be sold: Enquire said* Oliver.

The Boston Evening-Post, October 17, 1743; November 7, 1743. See The Boston Evening-Post, June 9, 1740, and The Boston Evening-Post, January 9, 1744.

RAN-away on the 12th Instant from the Widow *Sarah White* of *Haverhill*, a Negro Man named *Scipio*, aged about thirty, a well set Fellow of a middle Stature: He had on when he went away a new Felt Hat, a dark colour'd woollen Jacket, brown breeches and yarn Stockings; walks something limping. Whoever shall take up the said Negro and convey him to or give Notice of him so that his said Mistress may have him again, shall have *five Pounds* Reward old Tenor, & all necessary Charges paid.

The Boston Gazette, or Weekly Journal, October 18, 1743. See The Boston Weekly News-Letter, October 20, 1743.

RAN-away on the 12th Instant from the Widow *Sarah White* of *Haverhill*, a Negro Man named *Scipio*, about 30 Years of Age, a well set Fellow of middle Stature, had on when he went away, a new felt Hat, a dark woollen Coat with Pewter Buttons, light colour'd woollen Jacket, brown breeches and grey yarn Stockings: He limps a little as he goes.

Whoever shall take up the said Negro and convey him to his said Mistress in *Haverhill* aforesaid, shall have *Five Pounds* Reward, old Tenor, and necessary Charges paid.

The Boston Weekly News-Letter, October 20, 1743; October 27, 1743; November 3, 1743. See The Boston Gazette, or Weekly Journal, October 18, 1743.

RAN-away the 24th September, *from his Master* Joseph Guile *of* Scituate, *in the County of* Providence; *a Negro Man Servant, named* Proiperous; *about Thirty Years of Age, of a middle Stature, but Slim; with Scars in his Face, and a large Scare* [sic] *on one of his Ankle Joints, speaks good English:—He had on when he went away, a Beaver Hat, a bluish gray Coat, fac'd with Red; a red Camblet Jacket, a fine white Shirt, dy'd Leather Breeches, and white Stockings, with some other Cloathes.—He carried away about Forty Pounds in Money with him.—Whoever shall take up the abovesaid Negro; and him safely convey to his abovesaid Master, shall have* Ten Pounds *old Tenor Reward, and all necessary Charges paid by* Joseph Guile.

N B. *if said Negro should be taken up in any of the neighbouring Governments, they are desired to secure him in his Majesty's Goal; and*

give Notice to said Guile, *or to* Robert Gibbs, *Esq; in* Providence *who will be speedy in sending for him.*
The Boston Weekly Post-Boy, October 24, 1743; October 31, 1743.

R*AN-away from Capt.* Philip Wheeler *of Rehoboth the* 28 *Instant, an Indian Fellow, nam'd* Nathan Harris, *about* 19 *Years of Age, a stout well set Fellow, has short Hair, one of his Fingers crooked; he had on a blue worsted Jacket lin'd partly with blue Shalloon; & partly with striped Flannel, also two Flannel Jackets striped blue red & white, took with him two Shirts, one Toe & Linnen, the other checker'd blue & white Cotton & Worsted, Leather Breeches, worsted Stockings, new Shoes, felt Hat the brim crop'd. Whoever shall take up said Indian, & bring him to his Master in Rehoboth, or secure him so that he may be had again, shall have* three Pounds *Reward old Tenor, and necessary Charges paid.*
And all Masters of Vessels are caution'd against carrying off said Servant, on Penalty of the Law. Rehoboth, *Octob.* 29. 1743,
The Boston Gazette, or Weekly Journal, November 1, 1743.

DEserted from the Ship *Molly, William Coupland* Commander, Two Irish Servant Boys, viz. *James McCannon*, about 20 Years of Age, pretty tall, wears a black Wigg, and *Bryan O'Cannon*, about 19 Years old, middle siz'd well set wears a Wigg. Whoever apprehends said Servants or either of them, and brings them to Capt. *George Nicholson*, or to Messi. *Gough* and *Noye's* Warehouse on the Town-Dock, shall be satisfied for their Trouble.
Boston, November 8, 1743.
The Boston Weekly News-Letter, November 17, 1743; November 25, 1743; December 1, 1743.

R*AN*-away on Saturday last 20th Instant, from Capt. *Jonah Casker* now residing in *Boston*, a Welsh Man-Servant, named *George Carrow*, about 18 Years of Age, middle Stature, brown Complection. He had on when he went away, a brown cloth Jacket, large Oznabrigs Trowsers, yarn Stockings, and a Pair of Pumps.
Whoever shall take up the abovesaid Runaway, and bring him to his said Master, on board the Ship Milk-River at *Clark's* Wharff, or Mr. *David Evans* near the *T*own-House, shall have Five Pounds Reward, old *T*enor, and all necessary Charges paid.
And all Masters of Vessels are hereby caution'd against carrying off said Servant on Penalty of the Law.
The Boston Weekly News-Letter, December 1, 1743; December 8, 1743; December 15, 1743.

ON Monday Evening, the fifth of this Instant *December*, escaped out of his Majesty's Goal in *Charlestown*, by a false Key, the noted *Thomas Bell*. He is about 30 Years of Age, of a midling Stature, of a ruddy Complexion, of a pleasant Countenance, and has a handsom Set of Teeth, and shows his upper Teeth when he speaks. He has a variety of Cloaths, and appears sometimes in one Dress, and sometimes in another; he also goes sometimes by one Name and sometimes by another; he also goes sometimes by one Name and sometimes by another. His Discourse is polite, and he is of a spritely Look and Gesture.

Whoever shall take up the said *Thomas Bell*, and convey him to his Majesty's Goal in *Charlestown* aforesaid, shall have a Reward of *Fifteen Pounds*, Old Tenor, paid by *John Chamberlain*, Keeper of said Prison.
December the 6th. 1743.
The Boston Evening-Post, December 12, 1743; December 19, 1743. See *The Pennsylvania Gazette*, June 23, 1743, *The Pennsylvania Gazette*, July 14, 1743, and *The Boston Weekly Post-Boy*, August 22, 1743.

RAN away from the Ship *Providence, John Parr* Master, on the 9th of *December*, 1743. *John Scudder*, who if he will return to his Duty on board the said Ship in five Days from the Date hereof, he shall be kindly received, but if not, he shall be deemed a Deserter, and treated accordingly.
The Boston Evening-Post, December 26, 1743; January 2, 1744.

1744

R*AN away from Capt.* James Oliver *of* Boston, *a Negro Man named* Cambridge, *about* 27 *Years old and Pockbroken, that has been used to work at the Baker's Trade. He had on a new double breasted light coloured Cloth Jacket, with flat Metal Buttons, lined with blue Bays, and a great Coat and Breeches of the same Cloth, or else a pair of blue Cloth Breeches, and a Seal-skin Cap. Whoever takes him up, and brings him to his abovesaid Master, shall have* 40s. *Reward, old Tenor, and all necessary Charges. And all Masters of Vessels are forbid carrying him off at their Peril.*
The Boston Evening-Post, January 9, 1744. See *The Boston Evening-Post*, June 9, 1740. See *The Boston Evening-Post*, October 17, 1743.

WHEREAS Jane Williams *the Wife of* Jonathan Williams *of said* Beverly, *hath run him in Debt, and squander'd away a considerable Part of his Estate;*

THIS is to caution all Persons whatsoever against trading with her, and to inform them, that her said Husband will not pay any Debt she shall contract after this Date, as witness my Hand,
Jonathan Williams.
The Boston Weekly Post-Boy, January 9, 1744; January 16, 1744.

RAN-away from Mr. John Pullen, a Portugueze Molatto Man Servant, named *Emanuel Mashatbe*, about 20 Years of Age, of middle Stature, black Hair, a dark colour'd Bearskin Coat with brass Buttons, green Jacket, light colour'd worsted Stockings, and a pair of thick Shoes. He went away on Saturday Night last the 7th Instant. Whoever shall take up the abovesaid Run-away, and him safely convey to his abovesaid Master in *Boston*, shall have *Three Pounds* Reward, old Tenor, and all necessary Charges paid. All Masters of Vessels are forbid carrying off said Servant on Penalty of the Law.
The Boston Weekly News-Letter, January 12, 1744; January 19, 1744.

RAN-away from his Master *John Gardner*, Commander of the Brigt. *Sarah*, lying at the North End of *Boston*, the 15th Instant, an English young Man Servant named *Jacob Wood*, about 18 Years of Age, wears a Cap, and had on when he went away, a blue Cloth Coat with white Mettal Buttons, a white Jacket and Breeches, speckled Shirt, but took with him several other Sorts of Cloathing, something bandy Legged, and sharp'd Ey'd. He is a thick well set Fellow.

Whoever shall take up said Servant, and bring him to his said Master on board the said Brigt. or to Mr. *Thomas Greenough* at his Shop in Ann-street Boston shall have *Four Pounds* Reward, (old Tenor) and all necessary Charges paid.

All Masters of Vessels and others are hereby caution'd against harbouring concealing or carrying off said Servant, as they would avoid the Penalty of the Law in that Case made and provided.
Boston, Jan. 16. 1743,4.
The Boston Gazette, or, Weekly Journal, January 17, 1744.

R*An-away from* Joseph Inches, *Master of the Brigantine* John, *lying at the Long Wharf in* Boston, *on the 20th Instant, a likely Servant Boy named* William Bailey, *about 14 Years of Age, small of Stature, and of a fair Complexion, born in* Somersetshire, *in* England, *speaks quick, and has a Scar in his Forehead. He has on when he went away, two blue Jackets, the upper on a Pee Jacket, double breasted, with Leather Buttons, an old worsted Cap, a Felt Hat, an old pair of Trowsers, a pair of blue Breeches, a pair of light blue worsted Stockings, Shoes half worn, and a large pair of Steel Buckles. Whoever shall take up the said Servant, and safely convey*

him to his said Master, shall have Forty Shillings *Reward, Old Tenor, and all necessary Charges paid. And all Masters of Vessels and others are cautioned against concealing or carrying off said Servant, as they will avoid the Penalty of the Law.*
   The Boston Evening-Post, January 23, 1744; January 30, 1744.

RAN away on the 7th Instant, from Mr. *Thomas Dean,* of *Dedham,* a young Man Servant, named *Elijah Galliver,* about 18 Years old, lusty thick Fellow, short Hair, but may wear a Cap with plain Pewter Buttons, took four Shirts. Whoever takes and conveys said Servant to his Master, shall have £3 old Tenor and necessary Charges. And all persons are forbid entertaining or carrying off said Servant.   Boston Febr. 10, 1743,4
   The Boston Gazette, or, Weekly Journal, February 14, 1744.

Boston, March 7. 1743,4.
DEserted this Day from the Ship *Leghorn Galley, David Ellis* Commander, *Andrew Fletcher,* a Dutchman, Carpenter of said Ship, a lusty well-set Man, of a dark Complexion, speaks broken English. He is hereby notified, that unless he returns to the said Ship, or the Commander thereof by To-morrow at 12 o'Clock, he will be deemed a Deserter.
   The Boston Weekly News-Letter, March 8, 1744.

DEserted two Days ago from the Ship *Britannia, Jeremiah Fones* Commander, *Francis Kidwill,* a Sailor. This is to notify him that unless he returns to his Duty on board said Ship within three Days he will be deem'd a Deserter.
   The Boston Weekly News-Letter, March 8, 1744.

RAN *away from his Majesty's Goal in Providence, one* Ezekiel Brock, *late resident in* Scituate, *in the County of* Providence. *He is inclining to tall, about* 35 *Years of Age; had on when he went away, a blue homespun Coat and Jacket: He wears his own Hair, black and curled, and is hard of hearing.* N. B. *He absented himself on Wednesday Evening the* 28*th of this Instant. Whoever shall take up said Runaway, and him safely convey to said Goal, shall have* Five Pounds *Reward, (Old Tenor,) and all Necessary Charges paid.   Per* Samuel Westcot, *Goal-Keeper.*
                                         Providence, March 29th. 1744.
   The Boston Evening-Post, April 9, 1744; April 16, 1744; April 23, 1744.

RAN away from his Master *Joseph Abbe,* of *Ipswich,* on the 17th Instant, a white Servant *M*an, named *John Wells,* aged about 18 Years, a short thick Fellow. He had on when he went away, a blue Coat with hard *M*ettle

Buttons, and a double brested red Waistcoat trim'd with Black, or a grey whal'd Waistcoat double brested, trim'd with hard *M*ettle Buttons, a short dark Peruke, brown Breeches, grey yearn Stockings, and a white Shirt. Whoever shall take up said Servant, and safely convey him to his said *M*aster at *Ipswich*, or secure the said Fellow in *Boston*, shall have five Pounds old Tenor Reward, and all necessary Charge paid.

All Masters of Vessels are others are caution'd from concealing or carrying off said Servant, as they would avoid the Penalty of the Law.

The Boston Weekly Post-Boy, April 14, 1744; April 23, 1744; April 30, 1744; May 14, 1744.

STollen and carried away out of the House of *Jonathan Lawrence* of *Norton* in the County of *Bristol*, on the 15th Instant, a blue Broad Cloth Coat, with Hair Buttons, one yard and half of black Broad Cloth, one pair of worsted Stockings, a Holland Shirt, ruffled, one Linen check'd Shirt, a black Wig, a fine Holland Jacket, and it's thought sundry other Things yet unknown. The aforesaid Things were taken away and carried away by an *Irish* Man of about 30 Years old, of midling Stature; he had on a brown Camblet Coat, much wore, a black Wig, a small brim'd Hat, black Plush Breeches, thick Leather Shoes, with Brass Buckles, and generally wears a black Velvet Band or Stock about his Neck. He is a thin faced Man, of a dark Complexion, and has been one of those called *New-Light* Preachers, and still inclines to be so. He has a liberal Education, writes well, and has a very smooth and deceitful Tongue. He calls himself by several Names, viz. *John St. Ambrose*, or *John Ambrose*, but changes his Name as suits him best. Whoever will take up the said *John*, and bring him to the said *Jonathan Lawrence*, shall have *Six Pounds*, old Tenor Reward, and all necessary Charges paid, by   Jonathan Lawrence. *April* 16, 1744.

The Boston Evening-Post, April 15, 1744; April 23, 1744; April 30, 1744.

RAN-away from his Master *John Henderson* of *Boston*, on the 12th Instant at Night, a bought Irish Servant Man, named *Charles McGlocklin*, aged about Twenty-five Years, streight Limb'd, of a fair Complexion. He had on when he went away, an old Castor Hat, a white Cap or an old light Wigg, his Head lately shav'd, a blew Cloth Waistcoat with Mettal Buttons a great Coat and a Pair of Breeches of the same, with a Pair of dirty brown Holland Breeches over them, an old Pair of blew worsted Stockings, a good Pair of Shoes, a Pair of Steel Buckles black'd over. Whoever shall take up said Servant, and safely Convey him to his said Master living near Summer-Street, shall have *Three Pounds* old Tenor Reward, and all necessary Charges paid.

All Masters of Vessels and others are hereby caution'd from concealing or carrying off said Servant, as they would avoid the Penalty of the Law.   *Boston April* 16, 1744.

The Boston Weekly Post-Boy, April 16, 1744; April 23, 1744; April 30, 1744.

RAN-away from Mr. *James Bailey* of *Watertown an* Scots Man Servant named *James Gall* about 20 Years of Age, thin Face, long Visage, dark Complection, has a Coat on with Pewter Buttons with Admiral *Vernon* two and two with Feet to Feet. Whoever takes up and brings him to his said Master or to the Printers, shall have *five Pounds* old Tenor, and all other Charges. And all Masters of Vessels are forbid carrying him off.
    April 13. 1744.

The Boston Gazette, or, Weekly Journal, April 24, 1744; May 1, 1744.

RAN-away from Mrs. *Eleanor Pullen*, on Monday the 9th of this Instant *April*, a Negro Woman named *Cuba*, about 36 Years of Age, a well-set Wench, with a Scar over one Eye-Brow, has lost one or two of her fore Teeth, and speaks good English. She had on when she ran away, a striped homespun Jacket and Petticoat, a quilted Petticoat, two Strings of black and white Beads about her Neck, a Cotton & Linnen Shift, a Mob, a coarse Apron, Stockings, and Shoes with Buckles.

Whoever shall take up the said Run-away, and bring her to Mrs. *Pullen*, living in Corn-Court, near *Faneuil-Hall*, shall have *Twenty Shillings* (old Tenor) Reward, and all necessary Charges paid. All persons are hereby notified not to harbour, conceal, or carry off said Negro, as they would avoid the Penalty of the Law.

The Boston Weekly Post-Boy, April 30, 1744; May 7, 1744; May 14, 1744. See *The Boston Gazette*, From January 17, to January 24, 1737, *The Boston Weekly Post-Boy*, July 9, 1744, and *The Boston Weekly Post-Boy*, August 6, 1744.

    Boston, May 3d. 1744.
RAN-away on Tuesday Night last, a Man-Servant about 19 Years of Age, named *Abraham Stillwell*, of a thick, short Stature, full fac'd, fresh colour'd, having on an old ragged Coat, a good check'd Shirt and Trowsers, a Pair of black Callamanco Breeches, a Pair of grey Yarn Stockings, and a new Pair of Shoes. Whoever shall take up the said Servant and convey him to his Master *Josiah Jones*, living in Fleet-Street near the Rev. Mr. *Mather's* Meeting House, shall be well rewarded by me *Josiah Jones*.

The Boston Weekly News-Letter, May 3, 1744; May 17, 1744; May 24, 1744.

Province of New-Hampshire, London-derry, May 2. 1744.
A Stray Negro Woman about 24 Years of Age, middle Stature cloathed with a striped Cotton and Linnen Gown, a Flesh colour'd Petticoat, born as she says at *Long-Island,* and free, served her Time in *Connecticut* Government, and is now in the House of the Rev. Mr. *David MacGregory* in said Town, where she may be delivered to the right Owner paying all necessary Charges.
The Boston Weekly Post-Boy, May 7, 1744; May 21, 1744.

RAN-away from Mr. *Samuel Lock* of *Cambridge*, a Scot Man Servant named *Daniel M'Pherson,* about 20 Years of Age a short thin Fellow, black Hair, pock-broken; had on when he went away a Sea green Camblet Waistcoat, a blue half thick ditto, a pair of wash Leather Breeches, with white Mettal Buttons, black yarn Stockings, old Shoes, and an old Beaver Hat. It's tho't he will cut off his Hair and disguise himself. Whoever shall take up the said Runaway, and bring him to his said Masters in *Watertown* and *Cambridge,* shall have *ten Pounds* Reward (old Tenor) and all necessary Charges paid. All Masters of Vessels are hereby caution'd against carrying off said Servant, on Penalty of the Law.
Boston, April 30. 1744.
The Boston Gazette, or Weekly Journal, May 8, 1744.

R*AN away from his Master Mr.* James Raymar *of* Boston, *Cordwainer, on the 8th of this Instant* May, *a Servant Man named* Elias Bellow, *aged about Nineteen Years, of a middle Stature, of black Complexion, has black Eyes, and short black Hair. He had with him when he went away, an old Cloth coloured great Coat, a light blue Jacket, and a Cloth coloured Duroy Jacket under it; Leather Breeches, and had with him both blue Worsted and gray Yarn Stockings, and an old pair of Shoes: one of them mended in the upper Leather at the Toe.*
Whoever shall take up the said Servant, and him safely convey to his abovesaid Master, living in Marlborough-Street *towards the South End of* Boston, *shall have* Five Pounds *Reward, Old Tenor, and all necessary Charges paid.* N. B. *All Masters of Vessels and other Persons are hereby cautioned against harbouring, concealing, or carrying off the said Servant, as they would avoid the Penalty of the Law in that Case made and provided.*
Boston, May 11, 1744.
The Boston Evening-Post, May 14, 1744; May 21, 1744; May 28, 1744.

WHEREAS *Honour Rook,* the Wife of *James Rook,* hath by divers notorious Actions greatly injured the said *James Rook* in his Business and Interest, in so much that the said *James Rook* is oblig'd to break up his

Family to prevent further Charge and Difficulty. Therefore he forbids hereby all Persons to trust his Wife for any Thing on his Account, for he now declars that he will not pay any Debts whatsoever that she shall contract after the Date hereof.
      James Rook.   *Boston, May* 12. 1744.
 The Boston Evening-Post, May 14, 1744; May 21, 1744; May 28, 1744.

RAN-away from Mr. *Jeremiah Dexter,* of *Walpole,* on the 11th Instant at Night, an Irish Lad Servant nam'd *Morgan Sweney,* about 16 Years of Age, middling Stature, something freckled, and has a Scar on one of his Legs a little below his Knee; He had on when he went away an old Felt Hat, a Cotton & Linnen Cap, a Tow Shirt, a Cinnamon colour'd Jacket, with white Mettle flower'd Buttons, an old black Coat, much torn, Linnen Breeches grey Yarn Stockings, round to'd Shoes with Strings.
 Whoever shall take up the abovesaid Runaway, and bring him to his said Master at *Walpole,* or secure him in *Boston* Bridewell, shall have *Three Pounds* (old Tenor) Reward, and all necessary Charges paid. All Masters of Vessels and others are hereby caution'd against concealing or carrying off said Servant on Penalty of the Law.   *Boston, May* 14th, 1744.
 The Boston Gazette, or Weekly Journal, May 15, 1744; May 22, 1744.
 See *The Boston Evening-Post,* May 9, 1743, for Swiny/Sweny

DEserted from on Board the Ship Mary, *Thomas Cornish* Master, a Scots Man Sailor, nam'd *John Robinson,* of middle Stature, wears a Wigg. Whoever will apprehend him and bring him on board said Ship, shall have 40*s.* old Tenor Reward.
 The Boston Gazette, or Weekly Journal, May 15, 1744.

RAN-away on the 10th Instant at Night, from his Master *William Dickson* Leather-Breeches Maker in *Boston,* a Servant Lad named *John Smith,* about 16 Years of Age, of middling Stature, a fair Complexion. He had on when he went away, a Coat of a dark blew Colour, mix'd with white, a pair of Leather Breeches, a check'd Shirt, yarn Stockings, a strip'd worsted Cap or a black Wigg, a Castor Hat, and a pair of Shoes half worn. He has a Scar on one of his Legs, a little below the Knee. Whoever shall take up the said Servant, and convey him to his Master in *Newbury-street, Boston,* shall have *Three Pounds* Old Tenor, Reward, and all necessary Charges paid.
 All Masters of Vessels and Others, are hereby caution'd against concealing or carrying off said Servant, as they would avoid the Penalty of the Law.
 The Boston Weekly News-Letter, May 17, 1744; May 24, 1744.

WHereas *Margaret Rust* the Wife of *Benjamin Rust* hath by diverse notorious Actions greatly injured the said *Benjamin*, in his Absence, and refuses to live with the said *Benjamin*, insomuch that he is obliged to break up his Family to prevent further Charge and Difficulty: Therefore he hereby forbids all Persons to trust his said Wife for any Thing, or to pay any Money to her upon his Account, for he now declares he will not pay any Debts, or allow any Accounts that she shall contract after the Date hereof.
     Benjamin Rust. Portsmouth, New-Hampshire,
                 May 17. 1744.
 The Boston Weekly Post-Boy, May 21, 1744.

We hear that the famous Mr. THOMAS BELL *was on Friday last lawfully discharg'd from his Confinement, and is now in this Town, having already waited on several Gentlemen of Ability and Character* (*whose Names he has personated*) *in order to make suitable Acknowledgements for so unworthy a Behaviour. We likewise hear he intended* (*by divine Assistance*) *effectually and intirely to reverse his past Conduct: Therefore 'tis to be hop'd all well dispos'd Persons will encourage him in so laudable an Undertaking, especially as he is well known to be a Person capable to improve or abuse his Liberty to the best or worst Ends and Purposes.*
 The Boston Gazette, or Weekly Journal, May 22, 1744. See *The Pennsylvania Gazette*, June 23, 1743, *The Pennsylvania Gazette*, July 14, 1743, *The Boston Weekly Post-Boy*, August 22, 1743, *The Boston Gazette, or, Weekly Journal*, September 20, 1743, and *The Boston Evening-Post*, December 12, 1743.

DEserted on the 18th Instant from the Ship Industry *Wm Curling* Commander, *Richard Fulford*, about 22 Years old, slight body'd, pale Complection, and in Sailor's Habit when he went away.
 As also *Jasper Bedeorn* about the same Age, well set, of a fresh colour, and is Sailor's Habit when he went away.
 If the said Sailors will return to their Duty they shall be kindly received, otherwise they will be deem'd Deserters.
 The Boston Gazette, or, Weekly Journal, May 29, 1744; June 12, 1744.

              Newport, May 21st, 1744.
R*AN away on the* 16*th of this Instant* May *in the Night, from his Master* Evan Mallbone *of* Newport, *a Negro Man named* Cuff, *he formerly belonged to* Thomas Borden *of* Portsmouth, *and used to tend said* Borden's *Ferry; he is a stout lusty Fellow, aged about thirty Years; had on when he run away, a speckled Shirt and an Ozenbrig Frock and Trowsers, pretty*

much tarred, and leather Breeches; and took with him a blue great Coat. He has but one Testicle.
  Whoever shall apprehend said Negro and convey him to his abovesaid Master, shall have five Pounds old Tenor Reward, and all necessary Charges paid.   Evan Mallbone.
  The Boston Evening-Post, June 4, 1744; June 11, 1744. See *The Boston Weekly Post-Boy*, June 11, 1744.

RAN-away on the 16th of this Instant *May* in the Night from his Master *Evan Malbone* of *Newport*, a Negro Man named *Cuff*, who formerly belonged to *Thomas Borden* of *Portsmouth*, and used to tend the said *Borden's* Ferry; he is a stout lusty Fellow, aged about 30 Years; he had on when he run away, a speckled Shirt and an Oznabrigs Frock and Trowsers, pretty much tarred, and Leather Breeches; and took with him a blue great Coat. He has but one Testicle. Whoever shall apprehend said Negro and convey him to his abovesaid Master, shall have *Five Pounds*, old Tenor Reward, and all necessary Charges paid.   Evan Malbone.
  Newport, May 21, 1744. *Province of New-Hampshire.*
  The Boston Weekly Post-Boy, June 11, 1744; June 18, 1744. See *The Boston Evening-Post*, June 4, 1744.

RAN-away from Mr. *Benjamin Barnard* of *Boston*, Cooper, on the 10th Instant at Night, two Men Servants; one nam'd *James Flin*, about 19 Years of Age, middle Stature, sandy Complection, he had on when he went away, a Kersey Coat fac'd with red, blue Jacket, Leather Breeches, a pair of Trousers, worsted Stockings, new Shoes. The other nam'd *Michael Clemons*, about 19 Years, well set, short Stature, dark Complection, much Pock-broken, he had on when he went away, much the same Cloathing with the other.
  Whoever shall take up the abovesaid Run aways, and them convey to the said *Benjamin Barnard*, shall have *Three Pounds* Reward (old Tenor) for each, and all necessary Charges paid.
  All Masters of Vessels are hereby caution'd against carrying off said Servants, on Penalty of the Law.
  The Boston Gazette, or, Weekly Journal, June 12, 1744.

RAN-away from Mr. *John Hunt* of *Watertown*, a Negro Man nam'd *Ben*, about 30 Years of Age, (he says 27) yellow Complection, round Face, speaks good English, a pleasant Countenance, middle Stature, treads light, understands Farming; he had on when he went away, a Drabb Cloth colour'd Jacket, near the Colour of his Complection, a Pair of black Sheep Skin Breches, his Wool was just cut off, he plays on a Violin. Whoever shall take up the abovesaid Run-away, and him convey to his said Master,

shall have *Five Pounds* (old Tenor) Reward, and all necessary Charges. All Masters of Vessels are hereby caution'd against carrying off said Servant, on Penalty of the Law.
The Boston Gazette, or, Weekly Journal, June 12, 1744.

RAN-away from his Master Stephen Clap, the 18th Instant, an Irish Man-Servant, named *Michael Reisdon,* being a short, well-set Fellow, with short Hair, about 18 or 20 Years of Age, of a sandy, redish Complection: He had on a blue Coat and Breeches of the same Colour. Whoever shall take up said Run-away and convey him to his said Master, near the Town-House in *Boston,* shall have *Forty Shillings* old Tenor Reward and all necessary Charges paid.
The Boston Weekly News-Letter, June 21, 1744.

RAN-away again from Mrs. *Eleanor Pullen* of *Boston,* on Monday the 2d Instant, a Negro Woman, named *Cuba,* about 36 Years of Age, a well-set Wench: She has a Scar over one of her Eye-brows has lost some of her fore Teeth, speaks good English: She had on when she went away, a new cotton and linnen Shift, a quilted Coat, and a Calico Apron: Whosoever shall take up said Negro, and bring her to her said Mistress in Corn-Court, near *Faneuil-Hall,* shall have *Twenty Shillings* Old Tenor, and all necessary Charges paid.
　　N. B. All Persons are hereby notified not to entertaining or harbour said Wench as they would avoid the Penalty of the Law in that Case.
The Boston Weekly Post-Boy, July 9, 1744. See *The Boston Gazette,* From January 17, to January 24, 1737, *The Boston Weekly Post-Boy,* April 30, 1744, and *The Boston Weekly Post-Boy,* August 6, 1744.

RAN-away together from their Masters *John Dean* of *Stonington,* and *John Douglass* of *Plainfield,* on the 18th of this Instant *July,* two Negro Slaves, the one named *Adam,* the other *Caesar*: *Adam* is about 17 Years of Age, pretty large of Stature, and of a very light Complexion, and presumes to call himself a Mollatto: *Caesar* is of middle Size, and a black Fellow, that had but a small Matter of Clothing, when they went away.
　　Whoever shall apprehend the said Fellows or either of them, to their said Masters, or secure them, so that they may have them again, shall have *Five Pounds* old Tenor, Reward, for each Fellow: and all necessary Charges 　　　　　paid by　　John Dean or *John Douglass.*
The Boston Weekly Post-Boy, July 23, 1744; July 30, 1744; August 6, 1744.

DEserted on Saturday the 21st Instant at Night, from on Board the Snow *Elizabeth* now lying in the Harbour of *Boston, James Hasty* Commander, a

Scot Man, nam'd *Alexander Glinn*, speaks broad Scot, about 22 Years of Age, a short well set Fellow, has a scar from his Lip to his Chin, and a Mole on his Lip. Whoever will bring the abovesaid Deserter to Capt. *Hasty*, shall have *Ten Pounds* Reward, old Tenor, and all Charges paid.
The Boston Gazette, or, Weekly Journal, July 24, 1744.

Last Night ran away from her Master *Thomas Drowne*, a very spritely Negro Girl, named *Violet*, of middle Stature, 20 Years old, speaks good English: Whoever shall take up the said Runaway and convey her to her said Master, shall have *Five Pounds*, Old Tenor, Reward, and all necessary Charges paid by   *Thomas Drowne.*
N. B. As she has been lately enquiring for a Passage to go off all Master of Vessels are more especially caution'd against concealing or carrying of the said Negro, as they would avoid the Penalty of the Law.
The Boston Weekly News-Letter, August 2, 1744.

RAN-away again from Mrs. *Eleanor Pullen*, on Monday the 2d of July, a Negro Woman, named *Cuba*, about 36 Years of Age, a well-set Wench, she has a Scar over one Eye-brow, and she lost one or two of her fore-teeth, speaks good English, she had on when she ran away a cotton and linnen Shift, quilted callico Petticoat, coarse Apron, and a Mob. Whoever shall take up said Run-away, & bring her to her abovesaid Mistress in Corn-court, near Faneuil-Hall, shall have *Forty Shillings* Old Tenor, Reward, and all necessary Charges paid. All Persons are hereby caution'd against concealing or entertaining said Negro as they would avoid the Penalty of the Law.
N. B. She was seen last Week in Town, and had on a strip'd Gown.
Boston, August 6. 1744.
The Boston Weekly Post-Boy, August 6, 1744; August 20, 1744; September 3, 1744; September 10, 1744; September 17, 1744; October 1, 1744; October 8, 1744; October 22, 1744. See *The Boston Gazette*, From January 17, to January 24, 1737, *The Boston Weekly Post-Boy*, April 30, 1744, and *The Boston Weekly Post-Boy*, July 9, 1744.

RAN-away on the 12th of this Instant *August*, from Mr. *Timothy Draper* of *Dedham*, an Indian Fellow, about 20 Years of Age, named *Thomas Scoggens*, of middle Stature, has short Hair, his Face something scabby: He had on when he went away, a light colour'd Duroy Coat, a striped Jacket, a linnen Shirt, Leather Breeches, yarn Stockings, round to'd Shoes, a felt Hat about half worn. Whoever shall take up said Servant, and convey him to his said Master in *Dedham*, shall have *Twenty Shillings*, old Tenor, Reward, and all necessary Charges paid.

All Masters of Vessels are hereby caution'd against concealing or carrying off said Servant, as they would avoid the Penalty of the Law.

Dedham, Aug. 18. 1744.\\
The Boston Weekly News-Letter, August 23, 1744.

RAn-away from his Master Stephen Pendergast of Durham in the Province of New-Hampshire, on the 28th of August last, a Negro Man Servant named Bristow; he is a tall Fellow, had on when he went away, a white woollen Shirt, a striped homespun Jacket, Leather Breeches, light colour'd yarn Stockings, round to'd Shoes and a Felt Hat. Whoever shall take up the said Run-away, and bring him to his said Master, shall have *Five Pounds* old Tenor Reward, and all necessary Charges paid.

Stephen Pendergast.
The Boston Weekly Post-Boy, September 3, 1744; September 10, 1744; September 17, 1744.

RAn-away from *Robert Temple* of *Noddles-Island*, two Irish Men Servants, on a short, thick, fresh colour'd Man, about 26 Years of Age, and carried with him a yellow and green Jacket, a blue Coat, striped Trowsers, new Shoes with large brass Buckles. The other, a stout clumsy strong built Man, round fac'd, & pock-broken, about 22 Years old, brown Complection, and carried with him a brown Drugget Coat, new turned, with Mettle Buttons, speaks very bad English. Whoever takes up said Men, and bring or send them to said Mr. *Temple*, shall have *ten Pounds* old Tenor Reward, or *five Pounds* for each or either of them.

The Boston Gazette, or, Weekly Journal, September 4, 1744.

Salem, September 8. 1744.
LAst Night broke out of His Majesty's Goal, *Joseph Boyce*, and *John Syas*, who were commited on Suspicion of counterfeiting Bills of Credit. They are good looking strong able bodied Men; *Boyce* wore his own Hair, which was short and black, *Syas* wears a Wig or Cap. They were both burnt in the Hand about two Years ago, mark'd with the Letter T, being then convicted of counterfeiting Bills of Credit.

Whoever will apprehend them, or either of them, and bring them to said Goal, shall receive *Ten Pounds*, Old Tenor, for each, and be paid their Charges.   JOHN WOLCOTT, *Sheriff.*
The Boston Evening-Post, September 10, 1744; *The Boston Gazette, or, Weekly Journal*, September 11, 1744. Minor differences between the papers.

BROKE out of Prison on Friday last, two Prisoners named *James Thompson & Daniel Byrn*, young Men between 20 & 30 Years of Age:

Thompson is a lusty, thick-set Fellow of a dark Complexion, of a dark Complexion, a large Eye-brow, a good set of Teeth, looks thin; he had on when he went away a pair of red Plush Breeches, and a pair of strip'd Draws, a narrow brim'd Castor Hat, and a white or light Wig: *Byrn* had on a blew fear-nothing double breasted Jacket, a pair of plush Breeches, looks pale and pockfret, has two Scars in his Forehead, is branded with the Letter T. in the Ball of his left Thumb, has an old Hat, and white Wigg, his Knees bends in, was born in Ireland, speaks good English. Whosoever shall take up said *Thompson* and *Byrn* and convey them to his Majesty's Goal at *Portsmouth, New-Hampshire*, shall have Twenty Pounds, old Tenor for each, and all necessary Charges paid.
      THOMAS PACKER, *Sheriff.*
 The Boston Weekly Post-Boy, September 10, 1744; September 17, 1744; September 24, 1744; October 1, 1744; October 8, 1744.

RAN-away from *Robert Temple* of *Noddles-Island* on the 2d Instant at Night, two Irish Men Servants, one named *John Croney*, about 26 Years old, a short thick fresh colour'd Man, and carried with him a yellow and green Jacket, a blue Coat, striped Trozers, new Shoes, with broad brass Buckles. The other named *Edward Ore*, about 22 Years old, a stout, clumsy, strong Man, round fac'd, brown Complection, pock-broken, and carried with him a brown Drugget Coat, new turn'd, with mettal Buttons, and speaks bad English.
 Whoever shall take up the said Servants, and bring or sent them to Capt. *Temple*, shall have *ten Pounds* old Tenor Raward, or *Five Pounds* old Tenor for each or either of them, and all necessary Charges paid.
 All Masters of Vessels are hereby caution'd against carrying off the said Servants as they would avoid the Penalty of the Law.
 The Boston Gazette, or, Weekly Journal, September 18, 1744.

RAN-away from her Master *George Tibbits* of *North-Kingstown*, a Mustee Servant Woman named *Phelice*, of a short Stature, fat of Body, very crooked Legs, about 30 Years of Age; he hath taken away with her two Gowns, one a striped Cotton, the other striped black and white Drugget, a quilted Coat, and a striped Flannel Coat, two Shirts two old Tow and one a Flannel; she went away the 13th of this Instant in the Night in Company with a Mustee Man named *Benjamin*: They have taken sundry Things from said *Tibbits*.
 Whoever shall take up said Servant Woman, shall have *Three Pounds* old Tenor and *five Pounds* for both of said Runaways, and all necessary Charges paid, they conveying them or either of them to said *Tibbits*, or securing them so that said Runaways may be had again.
    George Tibbits.   *Septemb.* 14th 1744.

The Boston Gazette, or Weekly Journal, September 25, 1744.

RAN-away on the 29*th* ult. from *William Clift*, on Board the Sloop *Evans* lying at Capt *Gould's* Wharffe in Boston, a white Servant named *John Tomson*, of a middling Stature, light Complection, very much pock-broken, short Hair, a Handkerchief for a Cap, a Felt Hat, a pair of Trowsers, a pair of yarn Stockings, a pair of turn'd Pumps, both of them wore out at the Toes: And when he went away stole three Dear [*sic*] Skins, and other Things out of said Vessel. Whoever shall take up the said Servant and bring or send him to Mr. *Joseph Sherburne*, Brazier; shall have *five Pounds* Reward, old Tenor, and all necessary Charges paid.

Boston, October 1st. 1744.
The Boston Gazette, or, Weekly Journal, October 2, 1744; October 9, 1744.

RAN away from *Samuel Willis* of *Middletown* in *Connecticut*, a well set Angola, Negro Fellow aged about 20 Years, a little bow-Leg'd, and his Toes spread pretty much, he has small Scratches each side of his Face, sometimes has a Bobb in his Ear, and is a good Cook, he carry'd away with him several Sut's of striped and white Vests, and a brown Holland fly Coat an old pair of Pumps a Pair of Worsted Stockins, a Worsted Cap or two, some Silver Money, a black Velvet Stock, with a Silver Clasp, a Pair of Knee Buckl's, whoever takes up said Negro, and brings him to his Master, or secures him so that he may be had again, shall have forty shillings Reward, and all Reasonable Charges
        paid by   *Samuel Willis.*
The New-York Gazette, October 29, 1744; *The New-York Evening Post*, December 24, 1744; December 30, 1744; January 7, 1745.

DESERTERS from Castle *William.*
The following nam'd Soldiers belonging to Brigadier
PHILLIPS's *Regiment;*
William Firkin a small black Man about 22 Years of Age, born in *England*, middle Size. *Andrew Peterson*, an Englishman about 35 Years old, a fair Man. *Amos Jefferson*, an Englishman, a little brown Pock-fretten Fellow, about 25 Years old. *John Thomas*, a middle siz'd square shoulder'd stout young Fellow, limps in his walking, an English Man. *John Gould*, a little chattering Fellow, about 40, an Irish Man, very ragged. *John Mixter*, a little thin brown Fellow, an English Man. *Richard Collis*, a short lusty strong young Fellow about 30 years of Age, an Englishman. *John Jesop*, a black swarthy Fellow, about 22 Years of Age, an English Man. *James Hankins* about 35 Years of Age, a fair grave looking Man, plays upon the Hautboy.

Whoever takes up one of more of the above Deserters and brings them to the House of Capt. *Hamockin*, Exchange Alley, *Boston*, shall receive *Ten Pounds* old Tenor for each, and travelling Charges paid.

The Boston Weekly Post-Boy, November 19, 1744; *The Boston Gazette, or Weekly Journal*, November 20, 1744.

RAN away from *Samuel Morgareidge* of *Newbury*, Shipwright, a Negro Fellow called *Primus*, alias *Isaac*, near 6 Feet high, well set, strait lim'd, speaks good English; had on when he went away, a scarlet Waistcoat with white metal Buttons, a blew out-side Jacket pretty much worn, and Leather Breeches, new Shoes and Hose, and a check'd wollen Shirt, no Hat or Cap. Whosoever shall safely convey him to his abovesaid Master, shall have *Five Pounds*, old Tenor, Reward, and all necessary Charges paid them

by me, *Samuel Morgareidge*   Newbury, Nov. 21*st*. 1744.

*The Boston Weekly Post-*Boy, November 26, 1744; December 3, 1744; The *Boston Evening-Post*, December 3, 1744; December 10, 1744.

Rippon's Prize, November 26, 1744.

DESERTED from on board His Majesty's Ship *Rippon's-Prize*, on Monday the 19th and Thursday the 22d Instant, the following Persons, *viz*.

William Delany, about twenty-two Years of Age, fresh colour'd, about five Feet six Inches high.

John Johnson, a Jersey Man, about thirty Years of Age, round Visage, has a Cast with one Eye, and is about sx Feet High.

David West, about twenty-six Years of Age, long Visaged, and about five Feet seven Inches high.

John Ryan, about twenty-three Years of Age, round Visaged, part of his under Lip bit off, about five Feet four Inches high.

John Francis, about thirty Years of Age, thin Visaged, and about five Feet six Inches high.

John Caine, about twenty-six Years of Age, round faced, pretty lusty, and about five Feet five Inches high.

Richard Gold, about twenty-two Years of Age, round faced, and about five Feet four Inches high.

William Darby, about thirty-five Years of Age, thin Visaged, about five Feet four Inches high.

Eleazer White, about twenty-four Years of Age, thin Visaged, and about five Feet eight Inches high.

Michael Ellis, about twenty-three Years of Age, round Visaged, about five Feet six Inches high.

Daniel Fitzpatrick, about twenty-four Years of Age, round Visage, and about five Feet five Inches high.

William Hartwell, about twenty-two Years of Age, thin Visage, about five Feet four Inches high.

James Hogg, about twenty-five Years of Age, thin Visage, about five Feet seven Inches high,

John Powell, about twenty-two Years of Age, round Visage, about five Feet four Inches high.

Whoever shall secure them in His Majesty's Goal in *Boston*, or bring them on board the said Ship, shall have *Ten Pounds*, old Tenor, Reward, for each Man.   *Samuel Graves.*

The Boston Weekly News-Letter, November 29, 1744; *The Boston Weekly Post-Boy*, December 3, 1744.

D*eserted from the ship* Swan, Thomas Dudding *Commander, the following Seamen, viz.* Alexander Malcum, John Nickson, *and* Steven Grant. *These are to inform the said Deserters, that if they will return to their Duty on board the said Ship in Six Days Time, they shall be kindly received, or otherwise they will be prosecuted according to Law.*

Boston, December 3 1744.
The Boston Evening-Post, December 3, 1744; December 10, 1744.

T*hese may Certify all Persons whom it may Concern, That on the twenty third Day of* November *last, Negro Man of about* 30 *Years of Age, being a small slender Fellow, having on a light coloured Duroy Jacket, with an old Kersey Ditto, with part of a Linnen Frock, without Hat, Cap, Coat, Shirt, Breeches, Stockings, or Shoes, was taken up in the Woods in the Township of* Kingston, *in the County of* Plimouth, *said Negro appears to be lately imported into the Country, talks little or no* English, *and was first taken up, almost famished for want of Food, and something Froze; and any Person to whom the said Negro belongs, paying the Charges, &c. may have him by applying themselves to the Subscriber, as Witness my Hand this* 27*th of* November, *A. D.* 1744.   David Sturtevant.

The Boston Evening-Post, December 10, 1744.

RAN-away on Tuesday the 11th Instant, from Mrs. *Ann Philips*, living near the Orange-Tree in *Boston*, a Negro Girl about 14 Years of Age, named *Violet*, pretty lusty; she had on when she went away, a black Linsey Woolsey Coat and Jacket, a strip'd Callimanco Petticoat under it; and had also with her a new blew Bays Jacket, and a Callico Petticoat, lin'd with a seersucker. Whoever shall bring the said Girl to her Mistress, shall be well Rewarded, and have all necessary Charges paid.

The Boston Weekly News-Letter, December 13, 1744.

Salem, December 16*th*. 1744.

R*AN away from the Hon.* Benjamin Lynde, *Jun. of* Salem *Esq; on the* 15*th of this Instant* December, *a Negro Man named* Cicero, *about* 20 *Years old, pretty slim but tall. He had on when he went away, a blue great Coat, and an Olive-coloured Cloth Coat under it, a striped homespun Jacket, dark coloured Cloth Breeches, a speckled Shirt, gray Yarn Stockings, double soled Shoes, a Worsted Cap, and a Castor Hat. Whoever shall take up said Negro, and him safely convey to his abovesaid Master in* Salem, *shall have* Five Pounds, *Old Tenor, Reward, and all necessary Charges paid.*

The Boston Evening-Post, December 17, 1744. See *The Boston Weekly Post Boy*, December 17, 1744.

R*UN-away from Benjamin Lynde, Esq; of Salem, a Negro Man, named Cicero, about* 20 *Years old; he had on when he went away, a blew great Coat, and underneath an Olive colour'd Cloath Coat with plate Buttons, a strip'd homespun Jacket, a pair of colour'd cloath Breeches, grey Yarn Stockings, double sol'd Shoes, a Worsted Cap, and a Castor Hat: Whoever shall bring the said Negro to his abovesaid Master, shall have Five Pounds, old Tenor, Reward, and all necessary Charges paid.*

The Boston Weekly Post Boy, December 17, 1744; December 24, 1744; December 31, 1744. See *The Boston Evening-Post*, December 17, 1744.

1745

R*AN away from the Brigantine* Happy Return, Richard White *Master, two Indian Men, the one named* Samuel Attakin, *the other* Jacob Harry. *This is to give Notice, that if the said Indians will return to their Duty on board the sail Vessel at Col.* Hutchinson's *Wharf at the North End, they shall be kindly received, otherwise deem'd as Deserters.*

Boston December 29*th*, 1745.

The Boston Evening-Post, January 21, 1745.

R*UN-away on the* 11*th of January* 1745, *from their Master John Martin of Jamestown, two lusty Fellows, one a Mustee, named James, about* 20 *Years of Age, had on when he went away two dark coloured thick Jackets, a flannel Shirt, a pair of buck Skin Breeches under his Trowsers: The other a Negro named Glasgow, about* 25 *Years of Age, had on when he went away, a Kersey Jacket, and a Duroy One under it, two flannel Shirts. Whoever shall apprehend said Servants, and bring them to their said Master, or secure them in some Goal so that he may have them again, shall have Ten Pounds old Tenor Reward, or Five Pounds for each, and all necessary Charges paid by me* John Martin.

The Boston Weekly Post Boy, January 24, 1745; February 11, 1745.
See *The Boston Evening-Post,* July 15, 1745, for Glasgow.

WHereas my Wife *Hannah Ball* has eloped from me, and supposed to be gone with one *John Munro* of *Bristol,* to some Part of *Connecticut*; these are therefore to forewarn all Persons from trusting or crediting her the said *Hannah* on my Account, for I do hereby declare that I will not pay one Farthing for any Debt which she shall contract. In Witness whereof I have hereunto set my Hand this 25th Day of *January, A. D.* 1744.5.
                Benjamin Ball.
The Boston Weekly Post-Boy, January 28, 1745.

RAN-away from Mr. *David Snoden* of *Boston,* on the 25th ult. a Negro Man named *Peter,* about 30 Years of Age, speaks good English, in a Chimney-Sweeper's Dress, and generally employ'd in that Business. Whoever shall take up said Negro, and bring him to his said Master, shall be well rewarded. And all Masters of Vessels are hereby warn'd against carrying off said Servant.
    The Boston Gazette, or Weekly Journal, March 12, 1745; March 19, 1745.

WHereas Jane, *the Wife of* Henry Wright, jun. *of* Springfield *in the County of* Hampshire, *hath lately eloped from her said Husband and refuses to live with the said* Henry *as his Wife ought to do:*
    These are therefore to notify and warn all Persons against trusting or crediting the said *Jane* with any Money, Goods or other Thing whatsoever on Account of the said *Henry*: And I do heregy forbid any Person to entertain her on my Credit; and that I will in no wise pay any Debt whatsoever that she shall contract.
          Henry Wright, jun.   *Springfield, March* 1. 1744.
The Boston Weekly News-Letter, March 28, 1745.

DEserted from his Majesty's Store Ship *Beien Aimê,* under the Command of Capt. *Clark Gayton,* at *Boston, Malachy Allen* of Manchester, *Roger Parker* of Portsmouth in New-Hampshire: This is to give Notice, that whosoever will bring either of the said Deserters to Boston to their Duty, shall receive *ten Pounds* old Tenor Reward, and all necessary Charges paid. Given under my Hand at *Boston* this first Day of *April* 1745.
          Clark Gayton.
The Boston Gazette, or Weekly Journal, April 2, 1745; April 9, 1745.

O*N the* 9*th of* April, 1745. *Whereas* Thomasine Clayton, *Wife of* John Clayton, *Hat-maker, late of* Newport *on* Rhode-Island, *hath eloped from*

her Husband, therefore I the said John Clayton *do forewarn all or any Person or Persons to trust or credit her to the Value of Four Pence, for I will not pay any Debt for her that she contracts.*
    John Clayton.
 The Boston Evening-Post, April 22, 1745.

RAN-away from his Master Mr. *James Howell* of *Boston,* an Indian Molatto Man, aged about 20 Years, he had on when he went away a green Jacket, and yellow Leather Breeches, he left his Hat behind him, but I am inform'd he has got two Hats since. Whoever shall take up said Runaway, and bring him to *Alexander Thorpe's* near the Common shall receive *Three Pounds* Reward, Old Tenor, and all necessary Charges paid by me,
    James Howell.
 The Boston Weekly News-Letter, May 16, 1745; May 23, 1745.

R*UN away from his Master* Jeffery Lany, *Goldsmith of* Salem *some time in the Month of* April *last, a Man Servant named* Nathaniel White, *between nineteen and twenty Years of Age, of a Middle Stature and of a dark Complexion. He had on when he went away a dark colour'd Drugget Coat and Jacket, Leather Breeches and a Castor Hat. This is to forewarn all Persons of entertaining, harbouring, trusting or trading with said Servant upon peril of the Law in that Case made and provided. It is thought he is gone towards* Piscataqua. *If any Person will give Intelligence to his said Master where he is, they shall be Rewarded for their Trouble.*
    Jeffery Lang.   Salem, May 25, 1745.
 The Boston Evening-Post, May 27, 1745; June 3, 1745; June 10, 1745.
 The second and third ads show the advertiser's name as Lang.

ABraham Stamper, *deserted from the Ship* New-Hampshire, May 27, *Capt.* Henry Grant *Master, a Man of a brown Complexion and well set, wearing a Wig or a Cap. If returned in* 24 *Hours shall be received after the third of* June 1745.   Mast-Ship.
 The Boston Evening-Post, June 3, 1745.

RUN away from Capt. *Henderson* Master of a Sloop belonging to *Dover* in *Piscataqua,* a Negro Man named *Adam,* aged 30 Years, middle Statue, belonging to *Thomas Wallingford* Esq; of said *Dover*: He had on when he went away, a woollen Shirt, a pair of old Plush Breeches, a grey Kersey Jacket, a bev [sic] great Coat, an old Beaver Hat, a pair of grey yarn Stockings, and a pair of old Shoes, one of his Legs in bigger than the other, he speaks pretty good English. Whoever apprehends said Negro and secures him in any of his Majesty's Goals, so that the Owner may have him again

shall have *Six* or *Seven Pounds* Cash, old Tenor Reward, and all necessary Charges paid for. *Thomas Wallingford.* *Newport, June* 1, 1745.
The Boston Weekly Post-Boy, June 3, 1745; June 10, 1745.

WHEREAS Judith, *the Wife of* Samuel Larrabe, *hath eloped from her Husband, and refuses to live with him, and this is to give Notice to all Persons both in Town and Country, not to trust nor harbour the said* Judith, *for he will not pay any Debt that she shall contract; and if any Person or Persons entertain and harbour the said* Judith, *they may expect to suffer the Penalty of the Law, as Witness my Hand,* Samuel Larrabe.
The Boston Evening-Post, June 17, 1745; June 24, 1745.

RAN-away from his Master *David Wallis* of *Woodstock,* on the 22d of *May* last, a Negro Man named *Jammey,* speaks good English, but stutters something, he is of a middling Stature and well set; had on when he went away, a good beaver Hat, a blue strait bodied Coat, with brass Buttons, duroy Jacket, and breeches of a light blue trim'd with Mohair of the same Colour, blue Stockings and new Shoes; carried with him five Shirts, two Woollen and three Linnen, and two pair of Leather Breeches, and a Hanger, a blue great Coat. Whoever shall take up said Runaway and bring him to his said Master, or secure him in any Jail, so that his Master may have him again, shall have *five Pounds* Reward, old Tenor, and all reasonable Charges paid by *David Wallis.*
And all Masters of Vessels and others are hereby caution'd against concealing or carrying off said Servant, on Penalty of the Law.
The Boston Gazette, or, Weekly Journal, June 18, 1745. See *The Boston Gazette, or Weekly Journal,* September 24, 1745.

WHEREAS Abigail, *the Wife of me the Subscriber,* James Remick *of* Charlstown, *in the County of* Middlesex, *Mariner, hath for a long Time liv'd in repeated, notorious Breaches of the Marriage Covenant and Duty, and thereby rendered it improper for me to treat her any long as my Wife; she having also in my Absence at Sea, embezel'd and wasted my Estate:* I do hereby Caution all Persons from trusting or crediting the said *Abigail Remick* on my Account, thereby decling that I will not pay any Debts whatsone which she shall contract, As Witness my Hand,
JAMES REMICK.
The Boston Gazette, or Weekly Journal, July 2, 1745.

RAN away from his Master, Mr. *Henry Price* of *Boston,* on Thursday *July* the fourth, an *Irish* Man Servant named *John Finly,* a Taylor by Trade. He goes lame, with a Crutch, and cannot straiten his Knee. The lame Leg is much less than the other. He wears a Wig, and a dark Cloth Coat, turned,

and is aged about twenty three Years. He is five Feet eight Inches high, or thereabouts. Whosoever will take up the said Runaway, and bring him to his Master in King-Street, shall have *Ten Pounds* Reward, old Tenor, and all other necessary Charges paid them, as witness my Hand,
   this Eighth Day of July, 1745. HENRY PRICE.
The Boston Evening-Post, July 8, 1745; July 15, 1745.

               Boston, July 7, 1745.
DEserted from on Board his Majesty's Ship *Bein Aime*, Capt. *Richard Farrish* Commander, this Morning, being the 8th of *July*, the ten following Persons, (who took with them a six Oar'd Boat belonging to said Ship), viz. *William Taylor, Richard Freeman, William Fitzgarell, Archibald Reding, William Christopher, Thomas O'Bryant, David Akins, Edward Cogan, John Baker,* and *Daniel Larey.*
 Whoever shall apprehend the said Deserters or either of them, and safely convey to said Ship, or commit to his Majesty's Goal in *Boston*, shall have *ten Pounds* (old Tenor) Reward for each, and all necessary Charges
    paid by me *Richard Farrish.*
The Boston Gazette, or Weekly Journal, July 9, 1745.

RAN-away from Capt. *Joseph Hale* of *Newbury*, a Negro Man named *Cato* the 6th Instant, about 22 Years of Age, short and small, speaks good English, and can read and write, understands farming Work, carry'd with him a striped homespun Jacket & Breeches, and Trousers, and an outer Coat and Jacket of home-made Cloth, two pair of Shoes, sometimes wears a black Wigg, has a smooth Face, a sly Look, took with him a Violin, and can play well thereon. Had with him three Linnen Shirts home-made pretty fine yarn Stockings. Whoever shall bring said Negro to his said Master, or secure him so that he may have him again, shall have *five Pounds* Reward, and all necessary Charges
    paid by me. *Joseph Hale. Newbury,* July 8*th* 1745.
The Boston Gazette, or Weekly Journal, July 9, 1745; July 16, 1745.

RAN-away from *Ebenezer Gray* of *Lebanon* in *Connecticut*, on the 28th Day of *June* last, at Night, a Negro Man named *Hector*, about 24 Years of Age, speaks pretty good English, he is a lusty, stout, well-sett, square-shoulder'd, well-featur'd Fellow, of a middle Size for Stature, and has a well-proportioned Leg, about 4 Years ago he was Servant to one Mr. *Swift* of *Sandwich*, and sold by him to *Zebulon West*, Esq; of *Tolland*: He had on when he went away a dark-colour'd homespun Coat, a lightish colour'd fustian Jacket, with the Sleeves cut off, a tow Cloth Shirt and Trowsers, yarn Stockings, and a good Pair of Shoes, a yellow and white strip'd muslin Handkerchief, he carried away with him also a blew and white homespun

checker'd flannel Shirt, and a Pair of very good cloth colour'd Buckskin Breeches, with a Watch Pocket in them, and the Buttons covered with Leather. Whoever shall take up said Negro and him convey to said *Gray* in *Lebanon* aforesaid, shall have a Reward of *Three Pounds*, old Tenor, and all necessary Charges paid them by   *Ebenezer Gray.*
The Boston Weekly News-Letter, July 11, 1745; July 19, 1745; July 25, 1745.

R*AN away from* John Martin *of* Jamestown, *near* Newport, Rhode-Island, *on the* 19*th of* June, *a Negro Man named* Glasgow, *about 27 Years of Age. Had on a brown full'd Cloth Jacket, and a white one under it, a pair of Buckskin Breeches, a Bever Hat, and Flannel Shirt. Whosoever shall apprehend said Runaway, and bring him to his Master, shall have* Ten Pounds, *old Tenor, Reward, and necessary Charges*
         paid by me.   John Martin.
The Boston Evening-Post, July 15, 1745. See *The Boston Weekly Post Boy*, January 24, 1745.

R*AN away from* Thomas Fleet *of* Boston, *Printer, last Night, the 18th Instant, a Negro Fellow named* Newport, *about 20 Years old. He is a sly cunning Rogue, of middle Stature, but pretty slim and spry, and has a large Scar over his right Eye, occasion'd by the Kick of a Horse. He had on a Cotton and Linen Shirt, and striped homespun Jacket and Breeches.*
   Whoever shall take him up, and bring him to his Master, at the Heart and Crown in Cornhill, shall have Five Pounds *Reward, Old Tenor, and all reasonable Charges paid.*
   N. B. *He will endeavour to get of by Sea, therefore all Masters of Vessels and others are cautioned against harbouring, concealing or carrying him off on any Pretence whatever, as they would avoid the Penalty of the Law.*
The Boston Evening-Post, July 22, 1745; July 29, 1745.

                                              Newport, July 15. 1745.
W*Hereas* Valantine Kennedy, Euen Griffith, Luke Scallin, Isaac Tucker, *and* John Ward, *Mariners, who inlisted themselves in his Majesty's Service to enter on board the Ship* Vigilance, *in the Hon. Commodore* Warren's *Squadron off* Louisbourg, *have deserted said Servnce and gone off with the Bounty-Money given by this Colony; I the Subscriber do hereby promise a Reward of* Five Pounds, *Old Tenor, for each of the abovesaid Persons that shall be apprehended and delivered to me: And all Persons are hereby cautioned not to conceal or carry off any of the aforesaid Persons.*

BENJAMIN WICKHAM.
The Boston Evening-Post, July 22, 1745; July 29, 1745; August 5, 1745; August 12, 1745; *The Boston Weekly Post-Boy*, July 22, 1745. Minor differences between the papers,

RAN away from her Mistress Margaret Robinson, on the 2d Inst. *Nancy*, a Negro Girl of a middling stature, mark'd on her Face with the Small-pox: Se had on when she went away a white Linnen Jacket, and a large check'd Petticoat: Whoever shall take up said Run-away and convey her to her Mistress at Mr. Joseph Marion's opposite to the North Door of the Town House, Boston, shall be well rewarded and have all necessary Charges paid.—All Masters of Vessels and others are hereby forbid harbouring or carrying off said Negro.
The Boston Weekly News-Letter, August 8, 1745; August 15, 1745; August 22, 1745.

The famous Tom Bell went into the Country yesterday; he was apprehended here a few Weeks ago, and committed to the Workhouse, but nothing appearing against him, he has been since discharged.
The Boston Weekly Post-Boy, April 8, 1745. See *The Pennsylvania Gazette*, June 23, 1743. See *The Pennsylvania Gazette*, July 14, 1743, *The Boston Weekly Post-Boy*, August 22, 1743, *The Boston Gazette, or, Weekly Journal*, September 20, 1743, *The Boston Evening-Post*, December 12, 1743, *The Boston Gazette, or Weekly Journal*, May 22, 1744, and *The Boston Weekly Post-Boy*, October 5, 1747.

WHereas on Monday Evening in 11th Instant *Richard Acton*, a lad of about 12 Years of Age, of a fair Complection, wearing a Cap or Wigg, ran away from the Ship *Abigail*, now lying at Capt. *Cheever's* Wharff at the North End, *Henry Holloway* Master: He had on when he went away a blew freize Coat with Brass Buttons, a pair of Trowsers and a strip'd worsted Cap. Whoever will bring Intelligence of said Lad, so that he return to said Ship, shall have *Twenty Shillings* old Tenor Reward. Whoever harbours or entertains him to their Peril be it. *N. B.* Said *Holloway* is to be spoke with on board the Ship, or at Mr. *Tyler's* Shipwright at the North End.
The Boston Weekly News-Letter, August 15, 1745; August 22, 1745.

RAN-away from Mr. *Daniel Lyon* of *Woodstock*, a Negro Man named *Cuffey*, aged about 35 Years, middle Stature, had on a double breasted light colour'd broad Cloth Jacket, &c. speaks good English, a sensible understanding Fellow, and can tell a fair Story. Whoever takes up said Negro, and shall bring or send him to his Mastor, shall have *five Pounds*, old Tenor Reward, and all necessary Charges.

And all Persons, are hereby warned against concealing or carrying off said Servant. *Woodstock, July* 25, 1745.
The Boston Gazette, or Weekly Journal, August 20, 1745; August 27, 1745; September 3, 1745; September 17, 1745.

R*AN away from Doctor* Thomas Waite *of* Boston, *about a Fortnight ago, a Negro Man named* Cuffee, *about* 37 *Years old, a stout well set Fellow, that speaks very good English, and has lost two of his upper Fore-Teeth. He had on when he went away, a blue Jacket and a striped Jacket, a pair of square toed Shoes, a pair of black Stockings, and a pair of tarred Trouzers. Whoever shall take up the said Run-away, and give Notice to his Master, shall have* Five Pounds *old Tenor, Reward, and necessary Charges paid. All Masters of Vessels and others are forewarned of carrying off the said Servant, as the Penalty of the Law in that Case made and provided.*
Boston, Aug. 22, 1745.
The Boston Evening-Post, August 26, 1745; September 2, 1745; September 9, 1745.

RAN-away from Mr. *David Wallis* of *Woodstock,* the 24th ult. a Negro Man named *Jemmy,* speaks good English, but something stuttering, middle Stature, well set, had on and took with him two Shirts one Check Holland the other a tow, two Jackets of a blewish Colour, old Trousers, worsted Cap, and a pair of Pot-Hooks about his Neck. Whoever shall take up said Servant, and bring him to his Master or secure him in Bridewell or Goal, so that his Master may have him again, shall have *five Pounds* Reward, old Tenor, and necessary Charges
paid by   *David Wallis.*
The Boston Gazette, or Weekly Journal, September 24, 1745; October 8, 1745. See *The Boston Gazette, or, Weekly Journal,* June 18, 1745.

RAN away from her Master *Thadeus Mason* of Charlestown, on the 22d Instant at Night or the next Morning, a Negro Woman named *Jenny,* about thirty Years of Age, middle Stature well set, and speaks good English; she carry'd away with her a black Crape Gown, a strip'd Holland and flower'd Callico, and a Cotton and Linnen ditto, also a homespun Gown much worn, with sundry other Cloaths in a wooden Box, and a Pillow Case.

Whoever shall take up the said Run-away, and convey her to her said Master, shall have *Three Pounds,* old Tenor, Reward, and necessary Charges paid.

And all Persons are caution'd against harbouring, concealing or carrying off said Negro. *Charlestown, Sept* 23d. 1745.
The Boston Gazette, or Weekly Journal, September 24, 1745.

RUN away from Deacon *Thomas Wilson* of *Exeter*, on the 24th Instant, a Negro Slave named *Cato*, about Forty Years of Age, pretty slender body'd and about five Foot eight Inches high, walks with his Toes standing outward, has lost some of his upper fore Teeth; he carry'd away with him a brown Camblet Coat and Jacket, a white half thick Coat trim'd with black, a greyish colour'd Duroy Coat cuffed with black, a greenish homespun Coat with large flat Buttons, a blue Ratteen Jacket with wash'd Buttons, and Ratteen Briches with flat Buttons, and a good pair of Boots; a black Callimanco Jacket and Briches, and a greenish colour'd great Coat with large flat Buttons; five linnen Shirts and two check'd Cotton and Wool Shirts, with sundry pair of Stockings of diverse Colours, and a good Bever Hat, Silver lac'd, and a good Felt Hat, with sundry other Things.
  Whoever shall take up said Negro, and bring him to his said Master in *Exeter*, shall have *Five Pounds* old Tenor as a Reward, and all necessary
    Charges paid, by me *Thomas Wilson.*
  The Boston Evening-Post, September 30, 1745; October 14, 1745.

RAN-away from *Thomas Disbrow* of *Fairfield* in Connecticut, on the 27th of last Month, a Negro Man named Newport, aged about forty Years, a tall slim Fellow, talks very good English: Had on when he went away, a homespun brown Jacket and Linnen Trousers; he also had with him a Leather Jacket and Breeches, two Coats, the one a blue Duroy fly Coat, and the other a Flannel one with brass Buttons, four Jackets one of them streaked, three Shirts two of them chequer'd and one new tow Frock, two pair of woollen Stockings. Whoever shall take up said Run-away, and bring or secure him, so that I have have him again, shall have *five Pounds* Reward, old Tenor, and all necessary Charges paid,
    by me *Thomas Disbrow.*
  And all Persons are caution'd against harbouring, concealing, or carrying off said Negro.   *Fairfield, Sept.* 20th 1745.
  The Boston Gazette, or Weekly Journal, October 8, 1745; October 15, 1745.

  WHereas *John Regeway* born in *Cheshire*, and speaks pretty broad, about 40 or 50 Years of Age, lately work'd at the North Mills, and is now absented, and took with him a blue Great Coat with a binding of Velvet round the Collar, belonging to me the Subscriber; and also took with him several other Things. The said *Regeway* had on when he went away a long brown Holland Wastecoat, Ozenbrigs Trousers, yarn Stockings, old red Great Coat, and is a lusty fresh colour'd Man. Whoever shall take him up and bring him to *Jonathan Bowman* Shipwright at the North End of Boston, that he may be brought to Justice, shall have 5 l. Reward, old Tenor, and all necessary Charges paid by me

Jonathan Bowman. Boston, October 7th 1745.
And all Masters of Vessels are forbid carrying him off.
The Boston Gazette, or Weekly Journal, October 8, 1745; October 15, 1745; October 22, 1745.

Middlesex, ff. Charlestown, Oct. 7. 1745.
LAst Saturday Night was committed to Goal two vagrant Women, on Suspicion of Theft, and this Day were further Examined, who say their Names are *Mary Williams* and *Deborah Boyd*. They had with them several Bundles and large Pockets, with sundry Goods, suspected to have been stolen, *viz.* Children's Shoes, four Pieces None-so pretty, several Knotts and flower'd Girdles, Cotton Yarn, coloured Sheep-skins, one Piece Blue Padufoy Ribband, Necklaces, Women's *New-England* Gloves, a Cambrick Handkerchief, a Lutestring Bonnet lined with a Peach-Blossom, a Silver Tea-Spoon, a Quantity of Mohair, sundry Silk Laces, a Pair of Green Silk Stockings, &c. The Persons are meanly habited, but have a considerable Quantity of Silver and Paper Money: They are to be confin'd 'till Thursday new Two o'Clock, that so any Persons claiming any of said Goods, may make it appear to be their's.
Thomas Jenner, Justice of the Peace.
The Boston Gazette, or Weekly Journal, October 8, 1745.

R*AN away from his Master, Mr.* Daniel Rea, *of* Boston, *Tailor, some Weeks ago, a Negro Boy named* Prince, *about* 16 *Years of age. He had on when he went away, a dark Cloth Jacket, Leather Breeches, and a check'd Shirt, but no Stockings or Shoes. Whoever shall take up the said Negro, and bring him to his said Master, shall have* Forty Shillings *Reward, Old Tenor, and all necessary Charges paid.*
N. B. *All Masters of Vessels and others are cautioned against harbourng, concealing, or carrying off said Negro, as they would avoid the Penalty of the Law.* Boston, October 14. 1745.
The Boston Evening-Post, October 14, 1745; October 21, 1745; October 28, 1745.

W*Hereas* Mary Donnaley, *about* 13 *Years of Age, an indented Servant to Mr.* Robert Reed, *Yeoman, of* Nottingham *in the Province of* New-Hampshire, *did on the* 10th *of* September *last, absent herself from her Master's Service, and 'tis supposed is secreted and entertained by some Person in or about* Portsmouth. *These are to give Notice, to any Person who will bring the said Servant Girl to her Master at* Nottingham *aforesaid they shall have* Forty Shillings *old Tenor, Reward and all necessary Charges paid; and all Persons are forbid harbouring or entertaining said Servant at their peril. N. B. She is a Girl of thin Visage, has brown curl'd*

Hair, she had on a Linnen Woolsey Gown, strip'd black, blue and white, a pair of Leather-heel Shoes.
The Boston Weekly News-Letter, October 24, 1745; November 14, 1745; November 28, 1745.

WHereas Annabella Holman *of* Newport *in the Colony of* Rhode-Island *in* New-England, *Wife to me* John Holman *of* Bridgewater *in the Province of the* Massachusetts-Bay, *absolutely refuses and declines to cohabit with me at my House in said* Bridgwater, *but keeps still at* Newport, *where she is continually running me in Debt, and exposing me to many Law Suits, of which I have had some late Experience.*
This is therefore to warn and caution all People whatever, more especially the People of that Colony, from intrusting her with any kind of Goods or Workmanship for any Sum on my Account, for I hereby declare I will not pay them if they do. John Holman.
The Boston Weekly Post-Boy, November 11, 1745; November 18, 1745.

DEserted his Majesty's Fort George, *in the Colony of* Rhode-Island, *on Saturday the tenth of* November, John Briant, *an inlisted Soldier in said Fort. He is about five Feet ten Inches high, about* 24 *Years of Age, of a swarthy Complexion, cloathed with a red Duffles great Coat, a homespun Jacket, with Metal Buttons, a dark pair of Buck-skin Breeches, with Brass Buttons. Whoever shall apprehend said Deserter, and bring him to* Newport, *shall have* Fifteen Pounds, *Old Tenor, Reward, and all Charges paid by me* Walter Chaloner.
The Boston Evening-Post, December 2, 1745; December 9, 1745.

Taken out of my Pasture a Bay Mare 14 Hands high, a natural Pacer, has a Starr in her Forehead, her near hind Foot has some White, she is about 8 Years old. At the same Time ran-away from his Master, a Negro Fellow named *Bridgwater,* well known in *Boston,* not for his Honesty: He had on when he went away a blue Cloth Coat and Jacket, and an old green great Coat: Whoever brings either the Mare or Negro to me, shall be well rewarded and Charges paid by Peter Luce.
N. B. *The said Negro will tell a fair Story, but believe him not for he is a great Lyar.*
The Boston Weekly Post-Boy, December 2, 1745; December 9. 1745; December 23, 1745.

WHEREAS John Case *of* Hartford, *and* Elisha Knowles *of* Haddam *in the Colony of* Connecticut, *upon the Evening of the* 15*th Instant, deserted the Province Hospital on* Rainsford's Island, *where they had been confin'd for* *some Time by Reason of the* Small-Pox; *the said* John Case *being but just recovered from said Distemper, and the said* Elisha Knowles *suspected to have the Symptoms of it now upon him: They are both tall Men, had each of them a new red duffle Great Coat, yarn Stockings, and new Shoes, and otherwise but poorly Cloath'd; and it's probable said* Case *hath a red Complection as he is but just recover'd from the* Small-Pox.

These are therefore to Caution all Persons from harbouring or concealing the said *John Case* and *Elisha Knowles*; and whoever shall take up the said Persons, or either of them, and bring them to the Fortification upon *Boston* Neck, and deliver them to the Select Men of *Boston*, or their Order, shall receive *Ten Pounds* old Tenor Reward for each of them, and have all necessary Charges paid.

By Order of the Select-Men,
Ezekiel Goldthwait, Town Clerk:

N. B. The said *Case* and *Knowles* stole the Boat belonging to the Hospital, and it's supposed went over to *Hull*, and design to travel to *Connecticut.*

Province of the Massachusetts Bay,
Court of the Vice Admiralty   Boston, December 14. 1745

The Boston Weekly News-Letter, December 19, 1745; December 26, 1745; *The Boston Weekly Post-Boy*, December 23, 1745; *The Boston Gazette, or Weekly Journal*, December 24, 1745. Minor differences between the papers. The *Post-Boy* has "Boston, December 17th. 1745." at the top, and ends after "travel to *Connecticut."*

STolen out of *Nathanael Moore's* Stable in *Worcester*, on the 15th Day of *December* Instant at Night, a Bay Horse about 8 or 9 Years old, 3 white Feet, the other Foot partly while, with a white Face, a small white Spot on his left Shoulder blade, one silver Eye, no Brand or Ear-mark, Paces well, suspected to be stolen by one *Israel Hilton*, a Man of middle Stature, round shouldered, he had on when he went away a blue Broad cloth Coat, a striped jacket, blue Plush Breeches. Whoever takes up either the Man or Horse, shall have *Five Pounds* Reward, and all necessary Charges paid.

The Boston Weekly News-Letter, December 19, 1745; December 26, 1745; January 9, 1746.

1746

BOSTON.
By His Excellency *WILLIAM SHIRLEY,* Esq; Captain General and Governor in Chief, in and over His Majesty's Province of the *Massachusetts-Bay* in *New England.*
A PROCLAMATION.

WHEREAS Capt. John Rouse, *Commander of His Majesty's Ship the* Shirley, *has represented to me that* John Turner, *Boatswain of the said Ship*, Joseph Breed, *Carpenter, and* John Elmes, Jacob Pyam, Jeremiah Fones, Samuel Webber, William Ingerson, Darby Solovan, Benjamin Cook, Richard Philips *and* George Chilmark, *Seamen, belonging to the said Ship have deserted to the great Detriment of his Majesty's Service, and the Hindrance of the said Capt.* Rouse *in proceeding one his Cruize for the Protection of this and the neighbouring Governments, and the Annoyance of his Majesty's Enemies.*

I have thought fit, with the Advice of his Majesty's Council, to issue this Proclamation, hereby strictly commanding, in his Majesty's Name, all his Majesty's Officers within this Province, to assist the said Capt. *Rouse* in making diligent Search in their respective Precincts for the said Deserters, and every of them; and then or any of them finding to apprehend and safely convey to the said Capt. *Rouse*, or his Order.

And I do further strictly forbid all and every Person and Persons whatsoever to entertain, harbour, conceal or convey away any of the said Deserters, as they will answer the same at their utmost Peril.

Given at the Council-Chamber in *Boston* the first Day of *January* 1745. [sic] In the Nineteenth Year of the Reign of our Sovereign Lord *GEORGE* the Second, by the Grace of GOD of *Great Britain, France* and *Ireland.* KING, Defender of the Faith, &c.

By Order of his Excellency the Governour, with the Advice of the Council,
J. Willard, *Secr.*   *W. SHIRLEY.*
            GOD save the KING.
The Boston Gazette, or Weekly Journal, January 7, 1746.

ON the ninth of *January* Instant, one *Jonathan Black*, broke out and ran away from his Majesty's Goal in York, in the Province of the *Massachusetts Bay*, who stood convicted upon a Conviction of Theft, and upon an action of Debt. He is a Molatto Fellow of a middle Stature, pretty thin and spare in his make, of a swarthy Complexion, black Eyes and Beard, about twenty eight Years of Age: He had on when he went away an old red duffle Great Coat. Whoever shall apprehend said Fellow and secure him, so that he may be retaken, shall have *ten Pounds* old Tenor Reward, and all reasonable Charges paid.

     Joseph Plaisted.   York, January 10, 1745. [sic]
The Boston Gazette, or Weekly Journal, January 21, 1746; January 28, 1746; February 4, 1746.

R*AN away from Capt.* Thomas Homans *of* Watertown, *a Negro Man named* Constant, *about Twenty Seven Years old, of thin Visage, and midling Stature, has a Scar under his Right Eye and speaks good English. He had* *on when he went away, a blue Coat with small Brass Buttons, and a Leather Jacket, double breasted, with round Metal Buttons, and a Leather Apron. Whoever takes up the said Negro and secures him so that his Master may have him again, shall have* Three Pounds *Reward, Old Tenor, and all reasonable Charges paid.*

N. B. All Masters of Vessels and other Persons are hereby cautioned against harbouring, concealing, or carrying off the said Negro, as they would avoid the Penalty of the Law in that Case made and provided.
Boston, Jan. 23. 1745,6.

The Boston Evening-Post, January 27, 1746.

WHEREAS the under-written Seaman and Servants have deserted from the Diamond *Transport,* William Sherwill *Master, now employed in His Majesty's Service, and lying in the Harbour* of Boston: If they will return to their Duty they will be kindly receiv'd; if not, whoever will bring them or either of them to the said Ship, or give Information to the said *William Sherwill* where they may be found, so that he may have them again, shall receive as a Reward for each Five Pounds old Tenor. And all Commanders and others, are hereby desired not to harbour or conceal them, as they will answer for it according to Law.
Seamen.

Thomas Jenney born at *Leghorn*, aged about twenty Years, about five Foot and three Inches in Stature, ruddy Complection, in Sailors Habit, wearing a Cap, and speaks broken English.

Robert Gellepsy, born at *Perthshire,* in *Scotland,* aged about twenty-six Years, in Stature about five Foot five inches, fair Complection, in Sailors Apparel, and wears a Cap.
Servants,

Michael Whitehead, born at *New Castle,* aged about twenty Years, five Foot six inches in Stature, in Sailors Apparel, wore a Cap of Furskin when he went away, his Fingers were also sore with the Frost.

Robert Stimpson, born at *Stockton,* in *Yorkshire,* aged 17 Years, about five Feet high, in Sailors Apparel, wearing a Fur Cap.

Robert Nickson born at *New-Castle,* aged 17 Years, Stature about five Feet, in Sailors Apparel, wears his own Hair.

Note, These Three have the North County Accent on their Speech.

The Boston Weekly News-Letter, January 30, 1746; February 6, 1746; February 13, 1746.

R*AN away from* John Craister *of* Boston, *a Negro Man named* Will, *about Thirty Years old, a thick short Fellow, speaks bad* English: *He had on when he went away, a Frock over a Cloth Jacket, and a red pair of Breeches. Whoever takes up the said Negro, and brigs him to his said Master, at the*

South End, shall have Forty Shillings *Reward, Old Tenor.* N. B. *All Masters of Vessels and other Persons, are hereby cautioned against harbouring, concealing, or carrying off the said Negro, as they would avoid the Penalty of the Law in that Case made and provided.*
Boston, February *the* 1*st.* 1745,6.
The Boston Evening-Post, February 3, 1746.

DEserted from his Majesty's *Castle William*, the Night last past, two Soldiers belonging to General *Philipps*'s Regiment, and were bound to *Annapolis Royal*, to recruit the Regiment here, viz. *Andrew Simson*, aged about 29 Years, a strait made Man of a dark Complexion, about 5 Feet 8 Inches, a Carpenter by Trade. *William Rose*, aged about 25 Years, of a brown Complexion, a strait well made clean limb'd Man, about 5 Feet 8 Inches, wore his own Hair, and is a Cordwainer by Trade. They had with them their Regimentals, which is a red Coat with Buff Facing, red Wastcoat and Breeches, square toed Shoes, white Stockings and Felt Hats; and said *Simson* over and above his Regimental had a Fustian Frock and brown Wastcoat, and had also his Wife with him, who is a small Woman. They were all born in *England*, and never before in this Country

And a few Days since, from the Store Ship *Diamond*, *William Casey*, aged about 27, about 5 Feet 4 Inches, with a great Impediment in his Speech, born in *Ireland*, and has the Accent of that Country.

Whoever shall apprehend the said Deserters or either of them, and return then to the commanding Officer at the Castle, or secure them in any of his Majesty's Goals in this or the neighbouring Governments, so that them may be return'd to their Officers, shall have *Ten Pounds*, Old Tenor, Reward, for each or either of said Soldiers, and all necessary Charges paid, and all Persons are forbid to conceal or entertain them, under the Penalty of the Law. *N. B.* Perhaps they may have altered their Cloaths.
JOHN WINSLOW. Dated at *Boston, Feb.* 8. 1745. [*sic*]
The Boston Evening-Post, February 10, 1746.

R*UN-away from his Master, Capt.* John Steel, *at the North End of* Boston, *the* 17*th Instant, a young Negro Fellow named* Pompey, *speaks pretty good English, is about* 19 *or* 20 *Years of Age, is short in Stature and pretty long Visaged, has been used to change his Name; he had on a green satteen Coat, Waistcoat and Breeches, the Coat pretty old, with white Metal Buttons, a cotton and linnen Shirt, an ordinary worsted Cap, and gray yarn Stockings; he took with him an old Hat, and a Leather Joky Cap, a pair of old black Stockings, and a new Ozenbrigs Frock, and an old pair of Boots. He had made several Attempts to get off in some Vessel, therefore all Masters of Vessels are caution'd not to entertain him. Whoever shall*

apprehend the said Negro, and convey him to said Master shall have Five Pounds, *old Tenor, and all necessary Charges paid by*
        John Steel.   Boston, Feb. 19. 1745,6.
The Boston Weekly News-Letter, February 20, 1746; February 27, 1746; March 14, 1746; *The Boston Evening-Post,* February 24, 1746; March 3, 1746; March 10, 1746; *The Boston Gazette, or Weekly Journal,* February 25, 1746; March 4, 1746; March 11, 1746; Minor differences between the papers.

RAN-away from his Master *Richard Smith,* of *Boston* Innholder, on Saturday the 25th Instant, a Negro Man Servant, named *Cato;* about 23 Years of Age. He had on when he went away a light colour'd Cloth Coat with Mohair Buttons, a pair of homespun Breeches, two homespun Jackets, a pair of yarn Stockings, and round to'd Shoes; speaks pretty good English but shows his Tongue when he speaks. He is a Shoemaker by Trade, and can both read and write.
    Whoever shall take up said Servant, and bring him to his said Master at the Sign of Admiral Vernon in Kingstreet, or secure him on any of His Majesty's Goals, shall have *five Pounds* Reward, old Tenor, and all
                  necessary Charges paid,   by *Richard Smith.*
    All Masters of Vessels and others are hereby caution'd against concealing or carrying off said Servant, on Penalty of the Law.
                                  Boston, February 28. 1745,6.
The Boston Gazette, or Weekly Journal, March 4, 1746; March 11, 1746; *The Boston Weekly News-Letter,* March 6, 1746. Minor differences between the papers.

Deserted from His Majesty's Castle William, *the Night last past, five Soldiers belonging to General Phillips's Regiment, and were bound to* Annapolis Royal, *to recruit the Regiment there.*
    Thomas Burton, *aged about 35 Years, a stout lusty and well limb'd Man of a fair Complexion, about 5 Feet 8 Inches, a Shoemaker by Trade, and wears a Wig.*
    Thomas Rock, *aged about 35, a short squat Man, of about 5 Feet 5 Inches, a Brushmaker by Trade, had short Hair, or a Cap.*
    William Smith, *aged about 21, a strait made Man, about 5 Feet 6 Inches, a Mason by Trade, of a light brown Complexion, wears his own Hair, pretty short and strait; all three born in* England.
    James Mullin, *aged about 30, a stout made Man, of a sour Complexion, and pretty dark, wears his own Hair, and is about 5 Feet 9 Inches; an* Irishman.
    James Linum, *aged about 25, a strait thin Man, of a dark Complexion, of about 5 Feet 11 Inches, wears his own Hair; also an* Irishman.

They had with them their Regimentals, which is a Red Coat with Bugg Facings, and Felt Hats, with a worsted white Lace on them. They were never in this County before.

Whoever shall apprehend the said Deserters, or either of them, and return them to the commanding Officer at the Castle, or secure them in any of his Majesty's Goals in this or the neighbouring Governments, so that they may be return'd to their Officers, shall have Ten Pounds, *Old Tenor, Reward for each or either of said Solders, and all necessary Charges paid, and all Persons are forbid to conceal or entertain them, under the Penalty of the Law.*

N. B. Perhaps they may have altered their Cloaths.

The Boston Evening-Post, March 24, 1746; March 31, 1746.

W*HEREAS an unhappy Difference has for many Years subsisted between me* John Charnock, *the Subscriber, and* Emma Charnock *my Wife, and her Carriage and Behaviour towards me has been so unkind and ungrateful, that I have been obliged for Peace sake to separate myself from her; these are to forbid all Persons to make use of my Name in crediting her for any one thing whatsoever; for I will not pay any Debts contracted by her, after the Date hereof, as Witness my Hand,* John Charnock.

Boston, March 24, 1745-6.

The Boston Evening-Post, March 24, 1746; March 31, 1746.

R*AN away from his Master* Stephen Sawyer, *jun. of* Newbury, *on the 21st. of this Instant March, a Molatto Man-Servant named* Peroe, *aged 25 Years, of middling Stature: He has a Notch in his Fore Teeth, a full brisk Eye, a Scar on one of his Legs; He took with him a wool and castor Hat, a green worsted and a white Fustian Cap, two brown Wigs, several Shirts woollen and linnen, a blew drugget Coat and a dark colour'd home-made Fustian Coat, plain without Pocket-Flaps, a brown camblet and a white striped Jacket, two Pair of Breeches, one of Buck-Skin, and the other Cloth, and a Pair of double stitch'd Pumps, a Pair of new and a Pair of old Shoes.*

Whosoever shall take up said Run away and bring him to his Master, shall have Five Pounds *old Tenor Reward besides all necessary Charges.*

Stephen Sawyer.

The Boston Weekly Post-Boy, March 24, 1746; March 31, 1746; April 21, 1746.

DEserted from the Ship *Katharine* and *Ann, Edmund Agars* Master, on Friday Night last the 21st Instant, a Servant Lad named *James Gutry* late belonging to the Orkneys, aged about 18 Years of Age, of a sanguine Complection, red Hair, about five Feet high, speaks broad Scotch, wearing a light colour'd Coat, and Seamens Cloaths. Also deserted at the same time a Seaman named *Isaac Wilson*, aged about 20 Years, pretty fair Complection, about five Feet high, wearing a Seaman's Apparel when he went away.

If any Person will apprehend said Deserters, they shall receive *five Pounds* old Tenor, for each of them or if they will return to the Ship within 48 Hours, they shall be well accepted.

N. B. All Masters Officers and others and others are hereby caution'd against carrying off, shipping or harbouring the said Servants, as they would avoid the Penalty of the Law in that Case made and provided.

The said Master may be spoke with on board the said Ship at the End of the Long Wharff Boston.

The Boston Gazette, or Weekly Journal, March 25, 1746.

B*Roke out of* Salem *Goal last Night, and absconded,* John Webb, *Jun. of said Salem: He is a middle statured, well set Man, of about Thirty Five Years of Age, and wears a Wigg, or Cap. Whoever shall take up said* Webb, *and bring him back to said Goal, or otherwise secure him, or shall discover such as assisted his Escape, so that they may be convicted thereof, in either Case, shall be paid* Twenty Pounds, *Old Tenor, and all necessary Charges,*
          by me   Robert Hall.   Beverly, March 20, 1746.

The Boston Evening-Post, March 31, 1746; April 7, 1746; April 14, 1746; *The Boston Weekly News-Letter*, April 3, 1746; April 10, 1746; April 17, 1746; *The Boston Weekly Post-Boy*, March 31, 1746; April 7, 1746; April 28, 1746. Minor differences between the papers. See *The Boston Weekly News-Letter*, April 5, 1754, and *The Boston Weekly News-Letter*, July 18, 1754.

RAN-away from his Master Dr. *Nathaniel Ames* of *Dedham*, a Negro Man Servant named *Cato*, a lusty Fellow, aged about 21 Years, speaks good English, had on a pale-dy'd Cloth colour'd Great-Coat and small Coat of the same, sheep skin Breeches, &c. He has endeavour'd to enlist to go to *Cape-Breton*. Whosoever shall take up said Negro and commit him to his Majesty's Goal in Boston, or convey him to his Master in *Dedham*, or give Intelligence of him so that he may be had, shall have *Five Pounds*, old Tenor, Reward, and all necessary Charges paid. All Persons are desired not to harbour said Negro; and all Masters of Vessels are caution'd not to take said Negro on board their Vessels upon the pain and penalties of the Law.
          Nathaniel Ames.   *Dedham, April* 15. 1746.

The Boston Weekly News-Letter, April 17, 1746.

RUN-away from his Master *Thomas Shearman* of *Portsmouth* on *Rhode Island*, the 12th of this Instant *April*, a Negro Man about 30 Years of Age, named *Prince*, a pretty likely Fellow, short Stature, who had on when he went away a blew Drugget Coat, a greenish Jacket, full Cloth Breeches, Castor Hat, Shoes and Stockings. Whoever shall secure or bring the aforesaid Negro to his Master, shall have *Five Pounds* old Tenor Reward and all necessary Charges

     paid by me *Thomas Shearman.*

The Boston Weekly Post-Boy, April 21, 1746; April 28, 1746; May 5, 1746.

       [Three Pounds to be got]

R*AN away from* Thomas Fleet *of* Boston, *Printer, on Tuesday the* 22*d Instant, a Negro Fellow named* Newport, *about 21 Years old, of a Middle Stature, but spry and slim, and has a large Scar over his right Eye. He is a cunning prating Fellow, pretends to be free, and has a great Inclination to go to Sea.*

  He had on a Cotton and Linen Shirt, a striped homespun Jacket, and a thick blue Jacket over it, and thick Leather Breeches.

  Whoever shall take him up, and bring him to his Master, at the Heart and Crown in Cornhill, shall have Three Pounds *Reward, Old Tenor, and all reasonable Charges paid.*

  N. B. He will endeavour to get off by Sea, therefore all Masters of Vessels and others are cautioned against harbouring, concealing or carrying him off on any Pretence whatever, as they would avoid the Penalty of the Law. Boston, April 23, 1746.

The Boston Evening-Post, April 28, 1746; May 5, 1746; May 12, 1746.

RAN-away on the 28th Instant from Mr. *Robert Galton* in *Boston*, a Welch Boy of about 14 Years of Age, named *Thomas Watkins*, belonging to the Ship Duke of Devonshire, has on a blue Jacket, black Wigg, high Heel Shoes. Whoever shall apprehend the said Servant Boy, and bring him on Board said Ship, or to the above *Robert Galton* at the Corner of Cold Lane, shall have *five pounds* old Tenor: And all Masters of Ships are caution'd not to entertain or carry him off. Boston, *April* 28*th*, 1746.

The Boston Gazette, or Weekly Journal, April 29, 1746.

RAN-away on the 9th Instant, from his Master *John Barrell*, of *Boston*, a Negro Man named *Pompey*, about 20 Years old, well shap'd of a middling Stature, had on when he went away a blue Jacket, white Shirt, leather Breeches, white worsted Stockings. Whoever shall apprehend the said Runaway and bring him to said *Barrell's* House in *Sudbury* Street, shall have *Three Pounds* old Tenor, Reward, and all necessary Charges paid.

And all Masters of Vessels and others are hereby caution'd not to entertain or carry off the said Negro, upon Penalty of the Law, in that Case made and provided.
The Boston Weekly Post-Boy, June 9, 1746; June 16, 1746; *The Boston Gazette, or Weekly Journal*, June 10, 1746; June 17, 1746.

I *The Subscriber,* Cornelius Wotton *of* Boston *in* New-England, *Mariner, having lately had the Misfortune of a Gadding Wife, who is resolved to waste my Estate as far as in her Power, do hereby forbid any Person whatsoever to trade with or trust her for any Matter or Thing whatsoever upon my Credit, for I will not hereafter pay any Debts whatsoever that she may hereafter so contract; as Witness my Hand this fourteenth Day of* June, *A. D.* 1746. Cornelius Wotton.
The Boston Evening-Post, June 16, 1746.

Deserted from His Majesty's Regiment of Foot, Commanded by the Hon. Sir *William Pepperrell* Baronet, and from on Board the Britania Schooner, Capt. *Greyvll* Master, who put into *Boston* Harbour on his Way from *Philadelphia* to *Louisbourg,* viz.

John Smith, six Foot High, slender of Body, brown Hair, aged twenty four Years, had on a short green Wastcoat, buckskin Breeches, had with him a short pair of Trousers, blue worsted Stockings.

James Howell, five Foot nine Inches high brown Complection, black Hair, had on a Camblet Coat and Wastcoat, Buckskin Breeches blue worsted Stockings, old Shoes &c.

Whoever will secure said Deserters or give Notice of them to Messirs. *Colman* and *Sparhawk* of *Boston* so as that they may be taken, shall have twenty Pounds old Tenor for each Deserter, paid immediately by said Gentlemen.
The Boston Gazette, or Weekly Journal, June 17, 1746.

RAN-away from his Master *Jonathan Dwight,* of *Boston,* Innholder, on the 15th at Night, a Negro Man named *Newham,* lately owned by Mr. *Luke Vardy,* had on a blue Coat, red Lining, and blue ribb'd Stockings. Whoever will inform of or bring him to his said Master, shall be well Rewarded therefor; and all Persons are hereby caution'd against entertaining or concealing him.
The Boston Weekly-News-Letter, June 19, 1746.

WHEREAS Mary Foulsham, *the Wife of Lieutenant* John Foulsham *of* Exeter, *in the Province of* New-Hampshire, *has for some time past absconded herself, refusing to cohabit and dwell with her Husband: This is therefore to warn and caution all People whatever from entertaining her, or*

trusting her with any Thing on my Account, for I hereby declare I will not pay any Thing for her after the Date hereof
      John Foulsham.   Exeter, July 11,1746,
The Boston Weekly Post-Boy, July 14, 1746; July 21, 1746; July 28, 1746. See *The Boston Weekly Post-Boy,* August 25, 1746.

RAN away from his Master Capt. *John Leppington* of *Charlestown* on Tuesday Evening the 8th. Instant, a Negro Man named *York,* a tall stout Fellow, about Twenty Years of Age, he had on when he went away a strip'd homespun Jacket, a blue Cloth Breeches, and Cotton and Linnen Shirt, worsted Cap, no Hat Shoes nor Stockings, Whoever shall take up the abovesaid Runaway and him safely convey to his said Master in Charlestown, shall have *Five Pounds* old Tenor Reward, and all necessary Charges paid.
  And all Masters of Vessels are hereby warned against carrying off said Servant, on Penalty of the Law in that Case made and provided.
                    Boston July 12. 1746.
The Boston Gazette, or Weekly Journal, July 15, 1746.

RAN away on the 3d instant, a Negro Man named *Portsmouth,* aged about 40 Years, of middle Stature, walks Limping and Spla-footed, talks good English, and plays on the Fiddle, he carried with him an Orange colour'd Coat with yellow Metal Buttons, a Wast Coat of thin Stuff, and Cloath Breeches.
  Whoever takes up said Fellow is desired to convey him to *Robert Temple* at his House in *Charlestown,* and they shall have *Five Pounds* Reward old Tenor, and all necessary Charges paid.
The Boston Gazette, or Weekly Journal, July 15, 1746.

RAN away on Tuesday the 8th Instant from his Master *James Collingwood,* a Jersey Boy named *John Leveston,* about 15 Years of Age, he had on when he went away a Tarry Frock. a pair of Trousers, he is a short well set Boy. Whosoever shall take up said Runaway and bring him to said *James Collingwood,* or to the Printer hereof, shall have *three Pounds* Reward, old Tenor, and all necessary Charges paid.
  And all Masters of Vessels and others are hereby caution'd against concealing or carrying off said Servant on Penalty of the Law in that Case made and provided.
       James Collingwood.   *Boston* July 15th 1746.
The Boston Gazette, or Weekly Journal, July 15, 1746.

RAN *away from his Master, the Hon.* John Alford, *Esq; of* Charlestown, *on Monday the fourteenth of July Currant, a Negro Man Servant named*

Boston, *about* 23 *or* 24 *Years of Age, speaks broken English, is a well made comely Fellow, between a middling and a tall Stature. He had on when he went away, a Jocky Cap, a blue double breasted close Coat, with close Sleeves, and white flat metal Buttons, some of them broke, a Cotton and Linen Shirt, strip'd blue and white Cotton and Linen Breeches, Yarn Stockings, a pair of very handsome new fashion'd large Silver Buckles in his Shoes. Whoever shall bring him to his said Master, shall have* Three Pounds, *Old Tenor, Reward, and all necessary Charges paid.*
                                                     Charlestown, 21*st*. July 1746.
    The Boston Evening-Post, July 21, 1746; July 28, 1746.

RAN *away from his Master Col.* Joseph Buckminster, *of* Framingham, *on the* 22*d Day of* June *last past, a Negro Man Servant, named* Cobbo, *alias* Pompey, *about* 25 *Years of Age, speaks very broken English, of middling Stature, well-set, full-fac'd, something Pock fretten. He had on a Cap, an old Hat, a good Tow cloth Shirt, woollen cloth colour'd Jacket, Camblet Breeches, yarn Stockings the Feet newly stock'd. Whoever shall take up the said Negro and convey him to his Master at* Framingham, *or to Mr.* William Cowell, *Goldsmith in* Boston, *shall have* Five Pounds *old Tenor Reward, and all necessary Charges paid.*
    The Boston Weekly News-Letter, July 24, 1746; July 31, 1746.

DEserted from the Regiment now raising for his Majesty's Service for the Expedition to *Canada, Nath. Clark* of Great Britain, inlisted the 14th of June last, about five Foot eight Inches, ruddy Complection, and pitted with the Small Pox; as also *Benjamin Taplin* of Roxbury: Whoever will bring either of these Persons to Mr. *Hibbert Newton* of Boston in Marlborough-street, shall have *five Pounds* old Tenor Reward, and all Charges paid.
    The Boston Gazette, or Weekly Journal, July 29, 1746; August 5, 1746.

RAN-away from his Master *Gilbert Brook* of *Weymouth* in the County of *Suffolk*, Shipwright, on the 24th of June last, an Apprentice Lad, about 18 Years of Age, tall and slim; has a Scar on the outside of one of his Legs; had on when he went away a blue homespun Coat & Jacket, Cloth colour'd Leather Breeches, woollen Shirt, old Stockings and Shoes, a Beaver Hat, Wigg and Cap His Name is *Zechariah Bicknel*. Whosoever shall apprehend said Runaway, and convey him to his said Master shall have *five Pounds* old Tenor Reward, and all necessary Charges paid. And all Masters of Vessels are hereby caution'd against carrying off said Apprentice, as they will answer the same, on Penalty of the Law.   Boston, *July* 18 1746.
    The Boston Gazette, or Weekly Journal, July 29, 1746.

WHereas Abigail Livermore, *the Wife of* John Livermore *of* Framingham, *hath eloped from her said Husband.*

These are to forbid all Persons entertaining her the said *Abigail,* as they will answer it at their Person; and all to caution all Persons against trusting of her, for he will pay none of her Debts.

    John Livermore.   Framingham, *July* 22 1746.
The Boston Gazette, or Weekly Journal, July 29, 1746.

ON Monday the 21st of *July* a young Man of about 19 Years of Age, inlisted with *Bartho. Green,* by the Name of *John Debenport,* receiv'd 8 £. in Part of his Bounty, and has since deserted. He is of middle Stature, down look, round shoulder'd, pale Complection, has a large Nose. Had on a blue Jacket, cotton & linnen Shirt, Trowsers and old Shoes. He says he was born in *Brantree,* but of late liv'd in *Dedham.* Whoever will apprehend the said Deserter, and convey him to the abovesaid *Green,* at the South End of *Boston,* shall have *Ten Pounds* old Tenor Reward.

N.B. He has with him a Flute, and 'tis tho't will change his Name.

The Boston Weekly News-Letter, July 31, 1746; August 7, 1746.

WHEREAS Philip Smith *of* Warwick *in the Colony of* Rhode-Island, *on the 27th of* June *last, and one* Phinehas Loomis *of* Lebanon, *in the Colony of* Connecticut, *in the Month of* July *last, did enlist themselves under me for the intended Expedition to* Canada, *and receiv'd the Bounty allowed by the Province of* Massachusetts Bay *for that Service; but have since deserted and conceal themselves, and keep from attending their Duty in that Respect:* Therefore whoever will take up the said Deserters and convey them to *Boston* that they may be on their Duty, shall have *Ten Pounds* old Tenor Reward, for each of either of them, and all necessary Charges paid. The said *Smith* is a tall Man of black Complexion, slow of Speech, and follows the Trade of a Tinker.

    JONATH. LAWRENCE.

The Boston Weekly News-Letter, August 15, 1746; August 21, 1746; August 28, 1746; *The Boston Evening-Post,* August 25, 1746; September 1, 1746. Minor differences between the papers.

R*AN away from his Master,* John Horswell *of* Little Compton, *on the* 8*th of this Instant* August, *a Negro Man named* Prince, *about* 30 *Years old, of a midling Stature, and some Words he cannot speak plain. He had on a new Castor Hat, Linen check'd Shirt, a double breasted Linen striped Jacket, a gray Jacket with Pewter Buttons, one pair of check'd Trowzers, and another pair of white, two pair of Stockings, one of Yarn and the other Worsted, of a bluish Colour, and a pair of single soled Calf-skin Shoes. Whoever shall take up said Negro, and bring him to his said Master, shall have* Five

Pounds *Reward, Old Tenor, and all necessary Charges paid.*
Aug. 15. 1746.
The Boston Evening-Post, August 25, 1746; September 1, 1746; September 8, 1746.

To the Publisher of the Boston Week'y Post-Boy.
Sir,
IN your paper of the 21st of July last No. 609) I find an Advertisement, signed by *John Foulsham,* who tells the Word, *That* Mary *his Wife has for some Time past absconded herself, refusing to cohabit and dwell with her said Husband;* and thereupon forbidding all Persons to entertain her, &c.

Now please to let the said Mr. *Foulsham* and the World know, That his said Wife is ready and willing to return to his House, cohabit and discharge all Conjugal Duties incumbent on her, provided she may live in Peace without indangering Life or Limb, and have reasonable Security or Assurance that she shall not be either knock'd down, horse-whipt, or kick'd without any Cause or Reason.—For as she liv'd in Peace, Credit, and Reputation with a former Husband, she is still fond of that kind of Life, and would chuse to maintain till Death that Character which she heretofore had, of a dutiful, frugal, faithful Wife. In her Behalf,
I am your humble Servant, Samuel Joy.
The Boston Weekly Post-Boy, August 25, 1746. See *The Boston Weekly Post-Boy,* July 14, 1746.

LATELY deserted from His Majesty's Service, out of a company of Foot under the command of Capt. *Charles Mackintosh,* designed on the Expedition against *Canada,* the following Persons, viz....

Amaziah Bush, New-England born, about six Foot High, a likely well-set Man, aged about 30 Years, wears a blew cloath Coat, red plush Breeches, and short black curl'd Hair.

Thomas Wiswal, also a *New-England* Man, about five Foot ten Inches high slender Body'd, has lately had the small Pox, and much pitted with it, aged about 25 Years.

Whosoever takes up said Deserters, or either of them, and delivers them to *Stephen Bayard,* Esq: at *New-York,* or to their said *Company* at *Albany,* shall have 4 Pounds Reward and all reasenable Charges
paid by *Charles Mackintosh.*
The New-York Evening Post, September 1, 1746; September 8, 1746; September 15, 1746; September 22, 1746; September 29, 1746; October 6, 1746; October 13, 1746; October 20, 1746; October 27, 1746; November 10, 1746; November 17, 1746; November 24, 1746; December 1, 1746; December 8, 1746; December 15, 1746; December

22, 1746; December 29, 1746. The ads from November 24 on do not list Wiswal.

B*Roke out his Majesty's Goal in* Salem, *last Night, one* John Siah, *committed for counterfeiting* Rhode Island *Bills. He is of midling Stature, and of a brown Complexion, and Pockfretten; he wears a Wigg or Cap, and has been branded with the Letter* T *on the Ball of his right Thumb. Whoever shall apprehend and secure said* Siah, *so that he may be conveyed to said Goal, shall have* Fifty Pounds, *Old Tenor, Reward, and all reasonable Charges paid by me,* ROBERT HALE, *Sheriff of the County of* Essex. Beverly, Sept. 4. 1746.

The Boston Evening-Post, September 8, 1746; September 15, 1746; September 22, 1746; *The Boston Gazette, or Weekly Journal*, September 9, 1746; September 16, 1746; September 23, 1746; *The Boston Weekly News-Letter*, September 11, 1746; September 18, 1746; September 25, 1746. Minor differences between the papers.

D*Eserted from Capt.* Nathaniel Richard's *Company of Foot design'd on the Expedition against* Canada, *the following Persons, viz.*

Samuel Donum, *New-England born aged 25 Years well set about 5 Feet 9 inches high a Sailor....*

Whoever apprehends the said Deserters or either of them, and secures them so that they may be had again shall receive Four Pounds Reward for each, and all reasonable Charges paid by me, Nathanial Richards.

The New-York Evening Post, September 8, 1746; September 22, 1746; September 29, 1746; October 6, 1746; October 20, 1746; October 27, 1746; November 10, 1746; November 17, 1746.

W*Hereas* Thomas Twigg *and* William Boyd, *Mariners, belonging to the Ship* Fisher, Philip Baker, *Master, now in the port of* Boston, *have absented themselves from the Service of the said Ship; if they will return to their Duty, they shall be kindly received, otherwise they shall be deemed Deserters.*

The Boston Evening-Post, September 15, 1746; September 22, 1746.

T*His is to give Notice to all Persons, that the Wife of Doctor* John Hoyle *of* Providence, *which was formerly the Widow of Capt.* Samuel Wett *of* Malden, *has left her Husband; I do forbid any Person trading with her, for I shall not pay any Debts she shall contract, till after she returns home to her Husband at* Providence. John Hoyle.

The Boston Evening-Post, September 22, 1746. See *The Boston Evening-Post*, October 6, 1746.

WHereas George Palmer *of* Boston *late of* Lancaster *in the County of* Worcester, *did inlist with me the Subscriber on the* 18*th Day of* August *last, for the intended Expedition, and received* thirty Pounds *old Tenor Bounty Money, but has since deserted, and kept from attending his Duty in that Respect:*

Whoever shall take up the said Deserter, and convey him to the Subscriber at *Malden*, shall have *ten Pounds* Reward old Tenor, and all necessary Charges paid. The said *Palmer* is a thick Fellow, fresh Complection about 50 Years of Age, and follows the Trade of a Tinker.
    Joseph Wilson.   *Malden Sept* 19*th* 1746.
The Boston Gazette, or Weekly Journal, September 23, 1746.

  W*Hereas* Mary, *the Wife of* Philip Mahaney *of* Boston, *Truckman, has run him in Debt: These are therefore to warn all Persons not to Credit her on any Account, for I do hereby declare I will pay no Debt she shall contract after the Date hereof. Witness my Hand,*
    Philip Mahaney.   Boston, Sept. 22d. 1746.
The Boston Gazette, or Weekly Journal, September 23, 1746.

WHEREAS *Stephen Greenleaf,* a Carpenter, belonging to the Ship *Good Intent, Benjamin Mulberry,* Master, now in the Port of *Boston,* hath absented himself from the Service of said Ship: If he will return to his Duty, he shall be kindly received, otherwise he shall be deemed a Deserter.
The Boston Weekly News-Letter, September 25, 1746.

WHEREAS John Colby *of* Marlborough, *lately living at the* New-Meadows, *did sometime since, at* Haverhill, *inlist himself in his Majesty's Service in the Expedition against* Canada, *in the Company of Mr.* John Marston, *and at the same Time receive* Thirty Pounds *enlisting Money:*

These are to require the said *Colby* forthwith to appear of at the House of the said *Marston* at *Boston,* as he will answer the contrary at his Peril.
    John Marston.
The Boston Weekly News-Letter, September 25, 1746.

WHEREAS John Kelly *and* James Wilson, *did on the* 30*th of* August *last enlisted with me the Subscriber in the present Expedition against* Canada, *and having absented themselves for several Days past:* Whoever will secire said Persons or give me Informaton so that I may secure them, or either of them, shall have *Ten Pounds* old Tenor Reward for each
    paid by me *John Soutback.*
N. B. The said *Wilson* also enlisted with Capt. *David Hills.*

The Boston Weekly News-Letter, September 25, 1746.

R*AN away from his Master, Col.* William Williams, *a lusty well set Negro named* Caesar, *(sometimes calls himself* Archalus*) near six Feet tall, speaks pretty good* English; *had on when he went away, a grey Jacket, Buff Breeches and a rusty Hat, the Brims cut narrow. Whoever shall apprehend said Negro, and bring him to his said Master in* Boston, *shall have* Five Pounds, *Old Tenor, Reward,*
    paid by   William Williams.
Note, All Masters of Vessels and others are hereby cautioned against concealing, harbouring or carrying off said Negro, as they will answer the same.
The Boston Evening-Post, September 29, 1746.

W*Hereas* Louis Fillis *Mariner, dwelling in the Town of* Boston in the County of Suffolk, and Province of the Massachusetts Bay, has most unfortunately met with an extravagant Wife; for which, and other sufficient Causes, desires that no Person or Persons would credit her in and upon any Account whatsoever, for by proper Complaints being made to the Justices, he has obtained Leave to cry her down. *Given under my Hand this* 25*th of Sept* 1746.   *Louis Fillis.*
The Boston Gazette, or Weekly Journal, September 30, 1746.

D*Eserted from his Majesty's Service, a lusty well-set Indian Man, named* John Holborn, *aged 26 Years, wears his own Hair, and had on him a striped Jacket, and a wide pair of Trowsers: Whoever will take up said Deserter, and bring him to* Henry Wendell *in* Boston, *shall have* Ten Pounds, *old Tenor, Reward, and all necessary Charges paid.*
The Boston Weekly News-Letter, October 2, 1746; October 9, 1746; October 17, 1746.

September 27*th Day*, 1746.
T*his to give Notice to all Men, what was the Cause that I put my Wife in the Papers, being she had left me. The Law is plain she had Power to run me into Debt, but she never did any such Thing, and she saith she never intended to run me into any Debt, and I think my Wife's Word is to be credited.*   John Hoyle.
The Boston Evening-Post, October 6, 1746; October 20, 1746. See *The Boston Evening-Post*, September 22, 1746.

R*AN* away from his Master *Philip Caverly* of *Colchester* in Connecticut, on the 24th of April last, a Negro Man named *Japhet*, about 21 Years old, his Toes on one Foot froze off, and Part of the other: He had on when he went away a Great Coat of a brown Colour, and a close bodied Coat of the same colour, Linnen Breeches, gray Stockings; but I suppose that in this length of Time he may have chang'd his Cloaths: He passes himself for a Freeman. Whoever shall take up said Runaway, and convey him to his Master, shall have *twenty Pounds* old Tenor Reward, and all necessary Charges paid: And if taken up forty Miles from Home, commit him to the next Goal, and send me Word.

    Philip Caverly.   *Sept.* 29.
The Boston Gazette, or Weekly Journal, October 28, 1746.

DEserted from his Majesty's Service, on Tuesday Night last, from on Board a Schooner, in the Harbour of *Boston,* lately employ'd as a Flagg of Truce, from *Louisbourgh* to *Checbucta,* the following Men, *viz.*

 James Howarth, a Soldier, who went off in his Regimental Cloaths, red, with yellow Facings and Cuffs, about five Feet ten Inches high, fair and thin-fac'd, is about 26 Years of Age, has short black Hair, and had on a red great Coat when he went away.

 William Alland, a Sailor, about 40 Years of Age, about five Feet seven Inches high.

 William Edinburough, a Sailor about 24 Years of Age, and about five Feet nine Inches high, red hair'd.

 —— *Chilman,* a Sailor about 20 Years of Age, and about five Feet nine Inches high, Hair-lip'd.

 Whoever shall take up the said Deserters or any of them, and bring them to the Hon. Admiral WARREN, or secure them in any of His Majesty's Goals, shall have a Reward of Three Guineas for each, besides what is allow'd by Act of Parliament.

 The Boston Weekly News-Letter, October 30, 1746; November 6, 1746; *The Boston Evening-Post,* November 3, 1746; November 10, 1746; *The Boston Gazette, or Weekly Journal,* November 4, 1746; November 11, 1746. The *Post* and *Gazette* spell the third man's name as Edinburgh. The *Gazette* ends with:

N.B. The above Deserters took with them 2 Boats. Whoever will bring the said Boats to *Benjamin Hallowell* shall have *five Pound* old Tenor Reward for each Boat, and all Necessary Charges paid.

***R**AN-away from her Master* Thomas Stone *of* Lovewell's *Island, an Indian Girl named* Ruth, *born at* Ipswich, *a short well set Girl, has a Scar over her right Eye, and another in her Throat; she went away with a light colour'd great Coat, without Cape or Cuffs, a bluish colour'd close body'd Coat, smoak'd Leather Breeches, yarn Stocking,* [sic] *brass shoe Buckles; and 'tis supposed she has the said Cloaths on, having some time since inlisted in the Expedition in such a Dress, but was soon discover'd and dismiss'd.*

Whoever shall take up and return the said Girl to her said Master on the Island, or to Elias Stone of Charlstown, *Jun.* [sic] *shall have* five Pounds *Reward, old Tenor, and all necessary Charges paid.*

The Boston Gazette, or Weekly Journal, November 4, 1746; November 11, 1746.

Portsmouth *on* Rhode-Island, November *the* 17th. *A. D.* 1746.
T*his is to give Notice to all Persons, that* Martha, *the Wife of* Michael Cory *of* Portsmouth *aforesaid, has left her Husband. I do forbid any Person or Persons trading with her, or trusting of her, to the Value of any Sum, for I will not pay any Debts she shall contract.*
Michael Cory.

The Boston Evening-Post, December 1, 1746.

L*Ately Ran away from the Snow* Grand Duke, John Taylor *Commander,* William Torrington, *a Servant to Mr.* James Russel *of* Boston. *Whoever shall take up the said Servant, and bring him to his said Master, or to Capt.* Taylor, *shall have* Twenty Pounds *Reward, Old Tenor, and all necessary Charges paid. And whoever shall Harbour, conceal or carry him off, may expect to be prosecuted with the utmost Severity of the Law.*

The Boston Evening-Post, December 8, 1746; December 15, 1746; December 29, 1746.

L*Ately ran the Snow* Grand Duke, John Taylor *Master,* William Talantire, *a Servant belonging to Capt.* James Russell, *about* 20 *Years of Age, was born at* Carlisle, *speaks something Broad, well set, five Feet 4 Inches high, fresh Complexion. Whoever will bring said Servant, or give Information so that his Master may have him again, shall have* 30 *Pounds, old Tenor Reward, and Charges paid; and whoever shall harbour, conceal or carry him off, may expect to be prosecuted with the utmost Severity of the Law.*

The Boston Evening-Post, December 15, 1746; December 29, 1746.

DEserted the 8th Instant from the Ship *Duke of Bedford,* James Collingwood Commander, a Sailor named *James Dogget*, belonging to *Rhode Island* Government: He is of a pale Complection and middle Stature; had on a dark Wigg, or a new worsted Cap, an old Pea Jacket blue, the Seams are cover'd with white Linen, or else he had on a new pea Jacket of a brown Kersey, lined with blue Duffle: he is broke out with Blotches on his Hands and Knees. And is suppos'd to be gone to *Rhode Island.* Whoever shall apprehend said Deserter, and bring him to said *Collingwood,* shall have *Ten Pounds* old Tenor Reward.

The Boston Gazette, or Weekly Journal, December 16, 1746.

Hatfield, Dec. 9th. 1746.
WHereas *Thomas Wilson, John Morey,* and *Isaac Whisk* all of the Colony of *Connecticut,* (enlisted by Lieut. *James Mitchell*) *Th*[   ] of said Colony, and *Nathaniel Davis* of this Province enlisted by myself for the Expedition against *Canada,* have not attended their Duty with the rest of their Fellow Soldiers in this Town; They are hereby order'd forthwith to repair to this Place, or otherwise they shall be treated as Deserters.
  Wm. Williams.
 The Boston Evening-Post, December 22, 1746.

COmfort Page, *an Indian Woman, Wife of* William Page *of* Newport, *have Elop'd from her Husband, and denies to live with him, therefore these are to desire all Persons not to Credit her, for he will not pay a Penny for her. Giveth under my Hand at* Newport, *the* 19*th of* December, 1746,
  William Page.
 The Boston Evening-Post, December 22, 1746; December 29, 1746; January 5, 1747.

1747

WHEREAS Oliver Darby *and* Ebenezer Severance, *Soldiers in his Majesty's Service at* Castle William, *who had Leave to be absent on Furlough, and the Time has long since expired: They are therefore hereby ordered to return directly to their Duty, or else they shall be treated as Deserted. Dated as his Majesty's* Castle William, *this fourteenth Day of* February, Anno Domini, 1746.
  John Larrabe.
 The Boston Evening-Post, February 16, 1747; March 2, 1747.

Broke out of His Majesty's Goal in Portsmouth in the Province of New-Hampshire, this fifth Day of February 1747, one Benjamin Littleton, a tall slim Man, about six Feet in length, had a large Nose, and as he said bred a Shoemaker, of a swarthy Complexion, and was born at Cape Cod or in Virginia, (he has said sometimes that he was born at Cape Cod, and sometimes that he was born in Virginia;) And one Wm Groster a Man of a middling Stature; he has had the Small Pox, of a low Voice, speaks broad Scotch; both young Men, and in Sailors Habits. Whoever shall take up the said Men, or either of them, and convey them, or either of them, to the Goal in the abovesaid Province, shall have for their Trouble Twenty Pounds old Tenor, for each of them.
  Thomas Packer, Shr. Portsmouth, *Febr.* 5. 1746.
  Province *of* New-Hampshire.
 The Boston Weekly Post-Boy, February 23, 1747; March 2, 1747.

Portsmouth, Febr. 5. 1747.
RAN-away in Company two Indian Women, one of them named *Experience*, Servant to *Aaron Eliot* of *Killingworth*, a large well-looking Wench, about 25 Years old, speaks pretty good English, a soft Voice, seemingly good-natured Behaviour; she carried with her two woolen Gowns of white Warp and striped in the filling with light Colours, one of them old, the other almost new, considerable or red, she hath since got a Blanket, The other named *Patience*, Servant to *Nathaniel Chapman* of *Saybrook*, about 27 years old, a short thick fat Wench, her Arms scar'd with burning for the Gout, speaks but little, seldom any English and that broken, had on a green woolen Gown, striped Coat, leather-heal'd Womens Shoes, carried with her a dark colour'd streaked Bed blanket: They came both from Nantucket, and are not likely to part; they went away in Company with a Negro Man. Whoever will take up said Run-aways and return them home, or secure them and inform so that they may be had, shall have Fifty Shillings, old Tenor, per Head, and all necessary Charges paid for them by their respective Masters.

The Boston Weekly Post-Boy, March 2, 1747; March 9, 1747; March 16, 1747. Second and third ads do not have the date and location at the top.

RAN away from Col. *Joseph Stafford* of *Warwick*, the 1st of *January* last, a Mulatto Man Servant named *Ben Peg*, alias *Ben Austin*, a lusty well set Fellow, who had on a light coloured Pea Jacket, old Shoes and Stockings, with a Scar on his Nose, and a large Scar on one of his Legs. Whoever shall take up said Servant, and send him Home, or secure him that he may he had, shall have *Five Pounds* Reward, *Old Tenor,* and all Necessary Charges paid by *Martin Howard* of *Newport*, or *Joseph Stafford*.

The Boston Evening-Post, March 16, 1747; March 23, 1747; March 30, 1747; *The Boston Weekly Post-Boy,* March 16, 1747; March 30, 1747. Minor differences between the papers.

Newport, Rhode-Island, March 4. 1746-7.
RUn away, on the 10th day of January last, in company, two English women servants, belonging to Robert Geltone, resident in Boston, New-England; one of them named Mandlin Westley, a short, thick set wench, of a fresh complexion, about 25 years of age, marked on one of her hands with the letters I G. The other named Anne Carrola Stockey, a well set wench, has black eyes, fresh complexion, dark hair, about 25 years of age. They both had on when they went away, red woolen gowns, and quilted petticoats; and one of them a black crape bonnet. They both came from Bristol, and 'tis not likely they will part. Mandlin Westley is a Welsh woman; they went away in company with two men. Whoever takes up said

servants, and secures them in any goal in the New-Jersey or Pennsylvania government, shall have Twenty Shillings reward for each, and reasonable charges, paid by Thomas Lightfoot in Philadelphia.
The Pennsylvania Gazette, March 16, 1747; March 24, 1747; April 9, 1747.

A Negro Fellow named *Moses*, about 24 Years of Age, Servant to the Rev. Mr. *Welsted*, left his Master's House last Evening, and is suppos'd to be conceal'd on board some Vessel. He had on a blue Coat and a Leather Jockey Cap, but is suspected to have furnish'd himself with Seaman's Cloaths. All Masters of Vessels and others are cautioned against carrying him off, and if any Person will give Information where he may be found, they shall receive Old Tenor, Reward.
The Boston Evening-Post, April 6, 1747; April 13, 1747.

BRoke out of his Majesty's Goal in *Taunton* in the County of *Bristol*, the last Night, an Indian Man named *Nathaniel Strum*, alias *Daniel James*, a short slim Fellow, with a very flat Nose and short Hair: He had on a brown Great Coat and a blue close bodied Coat, old gray Stockings and old Shoes, and a Check Shirt. He was committed to said Goal for Theft. Whoever shall take up said Fellow, and secure him so that he may be remanded back again to Prison, shall have *Five Pounds* old Tenor Reward,
paid by *Sylvester Richmond*,
Sheriff of the County of *Bristol.* April 10. 1747.
The Boston Evening-Post, April 13, 1747; April 20, 1747; April 27, 1747.

Deserted from on board a Vessel bound for Louisbourgh, on Thursday the 9th Instant, and cross'd over to Long Island, *James Howath*, of General Fuller's Regiment and Capt. Scott's Company; about 22 Years of Age, thin fac'd, somewhat inn knee'd 5 Feet 9 Inches high without Shoes, short dark brown Hair, has a thick undistinct Way of speaking; wore when he went off a light colour'd Frock and red Waistcoat. He robb'd his Captain and deserted from the Flagg of Truce which put into Boston about 5 Months ago: Whoever shall apprehend the said Howath, and give Information to Stephen Bayard, Esq; Mayor of New-York, shall receive Five Pounds Reward, and whoever harbours or conceals the said Deserter shall be prosecuted according to Law. *Hugh Scott.*
The New-York Gazette, Revived in the Weekly Post-Boy, April 13, 1747; April 20, 1747; April 27, 1747.

WHereas *Ruth* the Wife of me *Joseph Atkins* of *Marblehead*, Marriner, has unjustly absented herself from me; These are to desire all Persons not the

credit her on my Account for any Thing whatsoever, for I will not pay any Debt she shall so contract from the Date hereof.
    As witness my Hand, Joseph Atkins.
                   Boston, April 16, 1747.
 The Boston Weekly News-Letter, April 23, 1747.

                 Cambridge, April 24, 1747.
RUn away from me the Subscriber, about three Weeks past, a likely Negro Man named *Robin,* about 22 Years of Age, and had on when he went away, a short blue Jacket, and blue Breeches. Whoever takes up said Negro, and conveys him safely to me at *Cambridge,* shall have *Ten Pounds* (old Tenor) Reward, and all necessary Charges paid them. And all Persons are hereby forbid to harbour or carry off said Negro, as they would avoid being prosecuted with the utmost Rigour of the Law.
    HENRY VASSALL.
 The Boston Evening-Post, April 27, 1747; May 4, 1747; May 11, 1747.

 RAN away from *Samuel White* of *Haverhill* the 27th ult. a thick well set Negro Man named *Boston,* 25 Years of Age, with a lihtish colour'd Homespun Coat with Jacket Sleves, with a dark green Jacket, a striped Jacket and Breeches, large brass shoe Buckels. Whosoever shall take up said Negro, and return him to the Subscriber, shall have five Pounds old Tenor Reward, and all the necessary Charges
    defrayed by me Samuel White.
 N. B. *The Fellow above described has also a light colour'd great Coat a red Cap with a black Wig, and will doubtless, as is usual for Runaways, change and vary his Dress, as often as possible, that he may the more, effectually compleat his Design.*
 The Boston Gazette, or Weekly Journal, May 5, 1747; May 12, 1747.

DESERTED from on board Capt. *Philemon Saunders,* off the East End of *Long-Island,* in a Boat belonging to the Vessel, who therewith landed at *Montoge,* the following Recruits enlisted for Sir WILLIAM PEPPERRELL'S Regiment, viz *Luke Collens,* Serj. *Thomas Dunahoe, James McCaniel, Daniel O'Dowley, John Davis, Hezekiah Shaw, Robert Eiles, William Thompson, James Alexander, Charles Wiggins, John Wherton, William Dowhanty, James Mackadee, Cornelius Grimes, John Steward,* and *Edward Nutlees;* as also *James McBriage,* deserted from *Louisbourg.* Whoever takes up any of the said Deserters, and secures them in any of his Majesty's Goals, or will bring them to Messrs. *Colman* and *Sparhawk,* or Lieut. *Edmund Dwight* in *Boston,* or to any Officer belonging to the said Regiment, shall have a *Guinea* Reward for each and reasonable Charges paid.   *Edmund Dwight.*   *Boston, May* 19, 1747.

N. B. If any of the above Deserters will deliver themselves up to any Officer in said Regiment, so as to proceed to their Duty at *Louisbourg,* they shall be kindly received, and their past Offence forgiven.

The Boston Weekly News-Letter, May 21, 1747; June 4, 1747; June 11, 1747; *The Boston Weekly Post-Boy,* June 1, 1747; June 15, 1747.

D*Eserted from the* Greenwich *Frigate,* Wm. Donald *Commander, now laying in the Port of* Boston, Thomas Penny, *second Mate,* Alexander McDaniel, *and* Henry Gatety, *Seamen; if they will return to their Duty on board said Ship in Forty Eight Hours, they shall be kindly received, otherwise they shall be deemed as Deserters.*
          Wm. Donald.   Boston, June 6*th* 1747.
The Boston Evening-Post, June 8, 1747.

RAN-away from *William Molineux* of *Boston,* last Monday Night, a Negro Fellow named *Boston,* about 20 Years of Age, of a middle Stature, had on when he went away, a light colour'd pea Jacket, a red strip'd cotton and linnen Jacket, and Leather Breeches: All Persons are forbid harbouring or concealing said Fellow as they will answer it at their Peril. Whoever will secure said Fellow, and bring him to said *Molineux* shall be rewarded for their Trouble.   *Boston, June* 7, 1747.
The Boston Weekly Post-Boy, June 8, 1747; June 15, 1747.

W*HEREAS* Susanna, *the Wife of me the Subscriber utterly refuses to live with me, and notwithstanding I have used all Endeavours to perswade her to her Duty, and often promised to forget the many Indiscretions of which she had been guilty, yet she obstinately refuses, and declares her Intention to be to ruin me if possible, and that she married me with no other Design: This is therefore to warn all Persons not to trust her on any Account; for I hereby declare, that I will not pay any Debts that she shall contract after the Date hereof.*   Stephen Southard.   Boston, June 6. 1747.
The Boston Evening-Post, June 15, 1747.

BRoke from His Majesty's Goal in *Boston,* on Tuesday the 23d of June Instant, a Negro Man named *George,* belonging to *Robert Oliver,* Esq; of *Dorchester* committed for Theft: He is a pretty tall likely Fellow, very black, speaks good English; he had nothing on when he went away but a check'd Shirt, & a pair of Trousers.

Whoever shall apprehend the said Negro, and bring him to the said Prison in *Boston,* shall have *ten Pounds* old Tenor, Reward, and all
          necessary Charges paid,   by *Wm. Young.*

And all Masters of Vessels and others are hereby caution'd against concealing or carrying off said Negro, on penalty of the Law.

Boston, June 24th. 1747.
The Boston Gazette, or Weekly Journal, June 30, 1747; July 7, 1747; July 14, 1747; *The Boston Weekly Post-Boy*, July 6, 1747. See *The Boston Gazette, or Weekly Journal*, September 15, 1747.

W*Hereas* Rebeccah, *the Wife of me the Subscriber,* Robert Thompson, *Jun. of* Boston, *Tailor, has eloped from her said Husband, without any just Cause; and being apprehensive that she will run me in Debt; I do therefore forewarn all Persons against trusting her the said* Rebeccah *upon my Account; for I do hereby declare, that I will not pay any Debts contracted by her, after the Day of the Date hereof, as Witness by Hand,*
Robert Thompson, *Jun.* Boston, July 25, 1747.
The Boston Evening-Post, August 10, 1747.

R*An away from her Master,* Joseph Greenleaf *of* Newbury, *on the* 11*th Instant,* Mary Gooding, *a Servant. Whoever shall apprehend said* Mary, *and convey her to her said Master, shall have* Three Pounds, *old Tenor Reward.*
The Boston Evening-Post, August 24, 1747; August 31, 1747; September 14, 1747.

Norwalk, August 20*th.*
RUN away from *Nathan Nash*, junr. of *Norwalk* in Connecticut a Molatto Servant named *Peter* about 22 Years of Age, middle Size; had on when he went away, an old Felt Hat, poor Cloaths, speaks good English, has a Bunch on one side Born with him as large as two Hands, is a little above his wastband. Whoever shall secure said Servants so that he may be had again shall have 20 *Shillings* in New-York Money Reward, and all reasonable Charges. by *Nathan Nash*, junr.
The New-York Evening Post, September 7, 1747; September 14, 1747; September 21, 1747; September 28, 1747.

R*AN away from his Master, Capt.* Abraham Cary *of* Boston, *on the seventh Instant, an* English *Servant Boy named* Thomas Cox, *about thirteen Years old. He had on when he went away, a blue Pee Jacket, a striped Cotton Cap, a pair of Trowsers, and a pair of red Plush Breeches, but no Stockings or Shoes. Whoever shall take him up, and bring him to his said Master, shall have* Five Pounds *(Old Tenor) Reward, and reasonable Charges paid.*
The Boston Evening-Post, September 14, 1747; September 21, 1747; September 28, 1747.

BRoke from His Majesty's Goal in *Boston*, on Tuesday the 28th of June Instant, a Negro Man named *George*, belonging to *Robert Oliver*, Esq; of Dorchester, but formerly liv'd with Mr. *Joshua Thornton*, Housewright, committed for Theft: He is a pretty tall Fellow, very black, speaks good English: he had nothing on when he went away but a check'd Shirt, and a pair of Trousers.

Whoever shall apprehend the said Negro, and bring him to the Prison in *Boston*, shall have *twenty Pounds* Reward, old Tenor, and all necessary Charges paid, by *Wm. Young.*

And all Masters of Vessels and others are hereby caution'd against concealing or carrying off said Negro, on penalty of the Law.

Boston, Sept. 15th 1747.

The Boston Gazette, or Weekly Journal, September 15, 1747; September 29, 1747. See *The Boston Gazette, or Weekly Journal*, June 30, 1747.

RAN-away from his Master *Jacob Whitman* of *Providence*, Blacksmith, on the 19th Instant, a Negro Man Slave, named *Prince*, about 20 Years of Age, goes something stooping. Had on when he went away, a light coloured thick woollen Jacket, a Pair of Trowsers, Shoes, with large Brass Buckles, a Felt Hat, a striped woollen Cap, a tow cloth Shirt.

Whoever shall take up said Runaway, and him safely covey to this said Master in *Providence*, shall have *Six Pounds* Reward, Old Tenor, and all necessary Charges

paid by *Jacob Whitman.* Newport, Sept. 15. 1747.

The Boston Weekly Post-Boy, September 28, 1747; October, 12, 1747; October 19, 1747.

RAN away from the Rev. Mr. *Samuel Brown* of *Abington*, on the 26 of this Instant *September*, a Mulatto Fellow named *Cuffy*, about 20 Years of Age, of a short Stature, pretty well set, and has a Scar or two upon his Neck, under his Shirt Collar, which was occasioned by the King's Evil. He had on when he went away, a short brown double breasted Jacket, with a greenish Cast, and Pewter Buttons, and an under Jacket of striped Linnen and Wool, also Linnen Trowsers.

Whoever shall take up said Servant, and bring him to his said Master, or secure him so that his said Master may have him again, shall have *Three Pounds* Reward, old Tenor, and all necessary Charges paid.

Note, his Hair is cut off.

N. B. That all Masters of Vessels and other Person are hereby forbidden concealing or carrying off said Servant, as they would avoid the Penalty of the Law in that Case made and provided.

The Boston Evening-Post, October 5, 1747.

Yesterday the notorious Tom Bell was committed to the Goal of this City.
The Boston Weekly Post-Boy, October 5, 1747. See *The Pennsylvania Gazette*, June 23, 1743. See *The Pennsylvania Gazette*, July 14, 1743, *The Boston Weekly Post-Boy*, August 22, 1743, *The Boston Gazette, or, Weekly Journal*, September 20, 1743, *The Boston Evening-Post*, December 12, 1743, *The Boston Gazette, or Weekly Journal*, May 22, 1744, and *The Boston Weekly Post-Boy*, April 8, 1745.

BROKE out of Burlington *Goal, on the* 19*th of* September, *one* Jeremiah Carpenter, *who was committed for uttering counterfeit Jersey Money; he had on a grey homespun Jocky Coat with brass Buttons, old Leather Breeches, yarn Stockings, Linnen Cap, and old Hat; it is supposed that his Name is* Amos Fuller; *he is about six Foot high, and of a pale Complexion: Any Person that takes up the aforesaid Prisoner, and confine him in any of his Majesty's Goals, so that he may be had, shall have* TEN POUNDS *Reward, paid by me,* Jos. Hollinshead, *Sheriff.*
N. B. *He is a New-England Man.*
The New-York Gazette, Revived in the Weekly Post-Boy, October 12, 1747; October 19, 1747; October 26, 1747; November 2, 1747; November 9, 1747; November 16, 1747.

WHEREAS Jacob Blackstone, James Walker, Bartholomew Curry, Wm. Golson, and John Harrison, *belonging to his Majesty's Bomb* Comet, *did last Night rob Capt.* Leaver, *Commander of the said Bomb, & afterwards ran with the Boat & got ashore:*
This is to give Notice, that whoever apprehends the said Men or any of them, so as they make be taken and carried on board any of his Majesty's ships at *Nantasket,* shall have *Fifty Pounds* old Tenor, for each Man, to be paid them immediately by Admiral KNOWLES.
Jacob Blackstone is a tall well set Man pitted with the small Pox, with a Scar on the left Side of his Face near his Nose, had on a black Wigg and a dark brown Coat, and is about six Foot high, aged 30 Years.
James Walker, a thick well set Man upon the sandy Complection about 5 Feet 8 Inches, had on a brown Coat, woollen Cap, & Hat, and has some Freckles in his Face, about 26 Years of Age.
Bartholomew Currey, a middle size Man, swarthy Complection, had on a brown short Jacket, a woollen Cap, and Hat, about 5 Foot 5 inches high, aged 23 Years.
William Golson, a well set short Man, with a fresh Complection, had on a brown Jacket, and a Frock, with a woollen Cap, and Hat, about 5 Foot 9 Inches high, aged 24 Years.

John Harrison, a lusty well set Man, in his own black curl'd Hair, fresh Complection, in a blue Jacket, had on no Trowsers, about 5 Foot 10 Inches, and 26 Years of Age.

And whoever apprehends *John McMullen,* Carpenter's Mate of the Canterbury, shall have *two Hundred Pounds* old Tenor Reward.

Dated, Boston, October 12th 1747.

The Boston Gazette, or Weekly Journal, October 13, 1747; October 20, 1747.

DEserted from his Majesty's Ship *Canterbury,* three Mariners belonging to the Honourable Col. *James Cochrean's'* Regiment: Whose Names &c. are as follows, *viz.*

John Harris, who had on him when he went away from the Ship a Blue Jacket, Trousers, and a plain Hat, of a black swarthy Complexion, and pitted with the small-Pox, five Feet in Height.

James Gray, who had on a red Jacket, thin Canvas Breeches, and a plain Hat, thick set, of a fresh Complexion, short black Hair, about five Feet.

Richard Stanley, a blue Jacket, Trowsers, and a plain Hat, short and thick set, of a fresh Complexion, about the Height of the two former.

The abovemention'd Persons were seen last Wednesday Afternoon at Mr *Pierce's* at the Queen's Head near *Clark's* Wharffe.

Whoever shall apprehend the said Deserters or either of them, and convey them on Board his Majesty's Ship *Canterbury,* low lying in *Nantasket* Road, shall receive *Forty Pounds* old Tenor Reward.

Note. If the said Deserters will immediately return to their Duty on board the *Canterbury,* shall be kindly received.

Boston, October 19*th* 1747.

The Boston Gazette, or Weekly Journal, October 20, 1747.

RUN away from *John Bulkley* of *Boston,* living in Queen-street, on the 13th of last Month, a Negro Girl named *Billah,* a short thick Girl, about twenty Years of Age, has had the small Pox, speaks good English; had on when she went away a purple and white Callicoe Gown, a red and white Callicoe Petticoat, Wooden Heel'd Shoes. Whoever shall take up said Runaway, and convey her to her said Master as above, shall have *three Pounds* old Tenor Reward, and all necessary Charges paid. All Persons are cautioned against concealing or carrying off said Negro on Penalty of the Law.

The Boston Gazette, or Weekly Journal, November 3, 1747. See *The Boston Gazette, or, Weekly Journal,* June 7, 1743, and *The Boston Gazette, or Weekly Journal,* September 27, 1748.

In the Colony of Rhode-Island, Warren, Oct. 14. 1747.
STolen from Samuel Barns, *on the* 14*th Instant, a red Mare about three Years old, without Shoes; also a Saddle and Bridle snaffel Bitt, taken out of said Barns's House, the Saddle was mended on the Seam of the Seat, with a Housing and Mail pillion on the same, supposed to be taken by* Elijah Sabin, *who has sometimes called himself* Goulding: *Whoever shall take up said Mare, Saddle and Bridle, and convey them to said Barns, shall have* three Pounds *old Tenor Reward, and all necessary harges [sic]*
paid by Samuel Barns.
The Boston Weekly Post-Boy, November 9, 1747.

DEserted from *Georges Island,* in a large Canoe, belonging to his Majesty's Ship Lark, the five following Men, viz.
James Griffis, 5 Feet high, of a brown Complection, wears a black Wigg, aged twenty Years.
Robert Richardson, a slender Lad, of about 5 Feet 6 Inches, of a fair Complection, has a Mole under his Chin, wears a black Wigg, aged 22 Years.
John Bulger, 5 Feet 8 Inches, a hard Face much pitted with the Small Pox, a crooked Nose, wears a white Wigg, of a brown Complection, aged 29 Years.
James Sticks, 4 Feet 10 Inches, of a black Complection, very hairy, a shrill Voice, wears his own Hair, and a Leather Cap, aged 30 Years.
Whoever will apprehend any of the said Deserters, and deliver them on board the said Ship, shall have *twenty Pounds* old Tenor Reward for each Man. Boston, November 17, 1747,
The Boston Gazette, or Weekly Journal, November 17, 1747; November 24, 1747.

RAN away from Messieurs *Dean* and *Mason* of Boston, about the 10th Currant, a Negro Man Servant, named *Ned,* about 30 Years of Age, speaks good English and French, a tall slender well set Fellow, about 5 Foot 10 Inches high, had on a blew Jacket, and Breeches of the same, speckled Shirt, and appears as a Sailor.
Whoever shall take up said Run-away, and him safely convey to the said *Dean* and *Mason,* living in *New Boston,* shall have *five Pounds* old Tenor Reward, and all necessary Charges paid:
And all Masters of Vessels and others are hereby forbid concealing or carrying off said Servant on Penalty of the Law.
The Boston Gazette, or Weekly Journal, November 17, 1747; November 24, 1747.

DEserted from the Ship Defiance, *John Comrin*, Commander, lying at *Hutchinson's Wharffe*, the following Sailors, viz.
Jeremiah Smith, about 25 Years, fair Complection.
John James, about twenty five Years of Age, brown Complection;
Michael White, the Ship's Cook, about 40 Years of Age, dark Complection.
If the above Men will immediately return to their Duty on board said Ship, they shall be kindly received; or otherwise treated as Deserters.
Boston, Nov. 24, 1747.
The Boston Gazette, or Weekly Journal, November 24, 1747; December 1, 1747; December 8, 1747.

Province of the Massachusetts-Bay.   *Boston, Nov.* 30. 1747.
Court of Vice-Admiralty.
*W*Hereas Joseph Austell *Commander of the Ship* New-England Galley, *has exhibited a Libel in our said Court, setting forth that* Andrew Garnett, William Seatten, Thomas Fitzpatrick, *and* Michael Fitzpatrick, *Mariners, belonging to said Ship, have deserted the said Ship and their Duty on board her, praying that publick Monitions may issue for the said Defendants to appear in said Court, and that they may be ordered to return to their respective Duties on board said Vessel, or that the Waged due to each of them be decreed forfeited &c.*
These are therefore to notify said Marines to make their Appearances at a Court of Admiralty to be holden at *Boston* on Thursday next at ten o'Clock A. M. in order to shew Cause, if any they have, why the Prayer of said Libel ought not to be granted.
          Per Curiam.   *John Payne,* D. Reg.
The Boston Gazette, or Weekly Journal, December 1, 1747.

Newport, November 19. 1747.
DEserted from the Privateer Brigantine the *Prince Frederick,* Capt. *Ebenezer Trowbridge* Commander, *William Burn,* an *Irishman,* aged about 50 Years, 5 Feet 10 Inches high, wears a light colour'd Pea Jacket, also *John Hogan,* an *Irishman,* aged about 40 Years, midling Stature, wears a red Jacket and a blue Great Coat. Whoever takes up said Deserters, and conveys them safe to *John Channing* of *Newport,* or to *Gamaliel Wallis* in *Boston,* shall have for each Person *Ten Pounds* old Tenor.
The Boston Evening-Post, December 7, 1747; December 14, 1747; December 21, 1747.

R*An away from his Master* Joseph Buss, *jun. of* Portsmouth *on the* 28*th Day of* Nov. *last, a Negro Man named* Tobey, *about* 22 *Years of Age: Had on when he went away, an old Felt Hatt, a Worsted Cap, a grey Kersey Pea*

Jacket something patch'd, a dark Cloth under Jacket, a white Linnen Shirt, Leather Breeches, and Yarn Stockings. Whoever shall take up said Runaway, and him safely convey to his Master in Portsmouth, *shall have* Six Pounds *Old Tenor Reward and all necessary Charges paid, by* Joseph Buss, *jun.*

All Masters *of Vessels are hereby caution'd not to conceal or carry off said Negro on Penalty of the Law.*

The Boston Weekly Post-Boy, December 7, 1747; December 14, 1747; December 21, 1747; December 28, 1747.

RAN-away from his Master *Jonathan Brown* of *Reading*, on the 2d inst. a white Man Servant named *Manassah Marston*, a short thick well set Fellow, wears a Cap, had on when he went away a white Fustian Coat, blue Camblet Jacket, Leather Breeches, gray yarn Stockings.

Whoever shall take up the abovesaid Runaway and him safely convey to his abovesaid Master at *Reading*, shall have *ten Pounds* old Tenor Reward, and all necessary Charges paid.

All Masters of Vessels and others are hereby caution'd against concealing or carrying off said Servant on Penalty of the Law.

The Boston Gazette, or Weekly Journal, December 8, 1747; December 15, 1747.

NEW-YORK, December 7.

We have advice from Hackinsack, that on Monday last two men were apprehended there, and committed to Bergen county goal for uttering counterfeit New-Jersey bills of credit. On their being first apprehended, one of them made an excuse to go out, and going behind a barrack, was seen to stick something in it, and search being made, a large bundle of those bills were found there; which, together with some found upon them, made in all 102 bills of Fifteen Shillings each, whereof 36 were signed; 142 bills of Twelve Shillings each, whereof 9 were signed; and 89 bills of Six Shillings each, whereof 20 were signed; of the 6 Shilling bills there were some done in imitation of those dated 1743, and some of those dated 1746. They are all done from copperplate, and may be easily known when compared with the true ones, by the marks given in two of our late papers. One of the Men's names is Joseph Bradford, born in New London, and pretends to be a doctor; the other John Lummis, born in Narraganset, and is a blacksmith.

The Pennsylvania Gazette, December 15, 1747.

DEserted from the Ship *Molineaux*, Capt. *Jonathan Snelling*, Commander, on the 18th of this Instant *December*, two young Men Servants to the owner, one named *George Oliver*, the other *Henry Kenleaf.* If they will immediately return to their Duty on board the said Ship, they shall be

kindly received and excused, but if they do not, whoever shall apprehend them and deliver them to their said Master, shall have *Five Pounds* (Old Tenor) Reward for each of them. And all Persons are hereby forbid to harbour, conceal or carry them off, as they would avoid the Penalty of the Law.
 Boston Evening-Post, December 21, 1747; December 28, 1747; January 4, 1748. See *The Boston Weekly Post-Boy*, December 21, 1747.

DEserted last Friday Night from on board the Ship *Molineaux*, Capt. *Jonathan Snelling*, two young English Men Servants, one named *George Oliver*, the other Henry *Kinlief,* who took all their Cloathing with them. Whoever shall take up said Deserters and will bring them to the said Capt. Snelling, shall have Five Pounds old Tenor Reward. All Persons are caution'd not to harbour, conceal or carry off the said Servants, as they would avoid the Penalty of the Law.
 N. B. If the said *Oliver* and *Kinlief* will forthwith return to their Duty on board the said Ship, they shall be kindly received.
 The Boston Weekly Post-Boy, December 21, 1747. See *Boston Evening-Post*, December 21, 1747.

RAn-away from the Brigantine *Thomas* and *Mary*, Capt. *Rimer* now lying at *Minot's* T, two young Men, Servants to said *Rimer*, one named *Arundell Burten*, aged about 18 Years, of a low Stature, wears Red Breeches, or Fear-Nothing Trousers, the rest of his Cloaths dirty and ragged, the other *Joseph Winchester*, aged 17 Years middling Stature, wears Red Breeches, &c. Whoever will apprehend them and deliver them to their said Master, shall have ten Pounds old Tenor Reward. And all Persons are hereby forbid to carry them off, as they would avoid the Penalty of the Law.
               Boston, December 22, 1747.
 The Boston Gazette, or Weekly Journal, December 22, 1747.

WHEREAS Elizabeth *the Wife of me* John Fling *of* Boston, *Rope-maker, hath run me in Debt without my Knowledge, and likewise sold most Part of my Household Goods and wearing Apparel:*
 These are therefore to caution all Persons not to trust her upon my Account, for I will not pay any Debt she shall contract from this Date hereof. *Witness my Hand,* John Fling. Boston, Dec. 23. 1747.
 The Boston Weekly News-Letter, December 24, 1747; January 7, 1748.

               Boston, Decemb. 30. 1747.
RAN away the 25th Instant from *Mary Jackson* of *Boston*, a likely well-set young Fellow, named *Jeremiah Fones*: He had on when he went away a

Bear-skin Coat white flat Buttons a Pair of Pumps, and a large Pair of Silver Shoe Buckels. Whoever will apprehend the said Run-away, and convey him to his said Mistress, shall receive *Ten Pounds* old Tenor, and all necessary Charges paid.

All Persons are caution's not to harbour, conceal or carry off the said Servant, as they would avoid the Penalty of the Law.

The Boston Weekly News-Letter, December 31, 1747; January 7, 1748.

1748

RAN-away from *Ichabod Goodwin* of *Berwick*, a Negro Man named *Pompey*, a short thick-sett Fellow: Had on when he went away a Homespun double breasted, light colour'd Jacket plain pewter Buttons; one of his Ears cut: There went a white Boy of fourteen Years of Age with him, with little Hair and short, pretty slim and has a white Eye. Whoever shall take up said Negro and Lad and secure them so that I the said *Goodwin* may have them, shall have *Four Pounds* old Tenor Reward
     by me *Ichabod Goodwin.*
The Boston Weekly Post-Boy, January 25, 1748; February 1, 1748. See *The Boston Post-Boy*, July 23, 1750.

RAn-away from Mr. *Benanuel Bower's* Ship Yard in *Swanzey*, the 2d Instant, a Negro Man named *Caesar*, about 35 Years of Age; he is a tall well-set Fellow, had on when he went away, a double-breasted dark colour'd Kersey Pea Jacket, with yellow metal Buttons, a blue Devonshire Kersey Fly Coat, with large Copper Buttons, double breasted, without Lining, he carried with him a Variety of other Cloathing; he speaks indifferent English, is a cunning artful Fellow (a Negro of Mr. *Bower's* went off with him.) Whoever shall take him up, and bring him to his Master *John Banister* at *Newport*, shall have t*en Pounds* old Tenor Reward, and all necessary Charges paid, by *John Banister.*
The Boston Gazette, or Weekly Journal, January 26, 1748; February 2, 1748; February 16, 1748. *The Boston Weekly News-Letter*, January 29, 1748; February 4, 1748; February 11, 1748; Minor differences between the papers. The *News-Letter* spells Bower's first name as Benanael, and the runaway's name as *Caesar.*

RAN-away on the 26th of January from his Master, *Joseph Procter*, of *Boston*, a Negro Man named *Bristo*, about 26 or 27 Years of Age, a well set likely Fellow something Pock broken, speaks good English: he had on and carried away, a good blew Great Coat, a light kersey Jacket, and a black Jacket, a red under Jacket, grey Yarn Stockings and a pair of large Shoe Buckles. Whoever shall take up the abovsaid Negro, and safely convey him to his abovesaid Master, shall have *ten Pounds* old Tenor Reward and necessary Charges paid.

N. B. All Masters of Vessels and others, are hereby caution'd against concealing or carrying off the abovesaid Negro on Penalty of the Law.

The Boston Gazette, or Weekly Journal, February 2, 1748; February 16, 1748. See *The Boston Weekly Post-Boy,* February 8, 1748.

DEserted from the Ship Thomas, *lying at* Clark's *Wharf,* Philip Leigh *Master, a Sailor named* Frederick Fisher: *Whoever shall apprehend said Deserter, and bring him to said Master or to* Henry Atkins *Merchant in* Boston, *shall have* Twenty Pounds *old Tenor Reward, or if said Deserter returns to his Duty on board said Ship he shall be kindly receiv'd. All Masters of Vessels and others are hereby caution'd against harbouring or concealing the said Deserter, as they would avoid being proceeded against in the utmost Severity of the Law.* Boston, Feb. 3. 1747,8.

The Boston Weekly News-Letter, February 4, 1748; February 11, 1748.

RAN away from his Master, Joseph Procter, *a Negro Man named* Bristo, *about* 26 *or* 27 *Years of Age, a well set likely Fellow something Pock broken, speaks good English: he had on and carried away with him, a blue Great Coat, a light Kersey Jacket, a black Jacket, a red under Jacket, Plush Breeches, grey yarn Stockings and a pair of large Buckles. Whoever shall take up said Negro, and carry him to his said Master in* Boston, *shall have* Ten Pounds *Old Tenor Reward and necessary Charges paid.*

N. B. *All Masters of Vessels are hereby cautioned against concealing or carrying off the abovesaid Negro on Penalty of the Law.*

The Boston Weekly Post-Boy, February 8, 1748; February 15, 1748; February 22, 1748; February 29, 1748. See *The Boston Gazette, or Weekly Journal,* February 2, 1748.

RAN away from his Master *John Potter* of *South Kingston,* an Indian Boy named *James,* about 14 Years of Age, a slim Fellow, and has an Impediment in his Speech. He had on when he went away, a light coloured Cloth Jacket and Breeches. Whoever shall take up said Boy, and convey him to his said Master in *South Kingston,* shall have *Ten Pounds,* Old Tenor, Reward, and necessary Charges
        paid by me   *John Potter.*

The Boston Evening-Post, March 7, 1748; March 14, 1748; March 21, 1748.

RAN-away from the Brigantine Thomas *and* Mary, *Capt.* Matthew Rimer, *now lying at Mr.* Hubbard's *Wharffe,* William Wise, *of a tall Stature and fresh Complection, wears a light colour'd Coat with a Velvet Cape.*

Whoever will apprehend him and deliver him to his Master, the said Capt. Rimer, shall have Twenty Pounds *old Tenor Reward. And all Persons are hereby forbid to carry him off, as they would avoid the Penalty of the Law.*
    The Boston Weekly News-Letter, March 10, 1748; March 17, 1748.

WHereas Dorcas *the Wife of* Samuel Wheeler *of Acton, has eloped and refuses to dwell with me, I therefore hereby forbid all Persons from trusting or giving her Credit to the said* Dorcas: *for I will not pay any Debt she shall contract after this Date: I also forbid all Persons from Harbouring or Entertaining the said* Dorcas *upon any Account whatsoever; and if they do, they may expect to be Prosecuted for the same.*
    As witness by Hand the 15th Day of March. 1747. [sic]
            Samuel Wheeler.
    The Boston Gazette, or Weekly Journal, March 15, 1748.

RAn-away the 20th Instant from his Mistress *Ruth Clark* of Boston, a Negro Man named *Cambridge,* who formerly belonging to Mr. *Newhall* of Roxbury, had on when he went away a strip'd Homespun Jacket, blue Coat, with Pewter Buttons, and a blue Great Coat, Leather Breeches and Trowsers, yarn Stockings, round to'd Shoes and large buckles, white Shirt, check'd Handkerchief, bever Hat, strip'd worsted Cap, and took with him a drab cloth Jacket, a blue ditto, fine Garlix shirt, and a woollen check one. Whoever shall take up said Negro and bring him to the Printer hereof, shall have *three Pounds* old Tenor, and all necessary Charges paid.
    And all Masters of Vessels are hereby caution'd against carrying off said Negro on Penalty of the Law.   Boston, March 22. 1747,8.
    The Boston Gazetter, or Weekly Journal, March 22, 1748. See The Boston Gazette, or Weekly Journal, April 26, 1748.

RAN-away from *Benjamin Griffith* of *Killingworth* in *Connecticut,* an Irish Servant Man, named *Moses Cushon,* about 25 Years of Age, about five Foot ten Inches High, well set, sandy Complection, light Hair, wears a Cap, had on when he went away a light blue homespun Coat, Leather Breeches, an old Felt Hat, check Shirt, and a pair of Yarn Stockings, and I hear since has changed his Name. Whoever takes up the said Servant and secures him, so that his Master may have him again, or deliver him to Mr. *Mar[em]in Howard* of *Newport,* shall have *twenty Pounds* old Tenor, as a Reward paid
            by me,   *Benjamin Griffith.*   Newport, March 28. 1748.
    The Boston Gazette, or Weekly Journal, April 19, 1748.

RAN-away from *Jerathmeel Bowers* of *Swanzey,* on the 3d Instant, two Men Servants, *viz Robert Chambers,* about 23 Years of Age, of middling Stature, fair Complection, had on a green Ratteen Jacket lin'd with strip'd

Flannel, and took with him a light colour'd Cloth Coat something wore, check Shirt, light plush Breeches. The other named *Douglas Fosset*, about 19 Years of Age, a well set Fellow, not tall, had on a green Ratteen Jacket lin'd with strip'd Flannel, a pair of blue Breeches, and a check Shirt; wears his own light Hair.

Ranaway at the same Time from *Henry Bowers* of said *Swanzey* a Man Servant named *John Smith,* about 25 Years, pretty tall and spare, something pock-broken, had on an Orange colour'd broad Cloth Coat, lin'd with blue, about half worn, his right Ear deform'd and his right Cheek-Bone fuller than the other, which may serve for all other Descriptions.

They took with them several bever Hats, and other Goods to a considerable Value.

The above Servants were lately transported from *North Britain,* and speak broken English.

Whoever shall take up the abovesaid Runaway Servants, and them convey to their said Masters at *Swanzey* aforesaid, shall have *thirty Pounds* Reward, old Tenor, for the Three, or *ten Pounds* old Tenor for each or either of them, and all necessary Charges paid. And if any Person shall take them up and commit them to either of his Majesty's Goals, and send Word to their said Masters, so that they may have them again, shall have *twenty Pounds* old Tenor for the Reward, for the Three, and in Proportion for each or either of them.

And all Masters of Vessels and others are hereby caution'd against concealing or carrying of said Servants on Penalty of the Law.

The Boston Gazette, or Weekly Journal, April 19, 1748.

RAN-away on Tuesday Night, from the Snow *Isaac, John Woodhouse,* Master, a Servant Boy named *Edward Glancey,* aged about 15 Years, born in *Liverpool,* he had on a blue or a Snuff-coloured Jacket. Whoever will bring him to said *Woodhouse* on board said Snow lying at Capt. *Cheever's* Wharf, shall have *Five Pounds* old Tenor Reward, and all necessary Charges paid. All Masters of Vessels and others are cautioned against harbour, concealing or carrying off said Servant as the would avoid the Penalty of the Law.   April 7, 1748.

The Boston Weekly News-Letter, April 21, 1748.

RAN away from the Brig. *Dolphin,* at the *Winnesimet* Ferry Wharf in *Boston,* Capt. *Nicholas Boufford* Master, a lusty well set Seaman named *James Whalam*; had on a Great Coat, a Blue Jacket, brownish Breeches, with Leather Buttons on the Knees, wears a Cap, is supposed to be about 25 Years old. Whoever will bring out said Seaman so that said *Boufford* Master, or *Thomas Paine* of said *Boston,* owner of said Brig. may have him again, shall be pay'd *Twenty Pounds* old Tenor, and all necessary Charges,

by *Thomas Paine*
The Boston Evening-Post, April 25, 1748.

DEserted from the Sloop Lucretia, *Joseph Chase* Commander, on Saturday Night the 23d Instant, two Sailors, one named *Richard Moorey*, about 24 Years of Age, of middle Stature, well sett, clothed with Sailors Habit, the other named *William Pitman*, about 21 Years of Age, of short Stature and small Body. Whoever shall take up the above said Deserters, and bring them to Captain Chase on board his Vessel lying at *Minot's* T, shall have *five Pounds* old Tenor Reward for each of them, and all necessary Charges paid.
The Boston Gazette, or Weekly Journal, April 26, 1748.

RAn-away the 3d Instant from his Mistress *Ruth Clark* of Boston, a Negro Man named *Cambridge*, who formerly belonging to Mr. *Newhall* at Roxbury, had on when he went away a strip'd Homespun Jacket, blue Coat, with Pewter Buttons, and a blue Great Coat, Leather Breeches and Trowsers, yarn Stockings, round to'd Shoes and large buckles, white Shirt, check'd Handkerchief, bever Hat, red worsted Cap. Whoever shall take up said Negro and bring him to his said Mistress, shall be well rewarded.
    And all Masters of Vessels are hereby caution'd against carrying off said Negro on Penalty of the Law.   *Boston, April* 22 1748.
The Boston Gazette, or Weekly Journal, April 26, 1748. See *The Boston Gazette, or Weekly Journal*, March 22, 1748.

ON the last Day of *April* ran away from the Subscriber, a Scotch Man Servant, named *James Williamson*, he is about 25 Years old, of a ruddy Complection, well-set, down look, light coloured short Hair, he carried with him a dark coloured Coat, with white metal Buttons, blew Jacket, brown Leather Breeches with white metal Buttons almost new, a large red Handkerchief with yellow Flowers, two pair of Shoes, one of which is quite new, a Drab colour'd great Coat. Whoever takes up said Runaway, and delivers him to his Master, or in *Boston* or *Charlestown* Goals, shall have *Ten Pounds* old Tenor, Reward, and all necessary Charges
        paid by   *Robert Temple.*
    N B. All Masters of Vessels are hereby cautioned against carrying off said Runaway, as they would avoid the Penalty of the Law in that Case provided.
The Boston Weekly Post-Boy, May 2, 1748; May 9, 1748; May 16, 1748. See *The Boston Gazette, or Weekly Journal*, May 3, 1748.

RAN-away on the 30th of *April* from the Subscriber a Scots Man Servant, named *James Williamson*, he is about 25 Years old, a ruddy Complection, well set, down Look, light coloured short Hair, he carried with him a dark coloured Coat, with white metal Buttons, blue Jacket, brown Leather Breeches with white metal Buttons almost new, a large red Handkerchief with yellow Flowers, two pair of Shoes, one of which quite new, a drab colour'd great Coat. Whoever takes up said Runaway, and delivers him to his Master, or in *Boston* or *Charlestown* Goals, shall have *ten Pounds* old Tenor, Reward, and all necessary Charges

     paid by *Robert Temple.*

N B. All Masters of Vessels are hereby cautioned against carrying off said Runaway, as they would avoid the Penalty of the Law in that Case provided. *May* 2d 1748.

  The Boston Gazette, or Weekly Journal, May 3, 1748. See *The Boston Weekly Post-Boy*, May 2, 1748.

Deserted from on Board the Ship *Duke of Cumberland*, the 30th of March last, *John Bradford* Master from London, the following Persons, viz. *Darby Hally, James Keith, Lawrence Ogard, Francis Grimes, Charles Read, Mattal Dennel[y]:* Whoever shall apprehend the said Deserters, or either of them, and convey them on board said Ship lying at *Clark's* Wharffe, or to his Majesty's Goal in Boston, shall have *ten Pounds* old Tenor reward for each Person, and all necessary Charges paid.

  The Boston Gazette, or Weekly Journal, May 3, 1748.

RAN-away from *Daniel Dole* of *Newbury*, an Apprentice Lad named *Edmond West*: A likely Fellow; had with him a new Homespun round robin Coat, a Fustian Jacket lin'd with red, a worsted Cap; also an old Coat, and some old Sea Cloaths. Whoever will take up said Fellow, and convey him to said *Dole*, shall have *Five Pounds* old Tenor Reward, and all necessary Charges paid, by *Daniel Dole.* *Newbury, May* 10. 1748.

  All Masters of Vessels and others are hereby caution'd against concealing or carrying off said Apprentice, as they would avoid the Penalty of the Law.

  The Boston Weekly Post-Boy, May 16, 1748; May 23, 1748; May 30, 1748.

RAN-away from the Rev. Mr. *Warham Williams* of *Waltham*, on Tuesday the 19th of *May*, an English Servant Boy named *Samuel Smith*, about 19 Years of Age, short Stature, thick well set, he had on when he went away, grey Coat Jacket and Breeches, dark colour'd and Homespun yarn Stockings and a new pair of Shoes. Whoever shall take up the abovesaid Runaway, and bring him to his Master at *Waltham*, shall have *five Pounds* old Tenor Reward.

All Masters of Vessels and others are hereby cautioned against concealing or carrying off said Servant, on penalty of the Law.
The Boston Gazette, or Weekly Journal, May 31, 1748.

Deserted from the Ship Britannia, Jeremiah Fones *Commander, one* William Rosse, *a Sailor: If he returns to his Duty in two or three Days, shall be received, otherwise will be treated as a Deserter.*
The Boston Evening-Post, June 8, 1747.

THE Publick is hereby inform'd that three Persons, *viz. Daniel Weed, Timothy Davis,* and *William Worth,* who lately came from *St. Christopher,* in the brig Success, *James Brymer,* Commander, and for several Days were confin'd at the Province Hospital on *Rainsford* Island, on suspicion of being infected with the Small Pox, did, on Saturday Night last, take a Boat at said Island, and having put their Chests and Bedding on board, went away in her, and has not been heard of since, said *Weed* then having the Symptions of the Small Pox upon him, it's apprehended they are gone towards *Newbury* or other Eastern Parts, as they belong'd that Way; It's therefore desired that Enquiry may be made after the aforesaid Persons, and proper Care taken to prevent their Travelling; as there is great Danger to their spreading the Small Pox if they are not stopt, and confin'd in some suitable Place.   By Order of the Select Men,
        Ezekiel Goldthwait, Town-Clerk. *Boston, June* 20, 1747. [sic]
The Boston Weekly News-Letter, June 23, 1748; *The Boston Evening-Post,* June 27, 1748.

RAN away from his Master *Benjamin Bacon* of *Salem,* Wig-maker, *June* the 10th. his Apprentice Boy, *Samuel Dove,* aged 12 Years, who wears light coloured short Hair, having on when he went away, striped Jacket and Breeches, a check'd Shirt, and a Felt Hat. Whoever shall take up the abovesaid Runaway, and bring him to his said Master, shall have *Three Pounds,* Old Tenor, Reward, and all necessary Charges
        paid *per me*   *Benjamin Bacon.*
The Boston Evening-Post, July 4, 1748; July 11, 1748.

RAN away from his Master, a Negro Boy named *Cato,* the 30th June, lately belonging to *Dr. Stevens* of *Roxbury,* now of *Boston.* Had on when he went away, a white Cloth Coat, a white Flannel Waistcoat, without Sleeves, a white Shirt, a Bever Hat, about 16 Years old, speaks good *English,* and stutters at little. Whoever will bring said Negro to the Printer, shall have *Five Pounds,* Old Tenor, Reward, and all necessary Charges paid; and all Masters of Vessels and others are desired not to conceal or harbour him, upon Penalty of the Law.

The Boston Evening-Post, July 4, 1748; July 11, 1748; *The Boston Gazette, or Weekly Journal*, July 5, 1748.

RAN-away from the Widow Sarah Mason *and* Benjamin Jenkins *of* Durham *in* New-Hampshire, *Two Negro Men, the one between* 30 & 40 *Years of Age, is pretty slim, has very thick Lips, and one of his Legs has been broken; the other a French Negro aged* 20 *odd Years, named* Jeffry & John Battis: *Whosoever shall take up said Negroes and safely convey them to the said Widow* Sarah Mason *or* Benjamin Jenkins *shall have* Ten Pounds *old Tenor for each, and all necessary Charges paid.*
The Boston Weekly Post-Boy, July 4, 1748.

RAN away from his Master, *James Powner*, about 19 Years of Age, he is a stout lusty Fellow with light coloured short Hair, something Pock-broken, his left Foot has been cut, so that his great Toe falls down. He had on when he ran away, a striped Woollen Jacket, a striped Woollen Shirt, and a pair of old Ozenbrigs Trowsers. Whoever shall take up the said Run-away, and convey him to his Master, *Nathaniel Noyes* of *Falmouth* in *New Casco,* shall have *Five Pounds* old Tenor, Reward, and all necessary Charges paid.
    Nathaniel Noyes.   Falmouth, June 30. 1748.
The Boston Evening-Post, July 11, 1748; July 18, 1748; July 25, 1748.

***R**UN away from his Master* Eleazer Tyng, *Esq; at* Dunstable, *on the* 26*th* May *past, a Negro Man Servant call'd* Robbin, *almost the Complexion of an Indian, short thick square shoulder'd Fellow, a very short Neck, and thick Legs, about* 28 *Years old, talks good English, can read and write, and plays on the Fiddle; he was born at* Dunstable, *and it's thought he has been intic'd to inlist into the Service, or go to* Philadelphia: *Had on when he went away, a strip'd Cotton and Linnen blue and white Jacket, red Breeches with Brass Buttons, blue Yarn Stockings, a fine Shirt, and took another of a meaner Sort, a red Cap, a Beaver Hat with a mourning Weed in it, and sometimes wears a Wig. Whoever will apprehend said Negro and secure him, so that his Master may have him again, or bring him to the Ware-House of Messiers* Alford *and* Tyng, *in* Boston, *shall have a Reward of* Ten Pounds *old Tenor, and all reasonable Charges.*
 N. B. *And all Masters of Vessels or others, are hereby caution'd against harbouring, concealing or carrying off said Servant, on Penalty of the Law.*
The New-York Gazette, Revived in the Weekly Post-Boy, July 11, 1748; July 18, 1748; July 25, 1748.

WHEREAS about 3 *Weeks ago one* Benjamin Boylstone *came to the House of* Hugh Boyd *of* Bellingham, *and borrowed of him a Horse, Bridle and*

Saddle, to be return'd the next Day, but has not been heard of since: Whoever will apprehend the said *Boylstone* so as he may be bro't to Justice, and the said *Boyd* have his Horse again, shall have all the necessary Charges paid, and be well rewarded.

N. B. The Horse is about 3 Years old, of a dark brown Colour, has a white Blaze in his Face like an S. The said *Boylstone* is between 40 and 50 Years of Age, pretty lusty, wears a Wigg, and had on an old brown Coat.

The Boston Weekly News-Letter, July 21, 1748; July 28, 1748; August 4, 1748.

WHEREAS Elizabeth *the Wife of me the Subscriber has behaved herself very ill of late, and eloped from me, chusing rather to keep Company with other Men, and utterly refuses to live with me;* Therefore, in order to prevent her running me in Debt. These are to warn all Persons against trusting her on my Account, for I do hereby declare I will not pay any Debt she shall contract after the Date hereof.

    John Forrest.   *Boston, July* 21. 1748.

The Boston Weekly News-Letter, July 21, 1748.

ABsented himself from the Ship *Britannia, Jeremiah Fones*, Commander, on the 11th Instant, *William Rose*, Servant to Capt. *Samuel Carey* of *Charlestown.* If said Deserter will return to said Ship in 3 Days from the Date hereof, he shall be kindly received, or if any Person will deliver him to Mr. *Richard Carey* of *Charlestown*, shall have all necessary Charges paid, and Rewarded to Content.

The Boston Evening-Post, July 25, 1748.

DEserted *from the Ship* Defiance, John Comrin *Commander, lying in the Harbour of* Boston, *on the* 24*th of this Month, Four French Men, viz,* Moses Serran, John Torsine, Blaze Benrit, *and* John Percake, *who were taken out of Prison, and Bond given therefor by said* Comrin. *Whoever will take up said Deserters, and bring them to said Commander, or commit them to any of his Majesty's Goals, so as he may have them again, shall have* Five Pounds *old Tenor Reward for each, and all reasonable Charges paid. All Masters of Vessels and others are hereby caution'd against carrying off said Deserters, as they would avoid being prosecuted as the Law directs.*

  N. B *They can't talk English: Two of them are very lusty, the other two are but small of Stature.*

The Boston Weekly News-Letter, July 28, 1748.

RAN away from his Master, Mr. *Benjamin Hallowell* of *Boston*, Shipwright, on the 22d of *July* past, a young Negro fellow named *Paul*: He is tall and slim, and had on a blue and white speckled Shirt, a striped homespun Jacket, blue and white, a pair of blue Half Thick Breeches, with Metal Buttons, a pair of Pumps, and Brass Buckles, but no Stockings. Whoever shall take up said Servant, and bring him to his said Master, shall have *Ten Pounds*, Old Tenor, Reward, and all necessary Charges paid.

The Boston Evening-Post, August 1, 1748; August 8, 1748; *The Boston Weekly Post-Boy*, August 1, 1748. Minor differences between the papers.

RAN away from his Master, *John Allan*, Merchant of *Newton*, a Negro Man named *Quomino*, about 21 Years of Age, a likely Fellow, of a midling Stature, his Head shav'd half over, and speaks good English, carried away with him, an Olive coloured Cloth Coat with Buttons of the same Colour, a new Jacket and Breeches, dark Cloth Colour, homespun, with Pewter Buttons on, two pair of Trousers, two Tow Shirts, two Linnen Shirts, an old Bever Hat, and large Brass Buckles in his Shoes, &c. He also carried with him a Scythe.

Whoever shall take him up and return him to his said Master, shall receive of him the Sum of *Five Pounds*, and all necessary Charges, in Old Tenor Money: And all Masters of Vessels are upon their Peril forbid concealing or carrying off said Servant. *Newton, July* 26. 1748.

The Boston Evening-Post, August 1, 1748; August 8, 1748; August 15, 1748.

RAN away from his Master *Thomas Shepard* of *Boston* Innholder, at the Sign of the white Bear, at the South End, on the 30th of *July* last, a Servant Lad, named *John Leay*, about 15 Years of Age, of midling Stature; has a remarkable large Scar on the out side of his right Eye: He had on when he went away a striped homespun Jacket, a pair of Tow Trowsers: His Hair is of a brownish Colour, cut very short. There was a small white Dog which follow'd him. Whoever shall take up the said Runaway so as his Master may have him again, shall have *Five Pounds* old Tenor Reward, and all necessary Charges paid.

The Boston Weekly News-Letter, August 4, 1748. See *The Boston Weekly News-Letter*, Ocotober 27, 1748.

RAN-away from his Master *James Nicholl* of *Boston*, Peruke-maker, on the 2d Instant, a Young Man Servant, named *John Chambers*, about Sixteen Years of Age, a short well-set Lad, of a pale Complection, wears a Wigg, but sometimes a Cap, and had on when he went away, a light colour'd double breasted Jacket, Leather Breeches, and took with him a blue great Coat, several Shirts, and other Things. Whoever shall take up said Run away Servant, and him safely convey to his abovesaid Master in *Boston*, shall have *Five Pounds* old Tenor Reward, and all necessary Charges paid.

All Masters of Vessels and others are hereby caution'd against harbouring, concealing or carrying off said Servant, on Penalty of the Law.
The Boston Weekly News-Letter, August 4, 1748; August 11, 1748. See *The Boston Evening-Post*, August 8, 1748.

RAN away from his Master *James Nicoll* of *Boston*, Peruke-maker, on the 1st Instant, a Young Man Servant, named *John Chambers*, about Sixteen Years of Age, a short well set Lad, of a pale Complection, and has a large Scar on one of his Cheeks; he wears a Wig, but sometimes a Cap, and had on when he went away, a light colour'd double breasted Jacket, Plus Breeches, and took with him a blue Great Coat, several Shirts, and other Things. Whoever shall take up said Run-away Servant, and him safely convey to his abovesaid Master in *Boston* aforesaid, shall have *five Pounds* old Tenor, Reward, and all necessary Charges paid. And all Masters of Vessels and others are hereby caution'd against harbouring, concealing or carrying off said Servant, on Penalty of the Law.
Boston, August 2d. 1748.
The Boston Evening-Post, August 8, 1748.*The Boston Weekly News-Letter*, August 4, 1748; August 11, 1748. See

DEserted from his Majesty's Ship the *Norwich*, Capt. *Thomas Pye* Commander, now in *Nantasket* Road, the following Seamen, viz *Philip Mackmaners, Thomas Bone, Thomas Jenkins*, and *John Collins*. Whoever shall take up the said Deserters, and deliver them to their said Captain, or in his Absence to Capt. *Wheeler*, Commander of his Majesty's Ship *Boston*, shall have a Guinea Reward for each Man, and all reasonable Charges paid.
The Boston Evening-Post, August 15, 1748; August 22, 1748.

RAN away from his Master, Capt. *Andrew Craigie* of *Boston*, a Servant Boy named *John James*, aged 14 Years, lean fac'd, Pock broken, very small of his Age. Had on when he went away, a Hat and red Cap, blue Jacket, Leather pair of Breeches and speckled Shirt. Whoever shall apprehend the said *James*, and bring him to his said Master, shall have *Three Pounds*, old Tenor, and all necessary Charges paid. *N. B.* This is to caution all Masters of Vessels and others, not to harbour on carry away the said *James*, as they would avoid the Penalty of the Law.
The Boston Evening-Post, August 22, 1748.

DESERTED from the Ship *Industry*, Capt. *Graham*, and from the *Princessa*, Capt. *Bowes*, Four French Men (one of whom speaks English) two of them tall, and two of them of low Stature, named *Alexander Monnalt, Jeán Quandett, André Dubert*, and *Peter*, having stole over-board said Ships, new Hamocks, Blankets, &c. and wearing blue Jackets,

Trousers, and Felt Hats. Whoever apprehends and brings before any of his Majesty's Justices of Peace in *Boston,* them or any of them, shall have *Five Pounds,* old Tenor, Reward for each Person.
The Boston Weekly News-Letter, August 25, 1748; September 8, 1748.

RAN away from the Ship *Defiance, John Comrin,* Commander, on the 24th Instant, at one o'Clock in the Morning, *Timothy Long,* and carried with him a Yawl that Rowes with 4 Oars, from *Nantasket* Road. Whoever shall taken him up, and bring him to the said Commander, shall have *Twenty Pounds,* old Tenor, and all necessary Charges, besides *Ten Pounds* for the Yawl.
The Boston Evening-Post, August 29, 1748.

DESERTED from the Ship *Polly, Robert Hodge,* Commander, the 24th ult. at *Marblehead, Richard Prowse* and *Thomas Giles,* West-country-men and Mariners belonging to said Ship: *Prowse* is a tall, thin-fac'd Man, has a red sharp Nose, with Pimples on it, and used to wear a flower'd Holland Jacket. *Giles* is near six Feet high, of a brown Complection, full fac'd, a heavy logy Fellow, has a blue and brown Pea Jacket, and perhaps may lend one to *Prowse* who had none: *Prowse* sometime wore a Wigg, but *Giles* wore only a Cap.—They cut the Boat's Painter, run away with her, and left her adrift; the same Day sent unparallel'd menacing Letters on board, in express Words threatning to break the Bones of some, and to MURDER others belonging the said Ship— Whoever shall take up said Deserters, and bring them or either of them to said Captain on board said Ship now lying at *Clark's* Wharf in *Boston,* so that they may be brought to Justice, shall be paid *Fifty Pounds* old Tenor Reward, for the Two, or *Twenty Five* Pounds
for either of them. *Robert Hodge.*
The Boston Weekly News-Letter, September 8, 1748; September 15, 1748; September 22, 1748.

LAST Night broke out of the common Goal in *Worcester, Thomas Balderston,* who was committed for breaking up a Shop belonging to *Gardiner Chandler* in *Worcester,* and stealing from thence about Sixty Pounds, Old Tenor Bills of Credit. He is a short well set Fellow, suppos'd to be about thirty or forty Years old; his Hair is of a dark Colour, and very short, over which he wears a Cap. He had on a brown coloured Coat, a light coloured Jacket, old Leather Breeches, is a Blacksmith by Trade, and was a Transport.
Also a Woman who goes by the Name of *Elizabeth Richardson,* but her true Name is suppos'd to be *Mary Rogers,* and is a noted Thief, and was committed for several Thefts. She is a Woman of a midling Size, has with her a very beautiful Callico or Chintz Gown or Rode, pretty much on the dark, and also a Camblet one.

Whoever shall take up said Persons, or either of them, so that they are remanded back to said Goal, shall have paid them for each *Fifteen Pounds*, Old Tenor. By me *Luke Brown*, Goal keeper.

Worcester, Sept. 9 1748.

The Boston Evening-Post, September 12, 1748; September 19, 1748; September 26, 1748.

R*AN-away from his Master* Chadwallader Ford *of Wilmington, on the 16th Instant, a Negro Man named* Cyrus, *a lusty well set Negro, about* 29 *Years of Age, stammers in his Speech, full fac'd, had on when he went away a homespun Jacket with hard metal Buttons, Garlix and a tow Shirt, and took with him divers other Cloaths, viz a Coat & Jacket of red Camblet, a homespun Coat lin'd with red, and an old black Wigg, which he sometimes wears, a lac'd Hat something worn, blue rib Stockings and other worsted & yarn Stockings. The said Negro formerly liv'd with Col.* Chandler *of Worcester, then with Mr.* Hubbard *of Rutland, after that with Mr.* Ward *of said Worcester, and then with Mr.* Hunt *of Watertown. 'Tis suppos'd he has taken Worcester or Rhode-Island Road.*

Whoever shall take up said Servant, and him convey to his aforesaid Master at Wilmington, shall have ten Pounds *old Tenor Reward and all necessary Charges paid.*

The said Negro has been us'd to lie by a Days and travel in the Night; he took a Halter with him with a Design 'tis probable to steal a Horse.

And all Masters of Vessels & others, are hereby caution'd against concealing or carrying off said Negro on Penalty of the Law.

Sept. 20. 1748.

The Boston Gazette, or Weekly Journal, September 20, 1748.

R*AN-*away last Night, being the 19th Inst. from his Master *John Johnson* of *Boston,* Jack-maker, a Negro Man Servant named *Jo,* about 23 Years of Age; a likely Fellow, who had on when he went away, a dark coloured Fly Coat with flat white Metal Buttons, a Swan-skin double-breasted Jacket, Leather Deer-Skin Breeches, a pair of high heel'd thick sol'd Shoes. He can play well on a Flute. He has a large Scar on his upper Lip. Whoever shall take up the abovesaid Runaway, and him safely convey to his abovesaid Master in *Boston* aforesaid, shall have *Ten Pounds* old Tenor, Reward, and all necessary Charges paid. And all Masters of Vessels and others, are hereby caution'd against harbouring, concealing, or carrying off said Servant, on Penalty of the Law. Sept. 20.

The Boston Weekly News-Letter, September 22, 1748; October 6, 1748; October 13, 1748. See *The Boston Evening-Post,* September 26, 1748.

RAN away on the 19th of this Instant *September*, from his Master *John Johnson* of *Boston*, Jack-maker, a Negro Man Servant named *Jo*, about 23 Years of Age, a likely Fellow, who had on when he went away, a dark coloured Fly Coat, with flat white Metal Buttons, a Swan Skin double breasted Jacket, Leather Deer-Skin Breeches, a pair of high heel'd thick soled Shoes. He can play on the Flute, has a Scar on his upper Lip, and speaks good *English*. Whoever shall take him up, and deliver him to his said Master, shall have Ten Pounds Reward, Old Tenor, and all reasonable Charges paid.—All Masters of Vessels and others, are hereby cautioned against harbouring, concealing, or carrying off said Negro, as they will avoid the Penalty of the Law.

The Boston Evening-Post, September 26, 1748; October 3, 1748; October 10, 1748. See *The Boston Weekly News-Letter*, September 22, 1748.

RAN-away from Capt. *John Bulkley* living in Queen-street, a Negro Girl named *Billah*, about 20 Years of Age, a short thick well set Girl, has had the small Pox, speaks good English: Had on when she shent [*sic*] away a blue Jacket, and a strip'd homespun Petticoat: Whoever shall take up the said Runaway, and convey her to her said Master, shall have 40 *s*. Reward, old Tenor, and all necessary Charges.

The Boston Gazette, or Weekly Journal, September 27, 1748; October 11, 1748; October 18, 1748. See *The Boston Gazette, or, Weekly Journal*, June 7, 1743, and *The Boston Gazette, or Weekly Journal*, November 3, 1747.

RAN away from his Master, Mr. *John Wakefield* of *Boston*, a Negro Man Servant named *Bonney*, about 23 Years of Age, who had on when he went away, a Bengall Coat, the Buttons of the same, lined with Blue, a striped homespun Jacket, with Pewter Buttons, a pair of blue Kersey Breeches, with Pewter Buttons, a pair of blue worsted Stockings, and a check'd Shirt. Whoever shall take him up, and bring him to his said Master, near the Rev. Mr. *Mather's* Meeting-House, shall be satisfied for their Trouble, and have all necessary Charges   paid, by   *John Wakefield.*

Boston, October 10. 1748.

The Boston Evening-Post, October 10, 1748; October 17, 1748; October 24, 1748.

RAN-away from Mr. *Joseph Burch* of *Boston*, on Wednesday the 5th of this Instant, a Negro Man Servant named *Quam*, about 23 Years of Age, a thick well set Fellow, plays on a Violin; he has a thick Under Lip. He had on when he went away, a speckled Shirt, white Waistcoat, also a homespun short strip'd Jacket, red, blue and white; the Stripes go round his *Body*; and

there are Holes to lace it, and also button Holes and Buttons; light colour'd blue Breeches, trim'd with Black; Yarn Stockings and a large Pair of white Metal Buckles in his Shoes. Whoever shall take up said Runaway, and his safely convey to his abovesaid Master at *Boston*, shall have *five Pounds* old Tenor Reward, and all necessary Charges paid. And all Masters of Vessels and others are hereby caution'd against concealing or carrying off said Servant on Penalty of the Law.
The Boston Gazette, or Weekly Journal, October 18, 1748.

DEserted from the Ship Warren-Frigate, *James Nevin* Master, the following Sailors, viz. *Thomas Churchill, John Hutchinson, Alexander Mackey, Christopher Copeland*, and *Philip Holbrook*: Whoever shall deliver either of said Sailors on board the said Ship, shall have *five Pounds* old Tenor Reward.
The Boston Gazette, or Weekly Journal, October 18, 1748.

RAN away from his Master *Joseph Clap* of *Scituate*, on the 29th of this Instant *September*, a Negro Man named *Primus*, being about Forty Years of Age; speaks good English, has a good set of Teeth, he looks up glaring with his Eyes, has a Wen on the Joint of one of his great Toes, which makes his Shoe stick out a little: He had on when he went away, a good Kersey Coat and Breeches, a Tow Shirt and Trowsers, a good Felt Hat, Stockings and Shoes: Whosoever shall take up said Negro and bring him to his said Master, or secure him so as he may have him again, shall have *Four Pounds* old Tenor Reward, and all necessary Charges paid.
   Joseph Clap.
The Boston Weekly News-Letter, October 20, 1748; October 27, 1748; November 10, 1748.

              Dedham October 18. 1748.
STolen out of the House of *Jeremiah Fisher* Esq: of *Dedham*, the thirteenth Instant, One Hundred and Fifty Pounds *old Tenor* in Money, the Thief is supposed to be one *John Coggin* of *Sudbury* who was hired by the said *Fisher* for a Month: He is a small slim Fellow: had on when he went away a yellowish out-side Coat with Red Lining, a green Jacket Goat-skin Breeches, and a red Cap. Whoever discovers said Theft, so that the Author thereof may be brought to Justice, and the Owner receive his Money again shall have Twenty Pounds old Tenor Reward,
   paid by *Jeremiah Fisher.*
The Boston Weekly News-Letter, October 20, 1748; October 27, 1748; November 3, 1748.

RAN-away from his Master *Thomas Shepard* of *Boston*, Innholder, at the Sign of the White Bear, a Servant Lad named *John Lay*, about sixteen Years of Age; had on when he went away, a strip'd homespun Jacket, a pair of Trowsers, and a pair of grissel'd Stockings: He has short Hair and a remarkable Scar on the out side of his right Eye. Whosoever shall take up said Run-away, and bring him to his said Master, shall have *Five Pounds* old Tenor Reward, and all reasoanble Charges paid. *N. B.* All Masters of Vessels and other Persons are forbid harbouring, concealing or carrying off said Boy, as they would avoid the Penalty of the Law.
Boston, October 26. 1748.
The Boston Weekly News-Letter, October 27, 1748. See *The Boston Weekly News-Letter*, August 4, 1748.

WHereas Prudence *the Wife of* Wm. Beard,
of Boston, *Mariner, has eloped from him, and run him in Debt to his great Damage:*
These are to caution all Persons against trusting her on my Account, for I hereby publish & declare, I will not pay any Debt she shall contract after the Publication hereof. As Witness by Hand.
William Beard. *Nov.* 1. 1748.
The above Advertisement comes properly certify'd by one of his Majesty's Justices of the Peace.
The Boston Gazette, or Weekly Journal, November 1, 1748.

RAN away from Messirs. *Dean* and *Mason,* the 31st of last Month, an Indian Man named *Justin*, had on a plaid under Jackett and an outside white Kersey jacket with brass Buttons figured with the Duke of *Cumberland's* Bust, both new; he is middle Aged, low sett, speaks good *French* and very little *English* Whoever will secure him so that his Masters may have him again, shall have *Six Pounds* old Tenor Reward and all reasonable Charges paid by Messi *Dean* and *Mason,* at their House near the Baptist Meeting.
All Masters of Vessels and others are desired not to harbour or carry him off at their Perils. *Boston November* 3. 1748.
The Boston Weekly Post Boy, November 3, 1748; November 10, 1748; November 17, 1748. See *The Boston Gazette, or Weekly Journal*, November 8, 1748.

WHereas *Warwick Hawkey, John Bundle, John Goulding,* and *Aaron Gosham*, (an *Indian*) have absented themselves from their Duty on board his Majesty's Ship *Boston,* for some Time; This is therefore to acquaint them, that if they will return to the said Ship, on or before the 10th Instant, that they shall be forgiven this their first Neglect; but if after the Publication hereof, they do not return at the Time limited, they may be assured that all possible Means will be made use of to have them apprehended and taken as Deserters, and that if any or either of them shall be so taken after the Time abovementioned, they shall be delivered to the Marshal of the Admiralty, who will have Orders to prosecute them as such, and he will be fully acquainted with every Circumstance of their Desertion, to prevent as much as possible, their escaping the utmost Rigour of the Law.

Dated on Board the Boston, *in* Nantasket *Road, the* 4*th of* November, 1748.
    E. WHEELER.

The Boston Evening-Post, November 7, 1748. See *The Boston Gazette, or Weekly Journal,* November 8, 1748.

WHereas *Warwick Hawkey, John Bundle, John Goulding, John Forrister, Partrick Kirke, Antonia Piraza,* and *Aaron Gosham,* (an Indian) have absented themselves from their Duty on board his Majesty's Ship Boston, for some Time; This is therefore to acquaint them, that if they will return to the said Ship, on or before the 13th Instant, that they shall be forgiven this their first Neglect; but if after the Publication hereof, they do not return at the Time limited, they may be assured that all possible Means will be made use of to have them apprehended and taken as Deserters, and that if any or either of them shall be so taken after the Time abovementioned, they shall be delivered to the Marshal of the Admiralty, who will have Orders to prosecute them as such, and he will be fully acquainted with every Circumstance of their Desertion, to prevent as much as possible, their escaping the utmost Rigour of the Law.

Dated on Board the Boston, *in* Nantasket *Road,* the 4*th of* November, 1748.
  E. WHEELER.   *Boston, N. E. Nov* 5 1748.

The Boston Gazette, or Weekly Journal, November 8, 1748. See *The Boston Evening-Post,* November 7, 1748.

RAn-away from Messieurs *Dean & Mason* at *Boston,* the 31st of last Month, an Indian Man named *Justin,* had on a Plaid under Jacket, and an outside white Kersey Jacket with brass Buttons figur'd with the Duke of *Cumberland's* Bust, both new; he is middle aged, of low Stature, speaks good French, and but very little English. Whoever shall secure him so that his Masters may have him again, shall have *twenty Pounds* old Tenor Reward, and all necessary Charges paid by Messieurs *Dean & Mason* at their House near the Baptist Meeting. And all Masters of Vessels and others, are hereby caution'd against concealing or carrying off said Servant on Penalty of the Law. *Boston, Nov* 12 1748.

The Boston Gazette, or Weekly Journal, November 8, 1748; November 15, 1748; November 22, 1748; November 29, 1748; December 6, 1748. See *The Boston Weekly Post Boy,* November 3, 1748.

RAN away from his Master Capt. *Samuel Partridge* of *Boston*, on the 5th of this Instant November, an English Servant Boy named *Francis Lang*, about 16 Years old, is a well set Lad, round Faced, and has short Hair: He had on when he went away, 1 blue Waistcoat, a check'd Shirt, a little Castor Hat, a pair of Ozenbrigs Trousers, Yarn Stockings, and a new pair of Shoes. Whoever shall take him up, and bring him to his said Master, shall have *Five Pounds*, Old Tenor, Reward, and necessary Charges paid.

N. B. All Masters of Vessels and others, are hereby caution'd against harbouring, concealing or carrying off said Servant, as they will answer it at their Peril.
The Boston Evening-Post, November 7, 1748.

RAN-away from his Master *Amos Peaslee* at *Haverhill*, the fifth of *November* Instant, a Negro Man named *Pomp York*, about 33 Years of Age, speaks good English, and can read, write and cypher; had on an old black Coat, speckled woollen Shirt, and had no Hat. The said Negro formerly belong'd to Major *Gilman* of *Exeter*, and ran away from him about three or four Months ago, and has since work'd at *Billerica* and *Brookline*. Whoever shall take up the abovesaid Negro, and him bring or safely convey to his abovesaid Master, *Amos Peaslee* at *Haverhill*, shall have *Five Pounds* old Tenor Reward, and all necessary Charges paid, And all Masters of Vessels and others, are hereby caution'd against concealing or carrying off said Servant on Penalty of the Law. *Novemb.* 7. 1748.
The Boston Gazette, or Weekly Journal, November 8, 1748; November 15, 1748.

DEserted on the 14th Instant from the Brigt. *Joanna, Wm. Morris* Master, lying in the Harbour of Boston, a Sailor named *John Little*, a tall slim Fellow, about 25 Years of Age, wears a light Wigg, and a blue Jacket, and has lately had the Small Pox, as that the Pus is fresh in his Face. Whoever shall take up said Sailor, and bring him to Mr. *Andrew Mc'Kenzie's* Warehouse, shall receive ten Pounds old Tenor Reward, and all necessary Charges paid. It is thought he has gone out of Town, he has taken the Road towards *Portsmouth*. Boston, *N.E Nov* 5. 1748.
The Boston Gazette, or Weekly Journal, November 15, 1748; November 22, 1748.

RAN-away from his Master Mr. *Samuel Miller* of *Boston,* Gunsmith, on the 28th Day of *May* last, a Negro Man named *Casar*, aged about 30 Years, a pretty sensible Fellow, well sett, of midling Stature has a Scar under his Throat, speaks very good English, had on when he went away, a grey broad Cloth Coat, and a blue Cloth double breasted Jacket ull [sic] trim'd and blue Breeches, has since his running away been Privateering out of *Rhode-*

Island, and has lately return'd. and calls himself *Jo Adams*, and may probably now appear in a Sailor's Habit

Whoever shall take up the abovesaid Runaway, and convey him to his Master aforesaid, shall have *thirty Pounds*, old Tenor Reward, and all necessary Charges paid, by *Samuel Miller.*

The Boston Gazette, or Weekly Journal, November 15, 1748; November 22, 1748.

RAN-away on the 20th Instant, from his Master, Capt. *Samuel Partridge*, a white Servant Boy, about 15 or 16 Years of Age, he had on when he went away, two blew Waistcoats, yarn Stockings, a small Castor Hat, short hair, speckled Shirt, round Fac'd, a small Scar in his Forehead, a thick well set Lad. Whoever will up, take [sic] the abovesaid Runway, and convey him to his Master aforesaid, shall have *five Pounds* old Tenor Reward and all necessary Charges paid. And all Masters of Vessels and others, are hereby caution'd against concealing or carrying off said Servant on Penalty of the Law.

The Boston Gazette, or Weekly Journal, November 22, 1748.

RAN-away from his Master Mr. *Rowland Robinson* of *South-Kingston*, on the 20th current, an Indian Boy Servant named *Caesar*, aged about eighteen Years, is a likely well looking Fellow, had on when he went away a coarse Kersey Jacket & Breeches of a Sheep's grey colour, Yarn Stockings of the same colour, an under Jacket of blue Duroy, lin'd with red, a new Felt Hat, and a strip'd worsted Cap. It is supposed he stole from his Master a dirty black colour'd Mare. Whoever will take up said Servant and convey him to his said Master in *South Kingston*, shall have *Fifteen Pounds* old Tenor Reward, and all necessary Charges
paid by *Rowland Robinson.*   *Novemb.* 25 1748.

The Boston Weekly Post Boy, December 5, 1748.

RAN-away on the 24th of *November* last from their Master *Timothy Stevens* at Boston, two Negro Man Slaves, both aged about 24 Years, one named *Cato*, a tall well set Fellow, speaks English pretty well, had on when he went away, a dark Great Coat something patch'd, a new Felt Hat, a pair of short Trowsers, blue rib'd Stockings, woollen check'd Shirt. The other named *London* a middle siz'd well set Fellow, speaks but little English, had on a dark Great Coat much worn, new Felt Hat, Waistcoat, black Leather Breeches, blue ribb'd Stockings, double Channel'd Pumps, steel Buckles, woollen check Shirt. Whoever shall take up said Runaways, and convey them to their Master, shall have *five Pounds* old Tenor Reward for each or either of them, and all necessary Charges
paid by me   *Timothy Stevens.*

The Boston Gazette, or Weekly Journal, December 6, 1748. See *The Boston Gazette, or Weekly Journal*, April 4, 1749, for Cato.

Boston, December 7. 1748.
Last Night ran from on board the *St. George, William Hutchinson* Commander, *John Blaney*, an Apprentice to *Peter Johnson* Mate of said Ship: He is about 16 Years of Age, fresh colour'd, has black Hair, wears a Cap or black Wig; is about 5 Feet high, a smooth fac'd well-looking Lad. He took with him a great Coat, a brown Wastcoat, a scarlet ditto, with a Gold Button, and a blue great Coat with a white fustian Waistcoat, made after the Spanish Fashion. *N. B.* He wears sometime a red Cap, turn'd up with black Fur. Any Person who will secure said Run-away, so that he may be returned to his Master, shall have *Ten Pounds* old Tenor Reward. All Masters of Vessels are caution'd against receiving him, as they would avoid the Penalty of the Law.
The Boston Weekly News-Letter, December 8, 1748; December 15, 1748.

Province of *New Hampshire, Exeter, November* 29. 1748.
WHereas *Mary Dudley*, the Wife of me the Subscriber, *Samuel Dudley*, of *Exeter* in the Province of *New Hampshire*, has eloped from me, and not only tool away my household Stuff, but has run me into Debt, several large Sums, greatly to my Damage; These are therefore to Notify and Warn all persons, that they have henceforward no Dealing with the said *Mary Dudley*, nor Credit her on my Accounts for any thing; for I will not pay any Debt that she shall contract with any Person for Time to come.
Samuel Dudley.
The Boston Evening-Post, December 19, 1748; December 26, 1748; January 2, 1749.

1749

RAN-away from his Master *Isaac Anthony* of *Newport*, A Negro Man, named *Newport*, speaks good English, about 30 Years of Age, has a Blemish in one Eye; had on when he went away a blue Kersey Jacket, a tar'd Hat with the Brims cut off: He is of middle Stature; and by Trade a Goldsmith. Whoever shall take up said Runaway, and convey him to his Master in *Newport, Rhode-Island*, shall have *Five Pounds* old Tenor, and all necessary Charges
paid by me   *Isaac Anthony.*
The Boston Weekly Post Boy, February 6, 1749; February 13, 1749; February 20, 1749.

RAN-away the 11th Instant from His Majesty's Billender the *Montague*, *John Connoly* Commander, one *Jacob Bridgham*, a short smock-fac'd Fellow, formerly a Shoe maker by Trade, about Twenty-five Years of Age. Whoever will take up said Deserter, and bring him to said *Connoly*, or to *Charles Apthorpe* or *Thomas Hancock*, Esqrs: in *Boston*, shall have Thirty Pounds Old Tenor, and all Charges paid.
    The Boston Weekly Post Boy, February 20, 1749; February 27, 1749; March 6, 1749.

RAN-away from her Master Richard Smith of Boston, on Sunday the nineteenth of February Instant, a Negro Woman named Diana, about twenty five Years of Age; she had on when she went away a homespun Gown, with a Patch on the Corner of another Sort; she carried away sundry other Cloaths with her. She formerly belonged to Mr. Billings.
    Whoever shall take up said Negro, and bring her to her said Master at Admiral Vernon's Head in King's Street, or secure her in any of his Majesty's Goals, shall have five Pounds old Tenor Reward, and all necessary Charges paid.
    And all Masters of Vessels and others are hereby caution'd against carrying off or concealing the said Negro, as they would avoid the Penalty of the Law, in that Case made and provided.   Boston, Feb. 27. 1748,9.
    The Boston Gazette, or Weekly Journal, March 7, 1749; March 21, 1749.

THIS is to Certfy all People, that *Martha*, the Wife of me the Subscriber, hath absconded herself from me, and still continues [   ]: Wherefor I forbid any Person or Persons to harbour, entertain, or trust her on my Accompt, for I will not pay a Farthing she shall contract after the Date hereof.   *Joseph Davis.*   *Boston, March* 8 1748, 49.
    The Boston Weekly News-Letter, March 9, 1749.

RAN-away on the 20th of *February* last, from his Majesty's Billander the *Montague, John Connolly* Commander, one *James Newman*, a short thick Fellow: Had on when he went away, a blue Jacket, and Trowsers, and Cap: Whoever takes up the said Runaway, and him safely convey to the said *Connolly*, shall have *Twenty Pounds* (old Tenor) Reward, and all necessary Charges paid.
    The Boston Weekly News-Letter, March 24, 1749; March 30, 1749; April 6, 1749.

RAN-away from his Master *Timothy Stevens* of *Boston*, on the 31st of *March* last, a Negro Man named *Cato*, a tall well set Fellow, Aged about 25 Years, speaks English pretty well, has lost all his Toes by the Frost in

Maryland, where he practiced running away for some Years, his Way is to hide in the Day Time, and travel in the Night in the Woods, and kill Fowls, Shoats &c. for his Support. He on when he went away, a red Kersey great Coat, Deerskin Breeches, yarn Stockings, double sol'd Shoes with Strings, double worsted Cap, and Felt Hatt. Whoever shall secure said Negro shall have *five Pounds* old Tenor Reward, and all necessary Charges paid by   *Timothy Stevens.*
The Boston Gazette, or Weekly Journal, April 4, 1749. See *The Boston Gazette, or Weekly Journal*, December 6, 1748, and *The Boston Weekly News-Letter*, July 20, 1749.

RAN-away from his Master *Nathanael Mendum* of *Portsmouth* in *New-Hampshire*, a Negro Man named *Will*, about 30 Years of Age, a well set Fellow has lost part of one of his little Fingers, he had on when he went away, a large blue Fearnothing Jacket & Breeches, Hat, and Cap: Whoever shall take up said Negro and secure him, or send him to his Master in *Portsmouth*, shall have Five Pounds *old Tenor*, and all necessary Charges paid by me,   *Nathanael Mendum.*
The Boston Weekly Post-Boy, April 10, 1749; April 17, 1749; April 24, 1749.

RAN away from his Master, the Honourable *Richard Saltonstall* of *Haverhill*, Esq; on the 10th of this Instant April, a white Man servant named *William Blare*: He is something freckled and Pock-broken, has a flat Nose, and black Beard on his upper Lip, otherwise he is smooth faced. He had on when he went away, a worsted Cap, a broad brim'd Felt Hat, his outer Garment was a double-breasted Robbin, with White-Metal Buttons, which Garment had several Gashes between his Shoulders made by carrying an Ax. Whoever shall take up the said Servant, and convey him to his said Master in *Haverhill*, shall have *Ten Pounds*, (old Tenor) Reward, and all necessary Charges paid.   *Haverhill, April* 18, 1749.
The Boston Evening-Post, April 24, 1749; May 1, 1749. See *The Boston Evening-Post*, February 4, 1751.

THIS is to give publick Notice, that *Abigail* the Wife of *Andrew Simpson* of *Nottingham* in the Province of *New Hampshire*, on the Fourth of this Instant, elop'd from her Husand, and carry'd off considerable of said *Simpson's* Substancel wherefore I the said *Simpson* hereby declare I will not pay any Debt she shall contract with any Person or Persons after the Date hereof.   *Andrew Simpson.*   *Nottingham, March* 8th, 1749.
The Boston Evening-Post, April 24, 1749.

RAN-away from his Master *Joseph Cottle* of *Newbury*, Shipwright, on the 11th Instant, a White Servant Boy, named *Richard Cuttler*, about Fourteen Years of Age: He is short and thick-set, with very thick Lips and brown strait Hair, and had on a white woollen Shirt, a Pair of new Shoes, woolen Breeches; but no Jacket nor Stockings. Whoever shall take up said Servant and bring him to his said Master shall have *Ten Pounds* old Tenor, and all Charges paid by me *Joseph Cottle.*

Newbury, April the 22*d* 1749.

All Masters of Vessels are forbid carrying off said Servant.

The Boston Weekly Post-Boy, April 24, 1749; May 1, 1749; May 8, 1749.

RAN-away from his Master *William Ellery* of *Cape Ann,* on the 14th Instant at Night, a Negro Man named *Cato,* is a very likely Fellow, speaks goog English has lost his left Hand little Finger, and the next to it is a little crooked; is about 30 Years of Age, had on when he went away, a Cloth colour'd Kersey Jacket, lin'd with blew Bays, and flat Pewter Buttons, an old Pair of red Cloth Breeches, a Pair of Trouses, black Stockings, and a Pair of large Brass Shoe-Buckels.

Whoever shall take up said Negro, and bring him to his Master at *Cape Ann* aforesaid, or secure him so that his Master may have him again, shall have *seven Pounds* old Tenor Reward, and all necessary Charges paid.

And all Masters of Vessels and others, are hereby warned against concealing or carrying off said Servant on Penalty of the Law.

Boston, April 27*th* 1749.

The Boston Gazette, or Weekly Journal, May 2, 1749.

Boston, April 26. 1749.

WHEREAS one *Joseph Wilson* who said he came from some Parts of *Old England,* has this Day in a clandestine manner left his Lodging at *John Swinnerton's,* lately a School-master in this Town, without paying for his Lodging; and is supposed to carry off with him a Pocket Book with Paper Money in it to the Value of £. 134 10 *s.* old Tenor, which the said *Joseph* is thought to have stolen out of a Trunk belonging to the said *Swinnerton*; as also three Pair of red Worsted Hose with thread Clocks: These are therefore to inform any Person that if they will apprehend the said *Joseph* and send or convey him to *Boston,* so as me may be brought to Justice, shall receive *Ten Pounds* old Tenor Reward, and all necessary Charges

paid by me *John Swinnerton.*

N. B. The said *Joseph* is about 50 Years of Age, of middling Stature; had on when he went away, a loose blue great Coat, with white Metal Buttons, a white Fustian Jacket, an old Pair of Trowsers with Cloth

Breeches under them, and has also a short black Wigg. The Buckles in his Shoes were not Fellows.
The Boston Weekly News-Letter, May 4, 1749.

RAN-away on the 27th of *April* past, from his Master *Jonathan White*, of *Weymouth*, a Negro Man Servant named Scipio, about 27 Years of Age, of middling Stature, had on a double breasted Jacket, gray colour, with flat Metal Buttons, and a blue under one, a new Check Shirt, small Bever Hat, a Pair of Trousers, and blue Breeches, under them, gray Stockings, and round to'd Shoes. Whoever shall take up said Runaway, and bring him to his abovesaid Master, shall have *ten Pounds*, old Tenor Reward, and all necessary Charges paid. And all Masters of Vessels and others, are hereby caution'd against concealing or carrying off said Servant on Penalty of the Law. *Boston. May* 5th. 1749.
The Boston Gazette, or Weekly Journal, May 9, 1749. See *The Boston Gazette, or Weekly Journal*, August 20, 1751, and *The Boston Post-Boy*, September 2, 1751.

RAN away from his Master, Mr. *Matthew Hopkins* of *Boston*, Sawyer, on the 13th of this Instant *May*, a stout well set Negro Man named *Herculus*, about 30 or 35 Years of Age, and speaks good *English*. He has a large Bump on his left Shin, and had on when he went away, a blue Cloth Jacket, stich'd up the Seams with Canvas, and an under Jacket laced up the Breast, a woollen check'd Shirt, a pair of Buck-skin Breeches, with plain metal Buttons, a pair of old Shoes and blue Yarn Stockings, but no Hat. Whoever shall take up the said Negro, and bring him to his said Master, shall have *Five Pounds* Reward, old Tenor, and all necessary Charges paid. *N. B.* All Masters of Vessels are cautioned against concealing or carrying off said Negro, as they would avoid the Penalty of the Law.
The Boston Evening-Post, May 22, 1749; May 29, 1749; June 5, 1749.

WHereas *Matthew Foster, David Moncrath, William Brown* and *John Colberson*, late Mariners on board the Snow *Grenadier, Roger Carling* Master, have at several times since the 7th of *May* Instant, absconded from the said Snow, contrary to Agreement; These are to require them to return to their Duty on board the said Snow, within two Days from the Date hereof, otherwise they will be treated as Deserters, and prosecuted according to Law,
by *Roger Carling.*   *Boston, May* 21. 1749.
The Boston Evening-Post, May 22, 1749.

RUNaway from (his Master) *Thomas Ivers*, Rope-maker of *Stratford* in *Connecticut*, an Apprentice Boy named *Peter Hepbron*, aged 17 Years or

thereabouts; he is a well sett sturdy Lad of a swarthy Complexion, gray Eyes. Had on when he went away, a Lead colour'd Pea-Jacket, a blue Vest, a striped Waistcoat, blue Camblet Breeches and a pair of Trowsers. Whoever takes up the said Apprentice and secures him so that his Master may have him again, shall have 20 Pounds Reward *old Tennor*, and all reasonable Charges paid by *Thomas Ivers*, or
   Henry De Foreest Printer in *New-York, Stratford, May* 1*st* 1749.
The New-York Evening Post, May 29, 1749; June 5, 1749; June 12, 1749; June 19, 1749; June 26, 1749; July 10, 1749; July 24, 1749; July 31, 1749; August 7, 1749.

THis Morning run-away from his Master *George Massey*, a Molatto Fellow, named *Pero*, about 28 Years of Age, strait, well-limb'd and of a middle Stature, his Hair is very short: He had on when he went away a Pair of Buckskin Breeches, Shoes and Stockings: Whosoever shall take up the said Run-away, and safely convey him to his Master shall have Ten Pounds old Tenor Reward, and all necessary Charges paid.
   George Massey.
  All Masters of Vessels and others are cautioned against carrying off said Molatto, as they would avoid the Penalty of the Law.
  The Boston Weekly Post Boy, June 5, 1749.

RAN-away from his Master, *John White*, of *Boston*, Baker, on the 15th Instant, a Negro Man Servant; named *Quaco*, about 22 Years of Age, speaks good English, well set Fellow, had on a striped homespun Jacket, leather Breeches, check Shirt, white cotton Stockings, good pair of Shoes brass Buckles, new worsted Cap new yallow Silk Handkerchief, Caster Hat about half worn.
  Whoever shall take up said Negro, and safely convey to his abovesaid Master in *Boston*, shall have *five Pounds* old Tenor Reward, and all necessary Charges paid.
  All Masters of Vessels and others, are hereby caution'd against concealing or carrying off said Negro, on penalty of the Law.
  The Boston Gazette, or Weekly Journal, June 20, 1749.

WHereas *Daniel Murphy* aged 28 Years 5 Foot 5 Inches high, dark brown Complection, red Hair, born in Ireland, single Man; *Thomas Storey* aged 26 Years, 5 Foot and 5 Inches high light colour'd, born in Boston, married; *David Hadley* aged 26 Years, 5 Foot 8 Inches high, fair, a large Scar on his left Leg, and very much pitted with the Small Pox, born in Bristol in England, single; *John Bargery*, aged 23 Years, 5 Foot 5 Inches high, light brown; a small Scar on the right Cheek, born in Gosport, single; *James Buredge*, aged 27 Years, 5 Foot 2 Inches high, light brown, born in St.

James's, London, married; *James Buckland*, aged 25 Years, 5 Foot 11 Inches high, light brown, a Cut over the left Ear, born in Londonderry in Ireland, single;

Have deserted from His Majesty's Sloop the Viper under my Command: I do hereby promise a Reward of one Guineas for each Man over and above the Sum of forty Shillings usually given on the like Occasions to any Person who shall take or apprehend them or any one of them, on their being delivered into the Custody of any Officer on board his Majesty's said Sloop. Dated on Board the said Sloop in Nantesket-Road this 19th Day of *June* 1749. *Cornelius Smelt.*

The Boston Gazette, or Country Journal, June 20, 1749 *The Boston Weekly News-Letter*, June 22, 1749; June 29, 1749. Minor differences between the papers.

DEserted from his Majesty's Billander *Montagu, John Connolly* Commander, *Joshua Winnock*, Sail-maker, about Twenty four Years of Age, of a low Stature, born in *Boston*. Whoever apprehends the said *Winnock* shall have *Twenty Pounds*, old Tenor, Reward.
John Connolly.
The Boston Evening-Post, June 26, 1749; July 3, 1749.

RAN-away on 17th of *June* from *John Hunt* of *Watertown*, a Negro Servant named *Caesar*, about 17 Years old, middling Stature for his Age, speaks English, but has a hoarse Voice constantly, understands Farming Business, and lived with Mr. *Nath. Battle* of *Dedham*, and is suppos'd his Intention was to go to a Township called *Naragansset* No. 4. Had on when he went away a dark striped Homespun Jackett and Breeches, a Pair of light Worsted Stockings, and new Pumps. Whoever shall take up said Runaway, and him convey to said *Hunt*, shall have *ten Pounds*, old Tenor, paid him by said Hunt, and all necessary Charges. And all Masters of Vessels and others are hereby caution'd, against concealing or carrying off said Servant, as they would avoid the Penalty of the Law.

The Boston Evening-Post, June 26, 1749; July 3, 1749; July 10, 1749; *The Boston Gazette, or Weekly Journal*, June 27, 1749. Minor differences between the papers.

DEserted from the Ship Fearon Capt. *Robert Anderson*, on Friday the 14th Instant, *James Davis, William Floyd, & Archibald McGenes*, Sailors belonging to said Ship, if the said Seamen will return to their Duty within two Days from the Date hereof, they will be will received, if not, they will be deem'd Deserters. Boston, *July* 13th 1749.

The Boston Gazette, or Weekly Journal, July 18, 1749.

RANaway from his Master *James Smith* Sugar-Baker in Boston, the 12th Instant, a Negro Man named *Francis*, a French Negro, speaks with a low Voice, middle Stature, well Featured, very black, smooth skin'd and a broad Nose, a down Look, cloath'd with a Jacket and Breeches, Shoes & Stockings. Whoever shall take up said Negro and deliver him to his Master, shall have *five Pounds* old Tenor, and all Charges paid. And all Masters of Ships are forbid to carry him off, on Penalty of the Law.
   James Smith.
 The Boston Gazette, or Weekly Journal, July 18, 1749. See *The Boston Evening-Post*, July 24, 1749.

RAN away from his Master, on the 18th Instant, a Negro Man named *Cato* who formerly belonged to Dr. *Stivens* of *Boston*, aged about 25 Years; a tall well-set Fellow, speaks pretty good English, hath lost all his Toes by the Frost: He had on a Shirt and Trowsers of check'd Linnen, (carried away with him a Bundle of the same) a red great Coat, and a pair of Leather Breeches. N. B. He is us'd to this Practice, and hath been often guilty of stealing Poultry, Shoats, Lambs, &c. hides in the Day Time and Travels in the Night.

 Whosoever shall secure the said Negro, and inform the Printer hereof, so as his Master may have him again, shall have *Five Pounds* Old Tenor Reward, and all necessary Charges paid.
 The Boston Weekly News-Letter, July 20, 1749; July 27; 1749; August 3, 1749. See *The Boston Gazette, or Weekly Journal*, December 6, 1748, and *The Boston Weekly News-Letter*, July 20, 1749.

RAN-away from *Ichabod Plaisted* of *Berwick*, A Negro Man, named *Pomp*, a short thick Fellow. 'Tis said he has changed his Clothes since he ran away. Whoever shall take up said Negro and safety keep him so that his said Master may have him again, shall have *Four Pounds* old Tenor, with all necessary Charges paid to those concerned,
   per Ichabod Plaisted.   *Newport, July* 21. 1749.
 The Boston Weekly Post-Boy, July 24, 1749.

LAST Night ran away from his Master *William Johnson* of *Worcester, Thomas Balderson*: He is a short well-set Fellow, suppos'd to be about thirty or forty Years old; his Hair is of a dark Colour, and very short, over which he wears a Cap. He is of a swarthy Complection, flat Nose, broad Face, and little Eyes. He had on a brown coloured Coat, with brass Buttons, a light coloured Jacket, new Leather Breeches, grey yarn Stockings, a pair of new Pumps; he is a Blacksmith by Trade, and was a Transport.

 Whoever shall take up said Person, and return him to his Master, shall have paid *Five Pounds*, old Tenor, paid them by me

Wm Johnson *Worcester, July* 14. 1749.
N. B It is supposed he has got two Gold Rings with him.
The Boston Weekly News-Letter, July 27; 1749; August 3, 1749.

WHereas a *French* Negro named *Francis*, ran away from his Master *James Smith* of *Boston*, Sugar Baker, on the twelfth Instant: Whoever will bring the said Negro to his Master, or secure him in any of his Majesty's Goals, shall have *Five Pounds* old Tenor, Reward, and necessary Charges. The said Negro is of middle Stature, well featured, very black, smooth skin'd, flat nosed, and speaks with a low Voice. Had on when he ran away, a white Cap and Frock, blue Jacket and Breeches, with Brass Buttons, Shoes and Stockings, and sometimes wears a Gold Ring in his Ear.
N. B. He was taken from *Martinico*, carried to *Louisbourg*, and brought to *Boston* by Sir *Peter Warren*.   *James Smith*.
   The Boston Evening-Post, July 24, 1749; July 31, 1749. See *The Boston Gazette, or Weekly Journal*, July 18, 1749.

RAN-away on the 13th Instant from his Master Mr. *Albert Dennis* of *Boston,* a Negro Boy named *Cato*, about Seventeen Years of Age, a slim likely Fellow, stammers some in his Speech, had on when he went away a light short Broadcloath Jacket, without Sleeves, brown Linnen Shirt, brown coarse Kersey Breches, no Stockings nor Shoes.
   Whoever shall take up said Runaway, and him safely convey to his said Master, in *Boston*, abovesaid, shall have *five Pounds* old Tenor Reward and all necessary Charges paid.
   And all Masters of Vessels and others, are hereby caution'd against concealing or carrying off said Servant on Penalty of the Law.
Boston, July 17th. 1749.
   The Boston Gazette, or Weekly Journal, July 25, 1749.

RAN-away on the 13th Instant, from his Master *David Nevins* of *Canterbury* in *Connecticut*, a Spanish Indian Man Servant, named *Cesar*, about 18 Years of Age, a tall well set Fellow, long Vissage, full fac'd, a dark brown Eye with short Hair, speaks good English; had on a check'd Flannel Shirt, old Leather Breeches, an old Felt Hat; without Shoes or Stockings.
   Whoever shall take up said Run-away Servant and convey him to his abovesaid Master at Canterbury aforesaid, or secure him in any of his Majesty's Goals, shall have *twenty Pounds* old Tenor Reward, and all necessary Charges paid by *Timothy Green* or *Jonathan Dwight* of *Boston*,
     or by me the Subscriber.   *David Nevins.*
   And all Masters of Vessels and others are hereby caution'd againg conceal [*sic*] or carrying off said Servant on Penalty of the Law.

The Boston Gazette, or Weekly Journal, August 1, 1749.

RAN-away from his Master, Mr. *John Read* of *Norwich*, on the 31st of *July* last, a Mulatto Man-Servant, a stout lusty Fellow, speaks good *English*; he hath been branded in the Forehead with the Letter B, and hath his right Ear cut. Whoever will secure said Servant, and him safely convey to his said Master, shall have *Ten Pounds*, old Tenor, Reward, and all necessary charges paid.

The Boston Evening-Post, August 7, 1749; August 21, 1749. *The Boston Weekly Post-Boy*, August 7, 1749; August 14, 1749. Minor differences between the papers.

RAN away from his Master Capt. *John Payson*, of *Woodstock*, a Servant Man named *Bryant Macdermant*, about 17 Years of Age, of a small Stature, had on when he went away a Brown all woollen Coat, a white Fustain Jacket, a Speckled Shirt and Trowsers, has a sore Head. Whosoever shall take up said Runaway, and bring him to his said Master in *Woodstock* aforesaid, or secure him, so that his Master may have him again, shall have *Five Pounds* old Tenor Reward, and all necessary Charged [*sic*] paid by me
          John Payson   Dated in *Woodstock, August* 8. 1749.

Also Ran away at the same Time from Mr. *David Wallis* of *Woodstock*, a Negro Man Servant, named *Christmas* alias *Quashe*, a short Fellow, about 30 Years of Age, who formerly belonged to Mr. *Samuel Jackson* in *Boston*; Whoever shall bring him to his Master, shall have Five Pounds *old Tenor* Reward.

All Persons are caution'd not to carry off either of the said Servants as they would avoid the Penalty of the Law.

The Boston Weekly News-Letter, August 10, 1749; August 17, 1749; August 25, 1749.

Deserted from the Ship *Hannah, John Evers* Commander, on Sunday Morning last, *Nathanael Bowes & William Walker*, Seamen: If the said *Bowes* and *Walker* will return to their Duty in three Days from the Date hereof, they shall be received kindly, otherwise deem'd Deserters.
         John Evers.   Boston, *August* 14th 1749.
The Boston Gazette, or Weekly Journal, August 13, 1749.

WHereas one Walter McDaniel, *who call'd himself by the Name of* John Davis *when he hired a Horse of the Subscriber of* Chelsea, *Saturday the* 1st *of* April *last to go to* Marblehead, *since which I am informed he went with said Horse to* Rhode-Island.

The said *Walter McDaniel* is an Irishman, and has the Brogue on his Tongue, a pretty great Talker and Singer, of a fair Complection; had on a blew Broadcloth Coat, white Fustian Jacket, yellow Buckskin Breeches, pair of large flower'd Silver Buckels, three Rings on his right Hand little Finger, one a Grape Ring, the other two plain; the Horse was about 14 Hands high, Sorrel, with some white in his Face, a bob Tail, he trots, paces and Hand-gallops; had a black Saddle with Ears, something torn, a Russet Housing.

Whoever shall take up the said Man and Horse, and bring them to me the Subscriber at *Chelsea* aforesaid, shall have *twenty Pounds* old Tenor, or *ten Pounds* old Tenor for the Horse only, with reasonable Charges,
     paid them by *Richard Watts.*
The Boston Gazette, or Weekly Journal, August 13, 1749.

RAN-away from his Master *Wm Bucknam*, of *Falmouth* in *Casco Bay*, on the 27th of *July* last, a Negro Man, named *Cuffe*, about 40 Years of Age, pretty tall of Stature, thin favour'd, with Scars on each Cheek: He had on a blue Broadcloth Coat lin'd with Red, a black Jacket, Trowsers and striped Breeches under them, yarn Stockings, thick Shoes, and a coarse Linnen Shirt.

 Whoever shall take up said Servant, and convey him to his said Master at *Falmouth* aforesaid or secure him in any of his Majesty's Goals, shall have *ten Pounds* old Tenor Reward, and all necessary Charges
    paid by *William Bucknam.*
And all Masters of Vessels and others are hereby cautioned against concealing or carrying off said Servant on Penalty of the Law.
             Falmouth, August 7th 1749.
The Boston Gazette, or Weekly Journal, August 15, 1749. See *The Boston Evening-Post*, September 11, 1749, *The Boston Evening-Post*, May 19, 1755, and *Boston Evening-Post*, June 30, 1755.

PEter Swan aged about 22 Years, a slight made Man of a swarthy Complexion, latey had the Small-Pox, about 5 Foot 9 Inches high, absented himself from the Ship *Falmouth, Henry Grant* Master, now lying in the River of *Piscataqua*: Whoever shall take up the said Person, and bring him to the said Master, or Mr. *Mark Hunking Wentworth*, Merchant in *Portsmouth*, shall have *Five Pounds* old Tenor Reward and all reasonable Charges allow'd them.
     Henry Grant. *Portsmouth, August 25th* 1749.
The Boston Weekly Post-Boy, August 28, 1749; September 4, 1749.

STolen from *Alexander Farquharson* in the Night after the 14th Instant, a drab great Coat, a Pair of Boots, 3 fine Holland Shirts, several Notes of Hand, a Moydore, an English Guinea, a Double-loon, a Piece of foreign coin'd Gold; a Quantity of Spanish Dollars, a Number of small Pieces of

Spanish Silver, *Eighty Pounds* old Tenor, and two small Trunks: The Person who has stole the said Goods and Money is one *John Smith*, about Twenty-one Years of Age, fresh Complexion, a short thick Fellow, a Leather Breeches-maker and Glover by Trade. Whoever apprehends the said *John Smith*, and brings him to Mr. *Benjamin Kent's* in *Boston*, so that the Owner may have his Effects again, shall have *Fifty Pounds* old Tenor Reward, and all Charges
    paid by *Alexander Farquharson.*
The Boston Weekly Post Boy, August 28, 1749; September 4, 1749; September 11, 1749.

RAN-away from Mr. *John Box* of *Boston,* Rope maker, on Thursday Night the 24th Instant, a Lad named *John Fullerton,* about 17 Years of Age, small Stature; he had on when he went away, a strip'd Waistcoat and a Pair of Trousers. Whoever shall take up said Servant, and convey him to his abovesaid Master, shall be well rewarded for their Pains. And all Masters of Vessels and others, are hereby caution'd against concealing or carrying off said Servant, on Penalty of the Law. *Boston, August* 29th 1748.
The Boston Gazette, or Weekly Journal, August 29, 1749.

RAN-away on the 29th of *August* from his Master *John Williams* of *Roxbury,* a Negro Man Servant, named *Sharper,* a lusty Fellow about 25 Years of Age, speaks good English, and is something battle-hamed: He had on when he went away, a check'd Woolen Shirt, a pair of white Trowsers, a pair of gray yarn Stockings, a pair of calf-skin Shoes, with large pewter Buckles, a striped blue and white Jacket, a small bever Hatt, and the Wool on the Top of his Head newly shaved; he also carried away with him a dark blue Jacket trimm'd with black, one fine Shirt, a Jocky-cap, a pair of dark blue worsted Stockings, and a pair of yarn Stockings, black and white, stock'd with grey a little above his Shoes. Whoever takes up said Servant, and conveys him to his said Master at *Roxbury,* shall have *Five Pounds* old Tenor Reward, and all necessary Charges
    paid by me *John Williams.*
The Boston Weekly News-Letter, August 31, 1749; September 7, 1749.

DEserted from the Ship *Gremy, George Hunter* Master, now lying in *Boston* Harbour, the 24th of *August* past, two Sailors, one *Patrick Ewing,* of a black Complexion, and *William Morres,* of a brown Complexion, and both middle Stature. If the said Sailors will return to their Duty on board the said Ship in 3 Days Time from the Date hereof, they shall be kindly received, otherwise they will be deem'd Deserters.
              Boston, September 4. 1749.
The Boston Evening-Post, September 4, 1749.

Left the Ship *John* and *William, Silvanus Carr* Commander, on the 30th of *August* past, the following Seamen, *viz. Griffice Morgen* and *William Long*, and on the 31st of the same Month, *Thomas Boats, Andrew Anderson, John Russey* and *Thomas Deall* absented themselves from their Duty on board the said Ship: These are therefore to inform the said Seamen, that if they will return to their Duty within Three Days from the Date hereof, they shall be kindly received, otherwise they will be deemed Deserters, and treated accordingly. *Boston, Sept.* 4. 1749.
The Boston Evening-Post, September 4, 1749.

DEserted from the Ship *Gremy, George Hunter* Master, now lying in *Boston* Harbour, on the 8th Instant, Matthew Small, a Sailor, of a black Complexion. If said Sailor will return to his Duty on board said Ship, within 24 Hours after the Date hereof, he shall be kindly received, otherwise shall be deemed a Deserter, and treated accordingly.
Boston, September 11. 1749.
The Boston Evening-Post, September 11, 1749; September 18, 1749.

RAN away from his Master, *William Bucknam*, of *Falmouth* in *Casco Bay*, in the Month of *July* last, a Negro Man, named *Cuffe*, aged about 40 Years, a pretty tall spare Fellow, who had on a blue Broad Cloth Coat, a black Jacket and striped Breeches and Trowsers, grey Stockings and thick Shoes, a Worsted Cap and a Felt Hat, He has Scars on each Cheek, and I hear he has with him a forged Pass, which he got with the Help of some evil minded Person, which protects him from being taken up. Whoever shall take up said Fellow, and convey him to his said Master in *Falmouth*, or to Capt. *Benjamin Blany* in *Malden*, shall have *Twenty Pounds* old Tenor Reward, and all necessary Charges
paid by me, *William Bucknam.*
N. B. He has been something used to the Sea, and will endeavour to get off; therefore all Masters of Vessels and other Persons are hereby cautioned against harbouring, concealing or carrying him off, as they would avoid the Penalty of the Law. *Sept.* 3 1749.
The Boston Evening-Post, September 11, 1749; September 18, 1749; September 25, 1749; *The Boston Weekly News-Letter*, September 14, 1749; September 28, 1749. See *The Boston Gazette, or Weekly Journal*, August 15, 1749, *The Boston Evening-Post*, May 19, 1755, and *Boston Evening-Post*, June 30, 1755.

W*Hereas* Elizabeth *the Wife of me the Subscriber often gadding about and running me into Debt, and being of an exorbitant Temper, so that I cannot lie with her:*

These are to warn all Persons not to harbour, trust or trade with her the said *Elizabeth* on my Accompt, for I will not pay one Penny for the during Life.
As witness my Hand, *Richard Manson.*
Dated *Sunbury, September the* 12th A, D. 1749.
The Boston Gazette, or Weekly Journal, September 12, 1749.

WHEREAS *William Dearing* of *Scarborough* in the County of *York,* was at the Court of Assize held at *York* for said County, in *June* last past. Convicted and Condemned for the Murder of his Wife; and in the Night following the fifteenth Day of *September* Inst. with the Assistance of some evil minded Persons, Broke the Goal in *York* and escaped; These are therefor to Notify all Persons of the same: And I the Subscriber Sheriff of the said County of *York,* do hereby Promise that any Person or Persons who shall apprehend and secure the said *William Dearing,* so that I may receive him again, shall have *Two Hundred Pounds* old Tenor Reward and all Necessary Charges paid. And any Person that Discovers and Informs of any of the Persons who were aiding and assisting to the said *William Dearing* in making his Escape so that the Person or Persons so doing may be Convicted thereof, shall have *Fifty Pounds* old Tenor Reward for the same.
N. B. The said *Dearing* is a middle aged Man, of middling Stature with full Eyes, black curled Hair: 'tis not supposed that he will wear the same Cloathing he had on in Goal.
Jos. Plaisted.   *York September* 16th 1749.
The Boston Weekly News-Letter, September 14, 1749; September 28, 1749; October 5, 1749.

WHEREAS *Abigail,* the Wife of the Subscriber, *Ebenezer Flynt* of *Reading,* quartus, has unjustly absented herself from me and my Family for near Five Months last past, and run me greatly in Debt during that Time; these are therefore to caution and forewarn all Persons whatsoever not to trust or give Credit to the said Abigail upon my Account, for I will pay no Debt she shall so contract from the Day of the Date hereof.
As Witness my Hand   *Ebenezer Flint,* quartus.
Sept. 10th 1749.
The Boston Weekly News-Letter, September 14, 1749; September 28, 1749.

WHEREAS *John Grundill,* has Absented himself from the Sloop Thankful, *Thomas Mattison* Commander: If the said *John Grundill* will Return to his Duty on board said Sloop in three Days from the Date hereof, he shall be kindly receiv'd otherwise he shall be deem'd as a Deserter.
Thomas Mattison.   Dated *Boston, Sept.* 9th 1749.
The Boston Weekly News-Letter, September 14, 1749.

Kittery, Sept 15. 1749

RAN-away from *Samuel Johnson* of *Kittery*, a Negro Man about 25 Years old; he had on when he went away a white woollen Shirt, a blue broad-cloth Jacket, an old Felt Hat, blue Yarn Stockings, and old Shoes. Whoever shall have up said Negro, and convey him to me, shall receive a Reasonable Reward, and have all necessary Charges
         paid by me   *Samuel Johnson.*
The Boston Weekly Post-Boy, September 18, 1749; September 25, 1749; October 2, 1749; October 9, 1749; October 16, 1749.

RAN-away from his Master, *John Salmon* and Company, the 15th Instant, a Spanish Negro Man Servant named *Andrew*, (but calls himself *Andress*) between 30 and 40 Years of Age, a thick square set Fellow, with a Scar on his Chin, talks broken *English*, had on when he went away, a strip'd worsted Cap, a Lead colour'd outside thick Kersey Jacket, with thick Metal Buttons on it, a strip'd homespun blue and white under Jacket, with the Stripes made cross Way, a speckled Linen Shirt, a pair of Buckskin Breeches (almost new) with Leather Buttons, a pair of gray or blue Worsted Stockings, and a pair of half worn Shoes, with a pair of broad Buckles. Whoever shall take up said Runaway, and him convey to his Masters in *Boston*, shall have *Ten Pounds* old Tenor, and all necessary Charges paid.
The Boston Evening-Post, September 25, 1749; October 2, 1749; October 9, 1749; *The Boston Gazette, or Weekly Journal*, September 26, 1749; *The Boston Weekly Post-Boy*, October 16, 1749. Minor differences between the papers.

RAN-away from his Master, *Joseph Barnard* of *Deerfield* a Negro Man named *Prince*, of middling Stature, his Complection not the darkest or lightest for a Negro, slow of Speech, but speaks good English; He had with him when he went away, an old brown Coat, with Pewter Buttons, a double-breasted blue Coat with red Cuffs and Cape, a new brown Jacket with Pewter Buttons, a Pair of new Leather Breeches, check'd linnen Shirt and Trousers, tow Shirt and Trousers, a red Cap, two Castor Hats, several Pair of Stockings, a Pair of Pumps, a Gun and Violin. Whoever shall apprehend said Fellow and convey him to his Master, shall have *Ten Pounds* old Tenor, and all necessary Charges
         paid by   *Joseph Barnard*   *Deerfield, Sept* 18, 1749.
All Masters of Vessels and others are caution'd not to conceal or carry off the said Negro, as they would avoid the Penalty of the Law.
The Boston Weekly Post-Boy, September 25, 1749; October 2, 1749; October 16, 1749; *The Boston Weekly News-Letter*, September 28, 1749; October 5, 1749; October 12, 1749.

RAN-away last Thursday Afternoon three white Servants, viz *Thomas Kemball*, about 18 Years old, tall and thin favoured, had on a red Cap, a blew Pea Jacket. Also *Robert Burchan*, about 17 Years old, much of the same Make and Bigness, had on an old Wig and a new Beaver Hat, a Pea Cloth colour'd Jacket, striped Woollen Waistcoat. Likewise *John Mitchell*, between 16 and 17 Years of Age, something tall than any of the other, a raw Bon'd Lad, had on a Cap and a strip'd Jacket, a Pair of Trousers: The others might have Trousers also. Whoever shall secure said Servants and convey them or either of them to their Master, *Samuel Barret*, Sailmaker of Boston, shall receive a Reward of *Ten Pounds* old Tenor for each, and all necessary Charges. Boston, Sept. 23d 1749.
N. B. Their being coloured with Tar may be a further Direction.
The Boston Gazette, or Weekly Journal, September 26, 1749.

RAN-away from his Master *Hezekiah Blanchard* in *Boston*, on the 19th Instant, a small Negro Man named *Bedford*, had on when he went away, a new worsted Cap, red Jacket, Leather Breeches. Whoever shall take up said Negro and him safely convey to his abovesaid Master, shall be well rewarded, and all necessary Charges paid.
The Boston Gazette, or Weekly Journal, September 26, 1749.

WHEREAS *Lewis Rowzier*, an east-Indian, of small Stature, has absented himself from the *Success* Man of War, on board which Ship he was Captain's Cook: Whoever will secure the said *Lewis Rowzier*, and return him to his Master, shall receive *Twenty Pounds* old Tenor as a Reward for so doing.
The Boston Weekly News-Letter, September 28, 1749; October 5, 1749.

RAN-away from his Master *Samuel Morgareidge* of *Newbury* on the 26th of *September* last, a Negro Fellow named *Primus*, a lusty Fellow, lame in his right Ancle, had on when he went away a check'd Woollen Shirt, a green Ratteen Jacket, and a large Pair of Trousers. Whoever shall take up said Fellow, and bring him to his said Master at *Newbury* aforesaid, shall have *three Pounds* Old Tenor Reward & all necessary Charges paid by his Master.
The Boston Gazette, or Weekly Journal, October 3, 1749. See *Boston Evening-Post*, October 9, 1749.

Success, in Boston Harbour, Octo. 3. 1749.
Henry Pattie, a Seaman belonging to his Majesty's Ship the Success, having absented himself from Duty without leave; a Reward of Thirty Shillings

Sterling, is promised to whoever will secure him, so as he may be returned on board his Ship.

N. B. As there are several Persons in the Town of Boston, indebted to the said *Pattie* for English Good which he has sold them; they are here b[eseech]ed, as they regard his Majesty's Service, not to pay him until they are assured he has returned to his Duty. This I shall esteem as an Obligation and shall be ready to return them equal Service when in my Power. If it is objected that a just Debt ought to be paid when demanded, I promise to take the whole Affair upon myself, and to bear the Expence and Trouble of any Prosecution which may arise from such a Denial.   COLVILL.

The Boston Weekly News-Letter, October 5, 1749; October 12, 1749.

RAN away from his Master *Samuel Morgareidge* of *Newbury*, on the 26th of *September* last, a Negro Fellow named *Primus*, a lusty Fellow, lame in his right Ancle; had on when he went away, a Chect Woollen Shirt, a Green Ratteen Jacket, and a large pair of Trousers. Whoever shall take up said Fellow, and bring him to his said Master at *Newbury* aforesaid, shall have *Three Pounds,* old Tenor Reward & all necessary Charges paid by his Master.

N. B. All Masters of Vessels and others are forbid carrying off said Fellow, under Penalty of the Law.

See *Boston Evening-Post*, October 9, 1749. See *The Boston Gazette, or Weekly Journal*, October 3, 1749.

RAN-away from his Master Capt. *John Bradford* of *Boston*, on the 8th Instant, a Servant Lad named *Benjamin Rust*, about 17 Years of Age, middling Stature, much pitted with the Small Pox, had on a Forest Cloth Coat and Breeches, red Waistcoat, wears a Wigg. Whoever shall take up the abovesaid Runaway, and bring him to his Master aforesaid, shall have 20 *l.* old Tenor Reward, and all necessary Charges Paid.

The Boston Gazette, or Weekly Journal, October 10, 1749; October 24, 1749.

RAN-away from his Master *Malcom McNeill* of *Boston*, Taylor, on Thursday the 12th Instant, at Night, a Yorkshire Man Servant, named *John Gambles*, about 5 Feet 4 Inches high, well-set, fair Complection, about 27 Years of Age, and has much of a Tone in his Speech; had on when he went away, a Felt Hat, a black Wigg, a dark brown fly Coat, lin'd with Shalloon of the same Colour, and a Horse-Hair Button, an Ash colour'd Waistcoat and Breeches, with white frosted Buttons: He also carried away with him, a Pair of rib'd Worsted Stockings, and a Pair of plain blue and white ditto, a Pair of double-channel Pumps, and Copper Buckles, a red Waistcoat with Mettle Buttons. He can work well at the Taylor's Trade.

Whoever shall take up said Servant, and bring him to his said Master, shall have *Twenty Pounds*, old Tenor Reward, and all necessary Charges paid by   Malcom McNeill.

All Masters of Vessels are hereby caution'd against carrying off said Servant, on Penalty of the Law.

The Boston Weekly Post Boy, October 16, 1749.

RAn-away from their Master *Edward Gray* of *Boston* Ropemaker, two likely streight limb'd Negro Men of about twenty five Years of Age, both talks good English, as they were brought up in the Country; they had on when they went away, strip'd cotton Caps, pea Jackets of a redish colour, with Mettle Buttons, Leather Breeches, and Trowsers, &c. Whoever shall take up said Negroes, or either of them, and safely convey them to their said Master, shall have *ten Pounds* old Tenor reward for each of them, & all necessary Charges paid. And all Masters of Vessels and others are hereby caution'd against concealing or carrying off said Servant on Penalty of Law.

The Boston Gazette, or Weekly Journal, October 17, 1749; October 24, 1749.

RAN-away from his Master Capt. *Nath. Gorham* of *Charlestown*, an Indian Boy named *Moses*, about 12 or 14 Years of Age, had on when he went away, a strip'd homespun Jacket, Cotton and Linnen Shirt, a pair of Trousers, Stockings and Shoes. Whoever shall take up the abovesaid Runaway, and safely convey him to his abovesaid Master, shall be well Rewarded for their Trouble.

The Boston Gazette, or Weekly Journal, October 17, 1749; October 24, 1749. See The Boston Gazette, or Weekly Journal, May 22, 1750.

RAN away from his Master Dr. *William Clark*, of *Boston*, on the 14th Instant, a likely strait lim'd Negro Boy, about 16 or 17 Years of Age, and speaks very good *English*. He had on a blue grey Broad Cloth Jacket, and a blue and white striped Swanskin Jacket under it, a Cotton and Linen Shirt, and a greasy pair of Leather Breeches. Whoever shall take up the said Runaway, and bring him to his said Master, shall have *Ten Pounds*, old Tenor, Reward, and all necessary Charges paid.

The Boston Evening-Post, October 23, 1749.

RAN away from her Master *Joseph Kidder* of *Boston*, on the 17th of *October* past, a tall slim likely Negro Girl, about 16 or 17 Years of Age, named Cloe, of a very black Complection, she has been about four Years in the Country, and talks English very well: She had on when she went away a blue and white homespun Petticoat, and an Oznabrigs Jacket. Whoever

shall take up said Runaway and will bring her to her Master or the Printer hereof, shall have *Four Pounds*, old Tenor, Reward, and all necessary Charges paid.   *Boston, November* 2*d.* 1749.
The Boston Weekly News-Letter, November 2, 1749; November 9, 1749; November 17, 1749.

RAN-away from his Master, on Monday Night last, A Negro Man named *Jack*, of a middling Stature, much Pock-freten: He had on when he went away, a cloth Colour Drugget Coat, with a Patch on the left Shoulder, of a different Colour, a strip'd Jacket, a worsted Cap and Leather Breeches. Whoever shall take up said Negro and bring him to his Master shall be paid *Five Pounds* old Tenor, and other necessary Charges,
         by me,   *Hopestill Foster.*   *Boston, November* 2. 1749.
The Boston Weekly News-Letter, November 2, 1749.

RAN away from his Master, *Seth Bartlet* of *Newbury*, an Apprentice, named *Joseph Preble*, who is required on his Peril to return to his Master forthwith.   *Seth Bartlett.*
The Boston Evening-Post, November 6, 1749; November 13, 1749.

D*Eserted from the Ship* Bethel *Frigate,* Alexander Ross *Commander, the following Persons, viz.* George Knott, Thomas Lysence, Joseph Dent, Ambros Perry, John Steeper, *and* James Arnie*: This is to therefore to inform them, that if they will return to their Duty on board said Ship by the* 10*th Instant, they shall be kindly received, otherwise they shall be deemed Deserters.*
     This is farther to give Notice, that if any Person or Persons shall apprehend the aforesaid James Arnie, *so as to bring him to Justice for sundry Insults to the officers of said Ship, they shall be handsomly*
         Rewarded   *By* Alexander Ross.
The Boston Evening-Post, November 6, 1749.

R*AN away from his Master* Walter Logan *of* Boston, *an Irish Man Servant named* Barnabas Donnellan, *aged about Twenty-three Years, about Five Feet eight Inches high, pretty slim, of a light Complection, speaks proper English, and seems to be a civil, complaisant likely Fellow; Had on when he went away, a white Fustian Coat, a strip'd Swan-skin Jacket, a pair of old greezey Leather Breeches, ribb'd blue grey Yarn Stockings, a white Cap flower'd with colour'd Worsted, large Brass Buckles in his Shoes, a Castor Hat, and a pair of light Blue Silk Ferret Garters below his Knees. Besides which he took with him a small Cotton and Linen Bag, containing a double brested light colour'd half thick Jacket, a blue ditto single Breasted, a pair* *of Trousers, two pair of plain grey worsted Stockings, a blue mill'd Cap, and a linen ditto, with a Cambrick Border.*

Ran away in Company with the above nam'd Barnabas, *another Irish Man Servant, named* Christopher Harvey, *belonging to* John McClery *of* Boston: *He is about Twenty Years of Age, a thick well set Fellow, about five Feet five Inches high, round Fac'd, of a fresh Complection, and speaks good English: Had on when he went away, a blue Coat, a double Breasted plaid Jacket, scarlet Breeches, with brass Buttons, a black Wigg, blue worsted Stockings, a pair of large brass Buckles in his Shoes, a new blue Silk Handkerchief about his Neck, a Felt Hat. He also took with him a mill'd Cap, and a flower'd Ditto, several pair of Stockings, and an old rusty Cutlash without a Scabbard.*

N. B. They both profess themselves Sailors. Whoever shall apprehend, and secure the said Servants or either of them, so that their Masters may have them again, shall have a Reward of Ten Pounds *old Tenor for each, and all necessary Charges paid. And all Masters of Vessels and others are hereby caution'd against carrying off the said Servants.*

        Walter Logan,   Boston, Nov. 7th, 1749.

The Boston Weekly News-Letter, November 9, 1749; November 17, 1749; *The Boston Evening-Post*, November 13, 1749; November 20, 1749; *The Boston Gazette, or Weekly Journal*, November 14, 1749. Minor differences between the papers. The *Gazette* spells that second owner's last name as McCleary.

Run-away *Friday last from the Subscriber, from the Sign of the* Horse and Cart *in this City, a Servant Man named James Fitch, born in New-England, aged about 28 Years, a pretty tall slim Fellow, long Visag'd, dark Eyes and Wore a Cap; Had on when he went away, an old pale blue Coat, a light colour'd Jacket and Breeches, white Stockings, and a large Beaver Hats; He lately had the Fever and Ague, and looks poorly.*

Whoever takes up and secures the said Servant in any of his Majesty's Goals, and gives Notice thereof to Mr. John Lake, *Merchant in* New-York, *or to the Subscriber living in* Canterbury, *in the County of* Windham, *and Colony of* Connecticut, *shall have Forty Shillings Reward, and all*
                  reasonable Charges paid by   DAVID NEVINS.

The New-York Gazette Revived in the Weekly Post-Boy, November 13, 1749; November 27, 1749.

RAN away from the Ship *Cannings Frigate*, now lying in *Boston* Harbour, *Andrew Dewar* Master, the six following Sailors, *viz. Michael Redman, Thomas Brown, Robert Walker, Ananias Wood, Henry Small,* and *Thomas Corphy*: Whoever shall apprehend the said Sailors, or any of them, and shall return them to their own Ship, shall receive *Forty Pounds,* old Tenor,

for each of them. And furthermore, if any of the said Sailors will return to their Duty in Six Days from the Date hereof, they shall be forgiven.
    ANDREW DEWAR. *Boston, November* 20. 1749.
The Boston Evening-Post, November 20, 1749.

WHereas *Mary Evans,* the Wife of *John Evans,* Jun. has eloped from her said Husband, and refuses to live with him; This is therefore to warn all Persons from entertaining or trusting the said *Mary Evans,* for I shall not pay any Debts she shall contract from this Day.
    John Evans.   Dated at *Woburn, October* 21. 1749.
The Boston Evening-Post, November 20, 1749.

RAN-away from *Almsbury,* a Negro Woman lately owned by *Isaac Merrel* of said *Almsbury,* sometime in *September* last, aged about 27 Years: she had on when she went away a striped Drugget Gown, a black quilted outside Coat, a white inside Coat, border'd with red; she goes a little lame: Whoever shall take up the said Negro Woman, and convey her to me the Subscriber living in *Stratham,* in *New Hampshire,* or send Word so that I may conveniently come at her, shall have *Eight Pounds* old Tenor Reward, and all necessary Charges paid by me
    Joseph Wiggins. *Stratham, Sept.* 23. 1749.
The Boston Weekly Post-Boy, December 4, 1749; December 11, 1749; December 18, 1749.

1750

WHereas *Joseph Nutting* born in *Andover, Alexander McCallister,* and *Thomas Tenton,* born in the Highlands of *Scotland,* and *Moses Cushman,* born in *Plimton,* in *New-England* having inlisted themselves in his Majesty's Service, as Soldiers for the Defence of his Majesty's Province of *Nova Scotia,* and have since deserted said Service. Whoever therefore shall apprehend said Deserters or either of them, and bring them to me the Subscriber in *Boston,* or commit them in any of his Majesty's Goals, shall have *ten Pounds* old Tenor Reward for each, and all necessary Charges paid.
  And all Masters of Vessels and others, are hereby caution'd against concealing or carrying off said Servants on Penalty of the Law.
    Joseph Gorham.
The Boston Gazette, or Weekly Journal, January 2, 1750.

WHereas a few Days past, *Alexander Walker* a Sailor, belonging to a Vessel called the *Mary, Gilbert Falconer* Master now lying at *Cheevers*'s Wharff, has absented himself without Leave. These are therefore to give

Notice to the said Walker, that if he will return to his Duty on or before the 26th Instant, he shall be received, otherwise he shall be deem'd a Deserter.
          Gilbert Falconer.   *Boston, Jan.* 22d 1749,50.
The Boston Gazette, or Weekly Journal, January 23, 1750.

RAN-away from *Newbury* about a Fortnight ago, a Man Servant named *Tho. Sall,* speaks broad West County, stoops in his Walking, he had on when he went away, a frize Pea Jacket, and his Hatt fasten'd up with copper Nails.
    Whosoever shall take him up, and convey him to Capt. *Samson Tyler* at *Newbury,* or inform the Printer where he may be had, shall have *ten Pounds* Old Tenor Reward, and
          all necessary Charges paid   *Isaac Smith.*
The Boston Gazette, or Weekly Journal, February 13, 1750.

ON Wednesday last the 14th of *February,* 1749, 50, a Man who call'd himself *Joseph Woodward,* of *Brookline,* and had on a homespun light grey Great Coat, a dark close-bodied Coat with yellow Lining, a Pair of yellow Leather Breeches almost new, a Pair of mix'd blue and white rib'd yarn Stockings; came to the Shop of *James Davenport* at *Waltham,* and brought an order forg'd in his Name for *eighty Pounds* old Tenor, sixty of which he receiv'd in the following Goods, viz.
    Near a Piece of dark colour'd Camblet, about half a Piece of Garlix, four large yellow & white check'd silk Handkerchiefs, two Linnen ditto, one Pair of Mens Hose, light colour'd; sundry Yards of blue Ribbon, half a Dozen of Butchers Knives with Sheaths, four Brass handled Penknives, three Cards of flower'd brass Buttons, two Dozen Womens Stayhooks, several Pair of Womens white Shoe-Buckles, sundry Cakes of Crown Soap, four Papers of Pins of two Sorts, a pair of Men's white Leather Gloves, a large polish'd Steel Tobacco Box; and *twenty Pounds* Cash, *seven Pounds* of which was in Copper, and put the same in a Shot Bagg, No. 3.
    The said *Woodward* is of a middle Stature, of a yellow Complection.
    Whoever will make Discovery of said Person, so that he may be brought to Justice, shall have *thirty Pounds* old Tenor Reward,
          paid by me   *James Davenport.*
The Boston Gazette, or Weekly Journal, February 20, 1750; February 27, 1750.

Deserted the 21st of *Febr.* Instant, from the Ship Defiance *Samuel Waterhouse* Commander, *Kimbal Bass,* aged about 24 Years, of a dark Complection, with a full black Eye, and pretty tall. Whoever will give Notice or secure him that he may be brought to Justice, shall receive *five*

Pounds old Tenor Reward, from the Subscriber or *Samuel Hughes* in Queen-street *Boston.*   *Samuel Waterhouse.*
The Boston Gazette, or Weekly Journal, February 27, 1750.

Deserted from the Ship *Patuxent* Merchant, *Purser Donors,* Master, the following Seamen, viz. *Edward Dodd,* Boatswain, *Crean Percevell, Richard Gordon, John Linare, David Williams.* If the said Seamen will return to their Duty on board said Ship in *Boston,* otherwise they may expect to be deem'd Deserters.   *Boston, March* 5. 1749. [*sic*]
The Boston Weekly News-Letter, March 8, 1750.

WHEREAS *Rebecca Harris,* the Wife of me the Subscriber, living at *Norton,* has unlawfully absented herself from me and my Family; and carried off sundry Effects to a considerable Value, and may endeavour to run me in Debt; These are therefore to caution all Persons whatsoever, not to entertain, trust or give Credit to her the said *Rebecca,* upon my Account; for I will not pay any Debt contracted by her during her continuing to absent herself.
    As witness my Hand, Joseph Harris.
    N. B. If she will return to my Family, and behave as a virtuous Wife ought to do, she shall be kindly received.
The Boston Weekly News-Letter, March 8, 1750. See *The Boston Gazette, or, Weekly Advertiser*, November 27, 1752.

WHEREAS an Indian Lad about 14 Years of Age, who was taken up at *Attleborough,* supposed to be a Run-away, goes by several Names, as *Tom. Sam. Moses,* &c. Whoever owns the said Lad may apply to *Thomas Foster* in said *Attleborough,* who will deliver him upon paying the Charges.
    March, 13. 1749,50.
The Boston Weekly News-Letter, March 16, 1750.

W*HEREAS on the first of this Instant* March, *the Sloop* Success, *burthen then about* 80 *Tons,* George M'Cobb *late Master, was carried away from her Moorings in* Kennebeck *River, by two Irish Men, whose Names are* Dominick Stinson *and* Morris Smith, *and 'tis supposed they intend to proceed with her to* Ireland, *unless for want of skill or by stress of Weather, they should be obliged to put into some other Port.*
    THESE are to give publick Notice, that if any Person shall recover the said Sloop, so that the Owners shall have her again, and the Persons concerned in this Piratical Action to be brought to Justice, he shall receive *fifty Pounds Sterling* as a Reward therefor, from either of us the Subscribers.
    Samuel Denny, John Parker, James M'Cobb. Of George Town.

George Town, March 6. 1749. [*sic*]

N. B. The Sloop is about 8 Years old, hath been painted Blue on her Quarters, but is pretty much worn off, hath one Jibb, one Foresail and two Mainsails, no Boom nor Anchors, and but one piece of Cable, hath a Chimney in her Steerage, and the Cabbin well finished.

Stinson and *Smith* are each of them about 22 Years of Age, came Passengers last Years in Capt. *Stinson* from *Ireland; Stinson* is a comely Man and he always said he was born and bred in *Dublin*, and his Father is now a considerable Shopkeeper in that City.

The Boston Evening-Post, March 19, 1750; *The Boston Weekly News-Letter,* March 22, 1750.

BROKE *out of his Majesty's Goal in* Salem, *the last Night, one* John Read, *who lately kept the* Beverly *Ferry, is of a fair Complexion, about twenty eight Years of Age, thick and well set; and one* Zechary Fowler, *of about thirty Years of Age, of a brown Complexion, but has a light full Eye.* [*sic*] *Whoever shall take up the said Prisoners, and return them to the said Goal, shall have for each of them Fifty Pounds, old Tenor, Reward, and all necessary Charges paid.*

by Robert Hale, *Sheriff of* Essex.

Beverly, March 23, 1749. [*sic*]

The Boston Evening-Post, March 26, 1750; April 2, 1750; April 9, 1750. See *The Boston Weekly Post-Boy,* March 26, 1750.

BROKE out of his Majesty's Goal in *Salem,* the last Night, one *John Read,* who lately kept the *Beverly* Ferry, is of a fair Complexion, about twenty-eight Years of Age, thick and well set; and one *Zechary Fowler,* of about thirty Years of Age, of a brown Complexion, but has a light full Eye. [sic]

Whoever shall take up the said Prisoners, and return them to the said Goal, shall have for each of them *Fifty Pounds,* old Tenor, Reward, and all necessary Charges paid. *Beverly, March* 23. 1749. [*sic*]

by Robert Hale, Sheriff *of Essex.*

Marblehead, March 26th, 1750.

The Boston Weekly Post-Boy, March 26, 1750; April 9, 1750. *The Boston Gazette, or Weekly Journal,* March 27, 1750; April 9, 1750. The *Gazette* does not have any dates or locations at the bottom. See *Boston Evening-Post,* March 26, 1750.

DEserted from the Schooner *Success, James Tresteene* Commander,— *Thomas Storey, Bryan Corney,* and *Nicholas Power*; If they or either of them will return to their Duty by the 29th Current, they shall be kindly received, otherwise they will be deem'd Deserters, and treated accordingly.

The Boston Weekly Post-Boy, March 26, 1750.

RAN away from his Master, Daniel Hewes *of* Wrentham, *on the 5th Instant, a Man Servant named* Obadiah Eddy, *a small slim Fellow, about 17 Years of Age, of fresh Complexion, a long and large Nose, small Eyes, of a sly malicious Cast, and of a light colour, and large Feet He carried with him a new Felt Hat, an old brown Wig, 2 or 3 Caps, one Holland with Ruffles, one striped Cotton one, 3 Shirts, one coarse Dowlas, the others check'd Cotton and Wool, a blue homespun Cloth Coat, that has been turn'd, with Brass Buttons, a Jacket of light coloured Cloth, new, with Pewter Buttons, Leather Breeches, and short Trousers.*

Whoever shall take up the said Servant, and convey him to his said Master at Wrentham, *shall have* Forty Shillings *Lawful Money, Reward, and necessary Charges*

   paid, by Daniel Hewes.   Boston, April 7. 1750.

The Boston Evening-Post, April 9, 1750; April 16, 1750. See *The Boston Gazette, or Weekly Journal*, April 10, 1750.

RAN away from his Master, Mr. *Samuel Hutchinson* of *Charlestown*, on the 3d Instant, a Servant Man, named *John Saval*, about 20 Years of Age: He had on when he went away a Hatt and Wigg, a gray double Breasted Jacket with Brass Buttons, and a blue one, with Leather Breeches, grey Yarn Stockings; he is stockey built, and very much freckled.

Whoever shall take up said Servant and convey him to his said Master in Charlestown, shall have *Forty Shillings* Lawful Money, and necessary Charges paid.

All Masters of Vessels, and others, are hereby cautioned against entertaining or carrying off said Servant, as they would avoid the Penalty of the Law.   *Boston, April* 4, 1750.

The Boston Gazette, or Weekly Journal, April 10, 1750.

RAN away from his Master, *Daniel Hewes* of *Wrentham*, on the 5th Instant, a Man Servant named *Obadiah Eddy*, a small slim Fellow, about 17 Years of Age, of fresh Complexion, a long and large Nose, small Eyes, of a sly malicious Cast, and of a light colour, & large Feet He carried with him a new Felt Hat, an old brown Wig, 2 or 3 Caps, one Holland with Ruffles, one striped Cotton one, 3 Shirts, one course Dowlas, the others checked Cotton and Wool, a blue homespun Cloth Coat, that has been turn'd, with Brass Buttons, a Jacket of light coloured Cloth, new, with Pewter Buttons, Leather Breeches, and short Trousers.

Whoever shall take up the said Servant, and convey him to his said Master at Wrentham, shall have Forty Shillings Lawful Money, Reward, and necessary Charges

   paid, by Daniel Hewes.

And all Masters of Vessels and others, are hereby caution'd against concealing or carrying off said Servant on Penalty of the Law.
The Boston Gazette, or Weekly Journal, April 10, 1750 See *The Boston Evening-Post,* April 9, 1750.

WHEREAS Frances *the Wife of* John Edwards *of* Attleborough, *hath eloped from me her Husband:* These are therefore to warn all Persons that they do not credit the said *Frances*, for if they do I will not pay them; and if any Person hath credited here since the Year 1747 they are desired forthwith to bring their Accompts if ever they expect to be paid.
    John Edwards.   Dated in *Attleborough*, March the 30th. 1750.
The Boston Weekly News-Letter, April 12, 1750.

WHereas *Elizabeth* the Wife of *Bethel Blair* of *Boston*, Mariner, has eloped from me the Subscriber her Husband. These are therefore to caution all Persons not to give her Credit or contract any Debt on my Account, for I shall not pay any Debt by her so contracted.
    Bethel Blair.   Dated at *Boston, April* 15th 1750.
The Boston Gazette, or Weekly Journal, April 17, 1750.

DEserted from the Ship *Empress Queen, John Dunn* Master, about four Days ago, lately from London, the following Sailors, *viz.*
 Patrick Burns, about 5 Feet 8 Inches, of a brown Complexion, wearing a Wigg or Cap.
 David Waters, about 5 Feet 8 Inches, of a sandy Complexion, and Freckles in his Face, thin favour'd, wearing a Wig or Cap.
 Richard Archdeacon, about 5 Feet 10 or 11 Inches, the Complexion and Looks of a Spaniard, with a Cast in his Eye wearing a Cap or Wig.
 George Oneut, about 5 Feet 7 or 8 Inches, a brown Complexion, well set, and a little pitted with the Small Pox, wearing a Cap or Wig.
 James Finch, 5 Feet 10 or 11 Inches, of a brown Complexion, thin favour'd, very much pitted with the Smallpox, and black short Hair, sometimes wearing a Cap.
 Thomas Hunt, about 5 Feet 5 inches, of a brown Complexion, wearing his Hair.
 N. B. If they will return to the Ship in two Days Time, no more shall be said, but if not, any Person who shall take them up, and bring them to the Goal in *Boston*, shall have 20*s* Lawful Money for each, and all necessary Charges paid.   *Boston, April* 30th 1750.
The Boston Gazette, or Weekly Journal, May 1, 1750.

DESERTED *from the Snow* Hopton *of* Glasgow, Robert Steel *Commander, now in* Boston *Harbour, the 4 following Sailors, viz.*

Allen McAlla, *a lusty tall Man, Pock fretted, has thick Lips, is of brown Complexion, and wears a Wig.*

Robert Miller, *of middle Stature, pretty thick, and of swarthy Complexion, has dark coloured Hair, and wears a Wig.*

David Anderson, *of middle Stature, o black Complexion, and wears a Wig.*

James Flin, *a Cooper, is thick and lusty of Body, full faced, and ruddy, has a thick under Lip, is an* Irishman, *and is supposed to wear a blue Jacket.*

N. B. *If the said Deserters will return to their Duty on board the said Snow by Wednesday next, they shall be kindly received, but if they do not, they will be treated as deserters; and whoever shall take the up after that Time, and bring them to the Printer of this Paper, shall have* Five Pounds *Lawful Money Reward for each of them.* Boston, May 7, 1750.

The Boston Evening-Post, May 7, 1750.

DEserted from the Ship Empress Queen *John Dunn* Master, late from *London,* the three following Sailors, viz.

William Dunkinson about five Feet ten Inches, of a brown complection, wearing a Cap or Wig.

James Cunningham, about five Feet nine Inches, a brown Complection, wearing a Wig, and pitted with the Small Pox.

John Thompson about five Feet five Inches, a brown Complection, wearing a Wig.

Whoever shall take up the said Deserters, & bring them to the Master on board said Ship, shall have *forty Shillings* Lawful Money Reward for each.

The Boston Gazette, or Weekly Journal, May 15, 1750.

RAN away from his Master Capt. *Nathaniel Gorham* of *Charlestown* on Friday the 18th Instant, an Indian Boy named *Moses,* about 15 Years of Age; had on when he went away, a homespun Kersey Coat, Cotton and Linnen Shirt, and a Pair of Trousers: No Hat, Cap, Stockings nor Shoes. Whoever shall take up said Runaway, and convey him safely to his said Master in *Charlestown* aforesaid, shall be well rewarded for their Trouble.

Charleston, May 21. 1750.

The Boston Gazette, or Weekly Journal, May 22, 1750. See *The Boston Gazette, or Weekly Journal,* October 17, 1749.

Success, Boston Harbour, May 21*st.* 1750.

WHEREAS the three Men, whose Names and Descriptions are underwritten, have absented themselves without Leave from his Majesty's Ship Success, *whereunto they belong.*

Whoever will secure any one of them so as he may be returned to his Duty shall have *Twenty Pounds*, old Tenor, Reward, or *Sixty Pounds* for the three.

James Rich, about 22 Years of Age, 5 Feet 7 Inches high, dark brown Complection, talkative, and swears much in Conversation, round faced, with a youthful Aspect, and a large Quid of Tobacco in his Mouth; had a blue Jacket on when he went away.

William Duncomb, about 34 Years of Age, 5 Feet 8 Inches high, round-shouldered, with an idiot maudling down Look, red hair'd and a red Beard, commonly slovenly and nasty.

Anthony George, about 20 Years of Age, 5 Feet 10 Inches high, speaks English with a French Accent, has a light brown Complection, smooth Face, and strong chearful Features.   COLVILL.

The Boston Weekly News-Letter, May 24, 1750; May 31, 1750; June 7, 1750.

BROKE *out of* New-York *Goal, last Saturday Night, two Prisoners for Felony; one of them named* James Green, *a likely well-set Man, born, and well known in* New-England; *the other named* James Leech: *Whoever apprehends and secures said Green, shall have Five Pound Reward,*
           paid by   JOHN AYSCOUGH, Sheriff.

The New-York Gazette Revived in the Weekly Post-Boy, May 21, 1750; May 28, 1750.

ABSENTED *from the Ship* Britannia, Jeremiah Fones *Commander, a few Days ago,* David Sanders, *a Sailor. If he will return to his Duty on board the said Ship, lying at Long Wharf, within three Days from the Date hereof, he shall be kindly received, otherwise he will be treated as a Deserter.*
                                                                Boston, June 4. 1750.

The Boston Evening-Post, June 4, 1750.

DEserted from on board the Ship *Barbadoes*-Pacquet, *John Evan*s, Commander, the 9th Instant, *John Hodges*, a West-Countryman, pock-fretten, round shoulder'd, pale-fac'd; had on when he went away a light-coloured grey Coat, red Jacket, a large pair of carved pewter Buckels, suppos'd to have taken away a green silk Jacket, a brown pair of broad-cloth Breeches: Whoever shall take him up and bring him to said *Evans* at *Clark's* Wharf, shall have *Ten Pounds*, Old Tenor, Reward, and all necessary Charges
           paid by   John Evans.   Boston, June 13th. 1750.

The Boston Weekly News-Letter, June 21, 1750; June 28, 1750.

RAN away from his Master, *Henderson Inches* of *Boston*, on the 24th of this Inst. *June*, an *Irish* Servant Lad named Martin Landers, about 17 Years of Age. He is a fellow of a light Complexion, with white Eye-Brows, large Teeth, and speaks with the Brogue. He had on when he went away, a Cloth coloured Jacket, a Check Shirt, Leather Breeches and a Cotton Cap. Whoever shall apprehend the said Servant, and safely convey him to his said Master, shall have *Ten Pounds* old Tenor, and all necessary Charges paid. And all Masters of Vessels and others are hereby caution'd against harbouring, concealing or carrying off the said Servant, as they would avoid the Penalty of the Law.

The Boston Gazette, or Weekly Journal, June 26, 1750. See *The Boston Evening-Post*, January 1, 1753.

RAN-away on the 21st Instant from *Daniel Amos* of *Boston*, an Indian Girl, goes by the Name of *Esther* or *Phebe*, aged 16 or 17 Years: Had on when she went away, a homespun Petticoat, a short Osnabrigs Gown or a Blue Calamanco one: Whoever will bring her to her said Master, shall have *Forty Shillings* old Tenor Reward.   Daniel Amos.

The Boston Weekly News-Letter, June 28, 1750; July 5, 1750; July 12, 1750.

RAN away on the 17th of June, 1750, from Ichabod Godwin of Berwick in the County of York, an Indian Woman Servant, about 20 Years of Age, named Sarah John, a fat thick short Woman; She carried away with her a silk Crape Gown, she was seen to pass through Hampton on the 22d Inst. Whoever shall take up the said Runaway and secure her so that he may have her again, shall have 5 Pounds old Tenor Reward, and all necessary Charges paid.

The Boston Post-Boy, July 2, 1750; July 9, 1750; July 16, 1750; *The Boston Weekly News-Letter*, July 12, 1750.

RAN-away from this Master Capt. *Daniel Colman* of *Boston*, on Thursday the 26th of *June* last, an English Lad about 16 Years of Age, small of Stature, named *John Lawne*, he had on when he went away, a new double breasted blew Jacket, a strip'd under one, speckled Shirt, red Breeches, light grey Yarn Stockings, a strip'd Worsted Cap, and a new Hat: He can Read and Write very well.

Whoever shall take up said Servant and return him to his said Master, shall have *five Pounds* old Tenor Reward, and all necessary Charges paid. And all Masters of Vessels and others, are hereby caution'd against concealing or carrying off said Servant on Penalty of the Law.

The Boston Gazette, or Weekly Journal, July 3, 1750.

BRoke out of Bridewell on the 8th Instant at Nigh, [*sic*] a Servant Lad named —— *Hagen*, about 17 Years of Age; an Apprentice to Capt. *Robert Steel*, Commander of the Snow Hopeton of *Glasgow*, now in the Harbour of Boston: had on a green Jacket, Pock-frecken and thick Lips. Whoever apprehends the said Lad, and will bring him to said Commander, shall have *Twenty Pounds* old Tenor Reward, and all necessary Charges paid.
Boston, July 9. 1750.
The Boston Gazette, or Weekly Journal, July 10, 1750; July 17, 1750.

ON Thursday last the *5th* of *July*, Absented his Masters Service, a young Man of a light Complection, about 18 Years of Age, well set, named *Hugh Surrage*, had on when he went away, a striped homespun Jacket, Check Linnen Shirt, Leather Breeches, gray yarn Stockings, old Shoes, and a Felt Hat.

N. B. One of his Legs is sore, and he has a loping Gate.

Whoever shall apprehend the abovesaid young Man, and safely conveys him to his Master *Peter Roberts*, opposite to the Sign of the Lamb at the South End, shall have *Five Pounds* (old Tenor) Reward and all necessary Charges paid.

All Masters of Vessels and others are hereby caution'd, not to conceal or carry off the said young Man, on Penalty of the Law.
Boston July 6. 1750.
The Boston Weekly News-Letter, July 12, 1750; July 19, 1750.

RAN away from Capt. *James Forbes*, on Monday the 9th Inst. a Negro Man named *Achilles*, alias *Hercules*, a short squat Fellow, about 24 Years of Age, has a pretty broad Face, and has a shaved spot on the crown of his Head; had on when he went away, a white Shirt and Trousers, and a Handkerchief about his Head, no Shoes, Stockings, Jacket or Hat. Whoever secures said Negro and will bring him to his Master, shall have *Five Pounds* old Tenor, Reward and reasonable Charges. All Masters of Vessels and others are hereby caution'd not to conceal, entertain or convey the said Negro away, as they would avoid the Penalty of the Law.
Boston, July 11. 1750.
The Boston Weekly News-Letter, July 12, 1750; July 19, 1750. See *Boston Evening-Post*, July 23, 1750.

RAN away on Monday the 9th Instant, a Negro Man named Achelles, alias Hercules, a short squat Fellow, about 24 Years old; hath a pretty broad Face, and has had his Head shaved since he ran away. He had on when he went away, only a white Shirt and Trowzers, and a Handkerchief about his Head, no Shoes, Stockings or Hat. Whoever secures said Negro, and brings him to his Master James Forbes, of Boston, shall have Twenty Pounds, old

Tenor, Reward, and reasonable Charges. All Masters of Vessels and others, are hereby cautioned not to conceal, entertain or carry off said Negro, as they would avoid the Penalty of the Law.

N. B. He speaks very good English, and chews Tobacco.

Boston, July 12. 1750.

Boston Evening-Post, July 23, 1750. See *The Boston Weekly News-Letter*, July 12, 1750.

RAN-away the 19th of *July*, from *Ichabod Goodwin* of *Berwick*, in the County of *York*, a Negro Man named *Pompey*, about 40 Years of Age, a short well-set Fellow, speaks good English, he had on a pair of Pot-hooks when he went away, a pair of Trowsers, a homespun Jacket, and a check'd woolen Shirt, and has one of his Ears cut. Likewise a tall slim young Fellow named *William Nason*, of light Complection and light Hair: Whoever takes up said Servants and delivers them to their Master, or secures them so that they may be had again, shall have *Ten Pounds* Old Tenor Reward, with all reasonable Charges

paid by *Ichabod Goodwin.*

N. B. All Masters of Vessels are hereby forewarned carrying them off, as they may expect to answer it at their Peril.

The Boston Post-Boy, July 23, 1750; July 30, 1750; August 6, 1750. See *The Boston Weekly Post-Boy*, January 25, 1748.

R*AN away from the Snow* Hopton, *of* Glasgow, Robert Steel *Master, now lying in* Boston *Harbour, a Servant Boy named* James Wilson, *about* 18 *Years old, of a middle Stature, swarthy Complexion, and wears a Wig. Whoever shall take up the said Servant, and bring him on board the said Ship, shall have* Five Pounds, *Lawful Money, Reward.*

Boston, July 11, 1750.

The Boston Post-Boy, July 23, 1750; July 30, 1750.

RAN-away from *Nathan Niles* of *Groton* in the Colony of *Connecticut*, on the 16th Instant, an Indian Boy named *Daniel*, about 16 Years of Age, had on when he went away a new Felt Hatt, a pair of light Duck Trowsers, and has lost two of his small Toes: Whoever shall secure the aforesaid Boy, so that his Master may have him again, shall receive *Five Pounds* Old Tenor Reward, and all Charges paid. *Newport, July* 18. 1750.

The Boston Post-Boy, July 23, 1750; July 30, 1750; August 6, 1750.

RAN away on the 7th Inst. from her Master *Epes Sergeant* of *Sale*m, Esq; an Irish Servant Girl, named *Molly Birk*, about 24 Years of Age, of a middle Stature, black Eyes, black Hair, very much pock broken, had on when she went away a blue stuff Gown; Whoever shall take up the abovesaid Runaway and bring her to her said Master, or secure her so that he may have her again, shall have Five Pounds old Tenor Reward, and all necessary Charges paid.

And all Persons are hereby caution'd against concealling, or any way harbouring the said Runaway.

The Boston Weekly News-Letter, July 26, 1750; August 2, 1750; *The Boston Gazette, or Country Journal*, July 30, 1750; *The Boston Post-Boy*, July 30, 1750; August 6, 1750. Minor differences between the papers.

RAN-away from *John Hains* of *Exeter*, on Friday the 27th of *July* last, an Irishman Servant named *Darby Carty*, aged about 17 Years, is tall of Stature; had on when he went away a blue Jacket turn'd up at the Sleeves, and one of the Pockets made of a worsted Cap, and a Pair of old Leather Breeches: He is of a pale Complection. Whoever will take up said Runaway and convey him to his said Master, shall have *Ten Pounds* old Tenor Reward, and all necessary Charges paid.

    John Haines.   *Exeter, August* 1*st.* 1750.

The Boston Post-Boy, August 6, 1750; August 13, 1750; August 20, 1750; August 27, 1750.

RAN-away from Capt. *Thomas Bloss*, last Night, Two Negro Men, one named *Phillip*, the other *Ned*, both Sailmakers. *Phillip* is a tall spare Fellow, and walks a little lame. *Ned* is a spry young Fellow of about 19 Years of Age: They both talk broken English: They carried away with them sundry Wearing Apparel that belong'd to some of the Hands of the Vessel from which they run, such as Jackets made of coarse Blanketing and strip'd Homespun, speckled Shirts, Trowsers and Breeches, Hats, &c. but have neither Stockings or Shoes, unless they have Mogizeens. Whoever shall take up said Negroes and bring them to their Master on board the Schooner *Success* lying at Col. *Wendell*'s Wharf, or Mr. *Benjamin Hallowell* in Boston, shall have FIVE POUNDS old Tenor Reward for each, and all necessary Charges paid.

All Masters of Vessels and others are hereby caution'd against harbouring, concealing or carrying off said Servant [*sic*] as they would avoid the Penalty of the Law.   Boston, August 20. 1750.

The Boston Post-Boy, August 20, 1750.

RAN-away on the 9th Instant from *Aaron Davis* of *Durham*, in the Province of *New-Hampshire*, a Negro Man named *Quam*, of a middling Stature, talks good English, he carried away with him, a Gun and Ammunition; he had on a grey homespun Jacket a white woolen Shirt, a Felt Hatt: Whoever will take up said Negro and secure him, so that he may

have him again, shall have TEN POUNDS old Tenor Reward, and all necessary Charges paid by me
    Aaron Davis.   Durham, August 23. 1750.
The Boston Post Boy, August 27, 1750; September 3, 1750; September 10, 1750.

RAN-away on the 9th of *August* from *Robert Thompson* of the Town of *Durham* in the Province of *New-Hampshire,* a Negro Man, named *John Batter,* of a midling Stature, speaks pretty good English, and can speak French: He carryed away with him a Gun and Ammunition; and had on a grey homespun Jacket a pair of Leather Breeches, a white woollen Shirt and a felt Hat. Whoever will take up said Negro and secure him so that he may have him again, shall have TEN POUNDS old Tenor and all necessary
    Charges paid by me *Robert Thompson.*
The Boston Post Boy, August 27, 1750; September 3, 1750; September 10, 1750.

RAN-away from his Master *Benjamin Hallowell* of *Boston,* a new Negro Man named *Cuffey,* has been in the County about ten Weeks: Had on when he went away, a dark colour'd strip'd homespun Jacket, and a mix'd Jacket, a speckled Shirt, a new double Cap, a beaver Hatt new drest, a pair of Shoes with brass Buckels, has no Stockings on, a pair of Oznabrigs Trowsers, he has a large Scarr on his left Leg, is pock-fretten: Whoever will take up said Negro so that his Master may have him again shall have TEN POUNDS old Tenor, Reward, and all necessary Charges paid.
            Boston, August 27, 1750.
The Boston Post Boy, August 27, 1750; September 3, 1750; September 10, 1750. See *The Boston Evening-Post,* September 3, 1750.

*R*AN *away from his Master Mr.* Benjamin Hallowell *of* Boston, *the* 10*th Instant, a new Negro Man named Cuffey, has been in the County about Ten Weeks. He had on when he went away, a dark colour'd stript Homespun Jacket and a mixt Jacket, a speckled Shirt, a new double Cap, a Bever Hatt new drest, a pair of Shoes with brass Buckles, has no Stockings on, a pair of Oznabrigs Trousers, a large Scar on his left Leg, is pockfreckled. Whoever will take up said Negro, so that his Master may have him again shall have* Ten Pounds, *old Tenor, Reward, and all necessary Charges paid.*
  The Boston Evening-Post, September 3, 1750. See *The Boston Post Boy,* August 27, 1750.

RAN-away Yesterday from Capt. *Francis Bramham,* a Negro Man, named *York,* of a low Stature, of about 26 or 17 Years of Age, a round Face, and some rotten Teeth: Had on when he went away, a green Ratteen Jacket, a

Cap, a pair of large white Trowsers, and a large pair of brass Buckles in his Shoes, use to sweep Chimneys in the Winter. Any one that brings said Negro to his Master, or to the Printer hereof, shall have FIVE POUNDS old Tenor, Reward, and all necessary Charges
     paid by *Francis Bramham.*

All Masters of Vessels and others are hereby caution'd against entertaining, harbouring, concealing, or carrying off said Negro, as they would avoid the Penalty of the Law. *Boston, September* 6. 1750.

The Boston Weekly News-Letter, September 6, 1750.

RAN-away on the 3d of *September*, from Doctor *John Ross* of *Portsmouth*, in the Province of *New-Hampshire*, A Negro Man, named *Pomp*, about six Feet high, about 28 Years of Age, speaks good English; He had on when he went away, a striped homespun under-Jacket, an old upper blue Jacket, a pair of Leather Breeches, has a Sore upon his left Shin and a Scar if not a Sore on his right Shin, another Scar on his left Cheek, near his Ear, which oftentimes issues Water: He designs for the Sea. Whoever will take up said Negro, and secure him so that his Master may have him again shall have TEN DOLLARS old Tenor Reward, and all necessary Charges
     paid by *John Ross.*

N. B. All Masters of Vessels and others are caution'd from concealing or carrying off said Negro, as they would avoid the Penalty of the Law.

The Boston Post-Boy, September 17, 1750; September 24, 1750; October 1, 1750.

RAN-away on the 12th Instant a Servant Boy named *Briant McDorment* about 18 Years of Age, of a small Stature: Had on when he went away a black Wigg, Frock and Trowsers, new check'd Shirt, old worsted Stockings, and old turn'd Pumps. Whoever shall take up said Servant, and convey him to the Sign of the Lamb, at the South End of *Boston*, shall have five Pounds old Tenor Reward, and all necessary Charges
     paid, by *Jonas Lenard.*

All Masters of Vessels and others, are hereby caution'd against harbouring, concealing or carrying off said Servant, as they'd avoid the Penalty of the Law. *Boston, Sept.* 13. 1750.

The Boston Gazette, or Weekly Journal, September 18, 1750.

RAN away from his Master, *Thomas Hodson*, of Boston, on Friday the sixth of this Instant *October*, a Negro Man named *Scipio*, with a Frock and Trouzers, and a Leather Jockey Cap. Whoever shall take up the said Negro, and bring him to his said Master, shall be well rewarded for their Trouble, and all necessary Charges paid.

N. B. The Fellow has been used to the Sea, and will probably attempt to get off. He had a Dog with him when he went away, which is very fond of him.

The Boston Evening-Post, October 8, 1750; October 15, 1750; October 22, 1750. The third ad does not have the lines after charges paid.

Philadelphia, October 15. 1750.
RUn away, last night, from Philip Marot, of Bordentown, an Irish servant man, named Abraham Magee, of middle stature, about 25 years of age, of a pale complexion, a taylor by trade, and a good workman, has black hair, and a red beard, but has his hair off, and wears a linnen cap: Had on when he went away, a light colour'd homespun drugget coat, a brown drugget jacket, two pair of breeches, one pair of fustian, the other buckskin, an ozenbrigs shirt, two pair of stockings, one pair blue worsted, the other thread, a castor hat, about half worn, a new pair of neats leather shoes, with brass buckles.

There also went away with him a New-England man, named John Clarke, of a middle stature, about 25 years of age, of a fresh complexion, a carpenter and joiner by trade; he rid off an iron grey mare, blind in one eye: Had on when he went away, a light colour'd coat and jacket, the coat lin'd with red, the jacket with green, a pair of purple plush breeches, a large beaver hat, good shoes and stockings. Whoever takes up and secures said servant, and said Clarke, so as the subscriber may have them again, shall have Four Pounds reward for both, or Forty Shillings for either of them, and reasonable charges,
    paid by PHILIP MAROT.
The Pennsylvania Gazette, October 18, 1750; November 1, 1750.

RAN-away from the Brigg *Eagle* lying at Mr. *Gridley's* Wharff, on the 21st Instant, *Michael Handly,* a Sailor aged 20 Years, wore a blew outside double breasted Jacket, with yellow Mettle Buttons, a blue inside Ditto, single breasted with yellow Buttons, a Leather Cap, and worsted Cap under it, course grey Yarn Stockings, high heel'd Shoes, and is about 5 Foot 3 Inches high, of a black Complection.

Daniel Frugere, a Spanish Lad aged 16 Years, talks very good English, is about 4 Foot 9 Inches high, wore a blue Jacket with Mettle Buttons, a Hat and Cap, both of them check'd Shirts and Linnen Handkerchiefs. Whoever will secure said Persons & bring them to *James Belson* on board said Vessel, or to Mr. *James Bois* on *Gould's* Wharff, shall have 20 *Pounds* old Tenor Reward, and all necessary Charges.

The Boston Gazette, or Weekly Journal, October 23, 1750; October 30, 1750.

RAN-away from his Master *William Noyes* of *Newbury*, Cordwainer, an Apprentice Boy, named *John Williams*, about nineteen Years of Age; he had on when he went away, a blue Coat and a plad Jacket, and a light-coloured Pair of Plush Breeches; he is of a middle Stature: Whoever shall take up said Runaway, and convey him to his Master, shall have *Thirteen Shillings and Four Pence* Lawful Money, and all necessary Charges
          paid by me   *William Noyes.*

N. B. All Masters of Vessels and others are hereby warn'd against entertaining the said *John Williams.*   *Newbury, October* 19. 1750.

    The Boston Post-Boy, October 29, 1750; November 5, 1750; November 12, 1750.

THIS may serve to Notify, that there was taken up on the 15th Instant, by me the Subscriber, a Negro Man, his Name unknown, speaks bad English, suppos'd to be about 30 Years of Age, and has a Scar near his right Ear; having on a blue knit Cap striped with white, an old patch'd Jacket, a pair of old Trowsers, a dark pair of Yarn Hose, a white woollen Shirt: The Owner upon Application to me, and paying all necessary Charges, may have him again.
          George Newmarch.   *Marblehead, October* 16. 1750.

    The Boston Gazette, or Weekly Journal, October 30, 1750; November 13, 1750. *The Boston Weekly News-Letter,* November 2, 1750; November 8, 1750; November 15, 1750; Minor differences between the papers.

RAN-away from his Master *William Brown* of *Framingham*, on the 30th of Sept. last, a Molatto Fellow, about 27 Years of Age, named *Crispas*, well set, 6 Feet 2 Inches high, short curl'd Hair, Knees nearer together than common; had on a light colour'd Bearskin Coat, brown Fustian Jacket, new Buckskin Breeches, blew Yarn Stockings, and a check'd Shirt.

    Whoever shall take up said Run-away, and convey him to his abovesaid Master at *Framingham*, shall have *Ten Pounds*, old Tenor Reward, and all necessary Charges paid.

    The Boston Gazette, or Weekly Journal, November 13, 1750; November 20, 1750.

ON the 18th Instant at Night deserted from the Ship Knowles, *Benjamin Hallowell*, Master, the two following Persons, viz.

    Benjamin Sheperd, an Irishman, tall & well proportion'd, about 30 Years of Age, a little pock-broken, & has commonly a large Quantity of Tobacco in his Mouth; had on a blue Jacket, and a pair of Duck Trousers, a Cap and no Hat.

The other named *James Minzie,* an Irishman, about five Feet 8 Inches high, a thin Visage, much afflicted with Boils, two of which are on his Wrists; he had on a blue Jacket, and a pair of narrow Trowsers, a black Wigg, and a small Hat. Whoever will bring them on board said Ship now lying at the Long Wharffe, shall have *thirty Shillings* Lawful Money for each or either of them,
      paid by *Benjamin Hallowell.*
The Boston Gazette, or Weekly Journal, November 20, 1750.

RAn-away from his Master *Josiah Stowell* of Watertown, on the 13th Instant, a molatto colour'd Servant, named *Edward Stanley,* between 16 and 17 Years of Age, about 5 Foot 4 Inches high: Had on when he went away, a light colour'd Duroy Coat with red Lining, a dark Cloth colour'd Jacket and Breeches, a white Linnen Shirt, light blue yarn Stockings, a Felt Hat, almost new, and a pair of thick Shoes with brass Buckles. He has thick bushy black Hair. Whoever shall take up said Servant, and convey him to his abovesaid Master in Watertown, shall have *ten Pounds* old Tenor Reward, and all necessary Charges paid. And all Masters of Vessels & others are hereby caution'd against concealing or carrying off said Servant, on Penalty of the Law.   *Boston, Nov.* 19, 1750.
The Boston Gazette, or Weekly Journal, November 20, 1750.

1751

RAN-away from his Master *Nathan Perry* of *Watertown,* on the 20th Instant, a white Servant Lad named *Daniel Maddocks,* about 15 Years of Age, a slim Fellow, and of light Complection; wears a Cap, and a Felt Hat, and also had on a light blue Fly Coat, with brass Buttons, dark blue Jacket, Leather Breeches, Cotton and Linnen Shirt; and went away with a Leather Apron on: He is known to have gone towards the Eastward. Whoever shall take up said Servant, and convey him to his abovesaid Master in *Watertown,* shall have *Ten Pounds* old Tenor Reward, and all necessary Charges paid. And all Masters of Vessels and others are hereby caution'd against concealing or carrying off said Servant, on Penalty of the Law.
The Boston Gazette, or Weekly Journal, January 1, 1751.

RAN-away from his Master *Daniel Oliver,* Peruke-Maker, the 13th Instant, a Servant Boy named *John Malan,* about 18 Years of Age: He wears a Wigg, and has a Scar in his Forehead, had on a Broad Cloth Coat with Brass Buttons, Leather Breeches, and grey Yarn Stockings; has took with him a light colour'd great Coat, and 3 check'd Shirts.
  Whoever shall apprehend the abovesaid Servant, and convey him to his Master in Kingstreet, *Boston,* shall have *ten Pounds* Old Tenor Reward

& all necessary Charges paid. And all master of Vessels and others are hereby caution'd against concealing or carrying off said Servant on Penalty of the Law. *Boston,* January 15th, 1750,1.
The Boston Gazette, or Weekly Journal, January 22, 1751.

RUN from *Abigail Walker* of *Portsmouth* in the Province of *New-Hampshire,* on Sunday the 20th Instant, A Negro Man Servant named *Cato,* about 40 Years old, the End of his Thumb on his right Hand has been cut off near the Root of the Nail, and one of his fore Teeth is out, and he is something bow knee'd: He had on when he run a black broad-cloth Coat with round cuffs, a grey homespun Jacket with large bell-mettle flat Buttons, a blue Under-jacket of Baize, pewter Buttons, the Button-holes work'd, with white black cloth [sic] Breeches, black yarn Buskins, a felt Hat, and a blue and white woollen Shirt. Whoever shall apprehend said Negro so that the said *Abigail* shall have him again, shall have FIVE POUNDS old Tenor Reward, and all necessary Charges
      paid by   *Abigail Walker. Portsmouth, January* 21*st.* 1750,1.
N. B. All Persons are caution'd against harbouring, concealing or carrying off said Servant, as they will answer the same at their Peril.
The Boston Post-Boy, January 28, 1751; February 4, 1751; February 11, 1751.

R*AN away from his Master the Honourable* Richard Saltonstall, *of* Haverhill, *Esq; on the 29th of* January *past, a Servant Man named* William Blair, *a short Fellow, Pock-broken, with large black eyebrows, and a flat Nose. He had on when he went away, and carried with him, a striped double breasted Jacket, with Brass Buttons, a Fly Cloth coloured Coat, with red Lining, and flowered Brass Buttons, and a brown Kersey Great Coat, with Mohair Buttons. Whoever shall take up the said Servant, and secure him in Prison, so that his Master may have him again, shall have* Ten Pounds, *old Tenor, Reward, and necessary Charges paid.*
      February 2, 1751.
The Boston Evening-Post, February 4, 1751; February 11, 1751; February 18, 1751. See *The Boston Evening-Post,* April 24, 1749.

South-Kingston, in the Colony of *Rhode-Island,* Feb. 26.
On Saturday last was discovered in a Creek or Cove some distance from the High-way, a dead Man, stript naked, having two Wounds in his Breast and one in his Neck, suppos'd to be made with a Hanger, and other Marks of Violence on his Body. The Coroner's Inquest brought in Wilful Murder against one Thomas Carter, who says he was born in Virginia, and married a Wife in Newport about Eighteen Months past: The Deceased appears to be one William Jackson, and to have come from Virginia with

Deers-Leather, and fell in Company with Carter upon the Road; had with him the Day before the Murder a Quantity of Silver and Paper Money, a Silver Watch, and a Hanger with a rough Back like a Saw (Part of which was found by the Body) wore a red Great-Coat, a Snuff-coloured Waistcoat, and wash-leather Breeches.
The Boston Post-Boy, March 4, 1751; *The Boston Gazette, or Weekly Journal*, March 5, 1751; *The Boston Weekly News-Letter*, March 7, 1751; *The New-York Gazette Revived in the Weekly Post Boy*, March 25, 1751. Minor differences between the papers. See *The New-York Gazette Revived in the Weekly Post Boy*, March 25, 1751, *The New-York Gazette Revived in the Weekly Post Boy*, April 8, 1751, *The Boston Evening-Post*, April 22, 1751, and *The New-York Evening Post*, April 22, 1751.

RAN away from his Master *John Morse*, Peruke-Maker, in *Cambridge*; a young Man Servant named *Henry Bathrick*, small in Stature, pale Complection, about 18 Years of Age: Had on when he went away, a blue Homespun Coat with large flat Brass Buttons; a blue broad Cloath Jacket with red Lining, a Cotton and Lining Shirt, a pair of greasy Leather Breeches, light blue Yarn Stockings, a pair of new double Channel Pumps, white Mettle Buckles, a brown Wigg, and an old Castor Hatt.

Whoever shall take up said Servant, and convey him to his abovesaid Master at *Cambridge*, shall have *Three Dollars* Reward, and all necessary Charges paid.

And all Masters of Vessels and others, are hereby caution'd against concealing or carrying off said Servant, on Penalty of the Law.

Boston, March 2. 1750,1.
The Boston Gazette, or Weekly Journal, March 5, 1751.

WHereas Mary *the Wife of me the Subscriber has run me greatly in Debt:* These are therefore to caution all Persons against trusting her on my Account, for I hereby declare I will not pay any Debt she shall contract from the date hereof.

   John Alexander.   Dated, *Boston, March* 7, 1750,1.
The Boston Weekly News-Letter, March 7, 1751.

      WHEREAS Sarah *the Wife of the Subscriber,* Francis Burnam, *has Rifled his House, and absconded from her said Husband.* This is to forbid all Persons not to entertain her the said *Sarah*, or credit her for Money or Goods or any other Thing upon the Penalty of losing their Debt. *Francis Burnam.* Jun. *Ipswich, March* 22. 1750 [*sic*]
The Boston Post-Boy, March 25, 1751; April 1, 1751; April 8, 1751.

Whereas there was, on or about the first Day of January *last, an horrid Murder committed on the Body of* William Jackson, *supposed to come from some Part of* Virginia, *and had with him a Quantity of Deer's Leather; And on View of the Body, the Coroner's Inquest brought in Willful Murder against one* Thomas Carter, *(who is also said to be a* Virginian) *and is now confin'd in his Majesty's Goal in* South-Kingstown, *in the Colony of* Rhode-Island, *ad is to have his Tryal (if not put off longer) the first Tuesday of* April *next: THESE are therefore to desire all his Majesty's liege Subjects, to be aiding in giving Notice to the Relations of the said Deceased, in order that some of them may appear at the Tryal, to give Evidence to some Goods (if they have any Knowledge of them) found on said* Carter, *and presumed to belong to said* Jackson, *being marked* W. I. *and to secure what Effects are, or may be found, that belong'd to the said Deceas'd.* Given under my Hand in *South-Kingston,* this 9th Day of *March,* in the 24th Year of his Majesty's Reign, Anno. Do. 1750, 51.
    JOSH. BABCOCK.
       C. Justice of his Majesty's Superior Court in said Colony.
The New-York Gazette Revived in the Weekly Post Boy, March 25, 1751. See *The Boston Post-Boy*, March 4, 1751, *The New-York Gazette Revived in the Weekly Post Boy*, April 8, 1751, *The Boston Evening-Post*, April 22, 1751, and *The New-York Evening Post*, April 22, 1751.

RAN-away from his Master *Johnson Jackson* of *Boston*, Distiller, on the 24th of March, a Negro Man named Titus, of a middle stature, born at *Nantucket*, speaks softly: He had with him when he went away, two Jackets, one of a light colour which he wore outside, with mettal Buttons and a Patch on the shoulder, the other Jacket of a reddish colour, and a pair of Breeches of the same, a pair of Leather Breeches with mettal Buttons, a pair of Trowsers of old Canvas, two pair of Stockings, one pair blue very fine, the other grey patched on the Feet, two Shirts, one check'd woollen, the other cotton and linnen, and a narrow Beaver Hat; it is suppos'd that a Negro Woman named *Hannah*, and pretends to be free is along with him, who goes lame; He has lately been seen in several Country Towns, and 'tis tho't he has got to work with some Farmer. He plays well upon a Violin.
    Whoesover will take up said Negro, so that his Master may have him again, shall receive TEN POUNDS old Tenor Reward, and all necessary Charges paid,   *Johnson Jackson.*
All Persons are hereby caution'd against harbouring, entertaining or concealing said Servant, as they would avoid the Penalty of the Law.
    The Boston Weekly News-Letter, April 4, 1751; April 11, 1751; April 18, 1751.

RAN-away from his Master *Samuel Bancroft*, jun. of *Reading*, on the 18th Inst. an Apprentice named *Joseph Trow*, about 19 Years of Age: He had on when he went away, an old light colour'd Great Coat, with flat Pewter Buttons, a Coat and Jacket of a brownish Colour, a Pair of Leather Breeches, a dark Wigg and white Cap, a Castor Hatt almost new, a lusty well sett Fellow.

Whoever shall take up the abovesaid Run-away, and him convey to his Master at *Reading*, or secure him so that his Master may have him; shall have *Five Pounds* old Tenor Reward, and all necessary Charges

    paid by me   *Samuel Bancroft*, jun.   *Reading, April* 5. 1750. [*sic*]
And all Masters of Vessels and others, are hereby caution'd against concealing or carrying off said Apprentice on Penalty of the Law.

The Boston Gazette, or Weekly Journal, April 9, 1751.

Broke out of his Majesty's Goal in *York*, the Night following the 16 of *Feb.* last, two Prisoners, one named *Samuel Ball*, aged about 25 Years, of midling Sature, [*sic*] well sett, full fac'd, ragged drest, wore a Cap; not Hat; he was taken up and imprison'd on Suspition of Murder: Whoever shall take up said *Ball*, and bring him to *Joseph Plaisted*, Sheriff of the County of *York*; shall have 6£. 13*s*. 4*d*. Lawful Money Reward, and all necessary Charges paid. The other named *Stephen Pierce*, a tall slim Fellow of a light Complection usually wore a Cap or Wigg: Whoever shall take up said *Pierce*, and bring him to said *Plaisted* in the County of *York*, shall have 1£. 6*s*. 8*d*. Lawful Money Reward, and all necessary Charges

    paid by me the Subscriber,   *Joseph Plaisted.*

The Boston Gazette, or Weekly Journal, April 9, 1751.

RAN-away from his Master *Job Chase* of *Smithfield*, in the County of *Providence*, on the 26th Day of *March* last past, an Indian Man Servant named *Jeremiah Commoson*, aged about 25 Years, of a middle Stature: Had on when he went away a good Felt-Hat one check'd and one white linnen Shirt, a pair of green Plush Breeches, yarn Stockings, square-toed Shoes, a light colour'd cloth Jacket, a striped double-breasted flannel Jacket under it.

Whoever shall take up the said Runaway and bring him to his said Master, or confine him in any of his Majesty's Goals, to that his Master may have him again, shall have SEVEN POUNDS, old Tenor Reward, and necessary Charges

    paid by me   *Job Chase.*   *Smithfield, April* 8. 1751.

The Boston Post-Boy, April 15, 1751; April 22, 1751; April 29, 1751.

    From the New-York Gazette, April 8.

Whereas it appears by the New-York *Gazette of* March 25, 1751, *that* William Jackson *was murdered in* February *last: The said Jackson was a*

Freeholder *in* Augusta County, *at* Jackson's River *in* Virginia, *and left a Wife great with Child last Fall; He had when he left my House in* Newark *the 30th of* November *last, about 184 Skins of Wash-Leather, one Shirt mark'd* W. I. *with white Ilet Holes; his Great Coat, Waistcoat, Breeches and Hanger, as is described in the said Gazette right; his Horse that he had when he went from us was of a ronish and sorrel Colour; as for his other Goods I can't give any particular Account. It would be very agreeable to me, and no doubt to all his Relations, to hear how the Trial went, and what Effects are or may be found for the Widow and Heirs of the Deceas'd. These are to intreat his Majesty's liege Subjects of* South-Kingston, *to be aiding either by publick or private Letter; the which if it comes to my Knowledge, I shall be as expeditious as I can to convey it to the Widow. Given under my Hand the 1st of* April 1751.   THOMAS BOWS.

    The New-York Gazette Revived in the Weekly Post Boy, April 8, 1751. See *The Boston Post-Boy*, March 4, 1751, *The New-York Gazette Revived in the Weekly Post Boy*, March 25, 1751, *The Boston Evening-Post*, April 22, 1751, and *The New-York Evening Post*, April 22, 1751.

C*Harles Low*, about 28 Years of Age, born in *North-Britain* an Indented Servant to Sir *Henry Frankland*, went away and has absented himself since the 16th Instant: He is about 5 Feet 7 Inches high, of a dark Complection, and had on or with him, a dark colour'd Broad-cloth Coat, a Pair of Sheep-skin Breeches, a red Jacket, a strip'd one ditto, two Shirts, one woollen the other linnen, two pair of Stockings, one pair black the other blue, a pair of Shoes and a pair of new double-channel Pumps, brass Buckles; and wears a Cap or Wigg. Whoever shall take up the said Servant and bring or send him to the Custom-House in *Boston*, shall have FOUR DOLLARS Reward and all necessary Charges paid,   Boston, April 18, 1751.

    The Boston Weekly News-Letter, April 18, 1751; April 25, 1751; *The Boston Post-Boy*, April 22, 1751; *The Boston Gazette, or Weekly Journal*, April 23, 1751. The *Post-Boy* and *Gazette* identify him as "a Scotch-Man" and do not mention "born in North Britain."

    And from *South Kingston*, in the Colony of *Rhode-Island,* that *Thomas Carter* has been tried and condemned to die for the Murder of *William Jackson*, late of *Virginia*, as mentioned some Time ago in this Paper. 'Tis said he is to be executed on the tenth of *May* next, and his Body to be afterwards hung in Chains near the Place where he committed the Murder.

    The Boston Evening-Post, April 22, 1751; *The New-York Gazette Revived in the Weekly Post-Boy*, April 29, 1751. See *The Boston Post-Boy*, March 4, 1751; See *The New-York Gazette Revived in the Weekly*

Post Boy, March 25, 1751, *The New-York Gazette Revived in the Weekly Post Boy,* April 8, 1751, and *The New-York Evening Post,* April 22, 1751.

From Rhode-Island we hear, that Thomas Carter, (formerly mentioned in this Paper) is sentenced to be executed at South-Kingston, in that Colony, and hung in Chains, on the 10th of May next, for the barborous Murder of one William Jackson; who, it is said has a Wife, and seven small Children in some Part of Virginia.
The New-York Evening Post, April 22, 1751. See, *The Boston Post-Boy,* March 4, 1751; *The New-York Gazette Revived in the Weekly Post Boy,* March 25, 1751, *The New-York Gazette Revived in the Weekly Post Boy,* April 8, 1751, and *The Boston Evening-Post,* April 22, 1751.

WEnt away from his Master *Paul Farmer* of *Boston,* Peruke-Maker, on the 16th Instant, a Servant Boy named *Joseph King,* 11 Years of Age, wears a Cap, an old Hat, yellow Camblet Coat, reddish Jacket, linnen Shirt, DeerSkin Breeches: Whoever will take up said Boy, and bring him to his Master aforesaid, shall be well satisfy'd for their Trouble, and all necessary Charges paid.
The Boston-Gazette, or Weekly Journal, April 23, 1751.

Marblehead, May 9, 1751.
R*AN* away from his Master Estes Hatch *of* Dorchester, *Esq; a young Man named* Francis Burdet, *about* 22 *Years old, of a middling Stature, formerly a Soldier at* Louisbourg: *Had on when he went away, a Bever Hat, a brown Bob Wig, a red Soldier's Coat lin'd with White, a white Flannel jacket, red Breeches, blue Stockings, large Brass Buckles in his Shoes; is suppos'd to have gone towards* Situate. *Whoever will apprehend said Burdet, and secure him or bring him to his said Master, shall have* Four Dollars *Reward, paid by said* Hatch.
The Boston Evening-Post, May 6, 1751; May 13, 1751.

R*AN* away the 17th *of this Instant* April, *from her Master* Daniel Marquand *of* Newbury, *a Molatto Servant Woman named* Peach, *aged about* 30 *Years. Whoever will take up said Runaway, and bring her to her Master, shall have* Four Dollars *Reward, and all necessary Charges paid them; and all Persoms are warned against concealing or entertaining the said Servant; and all Masters of Vessels or others that carry the said Servant away, may expect to be prosecuted according to Law.*
The Boston Evening-Post, May 6, 1751.

RAn-away last Night from the Ship Robinhood, *David Little John* Commander, *Robert Mc Gie,* a middle sized well set Man, aged about 26 Years, fresh Complection and smooth faced: Had on when he went away, a dark coloured short jacket, a pair of trousers, hat and brown wigg. Also *Patrick Smith*, a thick set Man round faced and fresh Complection, about 35 Years of Age, had on when he went away, a short fly frock, hatt and wigg: he was bred a Taylor, and is the Captains bought servant. Whoever will secure either or both of the above Men, are desired to apply to Mr. *Samuel Wetbred*, at the bunch of grapes tavern in *Boston*, and shall have a Reward of *Ten Pounds* tenor for each, and all necessary charges.

N. B. They went over *Charlstown*-Ferry, between 5 and 6 o'clock this Morning. *Boston, May* 4. 1751.

The Boston Post-Boy, May 6, 1751.

RAN-away on the 9th of *May* 1751, from his Master *John Richardson* of *Stonington* in the County of *New-London*, A Man Servant named *David Robinson*, of about 20 Years of Age, of a middling Stature, has a very large Scar over his left Eyebrow, he says he was born and bred at the Town called *Norton*, and pretends to be something of a Cooper: He had on when he went away a Felt Hat half worn, a strip'd woollen Shirt, a pair of leather Breeches, a brown coloured Cloth mix'd Coat of this Country made, without Lining.

Whoever will take up said Run-away and return him to his said Master at *Stonington*, or secure him so that his Master may have him again shall have FIFTEEN POUNDS, old Tenor, Reward, and all necessary Charges borne by me   *John Richardson* of *Stonington*.

Province of the *Massachusetts-Bay*.

The Boston Post-Boy, May 13, 1751; May 20, 1751; May 27, 1751.

ABsented May 13th and 14th from the Ship *Elizabeth, Edward Cahill* Master, from *London, William Ellis, John Gale, Maurice Caine, Pelex Fox, William Bane,* and *William Jones*: If the above Seaman will return on board the said Ship in two Days after the Date hereof, they shall be kindly received, otherwise shall be deem'd as Deserters.

Boston, May 10. 1751.

The Boston Evening-Post, May 20, 1751.

RAN-away on the 22d Day of May 1751, from his Master *John Tilton* of *Ipswich*, in the County of *Essex*, an Apprentice Servant named *Joseph Semons*, about 17 Years of Age, of a middling Stature, of a light, fresh comely Countenance, a Shoemaker by Trade: He had on or carried with him, a Felt Hat, linnen Cap, a fly Coat of black & blue mix'd cloth, the fore-parts lin'd with blue, and brass Buttons, and a Waistcoat of the same, a

pair of light-coloured homespun woollen Breeches, two pair of Trousers of new tow cloth, two chequered woollen Shirts, and a fine linnen one, a pair of of blue yarn Stockings, and a pair ditto blue Worsted. Whosoever shall take up the said Apprentice, and return him his said Master, shall have *Two Dollars* Reward and all necessary charges
    paid by *John Tilton.*
The Boston Post-Boy, June 3, 1751; June 10, 1751; June 24, 1751.

RAN-away from his Master *Richard Dodge* of *Wenham,* in the County of *Essex,* on Wednesday last, A likely Negro Man-Servant, named *Hazard,* of a yellowish Complection, middling Stature, about 30 Years of Age, speaks pretty good English, well-set: Had on when he went away, a white cotton and linnen Shirt, a homespun Coat mix'd with a cast of Blue, tow Trowsers, blue worsted Stockings, a dark Wig, a Beaver Hat, and a Pair of Pumps, with large silver Buckles mark'd D. H. He has a Scar across the middle of each of his Legs of two Inches long, cut by an Ax. He carried off with him a fire large Bay Horse, Fourteen Hands high, a Sore in the middle of his Back; the said Horse being the Property of his Master. Whosoever shall take up the said Servant and Horse and return them to the said *Dodge* in *Wenham,* shall have Five Pounds old Tenor Reward for each, and all necessary Charges paid per me,
   Richard Dodge,   *Wenham, May* 30th 1751.
 N. B. All Persons whatsoever are hereby caution'd against concealing or carrying off said Negro and Horse, as they would avoid the Penalty of the Law.
The Boston Post-Boy, June 3, 1751. See *The Boston Post-Boy,* June 10, 1751.

RAN-away from his Master *Christopher Gardner,* of *Boston,* Mariner, on the 2d Instant, a white Servant Lad, about 16 Years of Age, well set, brown Complection, black Eyes, and round Face: Had on when he went away, a new light grey Forest Cloth Coat, with metal Buttons, a blue Jacket, Pair of Trousers, check Shirt, black Stockings, and new Shoes, and carried with him several other Sorts of Cloathing.
 Whoever shall take up said Runaway, and him safely convey to his said Master in *Boston* aforesaid, near Wind Mill Point, or Mr. *Joseph Chew* of said *Boston,* Merchant, shall have *Ten Pounds* old Tenor, and all necessary Charges paid.
 And all Masters of Vessels and others, are hereby caution'd against concealing or carrying off said Servant, on Penalty of the Law.
The Boston Gazette, or Weekly Journal, June 4, 1751.

RAN-away from his Master *Richard Dodge* of *Wenham*, in the County of *Essex*, on Wednesday last, A likely Negro Man-Servant, named *Hazard*, of a yellowish Complection, middling Stature, about 30 Years of Age, speaks pretty good English, well-set: Had on when he went away, a white cotton and linnen Shirt, a homespun Coat mix'd with a cast of Blue, tow Trowsers, blue worsted Stockings, a dark Wig, a Beaver Hat, and a Pair of Pumps, with large silver Buckles mark'd D. H. He has a Scar across the middle of each of his Legs of two Inches long, cut by an Ax.

Whosoever shall take up the said Servant and convey him to his Master in *Wenham*, or secure him in any of his Majesty's Goals, so as he may have him again, shall have EIGHT DOLLARS Reward, and all necessary Charges
     paid by me, *Richard Dodge,*
N. B. All Masters of Vessels and others are hereby caution'd against concealing or carrying off said Negro as they would avoid the Penalty of the Law.   *Wenham, June* 5. 1751.
The Boston Post-Boy, June 10, 1751. See *The Boston Post-Boy,* June 3, 1751.

Now in the custody of Thomas Smith, Sheriff of Cape May county, a runaway Negroe man, who goes by the name of Jupiter Hazard, is about 27 years of age, not very black, of a middle size, and well built: Had on when taken up, a flannel shirt, leather breeches, with a fob in the waistband, shoes and stockings, both very good, the stockings of a blue colour, bath metal buckles, a good felt hat, and worsted cap; he speaks English like a country born Negroe, who has liv'd some Time among the Dutch. He had a bundle with him, which contain'd two white shirts, a demity jacket and breeches, a white handkerchief, a linnen cap, and a pocket book, with four dollars in it, and a pair of silver knee buckles, mark'd N.S. He seems to have travell'd pretty much, for he gives a good account of Rhode Island, New York, Philadelphia, Shrewsbury, and other places; says his master's name is John Bannister, and lives at Piscataway, in Rhode Island Government.
The Pennsylvania Gazette, June 13, 1751.

R*AN away the 9th Instant, an* Irish *Maid Servant named* Grizel Sullivan, *about* 20 *Years of Age, pretty tall and a long Visage, a pale Complexion, has very much of the* Irish *Brogue. She had on went she went away, a dark strip'd blue and white* English *Cotton and Linen Gown, blue Bays Pettycoat, a pair of Men's dark grey Stockings, and carry'd away with her a homespun stript Gown, two speckled Aprons, several Shifts, &c. Whoever shall take up said Run away, and bring her to me the Subscriber, shall receive two Dollars, and have all necessary Charges paid.*
     James Gooch.

The Boston Evening-Post, June 17, 1751; June 24, 1751.

RAN-away from his Master *John Battle* of *Dedham*, on the first of this Instant, an Indian Man Servant named *Joshua Ephraim*, about 17 Years of Age, of a middling Stature, had on when he went away, a grey Jacket, and a pair of striped Breeches, grey yarn Stockings, and a pair of thin Shoes.

Whoever shall take up said Servant, and convey him to his said Master at *Dedham*, or to *James Leonard*'s at the Sign of the Lamb in *Boston*, shall have *Three Pounds* old Tenor, and all necessary Charges paid.

All Masters of Vessels and others are hereby cautioned against concealing of carrying off said Servant on Penalty of the Law.
Boston, July 3. 1751.
The Boston Weekly News-Letter, July 4, 1751. See *The Boston Gazette, or Weekly Journal*, November 7, 1752, and *The Boston Gazette, or Weekly Advertiser*, January 30, 1753.

L*Ately ran away from his Master*, Richard Hunt *of Boston, a Negro Man named* Bristol, *very tall, and goes lame of his right Knee. He had on when he went away, a stone grey Duroy Coat, a scarlet Jacket, double breasted, a pair of light coloured Kersey Breeches, a pair of Yarn Stockings, and carried with him a black Callimanco Jacket, and sundry other Things. Whoever shall take up the said Negro, and bring him to his said Master, shall have* Four Dollars *Reward, and necessary Charges paid.*
The Boston Evening-Post, July 8, 1751; July 15, 1751; July 29, 1751.

RAN away from his Master *Robert Cole* Boat-Builder, a young Man Servant, named *William Norman*, a tall slender Fellow, had on when he went away a short brown pea Jacket, and a striped under Jacket. Whoever shall take up said Run-away and convey him to his said Master, shall have five Shillings Lawful Money Reward, and all necessary
Charges paid by me,   *Robert Cole.*
All Masters of Vessels are hereby caution'd not to carry said Servant away, as they will avoid the Law provided in such Cases.
The Boston Post-Boy, July 15, 1751; July 22, 1751; July 29, 1751,

RAN-away last Night being the 15th of *July* from his Master, Capt. *Hugh Williams*, from on board the Ship *Eaton*, now lying in *Boston* Harbour, a young Man named *Henry Preston*, about 18 Years of Age, a short thick well sett Fellow, brown Complection, he has on Sailors Apparel: Whoever shall take up the abovesaid Run-away Servant, and convey him to his abovesaid Master, shall have *Ten Pounds* old Tenor Reward, and all necessary Charges paid. And all Masters of Vessels and others are hereby

caution'd against concealing or carrying off said Servant on Penalty of the Law.
The Boston Gazette, or Weekly Journal, July 16, 1751.

RAN-away from his Master *James Pitts* of *Boston,* on the 10th Instant, an Irish Man Servant named *Michael McNeily,* of a middling Stature, about 35 Years old, has a very light grey Eye, and a very down Look: Had on when he went away, a light colour'd Kersey Coat, blue Cloath Jacket and Breeches, with Mettel Buttons, the Jacket lin'd with red Shalloon; he was seen at the House of Mr. *Man* of *Wyentham,* on the 14th Instant, travelling towards *Rhode-Island.*

Whoever shall take up the said Run-away and commit him to any of his Majesty's Goals, shall receive *four Dollars* Reward upon Advice of the same, and all necessary Charges paid.
The Boston Gazette, or Weekly Journal, July 16, 1751.

RAN-away from Capt. *William Stook,* Commander of the Brigt. *William,* an Apprentice Lad, named *George Lorane,* about 20 Years of Age, sandy Complection, pock-broken, wears a black Wigg, is dress'd like a Sailor, and has on both a blue and red Jacket, and is about five Feet 7 Inches high.

Whoever shall take up said Servant, and bring or convey him to his said Master on Board said Brigt. in *Boston,* shall have *ten Pounds* old Tenor Reward, and all necessary Charges.

And all Masters of Vessels and others, are hereby caution'd against concealing or carrying off said Servant on Penalty of the Law.

If the said Servant will immediately return to his Duty, he will be kindly received, otherwise dealt with in due Severity.
The Boston Gazette, or Weekly Journal, July 16, 1751.

WHereas Mary, *the Wife of* James Sharp *of* Boston, *Shipwright, has heretofore run him considerably in Debt, and threatens to run him in Debt more and more;* These are therefor to caution and warn all Persons whatsoever against trusting the said *Mary* on my Account; for I do hereby declare, that I will not pay any Debt contracted by her from the Day of the Date hereof, as Witness my Hand.
   James Sharp.   Boston, *July* 15. 1751.
The Boston Evening-Post, July 29, 1751.

             NEW YORK, July 29.
Friday last one Jonathan Woodman, a Native of Narraganset, was committed to our Goal, for uttering Counterfeit Twenty Shilling Bills of this Colony, in Imitation of the Impression dated December 10,1737: He confesses he has passed ten of them: They are done on a Copper Plate, and

may be easily distinguished by those who know the Difference of Copper Plate from common Printing Letters: But that the unskill'd may not be imposed on, it is noted, that the two xxs. near the Arms, are not of an equal Size in the Counterfeit, but are in the True, and the Word N. YORK in the Flourish, has no Point between the N. and YORK, as in the true Bills; also the Word EBORAC in the Arms, is EBORAO in the Counterfeit, and the whole Bill appears more irregular than in the true Bills: He says, there are two others concerned with him, one of whom was in Town when he was taken up, but immediately made off, and went by the Name of Dr. Dunsten, whom he believes to be the Signer of the Bills, and it is probable he has passed more of them, these two being just on going home when apprehended. There was found on him a Number of New Hampshire Four Pound Bills, which are supposed to be counterfeit, and which the Man himself confesses he believes to be so. The other Person concerned, he says, he does not know, but as he heard from his Accomplice, from whom he says he had the Bills; but as he often prevaricates in his Stories, we must leave it to Time to unriddle this Mystery of Iniquity.

The Pennsylvania Gazette, August 1, 1751. See *The New-York Gazette Revived in the Weekly Post-Boy*, August 5, 1751, and *The Pennsylvania Gazette*, August 8, 1751.

NEW-YORK, August 5.

Tuesday last one *James Bill*, alias *Bradford*, a Narraganset Man, was apprehended near Second-River in *New-Jersey*, and committed to our Jail, as one of those concerned with *Jonathan Woodman*, mentioned in our last, in counterfeiting the Twenty Shilling Bills of Credit of this Province: The other called Doctor *Dunsten*, is not yet taken. 'Tis said, this *Bill* had been taken up and committed to Jail at *Hackinsack* a few Years ago, for uttering counterfeit *Jersey* Bills, from whence he made his Escape; but tis hoped he will now meet with the Reward of his Ingenuity. Their Trials we hear, are put off till next Term.

The New-York Gazette Revived in the Weekly Post-Boy, August 5, 1751. See *The Pennsylvania Gazette*, August 1, 1751, and *The Pennsylvania Gazette*, August 8, 1751.

NEW YORK, August 5.
Tuesday last one James Bill, alias Bradford, a Narraganset Man, was apprehended near Second River in N. Jersey, and committed to our Jail, as one of those concerned with Jonathan Woodman, mentioned in our last, in counterfeiting the Twenty Shilling Bills of Credit of this Province: The other called Dr. Dunsten, is not yet taken. 'Tis said, this Bill had been taken up and committed to Jail at Hackinsack a few Years ago. for uttering counterfeit Jersey Bills, from when he made his Escape; but hoped he will

now meet with the Reward of his Ingenuity. Their Trials we hear, are put off till the next Term.
The Pennsylvania Gazette, August 8, 1751. See *The Pennsylvania Gazette*, August 1, 1751, and *The New-York Gazette Revived in the Weekly Post-Boy*, August 5, 1751.

RAN-away from his Master Capt. *Job Prince* of *Boston*, a Negro Man named *Sipeo*, aged about 27 Years, speaks good English; he was bred from 10 Years in *Nantucket*, lived since at *Hingham*, and at *Weymouth* with Mr. *Jonathan White*: He had on when he went away, a white Flannel Jacket, a pair of wide Trowsers, check Shirt. Whoever shall apprehend said Negro and convey him to his Master, or to *John Kneeland*, jun. in *Boston*, shall have Ten Dollars Reward, and all necessary Charges
        paid by   *John Kneeland*, jun.
All Masters of Vessels & others, are hereby caution'd against concealing or carrying off said Servant on Penalty of the Law.
N. B. Said Negro has been gone about a Month.
The Boston Gazette, or Weekly Journal, August 20, 1751. See *The Boston Gazette, or Weekly Journal*, May 9, 1749, and *The Boston Post-Boy*, September 2, 1751.

RAN away from the Ship *Nancy, John Capithorn* Commander, now lying in the Harbour of *Boston*, the following Persons, *John Carew*, Mate, *Thomas Doyle, Maurice Newman* and *Richard Spirin*, Seamen. If they will return to their Duty on board said Ship in Two Days, they shall be kindly received, otherwise shall be deem'd as Deserters.
        John Capithorn.   *Boston, August* 24th. 1751.
The Boston Evening-Post, August 26, 1751.

RAN-away from his Master *John Judkins* of *Kingstown*, in the Province of *New Hampshire,* Blacksmith, the 13th Instant, a Servant Man, came from *Ireland*, called *Cornelius Lynes* he is about 16 Years of Age speaks pretty good English is about 4 Feet [sic] and a half high, round Shoulder'd: Had on when he went away a Bearskin Coat, the Body lin'd with red Bayes, and the Sleeves with Ozenbrigs, brown Mohair Buttons, a Homespun Jacket, black and stript, W[   ] woven, with flat Pewter Buttons on it, a Pair of Deerskin Breeches, Beveret Hat narrow brim'd, a Cotton and Linnen Shirt blew Stockings, a Pair of Pumps with Brass Buckles in them, a yellow Barcelona Handkerchief.
Whoever shall apprehend said Servant and convey him to his Master, shall have *Five Pounds* old Tenor Reward, and all necessary Charges paid.
All Masters of Vessels and others, are hereby caution'd against concealing or carrying off said Servant on Penalty of the Law.

The Boston Gazette, or Weekly Journal, August 27, 1751.

RAN-away from his Master Capt. *Job Prince*, of *Boston*, the latter End of *July* last, a Negro Man named *Scipio*, aged about 27 Years, speaks good English; he was bred from 10 Years old in *Nantucket*, has lived since at *Hingham*, and at *Weymouth* with Mr. *Jonathan White*: He had on when he went away a white Flannel Jacket, a Pair of wide Trowsers, a check Shirt.

Whoever shall apprehend said Negro. and convey him to his Master, or to *John Kneeland*, jun. in *Boston*, shall have TEN DOLLARS Reward, and all necessary Charges
           paid by   *John Kneeland*, jun.

All Masters of Vessels and others, are hereby cautioned against concealing or carrying off said Servant on Penalty of the Law.

The Boston Post-Boy, September 2, 1751; September 9, 1751; September 23, 1751. See *The Boston Gazette, or Weekly Journal*, May 9, 1749, and *The Boston Gazette, or Weekly Journal*, August 20, 1751.

RAN-away from his Master *Elisha Jones* of Weston, on the 2d of this Instant, a Negro Man named *Cesar*, about 30 Years old, a tall stout Fellow, and speaks good English. He had on a mix'd homespun Coat with brass Buttons, one Garlix and two tow Shirts, a pair of Leather Breeches, bluish mill'd Stockings, and a pair of double channel Pumps, and an old bever Hat.

Whoever shall take up said Servant, and convey him to his said Master, shall have a Reward of two Dollars, with necessary Charges
           paid, by   *Elisha Jones.*

The Boston Gazette, or Weekly Journal, September 10, 1751. See *The Boston Evening-Post*, September 16, 1751.

R*AN-away from his Master,* Elisha Jones *of* Weston, *near* Boston, *on the 2d of this Instant, a Negro Man named* Caesar, *about 30 Years old, a tall stout Fellow, and speaks good* English: *He had on a mix'd homespun Coat with Brass Buttons, one Garlix and two tow Shirts, a pair of Leather Breeches, bluish mill'd Stockings, and a pair of double channel Pumps, and an old Bever Hat.*

Whoever shall take up said Servant, and convey him to his said Master, shall have a Reward of Four *Dollars, with necessary Charges*
           paid, by   Elisha Jones.

N. B. *He is supposed to be gone towards* Connecticut *or* New-York.

The Boston Evening-Post, September 16, 1751. See *The Boston Gazette, or Weekly Journal*, September 10, 1751.

RAN-away on the 12th Instant, from Capt. *Partrick Montgomery*, Commander of the Ship *Peggy*, two white Men Servants; the one named *Robert Scott*, about 22 Years of Age, red Hair, pock-broken, a well set Fellow in Sailors Dress. The other named *William Dawson*, about 21 Years of Age, dark swarthy Complection; dark Hair, pretty tall Fellow in Sailors Dress: Whoever shall take up the said Servants, and convey them to their abovesaid Master on board the abovesaid Ship in *Boston*, shall have *Fifty Pounds* old Tenor, or *Twenty five* Pounds old Tenor for each or either of them, and all necessary Charges paid. And all Masters of Vessels and others, are hereby caution'd against concealing or carrying off said Servants on Penalty of the Law.
    The Boston Gazette, or Weekly Journal, September 17, 1751; September 24, 1751; October 1, 1751.

RAN-away from Mr. *Francis Shaw* of *Boston*, this Morning, being the 17th of September, an Irish Maid Servant, named *Rose Anna M'Gown*, about 20 Years of Age, middle Stature, well set, black Hair, of a fresh Complection; she took with her three Stuff Gowns, one blue, another green, and the other Birds Eye. Whoever shall take up the said Run-away Servant Maid, and bring her to her Master aforesaid, shall have *Two Dollars* Reward, and all necessary Charges paid. All Masters of Vessels & others, are hereby warned of entertaining or carrying her off in Peril of the Law.
    The Boston Gazette, or Weekly Journal, September 17, 1751.

                                              Chester, 4th *Day of June*, 1751.
WHEREAS *Mary* the Wife of *Henry Herring*, has riffled his House, and has absconded from her said Husband: This is to forbid all Persons not to Entertain her the said *Mary*, or Credit her for Money or Goods or any other thing upon the Penalty of losing their Debt.
                Henry Herring.
    The Boston Post-Boy, September 23, 1751.

On Monday the 2d *Day of this Instant Sept. made his Escape from* Wm. Deare Esq; *High Sheriff of the County of* Middlesex.
ONE Newal Coomes, about 27 Years of Age, a short slim Fellow, had on, an old red great Coat, a blue Broad-cloth Coat lin'd with red and trim'd with a very light blue with a Boot Cuff, a Scarlet Jacket full trim'd without Sleeves, a Pair of old green Breeches with blue Knee-bands, Worsted Stockings, a Pair of Pumps, an English-Caster Hat half worn, he has a down Look and when he talks or laughs one Corner of his upper Lip turns up, and is an New-Englandman, pretends to be Doctor, and has with him a Pair of crooked probing Cizars, a Doctor's Book, and Certificate of his taking the Benefit of the Insolvent Act of Assembly with him, but was not cleared by

the Court, he often changes his Names in calling himself *Thomas Newal Coomes*, and sometimes *Doctor Pidgeon*. Any Person taking up said Fellow and securing him so that the Sheriff may have him again or brings him to *Perth-Amboy*, shall have Three Pounds Reward, and all reasonable Charges paid by   *John Waller*,   Dept. Sheriff.

The New-York Evening Post, September 23, 1751; September 30, 1751; October 7, 1751; October 28, 1751; November 4, 1751; November 18, 1751; November 25, 1751; December 2, 1751; December 16, 1751; December 23, 1751. The last seven ads begin *"ON Monday the 2d Day of September last,"*

R*AN away from his Master,* Benjamin Renken *of* Boston, *Taylor, on Tuesday Morning last, an* Irish *Lad named* James Hatherton, *but calls himself* James Smith. *He is well set, and of a midling Stature, has large Legs, and speaks pretty good* English. *Carried away with him a Gun, under Pretence of going to train. Had on when he went away, a Beaver Hat newly drest, and a worsted Cap, a blue Coat lined with Red, trim'd with yellow Metal Buttons, dark coloured Jacket and Breeches, with yellow Metal Buttons, the Jacket was double breasted, blue Yarn Rib'd Stockings, peeked toed turn'd Pumps, with white Metal Buckles.*

Whoever shall apprehend said Servant, and bring or convey him to his said Master in Boston, *near the Draw-Bridge, shall have Four Dollars Reward, and all necessary Charges*
paid by me   Benjamin Renken.
All Masters of Vessels and others, are hereby cautioned not to conceal, entertain or carry off the said Servant, as they would avoid the Penalty of the Law in that Case made and provided. Boston,   October 4. 1751.

The Boston Evening-Post, October 7, 1751; October 14, 1751; October 21, 1751.

R*UN away on Sabbath-Day the* 29th *of* September *last, from* Ebenezer Ellinwood *of* Beverly *Ferry, a Negro Man named* Caesar, *who has gone in the Ferry-Boat there for about two Years past: He is about thirty two Years old, is near Six Feet high, speaks good* English, *goes something stooping, and one of his Legs is much larger than the other. He had on when he went away, a whitish Cloth Coat, a Castor Hat, Worstead Cap, and black Yarn Stockings.*

Whoever shall take him up, and convey him to his said Master, shall have SIX DOLLARS *Reward, and all necessary Charges*
paid by me   Ebenezer Ellinwood. Beverly, October 3. 1751.
The Boston Evening-Post, October 7, 1751; October 14, 1751; October 21, 1751.

RAN away from the Ship *Wilmington, John Penny* Commander, lying in *Piscataqua* River, the following Seamen, viz. *John Knowles, John Bargary, James Brown, Francis Winship, Henry Neal, John Loverage, George Flint,* and *Nathaniel Dunn,* the last Fellow carried away with him a Yawl of about 17 Feet long.
    Whoever shall apprehend said Runaways, and bring them on board said Ship, or secure them in any of his Majesty's Goals, and give Intelligence thereof, shall be well rewarded for their Trouble, and necessary Charges paid by   *John Penny.*
The Boston Evening-Post, October 14, 1751; October 21, 1751; October 28, 1751; November 4. 1751.

WHereas Sarah, *the Wife on me the Subscriber,* Increase Billing *of* Groton in New-London *County, in the Colony of* Connecticut *in* New-England, *on the* 10*th Day of* September *Instant, eloped from me her lawful Husband, and refuses to return to me and my Family, neglecting all conjugal and parental Duty;* These are therefore to warn all Persons against delivering to the said *Sarah,* any Monies, Wares, or Merchandizes upon my Credit; and I do hereby Certify all Merchants, trading Men, and all other Persons whatsoever, that I will not pay any Thing she shall take on my Credit, from this Day.   *Increase Billing.*   *Groton, September* 20th A. D. 1751.
    The Boston Evening-Post, October 28, 1751; November 4, 1751.

RAN-away from the Ship *William, Andrew Dewar* Commander, now lying at *Hubbard's* Wharf in *Boston,* two Seamen, *viz Samson Winn* and *Peter Murray,* the former had on when he ran away, a blue Bonnet and a Cap, a short blue Jacket and Trowsers, aged about 22 Years, born at *North-Yarmouth.* The latter had on when he went away, a blue Jacket and green Waistcoat, with white Metal Buttons, a Hat, Wig and Trowzers, about 5 Feet high, aged about 20 Years, of dark Complexion, born in *North-Britain.* Whoever apprehends either of the above-named Mariners, and brings them to the said Ship, shall receive *Twenty Pounds* old Tenor, and all necessary Expences, of   *Andrew Dewar.*   *Boston, November* 13. 1751.
    The Boston Weekly News-Letter, November 14, 1751; November 21, 1751.

RAN-away on Saturday last at 2 o'Clock in the Afternoon, from the Subscriber, Two indented Servants; the one named *John Sanders*, about twenty Years of Age, was born in *London*, and pretends to be a Caulker by Trade, has four Years to serve; he is of slim Stature, thin faced, had had the Small-pox, his Nose sharp, had a Piece of Skin broke off the Top of it, of a sandy Complection, and speaks thro' his Nose: Had on when he went away a dark-coloured coarse Kersey Jacket, with a white cotton Vest under it laced, a Pair of light coloured Duroy Breeches with Metal Buttons, check'd Shirt, a Pair of good Shoes, and has with him a mill'd Bonnet.

The other is a Lad of about seventeen Years of Age, named *William Holmes*, was born in *London*, he can shave and dress a Wigg well, has had the Small-pox, he is pretty well set, light Haired, large grey Eyes, has lost some of his fore Teeth, walks slouchingly and treads his Toes inwards, on strict search is somewhat pot-bellied: Had on when he went away, a blue Half-thick Jacket, with a white cotton Vest under it, Breeches of the same, good Shoes or Pumps, with brass Buckles; they may have stolen Money and other Things and may change their Apparel.

It is likely they will pass for Sailors.

Whoever takes up said Servants, or either of them, and secures them that they may be had, shall have for their Reward TEN POUNDS old Tenor for each, and reasonable Charges
     paid by John Avery.   Boston, December 2. 1751.

N. B. All Masters of Vessels and others are hereby caution'd against entertaining, concealing or carrying off said Servants, as they would avoid the Penalty of the Law.

The Boston Post-Boy, December 2, 1751.

RAN-away from his Master *David Felton* of *Marlborough*, the 28th of *Nov.* last, a Servant Boy named *John Campbell*, about 18 Years of Age, he wears a Cap, is full fac'd, and about 5 Feet 7 Inches high; had on a brown Coat, striped Wastcoat and Leather Breeches, has took with him a Coat, Waistcoat, and a Pair of Leather Breeches, a Check Shirt, three Pair of Stockings, &c. Whoever shall apprehend the abovesaid Servant, and convey him to his Master, shall have *Two Dollars* Reward, and all necessary Charges paid. And all Masters of Vessels and others, are hereby caution'd against concealing or carrying off said Servant on Penalty of the Law.
                Marlborough, Dec. 2. 1741. [sic]

The Boston Gazette, or Weekly Journal, December 10, 1751.

BRoke out of His Majesty's Goal in *Boston*, on Saturday Morning the 7th Instant, *Ebenezer Richardson* of *Woburn*; he is a well sett Man, had on a light colour'd Great Coat, and a red Worsted Cap: Whoever shall apprehend him and bring him to said Goal, or give Information to the Sheriff of the County of *Suffolk*, so that he may be retaken, shall have *Twenty Dollars* Reward.

The Boston Gazette, or Weekly Journal, December 10, 1751.

F*Riday Night last absconded from his Master* William Knox, *of Boston, Mariner, a Man Servant named* Edward Hamilton, *about 22 Years of Age, of middle Stature; he had on a* Spanish *Grego, a dark coloured Ratteen Pea*

Jacket, with round Metal Buttons, and Breeches of the same, with flat Metal Buttons, a strip'd Flannel Jacket and check'd Shirt, a pair of Fishing Boots, and Worsted ribb'd Stockings, a Beaver Hat and a red Worsted Cap: He is a Joiner by Trade, but has been about a Year at Sea.

Whoever shall take up said Servant, and convey him to his said Master, shall have Four Dollars Reward, and all necessary Charges paid. And all Masters of Vessels and others, are hereby cautioned not to conceal, entertain or carry of the said Servant, as they would avoid the Penalty of the Law. Boston, December 30. 1751.

The Boston Evening-Post, December 30, 1751; January 6, 1752; January 13, 1752.

RAN away from his Master *Jonathan Green* of *Stoneham*, on the 30th of *Nov.* last, a Man Servant named *John Curtis,* a lusty thick well sett Fellow, about 16 Years of Age, of fresh Complection, a thick stubbed Nose, grey Eyes, of a malicious Cast; he carried with him a new Felt Hat, and a striped worsted Cap, a black and blue mixt colour'd double breasted Jacket, and another Jacket striped with blue and white, two white Shirts, a Pair of Cloth Breeches, blue Stockings and Calf Skin Shoes.

Whoever shall take up the said Servant, and convey him to his said Master in *Stoneham*, shall have *Five Shillings and four Pence* Lawful Money Reward, paid by Jonathan Green

The Boston Gazette, or Weekly Journal, December 31, 1751.

1752

RAN-away from his Master Mr. *Micah Havens* of *Framingham*, on the 1st of *Dec.* last, an Indian Man Servant, named *Jonath. Pequeen*, about 18 Years of Age, a well sett Fellow, had on when he went away, long black Hair, an old Beaver Hatt, homespun Coat of a brown Colour with mettle Buttons, a Fustian Coat trim'd with the same, a pair of Leather Breeches, yarn Stockings, and a pair of double Channel Pumps: He speaks good English. Whoever shall take up said Run-away, and convey him to his abovesaid Master, shall have *Two Dollars* Reward.

The Boston Gazette, or Weekly Journal, January 7, 1752.

RAN-away from his Master *Josiah [   ]* of Watertown, the 13th of December last, a Molatto colour'd Fellow, named *Edward Stanly*, about 18 Years of Age: He had on when he went away, a brown all wooll Waistcoat, check woolen Shirt, Leather Breeches, blew yarn Stockings, thick Shoes, & brass Buckles, wears a Cap, and a Pair of Pot-hooks about his Neck. Whoever shall take up said Run-away and convey him to his said Master, shall have one Dollar Reward and all necessary Charges paid. And all

Masters of Vessels and others are caution'd against concealing or carrying off said Servant, on Penalty of the Law.
The Boston Gazette, or Weekly Journal, January 7, 1752.

BOSTON.

Last Week *Ann Trotter* and *Mary Clary*, were committed to Goal in this Town, by Mr. Justice *Phillips*, for stealing Goods out of several Shops. They are both *Irish* Women, and came here some months ago from Philadelphia; and it plainly appears, that they have been very diligent *in the Way of their Business*, having collected together a great Variety of Shop-Goods, some of which have been owned, and others remain in the Justice's Hands, ready for Claimers. They dress'd in the height of the Mode, which screen'd them from Suspicion, and have approved themselves Adepts in their Profession, tho' they happen to be detected.
The Boston Evening-Post, January 27, 1752.

RAN-away last Night from his Master John Goldsmith, Perriwig-Maker, near Clark's Wharf, in Boston, a Servant Lad named Charles Short, aged 16 Years, and says he was born in Carolina; a short thick well set Boy, something Pock-broken, had on when he went away a thick Bear-skin Coat, Chocolate colour'd, yarn Stockings, Leather Breeches, check'd Shirt, a Cotton Handkerchief, about his Neck, a Felt Hat, his Head close shav'd, wears sometimes a Cap or Wigg, a blue double-breasted Jacket with Brass-Buttons.

Whoever will take up said Servant and convey him to his said Master shall have THREE DOLLARS Reward, & all necessary Charges paid.

All Masters of Vessels and others are hereby caution'd against concealing or carrying off said Servant, as they would avoid the Penalty of the Law.
Dated, *Boston, February* 6. 1752.
The Boston Weekly News-Letter, February 6, 1752. See *The Boston Gazette, or Weekly Journal*, July 21, 1752.

WHereas Mary, *the Wife of me the Subscriber, of the Town of* Roxbury, *has eloped from me and refuses to come and live with me as my Wife, and had also run me in Debt;*
THESE are therefore to forbid all Persons to entertain the said *Mary* or trust her on my Account, for I hereby declare I will not pay and Debt she shall contract from the Date hereof. As Witness my Hand.
John Lowder, Dated, *February* 6. 1752.
The Boston Weekly News-Letter, February 6, 1752.

WHereas my Wife Martha Hamlin, *has for some Time past withdrawn herself from my House and Company, and refuses to dwell with me:* THESE are therefore to desire all and every Person or Person not to entertain her or trust her on my Account, expecting Pay from he, for I hereby declare that I will not pay any Debt or Debts that she shall hereafter contract on my Account for Entertainment or otherwise. Dated at *Barnstable,* the 16th Day of *January,* 1752.
Shubal Hamlin, jun.
The Boston Weekly News-Letter, March 5, 1752.

R*AN away from his Master, Mr.* Nathaniel Cuningham, *on the* 11*th of this Instant, an* Irish *Man Servant nam'd* William Burk, *about* 25 *Years of Age, of a brown Complexion, about five Feet eight Inches high; had on a Castor Hat, and an old brown Wig, a blue Kersey Jacket with Brass Buttons, with the Duke of* Cumberland*'s Head,* 4 *Brass Buttons on the Top of the Jacket, a red Coat with white Metal Buttons, a Cotten and Linen Shirt, a pair of Ribb'd Yarn Stockings, and a pair of square Brass Buckles in his Shoes.*

Any Person who shall take up said Servant, and bring him to his said Master, at his Farm in Cambridge, *near the Sign of the Duke of* Cumberland*'s Head, shall have have all their Charges paid, and four Dollars Reward.*

All Masters of Vessels and others, are hereby cautioned not to conceal, entertain, or carry off the said Servant, as they would avoid the Penalty of the Law. Boston, March 14. 1752.
The Boston Evening-Post, March 16, 1752; March 23, 1752; March 30, 1752.

R*AN away on the* 11*th Instant, at Night, from his Master,* Anthony Brackett *of* Boston, *an* English *Man Servant, nam'd* Andrew Griffith, *about five Feet nine Inches high, and had on when he went away, a Pee Jacket, single breasted, of a Cloth Colour, with a strip'd Homespun one Ditto underneath it, a Homespun Shirt, with one Garlix Ditto, Yarn Stockings, Leather Breeches and Trowsers, round toed Shoes, and large Brass Buckles. Hath on a Cap and Hat, is mark'd with the Small Pox, and also mark'd on the right Hand with the Letters* A. G. *in iddian* [sic] *Ink.*

Whoever shall take up said Runaway and him safely convey to his Master in School Street, shall have Ten Pounds, *old Tenor Reward, and all necessary Charges paid.*

All Masters of Vessels and others, are hereby cautioned not to conceal, entertain or carry off the said Servant, as they would avoid the Penalty of the Law.

N. B. *The same Fellow hath tended the said* Brackett's *Stable for this Year or Fifteen Months past.*

Boston, March 13, 1752.
The Boston Evening-Post, March 16, 1752; March 23, 1752; March 30, 1752. See *Boston Evening-Post*, January 1, 1753, and the *Boston Evening-Post*, April 29, 1754.

DEserted from the Schooner Industry, in *Boston*, on the 14th Instant, *William Darby*, Commander, the three following Sailors, *viz.*

Thomas Mahony, of a sandy Complection, freckled Face, five Feet eight Inches high, and had on a light colour'd Pea Jacket, new Oznabrigs Trowsers, and a pair of Pumps.

Daniel Darling, about five Feet high, had on a light colour'd Pea Jacket, and a pair of Trowsers, new Boots, and a blue double mill'd Cap.

George Stevens, about five Feet six Inches high, had on a lightish Cloth Coat, new Oznabrigs Trowsers, old Hat & Wigg; pale Complection.

Whoever shall take up said Deserters, and bring them to the said Commander, on Board the aforesaid Schooner, or to Mr. *Benjamin Brandon*, Merchant, on Dock-Square, for each or either, and all necessary Charges paid.

And all Masters of Vessels and others, are hereby caution'd against concealing or carrying off said Deserters, on Penalty of the Law.

The Boston Gazette, or Weekly Journal, March 17, 1752.

DEserted from the Ship *John* and *William James Clarke* Commander, about the middle of February last, a Sailor, *John Harthorn*, about 27 Years of Age, he is short and thick, with a smooth Face, Sailors Dress.

Also Ran-away from the said Capt. *Clark*, about two Months since, a Servant Lad, named *Alexander Nelson*, about 17 Years of Age, well set Fellow, smooth fac'd, and went away in Sailors Dress.

Likewise Ran-away from said Capt. *Clark*, on the 2d Instant, another Servant Lad, named *John English*, about 17 Years of Age, he is also well set smooth'd fac'd, and in Sailors Dress.

Whoever shall take up and bring to the said Capt. *Clark* in Boston, the said Deserter and Servants, shall have Three Dollars Reward, and all necessary Charges paid, for each or either.

And all Masters of Vessels and others are caution'd against concealing of said Deserter and Servants in Penalty of the Law.

The Boston Gazette, or Weekly Journal, March 17, 1752.

DEserted from the Ship *Bassnet, Andrew Lessley*, Master, the 11th Instant, a Servant Man named *John Davis*, the 11th Instant, a Welchman born, and commonly goes by the Name of *Shonen*, he is aged about 19 or 20 Years, and is about 5 Feet 5 Inches high, with his own Hair, and speaks but indifferent English: He had on a blue Jacket and Canvas Trowsers, when he went away.

Whoever shall apprehend the said Servant, and deliver him on board the said Ship *Bassnet* at *Clark's* Wharf, or to *Charles Apthorp*, Esq; shall have TWENTY POUNDS old Tenor Reward
                paid them by me   *Andrew Lessley.*

All Masters of Vessels and others are hereby cautioned, that if they secret of detain the said Servant, they shall be prosecuted to the utmost of the Law.   *Boston, March* 16*th.* 1752.   *A. L.*
The Boston Weekly News-Letter, March 19, 1752; March 27, 1752; April 2, 1752.

RAN-away from *Amos Seavey* of *Rye*, in *New-Hampshire*, an Irish Servant, about 16 or 17 Years o Age, named *David Casey*, is a slim Lad, thin favour'd, his Speech something broken, he had with him a light blue Drugget Coat lin'd, black Buttons on the left side, two blue Jackets, two pair of Breeches, one pair light Kersey, the other grey homespun, two Shirts, one check woollen the other strip'd Linnen, two pair of Stockings, one grey the other blue, a felt Hat almost new, wears a striped Cap, a stampt India Handkerchief red and yellow. Whoever will take up said Runaway and convey him to his said Master, or secure him, they shall FOUR DOLLARS, Reward, and all Charges paid.
      Amos Seavey.   *March* 23. 1752.
The Boston Post-Boy, March 30, 1752; April 6, 1752; April 13, 1752.

RAn-away from Mr. *Daniel Chickering* of *Dedham*, the 28th Instant, an indebted Servant, named *John Ryan*, about 21 Years of Age, short of Stature, fresh colour'd, dark Eyes, his Head lately shav'd: He had on a Bearskin Coat with flat mettle Buttons, blue Drugget Jacket, an old pair of Leather Breeches, yarn Stockings, thick Shoes. Whoever shall take up said Runaway, and him convey to his said Master, or have him in Boston Goal, shall have *Ten Pounds* Old Tenor Reward,
        paid by,   *Daniel Chickering.*
The Boston Gazette, or Weekly Journal, April 21, 1752.

                                        Nantucket, April 8; 1752.
      RAN-away lately from this Island,—*John Barlo*, an English-man, about 20 Years of Age, Servant to Capt. *Paul Paddock*: He is of middling Stature, pale Countenance, and has had the Small-Pox; had on a green Jacket, lin'd with *English* Blanketing, Kersey-Breeches, a check'd Shirt; and Shoes with *English* Soles. Ran-away also, *Thomas Robertson*, an English-Man, Servant to *Elizabeth Swain*, of said Island.—He had on a grey cloth Jacket, and a striped one under it; and a

check'd Cotton Shirt: He is short of Stature and Pock-broken, about 26 Years of Age.—Five POUNDS *old Tenor* Reward, and all necessary Charges will be paid, for taking each or either of them up and conveying them to *Nantucket*, by the said Master, and Mistress,
   The Boston Weekly News-Letter, April 23, 1752; May 7, 1752; May 14, 1752.

Province of *New-Hampshire*.
ON Saturday Night the 18th Instant one *Timothy Johnson*, a Prisoner for Debt in his Majesty's Goal in said Province, by the Assistance of some Persons without, broke said Goal, and escaped out of close Confinement: He is a tall slim Man, of a fair Complexion, about 28 Years of Age, and is a Joyner by Trade. Whoever will cause him to be apprehended, and sent to me, or bring him within my Precinct, or inform where he is, if within the same, so that I or any Officer of mine may take him, he shall have TWENTY-FIVE Pounds, old Tenor, Reward, and all necessary
   Charges paid. *Thomas Packer*, Sheriff.   *April 20th.* 1752.
   The Boston Post-Boy, April 27, 1752; May 4, 1752; May 11, 1752.

Westerly, May 7th, 1752.
ON the 17th of *April* last past at Night *John Walker*, an hired Servant to *Nathaniel Crandall* of *Stonington*, run from his said Master, and stole from him the following Things, viz. one new Duroy Coat of a brown colour, lin'd with home-made worsted Cloth, trim'd with a hair-cover'd Button, also a Jacket of the same Duroy something faded, lin'd with a Red Shalloon, one striped flannel double-breasted Waistcoat, one pair of Stockings of a blewish colour, one check red and white silk Handkerchief, a Cutlass and red Belt, a pair of blue and white mix'd cloth Breeches, a new linnen home-made Shirt, a Calf skin, and a quantity of Sole-Leather: His own Cloathing was a white fustian Coat something soiled, a red flower'd knit Jacket, a large Felt Hat, a pair of Leather Breeches, with a cross placket, white Stockings, and turn'd Pumps: He is of a middling Stature, a light Complection, a likely Person, a red Mark or Scar on his lower Eye-lid; he said he was a Weaver by Trade, and pretends to be a Doctor, he is near 40 Years of Age, appearing to be an Irishman: Whoever shall take up and secure said Run-away, so as his Master may have him, shall receive as a Reward FORTY POUNDS, old Tenor *Rhode-Island* Currency, and
   necessary Charges from   *Nathanael Crandell.*
   The Boston Post-Boy, May 11, 1752; May 18, 1752; May 25, 1752.

D*Eserted on the* 18*th Instant, from the Snow* Molly, Eleazer Dothy *Master, now in the Harbour of* Boston, *the two following Seamen, viz.* Oliver Oldham *and* James Finney. *If they will return to their Duty on board the*

said Snow, they shall be kindly received, but if not, they will be deemed Deserters. Boston, May 25. 1752.
The Boston Evening-Post, May 25, 1752.

WHereas *Prudence* the Wife of *John Marston* of *Hampton* in the Province of *New-Hampshire*, Yeoman, behaves imprudently and spends my Money without my Knowledge, and runs me in Debt: This is therefore to warn all Persons not to trust said *Prudence* on my Account, for I will not pay any Debts by her so contracted after the Date hereof. Witness my Hand at *Hampton*, June 16th 1752.
    John Marston.
The Boston Post-Boy, June 22, 1752; June 29, 1752; July 6, 1752.

ON *the 7th Instant, ran away from his Master* Timothy Perkins *of* Middletown, *a Negro Man named* Pompey, *about* 30 *Years, of midling Stature and strait lim'd: He speaks good* English, *has had the Small Pox, and hath lost one of his little Fingers by means of a Sore; he carried away with him a homespun light coloured Drugget Fly Coat, a white Linen Jacket, a black homespun Jacket,* 2 *Woollen Shirts,* 1 *Linen Shirt and a pair of all Wooll homespun Breeches. Whoever will stop and secure the said Negro, so that his said Master may have him again, shall receive a Reward of Six Pounds, old Tenor, and all charges*
    paid by   Timothy Perkins. Middleton,   June 18. 1752.
The Boston Evening-Post, July 6, 1752.

RUN-away the 11th Instant from his Master Jeremiah Brown of South-Kingstown, in this Colony, a Mustee Fellow, named Simon, aged about 20 Years, something short of Stature, and round favoured. Had on when he went away, an old blue Coat, striped Flannel Jacket, pretty good Hat, black Wig, Linen Trowsers, white Yarn Stockings, and an old Pair of mended Shoes.
    Whoever shall take up said Run-away, and deliver him to his said Master, or secure him, so that he may be had again, shall have Twenty Pounds old Tenor Reward, and all necessary Charges
    paid by   Jeremiah Brown.
The Boston Post-Boy, July 6, 1752; July 13, 1752; July 20, 1752.

R*AN away from the Ship* Elizabeth, Edward Cahill *Master, from* London, June 18th 29th *and* 30th. Mark Cone, William Hull *and* William Humperson, *Mariners. They are desired forthwith to return to their Duty on board the said Ship, otherwise they well be deemed Deserters.*
    Boston, July 11th. 1752.
The Boston Evening-Post, July 13, 1752.

RAN-away from his Master *John Goldsmith* of *Boston*, Peruke-Maker, a Servant Boy named *Charles Short*; had on when he went away, a check'd Shirt, black Leather Breeches, yarn Stockings, doubled soal'd Shoes, of swarthy Complexion, and a little pitted with the Small-pox. Whoever shall take up said Runaway, and him safely convey to his Master opposite to the Queen's Head on *Scarlet's* Wharf, shall be well reward, & necessary Charges paid.

And all Masters of Vessels and others are hereby caution'd against concealing or carrying off said Servant on Penalty of the Law.

The Boston Gazette, or Weekly Journal, July 21, 1752. See *The Boston Weekly News-Letter,* February 6, 1752.

R*UN away last Night from* Thomas Brownell, *of Portsmouth, a Mustee Fellow named* Jack, *about 23 Years of Age, is a short thick Fellow, and had on when he went away, a half worn Bever Hat, a Linen Cap, a dark coloured Fly Coat, chequer'd like Diamonds, with Metal Buttons, a striped Flannel Jacket, a white Tow Shirt, striped Tow Trowsers, a pair of dark colour'd Yarn, and a pair pale blue Worsted Stockings, and a pair of Pumps.*

Whoever takes up the said Fellow, and delivers him to his Master, or secures him, so that he may be had again, shall have THIRTY POUNDS, *old Tenor, Reward, and all necessary Charges paid.*

by THOMAS BROWNELL.

All Masters of Vessels and others, are hereby forbid carrying off or concealing said Fellow, as they would avoid the Penalty of the Law.

The Boston Evening-Post, July 27, 1752; August 3, 1752.

R*AN away from Doctor* William Rand *of* Boston, *on the third Day of this Instant* July, *an indented* German *Servant Man, named* (in German) Jean Jacob Ducard, *but in his Indenture is called* George Ducart; *about* 22 *Years old, is well set, of a Brown Complexion, and has brown Hair. He took with him a Suit of blue Cloaths, with Metal Buttons, a Pair of Leather Breeches, Ozenbrigs Frock and Trowsers, and Yarn Stockings. He also took from his Master, a Silver hilted Sword, a Cross-cut Saw, and a fine* French *Gun.*

Whoever shall take up the said Servant, and return him to his said Master, or secure him in Goal, so that he may be had again, shall have Three Pistoles *Reward, aid by the Printer or this Paper; or return'd to* Boston *to his Master,* Three Pistoles *Reward, and all necessary Charges paid.*

N. B. *He is supposed to be gone to* Pennsylvania. Boston, July 27. 1752.

The Boston Evening-Post, July 27, 1752; August 3, 1752; August 10, 1752. See *New-York Gazette Revived in the Weekly Post-Boy,* September 25, 1752.

RAN away from *Benj. Bird*, Esq; of *Dorchester* on the 28th of May last, a Servant Man named *George Michael Hobbatt*, he is a short black Man with black Hair; had on when he went away, a white Woollen or check'd Shirt, a blew & white strip'd Jacket, & white Trousers.

Whoever shall take up said Servant and return him to his said Master again, shall have 20*S*. Lawful Money Reward, and all necessary Charges paid, by *Benj. Bird.*

And all Masters of Vessels and others, are hereby caution'd against concealing or carrying off said Servant on Penalty of the Law.

The Boston Gazette, or Weekly Journal, July 28, 1752; August 4, 1752; August 18, 1752.

RAN-away from Mr. *John Tudor* of *Boston*, Baker, on the 29th Instant, an Irish Servant Lad named *Jeremiah Donevan*, a fair Skin lusty Boy for his Age, which is about 17 Years; he took with him a Beaver Hat, half worn; a whiteish Coat almost new, a Jacket much the same with brass Buttons, thin Breeches, and a pair of Trousers, a pair of Yarn, and a pair of worsted Stockings, round-toed Shoes, with large brass Buckles, has no sign on the Small-Pox.

Whoever takes up the said Fellow, and will bring him to his said Master, shall have THREE DOLLARS Reward, and all necessary Charges paid by *John Tudor.*

All Masters of Vessels and others, are hereby forbid carrying off, or concealing said Fellow, as they would avoid the Penalty of the Law.

The Boston Weekly News-Letter, July 30, 1752; August 6, 1752; August 13, 1752.

RAN-away on the 28th of last Month from his Master, *Israel Hearsey* of *Boston*, Wharfinger, an Irish Servant Lad, named *Henry Jones*, about 18 Years of Age, of middle Stature, and has a sharp Nose: He had on a good Hat, a white Cloth Coat, blew Jacket without Lining, Buck Skin Breeches, worsted Cap, light colour'd Stockings, and a Pair of Pumps; and took with him some other Cloathing.

Whoever takes up said Runaway, and delivers him to his said Master, shall have *Five Pounds* old Tenor Reward, and all necessary Charges paid by *Israel Hearsy.*

All Masters of Vessels and others are herby forbid carrying off or concealing said Servant, as they would avoid the Penalty of the Law.

Boston, August 1*st*. 1752.

The Boston Gazette, or Weekly Journal, August 4, 1752; August 18, 1752.

R*AN away from his Master* Samuel Allison *of* Boston, *Truckman, on the 9th Instant, an* Irish *Man Servant named* James King, *about 24 Years old, a stout well set surly looking Fellow, had on when he went away, a Felt Hat, brown Waistcoat, and strip'd blue and white Shirt, blue Breeches, and grey Yarn Hose, and wears a Wig or Cap. Whoever shall take up the said Servant, and bring him to his said Master in* Boston *aforesaid, or confine him in one of his Majesty's Goals, and advise his Master of it, shall have* Six Dollars *Reward, and all necessary Charges paid. All Masters of Vessels and others, are hereby cautioned not to conceal, entertain or carry off the said Run-away as they would avoid the Penalty of the Law.*
Boston, August 17. 1752.
The Boston Evening-Post, August 17, 1752; August 24, 1752; August 31, 1752.

ON the 3d Day of this Instant absconded from their Masters, Two Servant Boys, Joseph Page *and* Moses George: *The said* Page, *Servant to* Timothy Greenleaf, *Blacksmith, of* Newbury, *is about 19 Years old; had on a dark Bearskin out-side Jacket with flat metal Buttons, grey Stockings, brown Camblet Jacket, Wool-Hat and Leather Breeches, was of a dark Complection, with black Eyes.—The said* George, *Servant to* Joshua Mitchel *of said Town, Shipwright, is about 20 Years old, had on a light-coloured Rateen Jacket, with yellow flower'd Buttons, blue Breeches, Wool-Hat, striped Shirt, light-coloured Stockings; he is of a light Complection, something tall and light Eyes.—Whoever shall take up the said Servants, or either of them, and convey them to their Masters shall have* TWO DOLLARS *for each, and all necessary Charges paid. And all Masters of Vessels and others are hereby cautioned not to conceal, entertain or carry off the said Servants as they would avoid the Penalty of the Law.*
Newbury, Aug. 14, 1752. Province of *New-Hampshire.*
The Boston Post-Boy, August 17, 1752; August 24, 1752; August 31, 1752.

*WH*ereas Susannah Hidden, *the lawful Wife of me the Subscriber,* Jonathan Hidden, *hath for several Years past, eloped and absconded from me, and refuses to live and behave as a Wife ought to do towards her Husband, and gives me great Reason that she intends to run me in Debt, and bring me into Difficulty, &c.* These are therefore to Notify all Persons whatever, not to trust or give Credit to the said *Susannah Hidden* on any Account, for I will not pay any Debt she shall contract in any Way whatever.
Jonathan Hidden.
June 17. A. D. 1752.
The Boston Evening-Post, August 24, 1752; August 31, 1752.

RAN-away from his Master *Robert Hendrey* of *Boston,* Horse-Shoer, An Irish Servant Man, named *John Glyen,* about 24 or 15 Years of Age, about five Feet eight Inches high, pretty much pitted with the Small-Pox, and of a pale Complection, a strait, well-built Fellow, and good Presence: He had on when he went away, a Suit of dark blue German Searge, with Lining the same Colour; the Coat had blue mohair Buttons, the Jacket flat Brass Buttons, with five Hearts and other carved Work on the Front: A Pair of blue yarn Stockings, a Pair of double sol'd Shoes with large carv'd brass Buckles, almost Square; a white Shirt, a handsome black cut Wig, a felt Hat, half wore, very large. He is a White-smith by Trade, or properly a Lock-smith; but can shooe Horses very well.—Whoever shall take up said Run-away, and deliver or convey him to his said Master, living at the Mill Bridge in *Boston,* shall have FOUR DOLLARS; and all necessary Charges

paid by me   *Robert Hendry.*

It is humbly required of my Brother Trades-Men, to have a sharp Look-out, for I judge he will change his Name: He is suppos'd to be done towards *Connecticut,* in the Way to *New-York*; but designs to work for some Time back in the Country:—He was seen going that Way.—All Masters of Vessels and others, are hereby caution'd against concealing or carrying off said Servant, as they would avoid being prosecuted in the severest Manner the Law will admit of.

The Boston Post-Boy, August 24, 1752; August 31, 1752; September 18, 1752.

R*UN away from Doctor* WILLIAM RAND *of* Boston, *on the third Day of* July *last, an indented* German *Servant Man, named* (in German) Jean Jacob Ducard, *but in his Indenture is called* George Ducart; *about 22 Years old, is well set, of a Brown Complexion, and has brown Hair. He took with him a Suit of blue Cloaths, with Metal Buttons, a Pair of Leather Breeches,* Ozenbrigs *Frock and Trowsers, and Yarn Stockings. He also took from his Master, a Silver hilted Sword, a Cross-cut Saw, and a fine* French *Gun. He is supposed to be gone towards* Philadelphia, *but 'tis said, has been lately seen in* New-York, *in the Employ of a Butcher.*

Whoever takes up said Servant, and secures him in Goal, shall have Three Pounds Reward, *paid by the Printer or this Paper; or return'd to* Boston *to his Master,* Three Pistoles *Reward, and all reasonable Charges.*

New-York Gazette Revived in the Weekly Post-Boy, September 25, 1752; October 2, 1752. See The *Boston Evening-Post*, July 27, 1752.

R*AN away from his Master, Mr.* Abraham Gale, *of* Weston, *in the County of* Middlesex, *Blacksmith, on the 29th Instant, an Irish Man Servant named* Robert Gordon, *about 17 Years old, a short spry Fellow, about four Feet* *and an half high.* [sic] *Had on when he went away, a blue Jacket, a white Woollen Shirt and Trowsers, grey Yarn Stockings, and a pair of Pumps patch'd at the Sides, and ty'd with Strings, and an old Bever Hat; he has short light Hair, and a red Scar in the upper Part of his Forehead. Whoever shall take up the said Servant, and bring him to his said Master in* Weston *aforesaid, shall have* Five Pounds *old Tenor Reward, and all necessary Charges paid. All Masters of Vessels and others, are hereby cautioned not to conceal, entertain or carry off the said Run-away, as they would avoid the Penalty of the Law.*

The Boston Evening-Post, October 2, 1752; October 9, 1752; October 16, 1752.

WHereas *Ann* the Wife of the Subscriber Joseph Brownell, has rifled his House, and has absconded from her said Husband: These are to forbid all Persons not to entertain her the said Ann, or credit her for Money or Good or any thing upon the Penalty of losing their Debt.

   Joseph Brownell.   Dartmouth, October 16. 1752.
The Boston Post-Boy, October 23, 1752; November 6, 1752.

RAn-away from his Master *John Battle* of *Dedham*, on the 4th Instant, an Indian Lad, named *Joshua Ephraim*, about 19 Years of Age, strait and tall, with long black Hair: had on a dark Coat & jacket, old Leather Breeches, yarn Stockings, old Shoes, and an old Felt Hat.

Also, Ranaway on the 5th Instant, from his Master *Daniel Chickering* of *Dedham* aforesaid, an Indian Servant Lad, named *John Wombscom*, about 17 Years of Age, a slim tall Lad, wears a Cap, Sky colour'd Coat & Jacket, with Pewter Buttons, Fustian Breeches, a pair of Trowsers, yarn Stockings, single sole Shoes, brass Buckles.

Whoever shall take up said Runaways, or either of them, and convey them to their Masters, shall have *Three Pounds* old Tenor for each of either of them, and all necessary Charges paid.

And all Masters of Vessels and others are hereby caution'd against concealing or carrying off said Servants on Penalty of the Law.

              Dedham, Nov. 6th 1752.
The Boston Gazette, or Weekly Journal, November 7, 1752. See *The Boston Weekly News-Letter*, July 4, 1751, and *The Boston Gazette, or Weekly Advertiser*, January 30, 1753, for Ephraim. See *The Boston Gazette, or Weekly Advertiser*, July 10, 1753, for Wombscomb/Wamscom.

        Boston, Novemb. 13th 1752.
RAN-away on Thursday last, from his Master *James Fairservice* of *Boston*, a Servant Lad, named *Wm. Thomas*, about 17 Years old, small of his Age,

short black Hair, black Eyes (he often bungs [*sic*] the same to the Grief and Damage of his Master,) was bred a Chimney-sweeper, and had been here employ'd in that Service, and went away in and with his Sweeper's Gears. Had on two dark Jackets pretty sutty; chews Tobacco plentifully, and chuses the best sort. Whosoever shall take him up & bring him to his Master, shall have two Dollars, and necessary Charges.

All Masters of Vessel are caution'd against carrying off; for he cost me 250 Pound old Tenor 6 Months ago.
    James Fairservice.
The Boston Gazette, or Weekly Advertiser, November 14, 1752.

RAN-away from his Master *John Graton* of Roxbury, on the 12th Instant, an Irish Man Servant, named *William Hagin*, about 21 Years of Age, well set, and of a fair Complection, speaks good English, wears a brown Wigg, had on a broad Cloth Coat, of a Cloth colour, Cloth Breeches, blue rib'd Stockings, and a white Shirt.

Whoever shall take up said Run-away, and him convey to his said Master, shall have *Five Pounds* old Tenor, and all necessary Charges paid.

And all Masters of Vessels and others are hereby caution'd against concealing or carrying off said Servant on Penalty of the Law.
The Boston Gazette, or Weekly Advertiser, November 14, 1752.

RUN-away on the 12th Instant, from the Sloop *Aurora, John Davis* Master, *William Hardnot*, alias *William Arnold*, an indented Servant, about five Feet three Inches high, pale Complection, thirty Years old, walks lame, carried off with him, a white knap'd Coat, a blue and red Wastecoat, a pair of new Pumps: Has a Cut on his great Toe on the right Foot. Whoever secures the said Servant, and brings him to Capt. *Isaac Freeman* in *Boston*, shall have *Ten Pounds*, old Tenor Reward, and reasonable Charges
   paid by *Isaac Freeman.*
N. B. All Masters of Vessels and others are hereby forbid carrying him off or concealing said Runaway, as they would avoid the Penalty of the Law.   *Boston, November* 18*th.* 1752.

The Boston Weekly News-Letter, November 17, 1752; November 23, 1752; November 30, 1752; *The Boston Evening-Post*, November 20, 1752; November 27, 1752; December 4, 1752; *The Boston Post-Boy*, November 27, 1752; December 4, 1752. Minor differences between the papers.

RAN away from the Bunch of Grapes in Kingstreet, *Nov.* 16th, an indented Man-Servant named *William Miles*, he is a thin Fellow about five Feet high, of a pale Complexion: Had on a Chocolate colour'd Cloth Coat, Frock Fashion, a strip'd Flannel Waistcoat, a white Shirt and Muslin Neckcloth, a

red worsted Cap, a pair of new Pumps, and brown and white worsted Stockings. Whoever shall take up said Runaway and convey him to the *Bunch of Grapes* Tavern in *Boston*, shall have *Ten Pounds*, Old Tenor, Reward, and necessary Charges paid.
  The Boston Evening-Post, November 20, 1752; November 27, 1752; December 4, 1752.

WHereas Rebecca Harris *the Wife of me the Subscriber, living at* Norton, *has again continued unlawfully to absent herself from me and out Family, and has sundry Effects to a considerable Value, and may endeavour to run me in Debt:*
  These are therefore to caution all Persons whatsoever, not to entertain her, upon Penalty of the Law, and not to trust or give Credit to her the said *Rebecca* upon my Account: for I will not pay any Debt contracted by her from the Date hereof.   As witness my Hand,
           Joseph Harris.   *November* 20th 1753.
  The Boston Gazette, or, Weekly Advertiser, November 27, 1752. See *The Boston Weekly News-Letter*, March 8, 1750.

RAN away from the Bunch of Grapes in Kingstreet, *Nov.* 16th, an Indented Man Servant named *William Miles*, he is a thin Fellow about five Feet high, of a pale Complexion: Had on a Chocolate colour'd Cloth Coat, Fock Fashin, a strip'd Flannel Waistcoat, a white Shirt and Muslin Neckcloth, a red worsted Cap, a pair of new Pumps, and brown and white worsted Stockings. Whoever shall take up said Runaway, and convey him to the *Bunch of Grapes* Tavern in *Boston*, shall have *Ten Pounds*, Old Tenor, Reward, and necessary Charges paid.
  The Boston Evening-Post, November 27, 1752; December 4, 1752.

R*AN away from his Master Mr.* Joseph Reynolds, *of* Bristol, *on the* 20*th Instant, a Molatto Boy, about* 15 *Years of Age, he had on when he went away, a homespun Jacket of a light Colour, with a mixture of black, a pair of Linen Breeches, a Felt Hat, a Linen Shirt and a pair of dark grey Stockings. Whoever shall take up said Runaway, and bring him to Mr.* Jeremiah Belknap, *of* Boston, *or to his said Master in* Bristol, *shall have* Five Pounds, *old Tenor Reward, and all necessary Charges paid.*
                      Bristol, November 26, 1752.
  The Boston Evening-Post, December 4, 1752; December 11, 1752; December 18, 1752.

R*UN away about three Weeks ago from* Daniel Comstock, *of* Norwalk, *in* Connecticut, *a Negro Fellow named* Dick, *aged about* 20 *Years, of a very black Complexion and slim; he talks good English, and can both read and*

write; he had on when he went away, a homespun Coat and Jacket of a dark Colour, Leather Breeches, a holland Shirt, a new Felt Hat, and white woollen Stockings: Whoever takes up said Negro, and returns him to his Master, shall have a reasonable Reward, and all necessary Charges,
    paid by Daniel Comstock.
The New-York Gazette, Revived in the Weekly Post-Boy, December 4, 1752; December 11, 1752.

R*AN* away from his Master *John McKnown*, Master of the Sloop Endeavour, now lying at *Boston*, on the 2d Instant, an Irish Man Servant named *Charles Horan*, above 18 Years of Age, a low thick well set Fellow, smooth'd Fac'd, speaks poor English, wears an old brown Wigg, and has short pale Hair, had on an old brown Pea Jacket, white Flannel under Jacket, dark small check'd Shirt, wide Oznabrigs Trowsers, Scarlet Breeches, new Shoes with brass Buckles, and an old Felt Hat. Whoever shall take up said Run-away, and him carry to his said Master, or to *Joshua Winslow,* Esq; or Mr. *William Heslop*, Merchant, near the Quaker's Meeting-House, shall have *Five Pounds* old Tenor, and all necessary Charges paid. And all Master of Vessels and others are hereby caution'd against concealing or carrying off said Servant on Penalty of the Law.
              Boston, December 4th 1752.
The Boston Gazette, Or Weekly Journal, December 12, 1752; December 19, 1752.

R*AN away from his Master* William Downe *of* Boston, *Esq; on the* 18*th Instant, a Negro Man Servant named* London, *about Thirty five Years of Age; he had on when he went away, a dark colour'd Bearskin Coat, a strip'd homespun Jacket, he wears a Cap, but went off without a Hat. Whoever shall take up the said Runaway, and convey his to his said Master, shall have* Two Dollars *Reward, and all necessary Charges*
    paid, by William Downe.
All Masters of Vessels and others are hereby cautioned against concealing or carrying off said Servant on Penalty of the Law.
              Boston, 25th December 1752.
Boston Evening-Post, December 25, 1753; January 1, 1753.

DESERTED from the Ship *Knowles, Benjamin Hollowell*, Master, *John Pearson*, a Mariner on board said Ship: This is to inform him, That if he returns to his Duty, he shall be kindley received, otherwise he will be deemed a Deserter.
    B. H.   *Boston, Decemb.* 27. 1753.
The Boston Weekly News-Letter, December 28, 1752.

1753

RAN away on the 27th Instant, at Night, from his Master, **Anthony Brackett** *of* Boston, an English *Man Servant, named* Andrew Griffith, *about five Feet nine Inches high, and had on when he went away, a Pee Jacket, singlebreasted, of a Cloth Colour, with a strip'd Homespun one Ditto underneath it, a Homespun Shirt, with one Garlix Ditto, Yarn Stockings, and light Cloth Breeches and Trowsers, round toed Shoes, and large Brass Buckles. Hath on a Cap, Hat and Wig, is mark'd with the Small Pox, and also mark'd on the right Hand with the Letters* A. G. *in indian Ink. Hath also with him a close bodied Duroy Coat and a Bever Hat. Whoever shall take up the said Runaway, and convey him to his said Master, in School Street, shall have* Ten Pounds, *old Tenor, Reward, and all necessary Charges paid. All Masters of Vessels and others, are hereby cautioned not to conceal, entertain or carry off the said Runaway, as they would avoid the Penalty of the Law.*

N. B. *The same Fellow hath tended the said* Brackett's *Stable for this Year or Fifteen Months past.* Boston, December 28, 1752.

The Boston Evening-Post, January 1, 1753. See *The Boston Evening-Post*, March 16, 1752, and *The Boston Evening-Post*, April 29, 1754.

RAN away from his Master, Henderson Inches *of* Boston, *on the 27th of December past, an* Irish *Servant Lad named* Martin Landers, *about* 20 *Years of Age, of a light Complexion, and is about* 5 *Feet* 9 *Inches in Stature. He had on when he went away, a brown Wig, a brown coloured Bever Cloth Coat, with a Velvet Cap and Brass Buttons, a green Waistcoat with Brass Buttons, a check'd Shirt, Leather Breeches, blue Stockings, and a new pair of Shoes. Whoever shall apprehend said Runaway, and safety convey him to his said Master in* Boston, *shall have* Three Dollars *Reward, and all necessary Charges paid.*

All Masters of Vessels and others, are hereby cautioned not to conceal, entertain or carry off the said Run-away, as they would avoid the Penalty of the Law.

The Boston Evening-Post, January 1, 1753. See *The Boston Gazette, or Weekly Journal*, June 26, 1750.

BROKE out of His Majesty's Goal in Boston, *on the Night of the Twelfth of* January *Instant,* Frederick Sturmey, Jeremiah Sullivan, Richard Carty, *and* Samuel Nott. *Whoever shall apprehend the aforesaid Criminals, or either of them, and cause them to be delivered to the Sheriff of the County, or his Prison-keeper, that such Prisoners he or they may be re-committed, then*

such Person or Persons who shall so take them, shall be generously rewarded.
The Boston Evening-Post, January 15, 1753; January 22, 1753.

WHEREAS a Woman named Mary Jones, *is lately arrived from the Colony of* Rhode-Island, *and assumes to call her self the Name of* Mary Smith, *pretending to be the Wife of me the Subscriber, which I utterly deny:*
These are therefore to caution all Persons from entertaining, trusting or crediting the said *Mary Jones* on my Account, for I declare I will not pay any Thing she shall be credited with on my Account.
    Wm. Smith.   January 23, 1753.
The Boston Gazette, or Weekly Advertiser, January 23, 1753.

RAN-away from his Master *John Battle* of *Dedham,* on the 4th of *November* last, an Indian Lad, named *Joshua Ephraim,* about 19 Years of Age, strait and tall, with long black Hair: Had on a dark Coat & Jacket, old Leather Breeches, yarn Stockings, old Shoes, and an old Felt Hat: Whoever shall take up said Runaway, and convey him to his Master, shall have *Four Dollars* Reward, and all necessary Charges paid.
And all Masters of Vessels and others, are caution'd against concealing or carrying off said Servant on Penalty of the Law.
            Dedham, January 29th 1752. [sic]
The Boston Gazette, or Weekly Advertiser, January 30, 1753; February 6, 1753. See *The Boston Weekly News-Letter,* July 4, 1751, and *The Boston Gazette, or Weekly Journal,* November 7, 1752.

WHereas a Portugueze *Boy* 12 *Years of Age, with a blue Jacket, worsted Cap and Woollen Shirt, came on Board the Snow* Rebecca, William Clark *Master, lying at the lower End of the Long Wharf. Any Person claiming the said Boy, may have him again by enquiring on board of said Snow, and paying the Charges.*
The Boston Evening-Post, February 5, 1753.

RAN away from his Master *Daniel Oliver,* of *Boston,* Peruke-maker, on the 18th Instant, a Servant Boy named *John Maylam,* about 19 Years of Age, he wears a Wigg, and has a Scar on the upper Part of his Forehead; had on a Fly Cloth colour'd Coat and Breeches, a blew Jacket, and grey rib'd Stockings. Whoever shall apprehend the abovesaid Servant, and convey him to his Master in Kingstreet, *Boston,* shall have *Ten Pounds,* old Tenor, Reward, and all necessary Charges paid
    Daniel Oliver.   *Boston, Febr.* 20th. 1753.
And all Masters of Vessels and others are hereby caution'd against concealing or carrying off said Servant on Penalty of the Law.

The Boston Gazette, or Weekly Advertiser, February 20, 1753; February 27, 1753; March 6, 1753; March 13, 1753; March 20, 1753. See *The Boston Post-Boy*, March 12, 1753.

RAN-away on the 18th Instant, from his Master *William Murry*, Peruke-maker in King-street, *Boston*, an Irish Man Servant named *David Fitz Garrald*: Had on when he went away a white Bearskin Coat, Green Wastecoat, white Plush Breeches, gray yarn Stockings, and a whitish Hatt much wore it the Powder; he is a short thick Fellow, has sore Eyes, and short thick Leggs. Whoever will take up said Run-away, and bring him to his said Master, shall have Ten Pounds old Tenor Reward, and all necessary Charges paid, by   *William Murray.*   Boston, *February* 20th 1753.

And all Masters of Vessels and others are hereby caution'd against concealing or carrying off said Servant on Penalty of the Law.

The Boston Gazette, or Weekly Advertiser, February 20, 1753; February 27, 1753; March 6, 1753; March 13, 1753; March 20, 1753.

S*TOLE from* William Burley *of Newmarket, in* New-Hampshire, *on the 15th Day of* February *last, a large yellow Mare, with a black Main and Tail, and a black List on her Back, could trot and pace, her near hind Foot white, and a few white Hairs in her Forehead: the Person that Stole her was a small black hair'd, thick spoken mean looking Taylor, and had on red Breeches, a Jacket and a blue Great Coat. Any Person that will apprehend said Thief and Mare, so that the said Owner may have them, shall have* Twenty Pounds, *old Tenor Reward, and all necessary Charges paid, or otherwise any Person restoring said Mare to said Owner, shall have* Ten Pounds *old Tenor paid by* William Burley.

The Boston Evening-Post, March 19, 1753.

RAN-away from his Master *Daniel Oliver*, of *Boston*, Peruke-maker, on the 18th of last Month, a Servant Lad named *John Maylam*, about Nineteen Years of Age; He wears a Wig, and has a Scar on the upper Part of his Forehead; had on a Fly Cloth colour'd Coat and Breeches, a blew Jacket, and grey ribb'd Stockings.

Whoever shall apprehend the abovesaid Servant, and bring him to his abovesaid Master in King-Street, *Boston*, shall receive TWENTY DOLLARS for their Trouble.   *Daniel Oliver.*

All Masters of Vessels and others are hereby caution'd against concealing or carrying off said Servant, as they would avoid the Penalty of the Law.

N. B. He is an artful Fellow, & may deceive those that apprehend him, but may be discover'd, upon search, by a Scar upon one of his Thighs, occasion'd by the Bite of a Dog.—He has been lately seen travelling the Southern Road from *Boston.*

The Boston Post-Boy, March 12, 1753; March 19, 1753; March 26, 1753; April 8, 1753. See *The Boston Gazette, or Weekly Advertiser,* February 20, 1753,

RAN away from his Master *Alexander Hunt,* Ship-builder, on the 27th of this Instant, a Scotch Servant Man named *Alexander Duncan,* about 23 Years of Age, a tall lusty Fellow, dark Complection; Had on when he went away, a dark German Serge Coat and Breeches, with Mettal Buttons, dark Sagathee Jacket, a Woollen Shirt, Yarn Stockings, turn'd Pumps, Brass Buckles, and Wears a Wigg.

Whoever shall apprehend the said Servant, and bring him to his said Master, in *Boston,* shall have Three DOLLARS Reward, and all necessary Charges paid.

All Masters of Vessels and others, are hereby caution'd not to harbour entertain, or conceal the said Servant, as they would avoid the Penalty of the Law.   *Boston, March* 28. 1753.

The Boston Weekly News-Letter, April 5, 1753; April 12, 1753.

RAN-away on the 19th ult. from her Master, the Rev. *Joseph Champney* of *Beverly,* a Servant Girl, named *Jane Blake,* aged 14 Years, of a dark Complection, resembling a Molatto, of small stature, short curl'd Hair: Had on when she went away, a strip'd Woolen short Gown, and Petticoat, likewise a short blue Riding-hood, a Pair of new Shoes, &c.

Whoever shall take up said Run away and bring her to her said Master in *Beverly,* or to Mr. ―― *Clark* of *Boston,* Taylor, shall be well Rewarded, and all necessary Charges paid.

The Boston Gazette, or Weekly Advertiser, May 1, 1753.

R*AN away from his Master, Capt.* Timothy McDaniel *of Boston, a Negro Man named* Homer, *aged about thirty Years, a slim Fellow about five Feet eight Inches high, speaks very broken* English; *had on when he went away a blue Sailors Jacket, red Breeches and a white Waistcoat, two odd Buckles in his Shoes, grey Yarn Stockings, and a red or blue Cap. The said Negro is very much pitted with the Small Pox. Whoever shall take up said Negro and bring him to his said Master's House at* New-Boston, *shall be well rewarded for their Trouble*

                   by me   Elizabeth McDaniel.   Boston, May 28. 1753.

The Boston Evening-Post, June 4, 1753.

WHEREAS Margaret Farrington, *the Wife of the Subscriber, having long absented herself from me, and hath run me in Debt, and to prevent her from*

doing the like any more, these are to Notify all Persons not to trust her, or give her any Credit on my Account; for I will not pay any Debt that she shall contract whatsoever.
            his
        John X Farrington.
         Mark
            Lynn, June 4, 1753.
 The Boston Evening-Post, June 11, 1753.

R*AN* away the 19th Instant from *Isaac Fowler*, of *North Kingstown*, a dark Mustee Fellow, named *Caesar* about 21 Years of Age, well-set, has a thick short Neck, and a down Look. Had on when he went away, an old Felt Hat, a striped Flannel Jacket, and a Full-cloath dark grey Jacket, Check Shirt, Leather Breeches, white Thread Stockings, and old Shoes; took with him a Frock and Trowsers. Whoever takes up and secures said Fellow, so that his Master may have him again, shall have TWENTY POUNDS Reward, and all necessary Charges, paid by *Isaac Fowler.*
 The Boston Post-Boy, June 18, 1753; June 25, 1753.

R*AN away from the Snow St.* Thomas, *at* Marblehead, *on the 29th of* June *past, a* Jersey *Lad named* Joseph Pikoa, *of about* 17 *Years of Age, he is short and well set, speaks broken* English, *round favour'd and of a pale Complection; had on a brown Pea Jacket, a red Cap, a Cotton strip'd or a Linen Check Shirt. Whosoever shall bring the said Lad to me at* Marblehead, *or Mr.* John Spooner *at* Boston, *shall be well rewarded for taking him up, and have all necessary*
    Charges paid. George St. Roche.
 The Boston Evening-Post, July 9, 1753; July 16, 1753; July 23, 1753.

RAN-away from his Master *Daniel Chickering* of *Dedham* on the 7th Instant, an Indian Man Servant, named *John Wamscom*, about 18 Years of Age, a slim Fellow, with short black Hair; had on when he went away, a Felt Hat, a Leather Sheepskin Jacket, white tow Shirt, white tow Trowsers yarn Stocking, [*sic*] but no Shoes. Whoever shall take up said Runaway and bring or safely convey to his said Master, shall have *four Dollars* Reward, and all necessary Charges paid. And all Masters of Vessels and others are hereby caution'd against concealing or carrying off said Servant, on Penalty of the Law.
 The Boston Gazette, or Weekly Advertiser, July 10, 1753. See *The Boston Gazette, or Weekly Journal*, November 7, 1752, for Wamscom/Wombscom.

RAN-away on the 3d Instant from the Ship *Mary*, now lying at *Falmouth*, in *Casco-Bay*, **Wm.** *Deverson*, Commander; the three following Seamen, viz.

    Robert Tomson, a well set Man, fresh colour'd, and wears a black Wigg.

    John Curling, a thin fac'd Man, of middle Stature, and wears a Wigg.

    Robert Spight, a middle size Man, pitted with the Small Pox, and wears his own black Hair.

    Whoever will secure them in any of his Majesty's Goals, shall be satisfied for their Trouble by *Samuel Hughes*, in Queenstreet, *Boston*, or if they will return to their Duty, they shall be kindly received

            by   *William Deverson.*

    The Boston Gazette, or Weekly Advertiser, July 24, 1753; July 31, 1753; August 7, 1753.

R*AN away the* 14*th Instant, from his Master* Eleazer Tyng, *Esq: of* Dunstable, *a Negro Man named* Pompey, *about* 40 *Years of Age, midling Stature, heavy eyed, one of his Fingers is reckoned to be so crooked that he cannot hold it out streight; he carried away with him a Homspun grey Coat with yellow Metal Buttons,* 2 *Jackets, one a scarlet Cloth with a pink coloured Lining, and white Metal Buttons, the other blue* German *Serge, Buttons of the same Colour, red Shalloon Lining, light blue* German *Serge Breeches, white Metal Buttons, a white Linen and a Woollen Shirt, grey Yarn Stockings, a Pair of Pumps, one Felt and one Bever Hat, and a white Linen Cap. He can play on a Violin. Whoever shall take up said Runaway, and convey him to his said Master at* Dunstable, *or to Mess.* Alford *and* Tyng, *Merchants at* Boston, *shall receive* Five Dollars *as a Reward, and all necessary Charges paid.* Eleazer Tyng.

    The Boston Evening-Post, July 30, 1753; August 6, 1753; August 13, 1753.

Stolen from the subscriber on Wednesday the 25th inst. at Night, by Robert Wall, *out of the house of Mrs.* Mary Braddick, *in* New-London, *in the colony of* Connecticut, *about* Fourteen Hundred Pistoles, *(chiefly* single Pistoles*), about* One Hundred and Fifty Pounds *old tenor, which he soon parted with for a horse; one pair of blue silk stockings, one pair of snuff colour'd ditto, and several pair of thread ones; a gold lace, which he ripp'd off a waistcoat, several shirts, and other things.*

    The said Robert Wall *was born in* Brunswick *county in* Virginia, *is about 21 years old, a tall spare well made man, about six foot high, of a fair complexion grey eyes, dark brown hair, wore a silver laced hat, a dark cut pigtail wig, a cloth colour'd fustian coat, very short, with velvet cuffs and collar, breeches of the same with strings, a scarlet Vest, a light colour'd*

duffle great coat, a pair of fine ribb'd worsted stockings to roll over the knee, no boots, a pair of small silver buckles in his Shoes, had a large dark bay horse, with a new english saddle and bridle; took with him a silver watch, which he had on tryal from a gentleman in New-London: No doubt he will change his name, part with the horse he had, and shift his cloaths as soon as possible. Any person or persons securing the said THIEF, so that the Money, &c. may be return'd to the subscriber, in New-London, and he brought to justice shall have a reward of Thirty Pistoles, *and if he is taken, and any of the money &c. made away with, a Reward in proportion, though not less than* Ten Pistoles, *and all reasonable charges,*
    paid by me, EDWARD LANGFORD.
           New-London, July 27, 1753.
 The New-York Mercury, July 30, 1753; August 6, 1753. See *The Maryland Gazette,* August 23, 1753.

RAN-away from his Master *John Crosley,* Rope-maker, in *Boston,* on the 4th Instant, a Servant Lad, named *Edward Hunt,* about 17 Years of Age, a well set sturdy Lad; had on a blue Kersey Jacket, a dark striped homespun jacket, a pair of Leather Breeches, Trousers, a worsted Cap, and Castor Hat; and took with him three white Shirts, two pair of yarn Stockings. Whoever shall take up said Runaway, and him safely convey to his said Master, shall have *five Pounds* old Tenor, Reward, and all necessary Charges paid. And all Masters of Vessels are caution'd against concealing or carrying off said Servant, on Penalty of the Law.   *Boston, August* 7. 1753.
 The Boston Gazette, or Weekly Advertiser, August 7, 1753.

RAN-away on the 5th Instant, from on Board the Ship Spencer, *Thomas Shaftoe,* Master, lying at *Hubbard's* Wharffe, suppos'd to have taken away a Long Boost that can row with six Oars, scrap'd and painted black and yellow, the three following Servants to said Ship, viz.
 Charles Watkinson, of low Stature, brown Complection, aged about 20 Years, in Seaman's Dress, wears a Cap or Wigg.
 Anthony Bell, aged about 16 Years, middle Stature, & pretty small, brown Complection, in Seaman's Dress, wears a Cap or Wig.
 William Rutherford, aged about 15 Years, pretty much pitted with the Small Pox, brown Complection, low and well made, wearing a Cap or Wigg, in Seaman's Dress.
 Whoever shall apprehend the said Runaways, and them bring or safely convey to Mr. *John Jones* Merchant in *Boston,* shall have five *Pounds* old Tenor Reward for each or either of them, and all necessary Charges paid.
 And all Masters of Vessels and others are hereby caution'd against concealing or carrying off said Servants on Penalty of the Law.
            Boston, August 7. 1753.

The Boston Gazette, or Weekly Advertiser, August 7, 1753; August 14, 1753.

RAN *away from his Master* Charles Hight *of* Portsmouth, *Sail-Maker, a Servant Lad named* Sargent Jackson, *about Nineteen Years of Age, of Middle Stature, dark Complexion and black Eyes; had on when he went away, a blue Jacket, check Shirt, and a large pair of Trowsers, and wears a Cap or Wig. Whoever shall apprehend the said Runaway, and convey him to his said Master at* Portsmouth, *or secure him in any of his Majesty's Goals, shall have* Ten Pounds, *old Tenor Reward, and all necessary Charges paid by* Charles Hight.
ALSO ran away from him, one *William Pittman*, a Servant to Capt. *Luke Mills* of *Portsmouth,* about the same Stature, pretty much Pock broken, and the Bridge of his Nose broke: He was born in *England.* Whoever shall take him up, and convey him to his said Master, shall have the same Reward as for the above-mentioned Servant.
 N. B. All Masters of Vessels or others are hereby cautioned against concealing or carrying off said Servants, as they would avoid the Penalty of the Law. *Portsmouth, August* 14. 1753.
 The Boston Evening-Post, August 20, 1753.

THIRTY PISTOLES REWARD.
STOLEN from the Subscriber, on Wednesday the 25th Instant, at Night, by *Robert Wall*, out of the House of Mrs. *Mary Braddick*, in *New London*, in the Colony of *Connecticut*, about *Fourteen Hundred Pistoles* (chiefly *single Pistoles*), about One Hundred and Fifty Pounds old Tenor, which he soon parted with for a Horse; one Pair of blue Silk Stockings, one Pair of Snuff colour'd ditto, and several Pair of Thread Ones; a Gold Lace, which he ripp'd off a Waistcoat, several Shirts, and other Things.
 The said *Robert Wall* was born in *Brunswick* County in *Virginia*, is about 21 Years old, a tall spare well made Man, about 6 Feet high, of a fair Complexion, grey Eyes, dark brown Hair, wore a Silver laced Hat, a dark cut Pigtail Wig, a Cloth colour'd Fustian Coat, very short, with Velvet Cuffs and Collar, Breeches of the same with Strings, a Scarlet Vest, a light colour'd Duffell Great Coat, a Pair of fine ribb'd Worsted Stockings to roll over the Knee, no Boots, a Pair of small silver Buckles in his Shoes, had a large Dark Bay Horse, with a new *English* Saddle and Bridle; took with him a Silver Watch, which he had on Trial from a Gentleman in *New London*. No doubt he will change his Name, part with the Horse he had, and shift his Cloaths as soon as possible.
 Any Person or Persons securing the said Thief, so that the Money, &c. may be return'd to the Subscriber, in *New London*, and he brought to Justice, shall have a Reward of Thirty Pistoles; and if he is taken, and any

of the Money &c. made away with, a Reward in Proportion, though not less than Ten Pistoles, and all reasonable Charges, paid by me
    EDWARD LANGFORD. New London, *July* 27, 1753.
 The Maryland Gazette, August 23, 1753. See *The New-York Mercury*, July 30, 1753.

R*AN away from the Snow* Thomas *and* Martha, Samuel Partridge *Master, on the third Instant, a Seaman named* John M'Grough, *and if he will return within five Days, he shall be kindly received, otherwise he will be deemed a Deserter.* Boston, September 13. 1753.
 The Boston Evening-Post, September 17, 1752.

R**An-away from his Master Capt.** *Benjamin Reed*, of *Lexington*, on the 14th of this Instant *September*, a Negro Man Servant, named *Sambo*, but calls himself *Samuel Hank's*, and pretends to be a Doctor, about 30 Years of Age, of a middling Stature, speaks good English. Had on when he went away, a brown homespud [*sic*] Coat with brass Buttons, a brown Holland Jacket, new Leather Breeches, a pair of blue clouded seam's Stockings, a new course Linnen Shirt, and a Holland one, Trowsers, and an old Castor Hat: has lost some of his fore Teeth. He carry'd with him a Bible, with (*Samuel Reed*) wrote in it, with some other Books.
 Whoever shall take up said Runaway Servant, and convey him to his abovesaid Master in *Lexington*, shall have *Four Dollars* Reward, and all necessary Charges paid.
 And all Masters of Vessels and others are hereby caution'd against concealing or carrying off said Servant on Penalty of the Law.
           Lexington, September 17. 1753.
 The Boston Gazette, or Weekly Advertiser, September 18, 1753.

R**AN-away from his Master on the 7th of** *October* Instant, a Negro Man called *Hazzard*, who formerly belonged to Deacon *Benjamin Wadsworth*, a well set Fellow, speaks good English, and can read: Had on when he went away, a Lead colour'd Pea Jacket, and linen Trowsers, and is known to have been Lurking about *Millton*, the first Week of his Absence, he was at several Huskings, he has a scar on one of his Arms, where he was Inoculated for the Small-Pox, he keeps in the Woods in the Day Time.
 Whoever shall secure said Run-away, and inform the printer hereof, so that his Master may have him again, shall have *five Pounds* old Tenor Reward, and all necessary Charges paid.
 And *all* Masters of Vessels and others are hereby caution'd against concealing or carrying off said Servant on Penalty of the Law.
              October 23. 1753.

The Boston Gazette, or Weekly Advertiser, October 23, 1753; October 30, 1753.

DEserted from Lieut. *Thomas Moncrieffe,* recruiting at *Boston,* for Capt. *Joseph Gorham*'s Company; *John Diggens,* born in *Waterford,* in the Kingdom of *Ireland,* aged 28 Years, about 5 Feet 7 Inches high, lank black Hair, thin visag'd, and a little pitted with the Small-Pox. Whoever will secure the said *John Diggen*s, so as he may be confin'd in any of His Majesty's Goals within this Province, shall have *Twenty Shillings* Sterling Reward.

N. B. He is supposed to be about *Lunenburgh* or *Nutfield,* as at the Time of his Enlisting, he produced several Orders from a Tavern-Keeper, at one of those Places, for the Receipt of Money.

   T. Moncrieffe.   *Boston, October* 25, 1753.

The Boston Weekly News-Letter, October 25, 1753; November 2, 1753.

R*AN away from his Master* Richard Rogers *of* Ipswich, *an* Irish *Boy about fifteen Years of Age, named* John Fitz-Patrick, *a short thick well set Fellow, pretty full of Talk, he wears a brown Jacket and a pair of* German *Serge old Breeches, new Shoes and Stockings, square Brass Buckles in his Shoes, an old Felt Hat, and a new worsted Cap. Whoever shall take up said Fellow, and convey him to said* Rogers, *shall have* Three Dollars *Reward, and all necessary Charges paid by*

   Richard Rogers.   Ipswich, Nov. 2d. 1753.

The Boston Evening-Post, November 5, 1753.

RAN-away on the 16th of *October,* from his Master, *Stephen Turner* of *Hartford,* a Negro Man called *Primas,* about 37 Years of Age, a stout, tall well set Fellow, had on when he went away, a Brown double brested Jacket, with mettle Buttons, and a strip'd Holland jacket under it, a check'd Holland shirt, ruffled with the same, a pair of strip'd Trowsers, a pair of Blewish worsted Stockings, Calf skin Shoes with Buckles, a Caster Hatt, a white Holland Cap, has lost the first joint of one of his great Toes.

Whoever shall take up said *R*unaway, and secure him so that his Master may have him again, shall have *twenty Pounds* old Tenor Reward, and all necessary Charges paid by me,

   Stephen Turner.   *Hartford, November* 5. 1753.

The Boston Gazette, or Weekly Advertiser, November 13, 1753; November 20, 1753.

A Negro Man named *Pompey,* about 23 Years of Age, belonging to *John Wire* of Charlstown, went away of Friday Night last, from Mr. *Ridgaway,*

Bricklayer, in Boston, with whom he was labour'd the Summer past: He is a stout well set Fellow, and had on a blue under Serge Jacket, and an old patch'd one over it. Whoever shall give Intelligence of said Negro to his Master, or to Mr. *Ridgaway*, they shall be well rewarded.
    John Wire.   *Charlstown. Nov. 19th.* 1753.
The Boston Gazette, or Weekly Advertiser, November 20, 1753.

RAn-away from his Master Capt. *John Wakefield* of Boston, the 5th Instant, a Negro Man, named *Boney,* aged about 25 Years: He had on when he went away, a homespun under Jacket, a light colour'd Kersey Jacket, with Pewter Buttons, a speckled Shirt, a pair of old Pumps, a black sheepskin Wigg.
 Whoever shall take up said Runaway and bring him to his said Master, shall have *two Dollars* Reward. And all Masters of Vessels and others, are hereby warned against harbouring, concealing or carrying of said Servant, as they would avoid the Penalty of the Law.
    JOHN WAKEFIELD.   *Boston, November* 17. 1753.
The Boston Gazette, or Weekly Advertiser, November 20, 1753; November 27, 1753.

NOtice is hereby given, That Sarah *the Wife of* James Dwyer *of* Portsmouth, *in said Province, Truckman, lately the Widow Relict of* George Massey, *late of* Portsmouth, *aforesaid, deceas'd, on or about the 19th Instant eloped from the Dwelling House of said* Dwyer, *rifled the House by the Assistance of Persons to him unknown, carried away in the Night-Time all the Goods in the House, and secreted the same, as also, a Negro Man named* Scipio, *about* 26 *Years of Age, bred among the English, with four Cows, three Horses, and about* 26 *Sheep: All Persons are therefore hereby forbid to entertain the said* Sarah, *or to supply her on the Account of her said Husband (till she shall return to her Duty) as they would avoid the Consequences of a legal Prosecution—and any Person who will take up and bring the said Negro to him at* Portsmouth *aforesaid, or any of said Goals, or give him any Intelligence thereof, shall have a reasonable Satisfaction for the same, and all Charges paid.*
    James Dwyer.   Portsmouth, November 23. 1753.
The Boston Post-Boy, November 26, 1753. See *The Boston Post-Boy,* December 3, 1753.

    THE Publick is hereby informed of my
unhappy Case. I was left by my late Husband *George Massey,* late of *Portsmouth,* deceased, in plentiful Circumstances, with enough to maintain myself comfortably and besides a handsome Estate for my Child I have by him. *James Dwyer* late from *Ireland* (and then having not Estate save the Cloaths on his Back, that I even knew of) courted me, and by his Flatteries,

and thro' the Perswasions of some of his Countrymen, my pretended Friends; representing him to me as a Man of a good Education, great Ingenuity, and one that would make me a very good Husband, I was induced to marry him in *July* last.—But I soon perceived my Mistake, for in a very little Time after our Marriage he treated me with great Roughness and Violence, frequently with a Whip in his Hand held over me threatning to Horse whip me, afterwards got a Sword, and kept by the Bedside, threatning to run me thro' with it, took from me many valuable Things, and all my Case amounting to some Hundreds of Pounds, telling me that he would dispose of all the Estate I brought him, turn me out of Doors, leave the Country, and make me go a Washing for my Living; and about the 18th of *November* Instant, snapt two loaded Pistols presented to my Head and with the most profane Oaths and horrid Imprecations, swore he would kill me; the Night following attempted to choak me, and often wished Damnation to himself if he did not murder me; and all this base Usage I can say without the least Provocation or undutiful Behaviour to him on my Part. For which Usage of me as well for challenging a Man to fight a Duel with Pistols, he was apprehended and committed to Goal in *Portsmouth*, but is now out of Bail: And for my own Safety, and for the Safety of my Infant Child, which he frequently abused, and used to call my damn'd Bastard, I have left him.—And therefor am advertised by him in this Paper as an Eloper, and he has forbid all Persons to entertain me.—Let the World judge of my distressed Case.

Sarah Dwyer, late *Massey.*   November 30th, 1753.
The Boston Post-Boy, December 3, 1753. See *The Boston Post-Boy,* November 26, 1753.

1754

RAN-away from his Master *Robert Stone,* Innholder, living at the Royal Exchange Tavern in *Boston,* on the 11th Instant, a Negro Fellow named *Lan,* about 20 Years of Age, 5 Feet high, w well-set Fellow, much pitted with the Small-Pox, having lately hat it, has a very stern Countenance, and speaks good English, as born in *Plymouth* in *New-England*: Had on when he went away a red and white worsted Cap, an old Beaver Har, a dark Bearskin Pea-Jacket, with brass Buttons, and piec'd om the right Elbow, a red and white Swanskin Jacket, a white cotton and linnen Shirt, a blue and white strip'd Handkerchief, a pair of light Buckskin Breeches, a pair of mix'd Yarn Stockings, a pair of good Shoes and brass Buckles.

Whoever shall take up said Runaway, and him safely convey to his said master, shall have three DOLLARS Reward, and all necessary Charges paid: And all Masters of Vessels and others are hereby caution'd against harbouring, concealing, or carrying off said Negro, as they would avoid the Penalty of the Law.   *Boston, January* 14. 1754.

The Boston Post-Boy, January 14, 1754; January 21, 1754; January 28, 1754.

R*AN away from his Master* Giles Hosier, *living with Capt.* Clothier Pierce, sen. *in* Newport, *an Apprentice named* John Thomas, *about* 24 *Years of Age, pretty fair Complexion, about* 5 *Feet* 7 *or* 8 *Inches high: He had on when he went away, a flaxen Wig, a white Cloth Coat, let out an Inch of each side, a blue Waistcoat, the Sleeves of it longer than the Coat Sleeves, and a dark brown Pair of Breeches. Whoever shall take up and secure said Runaway, so that his Master may have him again, shall have* Ten Pounds, Old Tenor, *Reward, and all necessary Charges paid by me*   Giles Hosier.

N. B. *All Masters of Vessels and others, are hereby cautioned against concealing or carrying off said Servant, as they will answer it in the Law.*
Newport, January 13. 1754.

The Boston Evening-Post, January 21, 1754.

WHEREAS Sarah *the Wife of me the Subscriber,* Beriah Newton *of* Southborough, *has already run me in Debt without my Knowledge, and threatens still to do the same:*

These are to forewarn all Persons not to trust the said Sarah on my Account, for that I will not pay any Debrs she may contract on my Account as aforesaid.   Beriah Newton.   Southborough, *Feb.* 5. 1754.

The Boston Gazette Or, Weekly Advertiser, February 5, 1754; February 12, 1754; February 19, 1754.

DESERTED from on board the Ship *Bland*, John Hall Commander, on Sabbath-Day Night the 10th *February, Thomas Jackson*, about five Feet 7 Inches high, brown Complexion, had on a Cap; and *George Curtley*, about the same size, wears a Cap; both indented Servants, about twenty Years old: Whoever shall take up both or either of said Servants, shall have the Sum of FIFTEEN POUNDS old Tenor, Reward, and all necessary Charges paid: And all Masters of Vessels and others are hereby forbid to harbour, conceal or carry off said Servants, as they shall answer the same to the Extent of the Law.   John Hall.

The Boston Post-Boy, February 14, 1754; *The Boston Weekly News-Letter*, February 21, 1754; February 28, 1754.

DEserted from on board the Ship Bland, John Hall, *Master, on Friday Night,* Arthur Allen, *an Apprentice about 5 Feet 3 or 4 Inches high, dark Complection, and speaks very thick. Any Person that brings the said Person*

on board the said Ship, shall have a Reward of Ten Pounds *Old-Tenor, and all necessary Charges paid; or any Master of Ship, Vessel or others that shall take off the said* Arthur Allen *shall answer it as the Law directs.*
John Hall.
The Boston Evening-Post, February 18, 1754; February 25, 1754; *The Boston Weekly News-Letter,* February 28, 1754.

RAN away from the Sloop *Dove, William Mackey,* Master on Thursday the 13 Inst. A Servant Law named *William Osborne,* about five Feet four Inches high, a fresh Complection, short dark Hair; had on when he went away two blue Jackets and Breeches, with yellow metal Buttons, a whitish coloured fearnought great Coat, and had with him a blue Jacket and a white one besides; the white Jacket had Gold work'd Buttons: Whoever will take up said Runaway, and bring him to said *Mackey,* or to Mr. *Benjamin Hallowell* of *Boston,* shall have Five DOLLARS Reward, and all necessary Charges paid.
The Boston Weekly News-Letter, February 21, 1754; February 28, 1754; March 7, 1754.

RAn away from on Board the Sloop Shingle, *Joseph Rivers* Commander, on the 3d Instant at Night, an English Servant Lad, well set, of about nineteen Years of Age, wears pretty wide Trowsers, a thick blue or striped Cap; took with him two blue Jackets, and has a brown Dog with him named *Tray.* Whoever shall take up said Servant, and bring or safely convey to his said Master, or to Capt. *Samuel Hews* in Boston, shall have two Dollars Reward, and all necessary Charges. And all Masters of Vessels and others, are hereby caution'd against concealing or carrying off said Servant on Penalty of the Law.   Boston, March 1. 1754.
The Boston Gazette, or Weekly Advertiser, March 5, 1754.

ON the Night next after the 11th Instant, broke violently out of his Majesty's Goal in *New-London,* the following Persons, viz. *Thomas Stebbins,* a tall stammering Fellow, with dark brown Hair; *Judah Colman,* a tall likely Man with large light Eyes, a Joyner by Trade; *Ebenezer Howard,* jun. a young tall Man, has large black Eyes and Eye-brows, with large white Teeth; *James Mills,* a very thick large-bon'd Fellow, of a brown Complexion; *John Taylor,* a pretty likely Fellow, born in the *Isle of Man,* of the Seafaring Tribe, short and thick; *William Dent,* a young likely Fellow, of a middling Stature and brown: All the aforesaid Fellows were committed for stealing *Spanish* Gold, Silver and Indigo. Also at the same Time broke out of said Goal one *Nathaniel Keys* of *Kellingly,* a fat Man, of a sandy Complexion, committed for counterfeiting New-York Money; and the noted Horse Jockey *Stephen Potter* for Debt, all pretty well cloathed.

Whosoever shall apprehend one, or all of the aforesaid Persons, and secure them in said Goal, shall have FIFTY POUNDS, old Tenor, Reward for each (excepting *Potter* and *Dent*, for them Ten Pounds each) and all necessary Charges
    paid by, *Christopher Christophers*, [sic] Sheriff.
        Dated at *New-London, March* 12th. 1754.
The Boston Post-Boy, March 18, 1754; March 25, 1754; April 8, 1754.

WHereas one *John Webb*, sometimes residing in *Salem*, but generally trafficking about the Country, did, on the 30th of *March* last past, in a deceitful and clandestine Manner, obtain of me the Subscriber, a Note of Hand for £. 22 6 *s*. 8 *d*. lawful Money, and two Orders signed by me, one for *Seven Pounds*, and the other for *Two Pounds*, lawful Money each, as also an Account of Debt amounting to £. 67—15—0 old Tenor, due to me, which I had endors'd: For neither of which I have receiv'd any Consideration or Payment of the said *Webb*, and as he, the said *Webb*, has since absconded; these are to desire all Persons what so ever, not to purchase or answer the said Note or Orders in any Trade or Business.
  Wm. Wheeler.   *Boston, April 5th* 1754.
The Boston Weekly News-Letter, April 5, 1754; April 11, 1754; *The Boston Evening-Post*, April 8, 1754; April 15, 1754. See *The Boston Evening-Post*, March 31, 1746, and *The Boston Weekly News-Letter*, July 18, 1754.

R*AN away on the 26th Instant, at Night, from his Master* Anthony Brackett, *of* Boston, *an* English *Man Servant named* Andrew Griffith, *about five Feet nine Inches high, and had on when he went away, a dark Duroy Coat, with white Metal Buttons, and took with him two striped new homespun Jackets, one pair of Leather Breeches, and another pair of black worsted Breeches lined with Leather, two pair of Yarn Stockings, and two pair of black Worsted ditto, two pair of Shoes, and a pair of large Copper Buckles. He is mark'd with the Small Pox, and his right hand in mark'd with the Letters A. G. in Indian Ink. He took with him two Horses, with Bridles and Saddles, on a Sorrel Horse, about Fourteen Hands high, that paces and trots, the other a dark Bay that trots only.*
 N. B. The same Fellow hath tended the said Brackett's *Stable for about two Years past.*
 'Tis supposed that a Servant belonging to Mr. William Murray, *of* Boston, *Peruke-maker, is gone along with him: His name is* David Fitz-Gerald, *and is a short well set Fellow. Whoever shall take up the abovesaid Runaways, bring bring them to their said Masters in* Boston, *shall have* Ten Pounds, *old Tenor, Reward, and all necessary Charges paid.*

All Masters of Vessels and others, are hereby cautioned not to conceal, entertain or carry off the said Servants, as they would avoid the Penalty of the Law. Boston, April 25, 1754.
The Boston Evening-Post, April 29, 1754, May 6, 1754; May 13, 1754. See *The Boston Evening-Post*, March 16, 1752, and *The Boston Evening-Post*, January 1, 1753.

RAN-away from Dr. *Thomas Dean* of Exeter, *May* 1753, a Negro Man named *Quom*, suppos'd to be forty Years or upwards, a well set Fellow, something slow in Motion, a wrinkled Face and a Mouth full of Teeth, and a large Eye which he turns up when he is earnest in Speaking. He speaks brokenly, the Tops of two his Fingers are froze off. He had on when he went away a light colour'd Bearskin Coat, a striped Jacket, (the Stripes going round,) a white woollen Shirt and light Stockings.

Whosoever shall bring said Negro, to me the Subscriber in *Haverhill*, shall have 3 Dollars Reward, and all necessary Chages [sic]
paid by   John White, Junr.   Haverhill, May 8*th*, 1754.
The Boston Gazette, or Weekly Advertiser, May 14, 1754.

RAN-away from his Master Mr. *Lemuel Sturtevant*, of *Hallifax*, in the County of *Plymouth*, on April 25th 1754, a Mallatto Man Servant named *Shubal Lawrence*, aged 18 Years, a stout lusty Fellow, had on when he went away a Felt Hatt, and a curled Head of Hair a strait Bodied or mixed colour'd Great Coat with Pewter Buttons, a striped Jacket without Sleeves, white woollen Shirt, his Breeches the same with his Coat, light colour'd blue Stockings, and a Mark on his upper Lip, in form of Figure 3 something resembling an M:

Whoever shall take up said Servant, and bring him to his Master in *Hallifax*, shall have *ten Pounds* old Tenor Reward, and all necessary Charges paid.   Hallifax in the County *of* Plymouth, *May* 15. 1754.
The Boston Gazette, or Weekly Advertiser, May 21, 1754. See *The Boston Gazette, or Weekly Advertiser*, October 1, 1754.

TAKEN out of the Dwelling-House of the Subscriber on the 18th of this Instant *May*, a Coat and Breeches made of superfine Cloth of a pale Orange Colour, the Coat had an open Cuff with three Button-holes in it, a Flap in the Slip under the Cuff with three Buttons; the coat is work'd with a Barrell Hole, Hair Shapes and wadded, three Holes behind and three in each Flap: The Breeches lin'd with Leather; also, two Jackets, one a flower'd silk Grogram blue and white, with a white Taffity Lining, the other a fad Colour German Serge, trim'd plain, a Flap to button before; some white Thread and Stockings: It is supposed the Person that took them wore them away, who is an Irishman of a tall Stature, long Visage, a dark Complexion, a Scar on one

of his Cheeks, and a Lover of Sir Richard; also on his left Arm a little above his Wrist there is a Bunch caused (as he says) by a Bullet; has had the Small-Pox, he wears a dark Wigg. Whoever shall take up said Irishman, and convey him with the Cloaths to me shall have TEN DOLLARS Reward and all necessary Charges paid.
     Per SAMUEL ROGERS. *Marblehead*, May 25th, 1754.
N. B. Said Irishman left his old Duds at the Time of departing his Lodging, *viz* a homespun blue Coat, full trim'd with Pewter Buttons.
 The Boston Post-Boy, May 27, 1754.

*R*UN-*away on friday night the 5th inst. from Adam States of Horse-Neck, in Connecticut, a* German *servant man, named* Daniel Viscoup, *about 26 years of age, scarce 5 feet high, thick and well sett, broad face and large red nose, black strait hair about two inches long, speaks broken* English, *has been nine months in the county, and is a pot-baker by trade: Had on when he went away, a blue broad cloth coat and jacket, both double breasted, and had with him, a stript homespun jacket, with more blue in the fore parts than back, a fine white linnen shirt, stript breeches with black buttons, brown tread [sic] stockings, a pair of shoes newly soal'd, with different buckles, a felt hat, and had no money that his Master know of. Whoever takes up said servant, and secures him, so as his master may have him again, shall have FORTY SHILLINGS reward, and all reasonable*
     charges paid, ADAM STATES.
 The New-York Mercury, July 8, 1754; July 15, 1754; July 22, 1754; July 29, 1754; August 5, 1754; August 12, 1754; August 19, 1754.

*R*AN-*away from* Samuel Cooke *of* New-Haven, *a Servant Man, named* Caleb Pierce, *about 27 or 28 Years of Age, of middling Stature: Had on when he went away an old Hat and a Cap or Wigg, a brown Vest, check'd Shirt, old Leather Breeches, and a Pair of Yarn Stockings, half white half blue; he calls himself a Mason, and had a Trowel with him: Whoever shall take him up, and secure or convey him to said* Cooke, *shall have* TEN POUNDS *Reward, and all necessary Charges*
    paid by Samuel Cooke, New-Haven, July 16. 1754.
 The Boston Post Boy, July 22, 1754; July 29. 1754; August 5, 1754.

 We hear, that the famous John Webb, who has for some Years past been known in divers Parts of this Province as a crafty and common Cheat, and a Disturber of the Peace of His Majesty's good Subjects, was last week apprehended at Taunton, by virtue of a Warrant from His Majesty's Justices of the Superiour Court of Judicature, &c. and that he is committed to the Goal in Cambridge, in order to his being tried there at the next Assizes.

The Boston Weekly News-Letter, July 18, 1754. See *The Boston Evening-Post,* March 31, 1746, and *The Boston Weekly News-Letter,* April 5, 1754.

WHereas *Thomas Edwards, Charles Shannon, Alex. Cannon,* and *Robert Pottle,* have absented themselvesfrom their Duty of board the Snow Mermaid. Caliam, John*John Caliam* Master, bound for Europe: This is to order the said *Thomas Edwards, Charles Shannon, Alexander. Cannon,* and *Robert Pottle,* immediately to repair on board the said Vessel to their Duty, otherwise they will be deemed as Deserters,
    John Calkins.   Boston, July 29th 1754.
The Boston Gazette, or, Weekly Advertiser, July 30, 1754.

I The Subscriber hereby give Notice that *Elizabeth Fadre,* my Wife, hath eloped from me, and that therefore I will not pay any Debts that she shall contract: All Persons are therefore cautioned not to trust her on on Account. Witness my Hand this 3d Day of *August,* A. D. 1754.
   Benjamin Fadre.
The Boston Evening-Post, August 12, 1754; August 19, 1754.

*W*Hereas Elizabeth *the Wife of* Jeremiah Farington, *of* Lynn, *has eloped and run him in Debt, without his Knowledge, to his Damage*; This is to give Notice, that I will not pay any Debt she shall contract from this Date. Witness my Hand, *Jeremiah Farington.* Sept. 14*th* 1754.
The Boston Evening-Post, September 23, 1754.

R*AN away from his Master* Benjamin Sault, *of* Boston, *Cooper, on the 25th Instant, one* Thomas Fry, *a Boy about fifteen Years of Age, of short Stature, much Pock-broken, and has several Scars in his Head. He had on when he went away, a blue Ratteen Coat, with white metal Buttons, a striped red Homespun Jacket, red Cloth Breeches, with Trowsers over them, a check'd Cotton and Linen Shirt, blue ribb'd Stockings, Brass Buckles not Fellows. It is thought he has gone to* Middletown *in* Connecticut. *Whosoever shall take up said Apprentice, and bring him to his said Master in* Boston, *shall have* Three Dollars *Reward, and all necessary Charges*
   paid, by Benjamin Sault.
 N. B. *All Masters of Vessels and others, are hereby cautioned against harbouring, concealing or carrying off said Apprentice, as they would avoid the Penalty of the Law in that Case made and provided.*
        Boston, September 28. 1754.
The Boston Evening-Post, September 30, 1754; October 7, 1754; October 14, 1754. See *The Boston Post-Boy,* October 7, 1754.

RAN-away from his Master *Lemuel Sturtevant* of *Hallifax*, in the County of *Plymouth*, on the 27th of this Instant *September*, a Molatto Man Servant named *Shubael Lawrence*, about 18 Years of Age, a pretty thick set Fellow, with very short Hair, if any, and a Scar upon his upper Lip: He had on when he went away, an old Felt Hat, a white Flannel Shirt, a striped Jacket without Sleeves, a light colour'd pair of woollen Breeches. Whoever shall take up said Run-away and convey him to me his said Master, shall have *Five Pounds* old Tenor Reward, and all necessary Charges paid. Dated at *Hallifax, September* 26th 1754.   Lemuel Sturtevant.

And all Masters of Vessels and others are hereby caution'd not to conceal or carry off said Servant on Penalty of the Law.

    The Boston Gazette, or Weekly Advertiser, October 1, 1754. See *The Boston Gazette, or Weekly Advertiser*, May 21, 1754.

R*AN away from* John Blair, *of* Groton, *an* Irish *stout and lusty Servant Man about twenty one Years of Age, named* John Casey, *a Cooper by Trade: Had on when he went away a light Bearskin Coat with Brass Buttons, a striped Jacket, a pair of brown Cloth Breeches, with Mohair Buttons, and a pair of ribb'd Stockings. Whoever shall take up said Runaway, and bring him to his Master in* Groton, *or to Mr.* William Hall, *of* Boston, *Leather-Dresser, shall have* FOUR DOLLARS *Reward and all necessary Charges paid.*

    All Masters of Vessels and others, are hereby required not to conceal or carry off said Servant as they would answer it in the Law.

    The Boston Evening-Post, October 7, 1754; October 14, 1754; October 21, 1754.

R*AN-away from his Master* Benjamin Sault, *of* Boston, *Cooper, on the 25th of* September, *one* Thomas Fry, *a Boy about* 15 *Years of Age, of short Stature, much Pock-broken, several Scars in his Head: He had on when he went away, a blue Ratteen Coat, with white flat metal Buttons, a strip'd red homespun Jacket, red Cloth Breeches, with Trowsers over them, a check'd cotton and linen Shirt, blue ribb'd Stockings, brass Buckles, not fellows It is thought he has gone to* Middletown *or* Fairfield *in* Connecticut. *Whosoever shall take up said Apprentice, and bring him to his said Master in* Boston, *shall have* THREE DOLLARS *Reward, and all necessary Charges paid, by*   Benja. Sault.

N. B. *All Masters of Vessels and others, are hereby cautioned against harbouring, concealing or carrying off said Apprentice, as they would avoid the Penalty of the Law in that Case made and provided.*

                  Boston, September 28. 1754.

    The Boston Post-Boy, October 7, 1754. See *The Boston Evening-Post*, September 30, 1754.

RAN away from Henry Sherburne *Jun. of* Portsmouth, *Merchant, a Negro Man named* Cromwell, *about forty five Years of Age, of midling Stature, small Eyes, a running Sore in one Leg, almost if not quite dried up, talks good* English, *can read and write, and understands Husbandry Work. Had on and carried away with him, a blue Cloth Coat and Breeches, a Scarlet Cloth Jacket with Metal Buttons, and one pair of dark coloured Plush Breeches, also some white Oznabrigs Jackets and Breeches, Linen and Cotton Shirts, white Cotton and some Yarn Stockings, good Worsted Caps, &c. Whosoever will take up said Runaway, and him safely convey to his said Master in* Portsmouth, *shall have* Eight Dollars *for their Trouble, and all necessary Charges paid.*
     Henry Sherburne.   Portsmouth, October 3. 1754.
 The Boston Evening-Post, October 7, 1754; October 14, 1754; October 21, 1754; *The Boston Gazette, or Weekly Advertiser,* October 22, 1754. Minor differences between the papers.

RUN-away the 3d Instant from his Master *Joseph Dennis* of *Portsmouth,* on *Rhode-Island,* a Mustee or Molatto Man Servant, named *Pero,* about 27 Years of Age, very large of Stature; hath a Scar on each Thumb, which causes them to stand crooked, and a round large Scar on the outside of the Calf of his left Leg, resembling the Scar of a Burn. Had on when he went away, a Homespun full-cloth grey-coloured double breasted Jacket, with large flat Brass Buttons, notch'd or scollop'd round the Edges, a Pair of Tow Trowsers, and a Tow Shirt. Whoever takes up said Molatto, or secures him, so that his Master may have him again, shall have TEN POUNDS old Tenor Reward, and all necessary Charges,
    paid by me, *Joseph Dennis.*
 The Boston Post-Boy, October 14, 1754; October 21, 1754; October 28, 1754.

RAN away from *Joseph Trout, William Hogan,* a Boy about sixteen Years of Age, fair Complexion, wears his own Hair: Had on when he went away, a blue Serge Waistcoat, and Trousers. Whoever secures said Boy, and will bring him to Mr. *Edward Gyles,* Painter, shall have two DOLLARS Reward. All Masters of Ships and others are desired not to carry him away or entertain said Boy.
 The Boston Weekly News-Letter, October 24, 1754; October 31, 1754; November 7, 1754.

DESERTED from the Ship *Union-Galley, Jeremiah Walton* Master, lying at the Long-Wharf, lately from *London* and *Halifax,* the following Seamen, viz, *James Branscomb,* said to be born in *Piscataqua,* is about six Feet high,

of a swarthy Complection, and wears a Wigg. *Henry Mitchel* of *London*, about five Feet 7 Inches high, and pretty thick set:—And *William Hughes*, born in England, about five Feet six Inches high, wears a blue Bonnet; and were all of them in Seamens Habits; and have taken from on board the said Ship, a Pinchbeck Watch, Maker's Name *Neal*, Number forgot, some Money, a Silver-lac'd Hat, and a Pair of square silver Shoe-Buckles, very neatly wrought: Its thought they are gone towards *Piscataqua*, but not for certain: Whoever shall apprehend the above-mention'd Persons or either of them, so that they may be brought to Justice, and convicted of the same, shall have TWO GUINEAS Reward: And if either of the aforesaid Articles are offer'd to sale, pray stop them, and if already done you shall have your Money again with Thanks by applying to Mr. *Robert Stone* at the Royal Exchange Tavern in King-street, *Boston*.
       J. Walton.   November the 10th. 1754.
The Boston Post-Boy, November 11, 1754; November 25, 1754.

WHereas my Wife Mary Hill, *hath for some Time past eloped from me, and will not cohabit with me;* These are therefore to caution all Persons from trusting her or giving her any Credit, for I do hereby declare, that I will not pay one Farthing to any Person that shall trust her, as Witness my Hand,
       Joseph Hill.
       Present at Signng, *William Collins, Job Collins.*
The Boston Evening-Post, November 25, 1754; December 2, 1754.

RAN-away from Moses Marcy, *Esq; of* Sturbridge *in the County of* Worcester, *on the 8th Instant, an Indian Woman, named* Louis Wamscomb, *aged 22, speaks English, well sett, has a Scar under her Chin, had on a green & white Russell Gown, a red Cloak, and took with her other Apparel.*
    Whoever shal take up and convey said Servant to her said Master, shall have two Dollars *and all necessary Charges paid.*
       Sturbridge, Nov. 25, 1754.
The Boston Gazette, or Weekly Advertiser, November 26, 1754.

THIS is to warn all Persons from trusting Sarah *the Wife of me* John Worth *of* Hampton Falls, *in the Province of* New-Hampshire, *for that I will not pay any Debts she shall contract from the Date hereof, as Witness by Hand,*
       John Worth.   Hampton-Falls, November 11. 1754.
The Boston Evening-Post, December 2, 1754.

RAN away from Mr. *Philip Curtis* of *Stoughton*, on the 18th of *November* Instant, a Negro Man Servant about 24 Years old, named *Scipio Congo*, his Left Arm shorter than his Right, can read & write, of a Copper Colour, middle Stature, and with Teeth irregular: When he went away, he had on, an old Hat, a grey Woollen Coat, with Brass Buttons, a strip'd black and white Jacket, and white West coat laced round him, Linnen Breeches and Trousers, blue Stockings and old Shoes.

Whoever shall take up said Negro, and him safely convey to his Master aforesaid, shall have *Four Dollars* Reward, and handsomely paid for all necessary Charges.

P. S. And as he threatned to go to Sea, 'tis desir'd no Masters of Vessels would receive him, as they would shun the Penalty of the Law.

Stoughton, November 30*th* 1754.
The Boston Gazette, or Weekly Advertiser, December 3, 1754.

INDEX

Abbe, Joseph, 226
Abbot, John, 86
Abbot, Mrs., 86
Abraham, Paul, 176
Ackin, William, 180
Acton, Richard, 246
Adams, James, 205, 207
Adams, Jo, 300
Adams, Samuel, 29
Adolph, Dirick, 8
Agars, Edmund, 256
Aikman, Patrick, 25
Akins, David, 244
Alcock, Robert, 28
Aldin, John, 1
Aldroyd, Jonathan/John, 80
Alexander, James, 272
Alexander, John, 339
Alexander, Mary, 339
Alford, John, 260
Alford, Mr., 376
Allaen, Samuel, 94
Allan, John, 291
Alland, William, 267
Allen, Arthur, 383
Allen, David, 194
Allen, George, 83
Allen, Jabez, 156
Allen, Malachy, 241
Allen, Nehemiah, 204
Allin, Samuel, 68, 126
Allis, Samuel, 147, 150
Allison, Samuel, 365
Almy, Job, 125
Alsted, Thomas, 116
Ambrose, John, 227
Ambrose, Patrick, 94
Ame, John, 7
Ame, Mary, 7
Ames, Nathaniel, 257

Amos, Daniel, 329
Amy, John, 19
Anderson, Andrew, 313
Anderson, David, 327
Anderson, George, 93
Anderson, John, 221
Anderson, Robert, 307
Andover, George, 111
Anthony, Isaac, 301
Apthorp, Charles, 95, 166, 192, 198, 360
Apthorpe, Charles, 208, 221, 302
Archdeacon, Richard, 326
Archer, Henry, 61
Archer, Mary, 46
Arnie, James, 319
Arnold, Benedict, 136
Arnold, Philip, 87
Arnold, William, 368
Arthur, Robert, 8
Askin, Christopher, 138, 141
Astill, Benjamin, 123
Astills, Benjamin, 119
Atherton, Henry, 23
Atherton, Samuel, 118
Atkins, Henry, 283
Atkins, Joseph, 271
Atkins, Ruth, 271
Atkinson, Benjamin, 78
Attakin, Samuel, 240
Auchmuty, Robert, 52, 64, 119
Audoyer, George, 111
Austell, Joseph, 64, 279
Austin, Ben, 270
Austin, Capt., 66
Avery, John, 355
Aves, John, 204
Ayres, Jacob, 93
Ayres, Thomas, 59
Ayscough, John, 328

Babbidge, Benjamin, 218
Babcock, Josh., 340
Bacon, Benjamin, 288
Bacon, John, 204
Bacon, Josiah, 66
Bagnall, Benja., 203
Bailey, James, 228
Bailey, William, 225
Baker, James, 153, 154
Baker, John, 146, 244
Baker, Nathaniel, 6
Baker, Philip, 264
Baker, William, 177, 196
Balderson, Thomas, 308
Balderston, Thomas, 293
Baldwin, Thomas, 173
Ball, Benjamin, 241
Ball, Hannah, 241
Ball, Samuel, 341
Ballard, Daniel, 193
Ballentin, John, 9
Banclay, George, 92
Banclay, John, 92
Bancroft, Samuel, Jr., 341
Band, Nathaniel, 76
Bane, William, 344
Banister, John, 282
Banister/Bannister, John, 175
Barbeen, James, 50
Barbour, Peter, 24
Barbutt, William, 3
Barclay, George, 92
Barclay, John, 92
Bargary/Bargery, John, 306, 354
Barker, Capt., 12
Barlo, John, 360
Barnard, Benjamin, 232
Barnard, Joseph, 315
Barnes, Henry, 87
Barnes, John, 87
Barns, Andrew, 208
Barns, Samuel, 278
Barodell, Henry, 207

Barrel, Mr., 183, 210
Barrell, John, 258
Barret, Samuel, 316
Barrington, Thomas, 10
Bartley, Seth, 319
Barton, James, 141
Basham, Gilbert, 45
Bass, Kimbal, 322
Bass, Samuel, 72
Basset, Zephaniah, 173
Bathrick, Henry, 339
Batter, John, 333
Battis, Jeffry, 289
Battis, John, 289
Battle, John, 347, 367, 372
Battle, Nath., 307
Baty, Clousip, 63
Bayard, Stephen, 263, 271
Bayley, Robert, 44
Bazin, John, 183, 206
Bazin, Leonard, 202
Bazin, Mary, 202
Bazin, Sarah, 206
Beal, James, 147
Beal, William, 147
Beals, Morrice, 16
Beard, John, 111
Beard, Prudence, 297
Beard, William, 297
Beasley, George, 172
Beath, Adam, 20
Beath/Beat, Mrs., 196
Beats, Mary, 21
Becham, John, 197
Becks, Thomas, 112
Bedeorn, Jasper, 231
Bedgood, John, 170
Beetle, William, 163
Belcher, Andrew, 2, 3
Belcher, Mr., 46
Belden, John, 131, 132
Belden, Samuel, 103, 132
Belknap, Jeremiah, 369

Bell, Anthony, 377
Bell, Thomas, 231
Bell, Tom/Thomas, 214, 216, 218, 220, 224, 246, 276
Bellow, Elias, 229
Belson, James, 335
Bembridge, William, 49
Benkier, John, 100
Bennet, Caleb, 211
Bennet, John, 15
Bennet, Thomas, 177
Bennet, William, 116
Bennett, Ellys, 115
Benrit, Blaze, 290
Bent, Gilbert, 16
Bentley, Thomas, 136
Berry, James, 7
Betbune, Mr., 33
Beteille, Mr., 130
Bethel, Richard, 135
Bethell, Jarvis, 89
Bethil, Jarvis, 44
Bicknel, Zechariah, 261
Bill, Jack, 8
Bill, James, 349
Billing, Increase, 354
Billing, Sarah, 354
Billings, Ebenezer, 6
Billings, John, 109, 113
Billings, Mr., 302
Billings, Richard, 113, 188, 189
Billingsly, Thomas, 204
Binham, John, 141
Bird, Benj., 364
Birk, Molly, 331
Bissel, Job, 49
Bissel, Samuel, 30
Black, Jonathan, 252
Blacket, Edward, 21
Blacklock, Robert, 180
Blackmore, Capt., 9
Blackmore, George, 134
Blackstone, Jacob, 276

Blackstone, Peter, 38
Blair, Bethel, 326
Blair, Elizabeth, 326
Blair, James, 14
Blair, John, 27, 389
Blair/Blare, William, 303, 338
Blake, Andrew, 167
Blake, James, 208
Blake, Jane, 374
Blake, John, 77
Blanchard, Aaron, 91
Blanchard, Hezekiah, 316
Blaney, John, 301
Blany, Benjamin, 313
Blee, Peter, 54
Bleigh, Samuel, 65
Blish, Abraham, 68
Bliss, Peter, 107
Blood, Zachariah, 121
Bloss, Thomas, 332
Blowers, Mr., 82
Blowers, Pyam, 89
Boats, Thomas, 313
Bois, James, 176, 335
Boldeare, George, 149
Boman, Christopher, 103
Boman, Joseph, 79
Bond, Mr., 82
Bone, Thomas, 292
Bonnett, William, 83
Bord, John, 42
Borden, Thomas, 231
Borden, William, 24
Boreman, Mr., 22
Borland, Francis, 25, 67
Boufford, Nicholas, 285
Bourden, William, 30
Bourk, Michael, 160
Bourn, Benj., 39
Bourn, Sylvanus, 41
Bourne, Aaron, 154, 200
Bowdoin, James, 187
Bower, Benanuel/Benanael, 282

Bowers, Henry, 285
Bowers, Jerathmeel, 284
Bowes, Capt., 292
Bowes, Nathanael, 310
Bowman, Jonathan, 248
Bows, Thomas, 342
Box, John, 161, 312
Boyce, Joseph, 235
Boyd, Deborah, 249
Boyd, Hugh, 289
Boyd, Robert, 78
Boyd, William, 78, 264
Boydell, John, 130
Boyes, William, 51
Boyles/Boyls Thomas, 30
Boyles/Boyls, John, 30
Boylston, Mr., 94
Boylstone, Benjamin, 289
Brackett/Bracket, Anthony, 207, 358, 371, 385
Braddick, Mary, 376, 378
Bradford, James, 349
Bradford, John, 287, 317
Bradford, Joseph, 280
Braham, Francis, 333
Brand, John, 19
Brandon, Benjamin, 359
Branscomb, James, 390
Bratten, William, 180
Braydon, Gideon, 162
Breed, Amos, 45
Breed, Joseph, 252
Breed, Nathaniel, 45
Bremer, Martin, 77
Brennon, Timothy, 200
Brenton, Ebenezer, 121
Brenton, Jableel, 119
Brewer, Isaac, 167
Brewster, Mr., 199
Briant, John, 250
Bridge, Edward, 160
Bridge, John, 53
Bridger, Capt., 11

Bridger, John, 22
Bridgham, Jacob, 302
Bright, Thomas, 169
Bright, William, 8
Brock, Ezekiel, 226
Brock, John, 47
Brook, Gilbert, 261
Brown, Adam, 19
Brown, Elizabeth, 12
Brown, James, 76, 92, 93, 354
Brown, Jeremiah, 362
Brown/Browne, John, 123, 153, 192, 198, 221
Brown, Jonathan, 280
Brown, Joseph, 3, 80, 165, 203
Brown, Luke, 294
Brown, Major, 51
Brown, Nathaniel, 157
Brown, Patrick, 86
Brown, Peter, 162
Brown, Rachel, 165, 203
Brown, Richard, 41, 81
Brown, Ruth, 86
Brown, Samuel, 35, 78, 275
Brown, Thomas, 182, 320
Brown, Tom, 149, 164
Brown/Browne, William, 143, 144, 305, 336
Browne, Josiah, 214
Browne, Samuell, 78
Brownell, Ann, 367
Brownell, George, 174
Brownell, Joseph, 367
Brownell, Thomas, 363
Bryan, John, 138, 141
Bryant, Edward, 16
Bryant, Thomas, 25
Brymer, James, 288
Buckland, James, 307
Buckminster, Joseph, 261
Bucknam, William, 311, 313
Bulfinch, Adino, 60, 72
Bulfinch, William, 195

Bulger, John, 278
Bulkley, John, 83, 214, 277, 295
Bumpass, James, 170
Bumpass, Rachel, 170
Bundle/Bunale, John, 297, 298
Bunn, Matthew, 47
Bunn, Samuel, 47
Burch, Joseph, 295
Burch, Thomas, 157
Burchan, Robert, 316
Burdet, Francis, 343
Buredge, James, 306
Burk, John, 194
Burk, William, 358
Burkell, Thomas, 221
Burley, William, 373
Burn, William, 279
Burnam, Francis, 339
Burnam, Sarah, 339
Burns, Patrick, 326
Burr, Peter, 9
Burran, Edmund, 89
Burten, Arundell, 281
Burton, Thomas, 255
Bush, Amaziah, 263
Buss, Joseph, Jr., 279
Butler, Edmund, 141
Butler, Philip, 118
Butler, Thomas, 49
Butler, Valentine, 9
Byfield, Nathaniel, 4
Byles, Thomas, 48
Byrn, Daniel, 235
Cady, William, 60, 74
Cahill, Edward, 344, 362
Caine, John, 238
Caine, Maurice, 344
Calf, Joseph, 55
Call, John, 162
Callender, Joseph, 202
Cambpell/Campbell, Cornelius, 99, 108
Campbell, Charles, 19

Campbell, John, 1, 2, 5, 39, 355
Campbell, Thomas, 179
Cannington, Mr., 97
Cannon, Alexander, 388
Cantey, Anthony, 61
Capen, Samuel, 138
Capithorn John, 350
Carew, John, 350
Carey, James, 199
Carey, Samuel, 290
Carling, Roger, 305
Carlton, Samuel, 149, 163
Carnes, John, 81
Carpenter, Comfort, 83
Carpenter, Jeremiah, 276
Carr, John, 211
Carr, Silvanus, 313
Carrel, Daniel, 199
Carrow, George, 223
Carso, John, 221
Cartee, Charles, 164
Carter, E., 153
Carter, Edward, 153, 155
Carter, Thomas, 155, 338, 340, 342, 343
Carty, Darby, 332
Carty, Florence, 124
Carty, Francis, 31
Carty, Richard, 371
Cary, Abraham, 274
Cary, Nathaniel, 1
Casady, John, 173
Case, John, 250
Casey, David, 360
Casey, John, 389
Casey, William, 254
Casker, Jonah, 223
Cavenagh, Charles, 135
Caverly, Philip, 266
Cayrl, Catherine, 24
Chadock, Mr., 63
Chaloner, Walter, 250
Chamberlain, Alexander, 195

Chamberlain, John, 224
Chambers, Charles, 154
Chambers, John, 291, 292
Chambers, Robert, 284
Chambers, Thomas, 28
Champney, Joseph, 374
Chandler, Col., 294
Chandler, Gardiner, 293
Channing, John, 279
Chapman, Isaac, 92
Chapman, Lewis, 30
Chapman, Nathaniel, 270
Chappinter, Hugh, 25
Charles, Lydia, 68, 73
Charles, Silas, 177
Charles, Sylvester, 194
Charnock, Emma, 256
Charnock, John, 256
Chase, Job, 341
Chase, Joseph, 286
Checkley, Mr., 139, 142
Checkly, Colonel, 29
Cheever, Capt., 246, 285
Cheever, Joshua, 88
Cheever, Nathan, 88
Cheney, Samuel, 153, 154
Cheney, Wm., 219
Chesebrough, David, 67
Chew, Joseph, 345
Chickering, Daniel, 360, 367, 375
Child, Charles, 126
Chilman, Mr., 267
Chilmark, George, 252
Choat, Thomas, Jr., 139
Chorceman, More, 83
Christopher, William, 244
Christophers, Christopher, 385
Christophers, Joseph, 195
Church, Colonel, 7
Churche, Thomas, 62
Churchill, Thomas, 296
Clap, Joseph, 296

Clap, Stephen, 233
Clark, Elizabeth, 46
Clark, Henry, 47
Clark/Clarke, James, 147, 220, 359
Clark/Clarke, John, 3, 63, 70, 335
Clark, Mr., 374
Clark, Nath., 261
Clark, Ruth, 284, 286
Clark, Thomas, 213
Clark, William, 318, 372
Clarke, George, 195
Clarke, Wm., 182
Clary, Mary, 357
Claton, Alexander, 99
Clayon, Thomasine, 241
Clayton, John, 241
Clear, Mr., 152
Cleasby, Ezekiel, 24
Clement, Anna, 58
Clement, Jeremiah, 58
Clemons, Michael, 232
Clift, William, 237
Coates, Francis, 204
Cobb, William, 181
Cobbet, Nicholas, 84
Cobby, Thomas, 63
Cochrean, James, 277
Cockburn, Capt., 10
Cockrain, Samuel, 162
Coffee, Edward, 37
Coffee, John, 76, 79
Cogan, Edward, 244
Coggin, John, 296
Cogswell, Francis, 179, 193
Cojan, Laughlin, 31
Colberson, John, 305
Colby, John, 265
Cole, Caleb, 72
Cole, Elizabeth, 90
Cole, Robert, 347
Cole, Thomas, 60

Coleman, William, 133
Collens, Luke, 272
Collier, Anna Maria Barbarie, 9
Collingwood, James, 260, 268
Collins, Arnold, 62
Collins, Daniel, 102
Collins, John, 292
Collis, Richard, 237
Colman, Daniel, 329
Colman, John, 4, 7
Colman, Judah, 384
Colman, Mr., 53, 65, 272
Colston, John, 185
Colthurst, Henry, 203
Colvill, Mr., 317, 328
Comber/Combes, Richard, 159
Combs, Abel, 27
Comerford, James, 62
Commoson, Jeremiah, 341
Comrin, John, 279, 290, 293
Comstock, Daniel, 369
Cone, Mark, 362
Congo, Scipio, 391
Conner, Elioner, 213
Conner, Martin, 89
Connolly, John, 181, 183, 302, 307
Connoly, John, 302
Connor, Elioner, 212
Cook, Benjamin, 252
Cooke, Samuel, 387
Coomes, Newal/Thomas Newal, 352
Cooney, Nicholas, 187
Cooper, Ann, 158
Cooper, George, 109
Cooper, Ingram, 37
Cooper, Samuel, 126
Cope, Major, 81
Copeland, Christopher, 296
Copeland, Ephraim, 108
Copler, John, 19
Corbett, John, 101

Corkerry, John, 153
Corney, Bryan, 324
Corney, John, 17, 18, 107, 124
Cornish, Thomas, 230
Cornwall, Capt., 69, 72
Corphy, Thomas, 320
Cory, Martha, 268
Cory, Michael, 268
Cosly, Stephen, 55
Cotta, John, 23, 28
Cottle, Joseph, 304
Cottom, John, 187
Cotton, Grizel, 111
Cotton, Josiah, 180
Cotton, Rev., 79
Coughlan, Dennis, 152
Coulney, Darby, 204
Coupland, William, 223
Courtis, William, 194
Cowell, William, 261
Cox, Charles, 171
Cox, James, 53
Cox, Mary, 171
Cox, Thomas, 274
Cozens, Samuel, 217
Craddock, Thomas, 112, 134, 136, 139, 140, 142, 186
Crage, James, 12
Craige, Capt., 204
Craigie, Andrew, 292
Craister, John, 253
Crandall/Crandell, Nathaniel/Nathanael, 361
Cranston, William, 59
Crawford, Jonathan, 166
Cristofor, Rich., 54
Cromwell, John, 47
Croney, John, 236
Crosby, William, 210
Crosdale, Thomas, 215
Crosley, John, 377
Cross, Thomas, 34
Crouch, Charles, 41

Crowley, Dennis, 127
Crowly, Darby, 201
Crues, John, 128, 129
Cuffee, John, 83
Cullen, William, 37
Cullimore, Peter, 7
Cumberland, John, 33
Cundall, Joseph, 159
Cunningham, James, 327
Cunningham, John, 212, 213, 216
Cunningham, Nathaniel, 358
Curling, John, 376
Curling, Wm, 231
Curry/Currey, Bartholomew, 276
Curtis, John, 356
Curtis, Philip, 391
Curtis, William, 183
Curtley, George, 383
Cushman, Moses, 321
Cushon, Moses, 284
Cuthbertson, William, 123
Cutler, Dr., 158, 163, 204
Cutler, Thomas, 117
Cuttler, Richard, 304
D'Coster, John, 110
Dam, Elnathan, 59
Dameeby, Alexander, 25
Danbruuil, Philip, 145
Daniel, Alexander Mack, 181
Danworth, Daniel, 97
Darby, Oliver, 269
Darby, William, 238, 359
Darling, Daniel, 359
Darrell, John, 80
Darwell, Ralph, 59
Daugherty, Dennis, 123
Dauvergne, John, 31
Davenport, James, 322
Davis, Andrew, 171
Davis, Aron, 332
Davis, Daniel, 133
Davis, James, 307

Davis, John, 64, 66, 272, 310, 359, 368
Davis, Joseph, 302
Davis, Martha, 302
Davis, Mr., 123
Davis, Nathaniel, 269
Davis, Simon, 5
Davis, Thomas, 21
Davis, Timothy, 288
Davisson/Davison, John, 132
Dawson, William, 352
Day, James, 191
Deall, Thomas, 313
Dean, John, 233
Dean, Mr., 278, 297, 298
Dean, Thomas, 226, 386
Dear, John, 194
Deare, Wm., 352
Dearing, William, 314
Debenport, John, 262
Debuke, Thomas, 76
Decoster, Elizabeth, 146
DeForeest, Henry, 306
Deivo, John, 167
Delany, William, 238
Demsey, Joseph, 62
Dench, Roger, 96
Denham, Thomas, 103
Dennely, Mattal, 287
Dennis, Albert, 309
Dennis, Joseph, 390
Denny, Samuel, 323
Deno, John, 165
Dent, Arthur, 52
Dent, Joseph, 319
Dent, William, 384
Deverson, Wm., 376
Dewar, Andrew, 210, 320, 354
Dewy, George, 8
Dexter, Jeremiah, 230
Diamond, Joseph, 14
Dickings, Thomas, 56
Dickinson, Charles, 32

Dickson, Richard, 95
Dickson, William, 230
Diggens, John, 380
Dilling, John, 58
Disbrow, Thomas, 248
Divers, William, 53
Dixon, Adam, 123
Dixon, John, 60, 74
Dixwell, John, 22
Doane, Ephraim, 119
Dodd, Edward, 323
Dodge, Richard, 345, 346
Dogget, James, 268
Dolbeare, John, 175
Dolbeare/Dolbear, James, 218
Dole, Daniel, 287
Dole, Nath., 86
Dollinson, John, 125
Donald, Wm., 273
Donevan, Jeremiah, 364
Donnaley, Mary, 249
Donnellan, Barnabas, 319
Donors, Purser, 323
Donovan, Dennis, 114
Donum, Samuel, 264
Dopson, Thomas, 16
Doset, Henry, 125
Dothy, Eleazer, 361
Douglass, Alexander, 31
Douglass, John, 233
Douglass, Thomas, 105
Douia, James, 103
Dove, Catherine, 116
Dove, Henery, 116
Dove, Samuel, 288
Dowey, Robert, 52
Dowhanty, William, 272
Dowie, Davie, 28
Downe, William, 370
Downing, Harrison, 163
Downing, John, Jr., 163, 172
Downing, Patrick, 123
Downs, Samuel, 4

Dows, Jonathan, 20
Doyle, Thomas, 350
Draper, Richard, 20
Draper, Timothy, 234
Drowne, Thomas, 234
Drummey, John, 50
Dubert, André, 292
Ducard, Jean Jacob, 363, 366
Ducart, George, 363, 366
Dudding, Thomas, 239
Dudley, Mary, 301
Dudley, Samuel, 301
Dullowin, Michael, 150
Dumaresque/Dumerisq,
 Philip/Phillip, 93, 95
Dummer, William, 38, 41, 56
Dunahoe, Thomas, 272
Duncan, Alexander, 374
Duncomb, Wiliam, 328
Dungen, Edward, 196
Dunkinson, William, 327
Dunn, John, 326, 327
Dunn, Nathaniel, 354
Dunn, Samuel, 174
Dunn, William, 181
Dunsten, Doctor, 349
Durell/Durrell, Capt., 72, 156
Durham, Daniel, 106
Dwight, Edmund, 272
Dwight, Jonathan, 148, 259, 309
Dwyer, James, 381
Dwyer, Sarah, 382
Dwyer, Thomas, 146
Dyer, Barrat, 30
Dyer, Robert, 180
Dyre, Barrat, 45
Dyre, Elisha, 117
Dyre, Henry, 140
Earl, Jonathan, 103
Earl, Joseph, 103
Earland, Robert, 23
Eastman, Ebenezer, 84
Easton, John, 199

Eastwick/Eastwicke, Stephen, 192, 198, 208
Eaton, Thomas, 76, 79
Edderige, Thomas, 126
Eddy, Obadiah, 325
Edinburough/Edinburgh, William, 267
Ednale, Richard, 95
Edwards, Frances, 326
Edwards, John, 8, 326
Edwards, Samuel, 81
Edwards, Thomas, 388
Eiles, John, 6
Eiles, Robert, 272
Elbridge, Thomas, 17
Eliot, Aaron, 270
Ellery, William, 304
Ellinwood, Ebenezer, 353
Elliot, Walter, 9
Ellis, David, 207, 226
Ellis, Francis, 153, 154
Ellis, James, 109
Ellis, Matthew, 109
Ellis, Michael, 238
Ellis, William, 344
Elmes, John, 252
Elwerthy, Simon, 102
Elwood, John, 95
Emmes, Samuel, 201
English, John, 359
Ephraim, Joshua, 347, 367, 372
Erving, John, 121
Esmond, Thomas, 115
Evans, John, 328
Evans, John, Jr., 321
Evans, Mary, 321
Evelin, Richard, 37
Evens, David, 223
Everendine, William, 81
Evers, John, 187, 310
Ewing, Patrick, 312
Exeter, George, 93
Fadre, Benjamin, 388

Fadre, Elizabeth, 388
Faffenback, Lawrence, 78
Fairservice, James, 160, 367
Falconer, Gilbert, 321
Faneuil/Fanueil, Andrew, 3, 34
Faneuil, Peter, 62
Farington, Elizabeth, 388
Farington, Jeremiah, 388
Farmer, Paul, 343
Farquharson, Alexander, 311
Farrel, Mary, 58
Farrington, John, 375
Farrington, Margaret, 374
Farrish, Richard, 244
Fellet, James, 126
Fellows, Nathaniel, 150
Felton, David, 355
Fennel, Thomas, 71
Fiend, Capt., 45
Fillis, Louis, 266
Fillis, Mrs. Louis, 266
Finch, James, 326
Finly, John, 243
Finney, James, 82, 361
Firkin, William, 237
Fisher, Frederick, 283
Fisher, Jeremiah, 296
Fisher, Patrick, 151
Fisher, Robert, 64
Fitch, James, 320
Fitz Gerrald, John, 151
Fitzchgerald, William, 105
Fitzgarell, William, 244
FitzGarrald, David, 373
Fitzgerald, Catharine, 212, 213
Fitzgerald, David, 385
Fitzgerald, Jane/Jenny, 77
Fitzgerald, Mauris, 116
Fitzpatrick, Daniel, 238
Fitzpatrick, John, 380
Fitzpatrick, Michael, 279
Fitzpatrick, Thomas, 279
Fixhall, Capt., 10

Flagg/Flegg, Gershom, 197, 209
Fleet, Thomas, 245, 258
Fletcher, Andrew, 226
Fletcher, Mr., 80
Fletcher, William, 166
Flin, James, 232, 327
Fling, ElizabetH, 281
Fling, John, 281
Flint, Edward, 120
Flint, George, 354
Flood, Ann, 187
Flood, Francis, 54
Flood, James, Jr., 158
Flowers, John, 182
Floyd, William, 307
Flucker, James, 153, 154
Flynt/Flint, Abigail, 314
Flynt/Flint, Ebenezer, 314
Follangsby, Wm., 89
Follot, Edward, 38
Fones, Jer./Jeremiah, 123, 170, 226, 252, 281, 288, 290, 328
Forbes, James, 330
Force, John, 155
Ford, Chadwallader, 294
Ford, John, 123
Forrest, Arthur, 221
Forrest, John, 290
Forrester, John, 92
Forrgerty, Terrence, 172
Forrister, John, 298
Forster, William, 156
Fosset, Douglas, 285
Foster, Hopestill, 319
Foster, John, 92
Foster, Matthew, 305
Foster, Richard, 121
Foster, Samuel, 124
Foster, Tho./Thomas, 72, 323
Foulsham, John, 259, 263
Foulsham, Mary, 259, 263
Fountain, William, 152
Fowler, Isaac, 375

Fowler, John, 172
Fowler, William, 154
Fowler, Zechary, 324
Fox, Pelex, 344
Fox, Richard, 115
Foxcroft, Mr., 149
Francis, John, 238
Francis/Francisco, John/Jaun, 201
Frankin, Mr., 27
Frankland, Henry, 220, 342
Frankland, Thomas, 220, 221
Franklin, Francis, 33
Franklin, John, 135
Franklin, Joseph, 44, 135
Freebody, John, 201
Freeman, Isaac, 368
Freeman, Richard, 244
French, Alexander, 156
Frissel, John, 17, 18
Frost, Samuel, 76
Frugere, Daniel, 335
Fry, James, 134
Fry, Thomas, 388, 389
Fulford, Richard, 231
Fuller, Amos, 276
Fuller, General, 271
Fullerton, John, 312
Furdize, James, 4
Furnace, Beneto, 64
Gahoit, John, 138
Gale, Abraham, 366
Gale, Azor, 28
Gale, John, 344
Gall, James, 228
Galliver, Elijah, 226
Galton, Robert, 258
Gamble/Gambles, John, 31, 317
Gardner, Andrew, 211
Gardner, Christopher, 345
Gardner, James, 177
Gardner, John, 43, 169, 225
Gardner, Samuel, 25

Gardner, Sylvester, 135
Gardner, William, 10
Garnett, Andrew, 279
Gary, Timothy, 177
Gatety, Henry, 273
Gayton, Clark, 241
Gee, Joshua, 12
Gee, Rev. Mr., 203
Geerish, John, 8
Gellepsy, Robert, 253
Geltone, 270
George, Anthony, 328
George, Moses, 365
George, Simon, 69
Gerrish, Mr., 183, 210
Gerrish, Paul, 185
Gibb, Capt., 33
Gibb, William, 32
Gibbins, William, 106
Gibbon, henry, 127
Gibbs, John, 54, 56, 57
Gibbs, Robert, 223
Gibson, Andrew, 27
Gibson, Deacon, 64
Gibson, Mr., 196, 197
Giles, John, 110
Giles, Thomas, 293
Gill, Sarah, 11
Gillam, Carteret, 6
Gillam, Richard, 67
Gilman, Edward, 137
Gilman, Major, 299
Gilpen, Abigail, 217
Gilpen, Thomas, 217
Glan, William, 37
Glase, Redman, 46
Glashine, Edward, 144
Glen, George, 130
Glin, John, 75
Glinn, Alexander, 234
Glyen, John, 366
Goble, John, 154
Godfrey, Benj., 3

Godfrey, Caleb, 202
Godfrey, William, 79
Godwin, Ichabod, 329
Goff, Patrick, 182
Gold, Richard, 238
Goldsmith, John, 363
Goldthwait, Ezekiel, 251, 288
Goldwmith, John, 357
Golson, Wm., 276
Gooch, James, 199, 346
Gooch, James, Jr., 180
Gooch, John, 96, 199
Gooding, Mary, 274
Goodridge, Walter, 34
Goodwin, Edward, 32
Goodwin, Ichabod, 282, 331
Gordon, James, 119, 152
Gordon, John, 82
Gordon, Richard, 323
Gordon, Robert, 366
Gorham, Joseph, 321, 380
Gorham, Nath., 318
Gorham, Nathaniel, 327
Gorham, Shubal, 73
Gorman, John, 162
Gosham, Aaron, 297, 298
Goss, Richard, 19
Gough, Mr., 223
Gould, Capt., 237
Gould, John, 237
Goulding, Elijah, 278
Goulding, John, 297, 298
Goulding, Robert, 211
Gradey, John, 141
Graham, Capt., 292
Granding, Philip, 167
Grant, Henry, 242, 311
Grant, Patrick, 209
Grant, Steven, 239
Graton, John, 188, 189, 190, 368
Gravel, John, 185
Graves, Samuel, 239
Gray, Caleb Joseph, 148

Gray, Ebenezer, 244
Gray, Edward, 148, 318
Gray, George, 70
Gray, John, 44, 277
Gray, Mr., 208
Green, Bartho., 262
Green, Bartholomew, 74
Green, Elisha, 69
Green, James, 328
Green, Job, 65
Green, John, 184
Green, Jonathan, 356
Green, Joseph, 220
Green, Mr., 112, 179
Green, Timothy, 74, 309
Greenleaf, John, 75
Greenleaf, Joseph, 274
Greenleaf, Stephen, 151, 265
Greenleaf, Timothy, 365
Greenough, Thomas, 225
Gregory, Alexander, 100
Grenane, Mary, 101
Grennings, Thomas, 106
Greton, John, 147
Greyvll, Capt., 259
Grice, Samuel, 91
Griffin, James, 217
Griffin, John, 69
Griffin, Simon, 95
Griffis, James, 278
Griffith, Andrew, 358, 371
Griffith, Benjamin, 284
Griffith, Euen/Even, 245
Griffithm Andews, 385
Grimes, Archibald, 40
Grimes, Cornelius, 272
Grimes, Francis, 287
Groster, Wm., 269
Grumin, John, 22
Grundill, John, 314
Guerard, Mr., 3
Guile, Joseph, 222
Gullison, John, 39

Gutry, James, 256
Guy, Anna, 34
Guy, John, 34
Guynn, John, 201
Gyles, Edward, 390
Haberson, Daniel, 83
Hadley, David, 306
Hadwan, Robert, 60
Hagen, Mr., 330
Hagin, William, 368
Hains/Haines, John, 332
Hair, Michael, 146
Hakney, Edward, 205
Hale, Joseph, 244
Hale, Robert, 264, 324
Halfall, James, 50
Hall, Anthony, 166
Hall, John, 383
Hall, Philip, 67
Hall, Richard, 23
Hall, Robert, 257
Hall, Stephen, 141
Hallowell, Benjamin, 174, 210, 267, 290, 332, 333, 336, 384
Hally, Darby, 287
Hambleton/Hamilton, Peter, 146
Hamilton, Edward, 355
Hamilton, Frederick, 101, 104
Hamilton, John, 123
Hamilton, Mary, 157
Hamlin, Martha, 358
Hamlin, Shubal, Jr,, 358
Hammet, Benjamin, 198
Hamockin, Capt., 238
Hancock, Thomas, 302
Handly, Michael, 335
Hanes, George, 200
Hankins, James, 237
Hanks, Samuel, 379
Hannay, Wm., 49
Hardin, John, 17
Hardnot, William, 368
Harmon, Thomas, 151

Harris, David, 93
Harris, Elijah, 93
Harris, George, 221
Harris, John, 38, 91, 277
Harris, Joseph, 323, 369
Harris, Mr., 116
Harris, Nathan, 223
Harris, Rebecca, 323, 369
Harris, Robert, 118
Harrison, John, 276
Harrod, Benjamin, 134
Harry, Jacob, 240
Hart, James, 186
Harthorn, John, 359
Hartwell, William, 239
Harvey, Christopher, 320
Harvey, John, 127
Harvy, Peter, 34
Hasty, James, 233
Hatch, Estes, 343
Hatch, Nathaniel, 64
Hatherton, James, 353
Havens, Micah, 356
Haward, David, 165
Hawkey, Warwick, 297, 298
Hawley, Jehiel, 14
Hay, James, 220
Hayes, John, 95, 113
Hazard, Jupiter, 346
Hazelton, William, 64
Head, John, 34
Hearsey/Hearsy, Israel, 127, 364
Hefferland, Mary, 52
Heley, Thomas, 186
Henderson, Capt., 242
Henderson, John, 84, 214, 227
Henderson, Joseph, 40
Hendly, Samuel, 201
Hendrey/Hendry, Robert, 366
Henshaw, Daniel, 78
Hepbron, Peter, 305
Herrald, John, 102
Herrig, Mary, 352

Herring, Henry, 352
Heslop, William, 370
Heulet, John, 215
Hewes, Benjamin, 45
Hewes, Daniel, 325
Hews, Samuel, 384
Hickie, John, 108
Hicks, Humphry, 107
Hidden, Jonathan, 365
Hidden, Susannah, 365
Hide, William, 8
Higgins, Peter, 92
Hight, Charles, 378
Higins, Alexander, 51
Hill, John, 188, 189
Hillard, David, 28
Hillhouse, John, 16
Hills, David., 265
Hilton, Israel, 251
Hinkley, Thomas, 57
Hinsdell, Mahuman, 69
Hirst, Grove, 19
Hirst, William, 19
Hitchburn, John, 49
Hoar, Lawrence, 162
Hoar, William, 126
Hoare, Thomas, 125
Hobbatt, George Michael, 364
Hobbs, John, 118
Hobson, Peter, 156
Hodge, Robert, 293
Hodges, John, 328
Hodson, Thomas, 334
Hogan, John, 279
Hogan, William, 390
Hogg, James, 239
Holbird, Samuel, 63
Holborn, John, 266
Holbrook, Nathanael, 131, 161
Holbrook, Philip, 296
Holford, Richard, 39
Holland, John, 92
Hollinshead, Jos., 276

Holloway, Henry, 246
Hollowel, Samuel, 152
Hollowell, Benjamin, 370
Holman, Annabella, 250
Holman, John, 250
Holmes, George, 114
Holmes, Samuel, 8, 72
Holmes, William, 355
Holmes. James, 13
Holnans, John, 201
Holt, James, 193
Homans, John, 92
Homans, Thomas, 106, 120, 252
Hood, Moses, 91
Hooker, Jean, 216
Hooker, John, 53
Hooker, Joseph, 216
Hooper, Elias, 164
Hoorl, John, 100
Hopkins, Lieut., 125
Hopkins, Matthew, 305
Hopkins, Stephen, 215
Horan, Charles, 370
Horn, William, 51
Horsewel/Horswell, John, 118, 362
Hosier, Giles, 383
Hoskins, John, 125
Houghton, Rowland, 104
Howard, Ebenezer, Jr., 384
Howard, Elizabeth, 155
Howard, James, 155
Howard, Mar[em]in, 284
Howard, Martin, 177, 270
Howard, Matthew, 1
Howard, Philemon, 215
Howarth/Howath, James, 267, 271
Howell, Henry, 94
Howell, James, 242, 259
Howell, Nathan, 22
Hoyle, John, 61, 264, 266
Hoyle, John, Mrs., 264, 266

Hubard, Mr., 294
Hubbard, Ebenezer, 14
Hubbard, John, 91
Hubbard, Mr., 22, 283
Hubbart, Elzabeth, 102
Hughes, Clement, 32
Hughes, James, 73, 77
Hughes, Samuel, 323, 376
Hughes, Thomas, 187
Hughes, William, 32, 391
Hughs, William, 105
Hull, William, 362
Hump, Daniel, 5
Humperson, William, 362
Hunt, Alexander, 115, 164, 374
Hunt, Edward, 377
Hunt, John, 232, 307
Hunt, Mr., 294
Hunt, Richard, 347
Hunt, Thomas, 326
Hunter, Andrew, 97
Hunter, George, 312, 313
Hunter, Thomas, 120
Hurst, John, 32
Hussey, Obed, 112
Hutchinson, John, 182, 296
Hutchinson, Samuel, 325
Hutchinson, Thomas, 218
Hutchinson, Thomas, Jr., 110
Hutchinson, William, 301
Hyat, Joseph, 110
Hyde, Robert, 14
Inches, Henderson, 329, 371
Inches, Joseph, 225
Indians, Abraham, Paul, 176; Amareta, 29; Ame, John, 7; Ame, Mary, 7; Attakin, Samuel, 240; Baker, John, 146; Bristow, 49; Cesar/Caesar, 24, 83, 309, 351; Charles, Lydia, 68; Charles, Silas, 177; Charles, Sylvester, 194;

407

Indians, Chin, Desiah, 32; Choho, Rachel, 32; Commonson, Jeremiah, 341; Coocbuck, 204; Covy, 137; Cozens, Samuel, 217; Daniel, 331; Daniels, Jo., 66; Dinah, 202; Eiles, John, 6; Ephraim, Joshua, 347; Esther, 329; Experience, 270; Francis/Francisco, John/Jaun, 201; Furnace, Beneto, 64; George, Simon, 69; Gosham, Aaron, 297, 298; Grace, 3; Harris, Nathan, 223; Harry, 1; arry, Jacob, 240; Hector, 42; Holborn, John, 266; Hump, Daniel, 5; 108, 109; Jame, 29; James, 20, 86, 90, 206, 283; James, Daniel, 271; Jennings, Absalom, 211; Jenny, 111; John, 151; John, Sarah, 329; Justin, 297, 298; Kilborn, 178; Larrens, Beriheba, 69; Mary, 154; Milly, 28; Moll, 11; Moses, 318, 327; Moses, Eli, 211; Nero, 81; Page, Comfort, 269; Pallas, 83; Patience, 270; Paun, Betty, 183; Peas, Tobias, 176; Pegg, 7, 149; Pequeen, Jonath., 356; Peter, 14, 101, 117; Phebe, 329; Pitteme, John, 161; Pompey, 69; Primus, 139, 169, 178; Prince, 2; Pummatich, Isaac, 3; Put, Peter, 69; Quanomp. Silas, 107; Robin, 29; Rose, 12; Ruth, 267; Sabera, 33; Saffidillah, 48; Sarah, 6; Scoggens, Thomas, 234; Shute, Isaac, 47; Strum, Nathaniel, 271; Thomas, Moses, 177; Toby, 20; Tom, 74; Tom/Sam/Moses, 323; Toney, 12; unnamed, 2, 4, 10, 13, 30, 61, 112, 190, 242; Venus, 194; Waban, Joshua, 184; Wampum, Keziah, 94; Wamscom, John, 375; Wamscomb, Louis, 391; Wapuck, Hannah, 5; Warmick, 7 Warwick, Ann, 138; Wicked, James, 176; Will, 42; Wombscom, John, 367; Worrison, Pallas, 170; Wright, James, 171; Ziporah, 29; Zipporah, 37

Ingersol, Jonathan, 186
Ingerson, Joseph, 2
Ingerson, William, 252
Inman, Ralph, 182
Ivers, Thomas, 305, 306
Ivers, William, 73, 77
Jackson, Edward, 135, 136, 139, 141, 143
Jackson, Gabriel, 6
Jackson, John, 49
Jackson, Johnson, 340
Jackson, Mary, 281
Jackson, Mrs., 123
Jackson, Samuel, 211, 310
Jackson, Thomas, 383
Jackson, William, 338, 340, 341, 342, 343
Jackson, Sargent, 378
Jacobs, Jacob, 33
Jaffrey, George, 52
Jamain, Nicholas, 3
James, Daniel, 182, 271
James, John, 91, 279, 292
James, Mr., 219
James, Richard, 165
James, Wm., 54
Jannerkins, Thomas, 183
Jarvis, Benjamin, 57
Jean, Arthur, 178

Jeanvrin, George, 47
Jefferson, Amos, 237
Jefferson, James, 73
Jeffries, David, 14
Jeffry, James, 165
Jeffry, John, 58
Jeffs, James, 157
Jekyl/Jekyll, John, 14, 21, 26, 36
Jenkins, Benjamin, 289
Jenkins, John, 11
Jenkins, Philip, 221
Jenkins, Robert, 114
Jenkins, Sarah, 221
Jenkins, Thomas, 292
Jenner, Thomas, 249
Jenney, Thomas, 253
Jennings, Absalom, 211
Jesop, John, 237
Jeudwin, Stephen, 95
Jipson, John, 26
Johannot, Daniel, 63
John, David Little, 344
John, Sarah, 329
Johnson, Daniel, 161
Johnson, Isaac, 29
Johnson, John, 47, 203, 238, 294, 295
Johnson, Joseph, 114
Johnson, Peter, 301
Johnson, Rev. Mr., 83, 170
Johnson, Samuel, 315
Johnson, Thomas, 213
Johnson, Timothy, 361
Johnson, William, 308
Johonnot, Zachariah, 212
Joliff, John, 169
Jones, Elisha, 207, 351
Jones, Henry, 364
Jones, Jeremiah, 72
Jones, John, 50, 377
Jones, Josiah, 82, 228
Jones, Mary, 372
Jones, Robert, 54, 55
Jones, Samuel, 84
Jones, William, 100, 344
Jorden, Joseph, 47
Jordin, Edmund, 60, 74
Josselyn, Joseph, 172
Joy, Samuel, 263
Joyce, John, 113
Judkins, John, 350
Kall, Elizabeth, 129
Kall, Nathaniel, 129
Kane, Col., 10, 11
Kanney, Nathanael, 41
Kapen, James, 151
Karr, John, 152
Keebler, Thomas, 210
Keeler, Samuel, 98
Keeler, Timothy, 98
Keen, Robert, 12
Keen, Shadrach, 204
Keighley, Thomas, 111
Keith, James, 287
Kelley, George, 117
Kelly, John, 33, 265
Kelly, William, 136
Kemball, Thomas, 316
Kemp, George, 63
Kenleaf, Henry, 280, 281
Kennedy, David, 44
Kennedy, Valentine/Valentine, 245
Kennely/Kennelly, John, 101, 104
Kenney, James, 205
Kent, Benjamin, 183, 312
Kentey, Anthony, 130
Keys, Mr., 192, 198
Keys, Nathaniel, 384
Kidder, Joseph, 318
Kidwill, Francis, 226
Kilby, Gilbert, 136
Kimbel/Kimbal, Jane, 198
Kimbel/Kimbal, Jonathan, 198
King, James, 365

King, Joseph, 343
King, Peter, 48
Kinlief, Henry, 280, 281
Kirby, John, 46
Kirke, Partrick, 298
Knap, Ebenezer, 172
Kneeland, John, Jr., 350, 351
Kneeland, Mr., 112, 179
Knight, John, 32, 143
Knott, George, 319
Knowles, Admiral, 276
Knowles, Elisha, 250
Knowles, John, 354
Knowlton, Joseph, 80
Knox, Peter, 162
Knox, William, 355
Lacey, James, 168
Ladd, Joseph, 105, 106
Lafagette, John, 93
Lake, Benjamin, 47
Lake, Capt., 19
Lake, John, 320
Lambert, John, 154
Lambert, William, 73
Landers, Martin, 329, 371
Lane, Robert, 203
Lang, Francis, 299
Langdon, Edward, 84, 85
Langford, Edward, 377, 379
Langley, Peter, 211
Lany, Benjamin, 311
Lany/Lang, Jeffery, 242
Larabe, John, 269
Larbordee, Lewis, 43
Larey, Daniel, 244
Larrabe, Judith, 243
Larrabe, Samuel, 243
Larrance, James, 31
Larrens, Beriheba, 69
Lathrop, Barnabas, 5
Lauchlen, Thomas, 48
Lauchlin, Thomas, 65
Laughton, Henry, 74

Lawne, John, 329
Lawrence, Bethiah, 164
Lawrence, Daniel, 164
Lawrence, Jonathan, 227
Lawrence, Shubael/Shubal, 386, 389
Lawrence, William, 103
Lawton, Henry, 59
Lawton, Robert, 190
Lawton, Thomas, 109
Le Mercier, Andrew, 208
Leach, Robert, 66
Leach/Leech, John, 178
Leander, Hugh, 78
Leaver, Capt., 276
Leavitt, Mr., 85
Leay/Lay, John, 291, 297
Ledyard, John, 147
Lee, Mr., 128
Lee, Samuel, 186
Leech, James, 328
Leech, John, 187
Lefeaver, Thomas, 124
Leigh, Philip, 283
Lenard, Jonas, 334
Lendall, James, 12
Lenox, William, 162
Leppington, John, 260
Lessley, Andrew, 359
Letten, James, 16
Leveston, John, 260
Lewis, Job, 205
Lightfoot, Thomas, 271
Linard, Ann, 219
Linard, Henry, 219
Linare, John, 323
Linum, James, 255
Lithered, John, 95
Little, Isaac, 8, 61
Little, John, 161, 299
Littleton, Benjamin, 269
Livermore, Abigail, 262
Livermore, John, 262

Livingston, Christopher, 169
Livingston, Lieut. Col., 21
Lloyd, William, 194
Lock, John, 204
Lock, Samuel, 229
Lockman, Major, 210
Logan, Walter, 319
Logen, John, 1
Long, Capt., 12
Long, John, 111
Long, Richard, 92
Long, Robert, 157, 163
Long, Timothy, 293
Long, William, 313
Looby, Victorius/Victorious, 33, 75
Lorane, George, 348
Lovell, Thomas, 76
Loverage, John, 354
Lovett, Eleanor, 219
Lovett, Joseph, 219
Low, Arthur, 47
Low, Charles, 342
Lowder, John, 207, 357
Lowder, Mary, 357
Lowder, William, 26
Lowlor, Thomas, 101
Loyd, John, 115
Lubbuck, James, 65, 67
Lucas, Augustus, 5
Lucas, John, 73
Lucas, Wm., 45
Luce, Mr., 140
Luce, Nicolas, 136
Luce, Peter, 64, 250
Lumbart, John, 16
Lummis, John, 280
Lynde, Benjamin/Benjamin Jr., 240
Lynde, Judge, 78
Lyndes, Samuel, 5
Lyndsie, Archibald, 92
Lynes, Cornelius, 350

Lyon, Daniel, 246
Lyon, John, 51
Lysence, Thomas, 319
Maccarty, Alexander, 146
Maccarty, Florence, 14
Maccarty, John, 146
Maccowloss, Jeremiah, 142, 143
Macdermant, Bryant, 310
MacGregory, David, 229
Mackadee, James, 272
MacKeel, William, 104
Mackenzie, Kennet, 36
Mackey, Alexander, 296
Mackey, William, 384
Mackgee, William, 132
Mackintosh, Charles, 263
Mackmaners, Philip, 292
Macknall, James, 213
Macmanara, Cornelius, 49
MacMillon/Macmillion, John, 115
MacNeil, John, 104
Macphedris, Archibald, 52
Macres, Joseph, 159
Macres, Mary, 159
Madden, Timothy, 143
Maddocks, Daniel, 337
Magee, Abraham, 335
Magill, David, 25
Magrath, Matthew, 181
Mahaney, Mary, 265
Mahaney, Philip, 265
Mahony, Thomas, 359
Mainzes/Mainzies/Meinzies, John, 31
Major, Peter, 63
Malan, John, 337
Malcum, Alexander, 239
Maley, John, 33
Mallary, Ebenezer, 42
Mallbone/Malbone, Evan, 231, 232
Malony, Thomas, 140

Man, Hugh, 63
Man, Mr., 348
Manchester, William, 100
Mandevell, William, 22
Manning, Mical, 116
Manning, Thomas, 146, 151, 155
Mansfield, Joseph, 117
Mansfield, Mary, 212, 213
Manson, Elizabeth, 313
Manson, Richard, 314
Manuel, Thomas, 162
March, John, 169, 178
Marchell, David, 221
Marcy, Moses, 391
Marion, Joseph, 246
Marot, Philip, 335
Marquand, Daniel, 343
Marriner, James, 26
Marshall, Michael, 50
Marshall, Samuel, 92
Marshell, George, 27
Marston, John, 265, 362
Marston, Manassah, 280
Marston, Prudence, 362
Martain, John, 194
Martin, Daniel, 106
Martin, Ja., 200
Martin, John, 240, 245
Martin, Rebeccah, 106
Martin, Thomas, 92
Marwood, Capt., 69
Marwood, Thomas, 72
Mascarene, Major, 127
Mashatbe, Emanuel, 225
Masieling, John, 60
Mason, Alexander, 25
Mason, John, 93, 118
Mason, Mary, 25
Mason, Mr., 278, 297, 298
Mason, Sarah, 289
Mason, Thadeus, 247
Massey, George, 306, 381
Massey, Sarah, 382

Mather, Mr., 228, 295
Mathers, Thomas, 208
Mathes, Benjamin, 220
Mathews, John, 55
Mattison, Thomas, 314
Mattocks, Samuel, 71
Maxwell, James, 161
Maxwell, John, 104
Maxwell, Wm., 42
Mayby, Thomas, 146, 151
Maylam, John, 372, 373
Mayo, George, 39
Mcalkin, Charles, 105
McAlla, Allen, 327
McBriage, James, 272
McCallister, Alexander, 321
McCan, Hugh, 140
McCaniel, James, 272
McCannon, James, 223
McCarrol, John, 129
McCarty, Carter, 162
McClean, James, 193
McClery/McCleary, John, 320
McClewer, Samuel, 181
McCobb, George, 323
McCobb, James, 323
McCornrick, John, 127
McCoy, Francis, 219
McCulluch, George, 211
McDaniel, Alexander, 273
McDaniel, Elizabeth, 374
McDaniel, Timothy, 207, 374
McDaniel, Walter, 310
McDorment, Briant, 334
McGee, William, 120
McGenes, Archibald, 307
McGenissy, Francis, 91
McGie, Robert, 344
McGlocklin, Charles, 227
McGown, Rose Anna, 352
McGregor, Alexander, 107
McGrough, John, 379
McHard, James, 181

McKenny, William, 140
McKenzie, Andrew, 299
McKnown, John, 370
McMullen, John, 277
McNeill, Malcom, 317
McNeily, Michael, 348
McNemarer, Daniel, 99
McPherson, Daniel, 229
Mead, Capt., 24
Mead, Jabez, 156
Meinzeis, John, 35, 40
Melledge, John, 48
Mellens, Benj., 52
Melvill, David, 29
Men, unnamed, 38, 97, 103, 107, 112, 183, 235, 282, 300, 345, 372, 373, 386
Mendum, Nathanael, 303
Menzeis/Menzies, John, 36, 68, 73
Merky, David, 209
Merrel, Isaac, 321
Merret/Merrett, Mr., 80, 116
Merrett, John, 118
Merrit, Major, 78
Messervey, Nathaniel, 155
Metcalf, Joseph, 40
Michael, Michael, 191
Milburn Jonathan, 1
Miles, William, 368, 369
Millar, James, 52
Miller, Francis, 30, 57
Miller, Henry, 25
Miller, Mr., 54, 55
Miller, Robert, 327
Miller, Samuel, 99, 299
Miller, William, 152
Millins, Benjamin, 52
Mills, James, 384
Mills, Luke, 378
Minzie, James, 337
Mirick, William, 132
Mitchel, Henry, 391

Mitchel/Mitchell, James, 148, 167, 269
Mitchel, Joshua, 365
Mitchell, John, 316
Mixter, John, 237
Moffat, Mr., 19
Moffet, Thomas, 18
Mograch, Patrick, 173
Mohegin, Denies/Ned, 102
Molinuex, William, 273
Moncrath, David, 305
Moncrieffe, Thomas, 380
Monk, George, 78, 82
Monk, James, 200
Monnalt, Alexander, 292
Montgomery, Partrick, 352
Moody, Ebenezer, 142
Moody, Samuel, 202
Moore, Alexander, 47
Moore, Nathanael, 251
Moore, Thomas, 136
Moorey, Richard, 286
More, John, 9
More, William, 8
Morecock, Mr., 22
Morey, John, 269
Morgareidge, Samuel, 238, 316, 317
Morgen, Griffice, 313
Morres, William, 312
Morris, James, 22
Morris, Matthew/Mathew, 188, 189, 190
Morris, Nicholas, 169
Morris, Robert, 218
Morris, Wm., 299
Mors, Obadiah, 198, 200
Morse, John, 339
Mortimer, Philip, 148
Mortimore, William, 113
Moseley, Anthony, 166
Moses, Eli, 211
Moses, Mark, 49

Mouleworth, Edw., 54
Mountfort, Jonathan, 7
Moverly, William, 89
Mower, Ephraim, 67
Mulberry, Benjamin, 265
Mullin, James, 255
Mumford, John, 33
Munden/Mundell, Patrick, 35, 36, 40
Munro, John, 241
Murfee, Cornelius, 124
Murfey, John, 204
Murphy, Daniel, 306
Murphy, Edward, 134, 136, 139
Murphy, James, 160
Murray, Peter, 354
Murry/Murray, William, 373, 385
Musgrave, Philip, 39, 41, 44
Mustees, Abel, 121; Benjamin, 236; Caesar, 375; Jack, 363; James, 240; Pero, 390; Phelice, 236; Simon, 362
Muzzy, Benj., 64
Muzzy, John, 64
Nash, Nathan, Jr., 274
Nash, William, 187
Nason, William, 331
Neal, Henry, 354
Negroes, Achilles/Achelles, 330; Adam, 233, 242; Adams, Jo, 300; Aesop, 61; Andrew/Andress, 315; Anser, 167; Archalus, 266; Austin, Ben, 270; Bass, 91; Batter, John, 333; Battis, Jeffry, 289; Battis, John, 289; Bedford, 316; Ben, 100, 204, 232; Bess, 90; Bill, Jack, 8; Billah, 214, 277, 295; Black, Jonathan, 252; Blow, Charles, 72; Boney, 381; Bonney, 295; Boston, 58, 78, 261, 272, 273; Brazill, 196; Bridgwater, 250; Bristo, 282, 283; Bristol, 53, 144, 347; Bristow, 235; Briton, 180; Brown, Tom, 149, 164; Caesar, 36, 71, 96, 97, 109, 128, 158, 166, 169, 175, 233, 266, 307, 353; Cajo, 119; Cambridge, 149, 171, 221, 224, 284, 286; Casar/Caesar, 282, 299; Cato, 77, 192, 205, 244, 248, 255, 257, 288, 300, 302, 304, 308, 309, 338; Ceasar/Cesar, 56, 78; 56; Charles, 125, 214; Christmas, 76, 310; Cicero, 205, 207, 240; Cloe, 318; Cobbo, 261; Coffe, 147; Coffee, John, 76, 79; Coffy, 202; Congo, Scipio, 391; Connungo, Jemy/Jemmy, 54, 56; Constant, 252; Crispas, 336; Cromwell, 390; Cuba/Cuber, 122, 228, 233, 234; Cuff/Cuffe, 93, 152, 157, 134, 171, 206, 231, 232; 311, 313; Cuffee, 57, 80, 98, 100, 133, 150, 247; Cuffee, John, 83; Cuffey/Cuffy, 94, 246, 275, 333; Cyrus, 294; Daniel, 15, 23, 166; Diana, 302; Dick, 369; Dinah, 109; Dorus, 217; Emanuel, 125; Exeter, 188, 189; Felix, 215; Francis, 308, 309; Franklin, 14; George, 1, 57, 80, 95, 109, 273, 275; Glasgow, 240, 245; Green, Joseph, 220; Hall, Philip, 67; Hanks, Samuel, 379; Hannah, 340; Harmon, Thomas, 151; Harry, 13, 14, 18, 96, 127; Hazard/Hazzard, 345, 346, 379; Hazard, Jupiter, 346; Hector, 174, 244;

Negroes, Hercules, 330; Herculus, 305; Homer, 374; Isaac, 118, 238; Jack, 9, 32, 62, 81, 84, 85, 131, 132, 145, 151, 174, 178, 192, 196, 198, 319; Jacl, 156; Jammey, 243; Janto, 168; Japhet, 266; Jean, 196; Jemmy, 59, 67, 247; Jenny, 247; Jersey, 11; Jethro, 35; Jim, 153; Jo, 4, 138, 197, 294, 295; Jocco, 146; John, Peter, 145; Juba, 78, 161, 179; Juno, 124; Jupeter/Jupiter, 63, 185; Lan, 382; Lawrence, Shubal, 386; Lester, 13, 18; Letitia, 152; Lewis, James, 10; London, 300, 370; Lymas, 39; Mallott, John, 71; Mary/Mary Ann, 175; Mashatbe, Emanuel, 225; Maximus, 144; Melech, 119; Mercy, 156; Millet, 149, 163; Mimbo, 123; Mingo, 28, 41, 98, 202; More, John, 9; Moses, 271; Nancy, 246; Ned, 278, 332; Nero, 184, 201; Nevis, 199; Newham, 259; Newport, 72, 245, 248, 258, 301; Obed, 196; Paul, 210, 290; Peach, 343; Peg, Ben, 270; Penelope, 1; Pero/Peroe, 35, 256, 306, 390; Peroe, 256; Peter, 2, 14, 22, 50, 133, 178, 187, 241, 274; Phillip, 204, 332; Phillis, 96, 165; Plumb, 188; Pomp, 308, 334; Pompey/Pompy, 27, 57, 64, 147, 179, 191, 193, 209, 254, 258, 261, 282, 331, 376, 380; Port, 190; Portsmouth, 88, 260; Primas/Primus, Primus, 7, 70, 75, 238, 296, 316, 317, 380; Prince, 249, 257, 262, 275, 315; Proiperous, 222; Quacco, 41; Quaco, 145, 306; Quam, 295, 332; Quambe, 220; Quan, 219; Quashe, 310; Quoddy, 175; Quom, 386; Quomina, 189; Quomino, 165, 291; Rinah, 110; Robbin, 289; Robin, 76, 216, 272; Roger, 75; Rose, 218; Saco, 34; Sam, 107; Sambo, 53, 202, 379; Sampson, 214; Samson, Toney, 163; Sandy, 45; Scipio/Scippio, 50, 76, 157, 222, 334; Scipio/Sipeo, 305, 350, 351; Scipio, Tom, 120; Sharper, 179, 312; Stanley, Edward, 337; Swift, Caesar, 69; Timothy/Tim, 63, 65, 184; Titus, 340; Tobey, 279; Tom, 74, 82, 89, 120, 152, 197, 203; unnamed, 4, 5, 6, 10, 26, 65, 67, 82, 92, 131, 143, 190, 201, 209, 229, 237, 239, 310, 315, 318, 321, 336, 369; Venus, 185; Violet, 98, 234, 239; Will, 83, 143, 144, 253, 303; York, 191, 260, 333; York, Pomp, 299; York, Pompey, 197

Nelson, Alexander, 359
Nelson, James, 150
Netherton, William, 17
Nevin, James, 296
Nevins, David, 309, 320
Newell, John, 46, 157, 163
Newhall, Mr., 284, 286
Newing, Stephen, 89
Newman, James, 302
Newman, Maurice, 350
Newman, Michael, 191
Newmarch, George, 336
Newton, Beriah, 383

Newton, Hibbert, 261
Newton, Mr., 137
Newton, Sarah, 383
Nicholas, Anthony, 47
Nicholl/Nicoll, James, 291, 292
Nichols, James, 156
Nichols, John, 169
Nichols, John, Jr., 191
Nichols, Mary, 191
Nicholson, George, 223
Nickson, John, 239
Nickson, Robert, 253
Niles, Henry, 53
Niles, Nath./Nathaniel Jr., 4, 6
Niles, Nathan, 331
Niles, Nathaniel, 1, 191
Niles, Samuel, 2, 4
Noble, Arthur, 175
Noble, Humphry, 92
Nolan, James, 146
Nolan, Jaques, 145
Norden, Nathaniel, 12, 33
Norman, William, 347
Norris, Jonathan, 184
Norton, John, 165
Norton, Thomas, 177
Nott, Samuel, 371
Noye, Mr., 223
Noyes, Nathaniel, 289
Noyes, William, 336
Nucall, David, 92
Nutlees, Edward, 272
Nutting, Joseph, 321
O'Bryant, Thomas, 244
O'Cannon, Bryan, 223
O'Dowley, Daniel, 272
Odinell, John, 148
Odlin, Elisha, 23
Ogard, Lawrence, 287
Okeden, Mr., 66
Oldcraft, Mary, 119
Oldham, Oliver, 361
Oliver, Bratle, 58

Oliver, Daniel, 337, 372, 373
Oliver, George, 280, 281
Oliver, James, 171, 221, 224
Oliver, Robert, 273, 275
Oliver, William, 122
Olivey, Joseph, 123
Oneut, George, 326
Ore, Edward, 236
Orrok, David, 103
Osborne, William, 384
Osgood, William, 216
Otis, John, 5
Oulton, John, 13, 18
Owen, Nathanael, 107
Owen, William, 104, 105
Packer, Thomas, 236, 269, 361
Pacqueran, Mr., 3
Paddock, Paul, 360
Page, Comfort, 269
Page, Joseph, 365
Page, William, 269
Paige, Nicholas, 8
Paine, Thomas, 285
Painter, Obadiah, 198
Palin, James, 33, 37
Palmer, George, 265
Palmer, John, 42
Palmer, Thomas, 13, 18
Papillon, Peter, 53
Parker, John, 323
Parker, Roger, 241
Parker, William, 27
Parkes, Thomas, 217
Parkeson, Timothy, 221
Parkman, Alexander, 166, 169, 175
Parris, Charles, 16
Parsons, Joseph, 98
Parsons, Robert, 43
Partridge, Samuel, 299, 300
Pate, Christopher, 118
Paterson, John, 121
Paterson, Thomas, 67

Pateshall, Robert, 75
Patridge, Samuel, 379
Pattie, Henry, 316
Pattin/Patten, William, 87
Paun, Betty, 183
Paxton, Charles, 169
Paxton, Wentworth, 42
Payne, John, 279
Payne, Margaret, 145
Payson, John, 310
Peach, Emm, 27
Peagrum, John, 112
Pearl, Anthony, 23
Pearson, John, 370
Pearson, Mr., 81
Pearson, Thomas, 128, 150
Peas, Tobias, 176
Peaslee, Amos, 299
Peaslee, Nathanael, 84
Peck, Joseph, 47
Peg, Ben, 270
Pembroke, Elkanah, 21
Pembroke, Henaretha, 21
Pendergast, Stephen, 235
Penny, John, 354
Penny, Thomas, 273
Pepperel, Mr., 22
Pepperel, Wm., 45
Pepperel/Pepperil/Pepperrell/
   Pepperell, William/Wm., 2, 39,
   45, 259, 272
Pequeen, Jonath., 356
Percake, John, 290
Percevell, Crean, 323
Percivall, F., 169
Perkins, Edmund, 178
Perkins, Lydia, 76, 79
Perry, Ambros, 319
Perry, James, 7
Perry, Joseph, 184
Perry, Nathan, 337
Perry, Robert, 24
Peterson, Andrew, 237

Peterson, Peter, 103
Pharour, John, 216
Philipps, Caleb, 176
Philipps/Phillips, General, 237,
   254, 255
Philips, Ann, 239
Philips, Richard, 252
Philips. John, 196
Phillips, Christopher, 77
Phillips, George, 14
Phillips, John, 113, 210
Phillips, Justice, 357
Phips, William, 167
Pidgeon, Doctor, 353
Pierce, Caleb, 387
Pierce, Clothier, 383
Pierce, Mr., 277
Pierce, Stephen, 341
Pigeon, Henry, 190
Pigot, Mrs., 158
Pigot, Rev. Mr., 94, 158
Pigott, George, 83
Pikoa, Joseph, 375
Pinder, John, 188
Piraza, Antonia, 298
Pitman, Mark, 183
Pitman/Pittman, William, 45,
   286, 378
Pitteme/Pittome, John, 131, 161
Pitts, James, 5, 348
Plaisted, Ichabod, 308
Plaisted, Jos., 314
Plaisted, Joseph, 197, 252, 341
Plaisted, Tho., 196, 197
Plaisted, Thomas, 20
Plastead, Daniel, 221
Pomrey, James, 66
Poole, Benj., 64
Poor, Joseph, 187
Poor, William, 220
Porter, Samuel, 43
Porter, Thomas, 90
Potter, John, 283

Potter, Stephen, 384
Pottle, Robert, 388
Pougher, Daniel, 39
Povey, Thomas, 1
Powell, John, 27, 239
Power, James, 182
Power, Nicholas, 324
Powner, James, 289
Pratt, Mrs., 210
Pray, Ephraim, 6
Pray, John, 47
Preble, Joseph, 319
Preston, Henry, 347
Prey, John, 63
Price, Henry, 243
Price, John, 25
Price, Mr., 130, 131
Price, Rev. Commissary, 199
Prince, Capt., 133
Prince, Job, 350, 351
Procter, Joseph, 282, 283
Procter, Obadiah, 53
Proctor, Richard, 30
Prout, Timothy, 62
Prowse, Richard, 293
Pue, Jonathan, 138
Pullen/Puller, Eleanor, 122, 228, 233, 234
Pullen, John, 225
Put, Peter, 69
Pyam, Jacob, 252
Pye, Thomas, 292
Quandett, Jeán, 292
Quincy, Edmund, 168
Raby, James, 169
Rackwood, John, 97
Ragan, Darby, 8
Rand, William, 363, 366
Rathwell, Joseph, 106
Rawlings, Jeremiah, 185
Raymar, James, 229
Raymond, Jonathan, 147
Rea, Daniel, 249

Read, Charles, 287
Read, Daniel, 155
Read, John, 310, 324
Read, Thomas, 20
Redford, Thomas, 16
Reding, Archibald, 244
Redman, Michael, 320
Redshaw, Christopher, 17
Reed, Benjamin, 379
Reed, Jonathan, 122, 129
Reed, Robert, 249
Reed, Stepen, 221
Reeves, Cockrell, 143, 144
Regane, David, 154
Regeway, John, 248
Reisdon, Michael, 233
Remick, Abigail, 243
Remick, James, 243
Renken, Benjamin, 353
Reteille, Mr., 131
Reynold, Joseph, 369
Reynolds, John, 140
Rian, Michael, 209
Rich, James, 328
Richards, Edward, 45
Richards, Nathaniel/Nathanial, 264
Richardson, Caleb, 164
Richardson, Ebenezer, 355
Richardson, John, 344
Richardson, Pierson, 153
Richardson, Robert, 278
Richardson, John, 93
Richarson, Elizabeth, 293
Richbrook, Thomas, 30
Richey, Francis, 140
Richmond, Silvester/Sylvester, 62, 271
Riddell/Riddel, Joseph, 13
Ridgaway, Mr., 380
Riggin, Peter, 16
Rimer, Capt., 281
Rimer, Matthew, 283

Rintoul, John, 92
Rivers, Joseph, 384
Roach, David, 101, 104
Roberts, Peter, 330
Robertson, Rhomas, 360
Robertson, Robert, 141
Robie, John, 70
Robinson, David, 344
Robinson, Elias, 208
Robinson, George, 4
Robinson, John, 230
Robinson, Margaret, 246
Robinson, Rowland, 300
Robinson, William, 81
Robison, James, 24
Roch/Rock, Morris, 130, 131
Roche, James, 166
Rock, Thomas, 255
Rogers, James, 153
Rogers, Mary, 293
Rogers, Richard, 81, 380
Rogers, Samuel, 387
Rogers, Thomas, 203
Rook, Honour, 229
Rook, James, 229
Rose, David, 13
Rose, Mrs. William, 254
Rose, William, 254, 290
Ross, Alexander, 319
Ross, John, 334
Ross, Laurence, 26
Ross, Seth, 210
Ross, William, 118
Rosse, William, 288
Roth, Richard, 44
Rothman, John, 165
Rouse, John, 252
Row, John, 208
Row, Stephen, 16
Rowlandson, Francis, 106
Royall, Jacob, 203
Ruggels, George, 194

Ruggels/Ruggles, Elizabeth, 114
Rullo, John, 162
Rumsey, Robert, 9
Russel, Chambers, 154
Russel/Russell, James, 268
Russell, Gyles, 179
Russell, Nath., 216
Russey, John, 313
Rust, Benjamin, 231, 317
Rust, Margaret, 231
Rutherford, William, 377
Ryan, Edmund, 112, 140, 142
Ryan, John, 193, 238, 360
Ryan, Thomas, 177
Ryan, William, 43
Rymes, Christopher, 102
Rymes, Samuel, 2
Sabin, Elijah, 278
Sale, John, 91
Sall, Tho., 322
Salmon, John, 315
Saltar, John, 104, 105
Salter, Thomas, 29, 80, 95, 109
Salter, Zebulon, 87
Saltonstall, Richard, 303, 338
Sampson, Tony, 60
Samson, Toney, 163
Sanders, David, 328
Sanders, John, 354
Sanford, William, 166
Sanford, Wm., 166
Sault, Benjamin, 388, 389
Saulter, William, 12
Saunders, Philemon, 272
Savage, Arthur, 16
Savage, Col., 195
Savage, Habijah, 71
Savage, Richard, 49
Saval, John, 325
Savell, John, 40
Sawyer, Stephen, 101
Sawyer, Stephen, Jr., 256

Scallin, Luke, 245
Schuyler, Peter, 3
Scipio, Tom, 120
Scoggens, Thomas, 234
Scolley, James, 54, 62
Scott, Hugh, 199, 271
Scott, John, 23
Scott, Robert, 50, 352
Scott, Silvanus, 76
Searle, Joseph, 41
Seatten, William, 279
Seaver, Jonathan, 121
Seavey, Amos, 360
Sebear, John, 54
Sebear, Mr., 55
Seeth, James, 201
Segourney, Mr., 77
Selby/Silby, Thomas, 28, 31
Semons, Joseph, 344
Sergeant, Epes, 331
Serran, Moses, 290
Sever, Jonathan, 88
Severance, Ebenezer, 269
Sewall, Judge, 46
Sha, Patty, 212
Shaftoe, Thomas, 377
Shainton, Richard, 53
Shangasseys, Patrick, 150
Shannon, Charles, 388
Sharp, James, 348
Sharp, Mary, 348
Sharp, William, 87
Sharpe, Ann, 106
Sharpe, Lewis, 106
Sharples, Robert, 106
Shaw, Francis, 352
Shaw, Hezekiah, 272
Shaw, Patrick, 212
Shaw, Samuel, 160
Shearbourne/Sherburn/
Sherburne, Henry, 22
Shearman, Thomas, 257

Shearrer, Thomas, 52
Sheffield, Nathaniel, 51
Shepard, Thomas, 291, 297
Sheperd, Benjamin, 336
Shephardson, William, 78
Sherburn, Henry, 87
Sherburne, Henry, Jr., 390
Sherburne, Joseph, 237
Sherrard, Thomas, 52
Sherwill, William, 253
Shimmans, Rodge, 53
Shirley, Mr., 85
Shirley, William, 251
Shore, George, 43
Short, Charles, 357, 363
Shotoro, John, 117
Shurkey, George, 77
Shute, Isaac, 47
Siah, John, 264
Sias, Joseph, 220
Sigourney, Andrew, Jr., 168
Sigourney, Capt., 151
Simmon, Richard, 172
Simon, Charles, 47
Simons, William, 92
Simpson, Abigail, 303
Simpson/Simson, Andrew, 254, 303
Simpson, John, 121
Simpson, Robert, 253
Sinclair, William, 45
Sisson, James, 140
Sivret, Matthew, 68
Skinner, George, 66, 88
Slapp, John, 11
Slattery, Darby, 207
Slonen, John, 359
Small, Henry, 320
Small, Matthew, 313
Smart, Capt., 38
Smelt, Cornelius, 307
Smibert, John, 133

421

Smith, Abiall, 168
Smith, Ebenezer, 168
Smith, Elizabeth, 125, 192
Smith, Isaac, 322
Smith, James, 53, 91, 308, 309, 353
Smith, Jeremiah, 279
Smith, John, 19, 47, 92, 192, 230, 259, 285, 312
Smith, John, Jr., 125
Smith, Margaret, 65
Smith, Mary, 372
Smith, Morris, 323
Smith, Mr., 216
Smith, Patrick, 344
Smith, Richard, 53, 255, 302
Smith, Samuel, 77, 88, 287
Smith, Thomas, 66, 346
Smith, William/Wm., 110, 255, 372
Smyth, Hannah, 94
Snelling, Jonathan, 280, 281
Snoden, David, 241
Solovan, Darby, 252
Soper, Benjamin, 168
Soule, Ichabod, 163
Soutback, John, 265
Southard, Stephen, 273
Southard, Susanna, 273
Southworth, Bridget, 189
Southworth, Edward, 189
Sparhawk, Mr., 272
Spaulder, Francis, 135
Spencer, Alexander, 52
Spight, Robert, 376
Spikeman, William/Wm., 96, 97
Spirin, Richard, 350
Spooner, John, 375
Spragg, William, 37
Sprague, Nicholas, Jr., 110
St. Ambrose, John, 227
St. Roche, George, 375

Stack, Robert, 119
Stacy, John, 213
Stafford, Joseph, 270
Stamper, Abraham, 242
Staniford, John, 15, 57
Staniford, Samuel, 107
Stanley, Edward, 337
Stanley, Richard, 277
Stanly, Edward, 356
Stanton, Henry, 29
Staples, Samuel, 93
States, Adam, 387
Stebbins, Thomas, 384
Steel, John, 254
Steel, Margaret, 120
Steel, Mr., 33
Steel, Robert, 326, 330, 331
Steel, Thomas, 48, 91
Steeper, John, 319
Sterling, James, 46, 59
Stevens, Dr., 288
Stevens, George, 359
Stevens, Joseph, 116
Stevens, Timothy, 300, 302
Steward, James, 83
Steward, John, 272
Stewart, Andrew, 148
Stewart, Edward, 177
Stewart, James, 24
Stewart, John, 63
Sticks, James, 278
Stillwell, Abraham, 228
Stinson, Capt., 324
Stinson, Dominick, 323
Stirling, James, 81
Stirman, Robert, 216
Stivens, Dr., 308
Stockey, Anne Carrola, 270
Stoddard, David, 43
Stokes, Joseph, 92
Stone, Elias, 268
Stone, Robert, 382, 391

Stone, Thomas, 267
Stone, William, 19
Stook, William, 348
Storey, Thomas, 306, 324
Story, Thomas, 34, 182
Stott, Thomas, 187
Stowell, Josiah, 337
Strum, Nathaniel, 271
Stuart, John, 191
Stuart, Mary, 191
Studley, Jonathan, 26
Sturmey, Frederick, 371
Sturtevant, David, 239
Sturtevant, Lemuel, 386, 389
Sullivan, Grizel, 346
Sullivan, Jeremiah, 371
Sullivan, John, 10
Sunderland Samuel, 166
Surrage, Hugh, 330
Sutcomb, Richard, 125
Sutton, Mary, 18
Swadell, Joseph, 13
Swain, Elizabeth, 360
Swan, Ebenezer, 211
Swan, John, 28
Swan, Peter, 311
Sweetser, Wigglesworth, 50
Sweetzer, Seth, 1
Swelling, William, 27
Swift, Caesar, 69
Swift, Mr., 244
Swinnerton, John, 304
Swiny/Swiney, Morgan, 212, 230
Syas, John, 235
Sylvester, Richard, 216
Symmons, Thomas, 45
Tabs, Carrel, 135
Talantire, William, 268
Tanton, William, 210
Taplin, Benjamin, 261
Tarp, John, 97

Taverner, William, 47
Tay, Deacon, 114
Taylor, John, 34, 268, 384
Taylor, Neal, 88
Taylor, Robert, 102
Taylor, William, 198, 244
Teber, William, 100
Temple, Capt., 208
Temple, Robert, 235, 236, 260, 286, 287
Tennant, Francis, 50
Tenton, Thomas, 321
Thacher, Josiah, 151
Thacher, Oxinbridge, 30
Thacher, Peter, 30
Thackster, Samuel, 3
Tharold, Francis, 38
Thayer, Mr., 96, 97
Thomas, David, 2
Thomas, John, 237, 383
Thomas, Moses, 177
Thomas, Nathaniel, 40
Thomas, Philip, 181
Thomas, Wm., 367
Thomlinson, Robert, 134
Thompsom, Rebeccah, 274
Thompson, Cornelius, 53
Thompson, David, 92
Thompson, Francis, 10
Thompson, James, 235
Thompson, John, 180, 207, 327
Thompson, Robert, 333
Thompson, Robert, Jr., 274
Thompson, William, 272
Thornton, Joshua, 275
Thorpe, Alexander, 242
Thwing, Nathanael, 160
Tibbits, George, 236
Tidd, Joseph, 220
Tidd, Martha, 220
Tilley, George, 98, 144
Tilton, John, 344

Tinsley, William, 44
Titmarsh, John, 141
Todd, Andrew, 44
Todd, William, 38
Tolman, Elisabeth, 159
Tolman, John, 159
Tompson, George, 82
Tompson, John, 83
Tomson, James, 103
Tomson, John, 237
Tomson, Robert, 103, 376
Tomy, Patrick, 99
Tonkin, Charles, 128, 129, 130
Toole, John, 179
Torrington, William, 268
Torsine, John, 290
Townsend, Job, 126
Trescot/Trescott, Zechariah, 113
Tresteene, James, 324
Trevelle, Peter, 26
Trevett, Richard, 57
Tripsack, Henry, 94
Trotter, Ann, 357
Trout, Joseph, 390
Trow, Joseph, 341
Trowbridge, Ebenezer, 279
Tuck, Joseph, 22
Tucker, Bethia/Bethiah, 152, 171
Tucker, Francis, 218
Tucker, Isaac, 245
Tucker, John, 111
Tuckerman, Daniel Jent, 219
Tuckerman, John, 177
Tudor, John, 364
Turell, Joseph, 55
Turner, Edward, 169
Turner, Francis, 64, 135
Turner, John, 60, 252
Turner, Lewis, 179
Turner, Stephen, 380
Turrell, Joseph, 54
Twehee, James, 186

Twigg, Thomas, 264
Tyler, Andrew, 39
Tyler, Mr., 246
Tyler, Samson, 322
Tyng, Eleazer, 289, 376
Tyng, Mr., 376
Tyson, Richard, 63
Underdown, John, 60
Usher, Hezekiah, 151
Valenton, Thomas, 180
Vardy, Luke, 259
Varley, Mathew, 47
Vassall, Henry, 272
Vassall, Lewis, 206
Vaughan, Nariar, 116
Vernon, Samuel, 30
Verry, Isaiah, 113
Vetch, Col., 12
Vetch, Governor, 9
Vickerman, Slack, 150
Vincent, Ambrose, 8
Vintiman, George, 22
Viorney, Thomas, 50
Viscount, Philip, 61
Viscoup, Daniel, 387
Waade, Samuel, 68
Waban, Joshua, 184
Wade, Arthur, 62
Wadge, Nicholas, 93
Wadsworth, Benjamin, 379
Waite, Return, 30
Waite, Thomas, 247
Wakefield, John, 295, 381
Waldo, Benjamin, 220
Waldo, Mr., 80
Waldo, Samuel, 144
Waldron, Rev. Mr., 202
Walford, John, 215
Walker, Abigail, 338
Walker, Alexander, 108, 321
Walker, James, 276
Walker, John, 31, 38, 79, 361

Walker, Robert, 320
Walker, William, 51, 79, 310
Wall, David, 64
Wall, Robert, 376, 378
Wall, William, 100, 154
Wallais, Thomas, 49
Waller, John, 353
Wallingford, Thomas, 242
Wallis, Benjamin, 17, 18
Wallis, David, 243, 247, 310
Wallis, Gamaliel, 279
Wallis, Mr., 76
Wallis, Oliver, 124
Walton, Jeremiah, 390
Walton, John, 126
Wamscom, John, 375
Wamscomb, Louis, 391
Wanton, Edward, 15
Wapuck, Hannah, 5
Warburton, James, 52
Ward, John, 245
Ward, Mr., 294
Ward, Richard, 199
Ward, Thomas, 105
Warren, Capt., 156
Warren, Commodore, 245
Warren, Peter, 309
Warton, Sarah, 9
Wass, John, 152
Wate, Nathaniel, 211
Waterhouse, Samuel, 322
Waters, David, 326
Watkins, Thomas, 258
Watkinson, Charles, 377
Watson, Joseph, 45
Watt, Capt., 160
Watt, James, 15
Watt, Mr., 75
Watt, Robert, 61
Watt, Wm., 209
Watts, Daniel, 70, 75
Watts, Edward, 41

Watts, Richard, 311
Watts, Samuel, 186
Wattson, Joseph, 78
Waughan, John, 79
Weare, Peter, 131
Webb, George, 35
Webb, John, 385, 387
Webb, John, Jr., 257
Webber, George, 101
Webber, Jonas, 79
Webber, Samuel, 252
Weed, Daniel, 288
Weeks, Mr., 97
Weeks, Thomas, 162
Welch, Henry, 89
Wells, John, 226
Welsted, Mr., 271
Wendell, Col., 332
Wentworth, Ebenezer, 14
Wentworth, John, 52
Wentworth, Mark Hunking, 311
Wentworth, Samuel, 6, 15
West, David, 238
West, Edmond, 287
West, Zebulon, 244
Westbrook, Thomas, 47
Westcot, Samuel, 226
Westley, Mandlin, 270
Weston, John, 49
Wetbred, Samuel, 344
Wett, Samuel, 264
Whalam, James, 285
Whaley, William, 102
Wheeler, Abijah, 108, 109
Wheeler, Capt., 292
Wheeler, Dorcas, 284
Wheeler, E., 298
Wheeler, Nathanael, 90
Wheeler, Philip, 223
Wheeler, Samuel, 284
Wheeler, Wm., 385
Wheelwright, John, 101, 104

Wheelwright, Samuel, 47
Wherton, John, 272
Whetstone, joseph, 122
White, Abigail, 185
White, Benjamin, 185
White, Eleazer, 238
White, Isaac, 124
White, John, 48, 306
White, John, Jr., 386
White, Jonathan, 305, 350, 351
White, Michael, 279
White, Nathaniel, 242
White, Patrick, 90
White, Richard, 240
White, Samuel, 272
White, Sarah, 222
White, Thomas, 26
White, William, 121
White, Wm., 88
Whitehead, Michael, 253
Whiteworth, John, 221
Whitford, Paskee, 206
Whiting, Benjamin, 174
Whiting, Pethuel, 83
Whitman, Jacob, 275
Whitney, Capt., 38
Wicked, James, 176
Wickham, Benjamin, 246
Wickham, Capt., 176
Wiggan, Benjamin, 126
Wiggins, Charles, 272
Wiggins, Joseph, 321
Wight, Thomas, 21
Wilcox, Jeremiah, 62
Wilcox, Robert, 62
Wildman, John, 81
Wiliams, David, 323
Wilks, Quartermaster, 45
Willard, J., 252
Willet, Framcis, 196
Williams, Benj., 118
Williams, Edward, 122, 129

425

Williams, Hugh, 347
Williams, James, 199
Williams, Jane, 224
Williams, John, 47, 203, 312, 336
Williams, Jonathan, 224
Williams, Joseph, 94
Williams, Lewis, 142
Williams, Louis, 126
Williams, Mary, 249
Williams, Peter, 191
Williams, Richard, 137
Williams, Talburt, 169
Williams, Warham, 287
Williams, William, 266
Williams, Wm., 269
Williamson, James, 286
Willis, John, 145
Willis, Samuel, 237
Willson, Jordan, 95
Wilmot, James, 10
Wilson, Isaac, 257
Wilson, James, 265, 331
Wilson, John, 43, 138
Wilson, Joseph, 180, 265, 304
Wilson, Robert, 52, 158
Wilson, Thomas, 248, 269
Wilson, William, 78
Wilson/Willson, Jane, 181
Wilson/Willson, John, 181
Winchester, Joseph, 281
Winchester, Stephen, 37
Wing, Robert, 105
Wingham, Robert, 49
Winn, Samson, 354
Winnock, Joshua, 307
Winship, Francis, 354
Winslow, John, 254
Winslow, Joshua, 85, 370
Winter, William, 135
Wire, John, 380
Wise, Joseph, 13

Wise, William, 283
Wiswal, Thomas, 263
Wlliams, Benjamin, 181
Wolcott, John, 235
Wombscom, John, 367
Wood, Amos, 133
Wood, Ananias, 320
Wood, Jacob, 225
Woodberry, Josiah, 196
Woodbridge, Ephraim, 27
Woodbridge, Mr., 220
Woodhouse, John, 285
Woodman, Jonathan, 348, 349
Woods, John, 158
Woodside, James, 101, 104
Woodward, Joseph, 322
Worrison, Pallas, 170
Worth, John, 391

Worth, Sarah, 391
Worth, William, 288
Wotton, Cornelius, 259
Wotton, Cornelius, Mrs., 259
Wotton, William, 181
Wreggon, Richard, 123
Wright, Henry, Jr., 241
Wright, James, 171
Wright, Jane, 241
Wright, Thomas, 29
Wroe, Joshua, 50, 51, 55
Yeals, Nehemiah, 29
York, Pomp, 299
York, Pompey, 197, 209
Young, John, 103
Young, Robert, 103
Young, William/Wm., 146, 162, 216, 273, 275
Youngman, Ebenezer, 57
Yowelen, John, 20

www.ingramcontent.com/pod-product-compliance
Lightning Source LLC
Chambersburg PA
CBHW072117290426
44111CB00012B/1690